THE KENNEDY PRESIDENTIAL PRESS CONFERENCES

Also in this series:

The Nixon Presidential Press Conferences

The Johnson Presidential Press Conferences
(2 volumes)

Vietnam: The Definitive Documentation of Human Decisions
(2 volumes)

SERIES EDITOR: GEORGE W. JOHNSON

THE KENNEDY PRESIDENTIAL PRESS CONFERENCES

John Fitzgerald Kennedy

Introduction by
David Halberstam

Earl M. Coleman Enterprises, Inc., Publishers
New York • 1978

Library of Congress Cataloging in Publication Data

Kennedy, John Fitzgerald, Pres. U.S., 1917-1963.
  The Kennedy presidential press conferences.

  Includes index.
  1. United States—Politics and government—1961-1963—Sources.
2. United States—Foreign relations—1961-1963—Sources. 3. Kennedy,
John Fitzgerald, Pres. U.S., 1917-1963. 4. Presidents—United States—
Press conferences. I. Title.
E841.K374 1978   973.922'092'4   78-1869
ISBN 0-930576-01-2

> **"**And so, my fellow Americans: ask not what your country can do for you—ask what you can do for your country." **"**
>
> —John F. Kennedy, Inaugural Address, January 20, 1961

The Kennedy Presidential Press Conferences

INTRODUCTION

Charles deGaulle, living in a society that had one state controlled television network, spoke for all chief executives in all free or partially free
societies. He used to say that all reporters were against him, but television,
television belonged to him. It was the classic statement of a politician about
journalism, even a politician who by and large received a generous treatment in
the press. It meant that print could somehow be too querulous, could include
too much journalistic analyzing of motive, could filter out too much of the
original message, could in sum spread too much doubt. But broadcasting and
particularly television, had none of that, it was powerful and it was direct,
and by and large it was the property of the chief executive. Which was certainly the way that John Kennedy regarded the media, he was suspicious of all
publishers, he by and large liked working journalists though he would become
angry at the best of them; but television was his, it was a means of reaching
the people directly without being filtered out by print reporters.

Besides, he was very good at it. So it was not surprising that he was our
first television President. He was in no small part nominated for the Presidency ahead of the wishes of professional party politicians because of television; in State after State he used, largely through television and the press,
the primary system to circumvent the choice of the party apparatus and to prove
to party professionals that he was, in fact, a winner. Then again during the
campaign, television was crucial on two major occasions. First in a televised
appearance before Protestant ministers in Houston where he helped diminish religious prejudice against him, and second in a series of televised debates with
Richard Nixon he was able to neutralize the advantage that Nixon as Vice President of the United States should have had as a senior and more experienced political figure. In those debates it was Nixon who seemed uncertain and anxious
and Kennedy who appeared deft and cool; in his own mind and that of most working
politicians he defeated Nixon because of the debates.

So it was not surprising that once elected, he turned to television as a
major political asset, and in a move of historic American political significance he decided to televise his press conferences live. Teddy Roosevelt had
called the Presidency the "bully pulpit," the best place from which to educate
a society; Kennedy now sought to take the bully pulpit and bring it into the
home of every American. The benefits for him and his programs were potentially
enormous, and he was aware of all the pluses and minuses. He was after all the
ideal television politician and he knew it. He was young and he was handsome
and his looks televised well. He was well read, and articulate and quick on his
feet, and if anything, television seemed to emphasize that, his ease with difficult questions, his ease, above all, with himself. He understood the medium
and he was at peace with it, confident of himself; as he liked himself, he assumed that the camera would too; he did not worry that the camera might detect

some fatal flaw, and he did not worry as other politicians did about which side of their face to project. He appeared completely unconscious of the camera, he neither feared nor preened for it. This was in contrast to most of his predecessors much older men deeply ill at ease with the interruption of their lives by the camera (Eisenhower had used television sparingly. Aides had had to put powder on his bald dome to keep it from shining; he found, not surprisingly, the entire business demeaning. Besides, his syntax was so awkward that the use of television at his press conferences had diminished rather than added to his popularity).

Kennedy was not only good at television, he understood it. He understood, and in this he was way ahead of most working politicians, that it was not just substance, but it was style, it was as much theatre as it was reality. People he knew did not so much remember his words in the debates with Nixon as they did his style, cool, confident, somewhat patrician. In addition, one of the reasons for his stunning success in the Houston ministers' meeting was not what he had said about honoring freedom of religion; he has said that all many times before. It had been the setting which he had added to the drama - the Protestant ministers so angry and controversial that by contrast his own quiet, intelligent answers were not only amplified, they were made more civil. The excesses of his adversaries had helped him.

So it was that he understood the value of the Presidential press conference in every way, that this was not just news, but theatre; in the public mind there would be the contest: the President pitted against hundreds of tough, hard-questioning reporters. Could he do it? Would they stump him? Would he stumble in mid sentence? There were, after all, so many of them and only one of him. Yet the odds were terrific and the dice were loaded; he could anticipate most of the questions and he knew most of the areas reporters would touch on. To the degree that they were rude or too harsh, he would become the beneficiary, the public would not like a President unjustly being badgered or jostled by rude reporters.

Besides, and this was crucial, he was very good with working reporters. It was a natural constituency for him. He was interested in the same things they were, had gone to the same schools, read the same books and shared the same analytical turn of mind. By and large he was more comfortable with reporters than he was with working politicians. His closest friends numbered several working journalists. He took them seriously, which was a form of flattery in itself; even when on occasion he squabbled with working reporters, that was a form of flattery too, it meant that he cared about what they were writing, something that was inconceivable during the Eisenhower administration. Because Kennedy, by and large, liked working with reporters, they in turn reciprocated; they gave him something that technically was not theirs to give, but which they gave to political figures on occasion. They gave him the benefit of the doubt. It was based on trust, and since in the early sixties Vietnam had not yet shattered the trust of the American Presidency, and the unofficial ground rules which had grown up during the Cold War still existed, they did not press him too hard, particularly on issues of what were alleged to be national security. Vietnam and Watergate would change all that, but a reader looking through these pages will be surprised how little hard questioning there is of the President on such matters as Vietnam and Cuba. The President gives his word, reporters largely accept it at face value.

When he first decided to televise his press conferences live, some members of his staff like Rusk and Sorensen were opposed, fearing a small *faux pas* might weaken the Presidency or bring the world to the brink of war. But Kennedy was sure of himself from the start, and confident that this was a powerful instrument for his Presidency. Previous Presidents had used the press conferences as a means of reaching and informing and listening to the country all at the same time. Kennedy took it one step further, he used it to build himself up personally. The politician not just as leader, but as star. He was absolutely true in his instinct, he used reporters as pawns to make himself look smarter, shrewder, better informed and more capable than he really was. In some way mastery of the press conference became a substitute for mastery of public affairs. If he seemed in control at his press conference then there was a logical assumption in the minds of the audience, that he was in control of the affairs of state as well. The Bay of Pigs for example was a total disaster and it was largely Kennedy's fault, but it was not a televised disaster. His response to the Bay of Pigs at a press conference however, was televised and he was at his best. He put off all questions about the planning of the mission on the grounds of national security and reporters let him have his way. Then in a marvelous *tour de force*, he took all responsibility for it (he might just as well have, there was not other President at the moment, but to reach out for the blame seemed a particularly grand gesture). His popularity in the wake of the press conference went soaring upwards.

It was all marvelous television. The nation was fascinated, it had a new and dashing young President who seemed to do these conferences so well. The ratings were astonishingly good. It helped personalize the Presidency, the mail went up, the national interest in him and his family went up. Television in building up Kennedy and the Presidency was changing the institutional balance of the country and helping to create what would soon be called the Imperial Presidency. It was diminishing the role of the political party system in general (by making it an obsolete route to the Presidency); it was diminishing the role of the Opposition party once in office (the President had total access to television, his televised press conferences became national theatre; by contrast cameras could not enter the halls of the Congress). But it was not just the Opposition party which was being diminished, it was in fact the co-equal branch of Government, the Congress which was losing as well. Television was changing the entire institutional balance. By televising his press conferences, Kennedy was in fact televising his Presidency. The Congress could not get comparable time. As it was not televised, it was not seen; as it was not seen, it did not exist; as it did not exist, it had less and less leverage against the President. The televising of Kennedy's press conferences was a crucial step in making America an increasingly presidential society.

The Opposition party tried to counter this, in a pathetic way. The two Republican leaders, Everett Dirksen and Charles Halleck, started holding a weekly press conference of their own, designed primarily for television. The problems were awesome; where Kennedy was carried in full, live, on all three networks simultaneously, Dirksen and Halleck were lucky if they got a minute or two on the evening news shows. Besides, Kennedy was classically a creation of a media age and Dirksen and Halleck were the reverse; they were not television age politicians. They had risen to power by different routes, mostly by avoiding the eye of the media, avoiding national exposure. One had a sense of two overblown, slightly overripe Shakespearean actors on the decline winking at the audience – The Ev and Charley Show, it became known as. They became a marvelous foil for Kennedy. They seemed tired and old and conservative; he was young and fresh and on the move. Thus the President was young and active, and the Congress, to the degree that it opposed the President, was old and tired. All in all, the Kennedy press conferences were a significant moment in the American political balance. They helped inform the nation as previous conferences had done, they were a marvelous theatre for a handsome young President, they helped add awesome new power to an already powerful Presidency, and, coincidentally, they helped to make television journalists more powerful as conduits for politicians than print ones.

David Halberstam
New York, New York
January, 1978

COPY

The media has always been deeply involved in political life. But only in the last forty years has electronic communication (as the 20th Century neolog of the written word) become an overwhelmingly dominant factor in the establishment of trends and attitudes in the minds of the American voter. From Franklin Roosevelt's fireside chats to contemporary efforts by President Carter to achieve constant visual exposure, radio and television have shaped public perception of elected officials. If there were a beginning to this new media mode, John Kennedy was largely responsible for initiating it. His relationship with all forms of the media but with television in particular set the tone for future media relationships. Certainly Kennedy fostered the harmony between himself and the press officials who had approached his administration with some reservations and uncertainty. But the seeming openness which Kennedy brought to the Presidency was obviously laden with a generous leavening of judicious caution, as we know after the events which took place during his term in office.

Kennedy's success in manipulating public opinion is demonstrated nowhere more accurately than in his press conferences where his charm as well as his intellect were effectively displayed. The news conference was the perfect medium, moreover, for establishing Kennedy's visible political profile, and on a subliminal level, showing the limitations of the executive office in terms of the distinction between closed poker and frankness. If only because we have come to view John Kennedy as a legendary figure, the news conferences herein printed are important for helping us to understand that his assessment of events, mood, and people led him to conceal information as well as use it as a political and simply informational tool.

George W. Johnson
January 1978

THE INAUGURAL ADDRESS OF JOHN FITZGERALD KENNEDY

JANUARY 20, 1961

(Delivered in person at the Capitol)

Vice President Johnson, Mr. Speaker, Mr. Chief Justice, President Eisenhower, Vice President Nixon, President Truman, Reverend Clergy, fellow citizens:

We observe today not a victory of party but a celebration of freedom – symbolizing an end as well as a beginning – signifying renewal as well as change. For I have sworn before you and almighty God the same solemn oath our forbearers prescribed nearly a century and three quarters ago.

The world is very different now. For man holds in his mortal hands the power to abolish all forms of human poverty and all forms of human life. And yet the same revolutionary beliefs for which our forbearers fought are still at issue around the globe – the belief that the rights of man come not from the generosity of the state but from the hand of God.

We dare not forget today that we are the heirs of that first revolution. Let the word go forth from this time and place, to friend and foe alike, that the torch has been passed to a new generation of Americans – born in this century, tempered by war, disciplined by a hard and bitter peace, proud of our ancient heritage – and unwilling to witness or permit the slow undoing of those human rights to which this nation has always been committed, and to which we are committed today at home and around the world.

Let every nation know, whether it wishes us well or ill, that we shall pay any price, bear any burden, meet any hardship, support any friend, oppose any foe to assure the survival and the success of liberty.

This much we pledge ¬ and more.

To those old allies whose cultural and spiritual origins we share, we pledge the loyalty of faithful friends. United, there is little we cannot do in a host of cooperative ventures. Divided, there is little we can do – for we dare not meet a powerful challenge at odds and split asunder.

To those new states whom we welcome to the ranks of the free, we pledge our word that one form of colonial control shall not have passed away merely to be replaced by a far more iron tyranny. We shall not always expect to find them supporting our view. But we shall always hope to find them strongly supporting their own freedom – and to remember that, in the past, those who foolishly sought power by riding the back of the tiger ended up inside.

To those peoples in the huts and villages of half the globe struggling to break the bonds of mass misery, we pledge our best efforts to help them help themselves, for whatever period is required – not because the communists may be doing it, not because we seek their votes, but because it is right. If a free society cannot help the many who are poor, it cannot save the few who are rich.

To our sister republics south of our border, we offer a special pledge – to convert our good words into good deeds – in a new alliance for progress – to assist free men and free governments in casting off the chains of poverty. But this peaceful revolution of hope cannot become the prey of hostile powers. Let all our neighbors know that we shall join with them to oppose aggression or subversion anywhere in the Americas. And let every other power know that this Hemisphere intends to remain the master of its own house.

To that world assembly of sovereign states, the United Nations, our last best hope in an age where the instruments of war have far outpaced the instruments of peace, we renew our pledge of support – to prevent it from becoming merely a forum for invective – to strengthen its shield of the new and the weak – and to enlarge the area in which its writ may run.

Finally, to those nations who would make themselves our adversary, we offer not a pledge but a request: that both sides begin anew the quest for peace, before the dark powers of destruction unleashed by science engulf all humanity in planned or accidental self-destruction.

We dare not tempt them with weakness. For only when our arms are sufficient beyond doubt can we be certain beyond doubt that they will never be employed.

But neither can two great and powerful groups of nations take comfort from our present course – both sides overburdened by the cost of modern weapons, both rightly alarmed by the steady spread of the deadly atom, yet both racing to alter that uncertain balance of terror that stays the hand of mankind's final war.

So let us begin anew – remembering on both sides that civility is not a sign of weakness, and sincerity is always subject to proof. Let us never negotiate out of fear. But let us never fear to negotiate.

Let both sides explore what problems unite us instead of belaboring those problems which divide us.

Let both sides, for the first time, formulate serious and precise proposals for the inspection and control of arms – and bring the absolute power to destroy other nations under the absolute control of all nations.

Let both sides seek to invoke the wonders of science instead of its terrors. Together let us explore the stars, conquer the deserts, eradicate disease, tap the ocean depths and encourage the arts and commerce.

Let both sides unite to heed in all corners of the earth the command of Isaiah – to "undo the heavy burdens... (and) let the oppressed go free."

And if a beach-head of cooperation may push back the jungle of suspicion, let both sides join in creating a new endeavor, not a new balance of power, but a new world of law, where the strong are just and the weak secure and the peace preserved.

All this will not be finished in the first one hundred days. Nor will it be finished in the first one thousand days, nor in the life of this Administration, nor even perhaps in our lifetime on this planet. But let us begin.

In your hands, my fellow citizens, more than mine, will rest the final success or failure of our course. Since this country was founded, each generation of Americans has been summoned to give testimony to its national loyalty. The graves of young Americans who answered the call to service surround the globe.

Now the trumpet summons us again – not as a call to bear arms, though arms we need – not as a call to battle, though embattled we are – but a call to bear the burden of a long twilight struggle, year in and year out, "rejoicing in hope, patient in tribulation - a struggle against the common enemy of man: tyranny, poverty, disease and war itself.

Can we forge against these enemies a grand and global alliance, North and South, East and West, that can assure a more fruitful life for all mankind? Will you join in that historic effort?

In the long history of the world, only a few generations have been granted the role of defending freedom in its hour of maximum danger. I do not shrink from this responsibility - I welcome it. I do not believe that any of us would exchange places with any other people or any other generation. The energy, the faith, the devotion which we bring to this endeavor will light our country and all who serve it - and the glow from that fire can truly light the world.

And so, my fellow Americans: ask not what your country can do for you - ask what you can do for your country. My fellow citizens of the world: ask not what America will do for you, but what together we can do for the freedom of man.

Finally, whether you are citizens of America or citizens of the world, ask of us here the same high standards of strength and sacrifice which we ask of you. With a good conscience our only sure reward, with history the final judge of our deeds, let us go forth to lead the land we love, asking His blessing and His help, but knowing that here on earth God's work must truly be our own.

1961

THE PRESIDENT'S NEWS CONFERENCE OF

JANUARY 25, 1961

The President: I have several announcements to make first.

I have a statement about the Geneva negotiations for an atomic test ban. These negotiations, as you know, are scheduled to begin early in February. They are of great importance and we will need more time to prepare a clear American position. So we are consulting with other governments and are asking to have it put off until late March. As you know, Mr. John McCloy is my principal adviser in this field, and he has organized a distinguished panel of experts, headed by Dr. James Fisk of the Bell Laboratories – and Mr. Salinger will have a list of the names at the end of the conference – who are going to study previous positions that we've taken in this field, and also recommend to Mr. McCloy, for my guidance, what our position will be in late March when we hope the tests will resume.

Secondly, the United States Government has decided to increase substantially its contribution towards relieving the famine in the Congo. This will be done by airlifting a thousand tons of food supplies, seeds, and hospital supplies from a number of African nations to the Congo. [1]

It is the intention of the United States Government to meet fully the emergency requirements of the Congo for rice, corn, dry milk and other foodstuffs in our surplus stocks. Assurances have been received from the United Nations that with the help of this program the flow of supplies will be adequate to relieve the distress. The United States Government will cooperate fully to help the United Nations prevent famine in the Congo.

Third, I am happy to be able to announce that Captain Freeman B. Olmstead and Captain John R. McKone, members of the crew of the United States Air Force RB-47 aircraft who have been detained by Soviet authorities since July 1, 1960, have been released by the Soviet Government and are now en route to the United States.

The United States Government is gratified by this decision of the Soviet Union and considers that this action of the Soviet Government removes a serious obstacle to improvement of Soviet-American relations.

Our deepest sympathy and understanding go to the families of the men of the RB-47 who gave their lives in the service of their country. At the same time, I am sure that all Americans join me in rejoicing with the Olmstead and McKone families. The families, as well as the men, comported themselves in these trying times in a way which is truly in the best traditions of the military services of the United States. Restraint in these conditions is obviously not easy. But they can be assured that they have contributed in large measure to the final achievement of the objective which we all sought – release of the men.

QUESTIONS

The RB-47 Case and Reconnaissance Overflights

Q: Mr. President, this RB-47 case was regarded by the Russians as an over-flight although we took a different position. In the light of this announce-ment, what will be your general policy on such things as the U-2 case, or the U-2 flights? Do you conceive of circumstances which might warrant resumption of such things as the U-2 flight?

The President: The Soviet Government is fully aware of United States Government views with respect to the distinction between the question of the United States Air Force RB-47 and the incident which occurred over Soviet territory on May 1, 1960, involving an American U-2 type aircraft. Flights of American aircraft penetrating the air space of the Soviet Union have been suspended since May 1960. I have ordered that they not be resumed.

Possibility of Khrushchev Visit to Washington, D. C.

Q: Mr. President, there have been reports that Mr. Khrushchev might come to the United Nations General Assembly for the resumption of the disarmament debates sometime in March. If this were to happen, would you welcome a visit by him to Washington for a get-acquainted meeting?

The President: I've not heard officially of any proposal by Mr. Khrushchev to come to the United States. I've merely seen newspaper reports and I feel that it would be more appropriate to wait until we had some indication of whether Mr. Khrushchev was planning to come to the United Nations.

Kennedy Role in the Release of the Fliers

Q: Mr. President, can you tell us something about what your role was, if you had one, in the release of these fliers? Did this come about as a con-sequence of some action you took?

The President: Well, this matter has been under discussion by the Ameri-can Ambassador and Mr. Khrushchev on one occasion and representatives of the Soviet foreign ministry since this weekend. The fliers were released as of 2 a.m. yesterday morning, but in the plane taking off there was a tire that was blown and therefore the plane did not take off. Our last information is that it took off at 5 o'clock our time this afternoon. It will fly to Amsterdam and then we expect the fliers to be brought to the United States tomorrow afternoon.

U. S. Position on Disarmament Negotiations

Q: Mr. President, one of your task forces recommended that you resist any early move toward general disarmament negotiations until a firm and fixed U. S. policy could be worked out. What is your reaction to that report and how much time do you think it might take to get a firm fixed U. S. position?

The President: Well, Mr. McCloy has responsibility over the area of disarmament as well as nuclear testing. He has, as I've said, set up this committee - advisory committee - on nuclear testing. We want to also get the American position clearer on general disarmament. There is not the same dead-line that we've been facing on the nuclear testing where we were supposed to resume in early February, but I can state that this was a matter which was discussed early this week by the Secretary of Defense and the Secretary of

State and Mr. McCloy and we are preparing clarification of American positions on disarmament.

Ambassador Thompson's Conversation with Premier Khrushchev

Q: Mr. President, what more can you tell us about the long conversation that Ambassador Thompson had with Mr. Khrushchev, including whether the tone of that conversation was anywhere near as friendly as that of the messages that Khrushchev has sent you?

The President: I would say the tone was friendly. And as a result of the conversations, as I've said, the decision was made to release the fliers. But the conversations were conducted in an atmosphere of civility.

Q: Could you give us any indication at all as to what other subjects were taken up in addition to the release of the RB-47 fliers?

The President: No. I think that I have to stand on my previous statement.

The Tenant Farmer Problem

Q: Does your administration plan to take any steps to solve the problem at Fayette County, Tennessee, where tenant farmers have been evicted from their homes because they voted last November and must now live in tents?

The President: We are - the Congress, of course, enacted legislation which placed very clear responsibility on the executive branch to protect the right of voting. I supported that legislation. I am extremely interested in making sure that every American is given the right to cast his vote without prejudice to his rights as a citizen. And therefore I can state that this administration will pursue the problem of providing that protection with all vigor.

Distribution of Food to the Unemployed

Q: Sir, would you please tell us how it was possible for you to do by Executive order what Mr. Benson always told us was impossible for him to do without more legislation? I refer to the order expanding the distribution of food to the unemployed and giving them more variety in the diet.

The President: Well, I would not attempt to comment on Mr. Benson. I don't think there's any question of our rights to issue the Executive order under the authority given to us by the Constitution and by legislative action. I think we're within our rights. It is a judgment as to what is the best use to make of the funds that are available - the funds are quite limited. The diet which is being provided for the people who are unemployed is still inadequate. But nevertheless we have used the funds that are available to the maximum. And I don't think there's any question that we were within our rights.

Release of the Fliers

Q: Mr. President, could you tell us how and when you learned that these fliers were going to be released?

The President: I learned as a result of the conversations which Ambassador Thompson had with the Soviet officials and therefore we were informed as to the date that they would be released - the time - yesterday.

Presidential Press Conferences

Q: Mr. President, there has been some apprehension about the instantaneous broadcast of Presidential press conferences such as this one, the contention being that an inadvertent statement no longer correctible, as in the old days, could possibly cause some grave consequences. Do you feel there is any risk or could you give us some thought on that subject?

The President: Well, it was my understanding that the statements made by the, by President Eisenhower, were on the record. There may have been a clarification that could have been issued afterwards but it still would have demonstrated, it still would have been on the record as a clarification, so that I don't think that the interests of our country are - it seems to me they're as well protected under this system as they were under the system followed by President Eisenhower. And this system has the advantage of providing more direct communication.

Reopening of Diplomatic Relations with Cuba

Q: On the question at issue would you consider reopening diplomatic relations with Cuba and are you considering such a step now?

The President: Well, at the - take the last part first - we are not considering such a step at the present time. I may say that the United States is interested, and I think that this administration is extremely interested in movements in Latin America and Central America, or the Caribbean which provide a better life for the people. And if American interests may be damaged by those movements - or revolutions, or whatever term you want to use - we feel that this should be a matter that should be negotiated. What we are of course concerned about is when these movements are seized by external forces and directed not to improving the welfare of the people involved but towards imposing an ideology which is alien to this hemisphere. That is a matter of concern particularly when that intervention takes the form of military support which threatens the security and the peace of the Western Hemisphere.

Now, I'm hopeful that governments will be established throughout all of Latin America and governments which are established will, and I think nearly all of them do, share the same view that we have to provide in this hemisphere a better life for the people involved, that we are interested in that, that we are concerned about it, that American policy will be directed towards that end. But we are also concerned that in the name of that peaceful revolution, when it's seized by aliens for their purposes, it's very difficult for the United States to carry on happy relations with those countries.

So in answer to your question we have no plan at present to resume diplomatic relations with Cuba, because of the factors which are involved in that island.

Expansion of the Rules Committee

Q: You said in the past, sir, that the President should be in the thick of the political battle, and I wondered, sir, if you could tell us what part you're playing in the effort to expand the Rules Committee and whether you feel your domestic program - whether the success of your domestic program in part depends on expanding the Rules Committee?

The President: Well, the Constitution states that each house shall be the judge of its own rules, and therefore the Speaker of the House, Mr. Rayburn, has been extremely anxious that the House be permitted to settle this matter in its own way.

But it's no secret that - I would strongly believe that the Members of the House should have an opportunity to vote themselves on the programs which we will present. That, I think, is the reason the people selected them to go to the House of Representatives and to the Senate and selected me as President, so that we could present programs and consider programs and vote on programs which are put forward for the benefit of the country.

Now I feel that it would be - I'm hopeful that whatever judgment is made by the Members of the House, that it will permit the Members to vote on these bills. This is a very difficult time in the life of our country. Many controversial measures will be presented which will be in controversy and will be debated. But at the end the majority of the Members of the House, the majority of the Members of the Senate, I hope, will have a chance to exercise their will, and that a small group of men will not attempt to prevent the Members from finally letting their judgments be known.

For example, we have the housing bill which is going to come before the Congress this year. We have an aid-to-education bill. We have legislation which will affect the income of farmers. Shouldn't the Members of the House themselves and not merely the members of the Rules Committee have a chance to vote on those measures? But the responsibility rests with the Members of the House, and I would not attempt in any way to infringe upon that responsibility. I merely give my view as an interested citizen. (Laughter)

The Cuban Refugee Problem

Q: Are any plans being made to implement the recommendations in the Voorhees report on the Cuban refugee problem? Secondly, do you plan to appoint somebody to continue Mr. Voorhees' work?

The President: We are considering the recommendations of Mr. Voorhees and the whole problem of the Cuban refugees, but I don't have any statement to make on it at this time.

The Portuguese Seized Ship

Q: Mr. President, what is the official Government position in regard to the Portuguese-seized ship? Can the Navy board it if and when it makes contact?

The President: Well, I believe that the location of the ship has been determined, and - (aside to Mr. Salinger) - perhaps we could give the location of it - at the present time the instructions are for the Navy to continue its accompaniment of the ship. The *Santa Maria* has been located by Navy P2V aircraft, and the position is approximately 600 miles north of the mouth of the Amazon River. It is headed on a course of 117, a speed of 15 knots, and the exact position at 10 minutes after 4 was 10-35 north, 45-42 west. It will be trailed by aircraft and picked up by the destroyers of our African task force.

Now, there are Americans involved; and their lives are involved. But we have not given any instructions to the Navy to carry out any boarding operations. Though, of course, we are concerned about the lives of the Americans involved. And also we are concerned because the ship belongs to a country with which the United States has friendly relations.

Khrushchev's Willingness To Release The Fliers

Q: Mr. President, in consequence of Mr. Khrushchev's apparent indication last weekend of willingness to release the American fliers, have you sent any communication to him through Ambassador Thompson or otherwise?

The President: Well - have I sent a message since the release of the fliers?

Q: Since his communication to us through Ambassador -

The President: We have had several exchanges with the Soviet authorities. I do not believe that one has taken place since the release of the prisoners but that's partially because there has been this delay about their leaving Moscow.

The Reciprocal Trade Agreements Act

Q: Mr. President, there is meeting here now a nationwide group of labor, agriculture, and industry which wants to abolish all restraints of the Reciprocal Trade Agreements Act. They say that it robs us of gold, robs American workers of jobs. What is your position on such a proposal?

The President: Well, I think that their meeting here is well within their rights as citizens of the United States and I think that we should listen to their views. This is a matter of great concern. I do think we should be conscious of the fact, of course, that the balance of trade has been substantially in our favor in the last year. But we are continually concerned about those imports which adversely affect an entire industry, or adversely affect the employment of a substantial number of our citizens. The present laws - peril-point and escape clause - of course, all take those matters into consideration. But I'm glad to have them here; I'm glad to have them express their views. I think the Congress should consider their views carefully, and I hope that in their consideration they will consider the whole problem of trade, and I do think we should realize that the balance of trade has been in our favor and the gold flow would have been substantially worse if we had not had this favorable balance of trade.

A Cutback in The Military Abroad

Q: Mr. President, in relation to the gold problem, the outgoing administration has ordered a cutback in the number of American military and civilian dependents stationed abroad in the so-called hard-currency nations. The day before your inaugural the outgoing Defense Secretary advised your incoming Defense Secretary in a manner urging that relief should be sought as soon as possible because of what the outgoing Defense Secretary termed the "adverse affect of the order on the morale of the military." Have you had a chance to make up your mind on that postion, sir?

The President: Mr. McNamara and Mr. Dillon have discussed the effect of this order on military morale, military strength, the rate of reenlistment. It's really a question of determining what alternative steps can be secured which would be less harmful but which would protect the flow of gold. I do expect to make some reference to this matter of gold outflow in the State of the Union Address. I will send within a 2-week period after the State of the Union Address a message to the Congress dealing with the gold outflow and our recommendations for meeting it and we will at that time come to some judgment as to whether a more satisfactory method of protecting our gold could be secured than providing for the return of the families of Americans serving abroad in the military.

I will say that our study so far has convinced us that the dollar must be protected, that the dollar can be protected at its present value, that exchange controls are not essential, but it is a most serious problem and it will be the subject of a message to the Congress.

The New York Democratic Party

Q: Mr. President, the State of New York gave you one of your handsomest majorities in the 1960 election campaign, but now the Democrats of New York are rather bitterly divided over leadership. As the leader of the Democratic Party nationally, are you going to take some steps to try and heal the splits in New York?

The President: Well the people in New York, the Democratic organizations in New York, who are interested in the success of the Democratic Party, they have to make their judgments as to what kind of a party they want to build there. I have asked Mr. Bailey, the new chairman of the Democratic Party, to lend a helping hand in attempting to alleviate some of the distress. (Laughter)

Federal Aid for the Unemployed

Q: Sir, do you have any plans for quick Federal aid for the unemployed?

The President: We are going to send a message to the Congress right after the State of the Union Address on what steps we think the Government could profitably take to provide protection for the unemployed and also to stimulate the economy. On the immediate question, I will discuss that in the State of the Union Address on Monday.

Chances for a Meeting With Khrushchev

Q: Mr. President, now that the Soviets have released the RB-47 fliers, will you estimate for us the chances of you meeting with Premier Khrushchev?

The President: Yes. There is no relationship, nor has there been, in the discussion between the two matters. And therefore I have no - there has been no change in my previous statement that there are no plans at the present time for meeting with Mr. Khrushchev.

Abuse of Executive Privilege

Q: Mr. President, will you tolerate the continued abuse of Executive privilege to suppress information which is needed by Congress? For instance, now that you are President, will you direct the USIA to give the Senate Foreign Relations Committee those prestige polls which you urged the previous adminis- tration to make available during the campaign?

The President: Well, let me say that I would have no objection at all to the polls, or at least the results of the polls, being made available. And I'd be delighted to check in and see what we can do about making it available to the Senate Foreign Relations Committee or the House Foreign Relations Committee, if they would like them.

Q: Mr. President, about the abuses regarding the privilege to suppress all sorts of information. What is your position on that?

The President: Well, that's a statement, really, not completely a question, in-

Q: Sir, but you yourself agreed.

The President: That's why I stated that I thought that it would be well to release these polls and that's why I said I'd be glad to release these polls. Now if other matters come up, we'll have to make a judgment whether it is an abuse or whether it is within the constitutional protections given to the Executive, and I would hope that we can within the limits of national security make available information to the press and to the people, and I do think that it would be helpful to release the polls which we discussed last fall.

Q: Mr. President, Press Secretary Salinger said today, indicated today, there might be a need for a tightening of information on national security. Doesn't the policy of deterrence require that the enemy have knowledge of our strength and the ability to carry them out and wouldn't there be a risk of possible miscalculation by tightening up information?

The President: Well, I think that the enemy is informed of our strength. I think Mr. Salinger in his statement today at lunch indicated his judgment based on his experience so far, that there had been very ample information given so that the enemy can make a determination as to our strength. I am anxious that we have a maximum flow of information but there quite obviously are some matters which involve the security of the United States, and it's a matter on which the press and the Executive should attempt to reach a responsible decision.

I could not make a prediction about what those matters will be, but I think that all of us here are aware that there are some matters which it would not be well to discuss at particular times so that we just have to wait and try to work together and see if we can provide as much information as we can within the limits of national security. I do not believe that the stamp "National Security" should be put on mistakes of the administration which do not involve the national security, and this administration would welcome any time that any member of the press feels that we are artificially invoking that cover. But I must say that I do not hold the view that all matters and all information which is available to the Executive should be made available at all times, and I don't think any member of the press does. So it's a question of trying to work out a solution to a sensitive matter.

Dean Rusk's Statement on Private Diplomacy

Q: Mr. President, in the past few days the Secretary of State, Dean Rusk, has issued statements - one with your name on it - to the effect that this country wants a return to quiet private diplomacy. Could you give us some idea of the meaning behind this, Mr. President? Are you trying to suggest to Khrushchev that you'd like to resort to this for the time being without offending him or making him go off the cordial path he's on at the present time?

The President: Would you — the last part of that —

Q: Are you trying to suggest to Mr. Khrushchev by the tone of these - by what you're saying in these statements - that you don't want a summit meeting now and you'd like to go through private channels, and trying to do this without offending him or getting him off the cordial path he's on now?

The President: Well, I would just say — without accepting the question completely as a premise - I would say that the Secretary of State is anxious to explore with interested countries what chance we have of lessening world tension which is - in some areas of the world - is quite high tonight. And therefore there are occasions when traditional exchanges between diplomats and the countries involved are in the national interest. And that, I think, is what Mr. Rusk is directing his attention to. And I'm hopeful that from those more traditional exchanges we can perhaps find greater common ground.

Surplus Food to Red China

Q: Sir, do you favor Senator Humphrey's suggestion that we send surplus food to Red China through the U.N. or CARE or some similar organization?

The President: Well, I'd say two things: firstly, Red China - the Chinese Communists - are exporting food at the present time, some of it to Africa, some of it going, I think, to Cuba, and therefore that is a factor in their needs for food from abroad.

Secondly, we've had no indication from the Chinese Communists that they would welcome any offer of food. I'm not anxious to offer food if it's regarded merely as a propaganda effort by the United States. If there is a desire for food and a need for food, then the United States would be glad to consider that need, regardless of the source. If people's lives are involved- if there is a desire for food - the United States will consider it carefully. I do say that in this case, however, there are these examples of food being exported during this present time or recent history and, secondly, there has been a rather belligerent attitude expressed towards us in recent days by the Chinese Communists and there is no indication, direct or indirect, private or public, that they would respond favorably to any acts by the United States.

Task Force Report on Space

Q: Mr. President, the task force report on space has been criticized as partisan opinion. There also has been criticism that the report was made without any contact with NASA officials, without any attempt at liaison during the transition period. And there is concern that no one has so far been named to head the agency. Could you comment on these charges, sir?

The President: Well, I don't - the task force was free to make the kind of report that in their best judgment the events called for. The task force was made up of men of broad experience in this field. I think it was really a blue-ribbon panel. They presented their views. I don't think anyone is suggesting that their views are necessarily in every case the right views. I am hopeful- we have appointed an acting director - and I'm hopeful that before that week is out we will have a director of NASA.

The Budget

Q: Mr. President, you have directed your departmental heads to take a new look at the Eisenhower budget. I wonder - with indications that you may have some partial revisions with this budget - can you now say whether you hope or expect to live within the $80,900 million spending figure which your predecessor laid down?

The President: I would - that study of the budget is now going on and I couldn't give you an answer yet. We haven't finished our study.

The Inaugural Address

Q: Mr. President, your Inaugural Address was unusual in that you dealt only with America's position in the world. Why, Mr. President, did you limit yourself to this global theme?

The President: Well, because the issue of war and peace is involved, and the survival of perhaps the planet, possibly our system. And, therefore, this is a matter of primary concern to the people of the United States and the people of the world.

Secondly, I represent a new administration. I think the views of this administration are quite well known to the American people, and will become better known in the next month. I think that we are new, however, on the world scene, and therefore I felt there would be some use in informing countries around the world of our general view on the questions which face the world and divide the world.

Crisis in Laos

Q: Mr. President, you have spoken of the situation where there are crises in the world now. One of these crises is Laos. Do you have any hope that a political settlement can be negotiated there?

Well, as you know, the British Government has presented to the Soviet Union - and to the best of my information an answer has not been received by the British - a proposal to reestablish the International Control Commission. We ought to know shortly whether there's any hope that that commission can be reestablished. As to the general view on Laos, this matter is of great concern to us. The United States is anxious that there be established in Laos a peaceful country - an independent country not dominated by either side but concerned with the life of the people within the country.

We are anxious that that situation come forward. And the United States is using its influence to see if that independent country, peaceful country, uncommitted country, can be established under the present very difficult circumstances.

Francis Gary Powers and 11 Other Missing Fliers

Q: Mr. President, in discussing with the Soviet Union the release of the RB-47 fliers, did we also take up with Mr. Khrushchev the fate of Francis Gary Powers, a U-2 pilot, and the 11 fliers who are missing from the C-130 which was shot down inside Armenia in 1958?

The President: The matter of the 11 fliers was discussed and Mr. Khrushchev - the Russians rather - have stated that their previous public statements on these fliers represent their view on the matter: that the newspaper - magazine story which was written by an East German does not represent the facts. So that that would - on the matter of Mr. Powers, we have not discussed him at this time because he is in a different category than the fliers that were released. One was an overflight and the other was a flight of a different nature.

Q: Did the Russians ask any quid pro quo or did we make any concessions to them in exchange for the release of these fliers? If not, how do you account for this remarkable turnabout in their relations with us?

The President: They did not. The statement which I have made is the statement which the United States Government put forward on this matter, which I read to you earlier in regard to overflights. I would not attempt to make a judgment as to why the Soviet Union chose to release them at this time. I did say in my statement that this had removed a serious obstacle in the way of peaceful relations between the Soviet Union and the United States and I would judge that they desired to remove that serious obstacle.

Q: Mr. President, did they accept a reassurance of no more overflights as an exchange?

The President: It is a fact that I have ordered that the flights not be resumed, which is a continuation of the order given by President Eisenhower in May of this year.[2]

Proposals for Electoral Reform

Q: Mr. President, your own election has stimulated renewed proposals for electoral reform. Do you have any objection to changing the present method of electing Presidents or do you favor any of the proposals?

The President: Well, I do have some thoughts on it. One, that in the first place, having been through the experience in '56, I think it was, of an attempt to substantially change the electoral college, it's my judgment that no such change can secure the necessary support in the House, the Senate, and in the States of the Union. The area where I do think we perhaps could get some improvement would be in providing that the electors would be bound by the results of the State elections. I think that that is a - would be a useful step forward.

The electors - after all, when the people vote they assume that the votes are going to be cast in a way which reflects the judgment of a majority of the people of the State and therefore I think it would be useful to have that automatic and not set up this independent group who could vote for the candidate who carried the State or not, depending on their own personal views. That would be the first thing.

Secondly, I'm hopeful that the Congress would consider the suggestions made, I think, first by President Theodore Roosevelt and later by Senator Richard Neuberger, of having the National Government participate in the financing of national campaigns, because the present system is not satisfactory. Perhaps it would be useful to go into that in more detail later because I do think it's a most important subject. But I would say for the present that this matter of the electors would be an area where I think we could usefully move.

The Problem of Succession

Q: Mr. President, on a related subject, without being morbid, have you given any consideration to the problem which President Eisenhower resolved with his Vice President - that is, the problem of the succession in case of injury, illness, or some incapacitation - some agreement with the Vice President such as your predecessor had?

The President: Yes. Well, I haven't developed that at this present time though I do think that President Eisenhower's decision was a good one, and I think it would be a good precedent. Nothing's been done on it as yet, but I think it would be a good matter on which we could proceed.

Reporter: Thank you, Mr. President.

[1] A White House release, dated January 25, describes more fully the Emergency Food Program for the Congo. The release is printed in the Department of State Bulletin (vol. 44, p. 218).

[2] See 1960-61 Volume of the *Public Papers of the President*, pp. 440-441.

THE PRESIDENT'S NEWS CONFERENCE OF

FEBRUARY 1, 1961

The President: I have several announcements to make.

First is one made at the request of Mrs. Kennedy. Since the election, the birth of our son, and the inauguration, Mrs. Kennedy and I have received over 100,000 letters and telegrams of congratulations and good wishes. They are now building up in available rooms at the White House. Unfortunately, it's not going to be possible for us to acknowledge and answer as we would like to answer each and every message, and therefore I wish to take this opportunity on behalf of Mrs. Kennedy and myself to thank everyone who has been so kind and generous.

Secondly, I'm happy to be able to announce that the restrictions recently imposed on travel abroad of dependents of service personnel will be lifted as soon as the necessary detailed arrangements can be made in the Defense Department. Secretary McNamara has been able to work out arrangements for equivalent savings in personnel costs abroad, so that this change does not imply any weakening of our determination to protect the value of the dollar.

This is a matter of great importance. The Chiefs of Staff have been most concerned about the effect of this order on morale and on the rate of enlistment, and therefore we have had to make a balanced judgment as to which actions in which areas would be in the national interest, and after giving this matter careful consideration, it is the judgment of the Defense Department that other savings can be made which will be more satisfactory to us and to the position of the Armed Forces.

Third, I'm announcing that there are going to be set up five pilot projects for foodstamp distribution, and that these will be in areas of maximum chronic unemployment. All the areas have not yet been determined, but one will be in West Virginia, one in Pennsylvania, one in southern Illinois, and the other in eastern Kentucky, with a fifth yet to be determined.

Next, the Veterans Administration has been instructed to speed up the payment of the National Insurance dividends. This is a sum of over $250 million, which would be paid out throughout this year. We're going to try to pay it out this winter in order to assist the economy at a critical time.

This, of course – the Veterans Administration fund has very ample reserves, very generous reserves. And I feel that this will be of some benefit.

Lastly, in order to lower the cost of housing credit and stimulate that sector of the economy, I've directed the Federal Housing Administration to reduce the maximum permissible interest on FHA-insured loans from 5-3/4 to 5-1/2 percent. Complementary action will be taken by the Federal National Mortgage Association.

In addition, I've asked the Community Facilities Administration to reduce interest rates on new loans to local public bodies for the construction of public facilities, and to broaden their eligibility requirements.

And I've instructed the Housing and Home Finance Agency to hasten those approved projects where a speedup can be effected without waste.

Thank you.

QUESTIONS

Possible Meeting with Premier Khrushchev

Q: Mr. President, as you know, Adlai Stevenson said the other day it was his guess that you would be happy to meet with Khrushchev if he should come to this country for the U.N. session. I wonder, was he correct in his guess that you would be happy to meet with Khrushchev?

The President: As Governor Stevenson - Ambassador Stevenson said, I have not discussed the matter with him. I have no idea whether Mr. Khrushchev is coming to the United States or not. There's been no indication, either publicly or privately, that he is planning a visit to the United States, and therefore I think it would be appropriate to wait in regard to what plans we might have as far as seeing him - it would be more appropriate to wait until we have some idea whether he is going to come or not.

Restrictions on the RB-47 Fliers

Q: Mr. President, could you tell us something of the reasoning and the background of the apparent restrictions on the RB-47 fliers in publicly discussing their experiences in Russia? We get the impression from the Pentagon that this blackout on any public interviews or discussions of the two fliers is to be more or less an indefinite thing. Now we are told at the Pentagon that this is in the national interest. First of all, I wonder if you could tell us why it's in the national interest, and second, what personal feelings you have in the matter on the reasoning behind this decision to keep these men quiet.

The President: Well I'll say that when they've finished their short leave and when they have been debriefed by the Air Force, and the Air Force has had an opportunity to have conversation with them, as far as I'm concerned I'd be glad to have them talk to the press. And therefore I would assume they would be available to the press as soon as that leave is over.

Military Officers and Administration Foreign Policy

Q: This may be a corollary question, but your administration has indicated that it expects officers of the military on active duty to support, in their public statements, or at least not to be hostile to the foreign policy of your administration. Does this project itself into other areas? What about the Atomic Energy Commission? What about economists working for the executive branch who may have differences about economic policy?

The President: I think that the procedure which we have established is a traditional one. I think that the Eisenhower administration made, according to the accounts that I have seen, over 65 known efforts to make sure that speeches by members of the military were in accordance with the general objectives of American foreign policy.

I think - we're going to continue to do that. If a well-known, high-ranking military figure makes a speech which affects foreign policy or possible military policy, I think that the people and the countries abroad have a right to expect that that speech represents the opinion of the National Government.

Now the speech of Admiral Burke which raised this question - when the speech was drafted Admiral Burke may not have known, nor did any of us, whether these fliers would be released, for example. Therefore, there is some value in coordinating statements made by high-ranking responsible officials of our national - involving national security - coordinating them, and making sure that the

State Department, the White House, and Defense are informed about the speeches and that they represent national policy.

That has been the policy followed by President Eisenhower; it is the policy which must be followed by this administration.

Now in the question Mr. Morgan asked, it's not intended that this will serve as a restraint on the ability of people in this administration to speak out, particularly when those speeches do not involve national security. I think the important point here is when they involve national security.

Business Slump and a Tax Cut

Q: Do you consider the current business slump serious enough to justify a tax cut?

The President: I do not at this time. I've stated that we're going to make another judgment on the state of the economy in 2 to 3 months and will then decide what action could be usefully taken. But I have not proposed a tax cut at this time nor do I intend to.

Federal Expenditures

Q: Mr. President, some critics stated that proposals of added Federal expenditures in your State of the Union Message may force us to "kick the bottom out of the money barrel." Could you give us an idea, sir, of how your proposed increased programs would be furnished and in connection with the previous question could it possibly mean an increase in income taxes?

The President: Well, I think that we can spell out our proposed proposals in the series of messages that we're going to send in the next 14 days. And as I said, the proposals that we will make will not of themselves unbalance the budget.

State of the Union Message

Q: Mr. President, your State of the Union Message was both praised and criticized. Some of the critics said that you painted the picture in dark colors so that should there be any improvement you would get the credit. Would you want to comment on that, sir?

The President: Well, I would - I painted the picture as I saw it - I also stated that in my judgment, in some areas involving the national interest the news would be worse before it gets better. And I think that the American people might just as well realize that. So that my statement stands as my view of the problems facing the United States at home and abroad at this time. To the best of my ability, it is an accurate presentation. I'm not a candidate for office for at least 4 years, so that there will be many ups and downs I suppose during that period, so that anybody who thinks that if things get better in the spring that we'll be able to say that they're the result of the administration policy and that's the reason that I painted them unnecessarily dark, misunderstands completely. They are painted accurately as I understand them to be, and anyone who makes the judgment that it was laid on thick for political reasons, I think is making a serious mistake and I hope would give us the benefit of the doubt of an honest view.

Now, other people may look at the same facts and come to a different conclusion. Obviously they have - before my speech and since my speech. But that represents my view as President.

Civil Rights

Q: Mr. President, in the spirit of your Los Angeles campaign speech, are you prepared to move soon by Executive action in the field of civil rights, and if so, in what fields would you make your first step?

The President: We have been considering what steps could be taken in the field of expanding civil rights by Executive action, and I'm hopeful that we will shortly conclude that analysis and have some statement to make on it. It's not completed as yet.

The Need for Public Sacrifice

Q: In connection with a couple of previous questions, you have stated several times since your election that the country was in for some substantial sacrifices, or that the year 1961 might be a difficult year to live in, and yet some of the measures you have announced seem to be intended to improve the lot of, let's say, more unfortunate sections of the population. Could you be more explicit on what you mean by sacrifices and the difficulties of living in 1961?

The President: Well, I would hope that a country as powerful as ours - I said it was the most resourceful industrialized country in the world - would not oppose efforts which we would take to make the life of people who live in these chronic depressed areas - make it easier. I do not feel that all the burdens of hardship should be placed on them. In addition, I do believe that we are heavily involved in critical areas of the world and I cannot today predict what the results will be of events in those areas of the world. I merely state that the tide has not been running with us, that we are heavily involved - heavily committed by public statements of the former administration, and therefore I felt that we should inform the people that there are hazards which lurk around us and which may place heavy burdens on us.

I will whenever I think that sacrifices of a particular nature are required, I will go to the people. At the present time, I merely suggest that the times are difficult.

Now, when we talk about five and half million people unemployed there are still over 60 million people employed. And I think that may be one of the reasons why there is some feeling that I overstressed the dark instead of the bright in my State of the Union Address. But it is the function, it seems to me, of the President to concern himself with that five and half million unemployed particularly when so many have been unemployed for such a long period of time.

Conditions in the Country

Q: Mr. President, some people have interpreted your address to the Congress as indicating that you found conditions very much worse upon taking office than you had anticipated. Is this interpretation correct? And, if so, can you give us some specifics?

The President: I think the situation is less satisfactory than it was last fall. And I don't - and I'm not convinced as yet that the tide in some of the critical areas in which the United States is involved has turned in our favor.

I think that anyone who reads the daily papers knows of the critical events in Laos, the Communist intervention in that area. I think they're aware of the fact that the situation in the Congo has deteriorated sharply recently, with a steady withdrawal of troops taking place by United Nations countries.

They're also aware of the steps which have been taken in recent months to increase the iron control of Mr. Castro on Cuba; the shipments of thousands of tons of arms to that country; the expansion of the militia. Those are all factors which affect the security of the United States.

U. S. Proposals and the Congo

Q: Mr. President, what proposals might the United States make in regard to the Congo now that you mentioned the situation there is deteriorating because of the pullout of troops?

The President: Mr. Timberlake is here for consultation in Washington now, Ambassador Brown from Laos is here, General Norstad, who's our NATO commander, is here in Washington, and Ambassador Thompson will be coming back next week, so that we are considering carefully what policies we should follow in all those areas of crisis. Particularly we are considering the matter of the Congo carefully and what useful steps might be taken which would prevent a further deterioration. I do not have anything further to say just at this time.

Labor-Management Relations

Q: Mr. President, do you plan any recommendations on the labor-management relations field in your future messages to Congress since you have not covered this subject in your addresses to date?

The President: I'd have to wait on that. We have no - it's not within the next 14 days.

Unemployment Compensation

Q: Sir, would you clarify your intentions in the field of unemployment compensation? Do you plan now to propose to Congress the establishment of Federal standards, wider coverage, higher benefits, and for their greater duration?

The President: Well, the first matter which we will address to the Congress will be the question of emergency payments to those unemployed who've exhausted their benefits.

Later in March, we will send to the Congress - or in April - proposals dealing with more permanent improvement in unemployment compensation standards, duration and benefits, because there isn't any doubt that, based on our experience in '58, in our experience this year, the unemployment compensation system has not met the needs of the country satisfactorily.

So we will be sending a second message dealing with the subjects which you discussed in your question.

Repeal of Directive on Military Dependents

Q: In connection, Mr. President, with your statement on the military dependents, is this to be a complete repeal of the existing directive?

The President: Yes.

Enlargement of the Rules Committee

Q: Do you agree with the general assessment that the narrowness of the House vote yesterday on enlarging the Rules Committee means rough going ahead for your legislative program?

The President: Well, the Speaker was successful yesterday and that does mean that the House will have an opportunity to vote on all these bills.

I do think that the House is closely divided on a good many matters which involve legislative proposals, and perhaps the country may be divided, too, but at least we will have a chance to have a vote. And I consider that the most important thing. If the House then doesn't want to support our proposals then at least I feel that the country has indicated its judgment and not the judgment of only a small number of Representatives.

But I would say that we're going to have a close debate in both the House and the Senate on a good many matters and which has always been true if the matters do anything, if they provide for any action, there is bound to be controversy about them. The only way we can get general agreement is when you confine yourself to general statements.

The Budget

Q: Mr. President, will you ask for the same new revenues that Mr. Eisenhower asked for in his Budget Message?

The President: I will. It is a fact, as I suggested in the State of the Union Address, that some of those proposals are generously estimated. For example, I believe that the President's budget calls for a - was it - $900 million deficit in the Post Office; I think the President's budget called for revenue action by the Congress of $843 million. In view of the fact that the Congress has been reluctant in the past I think we have to consider carefully whether we could expect the Congress to ever vote $843 million new revenue on mail and postage.

But nevertheless, we are going to go ahead in general with perhaps - there may be one or two changes but they'll be relatively minor - we are going ahead with the revenue requests of the previous administration.

Q: Have you thought of any new sources of revenue?

The President: We will be discussing the sources of revenue for any additional programs we suggest, because we will with every program we send suggest a source of revenue for it.

The President's Political Philosophy

Q: Mr. President, your predecessor in office called himself a political moderate - said he believed in a middle-of-the-road approach. What do you call yourself politically and how do you define your political philosophy?

The President: Well I don't call myself anything except a Democrat who's been elected President of the United States and I hope I am a responsible President. That's my intention.

Possible Meetings with Foreign Dignitaries

Q: Mr. President, are there plans afoot now for Prime Minister Macmillan or President de Gaulle or any of the others to meet with you personally in the next few months?

The President: I would not be able to answer that because any announcement on proposed visits should be timed with the countries that are involved and we have - we're not able to make that timing at this time.

Inflation

Q: Mr. President, in connection with your references to a sound dollar, will you give us your ideas as to whether there is any danger of inflation?

The President: There has been a steady inflationary rise in - throughout the history of the United States. I'm not able to make any judgment as to what would happen to the cost of living in the next 12 months.

We do have the problem - which is before us - of whether the only way we can prevent any increase in the cost of living is to have five and a half million people unemployed, and have only a limited - and have a substantial percentage of our capacity unused.

The question is whether we can maintain a reasonable balance between increase in purchasing power and the cost of doing business with full employment. That is the basic problem. I'm not satisfied to have the cost of living remain constant only by having the economy restrained.

What I was referring to is that we have no intention - two things: first, we have no intention of devaluing the dollar; secondly, we are concerned with price stability. And in all of the programs that we will put forward we will pay due care to the problem of preventing any stimulation of the economy resulting in an excessive increase in the cost of living.

Criticism of Eisenhower Military Policy

Q: Mr. President, your budget - your State of the Union Message to Congress was taken by some to mean a rather sharp criticism of President Eisenhower's military policy and judgment. Would you care to comment on that?

The President: We are making an assessment of whether the plans we now have for the defense of the United States are matched by the military strength to implement those plans. That preliminary judgment will be finished by the end of February. It may result in some different budget requests and some different command decisions. But until the Secretary of Defense completes that analysis I would not attempt to make any criticisms or suggest that we are going to have to change the plans made by President Eisenhower.

But I do think that the situation grows more serious. The Chinese Communist strength increases. The intervention by the Communists in these critical areas which I mentioned has grown greater and therefore we have to consider whether in the light of this additional threat the strength we now have, not only our nuclear deterrent but also our capacity for limited war, is sufficient. It's not intended as a criticism of any previous action by any previous administration. It merely is an attempt to meet our own responsibilities at this time.

Spending Proposals

Q: Mr. President, when you say that your spending proposals by themselves do not unbalance the budget, can you tell us whether you plan to spend more than Mr. Eisenhower proposed spending in fiscal 1962, and if so, how much more?

The President: I will send to the Congress when the Budget Bureau has completed its analysis our proposals, but they have not been completed as yet.

On Amending Section 315 of the Communications Act

Q: Mr. President, Senator Pastore during hearings held yesterday and today on amending section 315 of the Communications Act, raised the question of whether an incoming presidential candidate would agree to debate a so-called outsider on television. And the present Attorney General in postelection remarks expressed some doubt that one who is already President would agree to debate with one who wants to be president. Could you help us clear the air on this, sir, and tell us whether if you're a candidate in 1964 you would agree to debate?

The President: I would, yes.

Plans for a New Agricultural Program

Q: Mr. President, you described the agricultural problem as one of the most serious in our economy. And yet you didn't speak of it at any length in the State of the Union Message. Could you tell us what your present plans are for a new farm program?

The President: Well, we are going to send to the Congress within the next 7 days, I believe, legislation on feed grains and we're going to send to the Congress within the month of February legislation on wheat. And we are also - we had, of course, the meeting in New York; we had the meeting organized by the Secretary of Agriculture of various farm groups and we had our task force report yesterday on cotton, feed grains, and wheat and I must say that the Secretary of Agriculture is working overtime.

These two matters - feed grains and wheat - we are going to move ahead right away. The situation in cotton is different.

Increase of Price Supports

Q: Mr. President, will you increase price supports?

The President. I think we - I'd better wait until the Secretary of Agriculture sends the bill and we will then at that time announce what our decision will be on controls and also on what the dollar value will be of the price supports.

The Portuguese Liner *Santa Maria*

Q: Mr. President, can you explain what our policy and purpose is in connection with the Portuguese liner Santa Maria *and whether it goes beyond the safety of the passengers and whether you've had any notes from the Portuguese Government in connection with this?*

The President: Well, the Portuguese Government and the Ambassador, of course, have expressed their great interest in securing the control of the ship again. We've been concerned about the lives of the American passengers aboard. There are also other passengers aboard. We're concerned about their lives. We're also well aware of the interests of the Portuguese Government in securing control again of the ship and I'm hopeful that all these interests can be protected.

Now we have no information that the Portuguese Government has protested or threatened us with a withdrawal of our air rights in the Azores. I believe the Portuguese Government also has denied that, but they are most concerned about it and they've made their concern known to us.

Unanticipated Problems

Q: Mr. President, have you encountered any one particular problem in being the President that you had not anticipated?

The President: Well, yes, I've - I think the problem of course is the difficulty in securing the clear response between decisions that we might make here which affect the security of the United States and having them effectively instrumented in the field under varying circumstances. It's easier to sit with a map and talk about what ought to be done than to see it done. But that's perhaps inevitable.

The German and Berlin Question

Q: The Germans are reported to be somewhat unhappy because in your State of the Union Message, in speaking of critical areas, you did not mention Berlin or Germany, and this afternoon when you were talking of critical areas you did not mention Berlin and Germany. Is there any significance to your omission? In other words, last fall you anticipated the possibility of some new crisis in Berlin and Germany in the spring. I'm wondering if there has been some change in the situation that has altered your assessment of it?

The President: No, my view, and I think the United States Government's view, which is the same as the view expressed by the previous administration, remains constant. And it is very difficult to name every area. There is no change in our view on Berlin.

Americans Imprisoned in Cuba and China

Q: Mr. President, there are six Americans who have been convicted to 30 years' imprisonment in Cuba, and there are five Americans who have been jailed for more than 6 years in China. Could you say what efforts the United States might possibly make on behalf - what new efforts the United States might make on behalf of the six in Cuba and the five in Communist China?

The President: Well, we have asked - the Swiss Minister is representing our interest in regard to this trial. We've asked for complete information and we are going to attempt to, within the limits imposed by the nature of the regime in Cuba, to protect the interest of American citizens who are there.

Now, the previous administration on many occasions brought before the Chinese representative - in fact, there were many conversations in Geneva as well as in Warsaw, on the problem of the Americans who have been detained, some of them way back since 1951. This is a matter of continuing concern. And as long as those men are held, it will be extremely difficult to have any kind of normal relations with the Chinese Communists.

There are other matters which affect those relations too. But this is certainly a point of the greatest possible concern.

Now, we have asked for a delay in the meetings which take place in Warsaw, between the United States representative and that of the Chinese Communists, from February to March, because they have become merely a matter of form and nothing of substance happened.

But I'm going to make it very clear that we are concerned about those men in China. The Americans who have been detained in Cuba, and all the circumstances around their arrest, that is a matter which the Swiss Minister is continuing to keep us informed.

The Warsaw Talks

Q: Mr. President, does your statement about the Warsaw talks mean that you propose to have some matters of substance taken up there in March when the talks are resumed, and can you tell us in general what sort of matters you would deal with?

The President: No, it just meant that we had no business to discuss in the February meeting that made the talk at this time worthwhile.

Five-Point Program on Latin America

Q: Mr. President, what sort of reaction have you had from the Latin American countries to the five-point program that you proposed, that you outlined in your State of the Union Message to help the Latin American countries, and could you be a little bit more specific about when you expect your food-for-peace mission to sort of go into action in Latin America?

The President: Well, the food-for-peace mission will be leaving very - in the next few days. We have announced the appointment of Mr. Berle who's had long experience as head of that interdepartmental task force as an assistant to the Secretary. Mr. Berle headed the task force of ours during - between the election and January 20, and I'm very hopeful that under his leadership, of course with the Secretary and the Assistant Secretary, Mr. Mann, that we will be able to implement our commitments to Latin America.[1]

Acceleration of the Missile Program

Q: You said in your State of the Union Message, sir, that you planned to accelerate the missile program. I wonder within that framework if you could say whether that includes the possibility of providing funds in fiscal 1962 to start production on the Nike-Zeus antimissile missile?

The President: Well the Nike-Zeus - there are, of course, funds which have been spent in research on the general area of anti-missile missiles - that is a matter which is now being considered by the Department of Defense and also by the President's Science Advisory Committee - as to whether the amount of money which we are devoting, which is considerable. Unfortunately, in all of these weapons systems the amounts of money that become involved get into the hundreds of millions and then billions, so very careful judgments have to be made. And the - as a matter of fact, I discussed that particular matter with Mr. Weisner yesterday, so I can't give you a more precise answer than to say that we are considering it.

Policy on Juvenile Delinquency

Q: Mr. President, in your State of the Union Message, you spoke of juvenile delinquency. There is growing concern expressed by parents, clergy, and J. Edgar Hoover about the effect on young people of crime and violence in movies and on the air, and the Senate committee is investigating this. Is there anything you can do about it, or may you ask for legislation?

The President: I will have to wait, Mrs. Craig. We - as I said at the time in the State of the Union that we are considering what legislation could be enacted. Now when you get into movies, it's very limited - the amount of influence which the Federal Government can exert is quite limited, as you know - quite properly limited. But at least we are concerned with the general problem.

All the steps we take in urban renewal and housing also affect, of course, the kind of atmosphere, the kind of schools we have, the kind of housing we have, the kind of health conditions we have - all affect the atmosphere in which younger people grow up.

We are very much concerned with that area and we also have - are informed about what the Congress is doing. But this is a matter which goes to the responsibility of the private citizen. The Federal Government cannot protect the standards of young boys or girls - the parents have to do it, in the first place.

We can only play a very supplemental role and a marginal role. So that we can't put that problem on the - Mr. Hoover or on the White House or on the Congress. It rests with the families involved - with the parents involved. But we can do something about the living conditions and the atmosphere in which these children grow up, and we are going to do something about it.

Information to the Public

Q: Mr. President, in your State of the Union Address you said, "I shall withhold from neither the Congress nor the people any fact or report past, present, or future which is necessary for a free and informed judgment of our conduct and hazards." Does this apply, sir, to the Gaither report and will you make that available amongst other studies of a critical nature?

The President: I've been reading the Gaither report. I think there are two matters involved. First, some of its provisions are quite dated and rest on assumptions which are no longer valid. Secondly, some portions of it do involve security information. So that we will make a judgment, I hope, shortly, whether overall it would be possible to release those parts of it which would not adversely affect the security of the United States and which would assist us at our present time.

That is really the question. Does the release of this and the material in it, of a report 3 years old, benefit our security position today and help the people make a judgment on it? And I would have to finish the study of the Gaither report before we give you an answer on that.

New Ambassadors

Q: Mr. President, how soon do you expect to submit to Congress your slate of new ambassadors? I'm thinking of posts like London or Paris.

The President: We are - have of course informed the countries involved and asked for their agreement, which is customary, and as soon as those agreements come back to us we will send the names to the Senate.

Q: Do you plan to do that singly or in a bloc?

The President: As quickly as possible and if we can get the agreements back en bloc we'll send them en bloc.

Reporter: Thank you, Mr. President.

[1] A White House release of February 8 announced the departure of George McGovern, Director, Food for Peace, accompanied by Arthur Schlesinger, Jr., for Argentina and Brazil on February 13. The release also stated that another mission headed by James Symington, Deputy Director, Food for Peace, and Stephen Raushenbush, a staff member, would leave at the same time for discussions in most of the Latin American countries.

THE PRESIDENT'S NEWS CONFERENCE OF

FEBRUARY 8, 1961

The President: Good morning. I have several brief announcements.

One, I would like to announce that I have invited the Prime Minister of Canada, the Right Honorable John G. Diefenbaker, to make a brief visit to Washington, on Monday, February 20, for discussion of matters of mutual interest to our two countries. I particularly am glad he is coming. We will hold a luncheon in his honor at the White House. I think it is most important that harmonious relations exist between two old friends, and therefore I am glad to have this chance to visit with the Prime Minister.

Secondly, I do want to say a word or two about NATO. This is our central and most important defensive alliance, but in the larger sense it is much more. The members of NATO must be leaders also in and out of NATO itself, in such great causes as the integration of Europe and the cooperative development of new nations. We for our part mean to go on as full and energetic partners in NATO, and in particular we wish to maintain our military strength in Europe. Secretary Rusk is making an especially careful study of our policy in this great organization and I am delighted to say that he will have the help not only of Ambassador Finletter, but of an advisory group under the direction of one of the true founders of NATO, a distinguished former Secretary of State, Mr. Dean Acheson.

Three, with the approval of Secretary Ribicoff, I am directing the Surgeon General to organize and establish within the Public Health Service a Child Health Center, to deal with the special health problems of children. This is a matter of particular interest to me. Some 400,000 babies are born each year with congenital malformations. I don't think as a country, nationally, and as a matter of fact I don't think probably privately we have done enough on research into the causes of mental retardation. And while a good deal of effort is being expended in this country for the care of these children, I do think it is most important that we devote special effort in the coming months and years to research in the causes of it. I am therefore delighted that we are going to proceed ahead with Governor Ribicoff's strong support.

QUESTIONS

The Missile Gap

Q: Mr. President, in the past 24 hours there has arisen a somewhat hard to understand situation concerning the missile gap. An official of your adminis- tration, who was identified in some newspapers this morning as Secretary McNamara, has been quoted as saying that the missile gap which was expected and talked about so much did not exist, nor did he see prospects of it. Your press secretary, yesterday afternoon, denied this story. Now, I wonder if you can set the record clear, if you can tell us your version of what Secretary

McNamara said, and what your feelings are about the missile gap. Does it exist, and how and where does it exist?

The President: My only conversation with Mr. McNamara was not at any off-the-record meeting, if such a meeting took place, but was in a conversation which I had with him yesterday afternoon after the reports appeared.

Mr. McNamara stated that no study had been concluded in the Defense Department which would lead to any conclusion at this time as to whether there is a missile gap or not. In addition, I talked this morning to Mr. Hitch, who is the Comptroller of the Defense Department, who has been given the responsibility by the Secretary of Defense to conduct a review of our strategic weapons in the same way that Mr. Nitze is conducting a review of our tactical weapons. Mr. Hitch informed me that no study has been completed on this matter. He hoped to have a preliminary study completed by February 20th, but he did tell me quite specifically that as of today he is not prepared to make a judgment as to our capacity in strategic weapons.

There are many complicated problems involved. We have the realization that the United States will not strike first, and therefore, we have to consider what will be available to the United States if an attack took place upon us, not only in missiles, but also in the other arms of our arsenal, SAC, the Navy, Polaris, and all the rest.

So I think in answer to your question, the study has not been completed. It has not come, therefore, across my desk. There will be a study of how the budget for fiscal 1961 and 1962 should be changed in view of our strategic position, but that study will not be completed by either Mr. Nitze or Mr. Hitch, or come across Mr. McNamara's desk to be passed to me, for some days.

Q: Well, sir, during the campaign you seemed to feel very strongly that a serious missile gap did exist then. Do you now feel as strongly?

The President: Well, what I hope to do is to wait until the Defense Department who I have given this responsibility to, Mr. McNamara, and he has passed the responsibility to members of his department – I hope that we will have a clearer answer to that question. Of course, it is my hope that the United States is fully secure. I will be pleased if that is the result. If it isn't, I think it is important that we know about it, and I will say that we will then – I will then take on the responsibility of passing on to the Congress this collective judgment as to our position and what needs to be done.

So that without getting into the discussion of these stories this morning, I do want to say that it is my information that these studies are not complete and therefore it would be premature to reach a judgment as to whether there is a gap or not a gap.

News Briefings

Q: Mr. President, could you tell us what you think about the wisdom – the idea of these background news briefings where governmental officials do not identify themselves as distinguished from this type of wide-open news conference?

The President: Well, they are hazardous in many cases – (laughter) – and I think our Mr. McNamara might agree with that now. On the other hand, I will say that they are important, too. I'd hope it would be possible to work out some satisfactory system where reporters who are charged with covering matters which are particularly complicated, where they would have a chance to discuss with the responsible official on a background basis so that their stories would be more accurate. I believe there have been such conversations in this administration already and they have been, I think, useful. This one, evidently a controversy has risen from it, but I hope that it will be possible for the responsible officials and the reporters who are particularly concerned with that area, to work out ground rules so that they could be continued.

Meeting of the Heads of NATO

Q: Mr. President, in keeping with your statement about NATO, could you tell us how you would look upon a heads of government meeting of the NATO Council in the near future?

The President: Well, I would not be able to give you a response to that. There is a planned meeting I believe at Oslo, of the foreign ministers, in May. I have seen newspaper reports that it might be turned into a heads of state meeting. But I must say that there has been no judgment reached; I think it is fair to say that the matter is not as yet under consideration.

Danger to the U.S.

Q: Mr. President, you said during one of your recent messages that this Nation was rapidly approaching its hour of maximum danger or peril - I forgot the exact words. Some people have suggested that perhaps you were painting the picture blacker than it is for shock purposes. Could you perhaps spell out for us this morning what you have in mind, and whether you really sincerely feel that we are approaching this peril as you said?

The President: I sincerely believe what I said in my State of the Union Address about our position in the world. I hold this office for the next 4 years, and I believe that the next 4 years will be years in which this country and its capacity to maintain its position and security will be strongly tested. I think that anyone who looks at the globe and looks at the increasing power of the Communist bloc, the belligerency which marks the bloc, particularly the Chinese Communists, I would say would come to the conclusion that we are going to be severely tested in the next 4 years.

Desegregation of Public Schools

Q: Mr. President, 3 months ago a Federal court in New Orleans ordered two public schools there desegregated. Since then, what is apparently an organized campaign of intimidation has kept most white children out of those schools and effectively frustrated the court order.

During the campaign you spoke of using your moral authority as President in the civil rights field. Can you tell us what you plan to say or do to help the New Orleans families who evidently want to obey the Constitution but are afraid to do so?

The President: I will - at such time as I think it is most useful and most effective, I will attempt to use the moral authority or position of influence of the Presidency in New Orleans and in other places. I want to make sure that whatever I do or say does have some beneficial effect and, therefore, it is a matter which we are considering.

Q: But you do not have anything to say specifically about New Orleans to- day or about what has happened there - for example, last week the man who had tried to send his children to school and then in fear left town?

The President: We are going to - I will comment. As far as New Orleans goes, it is my position that all students should be given the opportunity to attend public schools regardless of their race, and that is in accordance with the Constitution. It is in accordance, in my opinion with the judgment of the people of the United States. So there is no question about that.

Now specifically, what we could most usefully do in order to provide an implementation of the court decision in New Orleans, that is a matter which we are carefully considering. On the general question, there is no doubt in my view: students should be permitted to attend schools in accordance with court decisions. The broader question of course is, regardless of the court decisions I believe strongly that every American should have an opportunity to have maximum development of his talents, under the most beneficial circumstances, and that is what the Constitution provides. That is what I strongly believe.

On the question specifically of what we can usefully do in New Orleans in order to provide a more harmonious acquiescence with the court decision, I would feel that we could perhaps most usefully wait until we have concluded our analysis of it.

Oversight of Regulatory Agencies

Q: Mr. President, the Congress has spent a good deal of time investigating regulatory agencies and Executive interference in them. Now, your assistant, Mr. Landis, has suggested that a White House office be set up to oversee these agencies. Do you feel this might lead to the same kind of Executive interference that the Congress has been investigating?

The President: Mr. Landis recommended such a White House office in his study. I have asked Mr. Landis to come to the White House, not to fill such an office, of course, which is not established, but merely to work with the White House and with the interested members of Congress who are concerned about improving our regulatory procedures.

He is going to stay some months and do that. I conferred yesterday with Congressman Harris, who has a special responsibility as Chairman of the House Committee on Interstate and Foreign Commerce, and we are going to continue to work together to try to speed up the procedures of the regulatory agencies and improve their actions.

Whether we should have such a White House liaison or center is a matter which we are going to consider. The Congress bears special responsibility for these agencies, and, therefore, I think it is probably not likely that major responsibility in this area would be released to the White House, and I am not completely sure it is wise.

The Presidential Retreat

Q: Sir, this question is a bit on the personal side. You have available to you at the Catoctin Mountains in Maryland a very fine weekend retreat that has been used by former Presidents. Sir, do you plan to use it and if so, do you plan to rename it back to Shangri-La? And also I believe you have two Government yachts at your disposal. Do you plan to use them, too, sir?

The President: I am not going to use the yachts at the present time. (Laughter) I don't plan to use Camp David very often. Now, I will keep - I think the name should be kept Camp David. But I doubt if I will go there very often. On the question of the yachts, we will have to wait and see what the situation is. I believe we have the Barbara Anne, and I am not familiar with the other yacht.

Acceleration in the Space Program

Q: Mr. President, there is a report from Australia this morning, quoting an American scientist as saying that we will have a man in space within 6 weeks. I wonder if you have ordered an acceleration of our space program, or if you consider it for psychological or other reasons that we are in a race with the Russians to get a man into space?

The President: No, in the first place, I don't know anything about that report. We are very concerned that we do not put a man in space in order to gain some additional prestige and have a man take disproportionate risk, so we are going to be extremely careful in our work and even if we should come in second in putting a man in space, I will still be satisfied if when we finally do put a man in space his chances of survival are as high as I think that they must be.

President's Action in the Rules Fight

Q: Mr. President, it has been rather reliably reported that you and some of your staff members and Cabinet members were quite active on the Hill by phone and otherwise in the recent rules fight. Could you give us your views as to what your activity and that of your Cabinet members and staff members will be in the coming legislative year, as far as getting your program going?

The President: We have a liaison officer, Mr. O'Brien, and he has Mr. Wilson who is liaison for the House and Mr. Manatos who is liaison for the Senate, and we will attempt to keep close contact between the White House and the House and the Senate in order to give our program the best possible chance that it has to pass. So we will keep very close contact with the Hill, and I hope that they will be harmonious.

Developments Prior to a Summit Meeting

Q: You said in the past that the release of the two fliers recently helped in our relations with the Soviet Union. Would you care to outline for us, sir, any developments you might hope to take place prior to any possible future summit meeting with Mr. Khrushchev?

The President: Well, I said that it removed a serious obstacle to harmonious relations with the Soviet Union, the release of the fliers. Mr. Thompson arrives back this week, and I am going to meet with Mr. Thompson on several occasions this week - Saturday morning with Mr. Thompson, Mr. Bohlen and Mr. Kennan - to help chart our future relations with the Soviet Union.

There are some things that I think could usefully be done, and must be done if our relations are going to continue to be fruitful. We are concerned, as I am sure they are, with the situation in Laos. We are concerned with the situation in the Congo, as I am sure they are, and I am hopeful that we can make our position clear to them, and accomplish some useful result.

Recognition of Mexican Americans

Q: Mr. President, the Mexican Americans are very concerned because you have not named one of them to a high place in your administration. They say that they are the only ethnic group that worked for you nationally, in the "Viva Kennedy" clubs and GI forums, that has not been recognized. I wonder if you plan to give them some recognition?

The President: Well, we have, I think, Dr. Garcia, from the State of Texas, who I believe has gone with Ambassador Whitney to Jamaica this weekend. We did offer a position of responsibility to an American of Mexican extraction who was unable to accept it, but it was a position of high responsibility.

I quite agree with you that we ought to use what I consider to be a great reservoir of talent, and I think this is particularly true in our relations with Latin America. So I will just say to you that it is a matter of interest and that we will continue to see if we can provide for - if we can associate them with our administration more closely.

Russian Rocket Launch

Q: Mr. President, last weekend the Russians launched a 7-ton satellite in orbit which they said was a test of a new rocket. This has led to worldwide speculation that there might have been a man aboard. What do we know about this Russian rocket and about the recent rumored Russian attempts to launch a man into space?

The President: Well, I have no information about - that there was a man involved. We have no evidence that there was a man in the rocket. We have, of course, some information, a good deal of which has appeared in the press, about the rocket. And it is a large one and it may be part of their experiments leading up to placing a man in space. But at least as of now we have no evidence that there is a man in there. But I am sure that they will continue these experiments leading up to placing one there.

Presidential Authority Over Domestic Interest Rates

Q: Mr. President, in your message to Congress on the gold problem, there was one passage in there in which you referred to interest rates on foreign funds which had a sentence that might lead to the presumption that perhaps you had in mind submitting legislation which would give you a little more authority over domestic interest rates in other fields. Is this a reasonable conclusion? Do you have any intention to expand the authority of the Presidency with respect to domestic interest rates?

The President: No. As you - we have had consultations with the Federal Reserve Board about what action should be taken to provide that the interest rate on short-term securities would not come down while the interest rate - which does affect the gold flow - while the interest rate on long-term securities remains high, which does adversely affect the economy.

But what, of course, we are interested in is to see the short-term rates remain high enough to protect our gold, while the long-term rates be reduced somewhat in order to stimulate the economy. But this is a matter under the control, of course, directly, of the Federal Reserve Board, with the Treasury having, of course, a direct interest in it.

But it is not intended, to answer your question, that we would propose any legislation or any Executive orders which would increase our control directly over long-term rates.

Nuclear Weapons and NATO

Q: Mr. President, in regard to NATO, have you looked into the problem or the recommendation of the previous administration that NATO be given its own nuclear weapons, or will this be left up to the Acheson group, and when will that group be expected to report?

The President: Well, that was one of the matters, of course, which General Norstad briefly discussed. It is a matter now which is being reviewed by Ambassador Finletter with the aid of Mr. Acheson. That is one of the, I would say, central matters of interest to us now, and both of these men will be working on it.

Q: When will that group report to you, approximately?

The President: I haven't got a time on it, but I think we ought to move with some speed in it.

Atomic Industrial Development by the States

Q: Mr. President, the States now can set their own safety and regulatory standards for atomic industrial development within their own borders. Critics of this do-it-yourself provision believe that it increases the danger of nuclear accidents and favor complete Federal control within these areas. Would you give us your views on it?

The President: Well, I will have to look into it. I am not informed about it.

West German Participation in Aiding Underdeveloped Areas

Q: Sir, in all the discussions about the gold problem, there keeps coming back West Germany doing more of its share in aiding underdeveloped areas and taking on more commitments in the common defense. Is your administration making representations either through the Treasury Department or through our Ambassador to get the Germans to do more in these fields?

The President. Yes.

Q: Could you elaborate on it, sir?

The President: Well, I think that the proposals that have been made, of course, in our opinion do not meet the problem or the opportunity, and I am hopeful that we can work out a more satisfactory arrangement with the West Germans.

Mr. von Brentano is going to be in the United States, the Foreign Minister, in the month of February. I do hope to see him. In addition, we are considering other methods which could put these negotiations on perhaps a more – a higher level.

Q: Just to follow that up, sir, could you spell out what you mean by "higher level"? Are you finding that you are running into problems with them because of their upcoming election?

The President: Well, they have a good many responsibilities and problems of their own. In addition to whatever they do in relation to us they have other responsibilities to the French and the British. So in fairness, I must say the matter is not wholly easy for the Germans. However, it is a matter of great importance and I therefore think it might be useful to provide that these discussions should take place on a higher level than they have in the past.

Success of the Administration

Q: Mr. President, you spoke during the campaign about the need of getting things moving again. I wonder if you could tell us how well you think you have succeeded so far in creating a new mood in Washington?

The President: As far as the domestic economy or as far as generally?

Q: Putting some urgency into it.

The President: Well, I think we have talented people in our Washington group who are giving it a great deal of time and attention. And therefore I am hopeful - though we have been in office only 2½ weeks - I am hopeful that before the snow is off the ground that we will have been able to stimulate action in a variety of areas.

Morality in Private and Public Business

Q: Mr. President, in your State of the Union Address, you remarked that morality in private business has not been sufficiently spurred by morality in public business. In the light of the economy-sized malpractice revealed by-carried on by some of the American leading corporations, would you care to comment on this situation and the impact of such private business morality or immorality on the community itself?

The President: Well, having participated in the investigation of improper practices in the labor-management field for 2 or 3 years, and having had a good deal of public attention given to it, I am hopeful that the Department of Justice, the Antitrust Division which was very effectively led in recent months, and other agencies of the Government will concern - and the Congress - will concern itself about the problem of conflicts of interest and monopolistic practices, as well as even more illicit practices conducted in the American business community. And I hope that the business community itself will consider what steps it could take in order to lift this shadow from its shoulders.

Q: Do you feel, sir, that perhaps business might well establish codes of ethical practice such as the trade unions have established?

The President: Yes. I am hopeful that the unions will live up to these ethical practices which state a very high standard for them; and I think it would be very beneficial if business groups today would consider what they could do to protect themselves from charges of conflicts of interest of the kind that we have recently seen, and also of the effort made by these large electrical companies to defraud the Government. And I must say I would be interested to watch what progress they can make in that area.

Admiral Burke's Speech and Appeasement and Unnecessary Friction

Q: Mr. President, Admiral Burke's speech was originally checked out and cleared of certain things which I believe Mr. Salinger said might have been sources of unnecessary friction with the Soviet Union. Some Republicans in Congress charged that this was appeasement. Could you sketch in for us the rather difficult ground between appeasement and "unnecessary friction"?

The President: No. All I would say is that I would hope that those who made speeches in the area of national security, Chiefs of Staff and others, and all others, would attempt to have those speeches coordinated with the Department of State and with the White House, so that we can make sure that those speeches represent national policy. I must say it seems to me that Theodore Roosevelt set a very good standard for us all, and one which I hope this administration will follow by speaking softly and maintaining ——

Cooperative Action with Other American Republics

Q: Mr. President, on Monday Mr. Rusk said that the United States was prepared to take cooperative action with the other American Republics to end tyranny, he said, against either the left or the right. Is it contemplated that we shall ask the other American States to join with us in some steps on the Cuban problem?

The President: The Cuban problem and the problem of tyranny throughout all of Latin America is a matter which is of course of special concern to Mr. Berle and his group - interdepartmental group - and they have not concluded their analysis as yet.

A New Cuban Radio Station

Q: Mr. President, Castro is reported to have built a new radio station, one of the largest in the hemisphere, which will begin operations within a few months to broadcast pro-Castro propaganda throughout Latin America. Is there anything we can do or plan to do to counter this?

The President: We are giving the matter of Cuba and its export of its revolution throughout Latin America a matter of high priority. I could not state what actions will be taken yet until Mr. Berle, Mr. Mann, and Mr. Rusk have concluded their deliberations, which are now going ahead very intensively.

Presidential Power to Cut Tax Rates

Q: Mr. President, one of your task forces recommended that you be given discretionary power within limits to cut tax rates as a counter-cyclical device. Can you tell us what you think of this idea?

The President: Well, in 1958 there were two proposals to cut taxes. One was made in March and I believe the other was made in June. I voted against it in March and voted for it in June, because it seemed to be, according to the economists I talked to, to be helpful. As you remember, I don't think it got more than 23 or 24 votes. The recession was serious and we ended up with a $12 billion deficit. Now we are going to take another look at the economy in April and make a judgment at that time whether we can expect an upturn in the spring or in the summer.

I will say that I am not convinced at the present time that Congress would entertain that proposal, and I would not make it at the present time because I do think we should have more experience and more perspective on the state of the economy before making a proposal which is quite far-reaching, and which would cost the Federal budget perhaps $4 or $5 billion, which is a serious matter and which would limit, perhaps, our ability to go ahead with other programs which in the long run may be more useful. If you have a tax cut, it may be 6 months, if the Congress should grant it, and you lose $5 billion, which is put back into the economy and expended. With $5 billion or $3 billion devoted to education or health or international security, you can produce a longer range result. So that this is a matter which must be considered from various perspectives. In any case, in April we will try to make another judgment on the state of the economy. What I am concerned about is that the economy will move along, using less than capacity, and it is extremely difficult to take steps which will provide quickly for it to operate at full capacity.

What we are concerned about is that with the tremendous increase in automation that it's possible for business profits to remain substantial and yet for employment to lag. The fact that the steel companies were able to maintain rather substantial profits at a time when they are operating at less than 50 percent of capacity does indicate the kind of problem we face with a good many more than 100,000 steel workers out of work.

In answer to your question specifically, we will come back to what further steps could be taken in April, but I do hope that the Congress will act on the proposals we have now made, which involve most especially the unemployment compensation payments and also the distressed area payments, as well as some improvements in social security. If we could move ahead on those we could get a better idea of perhaps what action should be taken in April.

Crisis in Laos

Q: Mr. President, the fighting in Laos is continuing. The Soviet airlift is now 2 months old. The Soviet answer to the proposal to revive the International Control Commission has been delayed for some weeks. I wonder if you can tell us how long this Government is prepared to wait before it proposes some new action to resolve this continuing crisis.

The President: There will be a meeting at the White House this afternoon on the subject of Laos and what new action we should now take. And I am hopeful that some proposal will be forthcoming from that meeting.

President's Position on Gerrymandering

Q: Mr. President, many States are now re-forming their congressional districts as a result of the 1960 census and inevitably this leads to charges of gerrymandering directed at both parties. Can you tell us where you stand on Chairman Celler's bill to control gerrymandering to a certain extent by such devices as making districts be contiguous and control a certain population within a State?

The President: Well, even if you could pass those proposals you could still have a good deal of gerrymandering. I represented a district which was about 5 to 1 Democratic, which was contiguous, which was geographically associated with an adjoining district, which was marginally Republican. Now it is very difficult for the Congress or for the Federal Government to enforce standards. What should have happened, of course, is probably under some standards is those two districts cut in a different way which would have provided instead of one Republican Congressman with a very marginal majority, while the Democratic Congressman got 5 to 1, it probably would have ended up with two Democratic Congressmen, which may or may not have been in the public interest. (Laughter)

But I do think it is very difficult for us to try to draw these lines. There isn't any doubt that they are unsatisfactorily drawn, not only for the Congress, which is not the worst offender, but the State legislatures, where we have very – and have had for many years – notorious examples of gerrymandering, but which is a responsibility for the States, not the Federal Government.

In any case, I am not familiar wholly with Congressman Celler's proposal and exactly what his standards will be, but I will look at it.

Q: Mr. President, in that same connection, could you tell us where you stand or do you have a position on increasing the size of the House of Representatives?

The President. Well, it is 435 Members now, which is a large body. Congressman Chelf and I believe other Congressmen have proposed increasing it, I think to 450. I will discuss that matter with Speaker Rayburn and get his views as well as the leadership of the House on both sides.

Reporter: Thank you Mr. President.

THE PRESIDENT'S NEWS CONFERENCE OF

FEBRUARY 15, 1961

The President: I have several statements to make first, and then I will be glad to submit to questions.

Ambassador Stevenson in the Security Council today has expressed fully and clearly the attitude of the United States Government towards the attempts to undermine the effectiveness of the United Nations organization. The United States can take care of itself, but the United Nations system exists so that every nation can have the assurance of security. Any attempt to destroy this system is a blow aimed directly at the independence and security of every nation, large and small.

I am also, however, seriously concerned at what appears to be a threat of unilateral intervention in the internal affairs of the Republic of Congo. I find it difficult to believe that any government is really planning to take so dangerous and irresponsible a step. Nevertheless, I feel it important that there should be no misunderstanding of the position of the United States in such an eventuality.

The United States has supported and will continue to support the United Nations presence in the Congo. The United States considers that the only legal authority entitled to speak for the Congo as a whole is a government established under the Chief of State, President Kasavubu, who has been seated in the General Assembly of the United Nations by a majority vote of its members. The broadening of the government under President Kasavubu is a quite legitimate subject of discussion, and such discussions have been going on in Leopoldville and in New York. But the purported recognition of Congolese factions as so-called governments in other parts of that divided country can only confuse and make more difficult the task of securing Congolese independence and unity.

The United Nations offers the best, if not the only possibility for the restoration of conditions of stability and order in the Congo.

The press reports this afternoon that Prime Minister Nehru has stated, and I quote, "If the United Nations goes out of the Congo, it will be a disaster." I strongly agree with this view. Only by the presence of the United Nations in the Congo can peace be kept in Africa.

I would conceive it to be the duty of the United States and, indeed, all members of the United Nations to defend the Charter of the United Nations by opposing any attempt by any government to intervene unilaterally in the Congo.

Secondly, I have a statement that we have today recognized the Government of El Salvador. It has announced its determination to bring about free and democratic elections in that country, and it seeks solutions for the economic and social difficulties which that country has faced. These objectives are in consonance with our goal of a free and prosperous Latin America. Manifestos of the government and its agencies have indicated a clear determination to improve the standard of living of the people of that country, particularly those engaged in agriculture. We hope to be able to assist El Salvador in reaching these goals under the spirit of the act of Bogota.

Thirdly, this country is most concerned about the very serious problem of unemployment which we have faced this winter and the more than five and a half million Americans who want to work and can't find a job.

We are particularly concerned about the more than 600,000 Americans who have exhausted their unemployment compensation checks and who are now on relief. We have sent to the Congress a program which we believe would be of assistance to the country and to them this winter. We do, as you know, provide for an extension of unemployment compensation benefits for those who have exhausted their benefits. We provide aid to unemployed workers. Today under the law a child of a worker who is out of work can only receive necessary assistance if his family splits up. We would correct that situation.

We sent a program up for aid to distressed areas.

We have sent up legislation to the Hill which will provide for an increase in social security benefits, and it will be followed by other programs as time goes on.

We have also provided for Executive action increasing the amount of food available in those areas of the United States where people live on these food packages.

I hope that we can get action on these programs as soon as possible. Today the Ways and Means Committee of the House held hearings on our program to extend unemployment compensation benefits. I am hopeful that we can move forward this winter so that some relief can be given to our fellow Americans.

In order to provide a stimulus to our economy I have provided, with the cooperation of the departments of the Government, for a speedup in programs using funds now available. Over $250 million, as we have said, will be distributed immediately under the GI dividend program. There are $4 billion for tax refunds which are coming due. As soon as those who are available for these refunds can put their applications in, we will attempt to stimulate and improve and quicken distribution of these funds.

We provided under the instructions given through the State of the Union Address for $700 million, committed this month for additional Polaris submarines and airlift capacity. In addition, we are providing through the Post Office a speedup in the programs to build post offices which had been authorized and approved by the Congress previously; but these programs would be developed in a more concentrated period than they would otherwise have been.

For farmers we have provided $75 million additional for loans to speed spring planting costs and also for farm home loans.

For the Federal highway construction program we are going to make $734 million to be available to the States this month. This program of course calls for action by the States and the local bodies. And we are sending, tonight, telegrams to all the State Governors asking if they also can provide for speedup in their programs.

I want to make it clear that we are going to continue to work in cooperation with the Governors and the Congress, all agencies of the Government, because we want to see the American economy get back on its feet. We want to see these people working again.

In addition, the Small Business Administration plans to increase by 25 percent the criteria for what small businesses there are that are eligible for defense contracts. By increasing this criteria we will make other small businesses eligible who happen to be in areas where there is high unemployment.

I am hopeful that these programs will all be of assistance. Mr. Goldberg's tour showed that in States like Michigan, nearly 350,000 people are out of work; 12 percent of the people in Gary, Ind. - over 200,000 steel workers; and they need our help.

I will be glad to answer any questions.

QUESTIONS

Impact of the Congo on Soviet-American Relations

Q: Mr. President, regarding the situation in the Congo and the crisis precipitated there by the Soviet Union, could you evaluate the impact on Soviet-American relations and your hopes that they might be improving?

The President: This statement was carefully drawn and represents the policy of the United States at this time on these matters, and I am going to confine myself, in all questions on the Congo, to the statement that we have made. I think this is the most effective way to deal with it.

Q: Mr. President, in a related field, however, Mr. Khrushchev this afternoon, I think in a message replying to you, said that he welcomed your proposal that you voiced in the State of the Union Message for pooling American-Soviet efforts in space exploration projects. Do you think this sort of pooling and cooperation you envisioned in your State of the Union Message will still be possible under the tense conditions that developed in the U. N. today?

The President: I hope it will be possible for the relations between the United States and the Soviet Union to develop in such a way that the peace can be protected and that it will be possible for us to use our energies along peaceful and productive and fruitful lines.

The development of space, preventing outer space from being used as a new area of war, of course, is of the greatest possible concerned to the people of this country. I am hopeful that it will be possible, if relations between our two countries can be maintained, can be channeled along peaceful lines; I am hopeful that real progress can be made this year. But it is my earnest hope that our relations can remain harmonious and that it will be possible for us to cooperate in peaceful ventures rather than be differing on matters which carry with them such hazards.

Meeting With Premier Khrushchev

Q: Along this line, sir, could you tell us how you would feel about a meeting at some time in the next few weeks or months with Mr. Khrushchev? Do you think it would be helpful or if it should be delayed?

The President: There are no plans nor have there been any plans for any meeting with Mr. Khrushchev. As I said earlier, I have not heard whether Mr. Khrushchev is planning to come to the United Nations meeting. There are no other plans for a meeting at this time.

President's Feelings About Recession

Q: Mr. President, you addressed a conference of businessmen here early this week and one of the officials of that conference noticed afterwards with some satisfaction that you hadn't used the word recession. He said he thought this was a good thing because in fact there was no business recession. Was your omission because you agreed with him or how do you feel about the word and about the economic situation?

The President: As you know, if you are unemployed and out of a job you think there is a recession. If you are working, perhaps the impact of the

economic slowdown doesn't hit you quite as hard. I think we have been in a
recession for some months and that we have not recovered fully from the
recession of '58, which is a matter, of course, of great concern.

We are concerned because while there was an economic slowdown in '49, and
'54, and '58, we now have an economic slowdown only 2 years after the '58
recession. So this compounds our difficulties. I think that - well, to - to
put it precisely to things, then I would call this a recession.

President's Comments About Admiral Burke

*Q: In line, sir, with your statement a moment ago that you hoped that the
relations between United States and Russia would improve, Admiral Arleigh Burke
is quoted in some newspapers today in an interview in which he makes some
rather sharp comments on American and Russian relations and among other things
says that the United States Navy would sail into the Black Sea if it so chose.
I am asking, sir, is this in line with your administration policy that all
high officials should speak with one voice?*

The President: I have been informed - and perhaps Mr. Salinger can correct
me - that that interview was given on January 12, which was before the administration took over January 20 and before we gave any indication that we would
like all statements dealing with national security to be coordinated. I would
say that this makes me happier than ever that such a directive has gone out.
(Laughter)

Trade Policy Toward Cuba

*Q: Mr. President, I would like to change the scene here to Cuba, if I may,
for a moment. A member of Congress has raised the issue of possible conflict
in our trade policy towards Cuba. He points out that under President Eisenhower's order all exports from this country to Cuba were barred. On the other
hand, we are now importing considerable quantities of Cuban goods. Specifically this member of Congress pointed out one liquor company has purchased
$12 million of Cuban molasses. Also we are importing considerable quantities
of Cuban fruit and vegetables. Have you done anything about it or are you
looking into this matter or contemplate doing anything about it?*

The President: The molasses has not been purchased as yet. It was
intended, as I understand, to be purchased during the next month, and that is
a private transaction. There are seventy, I think, or eighty million dollars
worth of fruit, tobacco, and so on which are coming in, mostly to Florida.
We are now making a study of what would be the most beneficial action we could
take in regard to that.

On molasses there is some question as to under what conditions we could
intervene in that transaction, but, of course, it has been my hope that that
transaction would not be consummated. I am not convinced that we are totally
without resources and we are considering what we could take to consider that
particular transaction. Twelve million dollars, I believe, is supposed to be
made into gin - and I am not sure that that is in the public interest.
(Laughter)

Space Gap Between the USSR and the U. S.

*Sir, on the space probe towards Venus made by the Soviets recently, do you
think this would point up any space gap between our two countries, and do you
see there is any need for a speedup in our efforts in that field?*

The President: The Soviet Union, as I said in the State of the Union, of
course, is ahead of us in boosters and there is an indication they are going

to be ahead of us for some time to come. This was, as I said in my statement at the time, this is a scientific achievement that is an impressive one. We have made exceptional gains in space technology, which may not be as dramatic as Sputnik or as a probe to Venus but which in the long run does, at least I think should, give all Americans satisfaction in the efforts that we have made.

Boosters, however, we are behind on and it is a matter of great concern. The Soviet Union made significant breakthrough in this area some years ago. They have continued to maintain their lead, and it explains why they were ahead of us in Sputnik and it explains why they have been able to put larger objects into space. We have to recognize their chances of continuing to do that unless we are able to make a breakthrough before the Saturn booster comes into operation. Unless we are able to make a scientific breakthrough we have to recognize that we are in a position - secondary position on boosters. It is a matter of great concern. We have sufficiently large boosters to protect us militarily, but for the long, heavy exploration into space, which requires large boosters, the Soviet Union has been ahead and it is going to be a major task to surpass them.

Status of the Dollar

Q: Mr. President, this is a question on the sound dollar. A relative of yours, a Republican relative, Mr. Bayard Auchincloss of Oklahoma City, has started a one-man campaign to regain - to restore the sound dollar. He has said that the public needs to be inspired by some forceful leadership in Washington to lead them in one major phase - and that is: fighting Government waste. Sir, do you propose to spark such leadership from the White House, or do you have other means in mind by which the public can assist you in regaining the sound dollar?

The President: Well, I don't want to deny kinship. But I - to the best of my knowledge, he is not related to me.

Q: Your step-second cousin. (Laughter)

The President: Well, then he is related to me. But we have not met; I have not heard from him directly. We want to - as a matter of fact, several members of the Congress - I was Chairman of the Subcommittee on Government Reorganization which attempted to put through some of the Hoover Commission recommendations - we are going to continue to work with a smaller staff beginning, of course, from the White House. And I am hopeful that all members of this Government will not consider now that they have been placed in position of responsibility that the test of their good work is the size of their staff. We are going to continue to try and will seek the cooperation of every citizen of this country in making sure that we get value for every dollar that the Government spends.

The Government spends a great deal of money. In fact, I asked, yesterday, Mr. Bell to talk to Senator Douglas and Congressman Hebert, who conducted hearings on waste in the Pentagon and have suggested it might be possible to save more than $1 billion, to meet with them. And we are going to continue to meet with every citizen, whether he is my relative or not - I would be glad to hear from Mr. Auchincloss. It is an important problem. When the Government spends over $80 billion we know we can do a better job in spending that money more wisely. And I would be delighted and I welcome the view of Mr. Auchincloss or any other citizen and all members of this administration to try to maintain a balance between revenue and expenditures.

Distribution of Surplus Food

Q: Mr. President, in regard to your program to distribute surplus foods to needy people in other countries, 2 weeks ago Dr. Fry, who is head of the World Council of Churches, advocated that this be done through Government channels and not through church or other private agencies. He said that the private agencies just can't insure that the food is going to reach the most needy, which our Government regulations require. Has your administration formulated a policy on this, or do you have a comment on it?

The President: Well, of course some does go through the governments and then we have relied upon private agencies. I would be very reluctant to abandon private agencies because they have done a first-class job in assisting us to get this food out.

I would be glad to see his comments and see what his suggestions would be. The alternative, of course, would be for us to distribute through the government involved, and we have never felt that that was better than having it done through voluntary groups. But Mr. McGovern is now in Latin American and he is looking at what we can do in that area, in food for peace, and I am sure that he will come back with some proposals on how we can make this distribution more effective.

Q: May I just say, excuse me, sir, Dr. Fry does not suggest clothing and so forth - he still wants that which is contributed voluntarily to be distributed through the church. But just our Government surplus food.

The President: We will look into that.

Possibility of State Department Collusion in the
Failure of the Cuban Operation

Q: Mr. President, have you determined whether any employee of our State Department was responsible or had any part in advancing the Communist foothold in Cuba, and if so, sir, will you take steps to remove them from office?

The President: I think that probably miscalculations were made by our country in assessing in Cuba, but I have no evidence that anyone did it out of any other motive than to serve the United States.

Arms Control Negotiations

Q: Mr. President, to clarify an earlier answer you made, is it your view that we can proceed in serious negotiations with the Soviet Union in such areas as arms control and nuclear test ban while they continue to agitate the situation in the United Nations and in the Congo? In other words, can we conduct relations with them in compartments?

The President: I am hopeful that all countries that are members of the United Nations will make a determination to operate in the Congo through the United Nations. I think that that is essential. As I said in my statement, unilateral intervention by one country or a group of countries outside of the United Nations, would endanger the United Nations and endanger peace in Africa. I am hopeful that that will come to be the judgment of all members of the United Nations. And if it does, I think that we will find ourselves with the prospects of peace increased.

Regarding the Economic Recession

Q: Following up Mr. Kent's question, Mr. President, the Republican Party as a whole seems to also take the view that your administration has overstated the economic recession. I wonder, sir, if you have given any thought to conferring with the Republican leaders in Congress in hopes of getting their support for your program to solve the economic recession, and if you have made available to them all the information that your administration has on the economic situation?

The President: To answer your second part, we have made available all the information that we have. I have described it. Everyone can look at these figures and come to the conclusion that - their own conclusion. I see no necessity or desirability of minimizing our problems. I think only by facing the problems with precision is it possible to get action.

I want the cooperation of the leadership on both sides and will make every effort that I can to seek the support of Members of the House and Senate on both sides of the aisle. But anyone who looks at the million cars in inventory today, who looks at the figures on unemployment, who looks at the steel capacity - who looks at the 600,000 Americans who have exhausted their unemployment compensation, who looks at five and a half million Americans who are out of work, who looks at our decline in economic growth since last spring, I would say would come to the same conclusion that I have: that it is necessary for us to take action.

The fact that a judgment was made the last year about what 1960 would be - 1960 was not the most prosperous year in our history as had been estimated earlier. We are now - find ourselves obliged to take action this winter. And by calling it a recession or calling it - saying it is not a recession, calling it a plateau - that's no excuse for not taking action. In my opinion it is essential that we move forward this winter because we don't want to find ourselves in the winter and the spring and the summer debating about our problem of whether we are in an economic recession or whether we have an economic decline and finding at the end of the congressional session that no action has been taken, only that all of my statements have had impact, I believe, of a snowflake in the Potomac, which was the description used by a distinguished Member of the Congress. I hope they have more effect than that.

President's Position on Distressed Areas

Q: Mr. President, your task force on distressed areas considers an independent agency with an administrator directly responsible to you the most efficient way of coping with this urgent problem. They are fearful that it might get fragmented if it were made a bureau in the Commerce Department. Do you have any objection to the creation of an independent agency under your authority?

The President: I believe that it would be most advantageous to have it in the Department of Commerce with all of the resources of the Department of Commerce to supplement its work. That would be my first choice. If the Congress makes a different judgment, however, I would accept that and say that an independent agency would be useful. But I do think that with Governor Hodges, who is committed to the program, with a Cabinet officer to represent their views at Cabinet meetings, and with the broad range of responsibilities which the Department of Commerce has, that this is the best place to put it. But this is a matter on which I would certainly listen to the Congress if they came to a different conclusion.

Troop Commitments to the U. N.

Q: Mr. President, if other nations become reluctant to assign troops to the U. N. for police work in the Congo, would you tell us whether we would consider contributing American units?

The President: Well, we are now hopeful that the policy which the Secretary General has followed, of securing troops for the Congo from Africa and Asia - we are hopeful that that is going to be successful. And until that fails - I don't think we should go under any assumption that he is going to fail, and if he does fail then we will have to make a new judgment. But I am hopeful that those countries which are most involved with maintaining the security and independence of the African countries and peace in Africa, that they will continue to respond to the Secretary General's appeal for support. And that is also true, of course, of Asian nations who are also concerned, particularly the smaller countries. We hope that they can maintain control of troop movements and not begin to have troops from larger countries with all of the hazards that that might bring.

Future Developments in the Congo

Q: Mr. President, in view of your remarks about the Congo and other world problems, do you regard the future developments in the Congo as a kind of good faith test for the prospect of improving the international atmosphere as a whole?

The President: Well, of course, if we fail - if the United Nations fails in the Congo, if we who are members of the United Nations fail, then of course the future usefulness of the United Nations will be impaired. And I think that this would be particularly serious for smaller countries.

As I said in my statement, the United States is not a small country. We can defend ourselves. Countries which I think must rely particularly upon the United Nations are smaller countries. The smallest country in the United Nations has the same vote in the General Assembly as the Soviet Union and the United States. And therefore I would think that they would be reluctant to see the United Nations fragmented, to see its usefulness impaired, to see the authority of the Secretary General, who represents all the members of the United Nations, to see it lessened. So I regard this as a most important test of the future effectiveness of the United Nations.

Liabilities of Membership in the U. N.

Q: Mr. President, do you find that the United States as a great power, as you have described, with legitimate interests all around the world, is sometimes hampered in the pursuit of these national interests by its membership in the United Nations? Could you conceive of a situation perhaps in Latin America where we would be hampered in a place where we had a vital interest by United Nations action?

The President: Well, I suppose it is possible always to conceive of situations, but I will say that the United Nations action in - for example, the fact that they maintained troops in the Gaza Strip for a number of years, I think, has been helpful in maintaining peace in that area. And the Congo has been an extremely difficult assignment and responsibility for the United Nations. But at least we have not had as yet massive unilateral intervention by great powers with all of the risks of war that that might bring, and with all the dangers to the peace that that might bring, because of the way the United Nations has met its responsibilities. So, I am a strong believer in the United Nations and while it is possible to say that they might interfere with some legitimate interest of ours in the future, I am prepared to say that their actions in the past, at present, and I believe in the future represent the legitimate common interest of all members of the United Nations.

Reporter: Thank you Mr. President.

The President: Thank you.

THE PRESIDENT'S NEWS CONFERENCE

MARCH 1, 1961

The President: I have three or four announcements which I will make.

We have extended an invitation to the Chancellor, German Chancellor Adenauer, to come to the United States, and he has accepted our invitation, and we are delighted that he is going to be here in Washington on April 12th and April 13th. I am looking forward very much to meeting him and having an exchange of views.

Secondly, I am writing to the Congress, to Congressman Vinson and to Senator Russell, a letter recommending that they consider legislation to restore former President Eisenhower to his military rank of General of the Army. President Eisenhower's outstanding military record and his long public service to our country in war and peace, I think, with that long experience it would be an appropriate act by the Congress if they should restore him to his former military rank.

Third, it is with some satisfaction that I am able to announce that the week ending today is the first week since last July that there has been no net outflow of gold from this country to foreign countries. While we realize that this complete halt is only temporary, I believe it does signify the confidence in the dollar throughout the world is being restored.

Fourth, our objective now is to help make effective at the retail level the influence of the Federal Reserve on the wholesale supply of money. We intend first to facilitate the flow of mortgage funds into the hands of prospective home buyers. I have requested Mr. Joseph McMurray, Chairman Designate of the Home Loan Bank Board, to meet with leaders in the savings and loan field, and to urge them to reduce mortgage rates so as to expand the flow of money into mortgages. His first such mission will be to California, where mortgage rates have been among the highest. We trust that his efforts here and around the country will mean real gains for home owners, the housing industry, and the economy.

And lastly, I have today signed an Executive order providing for the establishment of a Peace Corps on a temporary pilot basis. I am also sending to Congress a message proposing authorization of a permanent Peace Corps. This corps will be a pool of trained men and women sent overseas by the United States Government or through private institutions and organizations, to help foreign countries meet their urgent needs for skilled manpower. It is our hope to have between five hundred and a thousand people in the field by the end of this year. We will send Americans **abroad** who are qualified to do a job. We will send those abroad who are committed to the concept which motivates the Peace Corps. It will not be easy. None of the men and women will be paid a salary. They will live at the same level as the citizens of the country which they are sent to, doing the same work, eating the same food, speaking the same language. We are going to put particular emphasis on those men and women who have skills in teaching, agriculture, and in health.

I am hopeful it will be a source of satisfaction to Americans and a contribution to world peace.

QUESTIONS

Reappraisal of Defense Strategy

Q: Mr. President, you said in your State of the Union Message that you had ordered a reappraisal of our entire defense stragegy and that you would ask the Secretary of Defense to give you his conclusions by the end of February. Can you tell us what any of these conclusions are and would they involve any increased reliance on conventional as opposed to nuclear force?

The President: The Secretary of Defense has passed to me his conclusions, and at the end of, I would say, about 2 weeks I will have finished our study of it, my study of it, with him, and will then send our recommendations to the Congress.

Secondly, in answer to your question, part of his recommendation is to strengthen conventional forces.

Views on Economic Upturn

Q: Mr. President, some economists have voiced the opinion that perhaps the recession has reached a rockbottom and that the economy is on an upturn. Would you give us your views about that, and also answer some suggestions in your political opposition that perhaps some of your anti-recession legislation may not be needed because of this expected upturn?

The President: Well, I hope that an upturn does take place, but I must say that I think the Department of Commerce today is going to release some statistics and figures which do not indicate that an upturn is taking place as yet.

I would say there are still a great many hundreds of thousands of Americans who are dependent upon unemployment compensation. There are many – several millions of Americans who can't find work. Members of Congress and others with whom I have talked report from various sections of the country that they still face a most serious situation. I think it would be premature to make a judgment that our economy is on the rise and that therefore there's no necessity for action. I don't take that view at all. I think all of these programs are needed.

And I am hopeful that it will be possible – I am hopeful that we will see the economy move up in the spring and summer, but we can make no predictions about it. And there's not sufficient evidence at hand yet by any Government department to indicate an upturn has taken place as of today.

Situation in the Congo

Q: Mr. President, under the present U. S. troop command in the Congo, the pro-Communist Gizenga Government seems to be gaining ground, expanding its influence there almost daily. Is this Government satisfied with the conduct of that command and, if not, have we made any representations to Secretary Hammarskjold about it?

The President: Well, the situation is very uncertain in the Congo and it is not possible to wholly accept the premise upon which your question was based.

The United Nations resolution and, therefore, the new mandate given to the Secretary, is really only a week old. I am hopeful that the resolution will be carried out effectively. We are going to continue to concern ourselves, as members of the United Nations, with its successful implementation.

Role of Sargent Shriver in the Peace Corps

Q: Mr. President, what is the role of Mr. Sargent Shriver in the Peace Corps, sir?

The President: He has been working in organizing the Peace Corps.

Q: Will he continue in this - will he head it now that it is set up?

The President: Well, we are going to make a judgment about who will be the head and what its staff will be in several days. He has been working on a voluntary basis up to this time.

Withholding of Federal Funds from Universities

Q: Mr. President, back in January the Civil Rights Commission recommended that Federal funds be withheld from public colleges and universities that discriminate on grounds of race, religion, or national origin. How do you feel about this?

The President: Well, it is not part of the - this matter, this recommendation, as you know, is not included in the legislation that we sent to the Congress. As to whether we should by Executive order withhold funds from certain schools, that is a matter which is under consideration. It will be for - as a part of our general overall study of where the Federal Government might usefully place its power and influence to expand civil rights.

We hope in the next few days to have an Executive order forthcoming which will strengthen the employment opportunities, both in and out of the Government, for all Americans, and it will be followed as time goes on with other actions by the Federal Government to expand employment possibilities.

One of the areas which is being considered, of course, is the field of education; another is the field of housing. There are a great many areas where action might be taken. The one that will be taken first will be in the field of employment.

Food to Hungry People

Q: It has been suggested, Mr. President, that when we give food to hungry people in other countries, we put it into an international pool so they will not know where it comes from. My question is, if our system can produce an overabundance of food, and the Communist system is not able to produce enough sometimes for their own people, why should we not advertise this to the world and label it, "A gift of the American people"?

The President: Well, I think we should. And Mr. McGovern informed me - one of the matters I discussed with him was this question, and he told me that in his trip through Brazil, that on all the food that he saw being distributed which had originated in the United States there was clearly marked on it, "A gift of the people of the United States," which I was glad to hear.

The Algerian Peace Talks

Q: Mr. President, there is a great deal of interest abroad in your atti-tude and feeling toward the Algerian peace talks that are going on now. Would you comment, please, on what progress you feel might be made?

The President: Well, I would hope that they are fruitful.

Limitation on the Import of Fuel

Q: New England would like to know, sir, if your administration is going to take the limits off of the imports of residual fuel oil?

The President. Well, as you know, the Secretary of the Interior recently provided for an increase in the importation of oil or residual fuel oil, which I hope will be helpful.

Q: Do you think he will take the limits off completely? They say that is not sufficient to help New England.

The President: Well, we have to consider the needs of the coal industry and the domestic producers, the needs of New England, and we are trying to reach a balance which will protect the public interest.

One matter which has concerned me, of course, has been the sharp increase, 12 percent, in the cost of fuel in the East and Northeast United States. That increase has seem excessive and, as you know, several agencies of the Government are now investigating to find out what was the cause of that, what I would con-sider to be an excessive increase.

But in answer to your question, we are attempting to reach a balance.

Nomination of Charles Meriwether

Mr. President, on the nomination of Charles Meriwether, is there anything in this man's background that might embarrass your administration?

The President: No, I have sent Mr. Meriwether's name up there after reading the FBI report and other records.

Responsibilities of the Vice President

Q: Mr. President, there is a report that Vice President Johnson is setting up a special office across the street from yours. Does this indicate, sir, that you plan to place before him broader, perhaps unprecedented, Executive responsibilities?

The President: Well, we have already indicated that he is going to have special responsibilities in the field of space. We are going to recommend to the Congress shortly that the space agency be reconstituted, with the Vice President instead of the President as chairman. In addition, he will have responsibilities in the field of employment opportunities. And also he is concerned - as a member for many years of the Armed Services Committee of the Senate as well as Chairman of the Subcommittee on Preparedness, he has been concerned with national security matters generally. And, therefore, it would seem to me appropriate that he would have some offices in the Executive Office Building so that he could meet these responsibilities most effectively.

Public Response on Government Waste Question

Q: Mr. President, what sort of a response have you gotten from ordinary citizens as a result of your appeal a couple of weeks ago for ordinary people to write in about examples of waste in the Government spending that they have noticed, and have you any other examples which you could tell us about besides the $2,000 officers' club - $20,000; excuse me.

The President: We have received some letters, and their recommendations are being investigated to find out if the facts are as they state them. But we have none to announce as yet. The investigations haven't been completed.

Statements of the Roving Ambassador to Africa

Q: Mr. President, your roving Ambassador to Africa has been widely criticized for some of the statements he has made, that is, Mr. Williams, including the one of "Africa for Africans," and the like. Do you find any validity in this criticism, and would you consider that his tour of Africa has been a plus for the United States policy?

The President: Oh, I don't - I think Governor Williams has done very well. I am wholly satisfied with his mission. It's a very difficult one. Africa is not an easy matter to - the problems of Africa are not easy. And there are a good many conflicting forces that are loose in Africa as well as all parts of the world.

The statement "Africa for the Africans" does not seem to me to be a very unreasonable statement. He made it clear that he was talking about all those who felt that they were Africans, whatever their color might be, whatever their race might be. I do not know who else Africa should be for.

Status of the Air Force Missile Program

Q: Mr. President, Mr. Sheppard, who is Chairman of the House Appropriations Committee Subcommittee on Military Construction, stated that the Air Force missile base program, any way you look at it, is in a terrible mess, although he conceded there was some slight improvement in recent months. Do you care to comment, or will this forthcoming report that you mentioned before comment on that?

The President: Well, there are a great many difficulties. It is an extremely elaborate system to construct. A good many of the cost estimates were underestimated at the time. There are elaborate communications facilities that have to be developed, and it's not been proceeding altogether satisfactorily.

I think the congressional investigation was most helpful. And I think the Department of Defense will benefit from it, and we will attempt to improve the program.

Soviet Concept of Disarmament

Q: Mr. President, the Russians seem to have taken the position that Mr. McCloy's remarks the other day about the general and complete disarmament proposal of Mr. Khrushchev was a slogan, in McCloy's words. The Russians seem to take the position from this that your administration has now rejected this Soviet concept of disarmament. Is that a fact, or what is your attitude about that?

The President: Well, I think Mr. McCloy was pointing out that you have to, in addition to trying to work for disarmament, you also have to work for a mechanism which will permit an orderly settlement of disputes between nations, settlements which under present conditions might be settled by military action, but which in some future date, if the goal of disarmament was achieved, would have to be settled by another means.

Now, I think it would be premature to make any judgments on what progress can be made in the field of disarmament. It is going to be some time before we have completed our study of what the American position will be on disarmament.

We are proceeding immediately ahead, of course, on nuclear testing. But I did not read into Mr. McCloy's statement any broad position, any broad administration policy, because we have not reached that policy on disarmament.

Q: Do you accept, sir, the view that disarmament is really not a legitimate word for what we are trying to do, that really it's arms control that the West, including the United States, is after or should be after?

The President: Well, we want to proceed with arms control, leading to disarmament. But, of course, this complete disarmament in 4 years is a goal which has been talked about for a great many years.

I am somewhat familiar with the conversations which took place in Geneva under much less strained conditions from '28 to '29, through '33 and '34. It is extremely difficult to reach satisfactory agreements on disarmament. At that time the world was not divided as sharply as it is today, and yet rather limited progress was made. So this is an extremely difficult matter. I think the first area, of course, is in nuclear testing. That, I am hopeful, we can reach an agreement on.

But we also are going to be concerning ourselves with our position on disarmament. And I hope by this summer we will have completed that analysis. What progress can be made will depend upon the good will on both sides and their willingness to accept realistic inspection systems.

Split Between the USSR and Red China

Q: Mr. President, recently documents were made public indicating that the ideological split between Red China and Russia is perhaps greater than many people have thought. Do you feel that this split might be to the benefit of the United States? And to what extent? For example, do you think that this might bring Russia and the United States closer together, over the long run?

The President: Well, I wouldn't attempt to make a judgment about what our future relations are going to be. I am hopeful that we can work out a relationship which will permit us to live in peace and maintain our security and the security of those countries with which we are allied. That is our object.

I am hopeful that the Soviet Union will come to that conclusion also. What factors will be in their minds in making their policy, of course, can only be surmised. But we are attempting, and will be attempting in the coming months, to determine whether any effective agreements can be accomplished with the Soviet Union which will permit a relaxation of world tension. And we should know that in some months.

Disarmament and the Planning for Negotiations

Q: Mr. President, one of your campaign complaints was that fewer than a hundred people in the whole Federal Government were working in the field of disarmament and planning for negotiations. Can you tell us how many people you have working on that problem now and what progress you are making towards building up what you would regard as an adequate staff to deal with this question?

The President: We have, of course, the problem, and have had it, of going into the negotiations in late March. There have been voluntary groups, particularly one led by Dr. Fisk, which has been concerning itself with our position in those negotiations. I discussed with Mr. McCloy the setting up of a longer range operation on disarmament and nuclear testing, and we are now considering whether that should be established as a separate agency in the executive branch or in the State Department, with permanent personnel and a budget under a statutory action by the Congress. I am hopeful - Mr. McCloy is considering it, and we hope to be able to make a recommendation to Congress about the long-range buildup of our disarmament activities in some days.

President's News Conference on Russian Television

Q: Mr. President, what significance, if any, do you attach to the fact that the Russians put part of your news conference on their television, and would you welcome more of this?

The President: I would welcome more of it. And I am glad that they are doing it, and I hope that it can be expanded so that it gives an accurate reflection of the point of view of this country.

West German Aid to Underdeveloped Countries

Q: Mr. President, this last weekend, Vice Chancellor Erhard in Germany suggested that West Germany was not necessarily going to continue aid to under-developed areas beyond 1 year. Was it your understanding with the Foreign Minister, Herr von Brentano, when he left here, that this would be on a continuing basis?

The President: It is my understanding that it would be on a continuing basis, and I am sure that that would be the point of view of the German Government. As to how much they will be able to do on a continuing basis, that is a matter which they have to determine and I am sure will be a subject of discussion between the United States and the Germans and other interested countries. But my impression was very precise, that it would be a continuing basis. But I 'do not say that the figures which have been reported in the papers as to how much would be provided on a continuing basis, I did not have any understanding that those were the figures that they would finally reach. The idea of continuity was clearly accepted, and the idea of the figures is a matter of course which would be before the Germans and on which of course we will be talking with them.

Invitation of Soviet Space Scientists to the U. S.

Q: Mr. President, Congressman Anfuso has recommended that this country take the initiative and officially invite Soviet space scientists to meet with U. S. scientists to work out plans for cooperation and peaceful exploration of space in line with your own recommendations. Would you comment on this, and could you tell us what plans you may have now to achieve this end?

The President: We are attempting to improve our exchange program on a reciprocal basis with the Soviet Union - and have been engaged in that activity
for some time.

Q: *Yes, but have you defined any special areas in which you could cooperate
without any harm to our national security?*

The President: When we have been able to work out any successful exchanges
or new exchanges, we will announce them. But we are of course concerned that
they will be reciprocal, and national security will be protected, and also that
it would contribute to some useful purpose. We have, as you know, had recently
here in Washington a meeting which had been arranged some months ago on meteorology, in which the Soviet representative was unable to be here, which was a
source of regret. There are other proposals we have made for the long-range exploration of space, weather control, and so on, and we are going to continue to
attempt to engage the Soviet Union in a common effort in that kind of activity.

Financing the Education Program

Q: *Mr. President, you told an earlier press conference that for every new
program you set up, you would suggest a source of revenue. Does that mean, for
example, in the case of the education program that you are going to suggest some
special way of financing that?*

The President: No, what I said was that for the proposals that we would
make, we sould have a suggested source of revenue, and by the end of the month,
when we send up our completed budgetary recommendations for '61-'62, we will
also suggest sources of revenue.

Now, in the case of unemployment compensation, aid to dependent children,
social security, hgihways, and medical care for the aged, we did suggest the
appropriation.

On the suggestion of the appropriation on agriculture and on education there
is no direct tax link to those, but we will have some proposals to make before
the end of the month to bring that section of the budget which we have effected
in line with the revenues.

I have excluded, of course, from the beginning, what we do in the field of
national security.

Q: *A sort of an overall balancing out is what you have in mind in the case
of education, and not a specific source, but some general program for changing
the revenue?*

The President: I think as I have stated, we are going to suggest revenues
for any expenditures that we make which do not have by themselves or linked to
them a source of revenue as the other programs did.

Q: *Have you made any estimate whether there will be a deficit in fiscal
year 1962?*

The President: We will send to the Congress, I believe on March 23, our
view on what the '62 budget will look like. We have not completed our programs,
and we have not completed our analysis of tax revenues at this time.

Q: *Mr. President, there is a report that there is a billion and a half deficit in sight. Is that correct?*

The President: I would prefer to wait until we are able to complete our
programs because the amount of the budget is tied pretty much to what we recommend. All these programs, with the exception of defense, will be finished by
the 20th, and we will then be in a position to - of course the final budget

deficit will depend quite a lot on what we do in the field of national security. And I have not finished making a judgement on how much we should recommend in addition to the present '62 budget.

Burden Sharing on Defense and Foreign Aid in the Atlantic Community

Q: Mr. President, the aide memoire which was handed to Dr. von Brentano emphasized the need for burden sharing on defense and foreign aid in the Atlantic Community. Can you speak somewhat more precisely of your ideas on this burden sharing?

The President: Yes. I hope that all the members of the Atlantic Community will contribute according to their resources for the maintenance of NATO and for the assistance to the newly emerging countries, and that the burden will be commonly assumed, and the OECD discussions, the dicussions - the bilateral discussions with the Germans, discussions which are going to take place in March and in April in Europe - I am hopeful will lead to that result.

Federal Aid to Schools

Q: Sir, in view of the criticism that has occurred, could you elaborate on why you have not recommended Federal aid to public and - to private and parochial elementary and secondary schools?

The President: Well, the Constitution clearly prohibits aid to the school, to parochial schools. I don't think there is any doubt of that.

The Everson case, which is probably the most celebrated case, provided only by a 5 to 4 decision was it possible for a local community to provide bus rides to nonpublic school children. But all through the majority and minority statements on that particular question there was a very clear prohibition against aid to the school direct. The Supreme Court made its decision in the Everson case by determining that the aid was to the child, not to the school. Aid to the school is - there isn't any room for debate on that subject. It is prohibited by the Constitution, and the Supreme Court has made that very clear. And therefore there would be no possibility of our recommending it.

Q: But you are free to make the recommendations you have made which will affect private and parochial colleges and universities?

The President: Well, the aid that we have recommended to colleges is in a different form. We are aiding the student in the same way the GI bill of rights aided the student. The scholarships are given to the students who have particular talents and they can go to the college they want. In that case it is aid to the student, not to the school or college, and, therefore, not to a particular religious group. That is the distinction between them, except in the case of aid to medical schools, and that has been done for a number of years. Because that is a particular kind of technical assistance the constitutional question has not arisen on that matter.

Mr. Meriwether

Q: Mr. President, in regard to Mr. Meriwether, it has been alleged in the press and in Congress that he was campaign manager to former Admiral Crommelin. Now in fairness -

The President: In 1950.

Q: Yes. In fairness to Mr. Meriwether, can you state whether this is true and whether it entered into your thinking?

The President: Yes, he was campaign manager; had association with the campaign in 1950. That's correct.

Q: *Regarding your opening remark about the recommendation by the Defense Secretary to increase our conventional arms strength, would you please give us some of your thinking as to the rationale for this shift, if it is a shift, in our defense spending?*

The President: I would not say it is a shift. I would say it's - there are proposals made by the Secretary which talk about a general strengthening of our Armed Forces, including many areas. So I am not sure that the word "shift" is the most descriptive.

Q: *Mr. President, could you say whether any strengthening of our conventional forces will imply or mean a lessening of emphasis on nuclear weapons, or in our capacity to use them in a pinch?*

The President: I have not heard that. We have reached no decision which would indicate that there has been a change in our reliance. When - if we do reach a change in our reliance in new weapons, we will make it very clear. But no such change has been reached at the present time. What we are anxious to do, of course, is to see conventional forces strengthened not only in Western Europe but throughout the world. And that, it seems to me, was the gist of the Secretary's memorandum and his testimony yesterday and his public statements.

Reporter: Thank you, Mr. President.

THE PRESIDENT'S NEWS CONFERENCE

MARCH 8 , 1961

The President: I have several announcements to make.

First, I want to say a **word** on behalf of Radio Free Europe, which is now making its annual appeal for support from all of our citizens. For more than 10 years this enterprise has been reaching out to people in Europe - Eastern Europe; truth, devotion to liberty, is its message. For this radio is at work, with listeners numbering in the millions. The competition of ideas in these countries is kept alive. Individual Americans by giving to Radio Free Europe may be sure that they are bringing a beacon of light into countries to which millions of us are tied by kinship, and whose hope for freedom all of us must share.

This is a peaceful concern but a firm one. Radio Free Europe needs and deserves our generous help.

Secondly, Mrs. Kennedy and I are giving an afternoon reception at the White House next Monday for the Latin American Ambassadors to the United States, the Council of the OAS, as well as members of Congress concerned with Latin American affairs. I will take the opportunity at the close of the reception to make a major statement of some of my views about the problems of the Americas.

Third, pursuant to my instructions, each Federal department and agency has renewed its procurement and construction plans for the remainder of the current fiscal year, through June 30, 1961, for the purpose of speeding up its contracts and purchases with available funds. The total of obligations for the remainder of the fiscal year is now planned to be $660 million higher than before the directive. If this acceleration proceeds as planned by the agencies, direct Federal purchases of goods and services will be increased in the January-March quarter by an annual rate of about one quarter of a billion dollars, and in the April-June quarter by an annual rate of about three quarters of a billion dollars.

Next, I wish to announce that the Prime Minister of Sweden, Mr. Erlander, will make an informal visit to the United States for a period of 10 days, beginning March 28. The Prime Minister and I will meet together on the 29th, after which Mr. Erlander will visit other parts of the United States. I am very pleased with the prospect of meeting the Prime Minister, for we Americans have many close ties with Sweden and its people. And I extend a most hearty welcome to him.

It has been brought to my attention, next, that 5,000 Indian and Eskimo children under the jurisdiction of the Bureau of Indian Affairs of the Department of the Interior are not in school - cannot attend school until facilities are built for them. These children live on the Navajo Reservation in Arizona and New Mexico, in Alaska, and in the Choctaw Reservation in Mississippi. In addition, other thousands are housed in overcrowded and obsolete boarding and day facilities, some hazardous to their health and safety.

I have instructed the Secretary of the Interior, Mr. Udall, to submit to the Congress without delay plans to correct the situation.

I am announcing the appointment and scheduled departure this evening of a special mission to review the status and effectiveness of the United States economic policies in Bolivia. The chairman of the three-person mission is Dr. Willard Thorpe, and the other two members are Mr. Jack Corbett and Mr. Seymour J. Rubin. This mission will arrive in La Paz on March 9 and spend approximately 2 weeks before returning to Washington to report their recommendations for a plan of action to be followed by United States agencies in Washington and Bolivia. An adviser to the mission, Mr. Coerr, Deputy Assistant Secretary of State for Inter-American Affairs, has already arrived.

Finally, I want to say that in response to the first Executive order the number of people receiving surplus food has doubled from 3,500,000 in December to 6,100,000 at the present time. In addition, this has doubled the protein value of the direct distribution of food.

This is the last statement. The Cuban Red Cross, the American Red Cross, and U.S. Navy today combined in a three-way effort to combat a polio breakout in Guantanamo City, Cuba, some 31 miles from the naval base. Early today the Red Cross directorate at the U.S. naval base in south-eastern Cuba had a phone call from a male Red Cross nurse in Guantanamo City saying there was an outbreak of polio, with 3 children dead and 10 more stricken.

All available vaccine had been used by the hospitals in Guantanamo City. And aid was needed to give vaccine for at least 100 more children which they were unable to obtain. The Red Cross director at the base got permission from Adm. Edward J. O'Donnell to send all the vaccine which could be spared. She carried and sent enough vaccine for 160 first inoculations to the northeast gate, where she met the Cuban Red Cross ambulance where the transfer was made.

I want to take this opportunity and this incident to emphasize again that our differences of opinion on matters affecting Cuba are not with the Cuban people. Rather, we desire the closest, and harmonious and friendly, and most sympathetic ties with them.

QUESTIONS

The Missile Gap

Q: Mr. President, you told us last month that you expected to have an answer from the Defense Department about this time on whether there is or is not a missile gap. Are you able to say at this time whether there is or not?

The President: We are concluding our review of the recommendations which the Defense Department has made for changes in the Defense budget. I am hopeful that this survey can be completed in the next few days, and then we plan to send the results of our study to the Congress. And at that time we will indicate what I believe to be the relative defensive position of the United States and other countries and what needs to be done to improve it.

Presidential Press Conferences

Q: I am sure you are aware, sir, of the tremendous mail response that your news conferences on television and radio have produced. There are many American who believe that in our manner of questioning or seeking your attention that we are subjecting you to some abuse or a lack of respect. I wonder, sir, in this light, could you tell us generally your feelings about your press conferences to date and your feelings about how they are conducted?

The President: Well, you subject me to some abuse, but not to any lack of respect. (Laughter) I must say that I do know that there are difficulties, and I know that it places burdens on members of the press to have to stand up, particularly when I am not able to recognize them. On the other hand, if it were changed and one member stood up, then perhaps that would not be a satisfactory device. So I think that along with the old saying about "don't take down the fence until you know why it was put up," I would say that we should stay with what we now have.

Situation in Laos

Q: Mr. President, the approach to a peaceful settlement in Laos seems to have run into a dead end, with rejection by two of the proposed members of the three-nation neutral commission, and the Soviet Union apparently still insists upon the approach of an ICC[1] action there and an international conference. I wonder if in your review of the situation you have reached any conclusion as to what step the United States should now take to avoid the expansion of the war in Laos?

The President: Well, the United States had been hopeful that it would be possible to set up some procedures where neutral nations could guarantee the security of Laos and also isolate it from military pressures on both sides. We are going to have to consider what other procedures might be followed to achieve that goal. But this is a matter now of discussion with our friends and with others, and I am hopeful that we can achieve a result which will bring stability to Laos, permit it to maintain its independence, and bring peace to the area, and self-determination. Those are very difficult goals to achieve, given the situation which we found upon assuming our responsibilities. But we are going to continue and are now continuing to take every step that we can to achieve that goal.

What the People Can Do for the Country

Q: Mr. President, there has been considerable comment that your program up to now has illustrated what the country can do for the people. I think a lot of people have asked me and I am asking you, sir, at what point does your program tell what the people can do for the country?

The President: Well, we are trying to do two or three things in the domestic program. We are **trying** to protect and provide jobs for people - that is, I think, a matter of concern to all Americans. We are committed to that goal, and the programs which we have sent up to the Hill have that object in mind. We are also trying to strengthen our educational system, which needs to be strengthened over the long period in which we are going to be tested. We are trying to provide for more orderly and effective programs of medical care for the elderly. Now, these programs, in my opinion, are in the public interest, and they are being assessed in that regard.

I would say, as I have said from the beginning, that in time I have no doubt that all of us will find ourselves tested in our attempts to maintain the independence of the United States and the independence of those countries to which we are committed. These programs are an attempt to provide for a viable economy, which I think is essential for the security of the United States and for the security of those countries which are dependent upon it. It is also an effort to provide equality of opportunity to the extent that at least we can do so for all Americans because I think it is in the public interest.

Aid to Private Schools

Q: Sir, would you help to clarify the aid to private schools issue? The National Defense Education Act, passed in 1958, provides loans for private elementary and secondary schools for equipment. And existing provisions, as well as your recommendations, allow for construction loans for private colleges. I wonder if you would give us your view on proposals to add to your school bill provisions for loans, as differentiated from grants for private and parochial elementary and secondary schools.

The President: You have mentioned three rather different programs, which involve different purposes and different **constitutional** problems.

The first program was the National Defense Education Act, where loans were provided for nonpublic schools for specific purposes - languages, I believe, and also for science and engineering. Twenty million dollars was provided of which, interestingly enough, only about $1,300,000 has been used for loans. That was the first.

The second program we are talking about is loans to all colleges. And in my opinion - and also, of course, scholarship assistance to the students. That is in a differenct position, at least to the best of my judgment, from secondary education. Secondary education is compulsory. It is provided for every student, every citizen. Every citizen must attend school. We are providing a program which we have sent to the Congress, of grants for public schools. And, therefore, in my opinion, that is the program which I hope will be passed.

Now, the problem of loans to secondary education does institute serious constitutional problems. I do not think that anyone can read the Everson case without recognizing that the **position** which the court took, minority and majority, in regard to the use of tax funds for nonpublic schools, raises a serious constitutional question.

I have expressed my view on them. I think the Congress should consider carefully what its view is on them, and what kind of programs it wants to recommend in this area. The Congress, as I say, has recommended grants to private colleges in the past - I used, I think, a week or two ago, I gave that as an example - in the National Defense Education Act it used loans for specific purposes.

Whether across the board loans are constitutional is a question which, in my opinion, raises a serious constitutional question.

I am hopeful that the Congress will enact grants. If the Congress, the Congressmen, wish to address themselves to the problem of loans, which is a separate matter - we are not talking about, in this bill, loans to secondary education - then I am hopeful that it would be considered as a separate matter that the Congress will consider the constitutional problems and then consider what action it would want to take.

We will be glad to cooperate in every way. But I am hopeful that while that consideration is being given, that we will move ahead with the grant program.

Q: Mr. President, are you suggesting that Congress, if it wants to provide for long-term, low-interest loans for private and parochial schools, ought to have a separate bill?

The President: I definitely believe that we should not tie the two together. I think that there are sufficient constitutional questions which the members of Congress will have to consider. I believe in view of the fact that this act is directly, in its title and in its purpose, directed to giving grants to public schools, that we should proceed with that bill.

Now, any other matter, I think - seems to me should be taken up as a separate issue if we want to then discuss loans. I have given my view of the constitutional problems involved in across the board loans. As the questioner indicated, there have been some kinds of loans to nonpublic schools which have been supported by the Congress and signed by the President and about which no constitutional problem has yet been raised, and the National Defense Education Act is the best example.

But across the board loans, as this group knows, this matter was not brought up in the last - President Eisenhower sent several messages to the Congress dealing with Federal aid to education. I believe there were one or two times when it was voted upon in the House. I do not recall that there was a great effort made at that time to provide across the board loans to an aid to education bill. The only time, in my knowledge, that it was brought up was about the end of the last session in August, by Senator Morse, and then just in the Senate. But it was not made a matter of great interest at that time, and I am concerned that it should not be made an issue now in such a way that we end up the year with, again, no aid to secondary schools.

Q: Mr. President, you said last week, as I recall it, that there was no room for debate about this matter.

The President: That's right. There is no room for debate about grants. There is obviously room for debate about loans, because it has been debated. My view, however, is that the matter of loans, to the best of my knowledge and judgment - though this has not been tested by the courts, of course, in the sense that grants have been - but by my reading of the constitutional judgments in the Everson case, my judgment has been that across the board loans are also unconstitutional.

Q: Does that suggest that you would veto a bill that provided for across the board loans, Mr. President?

The President: I think I made my view very clear. I think it is always a mistake before we even have legislation to talk about what I am going to do. But I think it is very clear about what my view is of grants and loans across the board to nonpublic schools. Now, colleges are in a different category. Specific programs of grants, even to colleges which are nonpublic, have been supported by the Congress and signed by the President. Loans and even grants to secondary education under some circumstances might be held to be constitutional. But across the baord to all nonpublic schools, in my opinion, does raise a serious constitutional question which after reading the cases and giving it a good deal of thought, in my opinion - at least to my judgment would be unconstitutional.

Now, the President has an obligation, and the Congress to consider this matter very carefully. I am extremely sympathetic to those families who are paying their taxes for public education and also sustaining the rights - sustaining their children in non-public schools. They carry a heavy burden. But I have made my position very clear for many months and I have to make my position clear now, at least as long as I am here, on what I believe to be the constitutional problem. And I also point out that this matter was not made an issue in recent years until this time, except in the case of the the amendment offered at the end of the last session by Senator Morse which was just offered in the Senate and was not offered in the House of Representatives, to the best of my knowledge.

Civil Rights

Q: Mr. President, you have taken Executive action in the field of civil rights. Do you feel there is a need now for legislation in this area, and if so do you plan to offer any at this session?

The President: When I believe that we can usefully move ahead in the field of legislation, I will recommend it to the Congress. I do believe that there are a good deal of things we can do now in administering laws previously passed by the Congress, particularly in the area of voting, and also by using the powers which the Constitution gives to the President through Executive orders. When I feel that there is a necessity for a congressional action, with a chance of getting that congressional action, then I will recommend it to the Congress.

Changing of Indian Treaties

Q: Mr. President, you and the Democratic Party are on record in opposition to the changing of Indian treaties without the consent of the Indians. The Army Engineers are about to build a hugh conduit dam on the upper Allegheny River which will flood a third of a western New York Indian reservation in direct violation of a treaty that was signed by George Washington with the Seneca Indians. Have you any inclination at all to halt that project in favor of the so-called Morgan alternate project which would not violate the treaty?

The President: My recollection is that this matter has been tested in the courts, has it not?

Q: Yes, it has. The Supreme Court has upheld it.

The President: Well, I'm not - I have no plans to interfere with that action. [1]

President's Message to Khrushchev

Q: Mr. President, on the assumption that Mr. Thompson has by now caught up with Mr. Khrushchev, I wonder if you could tell us the contents of your message to the Soviet Premier and what thinking was behind this message at this time?

The President: Well, I would think that it would be more properly a matter that would best be left to Mr. Thompson and Mr. Khrushchev. It is a letter from me and I think it would be discourteous and unwise to reveal such a letter without any indication that it has been received and some response given. As As far as the purpose of the letter, the purpose of the letter was to give, in general, some of my views on the questions which are at issue now around the world, and also to indicate my strong confidence in Ambassador Thompson to speak for me and for our country at this time in any discussions he might have with Mr. Khrushchev.

Segregation, Religion, and Education

Q: Mr. President, back on the subject of education. There has been rising speculation that the openly developing fights over the issues of segregation and religion as they are involved in the legislation may well stop them before they start. How do you assess the possible damage of those issues as pertaining to your legislation on building schools and loans to teachers' salaries, and do you intend to carry the issue more strongly to the public directly?

The President: This matter, of course, these two, and of course other groups who are opposed to any action in this area, have all contributed to the fact that this matter has been debated for a number of years, passed the Senate at least two or three times, but we have never gotten legislation, so that, obviously, it is going to be a difficult matter to secure the passage of legislation this year. But I do not think that there is anything more important than to have good schools, well-trained competent teachers. When the Massachusetts Bay Colony was established, one of the first acts that were taken was establishment of a public school. The Northwest Ordinance, the land grant colleges, all indicate the long traditional interest which our Government and people have had in strengthening our education. We are as good in the long-range sense as our schools are and, therefore, I am extremely interested in seeing the country this year place additional emphasis on education - additional support to education.

In one area alone, as I mentioned some time ago, those people who were first thrown out of work are at the bottom of the educational ladder. The papers are filled with ads requiring scientists, technicians, engineers, on the west coast and all across the country. People who can't find jobs are people who were not well educated at the beginning. I think everyone should have a maximum chance to develop his talents. I do not believe that that can be done effectively without passage of this bill this year. I am therefore hopeful that however strong the feelings may run - and I am very conscious of them - on all these other matters, that the program of scholarships for college students, of loans to colleges, because we are going to have double the number of children in 1970 that we do today applying for admission to our colleges, and grants to public schools - I am hopeful that that will be passed this year.

Export Licenses for American Manufacturers to the Iron Curtain

Q: Mr. President, in order to avoid another snafu, as the one that involved the 45 peices of machinery that were originally scheduled to go to Russia, what instructions have you issued to the Departments of Defense and Commerce regarding export license for American manufacturers to Iron Curtain countries?

The President: Well, I am hopeful the procedures can be improved. There was a difference of opinion between the Commerce Department and the Defense Department, and there was a difference in emphasis in the Defense Department's position over a period of time, though they did take the view from the beginning that it was not in the national interest.

It has been, I think, quite unfortunate the way it was handled. I am hopeful that in the future we can set up better procedures so that a better judgment can be made.

But I must say that it is extremely difficult for those who are making the judgment. Caution tells them to send nothing and therefore - on the other hand, we are anxious to permit some degree of trade which does not weaken our security or increase our danger to be carried on with countries. After all, countries in Western Europe are carrying on very intensive trade with the Soviet Union, and some countries with Communist China. So what they cannot get here they get there. So we wish to bring some reason to it. It is a difficult matter. But after this experience, which has been not always satisfactory, Governor Hodges has given this matter close attention with Secretary McNamara to see if we can improve our procedures. This was not the best example of Government in action.

The RB-47 Fliers

Q: Mr. President, I have a two-part question on the RB-47 fliers. First, could you tell us now where and when and under what circumstances the fliers were shot down? And, second, are such flights being continued?

The President: I think the fliers discussed the matter quite fully with the press last Friday.

Economic Boycotts as the Answer to Import Competition

Q: Mr. President, in connection with trade, some domestic groups, including labor unions, are turning to economic boycotts as their answer to import competition. I wonder if you could state your position on this approach to international trade difficulties.

The President: Well, I am hopeful that those boycotts will not spread. It is not the - Congress has set up certain procedures by which those industries that are hard hit can protect themselves - the peril-point, escape clause, the procedures before the Tariff Commission. Congress is going to have an opportunity to consider the whole matter of reciprocal trade, I believe, next year. I recognize that these workers are hard hit. But they are not always able to make a judgment of what the total national need is and also the need - international need. I have seen some cases where boycotts have been suggested where the percentage of imports is fractional compared to the domestic market, 1 or 2 percent. Well, now, if we are not going to follow the procedures set down by the American people acting through their Congress, but instead every group is going to take it into their own hands, then, of course, we are going to have action taken against us in those countries. We sent abroad a good deal of important goods that employ hundreds of thousands and millions of people. And, as I have suggested before, the balance of trade has been in our favor by four or five billion dollars.

Two can play this game; and, therefore, unions in other countries can refuse to unload our goods. Pretty soon we will find ourselves with an exacerbated situation among friendly nations and also which will be harmful to the gold flow.

Problem of Communist China

Q: Mr. President, could you give us your thinking on the problem of Communist China in view of the latest word from the Warsaw negotiations, that is, that the Chinese will not consider the admittance of the 32 American correspondents and they will not consider the release of the prisoners? I believe there was some hope that if we could exchange correspondents with the Chinese that it might be a step towards more harmonious relations.

The President: Well, that was our hope and if they are unwilling to do that, of course that hope has been dimmed. They have been, as we know, extremely belligerent towards us, and they have been unfailing in their attacks upon the United States. But, of course, I think part of that has been because they recognize that the United States is committed to the defense of - committed to maintaining its connections with other countries, committed to its own defense and the defense of freedom.

But they have been extremely harsh in their attacks upon us and I would like to see a lessening of that tension. That is our hope from the beginning. But we are not prepared to surrender in order to get a relaxation of tension.

The Meriwether Nomination

Q: Mr. President, during the debate on the Meriwether nomination, Senator Morse raised some questions about whether this nominee had a police record and he said you had sent up to see him one of your legislative aides who had read certain notes from the FBI files. I wonder if you can enlighten us as to what are the facts so far as this -

The President: I informed the conference and the Senate that I looked over Mr. Meriwether's FBI record before I sent it to the Senate. Mr. Meriwether is now a member of the Export-Import Bank, confirmed by the Senate, by a rather large figure, and I am confident that he will do a good job.

The Peace Corps

Q: Mr. President, in regard to the Peace Corps, to do away with the objection of some countries which may not welcome American corpsmen, the suggestion has been made that you propose a United Nations corps of which the American corpsmen would be a part. Do you have a comment on that?

The President: Well, I think that that could usefully be considered. It is not intended that any member of the American Peace Corps would go to any country where he was not warmly welcome. In addition, as I have said from the beginning, we are putting our major emphasis, at the beginning, on teachers and I am hopeful that those countries which are interested in understanding our country and our traditions will welcome these young men and women. But they will be sent only **where** they are welcome and I would certainly feel that we should consider with the **United Nations** how we can bring our programs into harmony.

Reporter: Thank you, Mr. President.

---

[1]The President later reviewed the problems involved in the Kinzua Dam project. See his letter to the President of the Seneca Nation, Item 320 of the *Public Papers of the President.*

THE PRESIDENT'S NEWS CONFERENCE OF

MARCH 15, 1961

The President: I have several brief announcements to make.

First, the Secretaries of the military departments have been instructed by the Deputy Secretary of Defense to take steps to provide a greater percentage of defense contracts for small business. Specifically, the military departments have been asked to set a goal increasing individually in fiscal year 1962 small business participation by 10 percent over the year for fiscal 1960. Contracts for small business in fiscal year 1960 amounted to $3,440 million, or 16 percent. We are going to try to increase that by at least 10 percent.

In addition, we are going to provide an increase for small business participation in research and development contracts. During that year this category of contracting amounted to only $180 million, or 3.4 percent of the total. In addition, we are asking the Department of Defense to examine how additional contracts can be steered into distressed areas. At the present time we are not doing as much of that as I hope we can in the future.

Secondly, I am sending to Congress a request for funds to resume detailed planning of our largest remaining damsite in the Upper Columbia - the Libby Dam in Montana. It will be the first step in the development of the Columbia River Basin in coordination with Canada on an international basis. Yesterday the Foreign Relations Committee reported out unanimously the treaty that will make this dam possible. The Libby Dam will provide the power that we desperately need in the Northwest United States. It will help control the floods, that are devastating northern Idaho. And it will prevent the projected power shortage for that area.

The beginning of this project will give impetus to a new period of cooperation with Canada.

Next I want to announce that the Export-Import Bank is authorizing $25 million credit in favor of the Government of Israel, to purchase agricultural machinery in the United States, to help consolidate Israel's agricultural settlements, and electrical power equipment and construction items for the expansion of Israeli seaports.

This decision, I think, will help speed the development of Israel's economy.

And then lastly, I want to announce that we will hold a President's Conference on Heart Disease and Cancer, which will be held at the White House beginning April 22. The Department of HEW will then invite a number of distinguished medical leaders throughout the country to participate in this program.

Thank you.

QUESTIONS

Kennedy Appearance at the U.N.

Q: Mr. President, would you tell us, please, if you have any plans to appear personally at the United Nations General Assembly currently in session and, if so, when you might go up?

The President: I have no plans to and I do not expect to appear at the Assembly.

Possibility of Reaching an Arms Accord with the Soviet Union

Q: Could you give us your views, sir, about the possibiltiy of reaching some accord with the Soviet Union on general disarmament as well as nuclear test bans, and would you be willing to meet with Mr. Khrushchev face to face if you felt this was necessary to reach a truly genuine agreement?

The President: Well, as you know, this matter is now being discussed, at least the procedural matters leading up to what we hope will be progress in the area of general disarmament. It is now being discussed at the United Nations and Ambassador Stevenson has been discussing with the State Department the American position.

We — now that Mr. Dean has left to resume the discussions in Geneva, Mr. McCloy is working full time on developing an American position on disarmament. We have indicated before that we may not have completed our analysis until this summer, and we have suggested that we will be prepared to resume either the Ten-Nation Conference or some other similar structure, conference structure in, we first suggested, September, and now we have suggested August at the latest. So we are going to concentrate our attention on disarmament now. We hope progress can be made, and we will — I will consider what usefully could be done to advance progress.

Money for the Highways

Q. Mr. President, in addition to the $700-odd million in highway money that you have instructed the Commerce Department to make available to the States ahead of time, Governor Rockefeller has asked whether it would be possible for the States to get an advance on the money for highways for fiscal 1962. Have you any ideas on the subject?

The President: Yes. I received a letter from Governor Rockefeller and we are considering what action can be taken. We have to — the Congress has taken a very clear position on pay as you go, and we have to consider what funds can be made available between now and next July, and we have to consider what action the Congress is going to take on our request for additional funds in order to keep the program going.

So that all this is now being considered and an answer will be given to Governor Rockefeller after we have made a judgment as to what funds will be available, which depends in part upon what our response will be in the Congress.

Constitutional Issues in the School-Aid Fight

Q: Mr. President, you have stressed the constitutional issues in the school-aid fight. Regardless of the constitutional question, do you think it is wise public policy to make Federal loans to parochial and private schools below the college level?

The President: Well, I have stated my view in the previous White House conferences, and what I hope would be the procedure followed by the Congress, which continues to be my view. We will — when we see proposals, and what form they take, because as the previous press conference developed, loans take many different forms, and I indicated some fall within one category and some within another, and this administration will be glad to cooperate with the Congress in considering the matter.

60

But I am hopeful that, as I have said before, that the view taken by the administration of the desirability of passing the public school matter first — I am hopeful that that will be the decision which the Congress will adopt. But this is a matter that they are considering and we will consider with them.

Cardinal Spellman on School-Aid

Q: Mr. President, Cardinal Spellman in a statement this week indicated that tax exemptions for the parents who pay tuition for their children to go to private schools might be one possible approach. Do you think, sir, that this would be a constitutional way of perhaps compromising the issue?

The President: I think that all this matter should be examined carefully by the Congress. The Senator from Oregon, Mr. Morse, has asked the Secretary of HEW to send up a brief on all the various kinds of assistance which are given to nonpublic schools and colleges, which the Secretary is preparing to do. The committees then of the House and Senate, and the House of Representatives, can consider what kind of program they wish to put forward and at that time we can consider what the constitutional problems might be. But it is very difficult as new proposals are made for me or for anyone else to be giving constitutional opinions on each of them as they come up, without seeing the definite language. That obviously is not my function.

I would be glad to have the departments of Government participate in considering these matters with the Congress. But my view on procedures which I hope the Congress will follow are well known. I am hopeful we can get the program which we sent to the Hill out of the way. Then the Congress will have to consider what it wants to do in this other area. And the administration will be delighted to cooperate. But I could not possibly, unless I saw exactly what kind of language, give even a private opinion as to its constitutionality.

Ambassador Thompson's Meeting with Khrushchev

Q: Mr. President, are you able at this time to tell us something of Ambassador Thompson's report on his meeting with Premier Khrushchev?

The President: No, I have no statement on it at the present time.

Possibility of U.S. Increase in Aid to Laos

Q: Mr. President, Prince Souvanna Phouma, a representative of the Laotian rebels, said after a visit to the rebel area, that Moscow had provided 20 times as many weapons to the pro-Communist side as we have provided to the Royal Laotian Government. Can you tell us whether we are considering a step-up in such shipments as part of a new look at this?

The President: Well, we have been watching Laos with the closest attention. As I have frequently said, and as the Secretary has said, it is our hope that from all of these negotiations will come a genuinely independent and neutral Laos, which is the master of its own fate. The purpose of these discussions among the various people who participate in them at Pnom Penh is to make this possible. However, recent attacks by rebel forces indicate that a small minority backed by personnel and supplies from outside is seeking to prevent the establishment of a neutral and independent country. We are determined to support the government and the people of Laos in resisting this attempt.

Labor Unions and the Workweek

Q: Mr. President, labor unions want a shorter workweek to cope with the automation and unemployment. Your Secretary of Labor is against that. Are you for it and if so, would you prefer a shorter workday or a 4-day week? I don't mean yourself, personally, but the -

The President: I prefer it for myself - (laughter) - but I would say that I am opposed to a shorter workweek. I am hopeful that we can have employment high at 5 days a week and 40 hours, which is traditional in this country, and which is necessary if we are going to continue economic growth, and maintain our commitments at home and abroad.

So, I would be opposed to any arbitrary reduction of the workweek. And I am unhappy when I see the workweek reduced artificially, in the sense that the pressures of a declining economy reduce it so that we get averages of 38.5 hours a week instead of the 40 hours a week. In any case, to answer your question, I would be opposed to reducing the workweek.

Latin American Statement

Q: Mr. President, your Latin American statement the other day was quite sweeping in calling for political and social reforms in those countries. Have you had any indications before or since of how much acceptance there is in Latin American countries for this kind of reform?

The President: I think that it would be premature to make a judgment as to what the response will be in Latin America. I am hopeful it will be favorable; I am hopeful that we can begin discussions throughout the hemisphere which will lead to the kind of internal and external planning which will provide for a steady rate of economic growth throughout the hemisphere, which would be a cooperative effort. So that as of today I couldn't tell you what the response will be. I am hopeful it will be favorable, and I am hopeful that it will result in a joint effort of the kind that we saw in Western Europe in the late forties.

Presidential Popularity and Congressional Support

Q: Mr. President, recent public opinion polls and other reports indicate a high degree of public acceptance of your acts since you have become President, and of your program at the same time that certain basics of the New Frontier legislative program are in considerable trouble in Congress. How do you go about translating public approval into congressional support?

The President: Well, that is a matter, of course, on which every Member of Congress must reach his judgment. I think that the people are interested in high minimum wage, they are interested in improving our schools, they are interested in medical care for the aged, they are interested, I believe, in fiscal responsibility and the development of the highway program. Now, the problem, of course, is that there are - and they are interested in an agricultural program which provides some more adequate return for the farmer.

Now, I recognize that there are important and powerful and well-organized interest groups in this country which oppose all of these programs, and that they have been successful in developing mail campaigns of one kind or another which tend to give an impression that there is widespread opposition to increasing, for example, the minimum wage.

Now Mr. Gallup's poll the other day showed that over 75 percent of the people were in favor of increasing the minimum wage. I think that increase in the minimum wage is highly desirable. I don't think that anyone should be expected to work for 80 and 85 cents an hour in some of these jobs. We have seen them particularly in retail stores, in a business which makes over $1 million a year.

I think the more orderly way to finance medical care for the aged is through the social security system. I am hopeful that when these matters are brought to the floor of the House and Senate that a majority of the Members will support them. I think that a majority of the people support them.

I know, however, that we face very vigorous opponents who are well organized, and who bring a good deal of pressure to bear on this administration and on the Congress. But we are going to continue to work for these programs, and I am very hopeful that before the year is out they will have passed.

The members of the committees of the House and Senate, I think, have done very well. And I am hopeful that an opportunity will be given to each Congressman to vote on these programs this year, and then the people can make a judgment as to what - how their interests are being represented. But I am confident that we are going to get a favorable response.

Military Organizations of Side-Bar Corporations

Q: Mr. President, what do you think of the Air Force and other branches of Government organizing these side-bar corporations and using taxpayers' money to circumvent the Civil Service and pay large salaries to get scientists and others? Isn't this sort of incongruous with the call for volunteers for your Peace Corps?

The President: I think a subcommittee of the Congress has been looking into this matter. One of the problems, of course, is that valuable technicians are required to make a substantial economic sacrifice when they come with the Government. Therefore, the services, faced with this problem of where these men who are essential can secure much greater pay outside the Government than inside, have had to resort to the devices to which you refer. And we are looking at the matter, but I would not want to give an opinion today which would deny the services of these valuable scientists. On the other hand, we want to make sure that the way the matter is being conducted is in the public interest. So we will have to say, Mrs. McClendon, that it requires a further examination because it is not an easy matter to solve.

I don't know anyone who has come to work with the Government that I am familiar with that has not taken a - has not made a financial sacrifice in doing so. But most of them have been willing to meet that sacrifice. And we are going to examine the particular problem that you have suggested.

Religious Prejudice

Q: Mr. President, your election in November was widely hailed as among other things a victory over religious prejudice. Do you think, as some speculation has already indicated in print, that the seemingly inflexible stand on the part of some spokesmen for the Catholic hierarchy on the school legislation may provoke more religious prejudice?

The President: I am hopeful that it will not. I stated that it is a fact that in recent years when education bills have been sent to the Congress, we have not had this public major encounter. I don't know why that was, but now we do have it.

But everyone is entitled to express their views. The Catholic, Protestant, and Jewish clergy are entitled to take their views. I think it is quite appropriate that they should not change their views merely because of the religion of the occupant of the White House. I think that would be unfortunate if they - I think they ought to state what they think. They ought to express their views, they are entitled to do that. Then I will express mine, and Congress will express its.

I am very hopeful that though there may be a difference of opinion on this matter of Federal aid to education, I am hopeful that when the smoke is cleared there will continue to be harmony among the various religious groups in the country. And I am going to do everything that I can to make sure that that harmony exists because it reaches far beyond the question of education and goes in a very difficult time of the life of our country to an important ingredient of our national strength. So that I am confident that the people who are involved outside the Government, and Members of Congress and the administration, will attempt to conduct the discussion on this sensitive issue in such a way as to maintain the strength of the country and not to divide it.

A National Sales Tax

Q: Mr. President, there has been some speculation that in order to finance some of your aggressive programs you may possibly seek a national sales tax or even possibly a penny a bottle tax on soft drinks. Could you comment on that, sir?

The President. No, I have no such plan.

A Reasonable Expectable Level of Unemployment

Q: Mr. President, there has been a controversy in recent days between the Chairman of the Federal Reserve Board and the Chairman of your Council of Economic Advisers as to what constitutes a reasonable expectable level of unemployment. What is your veiw on this matter?

The President: Well, there has been - I am not so sure that the controversy is as significant as perhaps it has been reported in the paper. Mr. Martin has made the point that a good deal of structural unemployment exists and I think we have to say that in coal, steel, and perhaps some in aviation, it does exist, structural unemployment, and will continue to be a problem even if you had a substantial economic recovery. It would be far less if you had a substantial economic recovery. I do not see that there is a basic clash between these two views. But I think that they are both important and both ought to be considered. In other words, I do not think that regardless of whether the unemployment we now have is structural or not, and some of it is structural and some of it is not, I do not believe we should accept the present rate of unemployment as a percentage that we should live with. In other words, we have to reduce that percentage. I hope that we can reduce it down to 4 percent, but we are going to have to reduce it. But I do agree with Mr. Martin that even as we attempt to overcome unemployment in this country we are faced with a very serious and important structural unemployment which results from technological change, which the Canadians have also, and which even in good times would cause us serious concern.

In other words, even in eastern Kentucky, West Virginia, southern Illinois, and Pennsylvania, and even in 1959 and in 1957, you still had serious pockets of unemployment which were concentrated, even though the overall national figure was rather limited. It is my understanding that the Joint Committee on the Economic Report may call back Mr. Martin and Mr. Heller to discuss this further. I think that would be useful. It is a very important national problem, but I don't think from my conversations with both of them that there is a serious disagreement between them.

The Farm Bill

Q: Mr. President, in connection with the farm bill now in conference in Congress, the principal fight seems to be over the section which would allow the Secretary of Agriculture to sell grain into the market to hold the market price down. Do you feel that this enforcement feature is an absolute requirement in connection with the bill?

The President: Well, I am hopeful that the conference will reach a decision which gives the Secretary powers in this area, if not the specific language of title III, at least language which will protect, provide protection for the bill. If we don't - if the Secretary lacks power - this bill isn't going to be successful, and a good many people from the urban areas who voted for the program with title III in it, in the House of Representatives, have a right, it seems to me, to expect that the Secretary will be given sufficient powers to protect the program from noncompliers who, if they are - who may use the program, if title III is out, for speculative and exploitive purposes. So that I consider it most important that title III remain in, or otherwise some alternate language which will give the Secretary substantial powers provided in title III should be provided by the conference. Otherwise, we are not going to have any relief.

I am sorry to see the important agricultural leaders opposing giving us the protection which is required. You cannot have the Federal Government supporting agriculture in important ways unless there is some control over production and if there is some limitation, some provision for cross-compliance. Otherwise, the program will continue to cost a lot of money, the farmers' income will continue to drop, and we will have a gradual deterioration of agriculture in this country. The program we suggested and sent to the Hill in my opinion was one that was well balanced, and I am hopeful that a well-balanced program will come out of the considerations of the House and the Senate.

Labor-Management Conference

Q: Mr. President, this has to do with the labor-management conference which is scheduled for March 21. The past history of such conferences has shown a high percentage of failures, except at times of national crisis. Do you feel the present state of urgency is great enough to anticipate some success, and how do you plan to go about communicating that sense of urgency?

The President: Well, I think it is. One reason alone I think makes it extremely important, and that is the problem of our being able to be competitive abroad. There are some indications that last year's favorable balance of trade which protected to some degree our gold supply - that we may not have as successful a year abroad. And I would think both manufacturers and labor unions, and certainly the public, would want to see American industry remain competitive. If we are not able to be competitive with a very strong and thriving industrial economy in Western Europe, we are going to find ourselves in serious trouble. There are also serious domestic matters, automation, technological change, unemployment, the wage-price spiral. I am extremely concerned about all these matters. I am sure they are. They live with them. And I am hopeful that we can encourage a public interest philosophy among all the groups which will provide progress. We have not been successful in the past, but I don't - these are the only things we can do. We lack any other powers.

Q: Sir, may I ask whether you plan to have the first meeting of the labor-management conference at the White House?

The President: Yes. Yes.

Inspections Sites Within the USSR

Q: Mr. President, have you sent Ambassador Dean back to Geneva with authority to lower our demand for inspection sites within the Soviet Union, to bring it closer to the Soviet figure?

The President: Mr. Dean goes back to Geneva with the hope, the administration's hope, that it will be possible for the United States, the British and the Russians to come to an agreement on nuclear - for a nuclear test ban, which would provide adequate security to all the countries involved.

President's Views on Federal Aid to Schools

Q: Mr. President, is it a fair inference from your answer to Mr. Knebel's earlier question that the constitutional issue aside for the moment, you do not have a personal opinion as to whether it would be wise public policy to expend Federal funds on elementary and secondary nonpublic schools?

The President: Well, I have - my previous discussions have rested on the constitutional questions.

Q: And you do not wish to speak on the other question?

The President: Well, I would have to see what kind of loans they were, Mr. Roberts. As I said before, in 1958 I did vote the loans for education, science, and technology. I voted for that program. I voted against, as a Senator, across the board loans.

So that I have looked over recently the number of programs which the Federal Government has in these areas, impacted areas, aid to particular kinds of colleges - we sent up a program providing for actual grants to medical schools for private colleges, which could be sectarian. So that there is a whole spectrum of programs, some of which raise constitutional questions and some of which do not.

So it is difficult to give an across the board answer. Across the board loans, I have indicated the constitutional question which it raises. There may be other programs which do not raise a constitutional question which may be socially undesirable.

All I could say is that because of the complexity of the issue it would be better to consider this as a separate matter, and when we have an actual bill before us, this administration could give its views on both the constitutional and the socially desirable elements of the program.

Regulatory Responsibility for Atomic Industry

Q: Mr. President, a study was made recently by the Michigan Law School that recommended that the regulatory responsibility for atomic industry be under an agency other than that which is responsible for its development. The study indicates there is a dangerous paradox in allowing both regulation and development responsibilities to remain within the Atomic Energy Commission. What are your views on this? This has come up during your time in Congress, too, this question of separating health and regulation from -

The President: Health and regulation?

Q: - from development of the industry itself.

The President: Well, there has been some separation of the health with the Public Health having responsibilities in this area, and I think that members of the Atomic Energy Commission agree that there should be some external check on their research and development programs, and I think that there is a fair balance today. It was a matter which was discussed when I was at the Atomic Energy Commission.

President Eisenhower's Part in the Administration

Q: Mr. President, before your inaugural you expressed the hope that you would be able to use former President Eisenhower in some capacity in your administration. Are you still of that opinion, sir, and do you have any plans in that regard?

The President. I have no plans at the present time. I have not been – I have not discussed the matter with the President, and if we do have an area where he could be helpful and where he felt he could be helpful, then I would discuss it with him. At the present time I think he is still continuing his vacation, to which he is very much entitled.

Disposition of the Surplus Air Force Metal Extrusion Plant

Q: Mr. President, Adrian, Mich., is deeply concerned over what disposition the Government will make of the surplus Air Force metal extrusion plant there. Twice, when GSA has received bids, a firm which reputedly would dismantle the plant has been high bidder while the firm which ultimately might employ as many as 2,500 has been second highest. Appeals for retention of the plant for the local industry have been directed to you. Would you comment on what you have done or plan to do?

The President: Well, I have talked to Mr. Moore about it. I have expressed my hope that an arrangement could be worked out to transfer the plant so that employment can be permitted. One of the problems, of course, is that it would require the transfer of the plant at a price which – at least what is now being examined is whether the transfer of the plant could be made at a price which would be justified. But I quite agree that if it is possible to use this plant for employment, it should be done. I am hopeful, and I am glad that you reminded me of the matter. I am hopeful that we could perhaps get a decision out of Mr. Moore's agency this week, and I will press for that.

Reporter: Thank you, Mr. President.

THE PRESIDENT'S NEWS CONFERENCE OF

MARCH 23, 1961

The President: I want to make a brief statement about Laos. It is, I think, important for all Americans to understand this difficult and potentially dangerous problem. In my last conversation with General Eisenhower, the day before the inauguration on January 19, we spent more time on this hard matter than on any other thing. And since then it has been steadily before the administration as the most immediate of the problems that we found upon taking office. Our special concern with the problem in Laos goes back to 1954. That year at Geneva a large group of powers agreed to a settlement of the struggle for Indochina. Laos was one of the new states which had recently emerged from the French union and it was the clear premise of the 1954 settlement that this new country would be neutral - free of external domination by anyone. The new country contained contending factions, but in its first years real progress was made towards a unified and neutral status. But the efforts of a Communist-dominated group to destroy this neutrality never ceased.

In the last half of 1960 a series of sudden maneuvers occurred and the Communists and their supporters turned to a new and greatly intensified military effort to take over. These three maps (indicating) show the area of effective Communist domination as it was last August, with the colored portions up on the right-hand corner being the areas held and dominated by the Communists at that time; and now next, in December of 1960, 3 months ago, the red area having expanded; and now from December 20 to the present date near the end of March the Communists control a much wider section of the country.

In this military advance the local Communist forces, known as the Pathet Lao, have had increasing support and direction from outside. Soviet planes, I regret to say, have been conspicuous in a large-scale airlift into the battle area - over 100 - 1,000 sorties since last December 13th, plus a whole supporting set of combat specialists, mainly from Communist North Viet-Nam, and heavier weapons have been provided from outside, all with the clear object of destroying by military action the agreed neutrality of Laos.

It is this new dimension of externally supported warfare that creates the present grave problem. The position of this administration has been carefully considered and we have sought to make it just as clear as we know how to the governments concerned.

First, we strongly and unreservedly support the goal of a neutral and independent Laos, tied to no outside power or group of powers, threatening no one, and free from any domination. Our support for the present duly constituted government is aimed entirely and exclusively at that result. And if in the past there has been any possible ground for misunderstanding of our desire for a truly neutral Laos, there should be none now.

Secondly, if there is to be a peaceful solution, there must be a cessation of the present armed attacks by externally supported Communists. If these attacks do not stop, those who support a truly neutral Laos will have to consider their response. The shape of this necessary response will, of course, be carefully considered, not only here in Washington, but in the SEATO conference with our allies, which begins next Monday.

SEATO - the Southeast Asia Treaty Organization - was organized in 1954, with strong leadership from our last administration, and all members of SEATO have undertaken special treaty responsibilities towards an agression in Laos.

No one should doubt our resolutions on this point. We are faced with a clear and one-sided threat of a change in the internationally agreed position of Laos. This threat runs counter to the will of the Laotian people, who wish only to be independent and neutral. It is posed rather by the military operations of internal dissident elements directed from outside the country. This is what must end if peace is to be achieved in Southeast Asia.

Thirdly, we are earnestly in favor of constructive negotiation among the nations concerned and among the leaders of Laos which can help Laos back to the pathway of independence and genuine neutrality. We strongly support the present British proposal of a prompt end of hostilities and prompt negotiation. We are always conscious of the obligation which rests upon all members of the United Nations to seek peaceful solutions to problems of this sort. We hope that others may be equally aware of this responsibility.

My fellow Americans, Laos is far away from America, but the world is small. Its two million people live in a country 3 times the size of Austria. The security of all Southeast Asia will be endangered if Laos loses its neutral independence. Its own safety runs with the safety of us all - in real neutrality observed by all.

I want to make it clear to the American people and to all of the world that all we want in Laos is peace, not war; a truly neutral government, not a cold war pawn; a settlement concluded at the conference table and not on the battlefield.

Our response will be made in close cooperation with our allies and the wishes of the Laotian Government. We will not be provoked, trapped, or drawn into this or any other situation; but I know that every American will want his country to honor its obligations to the point that freedom and security of the free world and ourselves may be achieved.

Careful negotiations are being conducted with many countries at the present time in order to see that we have taken every possible course to insure a peaceful solution. Yesterday the Secretary of State informed the members and leaders of the Congress - the House and Senate - in both parties, of the situation and brought them up to date. We will continue to keep them and the country fully informed as the situation develops.

QUESTIONS

The Laotian Question

Q: Mr. President, can you tell us what reaction you may have had from the Russians, either directly or indirectly, perhaps through the British, with respect to the approach you suggest on this problem?

The President: The British have had a conversation with the Russians, but I think that it's impossible at the present time to make any clear judgment as to what the nature of the response will be. We are hopeful that it will be favorable to the suggestion that we have made - the suggestion that the British have made for a cease-fire and for negotiations of the matter.

State of the Economy

Q: Mr. President, a number - or several, rather - relatively highly placed economists in Government have said recently that the state of the economy is improving and that an upturn may be expected in April or May. How do you, sir, view the current state of the economy?

The President: Well, I think that there are evidences of some improvement in the economy. The question, of course, is whether the upturn which usually comes in the spring will be sufficient to reduce the unemployment percentage, which is high today, to a figure which is more in accordance with a full employment in our society.

We also have to consider whether the upturn will bring us to the use of our national capacity and whether that upturn will be the beginning of a sustained economic growth this year and in the immediate years to come. It is impossible to make any judgment at this time in March on these factors with any precision.

Troop Movements by the Navy and Marines

Q: Mr. President, there have been reports that some portions of our Navy, some portions of our Marines, have been alerted and are moving toward that area. Could you tell us something of that, sir, and would it be safe to assume that we are preparing to back up our words as you have outlined them here?

The President: I think that my statement is clear and represents the views I wish to express at the present time, and I'm hopeful that it will be possible for us to see a peaceful solution arrive in a difficult matter, and I would let the matter rest at this point with that.

Q: Is there any kind of indicated deadline or time limit by which this Government will consider that further action is necessary unless hostilities have ceased in Laos?

The President: No time limit has been given, but quite obviously we are anxious to see an end to overt hostilities as soon as possible so that some form of negotiations can be carried on. And we are - but there has been no precise time limit set.

Q: Sir, I did not mean an ultimatum. I did mean in terms of an indicated time limit in our own minds if this drags on for a week or two weeks or three weeks, is there some time in there?

The President: Well, I think the matter, of course, becomes increasingly serious as the days go by, and that's why we're anxious to see if it's possible at the present time to reach an agreement on a cease-fire. The longer it goes on, the less satisfactory it is.

Q: Mr. President, that map would indicate that the Communists have taken over a good part of Laos. Have your advisers told you what the - how dangerous the military situation is there? Is there a real danger that the Communists will take over the whole kingdom?

The President: Well, quite obviously progress has been made on the - substantial progress has been made by the Communists towards that objective in recent weeks. And the capital - royal capital of Luang Prabang - has been in danger, and progress has been made southward towards the administrative capital of Vientiane. So that it is for this reason that we are so concerned and have felt the situation to be so critical.

Q: Yes, sir. Is there any - do you know how much time the supporters of the Laos Government might have for diplomacy? In other words, is there a danger of a quick takeover by the Communists in a matter of ——

The President: I would say that we are hopeful that we can get a quick judgment as to what the prospects are going to be there. I think that every day is important.

Q: Mr. President, you mentioned earlier in your statement that there were dissident elements in Viet-Nam who were carrying on this warfare. There have been many reports of North Vietnamese troops involved. Do we have any intelligence or information that would bear out these reports?

The President: The phrase "dissident elements," I believe, referred to the internal group, and I also stated that there have been, has been evidence of groups from Viet Minh or North Viet-Nam who have been involved.

Meeting Between Kennedy and Khrushchev

Q: Mr. President, have the events of the past week changed your view on the advisability of a meeting between you and Mr. Khrushchev?

The President: No.

Compromise on the Minimum Wage Bill

Q: Mr. President, we're getting conflicting reports in the Capitol as to your willingness to accept a compromise on this minimum wage bill, particularly in regard to coverage. Can you give us a little information on what your position is on this?

The President: Well, I'm anxious - I've supported the bill that came out of the committee for $1.25 with the expanded coverage over a period of time and also expanded coverage of nearly 4 million. I'm hopeful that that bill will pass, or a bill as close as possible to it would pass.

I find it difficult to know why anyone would oppose seeing somebody, by 1963, paid $1.25 in interstate commerce. And in the new coverage we're talking about businesses which make over $1 million a year. And I find it difficult to understand how anybody could object to paying somebody who works in a business which makes over $1 million a year, by 1963, $50 a week. I think that anyone who is paid less than that must find it extremely difficult to maintain themselves and their family.

I consider it to be a very minimum wage. So that I'm hopeful that the House will pass legislation as close to the bill that came out of the committee as possible, and - because I must say we are talking about a standard for fellow Americans, and millions of them - and I must say I think that it is in the public interest to pass that bill as closely as possible to the House committee bill.

Importance of a Free Laos

Q: Mr. President, there appears to be some national unawareness of the importance of a free Laos to the security of the United States and to the individual American. Could you spell out your views on that a little farther?

The President: Well, quite obviously, geographically Laos borders on Thailand, to which the United States has treaty obligations under the SEATO Agreement of 1954, it borders on South Viet-Nam - or borders on Viet-Nam to which the United States has very close ties, and also which is a signatory of the SEATO Pact. The aggression against Laos itself was referred to in the SEATO Agreement. So that, given this, the nature of the geography, its location, the commitments which the United States has assumed toward Laos as well as the surrounding countries - as well as other signatories of the SEATO Pact, it's quite obvious that if the Communists were able to move in and dominate this country, it would endanger the security of all, and the peace of all, of Southeast Asia. And as a member of the United Nations and as a signatory of the SEATO Pact, and as a country which is concerned with the strength of the cause of freedom around the world, that quite obviouslt affects the security of the United States.

Q: Mr. President, the United States has made the position all the way through on this that we want a neutral Laos. But isn't it true that Laos has a nonviable economy and it can't exist as an independent country?

The President: Well, I think it can exist. That was the premise under which the 1954 agreements were signed. It may require economic assistance, but there are many countries which are neutral which have received economic assistance from one side or the other and many of those countries are in Southeast Asia and some of them are geographically quite close to Laos, so that I don't think that the final test of a neutral country is completely the state of its economy. The test of a neutral country is whether one side or another dominates it and uses it, a phrase I referred to, as a pawn in the cold war. We would like it to occupy a neutral category as does Cambodia.

Q: Mr. President, what is your evaluation of the theory that perhaps the Russians are so active in Laos to keep the Chinese Communists out?

The President: Well, I wouldn't attempt to make a judgment about a matter on which we have incomplete information. I think that the facts of the matter are that there has been external activity and that it has helped produce the result you see on the map, and this is of concern to us. I'm hopeful that those countries which have been supporting this effort will recognize that this is a matter of great concern to us and that they will be agreeable to the kind of proposals which we have made in the interests of peace.

Possibility of a Visit to Venezuela

Q: Mr. President, are you planning a visit to Venezuela or any other areas of Latin America within the next several months?

The President: To Latin America?

Q: Yes, sir.

The President: No, I'm not.

Q: Caracas?

The President: No, I have no plans for a trip.

The Civil War Commission and Blacks in the South

Q: Mr. President, the Civil War Commission has decided it has no authority to provide hotel rooms for Negroes who attend sessions in the South. What is your reaction to that decision?

The President: Well, the Centennial is an official body of the United States Government, Federal funds are contributed to sustaining it, there have been appointments made by the Federal Government to the Commission, and it's my strong belief that any program of this kind in which the United States is engaged should provide facilities and meeting places which may – do not discriminate on the grounds of race or color. I have received the response to my original letter to General Grant, and I am in contact, going to be in contact again with General Grant to see if we can work out a solution which recognizes the principle that I've just enunciated, because we cannot leave the situation as it is today.

Possibility of SEATO Intervention in Laos

Q: Mr. President, in the event that your strong efforts to reach a neutral Laos go unheeded, would you possibly consider it necessary then for SEATO to intervene, or would you spell out a little more clearly what would have to take place?

The President: I think a careful reading of my statement makes clear what the various prospects are and the critical nature of them.

Long-Term Borrowing and Foreign Aid

Q: Mr. President, your foreign aid message, particularly the provision for long-term borrowing, has had a rather mixed reception on the Hill. I wonder, sir, could you tell us, in view of the traditional congressional abhorrence of long-term commitments, what steps you are planning to persuade the country that this is necessary?

The President: Well, I think that it provides far more effective use of the funds that are available. It's very hard for us to say to x country that "We are prepared to join you in economic development if you will make the following contributions towards your own development: investment, tax changes, and all the rest," if we are only able to say that we can do this only on a 12-month basis. If we could say "We will join on a 5-month - over a 5-year period of development for the economy of this country which will give you some hope of improving the standard of living of your people and maintaining freedom," it seems to me that's a far more effective use of our money.

One of the reasons why so much money, I think, has been wasted in mutual security programs in recent years has been because they are financed on a year-to-year basis and no evident progress is made within the countries towards a viable economy. So that I must say that I recognize that the Congress has clear responsibilities for annual appropriations. We are only talking about long-term funding for loans. The Congress would still continue to have its annual appropriations for any other funds, including those which involve military grants. And I would feel that the kind of program we suggested offers the best use of the dollar in these areas. I think progress can be made this way. If we don't get it, I think we'll continue to see some of the drift we've seen in these programs in the past.

Coordination of Transportation to Save the Railroads

Q: Mr. President, what are your plans for coordinating our transportation to save the railroads and keep them running, especially to move missiles?

The President: I think - I've seen no evidences that the missile, the movement of missiles has been - is endangered at the present time or in prospect. The problem of commuters, the problem of the financial integrity of the railroads and their movement is in danger - is in critical position in some areas. It's a matter of concern to the Congress and this administration and we are examining what we can usefully do.

Segregation in Federal Housing Projects

Q: Mr. President, during the campaign you made a pledge, I believe, that if you became President you would issue an Executive order to ban segregation in Federal housing projects. I wondered if you had any plans to implement that pledge anytime in the near future?

The President: We are considering those areas. We've already, as you know, in one area, the area of employment by Government contractors, issued an extremely strong, the strongest Federal order that's ever been issued, with detailed facilities for implementation. We are considering other Executive orders that could be usefully issued. In addition, we are - the Department of Justice is moving ahead in carrying out the congressional mandate in regard to voting. So this matter of use of Executive authority in order to establish equality of opportunity in all areas is a matter which will have the continuing attention of this administration.

Laos and the Prospect of Improved Relations with the USSR

*Q: Mr. President, taking the aggressive Communist attitude on Laos togeth-
er with the negative Russian posture at the opening, the reopening of negotiations in Geneva on test ban, does this combination of circumstances disappoint
you about the prospect of really improved relations with the Soviet Union?*

The President: I am hopeful that it will be possible for the United States
to make progress towards lessening tension in our relations with the Soviet
Union. Quite obviously this is a critical area, and I think the kind of response that we get to our efforts for peace in this area will tell us something
about what kind of a future our world is going to have. We'll have to wait and
see what that response will be, and then I could perhaps give you a better answer as to what our long-range prospects will be after we see what happens
here.

*Q: Mr. President, if these responses aren't forthcoming and aren't favor-
able on your proposals here, would you - and we have to shoot - would you use
your Executive orders and authority, or is the purpose of Mr. Rusk going to the
Senators in preparation of asking for a declaration of war in case it really
becomes a shooting matter out there?*

The President: I think that it would be best to consider it as I stated it
in my statement. The prospects, alternative responsibilities - I've stated
them, I think, as clearly as today they can be stated. We will know a good
deal more in the coming days.

Communist Publishing and the "Book Gap"

*Q: Mr. President, concerning another aspect of this Communist threat, Rus-
sia and Red China publish an estimated 3 to 4 billion books a year, sending a
large proportion to the noncommitted nations, and an AP story says that our
USIA was able to send only a trifling fraction to these countries - last year,
I guess less than 5 million. Does this book gap - doesn't this present a tremendous obstacle to our winning the minds of the uncommitted peoples, and does
our administration plan to close this gap?*

The President: Well, I agree that both the Chinese Communists and the Russians have poured large sums of money into subsidizing cheap book publications
which have poured into many **sections** of the world and is a matter of concern.
I think the point is excellent. Mr. Murrow has been considering what we could
do in an expanded way in this area. There are other areas where they've also
made a greater effort, radio broadcasts to Africa and so on as well as exchanges. So that we have the whole problem of which books is a part, in this
struggle between freedom and control.

Laos and the Buildup of Conventional Forces

*Q: Mr. President, I have a question about conventional forces in relation
to the Laos situation. You have been reviewing the recommendations of your
Secretary of Defense on conventional forces. Have you come to any decision on
building them up, and have you found them adequate to deal with the Laos situation in case of ——*

The President: We will be sending a message on Monday or Tuesday on those
changes we are going to make in defense and at that time we'll give, I think,
a more adequate response than I could give here to your question, because we're
going to discuss the entire military budget. Quite obviously, we are stretched
around the world with commitments to dozens of countries and it does raise the
question of our - whether a greater effort should not be made.

Q: *Mr. President, could you tell us what in your opinion this country has obtained out of its roughly $310 million worth of aid sent in the past 6 or 7 years to Laos?*

The President: Well, Laos is not yet a Communist country and it's my hope that it will not be.

Further Meetings with Foreign Minister Gromyko

Q: *Mr. President, are you contemplating a further - a meeting with Soviet Foreign Minister Gromyko within the next week or have you one scheduled with him?*

The President: A further meeting? I've not seen Mr. Gromyko.

Q: *A meeting.*

The President: No, I have no plans for a meeting.

Q: *Mr. President, because it was such an obvious move, could you tell us what Mr. Salinger handed you just then? (Laughter)*

The President: Well, he handed me - I will not draw the cloak of Executive privilege around it. The point was made that Viet-Nam - these are the sort of things he knows - that Viet-Nam is not a signatory of the SEATO Pact, but is a protocol country of - under the SEATO Pact. (Laughter)

Secretary Dillon's Estimate of Corporate Profits

Q: *Mr. President, do you agree with Secretary Dillon's estimate that the corporate profits for fiscal '62 will be about $3 billion under President Eisenhower's estimate, and, if so, will your budget take these lower revenue estimates into account?*

The President: The budget estimates will be lower than were estimated in January, substantially lower than they were last October, and a good deal lower than they were estimated to be a year ago. We are sending a budget message up tomorrow which gives our opinion on what those receipts will be. But the economy, as it has slowed down, of course, the profit squeeze has been on, and the returns to the Government have been lessened, which have affected the budget picture.

Reporter: *Thank you, Mr. President.*

THE PRESIDENT'S NEWS CONFERENCE OF

APRIL 12, 1961

The President: I have several announcements.

Today is the 16th anniversary of the death of President Franklin D. Roosevelt. It is also the anniversary of the announcement of the vaccine which has been discovered to prevent paralytic polio. Today over 90 million Americans have been vaccinated with the Salk vaccine. Over 80 million remain unvaccinated. Almost 4,800,000 children have not been vaccinated and a majority of these are under 5 years of age. I hope that the renewed drive this spring and summer to provide vaccination for all Americans, and particularly those who are young, will have the wholehearted support of every parent in America. I hope that they will, knowing some of the long-range suffering which comes from an attack of polio, with this miraculous drug, I hope that everyone takes advantage of it.

Secondly, I wish to announce the formation of an advisory group, the members of which will be assisting Mr. Labouisse and other governmental officials in bringing about the much needed change in our foreign aid program which we announced in March. Mr. Eugene Black, President of the International Bank, and other distinguished members of the banking community who are familiar with the problems of development assistance abroad will be working with us. We have also secured the services of a distinguished member of the New York Bar, Mr. Theodore Tannenwald, who has agreed to assist us in the drafting of the new legislation; and Mr. George Gann of the Ford Foundation, who is giving us the benefit of his experience in the organizational aspects of the work. And finally, and in the most important phase of the effort, we are fortunate to have the services of Robert Blum of the Asia Foundation, William Dale of Stanford Research Institute, and Samuel P. Hayes, of the University of Michigan, Don Humphrey of the Fletcher School in Massachusetts, and Professor Arthur Smithies of Harvard, who will work with Dr. Max Millikan of MIT, and Mr. Frank Coffin, Director of the Development Loan Fund, to shift the aid to a sound and economical basis.

Thirdly, I wish to announce that the U.S. Naval Ordnance Plant at South Charleston, W. Va., will be sold to the Food Machinery and Chemical Corporation of New York City. The General Services Administration has accepted the bid of $4,320,000, and this company is proposing to provide a development which will, they hope, stimulate the economy in this area and in this State, which is a matter of particular interest.

QUESTIONS

U.S. Support for an Invasion of Cuba

Q: Mr. President, has a decision been reached on how far this country will be willing to go in helping an anti-Castro uprising or invasion of Cuba? What could you say with respect to recent developments as far as the anti-Castro movements in Cuba are concerned?

The President: First, I want to say that there will not be, under any conditions, an intervention in Cuba by the United States Armed Forces. This Government will do everything it possibly can, and I think it can meet its responsibilities, to make sure that there are no Americans involved in any actions inside Cuba.

Secondly, the Justice Department's recent indictment of Mr. Masferrer, of Florida, on the grounds that he was plotting an invasion of Cuba, from Florida, in order to establish a Batista-like regime should indicate the feelings of this country towards those who wish to re-establish that kind of an administration inside Cuba.

Third, we do not intend to take any action with respect to the property or other economic interests which American citizens formerly held in Cuba, other than formal and normal negotiations with a free and independent Cuba.

The basic issue in Cuba is not one between the United States and Cuba. It is between the Cubans themselves. I intend to see that we adhere to that principle and as I understand it this administration's attitude is so understood and shared by the anti-Castro exiles from Cuba in this country.

The Soviet's Man in Space

Q: Could you give us your views, sir, about the Soviet achievement of putting a man in orbit and what it would mean to our space program, as such?

The President: Well, it is a most impressive scientific accomplishment, and also I think that we, all of us as members of the race, have the greatest admiration for the Russian who participated in this extraordinary feat. I have already sent congratulations to Mr. Khrushchev, and I sent congratulations to the man who was involved.

I indicated that the task force which we set up on space way back last January, January 12th, indicated that because of the Soviet progress in the field of boosters, where they have been ahead of us, that we expected that they would be first in space. And, of course, that has taken place. We are carrying out our program and we expect to - hope to make progress in this area this year ourselves.

Fidel Castro as Communist

Q: Mr. President, your white paper,[1] last week, referred in very diplomatic language to the takeover by communism in Cuba. Is it your view that Fidel Castro is personally a Communist?

The President: Well, he has indicated his admiration on many occasions for the Communist revolution; he has appointed a great many Communists to high positions. A great many of those, I think, in the white paper - well, rather, the state paper - he indicated that two-thirds of those who had been members of his first government had fled Cuba, people who had a strong feeling for the revolution but who did not propose to see it come under the domination of the Communists.

So I would not want to characterize Mr. Castro except to say that by his own words he has indicated his hostility to democratic rule in this hemisphere, to democratic liberal leaders in many of the countries of the hemisphere who are attempting to improve the life of their people, and has associated himself most intimately with the Sino-Soviet bloc, and has indicated his desire to spread the influence of that bloc throughout this hemisphere.

The Problem of Red China and the U.N.

Q: Mr. President, in your talks with Prime Minister Macmillan, did you come to some common understanding on the best way to handle the problem of Red China in the United Nations next fall?

The President: Well, we discussed the problem. We also discussed the differing approach which the United States has followed. We discussed the problem of the admission of Red China. We also discussed the fact that there was a difference in approach between the British and ourselves. I made it very clear that the United States was going to continue to meet its commitments to the people on Formosa - the government on Formosa - and I also did discuss the fact that the vote on the moratorium was very close. And that we had no - cannot make a final judgment as to what the vote on the moratorium will be on the admission of Red China. But I must say that the report I saw this morning of that conversation from London was not accurate in that it indicated that the United States had changed its position on the moratorium. That we have not done. And I want to take this opportunity to emphasize that the United States supports the Taiwan, Formosa, Government in its membership in the United Nations and is exploring with all interested parties what the position will be in the discussions at the United Nations next fall. The Prime Minister made his own position clear and that of his government.

Unemployment and the Closing of Military Installations

Q: Mr. President, how do you reconcile your concern with unemployment in connection with the closing of about 50 military installations, which will throw thousands of civilian employees out of work?

The President: I might say just to make it perfectly clear, in response to Mr. Hightower's question, in conclusion I would say that the United States is opposed under present conditions - continues to be opposed under present conditions to the admission of Red China.

Now, on your question, we stated in the - we have asked for a substantial increase in expenditures for the national defense. This will affect, beneficially, employment. I think we said in our statement very clearly that we did not think that defense bases should be kept going when they no longer had a - when there was not longer a need for them in order to maintain the defensive strength of the United States. I think that is a traditional position and one which this administration will follow. We will attempt to the best of our ability to maintain jobs for the people who are involved, but we cannot get a strong national defense if we continue defense systems or bases which are archaic and outmoded, and which no longer represesent a real need. I am hopeful that the country's economy generally will be strong enough to absorb those who may be thrown out of work because of structural changes in our defense system. But I think it is a serious problem; as we change from planes to missiles you affect employment not only in the bases but in the defense industries themselves. This is a serious matter for the Government, but we cannot permit ourselves - we are paying in the $40 billions for national defense, which represents a heavy burden, and we have to make it as efficient as possible. So we will try to do that with due regard to the needs of people who are involved. But I am hopeful we can meet their needs on a broader national basis, and not merely maintaining bases for which we no longer have a need in our defense structure.

The Impending Release of Gary Powers

Q: Mr. President, do you have any indication that the Russians may be about to release the U-2 pilot, Francis Gary Powers?

The President: No, I do not. I have seen the story, but we do not have any information on the matter.

A Cease-Fire in Laos

Q: Mr. President, the Russians seem to be taking their time in replying to the urgent call for a cease-fire in Laos. In the meantime, there are reports that they have stepped up their airlift of weapons to the rebels. How long can you afford to wait before the Soviet reply?

The President: I am not sure that there is evidence that a step-up - there may have been an increase of 1 or 2 days, but over a period of 10 days or so, or 2 weeks, I don't think that there is any evidence that there has been very marked increase in their supplies. The supplies have continued, but I don't think it is fair to say, or accurate to say, that there has been a sharp step-up in the last few days.

I am hopeful that we are going to get an answer, I hope, this week, shortly, so that we can get a cease-fire and so that the supplying of forces on both sides could be ended. Our supplies to the government forces are continuing.

Bringing Down the Price of Medicine for the Aged

Q: Mr. President, Senator Kefauver and Representative Celler say that we must have legislation to bring down the prices of medicines for sick people and protect the purity of drugs. They have introduced legislation to do that by amending the patent and antitrust laws. Are you for that? Can you do anything executively, or can you do it through the Department of Justice?

The President: Well, I think that it may be that we can take some action executively without the Congress, and I will be glad to look into that. The Federal Trade Commission also, I am sure, will concern itself with this problem and with other related problems. Mr. Dixon was the counsel for that committee, who is the new chairman of the Federal Trade Commission.

I will be looking with interest to Mr. Kefauver's efforts in this area because the prices are high. I do think, moving away from your point, which I think is a good one, that all this effort would be useful and I think it would also be useful to provide medical care for the aged tied to social security as another facet of the problem of helping our people pay for - afford good health.

Support for William Blakley

Q: Sir, will you help, actively, Senator William Blakley of Texas to get elected? He is running in the primary on the Democratic ticket, and he has opposed your program quite a bit, and also opposed some of your nominees.

The President: He has been nominated by the party, but to the best of my knowledge I haven't heard - he hasn't asked for me, my assistance, as yet. If he does, I will certainly be glad to do what I think is useful. (Laughter) But I'm for Democrats in these fights between - I have read Mr. Tower's speech and so I think probably the people of Texas can decide these things. It isn't very useful, ordinarily, for people to come from out of State, whether it is the President or Senator Goldwater or anyone else, and I think probably the people of Texas can make a very effective judgment without external advice. But I would be glad to give it, if asked.

The Durability of the Communist System

Q: Mr. President, this question might better be asked at a history class than a news conference, but here it is, anyway. The Communists seem to be putting us on the defensive on a number of fronts - now, again, in space. Wars aside, do you think that there is a danger that their system is going to prove more durable than ours?

The President: Well, I think that we are in a period of long drawn-out tests to see which system is, I think, the more durable, not better, but more durable. And we have had a number of experiences with this kind of competition - a dictatorship enjoys advantages in this kind of competition over a short period by its ability to mobilize its resources for a specific purpose. We have made some exceptional scientific advances in the last decade, and some of them - they are not as spectacular as the man-in-space, or as the first sputnik, but they are important. I have said that I thought that if we could ever competitively, at a cheap rate, get fresh water from salt water, that it would be in the long-range interests of humanity which would really dwarf any other scientific accomplishments. I am hopeful that we will intensify our efforts in that area.

I think that if we could increase the techniques for improving education in uneducated sections of the world - by using the latest devices of science - that

that would be an extraordinary accomplishment. I do not regard the first man in space as a sign of the weakening of the free world, but I do regard the total mobilization of man and things for the service of the Communist bloc over the last years as a source of great danger to us. And I would say we are going to have to live with that danger and hazard through much of the rest of this century.

My feeling is that we are more durable in the long run. These dictatorships enjoy many short-range advantages, as we saw in the thirties. But in the long run I think our system suits the qualities and aspirations of people that desire to be their own masters. I think our system suits better. Our job is to maintain our strength until our great qualities can be brought more effectively to bear. But during the meantime, it is going to require a united effort.

The Strength of the Economy

Q: Mr. President, one aspect of the problem you have just been discussing is the strength of our economy. There has been increasing comment from both within your own administration and outside to the effect that even when we pull out of the current recession, we are going to be left with a very large, serious amount of unemployment. It has been suggested that measures quite different in character from what you have proposed, more far reaching, will be necessary to cure that. And I wonder whether you have anything further in mind?

The President: Well, in the first place, I would like to see the measures that we have suggested be passed. We haven't yet secured the passage of the depressed area bill. We haven't yet secured the passage of the aid to dependent children, which has passed the House and I hope will pass the Senate shortly.

We have not yet secured the passage of the social security changes, one of which provides for earlier retirement which will, I think, provide some relief. But these steps – the unemployment compensation which is going to begin to flow into the hands of people in need in the next week, the aid to dependent children, the early retirement, the aid to depressed areas – all these will be useful.

Now, we are also considering what longer range steps could be taken. In some of them which involve different changes in monetary policy, of course, we are rather limited because of the effect on the outflow of gold. Where for our domestic needs we might want to proceed differently, we are limited, because we don't want to start to stimulate the gold outflow again. But we are giving it a good deal of consideration.

These matters are not easy. You want to affect this hard core of unemployment which may continue after we have had a recovery without providing for inflation, without providing for an outflow of our gold. But we are now, in the administration, considering what other measures could be recommended to the Congress which would assist in this area. But I must say it is one of great complexity.

The Prospects of Catching the Russians in Space

Q: Mr. President, a Member of Congress said today that he was tired of seeing the United States second to Russia in the space field. I suppose he speaks for a lot of others. Now, you have asked Congress for more money to speed up our space program. What is the prospect that we will catch up with Russia and perhaps surpass Russia in this field?

The President: Well, the Soviet Union gained an important advantage by securing these large boosters which were able to put up greater weights, and that advantage is going to be with them for some time. However tired anybody may be, and no one is more tired than I am, it is a fact that it is going to take some time and I think we have to recognize it.

They secured large boosters which have led to their being first in sputnik and led to their first putting their man in space. We are, I hope, going to be able to carry out our efforts with due regard to the problem of the life of the man involved this year. But we are behind and I am sure that they are making a concentrated effort to stay ahead.

We have provided additional emphasis on Saturn; we have provided additional emphasis on Rover; we are attempting to improve other systems which will give us a stronger position - all of which are very expensive, and all of which involve billions of dollars.

So that in answer to your question, as I said in my State of the Union Message, the news will be worse before it is better, and it will be some time before we catch up. We are, I hope, going to go in other areas where we can be first and which will bring perhaps more long-range benefits to man-kind. But here we are behind.

Negro Photographers in the White House
News Photographers Association

Q: Mr. President, the White House News Photographers Association bars Negro members. Do you feel that a group attached to the White House should follow such a policy?

The President: No, I don't. I hope they will let everyone in. Everyone comes into the White House and I would hope that those who are involved in that organization - I am sure when the matter is brought to their attention that they will permit everyone who is accredited and is a photographer to come to the White House. Anyway, I'd certainly like to see it.

The Polish-German Frontier

Q: Mr. President, Mr. Gomulka said in a speech released yesterday that persons who are now high in your administration, unnamed, had given some assurance during the campaign last fall that if elected you would consider the present Polish-German frontier to be final. Have you given any such assurance?

The President: Well, I saw the story but I am not informed as to who had the conversation with Mr. Gomulka. In fact, I haven't been able to determine who that might be. But in answer to the - and quite obviously at that time we were not in any position - in any case I was not informed of any conversation then or since then. It may have taken place with Mr. Gomulka. In regard to the question itself, I think that the satisfactory solution of the line should be part of a general solution of the problem of Germany, of the question of Germany, involving the peace treaty with Germany and all the rest.

The Domestic Economy

Q: Mr. President, in connection with the domestic economy and the lag in Congress on the real problem, how do you feel that a greater sense of urgency can be developed among the American people generally? Apparently some Congressmen feel that back home at Eastertime there was not enough push and drive and interest among the people there to give them that interest in your program.

The President: Well, when you have 7 percent unemployed, you have 93 percent working, and therefore it is a fact that you have these pockets of unemployment, which are extremely serious. Some Congressmen can come back who represent West Virginia and some parts of Pennsylvania, and Gary, Ind., and southern Illinois, and all of the rest, and eastern Kentucky, and tell you that there is a great sense of urgency in this matter. Others who represent other areas may not feel it. But I think it is a serious matter. When you look at the rate of economic growth in Italy, Germany, and France this year, and our economic growth, I would say that it is a matter of the greatest urgency. And in addition, anyone who honestly is seeking a job and can't find it deserves the attention of the United States Government and the people, particularly those who are fortunate enough to work, and that includes us all.

French Attempts to Change the Structures of the U.N.

Q: Sir, the United States administration - your administration - had resisted with vigor, especially through its Ambassador to the U.N., Soviet attempts to change the structure of the world organization. Will the administration, now that General de Gaulle has indicated his displeasure with the structure of the U.N., resist with equal vigor any French attempts to change its structure?

The President: Well, we would not favor the change in the structure. I am not sure that there is an agreement - there is certainly not an agreement. They may both disapprove of the structure, but their disagreements are based on different factors, General de Gaulle and the Soviet. I would be opposed to changing the United Nations in the way the Soviets proposed. I support the United Nations and its present organization. We can, I think, perhaps provide more effective representation among the civil servants structure of the United Nations among all countries and all continents. And we also, I hope, can consider how the newly joined countries can play a greater, have a greater voice in the Security Council. But these are the kinds of improvements I would like to see in the United Nations - not tripartitism of the kind suggested by the Soviet Union, which would make it impossible for the United Nations to function. And I regret that this same principle has been suggested in the Geneva talks.

American Policy Regarding Cuba

Q: At the beginning of the news conference, sir, you told us what the United States cannot do in Cuba. Last night in the broadcast you said, "I think Latin America is in a more critical period in its relations with us. Therefore, if we don't move now, Mr. Castro may become a much greater danger than he is to us today." Can you explore, sir, what we can or are doing in the line of that now?

The President: Well, I think that we attempted to indicate some of the areas where I hoped we could take affirmative action, in the speech I made to the ambassadors in March. Mr. Dillon is in Rio at the meeting of the Inter-American Bank. And we are, in the months of April and May and June, going to attempt in other ways to implement the concept behind *alianza para progresso*. I hope that the Congress will appropriate as quickly as possible the $500 million suggested by the Act of Bogotá. That would be at least an important start. We will have other proposals to make, but I think that it's important that we seize the initiative and do not permit those who are not friends of freedom to become the spokesmen for the material aspirations of the people of Latin America. So that I hope we identify ourselves with both the social, political or the social and the material aspirations of the people of Latin America.

Q: Are we barred by our own neutrality acts or by the OAS treaty from giving any aid or arms to anti-Castro elements in the country?

The President: Well, there are, of course, as I stated - there is a revolutionary committee here which is, of course, extremely anxious to see a change in government in that country. I am sure that they have - that they are very interested in associating with all those who feel the same way. Mr. Castro enjoyed some support here in the United States and received some assistance when he was attempting to carry out his revolution. In fact, some Americans were involved in the military actions with him. That latter is what we are particularly anxious to ——

American Policy Regarding Disputes in Other Countries

Q: Would you say, sir, to what extent the United States can lend its good offices to disputes that arise between some of the new countries and their former colonial countries? I am thinking particularly of the West New Guinea dispute between Indonesia and the Netherlands.

The President: Well, we are going to see Mr. Sukarno, and I am sure that that will be one of the matters we will discuss. I did not have a chance to - that was one of the matters touched upon by the Foreign Minister of the Netherlands. It is rather difficult for the United States to offer its good offices unless we were asked by both parties to do so. To the best of my knowledge, we have not been asked by both parties to mediate that dispute.

Significance of the Texas Vote

Q: Mr. President, returning to that Texas election for a moment, what significance, if any, do you see in the vote there in terms of enacting your congressional programs? In other words, was this purely a local election or did it reflect some sort of a reaction to the administration?

The President: Well, I would think it would be probably unwise - I don't know how profitable it would be then, let's say that - to attempt to make a judgment. You could - each side can claim some comfort out of the Texas election. But I think that Senator Blakley runs as a Democrat, and I think that his prospects are - I think that he will probably run an active and vigorous campaign. And we will see what happens. But I wouldn't attempt, in the divided field with over 71 candidates, to make any judgments about which way Texas is going.

Reporter: Thank you, Mr. President.

[1]"Cuba" (Department of State Publication 7171, Inter-American Series 66, April 1961).

THE PRESIDENT'S NEWS CONFERENCE OF

APRIL 21, 1961

The President: Gentlemen, I have several announcements to make.

I know that many of you have further questions about Cuba. I made a statement on that subject yesterday afternoon. We are continuing consultations with other American Republics. Active efforts are being made by ourselves and others on behalf of various individuals, including any Americans who may be in danger. I do not think that any useful national purpose would be served by my going further into the Cuban question this morning. I prefer to let my statement of yesterday suffice for the present.

I am pleased to announce that the United States has offered concrete support to a broad scale attack by the United Nations upon world hunger. I have instructed the Food for Peace Director to offer $40 million in food commodities towards an initial United Nations reserve of $100 million. This will be administered by the United Nations Food and Agricultural Organization. I am informed that other United Nations members will also make similar contributions. The food will then be used to relieve hunger and to improve nutrition in underdeveloped countries of the world. Our participation in this project will complement rather than diminish our existing Food for Peace program.

Third, I am pleased to announce that the Veterans Administration will pay a special insurance dividend of $230 million, in a decision made this morning, to approximately 5 million holders of GI life insurance, beginning July 1. These dividends have been speeded up in order to assist the economy.

And lastly, I am pleased to announce that the Peace Corps is proceeding with its first project. At the request of the Government of Tanganyika, an African country that will gain its first independence on December 28, the Peace Corps will send to that country a party of surveyors, geologists, and civil engineers to help Tanganyika's own technicians map and construct roads. Twenty surveyors, 4 geologists, and 4 civil engineers will provide some of the skills needed to accelerate the development plan. There is nothing more important in Tanganyika than the development of roads to open up the country, and I am delighted that some Americans have volunteered to help in this important effort.

QUESTIONS

The President's Talk with Vice President Nixon

Q: Mr. President, can you tell us anything about your talk with Vice President Nixon last night?

The President: I brought - the Vice President came to the White House at my invitation, and I informed him of - brought him up to date, on the events of the past few days.

Economic Review

Q: Mr. President, can you tell us the status of the mid-April economic review you promised?

The President: Yes. I stated at a previous conference at the end of I think 75 days we were going to undertake a review of the economy. That is now under way under the direction of Dr. Heller, and I hope when that survey is completed that we will have a statement to make on it.

President's Decision to Continue Training Cuban Refugees

Q: Mr. President, respecting your feeling of not going beyond your statement of yesterday on Cuba, there still is in print this morning, quite widely distributed, a published report that you took the decision to continue training

Cuban refugees with arms provided by this Government and for releasing ships and fuel for launching the current operations in Cuba.

Furthermore, this report says that you reached this decision against the advice of Secretary Rusk and Mr. Bowles. Now, is this true?

The President: I think that the facts of the matter involving Cuba will come out in due time. I am sure that an effort will be made to determine the facts accurately. As for me, I am confining myself to my statement for good reason.

Q: Mr. President, this is not a question about Cuba; it is a question about Castro.

Could you tell us whether any intelligence that you have received can shed any light on the reports that the Prime Minister has been incapacitated, that he has not been heard from since Monday or Tuesday, or reports to that effect?

The President: No, I cannot. I saw some, I think some reference was on the ticker this morning that Mr. Castro was seeing some members of the press today, so I suppose we will have a better idea of that later on.

The Effect of Automation and Technological Improvements on Argiculture and Industry

Q: Mr. President, the leaders of House and Senate Republicans told us yesterday at a press conference that they are setting up special study committees on the effect of automation and technological improvements in agriculture as well as industry.

Are you hoping that your Democrats in Congress will set up similar study committees? Do you need them?

The President: Well, I do think that on the Subcommittee on Labor, a subcommittee headed by Congressman Holland, of Pennsylvania, has been conducting studies on the effect of automation for some months.

In regard to the effect of automation on agriculture, I think it is - some of our most serious problems which have arisen in agriculture have been because of research combined with automation, which have brought an extraordinary increase in production, with far less manpower, so that I know that this problem is a matter of substantial concern to all of us.

I am glad that the Republicans are conducting this study, because I think all the attention we can get by both parties into what I consider to be a genuine national problem, automation - what happens to the people who are thrown out of work - I think will be most useful. And agriculture, where we have a great increase in production, with around 4 million people less than we had several years ago, some years ago, in many ways is one of the most extraordinary and admirable facets of our national life.

I think it is unfortunate that we are not able to bring it more to the attention of the world where so many people, including in the Soviet Union and in China, are spending most of their time on subsistence agriculture, that we are able to have this extraordinary production with very few people. But like all blessings, they bring problems with them. And I am glad they are conducting the studies.

Cease-Fire in Laos

Q: Mr. President, at your last news conference you expressed hope that the Soviets would agree within a few days to a cease-fire in Laos. More than a week has gone by since then and the Soviets have not agreed yet. Could you tell us how much longer you will wait before contemplating other kinds of action?

The President: I understand that the British and the Soviets are conferring at the present time, using it in a general sense, and we are hopeful that a cease-fire can be obtained in Laos. We continue to be hopeful.

Campaign Promises

Q: Mr. President, Mr. Nixon, on the Ev and Charlie Show yesterday said that he was going to give you 10 days' grace to produce on your campaign promises that certain things would be done by 90 days. Did he go into this or other domestic politics in your White House meeting?

The President: No, there was nothing stated about - on politics. Mr. Nixon and I discussed matters of national concern, and it was done in a wholly nonpolitical way. Mr. Nixon's response was most helpful.

The Major General Ted Walker Incident

Q: Mr. President, I wonder if you would tell us what your grounds, your investigations of the Maj. Gen. Ted Walker incident in Europe - if you will please tell us what grounds you found for relieving him of his command for allegedly teaching troops anti-communist doctrine?

The President: When I saw the stories in regard to the things which had been said, or at least alleged to have been said in regard to General Walker, I called Secretary McNamara and asked him to investigate. Secretary McNamara then, I believe, suspended General Walker - and my term may not be precise - "pending a completion of investigation," but no decision has been made in regard to General Walker until the investigation has been completed, to find out exactly what was going on.

I do not believe that Secretary McNamara took even that limited action, however, merely because he felt that General Walker was teaching - talking against the Communists. That was not the ground for concern. But no final decision, to the best of my information, has been made on the matter of General Walker. He will be given every opportunity, and those who have been critical of him will be given every opportunity, to present their case. And a final decision will then be made by Mr. McNamara, who will then bring the matter to my attention and I will then review it, without prejudice to General Walker.

The Space Program

Q: Mr. President, you don't seem to be pushing the space program nearly as energetically now as you suggested during the campaign that you thought it should be pushed. In view of the feeling of many people in this country that we must do everything we can to catch up with the Russians as soon as possible, do you anticipate applying any sort of crash program, or doing anything that would ——

The President: We have added, I think it was $130 million to the budget on space several weeks ago, which provides some speedup for Saturn, some speedup for Nova, some speedup for Rover. And I will say that the budget for space next year will be around $2 billion. Now, we are now and have been for some time attempting to make a determination as to developing larger boosters, whether the emphasis should be put on chemical, nuclear rockets or liquid fuel, how much this would cost. And some of these programs have been estimated to be between 20 and 40 billion dollars.

We are attempting to make a determination as to which program offers the best hope before we embark on it, because you may commit a relatively small sum of money now for a result in 1967, '68, or '69, which will cost you billions of dollars, and therefore the Congress passed yesterday the bill providing for a Space Council which will be chaired by the Vice President. We are attempting to make a determination as to which of these various proposals offers the best hope. When that determination is made we will then make a recommendation to the Congress.

In addition, we have to consider whether there is any program now, regardless of its cost, which offers us hope of being pioneers in a project. It is possible to spend billions of dollars in this project in space to the detriment of other programs and still not be successful. We are behind, as I said before, in large boosters.

We have to make a determination whether there is any effort we could make in time or money which could put us first in any new area. Now, I don't want to start spending the kind of money that I am talking about without making a determination based on careful scientific judgment as to whether a real success can be achieved, or whether because we are so far behind now in this particular race we are going to be second in this decade.

So I would say to you that it's a matter of great concern, but I think before we break through and begin a program which would not reach a completion, as you know, until the end of this decade - for example, trips to the moon, may be 10 years off, maybe a little less, but are quite far away and involve, as I say, enormous sums - I don't think we ought to rush into it and begin them until we really know where we are going to end up. And that study is now being undertaken under the direction of the Vice President.

Q: Mr. President, don't you agree that we should try to get to the moon before the Russians, if we can?

The President: If we can get to the moon before the Russians, we should.

Q: Mr. President, isn't it your responsibility to apply the vigorous leadership to spark up this program?

The President: When you say "spark up the program," we first have to make a judgment based on the best information we can get whether we can be ahead of the Russians to the moon. We are now talking about a program which may be - which is many years away.

Q: The Saturn is still on a 40-hour week, isn't it, Mr. President?

The President: We have, as I say, appropriated $126 million more to the Saturn and we are attempting to find out what else we can do. The Saturn is still going to put us well behind. Saturn does not offer any hope of going to the - being first to the moon. The Saturn is several years behind the Soviet Union. I can just say to you that regardless of how much money we spend on Saturn, the Saturn is going to put us - we are still going to be second.

The question is whether the nuclear rocket or other kinds of chemical rockets offer us a better hope of making a jump forward, but we are second, and the Saturn will not put us first.

I want, however, to speed up, if we can, the Saturn, and the Vice President is now leading a study to see what we ought to do in this area.

The Medical Care Program

Q: Mr. President, do you anticipate that there will be a vote in both Houses of Congress this year on your medical care program?

The President: I don't know. If we had a vote in the House it would depend, of course, on the action of the Ways and Means Committee, so that I'm not - I haven't any information yet as to whether we will get a vote in the House. It is possible that there will be one in the Senate, which is not restricted by the same rules.

Q: There have been reports on Capitol Hill that this administration has reconciled itself to no vote on medical care this year.

The President: In either body; in either House?

Q: Yes, sir.

The President: Well, I haven't seen the reports and I would not make that assumption. I am hopeful that - we are dependent in the House on committee action. There can't be a vote in the House without action by the committee because of the rules of germaneness. In the Senate, however, there is a somewhat different situation, but there is no rule of germaneness.

So it's possible that somebody might offer the bill in the Senate as an amendment to another bill. I don't know that yet, but it is very possible that you could get a vote in the Senate this year.

The House is a different problem. You can't get a vote unless the Ways and Means Committee acts.

The John Birch Society

Q: Mr. President, your order to investigate General Walker suggests that you look askance at the teachings of the John Birch Society. Can you tell us how you feel about that organization?

The President: Well, I don't think that their judgments are based on accurate information of the kinds of challenges that we face. I think we face an extremely serious and intensified struggle with the Communists. But I'm not sure that the John Birch Society is wrestling with the real problems which are created by the Communist advance around the world.

I would hope that all those who are strongly concerned about it would address themselves to the kinds of problems which are created by Laos, Viet-Nam, by internal subversion, by the desperate life lived by so many people in this hemisphere and in other places which the Communists exploit.

These are the kinds of problems that we are dealing with. I said something about them yesterday. The use which the Communists make of democratic freedoms and the success which they are able to - once they have seized power - success with which they are able to maintain their power against dissent.

This seems to me to be the problem. We have talked about and read stories of 7,000 to 15,000 guerrillas operating in Viet-Nam, killing 2,000 civil officers a year and 2,000 police officers a year - 4,000.

Now there's been an election in Viet-Nam in which 75 percent of the people, or 80 percent, endorse the government. And yet we read how Viet-Nam is in danger because of guerrilla operations carried on by this small well disciplined, well supplied, across the border group of guerrillas.

How we fight that kind of a problem which is going to be with us all through this decade seems to me to be one of the great problems now before the United States. And I would hope all those who are concerned about the advance of communism would face that problem and not concern themselves with the loyalty of President Eisenhower or President Truman or Mrs. Roosevelt or myself or someone else.

Administration Dealing with the Russians

Q: Mr. President, was your speech yesterday before the editors intended to suggest another approach or a new departure in the administration's dealing with the Russians?

The President: No — I didn't — no.

Q: You have practiced what has been described as the quiet diplomacy approach and your speech yesterday seemed to suggest that you have perhaps decided upon another approach.

The President: No, I wouldn't attempt to make a judgment or response to that. I think that — I am concerned about the kind of problem which I just described. I don't feel satisfied that we have an effective answer to it yet and I think it's a matter of greatest possible concern to all of us because I think events have been moving with some speed.

The use which the Communists make of democracy, and then when they seize power, the effectiveness with which they manage the police apparatus so that dissent cannot arise and so that the people can no longer express their will — liquidation by gunfire of the opposition or by forcing them out of the country to be refugees — this suggests the kind of a problem which we are going to have in this decade.

And in my judgment it's an extremely difficult matter for the free nations to deal with. But I must say that it's a matter to which we must address all of our energy and all of our attention.

The President's Domestic Program

Q: Mr. President, how would you evaluate the present state of your domestic program in Congress?

The President: I think we've done better recently. Yesterday the Senate passed the $1.25 minimum wage. There was action on aid to dependent children and on social security. The vote in the Senate was very ample on the minimum wage. I think there were only 28 votes against it so I think that at least yesterday there was — we made progress.

Q: How much more, sir, do you think needs to be done in order to give you a satisfactory score on your hoped-for legislative program?

The President: Well, I'm hopeful that we can move ahead on the various other parts of the program, including education and housing. We are making progress on social security, distressed areas, and minimum wage. There may be other proposals which we might make to the Congress after we've considered — completed our review of the economy and made a judgment as to exactly what peak or plateau the economy is going to reach this year. And that is what we're attempting to do now and to see whether any additional Government programs may be necessary to encourage it.

Foreign Policy Information

Q: Sir, since last Saturday a certain foreign policy situation has given rise to many conflicting stories. During that time reporters in Washington have noticed that there's been a clamming up of information from formerly useful sources. To my knowledge the State Department and the White House have not attempted to take a representative group of reporters and say, "These are the facts as we know them," and this morning we are not permitted to ask any further questions about this foreign policy situation. In view of the fact we are taking a propaganda lambasting around the world, why is it not useful, sir, for us to explore with you the real facts behind this, or our motivations?

The President: Well, I think, in answer to your question, that we have to make a judgment as to how much we can usefully say that would aid the interest of the United States. One of the problems of a free society, a problem not met by a dictatorship, is this problem of information. A good deal has been printed in the paper and I wouldn't be surprised if those of you who are members of the press will be receiving a lot of background briefings in the next day or two by interested people or interested agencies.

There's an old saying that victory has 100 fathers and defeat is an orphan. And I wouldn't be surprised if information is poured into you in regard to all of the recent activities.

Now, I think we see some of the problems, to move from this particular case into the problem of space where in the Soviet Union no reports were made in regard to any experiments that they carried out on "our man in space." I saw in a national magazine about some student who said the Americans talk a good deal about their man in space, the Soviet Union says nothing and yet it wins. That is one of the problems of a democracy competing and carrying on a struggle for survival against a dictatorship.

But I will say to you, Mr. Vanocur, that I have said as much as I feel can be usefully said by me in regard to the events of the past few days. Further statements, detailed discussions, are not to conceal responsibility because I'm the responsible officer of the Government - and that is quite obvious - but merely because I do not believe that such a discussion would benefit us during the present difficult situation.

But as I say, I think you'll be informed and some of the information, based on what I have seen, will not be accurate.

Tax Investment Incentive Program

Q: Mr. President, have you any assurance your tax investment incentive plan will be supported in Congress?

The President: No, I think it will be a hard fight because the plan when it was sent up was intended to secure as much revenue as may have been lost because of the tax credit plan. The tax credit plan puts special emphasis on stimulating new industry and therefore new employment, but in order to make up the revenues we lost by the tax credit plan we have had to take control of other revenues, and of course those people are going to object - the expense accounts and the dividend credits and so on, so that I think we will have a hard fight.

Q: You asked for it at this session - do you think your educational program will be persuasive this session?

The President: I hope so because I really believe that the tax credit program, in fact, the whole tax bill, was carefully considered by people in the Treasury as well as the Council of Economic Advisers. It had the strong support of Mr. Dillon and others who have given this matter great consideration.

I am hopeful that Congress will respond favorably. But it is a technical matter, it involves important interests. And I think it will have a - be very soberly considered, which I hope it will be. But I am hopeful that it will pass and I think it would be useful if it would.

The President's Trip

Q: *Mr. President, are you contemplating visiting any other countries besides France on your trip at the end of May to see General de Gaulle?*

The President: I am planning - my only present plan is to go to France.

Q: *There had been some talk that you're going to London, I understand, to christen the Radziwill baby.*

The President: Well, that has been considered but I've not reached any judgment on it. I think there is some interest by the family and it would really be a question of whether we could - whether it would be the best thing to do.

The Charges Against the Russian Spy Melekh

Q: *Mr. President, would you explain the reason for the dropping of espionage charges in Chicago recently against the Russian spy Melekh, and was that a part of a bargain for the RB-47 fliers?*

The President: In answer to the last part of the question, it was not. There was no connection. The dropping of the charges was made after an examination of the details of the case and of the national interst and it was felt that it would be useful to take the action we took. I am sorry I can't be more responsive but I will say it was not in regard to the RB-47 fliers.

Funds for Communications and Meteorology

Q: *Mr. President, we have demonstrated a great capability in space and communications and meteorology. While these are not as dramatic as a man orbiting in space, there has been a strong feeling among scientists the world over that the country that would first develop a space telecommunications system to bring communications within the reach of every nation in the world at the price they could afford would make an even greater impact than the country that orbited man first in space.*

Are you considering putting more funds, because you have cut some, in both communications and meteorology - are you considering adding more funds to the budget?

The President: Yes, I believe that we have, or are about to, if we haven't already done so, put an additional - and I just have to go from memory now, of a decision made several weeks ago - I am under the impression that we decided to put another 25 to 27 million dollars into a communication satellite as part of this general program.

Q: *Yes, but industry also has been interested in putting its funds in it, and there was a statement by Mr. Webb that we weren't going to at this point put any of this program into industry's hands until we had investigated further. Since they're willing to spend money, are you considering perhaps allowing them to share the cost and advance this program?*

The President: Well, I don't know enough about the matter to give you a detailed answer, except I do know that we did put an additional sum of money for a communications satellite, amounting to the sum that I suggested there.

Now if there are any other further things that can be done, or if anyone else wants to put their money into it, I am sure that Mr. Webb would be agreeable. But I must say from examining this and other programs, I find that the Government puts most of the money into them.

Possibility of Vice-President Johnson Going to Southeast Asia

Q: Mr. President, do you intend to send Vice-President Johnson to Southeast Asia soon?

The President: We have been considering the Vice President going to Southeast Asia, and I think a decision will be reached on that in the next - perhaps over the weekend or the next few days.

Formal Agreements with the Soviet Union

Q: Given the stress that you've put this morning and in recent days on this problem of fighting the indirect Communist tactics, do you still - and also given the rather harsh language out of Moscow, including Mr. Khrushchev's note to you - do you still feel that it is useful to go ahead with efforts at the diplomatic level to negotiate formal agreements with the Soviet Government?

The President: Well, we still continue to hope that some agreement could be reached on the cessation of nuclear tests. We are, of course, very discouraged by the newest insistence of the Soviets on a veto. It's quite obvious that the Senate would not accept such a treaty nor would I send it to the Senate, because the inspection system then would not provide any guarantees at all.

Now, I noticed the language used by Mr. Khrushchev himself, not merely one of his representatives, in Mr. Lippmann's article, a strong insistence on the tripartite and on unanimous agreement in regard to the inspection system. I am hopeful that there may be a change in that. But if there isn't a change in that position, it is going to be very hard to get an agreement. But I believe that Mr. Dean should continue because if these test conversations should break up, then of course our hopes of getting any agreement on disarmament would be substantially lessened and we could look for a proliferation of atomic testing in other countries.

So that I feel that Mr. Dean should continue, though we have been discouraged by the Russian position.

Q: Do you feel, sir, that it is possible to have really a two-level operation here, an undeclared kind of warfare which you have been talking about, and yet a formalized effort not only in the test ban negotiations but in terms of exchanges and other types of negotiations? Are these two things compatible?

The President: The incompatability may rest in the fact that it's hard to get an agreement on any matter when there is suspicion between the two systems and when one of the systems are pressing their interest with great vigor around the world.

It makes the chances of getting any agreement far less. I thought the best hope was the nuclear testing, even though it was always true that the obstacles were large.

But if there is any chance at all of getting an agreement on a cessation of nuclear tests, regardless of what appear to be the obstacles, I think we should press on.

So in answer to your question, I still believe that Mr. Dean should continue to work at Geneva.

Reporter: Thank you, Mr. President.

THE PRESIDENT'S NEWS CONFERENCE OF

MAY 5, 1961

The President: I have several announcements to make.

This week Ambassador Arthur H. Dean has reported to me upon the status of the nuclear test ban conference at Geneva. On the opening day of the resumed conference, the United States in closest cooperation with the United Kingdom presented a series of new proposals, and on April 18, 1961, presented a complete nuclear test ban draft treaty. The new U.S. position represents an earnest and reasonable effort to reach a workable agreement. It constitutes a most significant overall move in these negotiations. Unfortunately, the Soviet Union has introduced a new proposition into the negotiations which amounts to a built-in veto of an inspection system.

The Soviet proposal calls for a three-man administrative council to direct inspection operations and other activities of the control arrangements. This proposal reverses a position to which the Soviet Union had previously agreed. In earlier negotiations before this session in Geneva, it had been agreed that the inspection system would be headed by a single administrator, operating within a mandate clearly defined in the treaty. The Soviet Union would substitute a directorate, representing the Communist bloc, the Western Nations, and uncommitted countries. Each member of this triumvirate would have to agree with every other member before any action could be taken. Even relatively detailed elements of the inspection system would be subject a veto or a debating delay.

We recognize that the Soviet Union put forward its proposition before it had considered our new proposals. It is now considering our draft treaty, and we hope it will do so in a positive manner, as of course we are most anxious to secure an agreement in this vital area - a responsible and effective agreement.

Ambassador Dean is leaving for Geneva today to resume the negotiations. The United States will continue to strive for a reliable and workable agreement. I have asked Ambassador Dean to report to me within a reasonable time on the prospects for a constructive outcome.

Secondly, I have asked Vice President Johnson to undertake a special fact-finding mission to Asia. The Vice President has agreed to do this. I consider this an extremely important assignment and I will be looking forward to receiving the Vice President's firsthand reports when he returns.

The Vice President will report directly to me upon his return. It is expected that the State Department will make public the itinerary and the technicians who will accompany the Vice President as soon as possible. It is anticipated that in the course of his trip the Vice President will consult with top governmental officials and conduct discussions on the highest level relating to the situations in those countries.

Next, I have today instructed the United States representatives on the Council of the Organization of American States to propose the convocation on July 15th of an extraordinary meeting of the Inter-American Economic and Social Council to be held at the ministerial level. The purposes of this meeting should be to initiate and develop planning and arrangements related to realistic economic development in the Americas, as well as to elaborate the objectives of the Act of Bogota in all key areas of economic and social betterment. This will be an important aspect of the cooperative program which I have set forth in the concept of the Alliance for Progress.

Finally, I was asked at a previous press conference what the Government was going to do about the aluminum extrusion plant that it owns in Adrian, Mich. I am pleased to announce that the General Services Administration has completed negotiations for the sale of the plant to the Harvey Aluminum Company of California and one of the conditions of the sale was that the plant be kept in production.

QUESTIONS

Efforts in the Space Field

Q: Mr. President, you said earlier today that today's space flight should provide incentive to everyone in our Nation concerned with this program to redouble their efforts in this vital field. Do you have any specific proposals as to how these efforts should be redoubled, and would you want more money for space now than you have already asked from Congress?

The President: The answer to the question is yes, we are going to send an additional request for appropriations for space, which I hope will have a beneficial effect on the program. We are going to make a substantially larger effort on the program. We are going to make a substantially larger effort in space.

The United States' Main Adversary

Q: Mr. President, in the speech prepared for delivery in Chicago last Friday which you did not read, you said that the principal adversary was not the Russians but rather our own unwillingness to do what must be done. Could you clarify for us your thinking on that and indicate some field in which the American people have not done what their governmental leaders asked?

The President: Well, the latter is not the correct - I said "our", not to make a distinction between the Government and the people. I was talking about the common problems of our free society.

I do wish that some of the speeches I give would get as much attention as the speeches which I do not give. (Laughter)

I do think there are a number of things that can usefully be done. We are going to require a larger effort in space. We are going to require a larger effort in other areas of the national security and we will be making our suggestions to the Congress.

I will say that this is a free society and it is not - it really requires a good deal of voluntary effort. On the matter of space, I've asked Secretary Goldberg to cooperate closely with Senator McClellan, to see if we can get a responsible, consistent effort by labor and management in the field of production of our missile program.

What is true there is true of other programs essential to our national defense. We have meetings at the White House, under the leadership of Secretary Goldberg and Secretary Hodges, a panel composed of the leading business and labor leaders of this country and public members, to see if we can persuade labor and management to come to useful national conclusions on problems of price and wages which will affect our balance of payments, and also address themselves to the problems of automation.

Now the Federal Government cannot compel that. All we can do is indicate the need. We are asking the people of this country to spend a good deal of money on mutual security and foreign assistance, which is not a popular program but which I believe to be essential. We have asked the people to support a greater effort - both of the National Government and in their own communities - to improve education. We are asking the people of this country to try, regardless of their own personal views, to reach - to come closer to the constitutional concept of equality of opportunity for all Americans, regardless of their race or creed.

There are a good many of these areas which are within the private sector where each person can contribute usefully to strengthen education, to improve the opportunity for all Americans, to pay heavy burdens as they do in taxation to maintain programs which they may not always wholly agree with but which at least many of us feel to be in the national interest. In their own private work they consider the national needs, and we will continue to try to point out where we need a national effort.

Q: May I ask one followup question, sir? When you use the word "our", are your suggesting that it's the unwillingness of Government and people to do what must be done?

The President: I had not subjected that sentence to the - but what I do think is a problem is to, in a free society, to attempt to come to actions which permit us to compete successfully with the discipline of the Communist state. And I think it's probably not only true using the "our" - I would use it not only in the national sense, but also in the international sense.

There isn't any doubt, reading today's news from one country and another, that the forces of freedom are in many areas on the defense, partly because they have not always been willing to take those progressive steps which will associate the governments with the progressive aspirations of the people so that when I use "our", I use it really in the sense of speaking of the common purpose of the free world, which affects other countries besides ourselves. But as time goes on, I think the point made in the question is a good one.

I think we should continue as much as we can to indicate where the people, other than in the payment of taxes or in their acceptance of military obligations, where they can usefully contribute to the advancement of the national interest. I have suggested several areas, and I will suggest others in time.

Forces in South Viet-Nam

Q: Mr. President, there have been reports that you would be prepared to send American forces into South Viet-Nam if that became necessary to prevent Communist domination of that country. Could you tell us whether that is correct, and also anything else you have regarding plans for that country?

The President: Well, we have had a group working in the Government and we have had a Security Council meeting about the problems which are faced in Viet-Nam by the guerrillas and by the barrage which the present government is being subjected to. The problem of troops is a matter - the matter of what we are going to do to assist Viet-Nam to obtain its independence is a matter still under consideration. There are a good many which I think can most usefully wait until we have had a consultation with the government, which up to the present time - which will be one of the matters which Vice President Johnson will deal with: the problem of consultations with the Government of Viet-Nam as to what further steps could most usefully be taken.

The Indian Chairman of the International Control Commission in Hanoi

Q: Mr. President, is the administration satisfied that the Indian Chairman of the International Control Commission in Hanoi has pressed as vigorously as he might have the right of the Commission to go to the Hanoi airfield, where the Soviet planes have been putting down on the way to Laos? Specifically, has he at times declined to have the Commission do that?

The President: There has been, as you know, some disagreement as to the authority of the International Control Commission. I would hope that - and after all, this is a matter which the British have, and the Indian Government, as well as the other two members of the Control Commission, the Canadians and the Poles - I would hope that they would use maximum influence to make the Control Commission as effective as possible. And we would be - this Government would cooperate in every way to make it effective.

The Training and Arming of Cuban Exiles

Q: Mr. President, is it anticipated that the United States will continue to train and arm the Cuban exiles in this country or elsewhere, or will that operation be disbanded?

The President: We have no plans to train Cuban exiles as a Cuban force in this country or in any other country at this time. There are, of course, Cubans who live in this country or have the opportunity to serve in the Armed Forces of the United States. But if your question means are we planning now to train a Cuban force, as I understand your question, we are not now training and are not now planning to train a Cuban force of the kind that your question would suggest.

Senator Fulbright on Foreign Policy

Q: Mr. President, are you embarrassed or is the Government harmed in any way by the rather frank statements that Senator Fulbright has made on foreign policy?

The President: Am I embarrassed - and what was the other word?

Q: Or is the Government harmed in any way in its foreign relations by a member of your party speaking as he has?

The President: No. Senator Fulbright and I spent an hour together last evening, and we've had - I've talked to Senator Fulbright, I think, at least on five different occasions in the last 4 or 5 weeks, and I expect to continue to confer with him. He is Chairman of the Senate Foreign Relations Committee and he is a valuable citizen, and I think his counsel is useful and I think that he should say what he thinks. And if he has indicated disagreement on occasions, then he has indicated general support on a good many other occasions, although that has not become as newsworthy.

The Conflict of Interest Laws

Q: Mr. President, about 10 days ago you sent a message to Congress on the conflict of interest laws and in that message you mentioned that public confidence is the basis for effective government, and that when that confidence appears to falter or does falter then we are in some sort of trouble. Since that time one of your Cabinet members, Secretary of the Interior Udall, has been involved in a situation in which one of his friends, believing to have acted on his suggestion, solicited members of the oil and gas industry for contributions to a $100-a-plate Democratic Rally.

Now, in this instance, do you believe that ethical standards have appeared to falter or have you had any advice for your Secretary in this case?

The President: Well, I know that the Secretary attempted, I believe, according to what I read of his press conference and the conversations that I have had with him myself, did - when he heard of the letter that had gone out which he had not envisioned - did attempt to have those letters recalled.

I think this whole question of trying to raise funds for campaigns is a very difficult one and it leads to embarrassments. I wish and I hope that before we get into another presidential campaign that we can work out some system by which the major burdens of presidential campaigns on both sides would be sustained by the National Government, as suggested by Theodore Roosevelt, as suggested by Senator Neuberger - Dick Neuberger - when he was here. Because, to try to raise $6 million or $7 million, which a presidential campaign must, from people, is a very difficult task and leads to embarrassing situations. I made it clear in the campaign, and I make it clear again, that no one should contribute - that while we are glad to have support, no one should contribute to any campaign fund under the expectation that it will do them the slightest bit of good, and they should not stay home from a campaign fund or dinner or campaign under the slightest expectation that it will do them a disservice.

I'm satisfied that that's Mr. Udall's view, from my knowledge of him. But I do think that every member of the Cabinet, every member of this administration, should bend over backwards to make sure that there are no misunderstandings of the kind that could have arisen from this incident.

Secretary Udall understands that. I hope everybody else does. But I think the best way to prevent an embarrassment to a Cabinet officer - and I think that Mr. Udall was embarrassed by this incident - and embarrassment to an administration, would be to try to work out some other way of raising funds for these presidential campaigns, because there isn't any doubt that people give - and I am talking now not about this incident, but about generally - under the expectation that they should, or it is expected of them. As long as we can't get broader citizen participation, I think it ought to be done through the National Government, and I would support that strongly if the Congress would move in that direction.

Q: *Have you spoken to Mr. Udall about this, sir?*

The President: I have.

An Embargo on Trade with Cuba

Q: *Mr. President, has the administration made any determination with respect to an embargo on trade with Cuba?*

The President: We had a meeting of the National Security Council in which we discussed the problems of Cuba. As you know, the only kinds of supplies that are now being sent to Cuba involve food and medicine, so that we have to consider carefully all of the implications of further action and that is being done.

Q: *Is a decision imminent?*

The President: That will be considered carefully.

The Successful Launching of an Astronaut into Space

Q: *Mr. President, in addition to the statement you issued earlier, will you here give your evaluation and reaction to today's successful launching of an American astronaut into space and back?*

The President: Well, I first would like to repeat what I said about Major Gagarin, which was that as a human accomplishment and as a demonstration of courage, I think everyone, whether they are citizens of this country or citizens of another country, take the greatest personal satisfaction in the accomplishment of another member of the human race.

As an American, I am, of course, proud of the effort that a great many scientists and engineers and technicians have made, of all of the astronauts, and, of course, particularly of Commander Shepard and his family.

We have a long way to go in the field of space. We are behind. But we are working hard and we are going to increase our effort. In addition, we are making available the scientific information which we have gathered to other scientists in the world community and people who share our view that the probe into space should be peaceful, and should be for the common good, and that will continue to motivate us.

Status of Foreign Policy

Q: Mr. President, leaving aside the matter of the space trip today, I think many of us are concerned by the relentless knelling of the gong of gloom and doom by some of the administration officials who participate in foreign affairs. I was wondering, sir, if you could tell us if there are any bright spots on the international horizon?

The President: Well, I think that we have grounds for encouragement. I am hopeful that NATO will be strengthened by the meeting in Oslo, and that we will make a more determined effort. I believe that as other situations become more difficult, that there is a common recognition of the need for closer collaboration. That is true of NATO.

Secondly, I am hopeful that our ties with Japan can become strengthened as the weeks and months pass, and I have a good deal of encouragement from the effort which India is making on its third 5-year plan, which if successful could make a tremendous difference in the cause of freedom throughout all of Asia.

Then I feel that there is a greater recognition in this hemisphere of - I don't think that there is any doubt about this - that there is a greater recognition of the urgency of a common hemispheric approach to the problems of poverty and a common hemispheric effort to improve the life of the people. In addition, I think there is a common hemispheric awareness now that there is cause for alarm in the determined effort which Communists are making to seize control of the liberal revolutionary movements which are endemic to the Western Hemisphere, and turn them to their own ends.

And, quite obviously, I think that we are happy about what happened this morning. I am not a pessimist about the future, but I think that we have a good many problems, but that doesn't ——

The Assertion and Support of Foreign Policy

Q: Mr. President, you have emphasized on several occasions in public the necessity to find new nonmilitary ways to assert and support our foreign policy. Can you suggest to us this afternoon any ways in the immediate future that we might do that in meeting the Communist threat in Southeast Asia, specifically?

The President: Well, I think the United States can play an important role. And I think in considering the problems in our own hemisphere we have to remember that the United States is holding back - is protecting the integrity by its guarantees of a good many countries which are in the direct line of hazard in the Middle East, in Asia, and in Western Europe - and that in itself is a substantial accomplishment. We can assist these countries by our guarantees or at least we can protect these countries by our guarantees against outright military invasion. We can assist them through economic assistance to improve the life of their people. We can assist them through defense support in strengthening their armed forces against internal guerrilla activity. But in the final analysis they have to - and we cannot do it for them - they have to organize the political and social life of the country in such a way that they maintain the support of their people.

There is a limit beyond which our efforts cannot go. I think that I have described what our efforts can do. In the final analysis, then, the responsibility rests with the people involved to maintain the support of the people, to identify their government with the people.

One of the reasons why it has been a satisfaction to have the President of Tunisia here, Mr. Bourguiba, is that he has done that. He has stood for freedom; he has identified himself with a common effort - national effort - by the people under freedom, and that's what we need to do around the globe.

The Preparation of Overseas Dependents

Q: Mr. President, what are you and the Defense Department doing to better prepare the one-half million dependents, more than half of whom are wives, sons, and daughters, of Peace Corps qualifications, for their roles while living overseas with their husbands, in the case of wives, and fathers, in the case of sons and daughters?

The President: Well, I don't think the Defense - did you say the Defense Department?

Q: I asked what you and the Defense Department, because I was referring primarily to Armed Forces wives and sons and daughters who are of Peace Corps qualification.

The President: Well, that really is a responsibility of the Peace Corps, which is to - I may not be ——

Q: Perhaps I did not make myself clear. (Laughter) We have at least 485,000 dependents of our Armed Forces ——

The President: In order to make themselves more effective?

Q: Yes.

The President: Well, I see. I think that is a good - I don't know whether we are doing enough. I am not informed about the matter. I think it is a good point, and I think that the Defense Department and the State Department and the White House should see if there is anything more effective we can do, so we will.

The Monroe Doctrine

Q: Mr. President, in view of the communistic declarations of Cuba's Castro, what is the position of the United States now on the Monroe Doctrine and how do we expect to enforce it?

The President: Well, the Monroe Doctrine and other treaties which the United States has committed itself to, of course, govern the foreign policy of the United States in this hemisphere. I have discussed the problem, and the Secretary of States has made other references to it. It is a matter of some concern now on an individual and hemispheric basis.

The President's First 100 Days

Q: Mr. President, how would you appraise your first 100 days in office?

The President: Well, I feel I can read what you gentlemen write about it and I wouldn't attempt to contradict you.

U.S. Ties with Japan

Q: Mr. President, speaking of ties with Japan, as you did, do you think it might still be useful for General Eisenhower to visit Tokyo in the fall, or is that still under consideration?

The President: Well, I think whatever the judgment would be of the President, I would accept, and ——

Q: The State Department has asked him not to, if I recall correctly.

The President: I have looked into it and it is - I saw that statement and I have talked to the State Department, and we are attempting to come to a more definitive conclusion as to what we might suggest to him, though, of course, what we would do is give him all the information we have and then see what his best judgment was. I think that President Eisenhower could **very usefully** travel abroad as an individual and also, of course, as a respected citizen of this country. When and where he should go is a matter on which he would make a judgment. But we would, in the meanwhile, provide him with all the information we had as to the appropriateness - as, really, to the wisdom of exactly when those trips should be taken and where. The final decision will be made by the President - President Eisenhower - but we will make **available** to him all the information that we have.

The Plight of Laundry Workers

Q: Mr. President, during the campaign you repeatedly mentioned the plight of laundry workers in some of our big cities, being paid substandard wages. How do you feel about both Houses having passed a minimum wage bill which specifically excludes them from coverage?

The President: I wish we could include them in the coverage. I am hopeful that we will not settle with what we now have, but that we will get the laundry workers in. One of the problems with laundry workers, of course, is that they are paid quite badly now. I would say they are among the lowest group - almost the lowest group in the American economy. Laundries are not a prosperous business at the present time. The passage of the minimum wage of $1.25 would increase the cost of the laundry owners by a substantial sum because manpower represents a high percentage of their cost, and they are competing with home laundries, which now have become a rather easy alternative in many cases, so that the argument is made that we would liquidate a substantial percentage of the industry and throw them out of work. So it is not the easiest problem. But, nevertheless, considering all that, in my judgment they should be covered. And that goes for hotel and restaurant workers, too - it was necessary to drop them in order to get the coverage we did. The coverage we passed, which was 3,600,000, is the first time that we expanded the coverage since 1938. It's a hard fight, but I am hopeful that we will come back to them and get those groups covered.

Spending in Public Works as an Attack on Unemployment

Q: Mr. President, does your administration have plans for further spend-ing in public works as an attack on unemployment, and do your remarks that a substantially larger effort is needed in the space program indicate that you prefer to channel any extra spending into the military field?

The President: Well I think we can make a judgment as to what additional efforts should be made in retraining or public works, and so on, based on our judgment of the economy, and also what other expenditures we have to make in the fields of national security and related - we are making a study of what greater effort should be made in the field of conventional forces at the pre-sent time. All these will be completed before the end of the month, and will be made public. So that we are trying to make a judgment on the state of the economy, of what usefully could be done, of the international and national needs. I cannot today give you an answer to the ———

The Availability of Russian Knowledge Regarding Space

Q: Mr. President, is there any evidence that the Soviet Union is making available to the scientists in other countries the knowledge which it recently acquired from its man in space?

The President: I have not heard it. Now, I don't want to be inaccurate. It is possible they have, but it has not been brought to my attention. And there was our statement this morning in which we spoke of the fact that we were going to disseminate it to other scientists. We did. It was suggested that others who have pioneered in this field have not made that information avail-able.

Coverage of the Space Shot

Q: Mr. President, in that connection, were you satisfied with the cover-age given today of the space shot, and if you were, and it was not a success-ful thing, would we be back in the orphanage?

The President: Back in the what?

Q: In the orphanage.

The President: I agree that if it had failed, having had some experience with that, it would be a very difficult time for NASA and for us all. But fortunately, it succeeded. I have not got the answer, however, to the ques-tion of the buildup.

What I think is somewhat unfair is when pressmen themselves, or editorial writers, criticize NASA for attempting a big buildup with all of the implica-tions it would have to our prestige and standing if there is a failure. We are not responsible, at least we are making every effort not to be responsible, for encouraging a press concentration on this event, because quite obviously if we fail we are humilated here and around the world.

But in a free society, if a newspaperman asks to be represented, and to come, then he can come. So I think everybody ought to understand that we are not going to do what the Russians did, of being secret and just hailing our successes. If they like that system, they have to take it all, which means that you don't get anything in the paper except what the government wants. But if you don't like that system, and I don't, then you have to take these risks. And for people to suggest that it is a publicity circus, when at the same time they are very insistent that their reporters go down there, does seem to me to be unfair.

What is fair is that we all recognize that our failures are going to be publicized and so are our successes and there isn't anything that anyone can do about it or should.

Reporter: Thank you, Mr. President.

REMARKS AND QUESTION AND ANSWER PERIOD AT THE PRESS LUNCHEON IN PARIS

JUNE 2, 1961

Distinguished guests, ladies and gentlemen:

I do not think it altogether inappropriate to introduce myself to this audience. I am the man who accompanied Jacqueline Kennedy to Paris, and I have enjoyed it.

I am also happy to have an opportunity to express publicly my appreciation to President and Mrs. de Gaulle for the hospitality and kindness which they have shown to us since our visit to Paris. I must say also, as I said to the General, that my most vivid impression of my visit here was not even the extraordinary spectacle which we all witnessed last night, which reminded us of the long reach into history which this country possesses, but rather was the sense of vigor and vitality and force possessed by the French people themselves. I do not say that riding in a car through rainy streets is the best method of making a determination of national character, but I have ridden through many streets and I must say it is a most effective method of determining the quality of the people. And I think any American who shared the experiences which we have had during the past 2 days in the sunshine on occasion, in the rain more often, would come away from this country with a feeling of confidence and hope.

I come on the same mission which occupied many of my predecessors, stretching all the way back to President Wilson at the conclusion of the First World War, and that is how it is possible to bind more intimately for the common interest France and the United States, Europe and the United States. This is not altogether a new effort. I recall in my first days in the Congress of the United States in 1947, '48, and '49, when the great steps which were proposed on a bipartisan basis by the American people to assist in the restoration of Europe were among the most foresighted and farsighted actions in which my country has been engaged, the Truman doctrine, the British loan, the aid for Greece and Turkey, the Marshall plan and later NATO. The United States, I believe, can be proud of these programs, and of the great results that they helped to produce. Without them it is possible that the whole history of Western Europe since 1945 would be entirely different. Even today the basic concepts suggested in these programs form the essential part of the foreign policy of the United States. But these concepts alone are not adequate for our European policies in the 1960's. All of the power relationships in the world have changed in the last 15 years, and therefore our policies must take these changes into account. First is the change in Europe itself. In the 1940's Europe - much of it was destroyed, its productive capacity liquidated, divided by a bitter war, inflation rampant, and only those who were optimists of the most extreme sort could have ever predicted the astonishing renaissance of Western Europe today. Its people have energy and confidence. Its economic growth rate is higher than that of the new world, either Canada or the United States. Its dollar shortages have been converted into balances which have even disturbed the monetary stability of the United States.

There are those who said that Europe after the war would be a prisoner again of its ancient rivalries. Today this continent offers the world the most outstanding examples of strength through unity. After 15 years of extraordinary creative effort and administrative invention, the development of the OEEC, the European Payments Union, the Coal and Steel Community, Euratom, the Common Market, and the OECD, and all of these have only laid the foundation for an even closer economic and political unity.

At the same time, the wise and sympathetic policies followed by France and Great Britain towards those countries which were formerly dependencies have strengthened the free world, the globe around us, and have also increased the prestige, influence, and stature of the countries themselves.

The second great change is the change in weaponry. The United States no longer has a nuclear monopoly. The Soviet Union's possession of atomic and hydrogen weapons has increased its willingness to test and probe and push the West. In addition, the intercontinental ballistic missile has made my own country vulnerable to attack and it has also reinforced our view that your defense and ours is indivisible, that in terms of potential destruction, Washington today is closer to Moscow than this city was to any other city in any other country before the outbreak of World War II. We must in short be constantly strengthening all of our forces of all kinds, at all levels, deterring war, and keeping the peace by making certain that those who would oppose us know that we are determined to resist aggression, whatever its force, and whatever kind of force is needed to resist it.

The new change in weaponry presents new challenges, with possession by both the United States and the Soviet Union of an atomic and hydrogen capacity, with the great masses of armies that are available to the Sino-Soviet bloc, to the close lines of communication which they have at their service in Western Europe, in the Middle East, in Asia, in Southeast Asia. It indicates the kind of difficult problems that we face in planning for a secure future. But while we keep our arms so strong that no antagonist can believe that he can secure an easy or shortcut road to world domination, man's inventive power for keeping the peace has not kept pace. We still have strong hopes that it will be possible for us to reach an agreement at Geneva on a cessation of nuclear tests. If we cannot reach an agreement on this subject, which is relatively easy to patrol because of the flow of radiation, how is it going to be possible for us to set up the kind of inspection system for the control of other weapons which could lead to disarmament, and, therefore, to a world peace?

I consider this to be a most essential, realistic step, and those of you who in this audience may have reported on the proceedings in Geneva in the 1920's and '30's, when many months and years and energy of a great many different countries were engaged in the subject under far better conditions of good will then prevailing, the subject of how to secure an adequate disarmament system which provided security, can judge how difficult it will be for us to do so in the future if we cannot make successfully this step.

Third and most important is the change in the location and the nature of the threat. The cause of freedom is under pressure all over the world. But because of the extraordinary rebirth of Western European strength, the struggle has been switched to other areas where the security of your countries and mine are now being directly threatened. The whole southern half of the globe where the attack potentially comes not from massive land armies but from subversion, insurrection, and despair. Europe has conquered her own internal problems. Those that remain are on the way to solution. The time has now come for us to associate more closely together than ever in the past in a massive and concerted attack on poverty, injustice, and oppression, which overshadow so much of the globe. When the threat of military aggression was the primary one, our posture was defensive. But where the contest is one of human liberty and economic growth - and I tie them both together as we must always do so because the slogans with which we have associated ourselves have significance and force when they are bound together with a recognition that economic growth and productivity and material well-being are the handmaidens of liberty - we have the resources in this most extraordinary section of the world, the oldest, and in many ways now among the youngest, allied with the United States and Canada, associated with the countries of Latin America and Africa and Asia, we have an opportunity in our time to fulfill our responsibilities.

In 1779, before France came into the War of Independence, someone said to Benjamin Franklin, "It is a great spectacle that you are putting on in America," and Benjamin Franklin said, "Yes, but the trouble is, the spectators do not pay".

We are not spectators today. We are all contributing, we are all involved, here in this country, here in this community, here in Western Europe, here in my own country, here all around the globe, where it is our responsibility to make a maximum contribution.

QUESTIONS

U.S. Intervention in Algeria

Q: In case of the failure of talks at Evian, would the United States be led to intervene more directly in settling the Algerian question, for example, in case of massive support by the Soviet Union and China?

The President: It is, of course, our hope that the talks now proceeding at Evian will be successful, and I can think of no useful purpose at the present time in planning for the eventuality which was suggested by the question. We should look forward to the present, we should look forward to the effort which is being made to work out a peaceful solution. If that effort should fail, then of course all of us who are concerned would be expected to participate in appropriate consultations. But for the present and certainly as we look to the future, we look with hope towards those talks.

Force Goals of the NATO Alliance's European Members

Q: Question from the Los Angeles Times: Will the President indicate how, and how soon he hopes to induce the negligent European member states of the North Atlantic Alliance to fulfill their accepted force goals for NATO's European shield forces?

The President: Without accepting the presumptions upon which the Los Angeles Times places the question, I am hopeful that all members of the NATO Alliance will fulfill the goals to which they are committed. I think it important that in making these goals we make them realistic, that we do not make plans that we have no intentions of keeping. So quite obviously I think it would be in the interests of all that we meet our commitments, and I can assure you that the United States of America will make every effort on its part to carry out its obligations. I will say also that I am interested in the effort which Western Europe and the United States and Canada are making through the OEEC, through DAG, to play a more substantial role in economic assistance to the southern part of the globe. This is a great challenge for Western Europe. So that we hope that all of us will be willing to bear the burdens that free people must in dangerous days.

The French Atomic Tests

Q: (In French) Did you discuss with General de Gaulle the French atomic tests and the attitude of France with regard to the Geneva conference on suspension of nuclear tests? At what stage of the atomic development of France will the McMahon law no longer prevent the President of the United States from giving her American secrets? Who in the United States is the judge as to whether this stage has been reached or not?

The President: In answer to the first part of the question, the answer is we have discussed these matters. In answer to the second, the determination or the interpretation of the McMahon Act is a matter of concern to the Executive and also a matter of great concern to the Joint Committee on Atomic Energy of the Congress. And I'm sure that if a question were raised in regard to the interpretations that the United States Government would attempt to make an appropriate determination.

The third part of the question is – to what degree – the responsibility falls most immediately on the President. It is a matter, of course, which – it's a statute of the Congress, it is a matter of great concern to many members of the Congress who have given this matter long attention. There are varying views on how it would be interpreted. And I would say that the United States Government would make a judgment if a judgment were required after consulting with our partners in the Congress.

May I say that on some of these matters my answers will be less than full and less than satisfactory to you. When this press conference was first planned, I expected to be at the end of my voyage. It comes at a time before General de Gaulle and I have concluded our talks, before a communique has been issued, and beginning tomorrow I face new responsibilities. Therefore, I hope that those who I leave less than satisfied will at least be sympathetic.

Aim of Meeting with Mr. Khrushchev

Q: Mr. President, a question by Serge Fleigers of the Hearst Newspapers: What in your opinion, Mr. President, is the principal aim of a meeting with Mr. Khrushchev at this time and do you feel that you are meeting him with enough cards in your hands?

The President: To answer the second part of the question first, I consider the power of the United States, plus those countries that are associated with it in the common defense, to give every form of encouragement to any Western leader who discusses matters which concern us with those who occupy positions of responsibility in other parts of the globe. I think Mr. Khrushchev has the same view. And to the first part of the question, I would say, as I have said before, that the purpose of this meeting is to permit me to make a more precise judgment on those matters which involve the interests of the United States, and the Soviet Union, and those countries which are members of the Sino-Soviet bloc. We are involved in two conferences at Geneva. We hope that more progress can be made at both of them. And if there is anything that may be said in the meetings Saturday and Sunday which may improve that prospect, then, of course, that makes the trip worthwhile. There are other matters also on which we have not come to an agreement with Mr. Khrushchev, and I think it's important that we understand fully his viewpoint and all of its implications, and that in return he has the same understanding of our viewpoint.

I said recently that in my lifetime I had been present, alive, during three world wars, and it is impossible to study the origins of each of these struggles without realizing the serious miscalculations which were made by the leaders on both sides. The most recent example was in our own experience in Korea, where the North Koreans did not seem certain that we would respond immediately upon the occasion of their invasion into South Korea, and where there was serious doubt on the part of the United States that the Chinese Communists would intervene as we moved to the north. In the experience of Europe, you have had similar circumstances. Therefore, when responsibility is pressed heavily on anyone to make a judgment, it seems to me useful to have as close an understanding of the view of each side as possible. I think that it is most valuable to talk to those with whom we are allied. I also think it is important that we talk to those who are separated from us, because in the final analysis, heavy decisions rest, constitutionally, upon the President of the United States. He must under some conditions make the final judgment himself, and if my judgment may be more lucid, may be based more on reality as a result of this exchange, then I think the trip will be useful.

Our Understanding with General de Gaulle on Berlin

Q: (In French) Would you interpret for us your understanding with General de Gaulle on Berlin? What is the real meaning and scope of this understanding?

The President: The matter of Berlin, of course, will be a matter, I am sure, of discussion tomorrow and Sunday and, therefore, I do not think that this is a particularly appropriate time to go into details on the position which we occupy in Berlin as it is a matter, of course, which will be discussed by Mr. Khrushchev and myself. Let me therefore sum it up by saying that I think that neither General de Gaulle nor I would feel it appropriate to have our rights, statutory rights, in West Berlin changed by force or the threat of force.

The Neutrality of Laos

Q: Crosby Noyes, Washington Evening Star: Mr. President, in view of the attitude shown by the Soviet and Chinese delegations at the Geneva conference on Laos, do you now feel that the neutrality and independence of that country can be established and insured by an international agreement?

The President: I think that the prospects are not easy of securing an independent and neutral Laos as we understand it, but we intend to continue to discuss this matter, and we will stay at the conference for as long as we feel that there is some hope of success. The Soviet Union has stated on occasions that it wishes a neutral and independent Laos. If we can come to an agreement on the exact, precise definition of these words, then our progress should be swift. I will say that the first and most essential step at the present time is to provide an effective mechanism for controlling the cease-fire. If we can secure a cease-fire, then we can move on to those other matters which must be settled by the conference. It is a difficult area. It presents us with many difficult decisions. But I cannot believe that anyone would imperil the peace by failing to recognize the importance of reaching an agreement in this country, by breaking up a conference and refusing to agree to a cease-fire and a government and a people which can maintain their neutrality against outside intervention from whatever source.

The Role of France in Europe

Q: (In French) Question of Mme. Genevieve Tabouis together with question annexed by a colleague: How does President Kennedy view the role of France in Europe? Do you think that closer consultations may take place between Washington, London, and Paris, on the political and military problems of the world?

The President: Yes, I do, and the reason I came to Paris was to participate in that kind of consultation. Consultation does not always, regardless
of how long it may go on, does not always provide unanimity at the end of the
consultation. But there is a more precise understanding of those areas where
there is agreement and there is a more precise understanding of the reasons
for positions which may be taken on which there is not agreement. So I regard conversations such as I have had for the last 2 days, and they have been
more than 8 hours with President de Gaulle, I regard them as most valuable.
And I believe that more than talking about consulting it is important to consult. And we have done that and will continue to do it, I hope with increasing
intimacy, in the months ahead.

Britain's Entry into the Common Market

*Q: Question of Thomas Cadett, of the BBC, and Christopher Johnson of the
Financial Times: Mr. President, did you discuss Britain's entry into the Common
Market with President de Gaulle, and what did he say? And does the United
States advise the French Government to facilitate the entry of Britain into
the Common Market as a full member?*

The President: I cannot believe that Mr. Cadett or Mr. Johnson have been in
Paris less time that I have, but nevertheless I am sure that even if they had
been here only in the last few hours they would know that on those matters
on which - regarding General de Gaulle's views, that the most authoritative
place to secure them is General de Gaulle.

The U.S. Role in the World

*Q: (In French) What can the United States and her allies do to be again
regarded in the world as a whole as the true defenders of liberty, of justice,
when in the eyes of underdeveloped countries they all appear today as the defenders of the unique privileges which the whites enjoy because of their high
standard of living? Can you tell us, for Africa and Latin America, what means
the United States is thinking of to help the peoples of these continents in
their revolution for peace, for equality - for an "independent order" as you
yourself have said?*

The President: I think the question suggests a basic problem which is not
easy to solve. We are a prosperous people. Some of us in the Atlantic Community have held colonial possessions and we, therefore, have not always experienced, in my own hemisphere, in Africa, or Asia, the happiest relations
with the people who are involved. But I will say on the other hand, that the
record of the last 15 years is an extraordinary one, as country after country
has gained its independence, by free means in many cases - in fact, in the
majority of cases - who were once held as colonial possessions. This is an
extraordinary record for the Western World and one not matched by the Eastern
World, which continues to hold areas under its control, not by free means. I
think that it is not enough, as I said in my speech, that we give our slogans,
though the slogans cloak very basic principles, but I feel we must make a
greater concerted effort than we have made in the past on a long-term basis,
to demonstrate to these people that through free choice they may be able to
solve their material problems. I do not want to see the United States, and I
am sure that those of you who are Europeans do not want to see Europe, associated with reactionary groups within these countries who seek only to maintain their own position. We want to assist and be associated with those groups
who look to the future, who are identified with the aspirations of their people. Otherwise, our days in some of these areas are on the yellow leaf. I
will say that one of the matters which I discussed with General de Gaulle was

the great hope which we had in the Western Hemisphere that Europe would play an increasingly larger role. Its traditional ties, its cultural affinities, its ties of language - of Latin America - are extremely intimate with Europe, and I believe that there is a great opportunity for Europe, not only to serve the general cause, not only in Africa and Asia, but also in the hemisphere of the Americas. And it was a source of great satisfaction to me that General de Gaulle, as he demonstrated in his speech of some weeks ago, shares strongly that view of the obligation of this area.

CIA Involvement in the April 22 Algiers Revolt

Q: Question by Joseph Barry, of the New York Post: Mr. President, has there been an investigation of the case of the reports circulated about alleged Central Intelligence Agency involvement in the April 22 Algiers revolt of the generals, and would you care to comment on this?

The President: I feel that the good will of this visit may be rapidly diminishing. Let me say that I have not been informed, and all my information is to the contrary, that there was any involvement by members of the CIA or any other members of the American Government. I think that the foreign minister discussed that matter quite clearly in his report of some weeks ago, and I think that the statements which our Government has made in regard to its association with this country and its government I think obviously answer it. So in answer to your question, I know of no basis for such a charge. I have never received information on it. I assume I would have and, therefore, I regard the matter as not in fact true.

The President's Impressions of France and General de Gaulle

Q: (In French) Mr. President, what impressed you most, first about France, and then concerning General de Gaulle?

The President: In France, as I said, I think the vitality of a very old race, which the French people are. In General de Gaulle, I am having a conversation with the only active figure who played a major role in the Second World War who is now involved in major policy matters affecting the security of the Western World. President Roosevelt, Prime Minister Churchill, Marshal Stalin have all disappeared from the positions of responsibility. General de Gaulle remains. And he is faithful to the same concepts of the strength of France and the unity of Europe as he has been for many years. It has been my hope in these conversations that he has a renewed appreciation of how seriously we consider our ties with France and Western Europe. I hope from our conversations that he understands how our new government in the United States is firmly committed to the security of this area and means to implement its commitments.

Normalization of Communist Chinese Relations with the West

Q: Question by L.E. Micey, of the United Press International: Mr. President, how can Communist China normalize her relations with the West and be admitted to United Nations membership?

The President: I would say that the normalization of relations which - of course, peaceful relations - which is in common interest of us all, between China and the West - I would hope that they would be brought about. But we desire peace and we desire to live in amity with the Chinese people. But I will say that since long before I assumed office and in the first days of our new administration, before really any actions were taken, the attacks upon our Government and the United States were constant, immediate, and in many cases malevolent. The debate which took place last fall between Communist parties indicated that the Chinese planned to take an extremely belligerent attitude and role towards us and those with whom we are associated. We hope that policy changes. We want good will. But it takes two to make peace, and I am hopeful that the Chinese will be persuaded that a peaceful existence with its neighbors represents the best hope for us all. We would welcome it. But I do not see evidence of it today.

The President's Reflections on Mr. Khrushchev

Q: (In French) If you were in the place of Mr. Khrushchev ——

The President: If I were - I suppose if I were in Mr. Khrushchev's place, it would be because I was Mr. Khrushchev and had I lived his life, and therefore I would look to the West and I would see a good deal of reports of disagreement. I would see where all Western leaders may not agree on every issue. I would see where distinguished American correspondents who speak with great influence take a different view on what actions the United States should take. I would see Mr. Kennedy under critical attack by many of his fellow countrymen, as well as those who live across the ocean. I would look at my own country, where everything on the surface is serene, where nobody criticizes or opposes, and everyone is united behind me. And, therefore, I would draw a conclusion that the tide of history was moving with me.

If I were Mr. Khrushchev, however, and had spent some time in the West, I would take a somewhat different view of the tide of history. I would read those distinguished spokesmen who had prophesied the imminent collapse of Europe in 1947 and '48. I would read those others who had felt it would be impossible for us to associate more closely together and I would also recognize that dissent and controversy brings a kind of vitality and also protects individual liberty. And I would consider that possibly we could improve Russian society. I will say that I don't agree very basically with one of the assumptions which a good many Communists put forward, and that is from the events of the last 15 years they have made the judgment that the tide is determined and in their favor. You cannot look at the relations between the countries behind the Iron Curtain. For example, the rather strange relationship between Albania and China, or between Yugoslavia and Albania and Russia, or between all the other countries of the bloc, to feel that if time were permitted to pass and the Communists were permitted to be successful, that there would not inevitably be the same rivalries which we now see already in evidence. The difficulty, of course, is that Caesar and Pompey and Antony and Octavius and the others did not fall out until they were successful. We cannot afford the luxury of permitting them the kind of success which will prove them wrong finally in the kind of world which they were witness. We have to maintain our position. And therefore, I hope Mr. Khrushchev is not misled by those signs of democracy which we understand but they do not, but instead recognizes that the United States of America, divided as it may be on many important questions, including governmental spending, is united in its determination to fulfill its commitments and to play the role that history and its own free choice have brought upon it in these years.

So I may say, as I said at the beginning, I go to Vienna with a good deal of confidence, and I go to Vienna with more confidence as a result of my last 2 days.

Reporter: Thank you, Mr. President.

THE PRESIDENT'S NEWS CONFERENCE OF

JUNE 28, 1961

The President: Good morning.

I want to first of all express my regret at the information I've just received in regard to the death of our colleague in these press conferences and a fine newspaper man, Ed Koterba, who, I understand, was killed in a plane crash last night.

He was a most - he was an outstanding newspaperman who was associated with Scripps-Howard, and we want to express our sympathy to members of his family and also to the papers with which he was associated. I want to say personally that I'm extremely sorry to have heard the news.

Secondly, I should like to comment briefly on Germany and Berlin.

Soviet and East German leaders have followed the recent Soviet aide memoire with speeches which were apparently designed to heighten tension. It is of the greatest importance that the American people understand the basic issues involved and the threats to the peace and security of Europe and of ourselves posed by the Soviet announcement that they intend to change unilaterally the existing arrangements for Berlin.

The "crisis" over Berlin is Soviet-manufactured.

The Soviets illegally blockaded the city in 1948 and lifted the blockade in the spring of 1949. From that time until November 1958, almost a decade, the situation in Berlin was relatively peaceful.

The peoples of West Berlin developed a thriving and vital city. We carried out our responsibilities and exercised our rights of access to the city without serious incident, although we were never completely free from irritating difficulties that were put in our way.

In November 1958, the Soviets began a new campaign to force the Allied Powers out of Berlin, a process which let up to the abortive summit conference in Paris of May last year.

Now they have revived that drive. They call upon us to sign what they call a "peace treaty," with the regime that they have created in East Germany. If we refuse, they say that they themselves will sign such a treaty.

The obvious purpose here is not to have peace but to make permanent the partition of Germany.

The Soviets also say that their unilateral action in signing a "peace treaty" with East Germany would bring an end to Allied rights in West Berlin and to free access for that city.

It is clear that such unilateral action cannot affect these rights, which stem from the surrender of Nazi Germany.

Such action would simply be a repudiation by the Soviets of multilateral commitments to which they solemnly subscribed and have repeatedly reaffirmed.

About the exercise of the rights of the principal powers associated in World War II: If the Soviets thus withdraw from their own obligations, it is clearly a matter for the other three allies to decide how they will exercise their rights and meet their responsibilities.

But the Soviets say that when we do so, we will be subject to the designs of the East German regime and that these designs will be backed by force.

Recent statements by leaders of this regime make it very plain that the kind of "free city" which they have in mind is one in which the rights of the citizens of West Berlin are gradually but relentlessly extinguished - in other words, a city which is not free.

No one can fail to appreciate the gravity of this threat. No one can reconcile it with the Soviet professions of a desire to coexist peacefully.

This is not just a question of technical legal rights. It involves the peace and the security of the peoples of West Berlin. It involves the direct responsibilities and commitments of the United States, the United Kingdom, and France. It involves the peace and the security of the Western world.

In the interests of our own vital security, we and other Western countries entered in a defense arrangement in direct response to direct Soviet moves following World War II.

These alliances are wholly defensive in nature. But the Soviets would make a grave mistake if they suppose that Allied unity and determination can be undermined by threats or fresh aggressive acts.

There is peace in Germany and in Berlin. If it is disturbed, it will be a direct Soviet responsibility.

There is danger that totalitarian governments not subject to vigorous popular debate will underestimate the will and unity of democratic societies where vital interests are concerned.

The Soviet Government has an obligation to both its own people and to the peace of the world to recognize how vital is this commitment.

We would agree that there is unfinished business to be settled as concerns Germany. For many years, the Western nations have proposed a permanent and peaceful settlement of such questions on the basis of self-determination of the German people.

Moreover, we shall always be ready to discuss any proposals which would give increased protection to the right of the people of Berlin to exercise their independent choice as free men.

The proposals which have now been placed before us move in the opposite direction and are so recognized throughout the world.

Discussions will be profitable if the Soviets will accept in Berlin, and indeed in Europe, self-determination which they profess in other parts of the world, and if they will work sincerely for peace rather than an extension of power.

I have a second statement. The Soviet Union's refusal to negotiate seriously on a nuclear test ban at Geneva is disheartening to all those who have held high hopes of stopping the spread of nuclear weapons and the pace of the arms race. It also raises a serious question about how long we can safely continue on a voluntary basis a refusal to undertake tests in this country without any assurance that the Russians are not now testing.

Consequently, I have directed that the President's Science Advisory Committee convene a special panel of eminent scientists to take a close and up-to-date look at the serious questions involved, including two questions in particular.

First, what is the extent of our information on whether the Soviet Union has been or could be engaged in secret testing of nuclear weapons?

Second, to the extent that certain types of tests can be concealed by the Soviet Union, what technical progress in weapons could be under way in that area without our knowledge?

These answers will be received and reviewed by myself, by the Joint Chiefs of Staff, and the National Security Council in the light of what they mean to the security of the free world.

In the meantime, our negotiating team will remain at Geneva, our draft treaty is on the table there, and I urge the leaders of the Soviet Union to end their intransigence and to accept a reasonable and enforceable treaty which is our wholehearted desire.

And lastly, Chairman Khrushchev has compared the United States to a worn-out runner living on its past performance and stated that the Soviet Union would outproduce the United States by 1970.

Without wishing to trade hyperbole with the Chairman, I do suggest that he reminds me of the tiger hunter who has picked a place on the wall to hang the tiger's skin long before he has caught the tiger. This tiger has other ideas.

Premier Khrushchev states that the Soviet Union is only 44 years old but his country is far older than that, and it is an interesting fact that in 1913, according to the best calculations I can get from governmental and private sources, the Russian gross national product was 46 percent of the United States gross national product.

Interestingly enough, in 1959 it was 47 percent. Because, while the Soviet Union was making progress and improving the material standards of her people in the ensuing years, so was the tired-out runner, and, on a per capita basis the Soviet product in 1959 was only 39 percent of ours.

If both countries sustain their present rate of growth, 3½ percent in the United States and 6 percent in the Soviet Union, Soviet output will not reach two-thirds of ours by 1970 and our rate will be far easier to sustain or improve than the Soviet rate, which starts from a lower figure.

Indeed, if our growth rate is increased to even 4½ percent, which is well within our capability, it is my judgment that the Soviet Union will not outproduce the United States at any time in the twentieth century.

This faster growth rate is a primary object of the various measures I've submitted and will submit in the future, tax incentives, education, resource development, research, area redevelopment, and all the rest.

Mr. Khrushchev obviously sees the future differently than we do and he has urged his people to work hard to develop that future. We in the United States must work hard, too, to realize our potential.

But I believe that we can maintain our productive development and also our system of freedom. We invite the U.S.S.R. to engage in this competition which is peaceful and which could only result in a better living standard for both of our people.

In short, the United States is not such an aged runner and, to paraphrase Mr. Coolidge, "We do choose to run."

QUESTIONS

Possible Mobilization of Forces in Berlin

Q: Would you care to comment on recurrent reports that the administration is considering a partial mobilization to meet the threat in Berlin?

The President: No such proposal has been placed before me at the present time. As you know this matter of what steps we would take to implement our commitments to Berlin has been a matter of consideration. Mr. Acheson, the former Secretary of State, was named to consider this matter in the middle of April. His report will be coming in - we're going to discuss it this week and we will be considering other proposals which might be put forward in order to make meaningful our commitment. But the proposals are still - have not still come to the White House officially and I'm therefore not able to comment because we have not seen any such proposal as you suggested at the present time, though of course we will be considering a whole variety of measures which might be taken.

The Cuban Tractor Deal

Q: Mr. President, in some retrospect, how do you now view the Cuban tractor deal? It seems pretty well off. What's the next move there? How do you plan to get those prisoners out of there now?

The President: Well, the tractors - the committee offered Mr. Castro, as I understand it, the 500 agricultural tractors which he mentioned in the original speech. Mr. Castro has not accepted these agricultural tractors but is insisting on a different kind of tractor - far larger, which could be used for other purposes besides agriculture. The committee has therefore felt that Mr. Castro is not interested in permitting these prisoners to be released in return for agricultural tractors and, unless he changes his view, the situation will remain as it is.

I wish the prisoners could be free. I wish that it had been possible to secure their release because they are, as I said at my first statement, men in whom we have great interest and who are devoted to the cause of freedom. But I think the committee did everything that reasonable men and citizens could do. They are motivated by humanitarian interests. I think that they demonstrated, by exploring with Castro in detail, exactly the nature of Castro's interest.

If the - our first response had been negative, it might have been possible for Mr. Castro to say that we had refused to send agricultural tractors in return for these men. This committee went to every conceivable length in order to demonstrate their good faith. Mr. Castro did not accept it.

The President's Health

Q: Mr. President, I think we'd like to hear you say how you are feeling now.

The President: Very well, very well. I'm feeling better, even, than Pierre Salinger.

General Taylor's Findings on Cuba

Q: Mr. President, with respect to the Cuban operation, would you tell us what General Taylor's findings were and what reorganization or adjustment in our intelligence activities you contemplate as a result of this report?

The President: General Taylor made an oral report to me, which I asked him to make and which I think will be useful to me. In addition, of course, General Taylor has been - is now a member of the staff of the White House as our military representative with special responsibility in the field of defense matters and intelligence and coordination in those areas.

Reorganization of Intelligence Activities

Q: Mr. President, will you tell us about the reorganization plan, if any, with respect to our intelligence activities because of his appointment?

The President: No, that matter will - has not been completely - completed. In addition, we - the Killian committee is looking at the same matter and when the Killian committee has finished its preliminary surveys, we may have some changes.

The Distribution of Low-Priced Textile Imports

Q: Mr. President, approximately 200 Members of Congress have protested to you regarding the Department of State plan for distributing low-priced textile imports among other Western nations. They urge abandonment of the plan because they feel it commits the United States to an unreasonably high level of low-priced imports in the future. Could you tell us whether this State Department plan has your unqualified support or whether you would favor modifying it to meet congressional objections?

The President: In the first place, there's no plan yet. No solution has been devised to this problem of how we're going to provide for an orderly flow of textiles from the newly emerging countries which concentrate on this kind of commodity and how we're going to provide for an orderly flow between those countries and the consuming countries so that we protect the interests of the producing countries and the consuming countries.

It's an extremely complicated task. No decision has been reached as to what the formula would be. It is proposed that we discuss the formula, and I think that the conference should go on and we should discuss it. If we come to any conclusion about what should be done, and we have not reached that conclusion, as yet, we will inform the American people and the members of the Congress.

I do want to point out that we do export nearly 7 million bales of cotton every year. We sell more cotton to Japan than we import in textiles from all over the world. This is not a matter on which we can say we'll take no imports and at the same time feel that we can continue to provide this tremendous outflow of cotton.

We export nearly 7 million bales of cotton every year. We import a total of about 600,000 bales of cotton, manufactured into textiles a year. So that we have to consider the economic interests of the United States as well as other people. We sell Japan - I think last year we sold them $150 million more than they bought from us, totally. So that while I'm concerned about, and I am concerned about the problem of the textile industry, which is one of the reasons why this conference was called, as a result of the protests which were made by members of Congress because the imports have increased in the textile industry, and it is hard hit. I think it came, it increased in recent months and recent years from around 4½ to 7 percent and therefore the trend is against, has been sharply - has provided for increases.

I do feel that we ought to take into account that this is a balance matter. In addition, some of the States which sell cotton overseas which may be adversely affected by textile imports - we also export a lot of textiles. We also, for example, export tobacco, which is an export product, so that we have to consider the general economic interest. We cannot expect that we're going to be able to cut off completely the importation of textiles and then think that we're going to have anything but ruin for our cotton exporters.

So it all has to be balanced, and one of the ways that the economic interests of all can be balanced is in this conference, and I support it.

The Maritime Strike

Q: Mr. President, without respect to the current maritime strike, do you plan to take any action on the American-owned flags of convenience, or runaway ships, as you once described them?

The President: Well, we are concerned about the - as I have said before - about the problem of runaway ships in the sense that ships who are put by American owners under other flags in order to avoid paying the wage scale which we have for our American merchant marine, the United States Government pays a large share of the bill for important segments of the American merchant marine, including these wages. So when these ships leave us and compete against us, in a sense it affects not only the welfare of the seamen involved but also affects governmental policy and governmental obligations. So we are concerned about the matter.

But in regard to the actual details, I would prefer for the present to wait until the Cole committee makes its report in regard to Taft-Hartley. And we are also considering what we could do to see if we can work out some solutions which will ease the burden of the people involved.

There is also an obligation, let me say, on the representatives of the American merchant marine, an obligation of Mr. Curran and Mr. Hall to make sure that the problems of the American merchant marine in its competition with other areas are taken into consideration. They cannot merely consider it isolated. This is a competitive business. And we could very well find, instead of flags of convenience or so-called runaway ships, that the ships were actually put under the - which, and in those cases the American, the United States Government has some control over the ships. They could actually put them under the flags or have contractual relationship with the British or the Norwegians and then we would not have the control in case of a national emergency and we would still be being undercut.

So it's an extremely complicated question to which Secretary Goldberg and the Secretary of Commerce and the members of the committee are giving a good deal of attention.

Some Consequences of Resuming Nuclear Testing

Q: Mr. President, in considering the resumption of nuclear testing, have you requested or do you propose to request a report and recommendation from the Federal Radiation and Council regarding the consequences of fallout that may result from such a resumption of tests?

The President: All these matters, of course, would be considered before any decision were reached.

Summit Meetings

Q: Mr. President, how do you feel now in retrospect about summit meetings and do you foresee any more of them in the future?

The President: Well I've never described the meeting in Vienna as a summit meeting. I think the meeting in Vienna was useful to - certainly to me in meeting my responsibilities, and perhaps it was also to Mr. Khrushchev. Because, as I've said from the beginning, these issues which we're now talking about are extremely serious issues which involve the well-being of a great many people besides even the people of the United States, and decisions have to be made on the basis of the best information we can get, and they involve the security of the United States and they involve also the peace of the world, and therefore if those decisions can be made more educated by such a meeting it was useful. Now there are no plans to have any further meetings that I know of.

Nixon on the Administration

Q: Mr. President, Vice President Nixon seems to be taking a dim view of your administration. He said in a speech yesterday that never in American history has a man talked so big and acted so little. Do you have anything to say about this?

The President: No, I wouldn't comment on Mr. Nixon. He has been engaged and busy and I sympathize with the traveling problems he has and his other problems but - (Laughter) - I don't have any response to make. We're doing the best we can and will continue to do so until 1964 and then we can see what the situation looks like. (Laughter)

The Country's Growth Rate

Q: Mr. President, you said that if the United States can attain a rate of growth of 4½ percent, that Russian will not catch up with us in the twentieth century. What is our rate of growth now, sir?

The President: Well, calling it from 1953 to today, it's about 3½ percent.

The Maintenance of a Growth Rate

Q: What are we doing to attain a rate of growth?

The President: Well, we're going to have a sharp - from the recession of 1960, winter of '61, we ought to have a substantial rate of increase. The big problem will be to sustain it over a period of time and that will require - I mentioned some of the things - a tax system which provides a stimulation to growth, education, and research, also the development of the natural resources of this country and also monetary and fiscal policies which will recognize the necessity of preventing a recurrence of these successive dips.

Now we had a recession in '54, we had a recession in '58, we had a recession in '60. The '60 recession came right on the heels of the '58 recession. Two of the reasons why it may have contributed - it was the movement from a $12 billion deficit in '58-59 to a prospective $4 billion surplus, which was a change of more than $16 billion in the potential receipts of the Government, which did have a restraining influence on the recovery.

Secondly, of course, the long-term interest rates were extremely high. Now we have to - the Federal Reserve will meet with Mr. Martin frequently. It's a very uncertain science, but we have to figure out what steps we can take - with this free economy - that will provide not only a recovery now, and we hope a reduced unemployment rate, but will also sustain it, not just through '62 but over a period of time. That we have to do it we're going to defeat Mr. Khrushchev, but it's within our potential and, therefore, I think, my judgment is that if the United States considers this problem and the people of the United States and the Government working together attempt to master this uncertain science in a more precise way, that we will remain not only ahead on a per capita basis but also on a national income basis in this century.

We have to recognize, of course, that the Soviet Union is working extremely hard and enjoys some advantages in being able to mobilize its resources for this purpose in the sense that a totalitarian society enjoys that advantage. What we wish was that they would do it under a system of freedom, but this is their decision.

The President's Handling of Inter-American Affairs

Q: Mr. President, there's been some criticism of our handling of inter-American affairs, particularly on grounds that you have a multiplicity of advisers in the White House duplicating and sometimes overruling people in the State Department. I wonder if you could define for us the relationship of policymakers on your staff as against those in State and perhaps in the Pentagon?

The President: Well, we have in the White House a number of people who have responsibilities in various areas. And one of the areas in which we're particularly interested is Latin America. Now I've read the - I think it's - I was sorry that we did not secure a replacement for Mr. Mann more quickly. I did talk to almost eight people. We had assurances in a number of cases which lasted some days, but we finally did not - in every case we were not successful. I think we were very fortunate to have Mr. Woodward and perhaps maybe we should have started with Mr. Woodward. That's the first point.

Secondly, we are particularly interested in Latin America. My experience in government is that when things are noncontroversial, beautifully coordinated, and all the rest it may be that there isn't much going on. I've never heard of any criticism of - I do not hear any criticism of our organizational structure in several areas of the world which I know are rather inactive as far as anything being done. So if you really want complete harmony and good will, then the best way to do it is not to do anything.

Now we haven't done so much in Latin America in the last decade. It has not been a matter of great priority. We are attemtping to do something about it. And we've been fortunate to have the services of Mr. Berle who is completing the work of his task force. Mr. Goodwin from the White House has given it a great deal of attention, particularly the meeting of the IAECOSOC in Montevideo through the end of July. The whole refinancing of the Brazil debt, which could have been a most serious crisis in that very vital country, was handled in cooperation between the Treasury, the White House, the State Department, the Export-Import Bank, Food for Peace and ICA. We've also given particular attention to the economic problems of Bolivia.

So we are attempting to do something about Latin America and there's bound to be a ferment. If the ferment produces useful results then it will be worthwhile. But I must say I don't think - my experience is you can't get very much done if - when things are very quiet and beautifully organized, I think it's time to be concerned, not when there is some feelings and interest and concern.

In addition, Governor Stevenson went down and made a tour there as a prelude to our meeting at Montevideo, which I think was useful. So I would say we have given more thought in this administration to the problem of Latin America than on almost any matter involving our foreign policy.

In answer to your question, when Mr. Woodward comes here next week he will be the responsible officer in the State Department and will work closely, I'm sure, with the Secretary of State and with me.

The Berlin Threat

Q: Do you feel that the Berlin threat is serious enough for you to plan a personal meeting with the British and French to map our strategy there if the situation becomes indeed very hot?

The President: It is a matter which we discussed with General de Gaulle and Mr. Macmillan. In addition, they've had - Lord Home was here - the French Government has had a representative, as well as the British Government, talking about the response in the aide memoire. I've no doubt that we will have close exchanges with Mr. Macmillan and General de Gaulle and when the matter reaches a point where a meeting would be useful, we would have it.

Acquiring Information on Soviet Testing

Q: On your statement this morning about a committee to go into the extent of information on Soviet testing, is there any suggestion here, sir, that we have an intelligence gap in this field? Or to specify, did not the Eisenhower administration and does not your administration pretty well know what the Soviets have been doing in nuclear testing during this ——

The President: No, there's - in what way?

Q: I just wondered if you had information about what testing they may have been doing.

The President: No, we do not - this is a matter which the committee will look into. But in answer to your question, I have not seen any information, nor did the previous administration have any knowledge, which would state that the Soviet Union had been testing - information either by seismography or by any other means. What is of concern is, is it possible to test without those evidences being secured? Is it possible to test underground, for example, without a determination being made that such a test is being carried on? That's the matter which we wish to have explored. But it would be inaccurate to state that we have information that would indicate to us what the Soviet Union is now testing. What we're concerned about is that our information is quite incomplete and we want to know whether it's possible that they could be testing without our knowing and what the chances are that that might be true.

The Laotian Situation

Q: It has been almost 6 weeks, sir, since the conference on Laos has been under way. There seems to have been little progress, at least little understanding, between the two sides. Do you consider it worthwhile to continue the conference?

The President: Yes, the cease-fire is generally in operation. What we're now concerned about are the details of the ICC's power, and I'm hopeful that we can secure effective instruction for the ICC, so that it can meet its responsibilities. I would continue the conversations to see if that can be obtained.

Public Support for the President's Stand on Germany

Q: Realizing that the Acheson and other contingency reports have not yet been finished, could you, nevertheless, give us at least a hint this morning in what areas the public may be involved in supporting your strong stand on Germany? I ask that question against this background: that it's generally considered that your words to Mr. Khrushchev in Vienna were highly impressive, but it's necessary to follow them up with decisions and deeds.

The President: Yes, well, that's the matter which is now engaging the attention of the United States Government; it is one of the matters which will be discussed at the Security Council tomorrow. But as of now, no report of the deliberations of the Pentagon and others as to what actions might be usefully taken have officially - have been finalized.

In addition, I would point out that we are talking about matters of extreme seriousness and I think that we should wait until a judgment has been reached as to what action we should take before it's useful to discuss it publicly. As of today, these considerations and recommendations have not yet come to the White House. One of the matters which will be discussed, as I say, tomorrow will be this matter at the Security Council.

Mortgage Bankers and the FHA System

Q: Mr. President, can something be done to require mortgage bankers to quit enriching themselves off of the FHA system to making loans? I refer to the many complaints that are coming in to the FHA on this matter from widows and poor people who - buyers and sellers - who are losing, say, several hundred dollars on the sale of a small house to these mortgage bankers who laugh at the people and say FHA and your Government condones this system whereby we charge side payments for financing these loans.

The President: Well, I think - I will look into it and Mr. Salinger will have a statement to make on it by tomorrow afternoon.

Reporter: Thank you, Mr. President.

THE PRESIDENT'S NEWS CONFERENCE OF

JULY 19, 1961

The President: I have a statement on Germany and Berlin. I'll read a few paragraphs of it and it will be available for distribution right after the press conference.

The Soviet aide memoire is a document which speaks of peace, but threatens to disturb it. It speaks of ending the abnormal situation in Germany, but insists on making permanent its abnormal division. It refers to the Four Power Alliance of World War II, but seeks the unilateral abrogation of the rights of the other three powers. It calls for new international agreements, while preparing to violate existing ones. It offers certain assurances, while making it plain that its previous assurances are not to be relied upon. It professes concern for the rights of the citizens of West Berlin, while seeking to expose them to the immediate or eventual domination of a regime which permits no self-determination. Three simple facts are clear:

1. Today there is peace in Berlin, in Germany, and in Europe. If that peace is destroyed by the unilateral actions of the Soviet Union, its leaders will bear a heavy responsibility before world opinion and history.

2. The people of West Berlin are free. In that sense it's already a "free city" - free to determine its own leaders and free to enjoy the fundamental human rights reaffirmed in the United Nations Charter.

3. Today the continued presence in West Berlin of the United States, the United Kingdom, and France is by clear legal right, arising from war, acknowledged in many agreements signed by the Soviet Union, and strongly supported by the overwhelming majority of the people of that city. Their freedom is dependent upon the exercise of these rights - an exercise which is thus a political and moral obligation as well as a legal right. Inasmuch as these rights, including the right of access to Berlin, are not held from the Soviet Government, they cannot be ended by any unilateral action of the Soviet Union. They cannot be affected by a so-called "peace treaty," covering only a part of Germany, with a regime of the Soviet Union's own creation - a regime which is not freely representative of all or any part of Germany, and does not enjoy the confidence of the 17 million East Germans. The steady stream of German refugees from East to West is eloquent testimony to this fact.

The real intent of the June 4 aide memoire is that East Berlin, a part of a city under four power status, would be formally absorbed into the so-called German Democratic Republic while West Berlin, even though called a "free city," would lose the protection presently provided by the Western Powers and become subject to the will of a totalitarian regime. Its leader, Herr Ulbricht, has made clear his intention, once this so-called "peace treaty" is signed, to curb West Berlin's communications with the free world and to suffocate the freedom it now enjoys.

The world knows that there is no reason for a crisis over Berlin today - and that if one develops it will be caused by the Soviet Government's attempt to invade the rights of others and manufacture tensions.

A city does not become free merely by calling it a "free city." For a city or a people to be free requires that they be given the opportunity, without economic, political, or police pressure, to make their own choice and live their own lives. The people of West Berlin today have that freedom. It is the objective of our policy that they will continue to enjoy it.

Peace does not come automatically from a "peace treaty." There is peace in Germany today even though the situation is "abnormal." A "peace treaty" that adversely affects the lives and rights of millions will not bring peace with it. A "peace treaty" that attempts to affect adversely the solemn commitments of three great powers will not bring peace with it. We again urge the Soviet Government to reconsider its course, to return to the path of constructive cooperation it so frequently states it desires, and to work with its World War II Allies in concluding a just and enduring settlement of issues remaining from that conflict.

Secondly, preliminary estimates of the gross national product in the second quarter of this year have been completed. The Nation's output of goods and services rose sharply to an annual rate of $515 billion, a $14 billion increase over the first quarter, reversing three consecutive quarters of decline.

Total personal income has risen steadily. In June it reached nearly $417 billion, $10½ billion above its recession low of last February, and as you know the Federal Reserve Board Index of Production increased 2 points in June to reach a level of 110.

There are still, however, serious problems of unemployment in this country. As I said some time ago, unemployment is bad enough when there's a recession, but it is intolerable when there is prosperity, and I believe it important, therefore, that the country, the administration, and the Congress remember as we move into a period of advance that there are still 5 million Americans who are unemployed, a million who are employed part time, and we have to develop programs and actions that will make it easier for them to secure their jobs.

Finally, as you know, I had hoped to be able to attend the forthcoming meeting of the Inter-American Economic and Social Council at Montevideo. However, during early August the Congress will be dealing with many of the most important issues of this session, including the foreign aid bill itself. Therefore, I consider it in the best interest of the Alliance for Progress that I remain here and work for those proposals on which our Latin American program and, indeed, our future relations with the entire free world so largely depend.

The delegation that I'm sending to Montevideo will be led by Secretary of the Treasury Dillon, and will consist of high-level, responsible people from other departments of the Government. They carry with them proposals to which I've given a good deal of personal attention and which have occupied the attention of the Government for some months, and which will, I believe and hope, mark an historic turning point in the life of the Americans.

Our task at Montevideo will be to build the framework of procedures and goals within which we can construct an American community of democratic states moving towards a better life for their people. This conference is the most important international gathering since the beginning of this administration, for on its success very largely depends the future of freedom in this hemisphere.

QUESTIONS

The Call-Up of National Guard or Reserve Units

Q: Mr. President, are you now considering a declaration of national emergency, limited or otherwise, in order to call up National Guard or Reserve units?

The President: We are concluding this afternoon our review of what actions we might take towards strengthening the military position of the United States. Those decisions will be brought to the attention of our allies this week, who also bear heavy responsibilities in this area. They will be part of a speech which I will make to the country next Tuesday evening, and will be presented to the Congress a week from today, and at that time the details of what we now plan to do will be made public.

The Increase of Conventional Forces by U.S. Allies

Q: Mr. President, some months ago you suggested that our allies could contribute to Western security by increasing the strength of their conventional forces. Since then, nothing much seems to have happened in this direction. Could you tell us whether you are satisfied with the pace of developments in this field?

The President: We will this week be talking with our allies about what we intend to do, and we will also have consultations with them about what we can in common do. There is going to be a foreign ministers conference in early August in Paris which will be preceded by preliminary consultations and at that time this will be one of the matters which will be before the foreign ministers. We have the problem of concerting our activities with 14 other countries.

Napoleon once said that he won all his successes because he fought allies. We are anxious that we make the consultations between our allies on all these questions - military, political, information, economic - that we try to work our procedures which will permit close harmony in the actions of all the countries which bear responsibility as members of NATO. Therefore, in answer to your question, we will be discussing - this will be one of the subjects which will be discussed in the next 2 weeks.

The Situation in Berlin

Q: Mr. President, in the note on Berlin yesterday, it said on several occasions that we are not wedded to the present situation in Berlin. In view of that, are we now planning to take an active lead in bringing about orderly and beneficial developments on Berlin, and specifically, how do you look upon the idea of an international peace conference on this subject?

The President: The statement of yesterday plus the statement of today represents the view I want to express at this time on Germany and Berlin, and other views will be expressed, of course, as the time moves on. But this is where I stand for the present.

Methods for Financing the Berlin Situation

Q: Mr. President, if your proposals for meeting the Berlin situation require substantial additional defense outlays, would you favor taxing to pay for this, rather than adding it to deficit spending? The Senate majority whip has suggested that we ought to meet this kind of cost with higher taxes.

The President: As you know, our budget - if the economy is proceeding at what we hope will be a steady rate of growth the present tax structure would bring in very substantial resources. I think we discussed at a previous conference that that tax structure is so strong that it contributed to strangling the recovery after the '58 recession. Therefore, the judgment on taxes and on expenditures will be made in light of what will produce the best economic situation for the United States in the coming months. We will make it clear at the time that we complete our review and announce then - as to what exactly we propose on taxes.

I will suggest, however, while we're on it, that both the previous administration and this administration recommended nearly $840 million of tax increase in postal payments. That amount has been steadily scaled down, and yet we've been unable to get a vote in the House of Representatives on the issue, and no hearings have been held in the Senate. This is a matter which I'm hopeful that Congress will deal with, because it represents an agreement between this administration and the last administration that we should not permit nearly $1 billion in deficit in the Postal Service. And a bill has just passed the Senate providing increased benefits for the employees, which will add another 60 or 70 million dollars to the deficit, which will take it over $1 billion if passed and signed by the President. So that here is at least one area, preliminary to a decisive answer to your question, which will come in the next few days, that I think we should move on.

School Legislation

Q: Mr. President, the whole bundle of your school legislation was torpedoed in the House Rules Committee yesterday, and it's clear that one of the things that largely helped to sink it was the religious issue. Will you discuss that problem, including the report that you have just about given up on passing school legislation in this first session of this Congress?

The President: Well, I know that we were defeated in the Rules Committee by a vote of 8 to 7. I will say that 7 out of those 8 votes came from members of Congress who were not sympathetic to the legislation nor supported me in the last election. They have, of course, their responsibility to meet. But the fact of the matter is that there are procedures available to the House of Representatives to adopt this bill, in spite of the action of yesterday, before the session ends.

Now the Senate passed it by a generous majority and it came out of the House Committee with support. I consider it to be probably the most important piece of domestic legislation. I'm hopeful that the members of Congress who support this will use those procedures which are avilable to them under the rules of the House to bring this to a vote, and that a majority of the members of Congress will support it. Every study that we make indicates the need for the legislation. There is broad general support, in my opinion, for improving our educational system. Anyone who has a child wants that child to educated to the extent of its talents. This program is most important.

In addition, included within that bill is a provision for the so-called impacted areas, and the July 1st date is past and those impacted areas are working on an emergency basis. So I feel that the impacted area part should stay in this bill, that it should be, I'm hopeful, considered by the House and that a majority of the members will vote "aye" or "nay" on it.

This matter has been involved. Education is a very important part of the life of this country and there are strong feelings - the matter of religion has been brought into it, other issues have. My view is that assistance for public education should be passed by this session. I'm hopeful a majority of the members of the House will agree, because I think it would be a most important step forward and I'm confident that Congressman Thompson and others in the House, Senator Morse in the Senate, who've been working on it, will continue to use all of their energies to get this bill by. I would sign it with the greatest possible pleasure.

Request for Defense Funds

Q: Mr. President, could you give us a broad estimate of approximately how much more defense funds you might be asking next week?

The President: No, Mr. Lawrence. We are meeting in the National Security Council this afternoon, at which time a final judgment will be reached; we do have an obligation to communicate our views to - particularly those who are involved with us in Berlin. It will be presented to the Congress early next week and to the American people early next week.

The Freedom Riders Movement

Q: Mr. President, will you give us your view of the Freedom Riders movement?

The President: I think the Attorney General has made it clear that we believe that everyone who travels, for whatever reason they travel, should enjoy the full constitutional protection given to them by the law and by the Constitution. They should be able to move freely in interstate commerce.

Now, I'm hopeful that that will become the generally accepted view, and if there are any legal doubts about the right of people to move in interstate commerce, that that legal position will be clarified. We naturally want those rights to be developed in a way which will permit them to be lasting and which will permit them to meet the needs of those people who have - who wish to travel.

In my judgment, there's no question of the legal rights of the freedom travelers - Freedom Riders, to move in interstate commerce. And those rights, whether we agree with those who travel, whether we agree with the purpose for which they travel, those rights stand, providing they are exercised in a peaceful way. We may not like what people print in the paper, but there's no question of their constitutional right to print it. So that follows, in my opinion, for those who move in interstate commerce.

So the basic question is not the Freedom Riders. The basic question is that anyone who moves in interstate commerce should be able to do so freely. That's a more substantive question, not the question merely of the Freedom Riders.

The Possibility of a Ground War in Europe over Berlin

Q: Mr. President, in your consideration of the military requirements now in dealing with the Berlin situation, and of the allied military reevaluation, are you basing your judgment on the assumption that it is conceivable that we might fight a ground war in Europe over Berlin?

The President: I'm making my judgment on what I consider to be the relative power balance between the Communist bloc and ourselves, the attitude which the Communist bloc is now taking, and what possible needs we might have in protecting our commitments and vital interest. I think that we have to realize that we are - our commitments are far flung. We operate at the end of a long supply line, and others in some cases operate at the end of a short supply line. All this indicates the needs, the very heavy burdens, placed upon this country. We have commitments in Southeast Asia and we have commitments in Berlin, and we are being very vigorously challenged.

Now, in answer to your question, I think that we'll make public - and you can make perhaps a better calculation after we give our figures - and as I said before those figures should not be discussed, in my opinion, until at least those who share this burden with us have a chance to be informed.

This alliance - NATO alliance - is going to move through very difficult periods in the coming months. Every country has its own strategic and tactical problems and carries particular burdens which other countries do not. If this alliance is going to move in concert, in my opinion we have to improve our consultation.

It took us, as you know, some time before we were able to come to a conclusion on the language of the aide memoire. We're going to have to improve our consultation so that we can come to decisions more quickly. But I think we should realize - as anyone who has studied the history of alliances - how enormous a task it is to have 15 countries moving down a stream all together over an issue which involves the security of them all. So we will inform them, and then the Congress, of what we plan to do, and the Congress will make the final judgment.

The President's Forthcoming Speech

Q: Mr. President, can you give us some details of the speech that you plan for the Nation next Tuesday?

The President: The speech will be a discussion of what our responsibilities are, and what our hazards are, and what I think the situation appears to be at the present time, what its consequences could be, and what we must do and what our allies must do to move through not merely the present difficulties but I would say we have to look forward to many challenges in the coming months and years.

So, we'll try to discuss at least the general problem that the United States faces in the security field in the summer of 1961, not merely that tied to Berlin, but generally.

Progress of the Space Program

Q: Mr. President, could you tell us whether the space program - the launching of a man into orbit - is going to come a bit faster than we might have expected in view of the fact that a second short ballistic flight was scheduled for today? I don't know whether it's come off or not.

The President: I'm not familiar with - that there's been any set-up in the previously announced schedule. If there has been I'll speak to Mr. Webb. But as I understood it, it was at the end of this year that we were talking about the orbit, but that may not be a precise date now. I'll have to look into it.

U.S. Foreign Aid

Q: Mr. President, many countries receiving foreign aid from us are concerned because their expanding populations nullify the aid. The President of Pakistan referred to this in his speech to the joint session of Congress and also in his speech at the Press Club. Since you are asking billions of dollars more in foreign aid, will you help countries control their expanding populations if they ask you?

The President: I've said before, Mrs. Craig, that this is a decision which goes very much to the life of a country, and it is a personal decision and a national decision which these nations must make. The problem is not altogether an economic one. We help countries which carry out different policies in this regard and it's a judgment, in my opinion, which they should make.

The President's Confidence in Secretary of State Bowles

Q: Although the White House has commented on the fact that Under Secretary of State Bowles is remaining in his job at this time, there still remains some doubt as to your own confidence in him, sir, and your own ideas on how the administration of the State Department is proceeding.

The President: Well, in the first place, I've never, contrary to some reports, never asked Mr. Bowles for his resignation, nor has he ever offered it. I have always expected that he would be part of this administration until it concluded its responsibilities.

I have a high regard for Mr. Bowles. He was my adviser on foreign policy last year. And all my conversations with the members of the State Department, the members of the Defense Department, and the members of the intelligence community have gone to the question of how we can best organize our talents - in the White House - how we can best organize our talents so that everyone is being used in a way which makes maximum use of their abilities.

Now, when General Taylor was appointed it was regarded as a diminution of the responsibilities of the Joint Chiefs, which it is not. But it came about as a result of conversations between the Joint Chiefs and Secretary McNamara. We have the Killian committee now examining the structure of the intelligence community. We have been talking about how we can make more effective the structure and the personnel of the State Department. We'll continue to do so, because they're faced with unprecedented hazards.

As I said, when Mr. Rusk is going to be meeting with the foreign ministers on the very vital question, Berlin, Secretary Dillon will be meeting at Montevideo and this puts great burdens on the Department of State, which is the arm of the President in foreign policy.

Mr. Bowles has my complete confidence. He is going on the trip which will take him to Africa and Asia, consulting with heads of states and with allies, and I expect that his trip will be most valuable and I'm confident that everyone who talks to him, Americans or heads of other states, will recognize that Mr. Bowles will be, I hope, a valuable part of this administration as long as it continues, and that he has the confidence of the President and the Secretary of State.

Q: Mr. President, does your answer mean that there is a possibility that he may be shifted, though, to some other responsibilities more in keeping with his talents?

The President: We have reached no judgment on how we're going to organize any of these departments or people. I've put the general principle forward that we are going to attempt to maximize the abilities of everyone working in the Government. If I came to the conclusion that Mr. Bowles could be more effective in another responsible position, I would not hesitate to ask him to take that position, and I am confident Mr. Bowles would not hesitate to take it.

My judgment is now that he should stay as Under Secretary of State and if there's going to be any change, I'll make it very clear at the time. But he will continue as Under Secretary of State, and I have no plan to ask him to assume a new responsibility. But any time I think that he or anyone else in the administration can do their job better in another way, I will certainly ask them, because as long as I'm going to bear the responsibility of the Presidency I'm going to attempt to make sure that it's implemented to the best, at least, of my ability.

Aid to Education Bills

Q: Congressman Powell said yesterday, sir, that it's your intention to veto any bill that may be passed for aid to education in federally impacted areas unless the general Federal aid bill is approved. Would you veto a bill for impacted areas if the general aid bill isn't ——

The President: My judgment is that the impacted school bill should be part of general public assistance. That's the position of the administration. Therefore, I'm hopeful that the Members of Congress who are anxious to secure the passage of this legislation should also recognize that we are not meeting our responsibilities if we merely pass the impacted area, that we should pass them both together and that's what we're working towards doing. As far as what action we'd take, of course, we have to wait until Congress has made its judgment. But my view is that the best way to secure the passage of that bill is to treat this as a unit, which I believe it is.

Self-Determination of the Peoples of Eastern Europe

Q: Mr. President, in your reply to the Soviet aide memoire, you stressed several times the lack of the right of self-determination among the peoples of Eastern Europe, and within the week you have issued a proclamation looking to the freedom of captive nations. Can you conceive in the event of any popular uprisings in Eastern Europe of a more active role for the United States in support of those uprisings than was the case in Hungary in 1956?

The President: I think - I'll stand on the statement which we made at this time.

Aid to Private Schools

Q: Mr. President, do you personally favor passage of aid to private schools as part of the National Defense Education Act, as part of the school package, which Congress should enact this year?

The President: Well, as you know - the bill which we sent to the Congress continued the previous assistance given to nonpublic schools to meet certain technical and defense requirements. The Office of HEW, I think, indicated to the House committee that the amendments which they added were not unconstitutional. Whether they are in public policy or not, and whether that would affect the final passage would be a judgment we would reach. They're not unconstitutional because they do not go across the board in a way which in my opinion is clearly unconstitutional. But the program which we support and which we hope the Congress will pass is the program we sent up there. Now, the Congress has to make its judgment on those bills. But in my judgment the best bills were the ones that - the most effective in meeting the problem was the legislation that we sent up there.

Public Opinion on Berlin

Q: Mr. President, Soviet Ambassador Menshikov is reported to have said that he did not think the United States people were either prepared or ready to go to war over Berlin. Do you think Ambassador Menshikov is sending back a correct assessment of the mood and temper of the American people?

The President: Well, I saw that this report came out of some function. I don't know how accurate it is, and whether that represents Mr. Menshikov's view. But I don't think that it's possible that anyone could read the aide memoire or the other statements which have been made by other governments and this Government without realizing that this is a very basic issue, the question of West Berlin, and that we intend to honor our commitments.

The Vicissitudes of the Presidency

Q: Mr. President, tomorrow as you doubtless know marks the end of your first 6 months in the Presidency. In view of Laos, Cuba, and now Berlin, I wonder if there is anything you would care to tell us about the vicissitudes of the Presidency.

The President: Well, I will say that we've had a - I think I said in the State of the Union address about the news will be worse instead of better. I would also say that Mr. Khrushchev would probably agree with that, in the sense that I think we are always conscious of the difficulties that we have. But there are a good many difficulties which should be taken into calculation in considering future bloc actions, in considering their own problems - whether it's the food shortage in China or the difficulties in other parts of the bloc empire, relations between certain bloc countries, and all the rest.

Now, as far as the United States, we've been pleased with the progress we've made internally, as far as the economy, the progress the country has made. We do feel we still have this problem of rather chronic unemployment. I'm glad that some of these bills which have been discussed for a number of years have passed. I'm hopeful that we can add education to that and long-term borrowing authority for foreign aid. My judgment is that the American people and this Government and the Congress must realize that we're in a long struggle which we'll be involved with for a great many years against very powerful countries, nearly a billion people in them, with strong economies in some cases, and that we cannot look for success on every occasion.

But I think if we have the patience and willingness to take some setbacks without taking unwise actions, recognizing that there are also other successes which may not be as dramatic to us but certainly come within Mr. Khrushchev's calculations, that we can move through this period, I hope, protecting our vital interests and our commitments and also maintaining the peace. But no one should think that it's going to be easy.

Reporter: Thank you, Mr. President.

THE PRESIDENT'S NEWS CONFERENCE OF

AUGUST 10, 1961

The President: Good morning. I have three announcements.

I read last week with great interest the statement by Prime Minister Macmillan, calling for negotiations looking toward Great Britain's entry as a full member in the European Common Market. I am gratified that this statement has been well received by the governments that are already members of the Common Market, and by the Commission of the European Economic Community. The United States Government, under the leadership of both parties, has steadfastly supported the political and economic integration of Western Europe. We are convinced that the continuing progress of this movement can bring new vitality to the Atlantic Community, and mounting strength to the free world. We welcome the prospect of Britain's participation in the institutions of the Treaty of Rome and in the economic growth that is the achievement and promise of the Common Market.

During the progress of the negotiations, the United States will of course give close attention to all developments affecting our own economic interests, and those of other friendly states in this hemisphere and elsewhere.

The enlargement of the European Community will necessarily result in some changes in the pattern of trade, but the necessary adjustments can be greatly facilitated if the European Community builds on the principle of broad and increasing trade relations with all other nations. It is our hope that progress towards this end can be made during the tariff negotiations under way in Geneva, in which both the European Economic Community and the United Kingdon are participating.

Secondly, I now have a report from the special panel on nuclear testing. This panel has examined a broad range of issues concerning our capabilities to detect and identify nuclear explosions. It has also gone into certain technical questions relating to nuclear weapons development. Although the report is made up of highly classified materials and cannot be released for that reason, I can say that as far as I am concerned this report has made me feel more urgently than ever that without an inspection system of the kind proposed by the United States and the United Kingdom at Geneva no country in the world can ever be sure that a nation with a closed society is not conducting secret nuclear tests.

In view of this report and in veiw of the deep longing of the people of the world for an effective end to nuclear testing, I am asking Ambassador Dean to return to Geneva on August 24 in an effort to ascertain whether the Soviet Union is now prepared to bring a safeguarded test ban agreement into being. It is my hope that he will succeed in convincing the Soviet representatives that the test ban treaty which we have proposed and stand to use as a basis for serious nego- tiations is a necessary and rational means of reducing the likelihood of nuclear war, and if we were successful, would be an admirable beginning in the long road towards general disarmament.

His return to Geneva is with our hopes and prayers, and I believe with the hopes and prayers of all mankind who are most concerned about further develop- ments of this deadly weapon. This meeting is most important, most critical, and I am hopeful that we will find a favorable response by those who will partici- pate in this negotiation.

Finally, I would like to say that while we face many problems about the world, one of the most encouraging features of recent months has been the whole- hearted response which so many young men and women have given to the proposal for the Peace Corps.

We have an opportunity, particularly in the area of teaching, to send hun- dreds and hundreds of young men and women who are skilled in this area through- out the world, teaching them English. And English opens up not only a key of communication, but also opens up all of the great cultural, historical, judicial areas which have become identified with the Anglo-Saxon world, and which are so vital in these difficult days.

I am hopeful, therefore, that the Congress will support this effort. It has had a most promising beginning, and we have an opportunity, if the amount re- quested by the Peace Corps is approved by the Congress, of having over 2700 volunteers serving the cause of peace in 1962, fiscal year.

QUESTIONS

Khrushchev and the German Problem

Q: Mr. President, in your reading of Mr. Khrushchev's recent speech and statements, have they increased, reduced, or left unchanged the changes for a peaceful settlement of the German problem?

The President: I thought Mr. Khrushchev restated the position which he took at Vienna and which he took in the Soviet aide memoire, and that there were no new proposals in that speech. He did state his desire, as I have done before, to have negotiations on these matters which are in dispute, and I can say that it is the strong conviction of the United States Government that every means should be employed, every diplomatic means, to see if a peaceful solution to this difficult matter can be achieved.

I think that we will, in the coming months, as I have said, use every device available to us to see if we can reach an equitable solution, and to see if we can get a more precise definition of the phrases and words and thoughts which the Soviet Union has expressed in the matter of Berlin, Germany, and Central Europe.

Q: Mr. President, I would like to ask your judgment on a passage in Mr. Khrushchev's speech. He says that in connection with a peace treaty between the Soviet Union and the East German Government: "We do not intend to infringe upon any lawful interests of the Western powers. Barring of access to Berlin, blockade of West Berlin, is entirely out of the question." Is there a catch in this, Mr. President?

The President: I think you have to read the speech in total. I believe it was stated that we should engage in negotiations with the East German Government in order to achieve the result which has been suggested. There have been a number of proposals about the rights of the East German Government to control access, and also to control the territory of West Berlin, and, therefore the speech should be read in total.

But I do believe that we should use, as I have said, every means available to us to make a determination whether a peaceful solution can be reached which will protect the rights of the people of West Berlin and our own rights.

Proposals to Increase the Size of the House

Q: As a former member of the House of Representatives and the Senate, sir, how do you feel about proposals to increase the size of the House from the present number of 437?

The President: Well, as a former member of the House, I would feel that it should be left to the members of the House of Representatives. (Laughter)

Arrangements in Case of President's Illness

Q: Mr. President, as a matter of prudence in these tense times, have you given any thought to making formal arrangements for the exercise of Presidential power in the event that you might become unable to function?

The President: Yes, I have entered into the same kind of an agreement with the Vice President that my predecessor, President Eisenhower, entered into with Mr. Nixon in the case of Presidential incapacity or inability to fulfill his constitutional functions, and I will ask Pierre if he could, at his noon briefing, put out a statement on what that agreement consists of.

Results of the Paris Conference

Q: Mr. President, recently you have appealed to our allies to make a greater effort in the conventional force field. In the light of that, are you satisfied with the results of the Paris conference which just concluded?

The President: Well, Mr. Rusk, after the Paris conference, went to Rome to talk to the Prime Minister of Italy, and I think was going to see Dr. Adenauer in Italy also and should be back very shortly, and then I think we could - I could give a precise answer.

That was one of the subjects which was discussed, and I think that I'll suspend any precise answer until Mr. Rusk has returned. In addition, those who participated at the Paris conference, the French Foreign Minister and, of course, Lord Home, have an obligation to report back to their governments to find out what the policy will be, as well as the members of NATO.

So I think it's still premature to make a determination. I am hopeful that the members of NATO will carry out the commitments which have been made in NATO on previous occasions, and particularly during these difficult days.

Resumption of Nuclear Testing

Q: Mr. President, in the event that Mr. Dean fails in his mission in Geneva, do you have in mind any deadline - any possibility of setting a certain date when you will decide to resume nuclear testing?

The President: I think we will be able to tell almost immediately whether the Soviet Union has made any change in its insistence upon the Troika, and therefore a unilateral veto on any inspection system. That of course is the fundamental issue which has up till now made it impossible to secure the acceptance of a treaty. Quite obviously, if that were written into any treaty, the treaty would be self-policing, and we would have no treaty, and as I've said in my statement, it's impossible to make a precise determination without inspection of whether nuclear testing is going on. We'll be able, therefore, to tell quite quickly whether there is any prospect for success, and if there is not, Mr. Dean will come home and I will then make the appropriate decisions.

Q: Is this our last try, then, Mr. President?

The President: We will try always if there's any genuine hope of success. But as I have indicated, this is probably a decisive meeting, because we will now find out whether there's any prospect of bringing an end to nuclear testing. And if we cannot agree on a system for effective inspection system on nuclear testing, which is really the easiest kind because of the various mechanisms that are available to determine testing - which is the easiest kind of disarmament in a sense, or at least limitations on arms, to police - how possibly can any country which will refuse to accept an effective inspection system on nuclear testing, how can they possibly say and argue in the General Assembly or anyplace else, that they're really for disarmament?

Military Role in Educating the Public About Communism

Q: Mr. President, there has been considerable argument in Congress in recent weeks about the proper role of military officers in educating the public on the dangers of communism. Senator Fulbright wrote a memorandum on it. There have been some orders issued in the Defense Department on the subject of proper conduct of military officers in this matter. I wonder if you could give us your views on this subject?

The President: Well, Senator Fulbright sent a memorandum to the Secretary of Defense and expressed his views about a matter which is of course of concern to the Department of Defense. The United States military, due to one of the wisest actions of our Constitutional Founders, have been kept out of politics, and they continue their responsibilities regardless of the changes of administration. I have no idea what the politics are of the members of the Joint Chiefs of Staff. I've appointed two of them since I've been President, and I have no idea what their views of politics are. This is a most important protection for our country, and it's equally important portection for the military. It prevents them from being exploited or discriminated by political people in either party. So therefore the problem always is, is how can the military remain removed from political life and how can civilian control of the military be effectively maintained and at the same time the military have the right and the necessity to express their educated views on some of the great problems that face us around the world. So I think this is a continuing matter which the Secretary of Defense is giving attention to. There is no desire to restrain or prevent any military man from speaking. What we are concerned about, however, always is that they not be exploited for any partisan purpose.

And I think basically it's for their own protection as well as the protection of the country. So in answer to your question, some of this arose because of an NSC decision in 1958, which placed special responsibilities upon them. And I think that it's therefore an obligation upon those who place those responsibilities upon them to clarify it in such a way that the common interest is protected.

So in my judgment, Senator Fulbright performed a service in sending his viewpoint to the Department of Defense and I am hopeful that every member of the Senate on this and every other matter will continue to give the administration the benefit of their judgment. That is why we are all up here.

East German Refugees

Q: Mr. President, some members of your administration and others have privately expressed concern that the continued large flight of East German refugees to the West might result in an act of violence. Senator Fulbright suggested that the border might be closed. Could you give us your assessment of the danger and could you tell us whether this Government has any policy regarding the encouragement or discouragement of East German refugees moving West?

The President: No, I don't think we have attempted to encourage or discourage the movement of refugees, in answer to the last part of the question. Of course, we're concerned about the situation in Eastern Germany, and really in Eastern Europe. There has been a tremendous passage from East to West which, of course, I know is a matter of concern to the Communists because this tremendous speedup of people leaving the Communist system to come to the West and freedom, of course, is a rather illuminating evidence of the comparative values of free life in an open society, and those in a closed society, under a Communist system. In answer to your question, however, the United States Government does not attempt to encourage or discourage the movement of refugees and I know of no plans to do so.

The Agreement at Punta del Este

Q: Mr. President, are you satisfied that the United States compromises in the agreement at Punta del Este on the public information program and the committee of experts will not weaken your Alliance for Progress program?

The President: Well, we haven't concluded the negotiations. So far I have been very satisfied with what has been done, and I have the greatest possible hopes for this meeting. I hope that all of us will not get so occupied with other matters occurring in this hemisphere that we forget that perhaps one of the most significant meetings in the history of the Western Hemisphere, in this century, is now taking place in Montevideo, and that if we can reach a successful conclusion we can come out of that meeting, all of these republics, with a real hope that we can move ahead in improving the life of the people of this continent. And that's where the great struggle is going on. If we fail there, and if we fail here in the United States to recognize that this is the issue to which we should now be devoting our attention, then the spread of communism is - and the failure of the free society - is going to be far more assured.

So I am hopeful that the meeting will be successful. I am hopeful that the country and the people of this hemisphere will look at what's going on there, because that is the most significant event of recent weeks.

U.S. Space Efforts

Q: Sir, have you asked your aides, or your science aides, to prepare for you some kind of a study on whether a greater focus can be put in our space efforts in some possible arrangement similar to the Manhattan project during the last war?

The President: We are now attempting to devote - we are spending as much money and devoting as large a percentage of scientific personnel, engineering and all the rest, as we possibly can to the space program. We are constantly concerned with speeding it up. We are making what I consider to be a maximum effort.

It may be possible to improve it as we go along and we will attmept to do so. But we asked for all the money for this program that those in positions of responsibility felt could be usefully employed for this purpose, because beyond this we begin to get into diminishing returns on personnel and all the rest.

We may be able to improve it and if we can, we will, but it is our hope to make the largest possible effort.

Possibility of War Breaking Out over Berlin

Q: Mr. President, if fighting should break out over Berlin, that is, if peace efforts fail, do you believe it can be limited to a conventional war or would it lead to the use of nuclear weapons?

The President: Well, we are hopeful that we would be able to reach peaceful solutions to these problems.

The Departments of State and Defense

Q: Mr. President, the Budget Director testified at the Captiol a week ago and said that your administration was a little unhappy with the policy planning and the generation of ideas in the State and Defense Departments and cooperation between them. Can you tell us what that problem is in a little detail and what is being done to improve the situation?

The President: Well, I think he also expressed satisfaction that some progress was being made. One of the problems, of course, is that nearly every international problem involves several governmental agencies: certainly the Defense Department, State, and in many cases at least one other agency. And therefore, the problem of coordinating these different agencies in an effective way represents a major problem of administration. We have, of course, as you know, on a number of the most important international problems that we faced, set up task forces which meet frequently and render at least weekly reports to the NSC, but it's a matter of constant concern, though I think we have improved our techniques recently.

Foreign Aid to Peru and Laos

Q: Mr. President, several congressional committees have issued reports that were quite critical of the handling of foreign aid in the past in Peru and Laos specifically, and they centered much of their attention on two or three individuals: Mr. Theodore Achilles, Mr. Rollin Atwood, Mr. Graham Parsons, who still have some positions of some responsibility in the Government. I wonder if you contemplate, or your administration contemplates, any action - removal of these individuals from positions of responsibility, or any studies of their role today, and do you have any specific plans for tighter administration of these programs in the light of the past record?

The President: Yes, I am hopeful, if we are able to secure passage of legislation now before the Congress, that our administration will be more effective. In addition, we hope to bring in, if we are effective in the Congress, 5 new area administrators, and between 45 and 50 new country heads, into the administration of foreign aid. Now, on the three names you gave me, I am familiar with two of them. One of them is an Ambassador now to Sweden, and the other is at work here in the State Department, and I am not informed about the third. I am not aware of anything in their records that throws any question, of course, on their integrity, and we are satisfied that they can meet the responsibilities which they now hold.

Plane Hijacking

Q: Mr. President, would you give us your views on the latest hijacking plane incidents involving –

The President: The Cuban one or the American one?

Q: Both. (Laughter)

The President: It's my understanding that the hijacking which took place yesterday of the American plane was done by a – at least the information I had before I came in – by a Frenchman who had been treated earlier this year for mental aberrations at Bellevue. The hijacking a week ago was done once again by two men, one of whom had also been treated for mental weakness. It does indicate that the lunatic fringe, those who are desirous of seeing their names in the paper, and all of the rest, have seized upon this technique.

I am, of course, wholeheartedly opposed to it. I am hopeful that we can make it possible to work out satisfactory procedures so that every government involved takes steps to prevent hijacking which endanger the lives of innocent people.

Now, let me say that we are – have ordered today on a number of our planes a border patrolman who will ride on a number of our flights. We are also going to insist that every airplane lock its door, and that the door be strong enough to prevent entrance by force, and that the possession of the key be held by those inside the cabin so that pressure cannot be put on the members of the crew outside to have the door opened.

In addition, I am hopeful that governments everywhere will use their maximum influence to discourage this kind of action which endangers the lives of the crew and of the people involved, and which is an exercise in futility. And that is the view of this Government and we will take every means that we can to prevent not only the hijacking of our own planes but the hijacking of other planes. I'm hopeful that all concerned will do the same. It just endangers the lives of people who should be protected.

Russians in Orbit

Q: Mr. President, there seems to be some doubt in the country as to whether the Russians really did put two men in orbit around the earth, as they have claimed. Are you satisfied from the evidence available to you that they did do what they said they did?

The President: Yes.

Q: Mr. President, after this latest Soviet space effort, Senator Long of Missouri, among others, said that the real problem was not our present space effort but the lack of young Americans going into science. He pointed out that the Soviets are still graduating three times as many scientists as we are. Can you, sir, see anything that the Government can and is doing to step up this problem?

The President: Well, we are hopeful that we can secure the passage of the Aid to Education Act as well as the NDEA, both of which offer scholarships to talented young men and women, and that we can increase the number of scientists who may be graduated.

In addition, of course, we have a good many very talented scientists, but we did not make a major effort in this area for many years, and we are now behind and paying the price of having the Soviet Union exploit a great propaganda advantage now on three separate occasions, with the flight of the Sputnik, the flight of Mr. Gagarin, and the most recent one. They are still, as I've said before, many months ahead of us. And therefore, we can look for other evidences of their superiority in this area. We are making a major effort which will cost billions of dollars. But we cannot possibly permit any country whose intentions toward us may be hostile to dominate space. What I would like to see at the United Nations and elsewhere is an effort made to have space insured for peaceful purposes. And the United States delegation to the General Assembly is going to make a major effort in that regard this year.

The Neutron Bomb

Q: Mr. President, there has been a lot of talk recently about the developments of a neutron bomb. Can you give us your estimate of the feasibility of developing a weapon which would destroy human beings without destroying real estate values?

The President: No.

The Test Situation

Q: Could you tell us, sir, whether your report from the experts on the test situation changes the general belief in this country that while we have no evidence that the Russians are cheating, we have no evidence that they are not cheating?

The President: I think my statement stated that we could not make a precise determination whether testing was going on in a closed society by present techniques.

Amendment of the Mutual Assistance Act

Q: Sir, I wonder what you think of a proposal by Senator Styles Bridges to amend the Mutual Assistance Act whereby we will deny any aid to any country exporting strategic goods to a country dominated by Russia?

The President: Well, that is a language somewhat similar to the Battle Act, and I'd have to look at the language of Senator Bridges and compare it to the Battle Act before I could give you a judgment on it.

Q: If it's an extension, I think it might hit at some of our allies, mightn't it?

The President: Well, I'll read the language –

The Immigration Laws

Q: Mr. President, when you were a Senator, you were actively in favor of legislation to broaden our immigration laws and establish a more liberal and equitable quota system. Under present laws, many of the foreign born scientists and scholars who contributed so largely to our national strength might not be admitted. What plans does the administration now have in this area of immigration?

The President: We have consulted with Congressman Walter and others as to what we can do to improve our immigration laws and we are going to continue to do so.

Because yesterday's hijacking aroused such great public excitement, and the week before, even though we now see that neither one of these hijackings was done by Cubans, does, it seems to me, make it important for us to act with the prudence which is worthy of a great power which bears responsibilities for the defense of freedom all around the globe, and not to make determinations on policy until our information is more complete.

In addition, we should realize that over 25 planes have come to the United States, 14 have been returned, 9 have been sold in response to a court order, and that, therefore, we should, I think, concern ourselves with procedures which will prevent a repetition and which will make sure that our own responsibilities are fully met in this regard.

The point I want to make is that what is going on in Montevideo is so important that we should not get overexcited about matters when our information is so faulty, so incomplete.

Summit Negotiations

Q: Mr. President, in connection with the Berlin crisis, there has been quite a bit of speculation about one or more summit conferences. Would you tell us what your attitude is at this time toward summit negotiations?

The President: Well, the attitude which I have held and still hold is that no summit between East and West is useful unless the groundwork has been laid beforehand which will insure some success. As far as a summit of Western leaders, I think that if it should prove important in coordinating our policy on any matter, Berlin, I think that that meeting should be held and would be prepared to do so.

Latin America and Self-Help Measures

Q: Mr. President, during the foreign aid debate, there has been some concern expressed by legislators based upon the reports from Montevideo that some of the Latin American nations are not, apparently, eager to institute the self-help measures which you've made a condition of your program, and that the administration may not insist upon those conditions. Do you intend to insist upon those conditions?

The President: We're prepared to make a major effort in this regard and we're hopeful that other countries who also have high living standards will do so. But of course it would be completely useless unless an effort were made by all concerned. One of the proposals which have been made in Montevideo which is of particular interest is that under the aegis of the Inter-American Bank, that a study by independent experts be made of each country's economic planning and progress and commitment, and it seems to me that this is a great basis for a hemispheric effort. We're not interested in making the contributions which

I think we have to make unless we feel that they're going to improve the life of the people. And, therefore, there's a responsibility on us all, for us to contribute to the success of this goal and for the countries involved to make sure that this effort helps the people, because otherwise the effort will fail and those societies will inevitably be wiped away - unless some real progress is made.

Reporter: Thank you, Mr. President.

THE PRESIDENT'S NEWS CONFERENCE OF

AUGUST 30, 1961

President Kennedy: I have several announcements to make.

First, I want to take this opportunity to congratulate Governor Vandiver of Georgia, Mayor Hartsfield of Atlanta, Chief of Police Jenkins, Superintendent of Schools Letson and all of the parents, students and citizens of Atlanta, Ga., for the responsible, law-abiding manner in which four high schools were desegregated today.

This was the result of vigorous effort for months by the officials of Atlanta and by groups of citizens throughout the community. Their efforts have borne fruit in the orderly manner in which desegregation was carried out - with dignity and without incident.

Too often in the past, such steps in other cities have been marred by violence and disrespect for law.

I strongly urge the officials and citizens of all communities which face this difficult transition in the coming weeks and months to look closely at what Atlanta has done, and to meet their responsibilities, as have the officials and citizens of Atlanta and Georgia, with courage, tolerance, and, above all, respect for the law.

Secondly, as agreed at their recent meeting in Paris, the Foreign Ministers of France, the United Kingdon, and the United States will again be joined by the Foreign Minister of the Federal Republic of Germany, and they will meet in Washington on September 14. This meeting will constitute a further stage in the process of continuing consultation by the four powers and our NATO allies with respect to Germany and Berlin in light of the Soviet challenge to our position there.

Three, I am appointing Gen. Lucius Clay to be my personal representative in Berlin with the rank of Ambassador. The situation in Berlin is a serious one, and I wish to have the advantage of having on the scene a person of General Clay's outstanding capacity and experience.

While this appointment will not change the existing responsibilities of our military and diplomatic officers in Germany and Berlin, General Clay will be in close touch with such men as Ambassador Dowling in Bonn and General Watson, our Berlin commandant, and the appointment adds to our resources of judgment and action by placing in a most important city an American in whom the Secretary of State and I have unusual confidence.

We are most grateful to General Clay for once again resuming his long career of public service. General Clay will take up his duties on September 15, will proceed then to Berlin, and will serve as long as this special arrangement seems desirable.

Lastly, I am sending the following message to the conference of unaligned states convening in Belgrade on September 1:

"It is always encouraging when responsible world leaders join together to consider the problems that beset mankind. We recognize that most of the countries at Belgrade do not consider themselves committed on certain of the issues which confront us today, but we do know that they are committed to the United Nations Charter. The people of the United States share this commitment.

"We know that those gathering in Belgrade are committed to finding a way to halt the waste of the earth's resources in the building of the implements of death and destruction, and the people of the United States have constantly pledged themselves to this goal.

"We believe that the peoples represented at this conference are committed to a world society in which men have the right and the freedom to determine their own destiny, a world in which one people is not enslaved by the other, in which the powerful do not devour the weak. The American people share that commitment, and we have pledged the influence of this Nation to the abolition of exploitation in all of its forms.

"The peoples represented at Belgrade are committed to achieving a world at peace in which nations have the freedom to choose their own political and economic systems and to live their own way of life, and since our earliest beginnings this Nation has shared that commitment.

"All this and much more the leaders at Belgrade have in common. This and much more the people of the United States have in common with them. So for myself, and I'm sure for the American people, I express the hope that their deliberations there will bring us all nearer these goals."

QUESTIONS

The Berlin Question

Q: Mr. President, there have been increasing statements on both sides about the prospects for Western negotiations with Russia on the Berlin question. Could you spell out in any specific terms just what areas there are for negotiations and what will you hope to gain in view of recent Communist words and actions?

The President: No, I don't think that it would be useful at this time to attempt to spell out the areas of negotiation.

We have indicated - and I've said before that we are prepared to participate in any exchange of views, to use all available channels which are open to us to see if a peaceful solution can be reached on the problems in Europe and in Germany - any solution which can provide greater guarantees to the people of West Berlin that they will have the right to live out their lives in a way of their own choosing and that we will be glad to participate in any conversations which we have hopes will advance that prospect. This is particularly true because the situation in this area is so fraught with danger.

Q: *Do you think, generally speaking, sir, that the crisis in Berlin has a better chance of being settled through negotiation, as you have suggested, rather than by force, as the Soviets have threatened upon occasion?*

The President: Well, I don't see that there could be any solution – which would serve the world – to Berlin by force, and therefore I'm hopeful that all people involved will realize that in these days of massive forces available on every side that – for the future of the countries involved and for the human race – that we should attempt to work out a peaceful solution and that neither side should attempt to impose its will by brute force because in that case it would be unsuccessful and disaster would be the common result.

The School Aid Measure

Q: *On a domestic question, Mr. President, in view of the House action today on your school aid measure, how do you view the future prospects for such legislation?*

The President: Well, it's very difficult because everyone is for education but they're all for a different education bill. And it's very difficult to get a majority who will support legislation that has a prospect of getting out of the House committee and the Senate committee – and through the House committee and through the Senate committee – and be signed by the President.

So that it's going to require a good deal of good will on all sides, because the only one who loses today is not the administration but school children who need this assistance.

So we will be back next year. But it's going to require a recognition by all groups that – and our experience this year shows it – that there has to be some recognition that what we're concerned about is advancing education of the young people of this country, which, of course, is our most important asset and responsibility.

I'm hopeful that before the session ends there will be an opportunity for the Congress to vote on our aid to higher education, because that is desperately needed. In the next 10 years we're going to have to build more school buildings than we have built since the beginning of this country.

And the Federal Government, since our earliest beginnings, has had a responsibility in this field. This responisiblity continues.

And therefore, though the defeat today was quite clear, and though the defeat today indicates it will be difficult to find a satisfactory formula, we will attempt to do so.

Dick Goodwin

Q: *Mr. President, could you give us your views on the wish of the Senate to question Dick Goodwin? Mr. Hatcher said this morning that he did not think the question of Executive privilege was involved.*

The President: No. I've – Mr. – I think Mr. Goodwin is going to be available to members of the Senate Foreign Relations Committee tomorrow afternoon at 5 in an informal meeting, and will be glad to discuss the entire report on the Punta del Este meeting, and all of its activities. And I'm sure other members of the delegation will be doing likewise.

Q: *Sir, if I may pursue that just one second. You spoke of an informal meeting. Does this meet the problem of Executive privilege and not –*

The President: The question of Executive privilege has not been raised.

Q: Would it not be raised if there were formal meetings is what I'm really getting at.

The President: Well, the question of Executive privilege has not been raised in the request that was made by Senator Morse for Mr. Goodwin to appear. And Mr. Goodwin attended the Punta del Este meeting as a member of the delegation, and I would be delighted, and I think it would be most helpful, if Mr. Goodwin appeared under the circumstances that I've described. Does that answer your question? (Laughter)

Mr. Nixon

Q: Mr. President, I would like to ask you a two-part question: Do you think that Mr. Nixon should run for Governor of California, and as a politician, Mr. President, what do you think of the advisability of a political party giving a defeated candidate a second chance at the Presidency?

The President: Well, I would think, in answer to your first question, if Mr. Nixon asked my view as a fellow practitioner of the - follower of the political profession - I'd be glad to give him my opinion, as I do have an opinion on the matter. (Laughter)

But, second, I think that history is filled with the case of men who have been defeated for offices who have continued their public service, and I think we've seen it very much in the last few years, and I'm sure we'll see it in the next years.

Charles Kamen

Q: Mr. President, do you think the Peace Corps should dismiss Charles Kamen because of the complaints that have been made about him?

The President: I think the Peace Corps, as Mr. Shriver has said, should make a judgment as they do. I don't think Mr. Kamen is as yet a member of the Peace Corps. He's in training, as a good many other men and women are, and then he will either be accepted or rejected. It's a matter which I'm sure the Peace Corps will deal with in a responsible way. And I've every confidence in the judgment of those who make the selections.

The Unemployment Problem

Q: Mr. President, there's a very hard core of unemployment still. Do you have any special plans now beyond those you've already suggested?

The President: Well, we are concerned still about unemployment, which is four and a half million and on a seasonally adjusted rate would be about five million, which is still too high.

We have had in the last 2 or 3 months a tremendous economic recovery, but population increases and because of productivity increases and technological changes, we still have a hard core, particularly in some of the major industrialized areas, as well as some of the areas which have had chronic unemployment, we still have this hard core.

I'm hopeful that as the economy begins to move ahead more that there will be a further decrease in the number of those unemployed.

In addition, I am hopeful that Congress will take action before they go home, on job retraining, because some of this is technological and even if we had a complete economic recovery you would still find some men left behind because of the change in skills.

So I do think that legislation would be helpful, and if these programs do not work, then we're going to have to consider what other steps we can take. But we have a large deficit and it's difficult to think that we could usefully increase that in order to effect employment without adversely affecting the cost of living. That's our difficulty there.

Republican Criticism on Berlin

Q: Mr. President, Mr. Nixon has called the movement of American troops into West Berlin a useless gesture, which Mr. Khrushchev might interpret as weakness rather than strength. At the same time, the Republican National Chairman has said that your administration's attitude in general is one of appeasement toward communism throughout the world. Do you have any comment on this criticism by top spokesmen of the opposition party?

The President: No, I don't. We are in a situation in Germany which is fraught with peril and I think that anyone who is aware of the nature of the destructive power that's available to both sides should, I would think, be careful in attempting to take any political advantage out of our present difficulties.

Now, in regard to the statement of the Vice President, I'm quite aware that Berlin is, from a military point of view, untenable, if it were subjected to a direct attack by the Soviet Union. What we hope will prevent that direct attack is the awareness of the Soviet Union that we mean to defend our position in West Berlin, and that American troops, who are not numerous there, are our hostage to that intent.

It would seem to me, and I think at the time, that the West Berliners would benefit from a reminder of that commitment, and it was for that reason that those troops were added to the garrison of West Berlin. I don't see really how that weakens our commitment. If troops were withdrawn, would that strengthen it?

Auto Negotiations

Q: Mr. President, in view of the fact that the economy is recovering, what steps is the administration prepared to take to prevent a breakdown in the auto negotiations in Detroit?

The President: Well, they're being carried on at the present time between the Auto Workers and the automobile industry, in the hope that they will come to a conclusion which will make it possible for work to be maintained and that it will make it possible for an agreement to be reached that will not provide for an increase in the cost of cars.

This is a matter in which the public interest is involved, quite obviously, but it's a matter which should be left, at this time, to the - those on both sides of the bargaining table, who are bargaining in a free economy.

Negotiations with the Russians

Q: Mr. President, I'm not clear from your answer to Mr. Spivak whether we are actively seeking negotiations with the Russians at this time on the question of Berlin, whether Mr. Thompson or any other official of the Government is trying to set a date, time, and place for talks on -

The President: Well, I think Mr. Thompson is going to be returning, under his regular schedule, in the next few days to Moscow and, as I have said, we will be using those means which are available to us to attempt to exchange views among all the parties that are interested, and see whether a satisfactory solution can be reached. And I feel I should leave it at that point.

Steel Price Hike

Q: Do you believe that there is anything the Government can or should do to try to head off a hike in steel prices? And if so, what would you plan to do?

The President: Well, I'm hopeful that the steel companies themselves will reach a conclusion that the October increase in wages can be absorbed without an increase in steel prices.

The inflation which marked our economy before 1958 was, I think, tied very closely to the increases in steel prices. Since 1958 the steel prices have remained relatively stable. And it is a fact that during that same period the cost of living has remained relatively stable.

Now my economic adivsers inform me that it would be possible for the steel companies to absorb the increase, wihtout increasing - the increase in wages - without increasing prices, and still insure to the steel companies, and their owners, a good profit.

I am concerned that an increase in steel prices would set off another inflationary spiral, and also make us less competitive abroad, serve as a brake on our recovery, and also affect our balance of payments.

So that I am very hopeful that these private companies will - and I'm sure they will - concern themselves with the public interests that are involved in their decision.

The Next Step in Nuclear Testing

Q: Mr. President, you described the present session of the Geneva nuclear test ban conference as critical. Does the Soviet reaction to our latest proposals bring us closer then to a resumption of tests, or what is our next step in this area?

The President: Well, Mr. Dean is going to continue during next week, and I would think that by the end of next week - I think they're meeting every other day - we should have a much - we'll have an answer as to whether it's going to be possible to reach an agreement.

He will then return home, and as I said before, we would then be expected to make the appropriate decisions.

Commitments for Development Lending

Q: Mr. President, the language adopted last night by the conference committee on the foreign aid bill gives you authority to make long-term commitments for development lending. If both houses approve this language, would you then think that there is at least a kind of moral obligation upon the part of the Appropriations Committee to honor those commitments with appropriations?

The President: No, I would think that the Appropriations Committee would have to make their own - meet their own responsibilities. But it would mean that - if the conference report is accepted by the House and Senate - that the House and Senate and those committees which have particular responsibility for foreign affairs have set this figure.

This figure does represent a cut in both economic assistance and military assistance. And as we do have heavy responsibilities in the coming years in these areas - we've accepted a particularly heavy responsibility and commitment, for example, toward the countries of Latin America - I am hopeful that the Appropriations Committees and the Congress will come as close as possible to the figures that the conference has set, because any cut would diminish by that much our ability to do the job.

I think the compromise, while of course not in the language which was originally suggested, I do think gives us a very valuable tool. And I'm therefore appreciative of the work that was done by the conference.

Khrushchev's Responsibility in Setting Off a War

Q: Mr. President, everything in the past 3 months that's been said by you and written about you indicates that you have a grave sense of your responsibility for involving this country and the world in a nuclear war over Berlin. Yet everything that's been said by Mr. Khrushchev and written about Mr. Khrushchev indicated he doesn't seem to share this grave responsibility.

Do you think there's been a failure in our diplomacy and our policy that he is not yet convinced about his responsibility in setting off a nuclear war?

The President: Well, every country operates under different systems and every - Mr. Khrushchev - there has been a good deal of brandishing of nuclear weapons, but I am hopeful, as I've said, that anyone - and I'm sure Mr. Khrushchev knows very well what the effect would be on the people of this world of ours if nuclear weapons were **exchanged** in a massive way between the countries which possess them - and I'm conscious of this and I'm sure Mr. Khrushchev is - and we will have to wait and see now whether from that consciousness on both sides peace can be achieved, which is our objective.

Castro and Brazil

Q: Mr. President, what is your view of the interference in the internal political affairs of Brazil by Castro in sending a message of encouragement to the leftist elements there, and what is your general view of the situation?

The President: I think it's a matter which should be left to the people of Brazil. It is their country, their constitution, their decision, **their** government, and I'm confident that they are going to solve the problem themselves without outside interference by any country.

The Part Played by **Our** NATO Allies

Q: Mr. President, in view of the Berlin situation and the common threat, you have called up 75,000 reserves and have called in aircraft and naval ships. Can you tell us whether you're satisfied with what our NATO allies are doing to increase their strength, and can you tell us what they are doing and what they are planning to do if you have any knowledge of that?

The President: There have been some increases, but we do not have a final judgment on what our NATO allies will do nor will we finally, I think, until the end of September. In addition, the United States is going to be considering what other steps it could take.

We have in the meeting of the foreign ministers in early August urged very strongly that the NATO countries commit larger forces to the defense of Europe. It involves their security and it involves peace in this area and I'm hopeful that all the countries that are involved will make the kind of effort which is required.

And I think if they do not, then, Europe has diminished to that degree. I am hopeful that we're going to meet our responsibility and we're asking them to meet theirs. And by the end of September we'll know whether that's going to be done.

Action on the Possible Steel Price Increase

Q: Mr. President, on steel do you have any thoughts or specific plans for meeting the situation if the steel industry does not seem to be persuaded by the arguments that you have been presenting against the price increase?

The President: Well, I'm hopeful that the view which has been expressed today, and been expressed on other occasions, and the problems - and the public responsibilities of people involved, I'm hopeful that they will have an effect, and I prefer to leave it at that for the present.

Access to East Berlin

Q: Mr. President, Ambassador Dowling has delivered a message to the Soviet Ambassador in Germany insisting - and that was the word of the note - that the Soviet Union take the necessary steps to insure continued unrestricted access to East Berlin without hindrance as to place or time. The East Germans have restricted some of the entry points into East Berlin for us and for the West Germans. Can you tell us how you intend to follow through on this?

The President: We - the communication between East and West Berlin is open. And the situation which you've described has existed for a number of days.

Q: Do I understand that we consider the present situation to meet these requirements of unrestricted access?

The President: We - I don't feel the situation in East Berlin is satisfactory in any way. And we have made clear that we have - do not consider it satisfactory. But it is also a fact that communication does exist between East and West Berlin, and that it's possible for those who have official responsibilities, as well as private citizens, to pass.

It is limited - it is not, in our opinion, in accordance with the agreements; but it does exist. What we are concerned about in addition, of course, is the whole question of access to West Berlin itself.

Q: Mr. President, on Berlin, if one takes the public statements of the two sides at face value, it would seem the U.S. and the U.S.S.R. are on something of a collision course here.

Do you have any feeling from private information, or other sources, that there is somewhere in all this wordage going back and forth, some room for diplomatic negotiation, and possibly a peaceful settlement of this problem?

The President: I do not have such information at the present time. Though I am hopeful that - as I have said - that negotiations can be successful. There have been some statements which have been made which would indicate that there would be a recognition under all conditions of the rights of the people of West Berlin. Other statements have not been precise.

So we will know as time goes on. As I've said before at a previous press conference, it was important that we try to get at the real meaning of words - dealing with access, and rights, and freedom and the rest.

But in answer to your question, I am - do not have information today which would make me wholly sanguine about present prospects.

Decisions in Matters of Defense

Q: Sir, there has been some indication that in the Cabinet, and elsewhere in the Government, that some of our top officials are deferring to the State Department for matters of decision involving the military and defense. There've even been papers sent from the Defense Department over to the State Department for clearance. I wonder if this is done at your order?

The President: Well, ma'am, if you would be more precise, I could perhaps tell you.

Q: Well, sir, recently at a press conference, Secretary McNamara was asked several questions about the future in Berlin. He said, I can't answer those questions, you'll have to go to the Secretary of State.

The President: Well, it depends what questions they were. If the questions dealt with matters which come under the competence of the State Department, then it seems to me Mr. McNamara was quite right.

My judgment and experience has been that Mr. McNamara is fully competent to deal with the military - his military responsibilities, and so does. And Mr. Rusk does.

There are a good many matters that overlap. This is a government which is supposed to communicate. And that's what they're doing. But I've never heard it suggested that Mr. Rusk - that Mr. McNamara was turning over his responsibilities to Mr. Rusk, or vice versa.

But I would think that it would be the height of folly not to have the most intimate communication on a matter as important as Berlin,

Letter From Chancellor Adenauer

Q: Mr. President, can you at this time discuss with us some of the contents of the letter you received from Chancellor Adenauer this morning?

The President: No, the main thrust of the letter was in regard to what measures might be taken by the countries which have responsibilities in the area to any further steps which might be taken by the Soviet Union or the East German regime to limit access of the people of West Berlin or our access to West Berlin, and it dealt with that matter of countermeasures.

The Democratic Primary in New York

Q: Mr. President, what is your view of the bitter Democratic primary fight in New York City, and do you favor one Democratic group over another?

The President: No. (Laughter)

Consultations on Berlin

Q: Mr. President, there has been some concern expressed over the amount of time it takes the allies to consult on the specific steps necessary to handle the Berlin situation. I think you, in one of your press conferences, recently indicated you weren't quite satisfied with the amount of time it took to draft a note. Could you tell us whether you are satisfied with the present tempo of such consultations?

The President: Yes, well they're meeting almost every day - in any case every other day - the ambassadors of the countries that are directly involved. There are four countries that are involved and there is also NATO, so quite naturally it takes a longer time.

When it's a matter of involving a direct interest of the United States, however, we have attempted to make our responses immediate. For example, last week, when there was some suggestion that air traffic might be interfered with, we did get out the same day our response, because we thought the matter was so important.

But there is very - there is daily consultation, and I'm hopeful that through that consultation and through advanced planning we can meet some of the problems that you suggest, but it's difficult to meet them all satisfactorily.

Secretary Rusk and the Cuban Invasion

Q: Time magazine today published a version of the Cuban invasion in which they say that Secretary Rusk canceled the air support for the landing force and that you supported his viewpoint. Could you comment on that?

The President: No, I said from the beginning that I would not comment or attempt to, on the matter because I didn't think it was in the public interest. I'll merely state that this is the most inaccurate of all the articles that have appeared on Cuba. (Laughter)

Q: Sir, in a recent interview with Senor Castro he told me that you have said in the inaugural speech that you would not fear to negotiate and will not negotiate in fear.

It was a question I could not answer and maybe you could give us an idea on it because he says that the United States negotiates with the Russians and big powers and seems to be afraid - that was his words - to negotiate with Cubans about all the problems that concern both countries.

The President: Yes. Well, I've expressed my view that as long as Cuba makes itself a willing - the Cuban Government makes itself a willing accomplice to the Communist objectives in this hemisphere, that we could not have successful negotiations. And that, in my opinion, is what their status is today.

Reporter: Thank you, Mr. President.

THE PRESIDENT'S NEWS CONFERENCE OF

OCTOBER 11, 1961

The President: I have several announcements to make.

You will recall that in my recent address to the United Nations General Assembly I expressed concern of this Government over the situation in southeast Asia, particularly in the attacks on the people of South Viet-Nam.

With this situation in mind I've asked General Taylor, with the wholehearted endorsement of Secretary McNamara and General Lemnitzer, to go to Saigon this week to discuss with the President and American officials on the spot ways in which we can perhaps better assist the Government of Viet-Nam in meeting this threat to its independence.

General Taylor will be accompanied by a small staff from the various departments of Government which are concerned.

Secondly, I have today announced my intention to appoint a panel of outstanding scientists, doctors, and others to prescribe a program of action in the field of mental retardation.

This condition strikes those least able to protect themselves from it. It affects not only the people involved but also the members of their family.

It is a serious personal matter to at least 1 out of every 12 persons, disables 10 times as many as diabetes, 20 times as many as tuberculosis, 25 times as many as muscular dystrophy, and 600 times as many as infantile paralysis.

At one time, there was practically no effective program in the field of mental retardation. Wherever possible the children were committed to institutions. They were segregated from normal society and forgotten except by the members of their family. Only in isolated cases was an effort made to bring them back into useful lives in the community. They suffered from lack of public understanding and they suffered from lack of funds.

The situation today is better. Most attempts still take the form of therapeutic research and treatment. The central problems of cause and prevention remain unsolved. And I believe that we, as a country, in association with scientists all over the world, should make a comprehensive attack. It is a matter of the greatest possible interest to me, and I am going to meet with the panel next week. Thank you.

QUESTIONS

Prospects for a Berlin Settlement

Q: Mr. President, at our last news conference you were hopeful but not, as I recall, wholly sanguine about prospects for a Berlin settlement. In the meantime, have there been any developments, including the Gromyko talks, or any new information in hand, to raise hopes for a solution?

The President: No. I would say that we are still anxious to have a solution which will lessen the threat of war and which, we would hope, could improve the security of the people of West Berlin. We have had not negotiations but exploratory talks - Mr. Rusk with Mr. Gromyko on three occasions, and I had a talk with him and the Prime Minister yesterday - in an attempt to determine the precise position of the Soviet Union on the various questions dealing with access, the free city, the question of boundaries, and all the rest. We have not, as I have said, carried out any negotiations, nor will we.

We will now continue the talks with Ambassador Thompson in Moscow, I hope. He is back here for that purpose and will be returning shortly. And we are going to be now in the process of consulting with our allies in order to determine a common Western position on these matters which are at issue.

So that I don't think that we can come to any conclusion as to what the ultimate outcome will be, though the talks which we had with Mr. Gromyko did not give us immediate hope that this matter would be easily settled.

Fallout Shelters

Q: Mr. President, I believe recently you spoke to a group of New Jersey publishers about your forthcoming plan involving fallout shelters that might be quite economical. In this general range of interest, sir, do you have personally fallout shelters in any of the residences that you frequently use? I'm thinking particularly of your house in Hyannis or in Middleburg or in Palm Beach or at Newport.

The President: Well, they're not all my residences, I'm sorry to say - (laughter) - but I would say that there are naturally provisions for the protection of those in the Presidency and in the Joint Chiefs of Staff and others who would have to maintain responsibility in case of a military action. Though of course there's no sure answer for anybody.

We - obviously you cannot build a shelter in the accepted sense of the word for the kind of money which we have talked about. But we can provide directions whereby a family can take steps to protect themselves on a minimum basis and give them - members of the family - some hope that if they're out of the blast area they could survive the fall out. And by the middle of November we hope to suggest some of the steps that every homeowner could take.

My own feeling is that these shelters are most useful and most important, and we're going to live through a long period of constant tension with these dangerous weapons which will be proliferating, and, therefore, anything that we can do to increase the chances of protection for our families ought to be done.

Public Attitude on the Possibility of War

Q: Mr. President, a recent public opinion poll showed that a majority of the American people are more worried about a war breaking out now than they have been in any time in recent years. Would you address yourself to this poll, sir, and whether you share that view or just how do you feel about it?

The President: Well, I think that they're naturally and quite correctly concerned because there is a collision in the points of view which the Western powers have taken in NATO with that of the Soviet Union and the Warsaw bloc countries over Berlin, and this area is extremely vital.

Western Europe is an area of great resources and the Soviet Union has long had policy ambitions in this area, so that this is a very, very serious matter unless we can reach a peaceful accommodation.

In addition, there are other areas where we can become involved. And as the weapons now are so annihilating, it causes the American people to be quite rightfully concerned.

Our ambition is to protect our vital interests without a war which destroys and doesn't really represent a victory for policy.

But we happen to live - because of the ingenuity of science and man's own inability to control his relationships one with another, we happen to live in the most dangerous time in the history of the human race.

Talks with Red China

Q: Mr. President, Communist China's Foreign Minister has indicated that high-level talks at the foreign minister level with the United States would be, as he says, acceptable, provided the United States took the initiative. How do you feel about this?

The President: Well I - we are, of course, having conversations at the present time at Geneva. The Chinese Communists are represented at the conference over Laos, and there are therefore many channels through which any exchange of views could flow.

We have been meeting periodically, for the last 3 or 4 years, for a period at Geneva and, of course, most recently at Warsaw in which we talked about the question of the exchange of prisoners, or rather the release of prisoners, and other matters. So that I would feel that these efforts will continue at Geneva and they will continue at Warsaw.

But we have not seen any evidence as yet that the Chinese Communists wish to live in comity with us, and our desire is to live in friendship with all people. But we have not seen that attitude manifested. In fact, just a few days ago there was a statement about Berlin that was quite bellicose.

Our Nuclear Deterrent

Q: There have been charges that we have not adequately maintained the strength or the credibility of our nuclear deterrent and that we also have not fully convinced the leaders of the Soviet Union that we are determined to meet force with force in Berlin or elsewhere. What is your reaction to those charges?

The President: Well, we have made many statements. I have made them and they've been as precise as I could make them. The Secretary of State, the Secretary of Defense, other Western people in positions of responsibility have all talked of our determination to maintain our vital interests in this area.

I think probably - aside from any domestic reasons for this kind of criticism - it's that everyone realizes that these weapons are, as I said, extremely dangerous and that the Soviet Union has a long-range bomber and missile capacity, as we do, and that, as I've said, we move through a period of maximum hazard. So that naturally anyone would be reluctant, unless all else had failed, to destroy so much of the world.

But we have indicated that we will meet our commitments with whatever resources are necessary to meet them and we also add that we hope it will be possible that accords can be reached which will protect the interests and freedom of the people involved without having to go to this - these extreme weapons.

Now I would like to point out two or three details about the effort we've made in the field of national security and national defense.

Since January, we have added more than $6 billion to the national defense budget, which is more than a 14-percent increase over the previous budget.

In strategic forces, which are the nuclear forces, we have ordered a 50-percent increase in the number of Polaris submarines to be on station - battle station - by the end of 1964; a 50-percent increase in the number of strategic bombers on 15-minute ground alert at the end of runways, which is already in effect; a 100-percent increase in our capacity to produce Minuteman missiles against the day when that production capacity may be needed, and a similar increase in Skybolt and other programs which affect our strategic arm.

Now to strengthen our nonnuclear forces - and I think this is important - we have called up two additional divisions and many thousands more - particularly in the air; we've increased by 75 percent our modern long-range airlift capacity; we've increased our antiguerrilla forces by 150 percent; we've stepped up the delivery of the M-14 rifle from a maximum of 9,000 a month to 44,000 a month and taken other steps to bring the Army, Navy, and Marine units to full strength in terms of manpower and equipment. And we still have someway to go.

But it does indicate our feeling that we should be stronger and also that there should be a balance in the forces that we have.

The President's Foreign Policy

Q: Mr. President, following up this same subject, sir, it has been reported that you have been angered or at least disturbed by what has been described as partisan criticism of your foreign policy.

It has also been reported that some members of your administration, possibly including yourself, have felt that sharp Republican warnings against appeasement have constricted the room that you may have to negotiate with the Russians. Would you discuss these points?

The President: No - I'm going to attempt to, as I have said, to protect our vital interests and see whether it's possible for us to reach an agreement in this matter which will not necessitate a war which could mean so much destruction for so many millions and millions of people in this country and elsewhere.

Now, I'm going to continue to do that and we'll do the best we can and we'll see what happens.

Everyone is free to make any attacks they want. I think what would be most helpful to the Nation today would be constructive and frequently critical alternatives - suggestions for alternative courses of action - and not merely rather generalized statements which throw very little light on very complicated and dangerous matters.

But I would never suggest that the battle of the mimeograph machines between the Republican Committee and the Democratic Committee should cease, only that it should perhaps be wiser.

Talks with Mr. Gromyko

Q: Mr. President, in your July speech you said that you didn't want to negotiate on a basis of what's mine is mine and what's yours is negotiable. In your talks with Mr. Gromyko, sir, what did you talk about that was theirs?

The President: Well, I don't think really it's particularly useful at this time to attempt to go into precise detail. Most of the - a good deal of the information in the talks has already been printed in the press. These talks, if they're not going to turn into merely exchanges of propaganda, should at least have the value of some degree of privacy.

I've stated that we have not been engaged in negotiations, no agreements have been reached but merely an attempt to explore what are the positions of the various powers.

I've already characterized my view of these talks and I think that with the information, which has been quite lucid and only slightly inaccurate, I think we can proceed on to additional talk.

The Viet-Nam Situation

Q: Mr. President, in reference to your decision to send General Taylor to Viet-Nam, there may be some interpretation of that decision as implying confirmation of reports that you intend to send American forces to Viet-Nam or to Thailand or to Laos. Can you give us your appraisal of the conditions under which you might find it necessary to send troops in?

The President: Well, we're going to wait till General Taylor comes back and brings an up-to-date description of the situation, particularly in Viet-Nam. As you know, in the last 2 or 3 months there has been a large increase in the number of forces that have been involved. There has been evidence that some of these forces have come from beyond the frontiers. And General Taylor will give me - and the Joint Chiefs of Staff - an educated military guess as to what the situation that the government there faces. Then we can come to conclusions as what is best to do.

A New Speaker of the House

Q: Mr. President, if it becomes necessary for the House to elect a new Speaker, would you be likely to express, either publicly or privately a preference for any candidate?

The President: The House has a Speaker; and the **House** will elect its next Speaker; and I would think it would be unwise for anyone outside the House to attempt to indicate a preference. This is a matter for the House. I'm sure they'll choose wisely.

The President's Domestic Program

Q: Mr. President, in addition to the criticism that's been heard in some quarters of your foreign policy, there's also been some criticism of your domestic program and it encountered some trouble in Congress. Does your decision to make speaking engagements in the West and the announced series of appearances of some of your Cabinet members indicate a feeling that it's now time to take your program to the country?

The President: Well, on the last part, we are having the members of our Cabinet speak at nonpartisan meetings upon invitation in various parts of the country to talk to them about some of the domestic programs that we have worked on and could work on in the future.

My own trip is very limited. I'm going to speak in Washington at the 100th anniversary of the University of Washington, and also at a dinner - the 25th anniversary of Senator Magnuson's service in the Senate - and will then go the next night to speak at the 50th anniversary of Senator Hayden's coming to the Congress, in Arizona. And those are my only speeches.

The Situation in Berlin

Q: Mr. President, going back to Berlin, I think the American people are confused by what they read and hear about Berlin. One day they read or they're told that American officials are encouraged by the outlook. Another day they read that they're not encouraged, that they're gloomy. One day we're going ahead, the next day we're going back. Mr. President, does the real situation fluctuate that much? As a one-time journalist who became President, how does it look to you?

The President: Well, a lot of journalists had bad luck - (laughter) - and I know these stories based on recent conversations that there have been, I think, from New York, exchanges between Mr. Rusk and Mr. Gromyko.

There seemed to be more hope in the stories that came out of my meeting with Mr. Gromyko.

I think it would be - I see no evidence as yet that there is any clear solution to Berlin. There still seems to - there still are very major differences of view.

Now I feel that the three talks he had and the talk I had at least helped to make more precise those differences.

We now will continue some more and in addition - and I think this is most important - the Germans will have a new government shortly and be able to participate with perhaps more vigor in making Allied policy with the other NATO countries, and then we can get a better idea as to how it's all going to end up.

There is - I would say that there have been, as I have said, no negotiations in the sense that we made proposals and they made them.

What there has been is a description of the kind of solution that they would like to see. And I must say that I have not found substantial changes in that policy as it was previously expressed some months ago.

There has been, and I think this may explain the stories, a desire to discuss these matters and a - statements about a desire to reach a peaceful accord. But on the substance we are not in sight of land.

Club Memberships for Members of the Administration

Q: Mr. President, do you have any feeling about whether members of your administration should belong to the Metropolitan Club here in Washington?

The President: It seems to me that where everyone eats and the clubs that they belong to - private clubs - is a matter that each person must decide himself, though I personally approved of my brother's action - the Attorney General.

The Foreign Aid Bill

Q: Mr. President, written into the foreign aid bill is a clause which says that there should be more stress on giving aid to friendly countries, countries that share our view on major world problems. In view of the decision to review aid to Ghana's Volta River project, could you elaborate on how far you think a country should go towards agreeing with us on these major issues?

The President: Well, I think that they should - what - we're not attempting to use our aid in order to secure agreement by these countries with all of our policies. The phrase that was used in signing the mutual security bill was that we should give particular attention to the needs of those countries which share our view of the world crisis.

Our view of the world crisis is that countries are entitled to national sovereignty and independence. That is all we ever suggested. That is the purpose of our aid - to make it more possible.

Now if a country has ceased to choose national sovereignty or ceased to choose national independence, then, of course, our aid becomes less useful. But that is a different matter from suggesting that in order to be entitled to our assistance, particularly as a good percentage of our assistance today is in the form of loans, that they must agree with us, because quite obviously these people in the underdeveloped world are newly independent. They want to run their own affairs.

They would rather not accept assistance if we have that kind of string attached to it. Therefore, I think we ought to make an educated guess. But it's not an easy matter. These countries are passing through very difficult times and they're going to swing one way and then another. But in general, our object is that they maintain their independence. We hope it's theirs.

The Possibility of Atmospheric Testing

Q: Mr. President, considering what we may know now about the - may have learned now from the Russians on nuclear shots and what we do know now about our own underground explosion, do you think it's probable, in order to keep up with the state of this art, that we'll have to go to atmospheric testing in the near future?

The President: Well, quite obviously if at the conclusion of this immediate series of tests, the Soviet Union was to propose an uninspected moratorium - that would not be very helpful in view of the experience we've gone through this

year. We will be glad to negotiate, but we will not feel that the moratorium
will be extended during the period of negotiation.

As to what kind of tests we will operate, we - I am extremely sorry that we
were not able to get the Soviet Union to accept the proposal to ban atmospheric
testing by the Prime Minister and myself.

They've made over 20 tests in the atomsphere, and we have to make a judgment
as to what is in the best interests of our security, and that is a matter which
is being studied. For the present, our tests are underground, and we feel
that's in accordance with our security.

Progress in Sending a Man to the Moon

*Q: Mr. President, do you feel that the Nation has reacted positively to
your May 25 appeal to send a man to the moon? And do you feel that progress is
being made on Projects Mercury and Apollo?*

The President: Well, until we have a man on the moon, none of us will be
satisfied. But I do believe a major effort is being made. But as I said before, we started far behind, and we're going to have to wait and see whether we
catch up.

But I would say that I will continue to be dissatisfied until the goal is
reached. And I hope everyone working on the program shares the same view.

U.S. Attitude on the Building of the Berlin Wall

*Q. Mr. President, did you make the decision for us not to use force to stop
the building of the wall in Berlin? And if you had it to do over again, would
you make the same decision? Or what would have been the alternative if you had
not made that decision?*

The President: As you know, Eastern Berlin and East Germany have been under
the control of the Soviet Union, really, since 1947 and '48. There's not been
four-power control and they have controlled this area.

There are many things that happen in Eastern Europe, as I said in my United
Nations speech, which we consider to be wholly unsatisfactory - the denial of
liberties, the denial of political freedom, national independence, and all the
rest.

And that is a matter of equal concern in the action which you described.
These are areas which the Soviet Union has held since the end of World War II,
for over 16 years.

*Q: Mr. President, you spoke of seeking a common Western position. Are we
far apart and at what level do we have to seek it?*

The President: Well, I think we're going to be meeting next week in Washington and by those who are particularly competent here among - we've had almost
daily conversations, and as I say I'm hopeful that when the new German Government assumes its responsibility we can come to more final conclusions as to
what our next approach should be to the Soviet Union.

I believe there are basic agreements among the Western Allied powers, but
these are matters which should be carefully explored and I think we can only
explore them with success since the talks with Mr. Gromyko because I think
they've helped illuminate the matters which we must decide.

Defense Expenditures

Q: We are told that your defense expenditures this year and next year will be vastly increased. Will they be increased so much that they will curtail your legislative program, especially for revision of the tax structure?

The President: Yes, in answer to the last part of your question, we had hoped before the Berlin crisis came out that we might have a, if business came back, we might have a $3 billion surplus which would have permitted a tax reduction. As you know since the July callup decision, which was $3,500 million we've lost that hope.

We still have a strong desire to balance our budget. But I cannot predict what extra military demands may be made in the next month or two which may lessen that chance. But our present intention is to balance our budget unless military increases – and only military increases – threaten that object.

Q: Mr. President, in your July speech on this same subject, you said that if it was necessary to balance the budget you would increase taxes. Do you still feel that way?

The President: I would, if we can – for example, there isn't any doubt that if we had been able to persuade the Congress to accept the $600 million or $700 million increase in postal rates it would have assisted us in our responsibility. We will increase – we will secure sufficient revenue to balance the budget unless there is excessive and substantial – and they may come, because of the events in southeast Asia or Western Europe.

Whether we should – at that time we will then make a judgment as to how much we can cut from nondefense expenditures and, secondly, how much of a tax burden can be sustained without strangling the recovery.

We don't want to – which I think is one of the difficulties – the recovery of '58 which was aborted in 1960, so that we don't want to provide a tax structure which already is very heavy – and brings in tremendous receipts at full employment – we don't want it to result in waste of resources and manpower. So that's the judgment we must make.

Economic Recovery and Unemployment

Q: Mr. President, could you give us your assessment of the vigor of the economic recovery, particularly in the light of statements by organized labor that we may have five and a half million unemployed by next February?

The President: Well, we've had a 10-percent increase in the second quarter and a 5-percent increase in the third quarter, and we are going to continue to have a substantial increase in the next quarter.

I think we're producing more cars this quarter probably than any year since 1950 and we've had less increase in the cost of living in a recovery than we've had in 10 or 12 years. So that the private sector is moving ahead.

The problem of unemployment continues because of technological changes and increases in the population and we do not have – unemployment is now at about 4 million. We do not – I am still as concerned as they are that we could have a great boom and still have the kind of unemployment they describe.

Possiblity of a Steel Price Increase

Q: Sir, do you believe your letter to the steel companies has had the desired effect that there will not be a steel price increase this fall?

The President: I think that the steel companies are going to make a judgment based on what they consider to be in the public interest and in line with
their own responsibilities, and I think it's their judgment and I'm hopeful that
they will make a judgment which will assist our economy.

Access of West Berliners to East Berlin

*Q: Mr. President, on Berlin, the Russians seem to be making a considerable
effort to cut any relationship between West Berlin and West Germany, even the
relationship which now exists. Do you consider that any settlement of the Berlin issue will have to include free access for West Germans and West Berliners
back and forth and other relationships between the city and the country as well
as access to the Allied forces themselves?*

The President: Well, I think that without going into the details, as I said
at the beginning, it's quite obvious that we're not only talking about the freedom of the city but also its viability, economic as well as political, and it
operates under the greatest possible difficulties, 100 miles within an area
controlled by the Soviet Union, so that this tie with the West - West Germany
and other sections of the West - is very vital to its remaining more than just
a shell, so that we will be concerned with the viability and vitality - economic
vitality - of the city in any agreement that we're able to make - if we can make
an agreement.

Reporter: Thank you, Mr. President.

THE PRESIDENT'S NEWS CONFERENCE OF

NOVEMBER 8, 1961

The President: Ladies and gentlemen, I have several statements to make.

I am delighted to announce that General Eisenhower has agreed to serve as
the first chairman of the board of trustees of a new people-to-people organization.   The purpose of the new organization will be, and I quote: "To foster
contacts between citizens of the United States and people of other lands in
every way possible."

The original people-to-people organization was formed in September 1956 by
a group of leading American citizens at a White House conference.

The new organization will provide a private, centralized coordination and
fund-raising leadership for the activities and projects of the people-to-people
program, which has been a matter of great interest to General Eisenhower.

I consider it a great honor to be able to serve as honorary chairman of
this outstanding citizens organization.

Secondly, General Taylor has returned and he and his colleagues have reported their findings to me and to other members of the administration. In the next
few days we shall be considering carefully the grave problems which have been
posed by both externally supported violence and the natural disaster of a great
flood in South Viet-Nam. Our concern is to find the most effective way of
sustaining the progress of the people of South Viet-Nam, and obviously this is
a matter on which we shall need to coordinate our activities with those of the
Government of South Viet-Nam.

Therefore General Taylor's findings will need review not only in this Government but discussion with the Government of South Viet-Nam, and at this stage I have no public announcement to make.

Third, finally, I want to comment on the success and significance of the first meeting of the joint United States-Japan committee on trade and economic affairs, which was held in Japan last week.

This joint Cabinet group was led by Secretary Rusk on our side and Foreign Minister Kosaka for the Japanese.

It succeeded in extending the concept of American-Japanese partnership to the economic and trade field and, I think, was a most important step forward in the relations between both of our countries.

Japan is our second largest trading partner and we are her largest trading partner.

Moreover, our merchandise export to Japan greatly exceeds the imports that we receive from her. In the first 6 months of this year, our merchandise trade surplus with Japan totaled $433 million.

In addition, Japan also plays a key role in the economy of Asia, and free world economic objectives depend to a very important extent on her cooperation.

This conference was characterized by a frank exchange of views, and I believe that economic cooperation between our two countries can be expanded by further meetings, and we are looking forward to the next annual meeting of the joint committee to be held in Washington in 1962.

Thank you.

QUESTIONS

Deterioration of Our Military Strength

Q: During the past campaign, the political campaign last year, specifically in October, you and others spoke of the serious deterioration of our military strength in relation to that of Russia. In recent weeks, however, you and the top officials of the Pentagon have spoken of our measurable superiority to Russia in military strength. I'd like to ask you, sir, what's happened since the campaign and now? Did you during the campaign possibly not have as much information as you derived later, or do you say, sir, that the improvement in our military position has resulted from the activities solely of your administration?

The President: Well, I think the phrase that I used in my announcement last week was that the United States would not trade places with anyone.

My statement to which you referred was echoed by a good many members of the previous administration as well as members of my own party. I think President Eisenhower himself said, and I quote him, that we are somewhat behind in the long-range missile field. General LeMay, in testimony before congressional committees, expressed concern that in overall military strength we would be behind in 1959. Admiral Radford expressed concern about the defense of the United States - the continental United States.

We have, as you know, since coming into office made requests for over $6 billion in increase in our national defense, and we have speeded up our Polaris program, our Minuteman standby capability; we've increased the number of SAC

which is on a 15-minute alert - now 50 percent of SAC - and we have made important contributions to strengthening our conventional forces.

We attempt to keep our information up to date, and we are doing so to the
best of our ability. And, based on our present assessments and our intelligence, we, in my words, would not trade place with anyone in the world. And
that represents our judgments as of now. But it's a matter to which we must
give continuing study.

We're going to ask for additional funds for defense next year, and we are
going to continue to maintain the most careful assessments of our intelligence
and capabilities and that of our adversaries, as well as our commitments, so
that statements that I made represented the best of my information based on
public statements made by those in a position to know in the last years of the
nineteen fifties.

The Recent Elections

*Q: Mr. President, would you give us your view of the elections Saturday and
yesterday - whether they may reflect public reaction to your administration or
to the part that you and Mr. Eisenhower took in them? Can this type of election
be a political barometer?*

The President: Well, I am always reluctant to claim that what happens in
one election with one set of candidates necessarily means it will happen again
at a later date with a different set of candidates. But as I believe if Mr.
Gonzalez and Mayor Wagner and Judge Hughes had lost, that it would have been
interpreted as a stunning setback for this administration. I will break my rule
and say that the fact that they all won constitutes a source of satisfaction to
us.

They won because they were effective candidates. But they all ran as Democrats. And I believe that it indicates that the American people believe that
the candidates and parties in those areas as well as nationally are committed
to progress, and that's what they're committed to. So I'm happy and I suppose
someday we'll lose and then I'll have to eat those words. (Laughter)

The Berlin Crisis

*Q: Can you give us the latest, sir, on the Berlin crisis, which seems to
have quieted down a bit, and also your views regarding the talk of possible
trips to the summit again to discuss this problem?*

The President: No. In answer to your last part of the question - I know
of no proposed trips to the summit. In the first matter, this is a matter of
continuing, of course, concern. And Chancellor Adenauer is coming to the United
States shortly and I think that his trip is of vital importance in our consideration of the entire matter of Berlin, Germany, Europe. We are anxious to get
his views. We are anxious to make sure that our policies are concerted, and
therefore I'm delighted that he is coming and I'm delighted that he's bringing
members of his new administration with him.

Assessment of the Issues of the President's First Year

*Q: Mr. President, this is the first anniversary of your election last year,
and in the campaign that preceded that election there was considerable talk on
the part of both candidates and both parties about a number of very specific
subjects - Cuba, for instance; the economic growth of the country; the prestige
of the Nation with other countries; hard-core unemployment, and an Executive
order to end racial discrimination in housing. I wonder if you could assess for*

us these issues in the light of your year in office and if we might know, if you were campaigning again today, if the emphasis of your campaign might be somewhat different?

The President: Well, it would be exactly what it was. We have met a good many of these commitments and I'm hopeful before our term is ended that we will meet the others. But we have passed a minimum wage of $1.25 an hour. We have made it possible for men to retire at age 62. We did pass the area redevelopment bill for areas of chronic unemployment - which had been vetoed twice. We did pass the most broad-range housing bill that had been passed since 1949. We did provide additional funds for pollution. And we did, I think, in a whole variety of areas, take actions which benefit the people.

The fact of the matter is that since we took office in January, our national income or gross national product has gone up from around $501 billion to - it is our calculation by the - within the two quarters immediately ahead, our gross national product will be $565 billion and - which represents a substantial increase and, I think, is of particular importance in sustaining our many burdens.

Unemployment in October now stands at 3,900,000. There are more people working than ever before - 67,800,000. The number of people in industry has gone up 2,000,000 since we took office in January - who have jobs.

Now I am not saying that these problems are solved because, in a sense, they're never solved. And there are areas which are still unfinished. Medical care for the aged, which we are going to recommend to the Congrss in the coming session.

We have, I think, made substantial progress in the field of civil rights. To conclude there have been more suits filed to provide for voting and there will continue to be a concentrated effort by this administration to make it possible for every citizen to vote under the laws and the directions provided by Congress.

We have put more people to work, under our Vice President's committee - unemployment - than there was ever done in the previous 8 years - in the last 8 months.

And I think that in voting, in the activities of the Justice Department, in education, in other areas, we are making substantial progress with a good deal left unfinished. And we'll meet our commitments before we're finished.

Justification of the Resumption of Nuclear Testing

Q: Mr. President, in view of our overall military position and your statement that you would not trade places, many people are wondering how you might eventually justify the possible resumption of nuclear testing in the atmosphere.

The President: Well, I've stated that I felt it incumbent upon us to maintain our lead; that we have not concluded as yet our analysis of Soviet tests, and if we felt that our present position in this very vital area has been endangered by Soviet tests, then we would have to take action to protect our security. So that, I also said, we would not test for political or psychological reasons unless we feel it militarily necessary. And, in the meanwhile, because there is a long time gap, we have ordered preparations to be made.

The Soviet Union tested while we were at the table negotiating with them. If they fooled us once, it's our own fault; if they fool us twice, it's our fault.

Q: On this question of nuclear testing, sir, Soviet officials have asserted in recent days that the United States in total has fired a larger quantity of megatons than of the Soviet tests. Is this statement true?

The President: The Soviet Union with the most recent tests have put into the air about 170 megatons, the United States and Great Britain combined about 125 megatons, France less than one megaton. What is significant in this area, of course, is the amount of megatons put in the air and the condition under which the bombs may be exploded as it might affect fallout. And I don't think that there is any doubt the Soviet Union is first in that very dubious category.

An Embargo on Imports from Cuba

Q: Last spring the Secretary of State indicated that an embargo was about to be imposed on imports from Cuba - sugar - not sugar, pardon me - tobacco, molasses, vegetables. Nothing has happened; that's months ago. Could you throw some light on that point, please, sir?

The President: Yes, when the limitations were put on trade by the previous administration, there was exempted food and drugs which amount to around $12 million a year. And it would be impossible for us to break, to stop, that trade unless we enforce the Trading with the Enemy Act.

This has been a matter continually before us, but we are not anxious to be in the position of declaring war on the Cuban people by denying them essential food and also denying them medicines, and therefore this administration, like the previous administration, has been reluctant to take that action, but it's a matter that will be before us continually, and if it seems like the proper action, we'll take it, but our dispute is not with the Cuban people but with the Communist control of Cuba.

The Frequency of Press Conferences

Q: Could you enlighten us, sir, as to why you're not having these press conferences more frequently, especially as to whether anything in particular you don't like about them or anything we might do on our part to encourage you to meet with us more often?

The President: Well, I like them. But - sort of - (laughter) - but I will - let me just say that I'll hold these - I'm anxious to hold press conferences as often as I believe it to be in the public interest. Now, we do hold - Mr. Salinger holds one or two press conferences a day. We put out a good many statements from the White House, members of the Cabinet speak around the country, we attempt to carry out communications to the extent possible. We're even having these regional meetings.

We are involved in a number of very sensitive matters on the question of Berlin, and I'm - I talk not only to the American people but also to our allies, to those who are opposed to us and our enemies, and those who are neutral, and, therefore, I feel that the schedule as we have recently had it is in the public interest. But I would have no objection to having them two or three times a week if I thought at that time it was in the public interest.

I had them nearly every week and I'm sure I will again when Congress is back. But most of the matters now before us deal with matters of foreign policy, and this seemed to be the most appropriate schedule in view of the public interest.

The Postmaster General's Statement

Q: Mr. President, how do you feel about the Postmaster General's statement that he yielded to political pressure to reinstate a postal employee considered unsuitable?

The President: Well, I think that Mr. Day probably feels that he would like to recast that statement, and, as I understand it, it was submitted to a board of review. The charges, although with the exception of one, were dismissed unanimously. One was considered and there was a 2-to-1 vote. It seems to me that that is the procedure that is best to follow without resort to political pressures of any kind. And I think that's what the Post Office and everyone else should do, and I hope they will. But - and I think that's Mr. Day's view.

The Rift Between Russia and Red China

Q: Mr. President, what significance to the West, in the course of the cold war, do you see in the current open rift between Red China and Russia?

The President: Well, I think that it's not - that none of us can talk with precision about the details of the relationships between Russia and China. It is a matter of surmise, and on this experts may differ. Therefore, I don't feel that it's probably useful now for us to attempt to assess it. I think we can judge better by actions. And we can - we'll have an opportunity to witness those actions in the coming weeks and months.

That's what really counts, not the - altogether the dialectics, but what result - the varying philosophies which animate the Communist world - what resultant actions - their different view of Marx and the different interpretation of the Communist doctrine; what action it brings them to, and what threats it poses to the free world. That will give us a more precise answer to your question.

Fallout Shelters

Q: Mr. President, there is a great deal of confusion among the public in regard to fallout shelters. Many people - people apparently aren't sold on building home shelters. Do you have any comment that might be helpful today on any aspect of this matter?

The President: Well, of course, as you know, none of us were really interested - I think that includes us all - in civil defense really until this summer and until we began to recognize the change in weapon technology which gave the Soviet Union the power to reach the United States with missiles as well as bombers, the destructive nature of the weapons, and also the fact that our two systems were in conflict in various areas.

We asked for additional appropriations, therefore, this summer for civil defense. We are - we asked for five times and received five times as much as we had the previous year.

Now, it's very difficult in a large country, with varying problems of geography, with 180 million people, to suddenly organize a civil defense program when so much depends on the cooperation between the Federal Government assigning it its proper responsibility, the State government, the local community, and the individual.

I stated that in July - that we were going to send a book giving the latest information that we had to every household, and I'm hopeful that that book will be completed before the end of this month.

But I'm - we are very conscious of the difficulties. We are very conscious of the desire of people to have accurate and precise information.

But it was not really in my opinion, until August that this became a matter of great public urgency. The responsibility for shelters was then transferred to the Department of Defense and I believe that the booklet will be helpful, but it will be a - must be recognized that each family, each community, each State, and the Federal Government are all going to have a role, and we desire to interpret that role with precision so that we are moving ahead on it.

The Persuasion of the Prime Minister of India

Q: Mr. President, some of the press in your country and India say that our Prime Minister is more pro-Communist and pro-Russian than he is Western. Now that your talks have concluded after the last 3 days, please tell us how you feel? Do you believe that he was either consciously or unconsciously against the interests of the United States or western countries? Do you believe that he was for the cause of world peace? And please give us some idea of your talk with him?

The President: In answer to your question, I have never thought, quite obviously, that - to use your phrase - the Mr. Nehru works consciously or unconsciously for the Communist movement, and I know of no rational man in the United States who holds that view. There are matters on which we differ, as the Prime Minister said in "Meet the Press" on Sunday, that "geography dictates a good deal of policy" as well as internal conditions, so that, quite obviously - and tradition, culture, the past, all this affects foreign policy.

So that there are areas where we differ, but I do not know any figure in the world, as I have said on other occasions, who is more committed to individual liberty than Mr. Nehru, and I think the people of India are committed to maintaining their national sovereignty and supporting liberty for the individual as a personal and cultural and religious tradition. We are going to disagree, but I'm sure it's possible for us to disagree in the framework of not charging each other with bad faith.

I have a high regard for the Prime Minister. It has become higher during our conversations. I've attempted to explain to him some of the areas of responsibility which the United States faces, and he has given me his views on a number of important questions, so I regard the talks as most valuable - (inaudible) - all matters affecting our countries and the personalities that may be involved.

The Recent German Crisis

Q: Mr. President, as you know, during the recent German crisis there's been a great deal of anxiety both in Germany and in this country about what our views are on the problem. Now that Dr. Adenauer has been invited to this country, can you give us a general idea of what you see as the future role of Germany, including East Berlin and East Germany, and also the question of rearming Germany or arming her with nuclear weapons?

The President: Well, I think that these are some of the matters which we will discuss with Chancellor Adenauer and involves his country and our country, and I think that it will be better to wait a few days when I will have a chance to see him.

On the question of arming them with nuclear weapons, as you know, Dr. Adenauer has stated West Germany does not intend to do so. And on the general matter of arms, I know that charges were made in regard to the remilitarization of Western Germany. Western Germany has almost no air force, very limited navy, has now nine divisions. Eastern Germany, which is far less in population, has substantially larger ground forces. And I think the effort to suggest that Dr. Adenauer, who is a distinguished European, who has brought about a reconciliation between France and Germany, who has brought the Common Market - helped bring the Common Market about, who has met his responsibilities under NATO, is a - represents a revanchist attitude, I think is wholly wrong. But on the details, I think this is what we should talk to Dr. Adenauer about.

U.S. Trade Policy

Q: Mr. President, recently there have been statements by several people inside and outside the Government that the United States needs a major change in its trade policy, a major liberalization in trade policy. We haven't heard from you on this score during this immediate period of policy formation. What is your feeling about the need for change and, specifically, do you feel that the administration should seek to have the change made next year.

The President: We have had several meetings in the administration about the matter and we'll be having others and will make recommendations to the Congress at the first of the year. I think that, quite obviously, we have to begin to realize how important the Common Market is going to be to the economy of the United States. One-third of our trade generally is in Western Europe, and if the United States should be denied that market, we will either find a flight of capital from this country to construct factories within that wall, or we will find ourselves in serious economic trouble.

On the other hand, we have obligations, for example, to Japan, and we have concern about our relations with Latin America, and what will happen to them, dependent as they are upon raw materials and on western European markets - where will they be left? These are all matters which we are now considering.

But I think that the people of this country must realize that the Common Market is going to present us with major economic challenges and, I hope, opportunities, and that this country must be ready to negotiate with the Common Market on a position of equality, as far as our ability to negotiate to protect our interests and the interests of those that are associated with us.

I think that one of our problems in the United States - and I think that it's illuminated by the statistics on Japan - we've read a good deal about the threat of Japanese goods coming into the United States, and I can understand where it is a concern. But here is a country where in the last 6 months a half billion dollars has been on our side, a balance of payments contributing to our dollar surplus and our gold balance.

Well, now we cannot just sell and never buy, and if all those who recognize the benefit to the United States - workers, industry - in an almost $5 billion to $6 billion surplus which we have every year, recognize how essential that is to our security, will speak as loudly as those who are hurt, we can get an adjustment, I think of the public interest.

But, in answer to your specific question, we are considering the matter and we will come to the Congress in January and make our recommendations. But the matter is by no means complete. The details of the Common Market, for example, and its effect upon us, will not be obvious probably until '63 or '64, and we have to attempt to go to the Congress at a time when we can be most successful. My judgment is that the time to begin is now, but as a matter of final decision, I think we'll have to wait about 2 or 3 more weeks.

Assurances to the Business Community

Q: Mr. President, how much more do you think you will have to do to assure American business leadership that you are not antibusiness and, in fact, do you think they need any special assurance?

The President: Well, if to be an - to stop them from saying we're anti-business we're supposed to cease enforcing the antitrust law, then I suppose the cause is lost.

There has been a - nearly a 10 percent increase, as I have said, in our gross national product. We have cut the flow of gold since January 1 even though we still have a serious dollar problem - it was almost $1 billion last year in gold lost, it's $76 million so far this year. We have had a very slight increase in the cost of living. In fact, wholesale prices are down. We've had less strikes than we've had any time in 20 years.

This country cannot prosper unless business prospers. This country cannot meet its obligations - its tax obligations and all the rest - unless business is doing well. Business will not do well and you will not have full employment unless they feel that there's a chance to make profit.

So that there is no long-range hostility between business and the Government. There cannot be. We cannot succeed unless they succeed. But that doesn't mean that we should not meet our responsibilities under antitrust, or that doesn't mean when we attempt to pass a bill on taxes to prevent tax havens abroad or a flood of capital which affects our gold balances - that doesn't mean we're antibusiness. It means that we have to meet our public responsibilities. So that I think in the long run that most businessmen know that we are allied - as we are with labor and the farmer - in trying to keep this country going.

U.S. Nuclear Testing

Q: On nuclear tests, in view of the fact that the Soviets have exploded 31 or more devices in the atmosphere, I think it's generally agreed that they're improving their nuclear weapons technology. Now this means that they're getting stronger in relation to the United States. Wouldn't it also mean that if we do not test in the atmosphere, that we're willing for the United States to become weaker with relation to the Soviet Union than we were, say, last summer?

The President: Well, I've stated that I thought that the United States was in a position that was powerful - Mr. Gilpatric said "second to none." I said it was our obligation to remain so. And that is what we intend to do. And therefore, as you suggest, these calculations will have to be made and a decision reached. And pending these calculations, we are making our appropriate preparations.

Q: Mr. President, Dr. Pauling said that the biggest Russian bomb would cause 40,000 gross mutations in the next three or four generations. This remark has been criticized by some scientists because he didn't say that this - if this was true - it would be spread over 34 billion people, and that this leads to an exaggerated fear of fallout. Do you think there is in the popular mind an exaggereated fear of fallout, because of statements like that?

The President: Well, I think that anyone feels that if one individual, whether it's among many billions, is - particularly an individual three generations from now - finds their life warped by radiation, of course it's a concern to anyone. And we should, therefore, approach atmospheric testing with the greatest caution and hesitancy, as I've already indicated.

On the other hand, of course, we have a responsibility to the freedom of hundreds of millions of people - including the citizens of our own country. So we cannot - we have to attempt to balance off our needs. But I've said we would never, because of the reason - whether Mr. Pauling's statistics are accurate or not, one is enough - that we would never test for political or psychological reason, but only if we felt that the security of the United States was endangered, and therefore the free world, which does affect this generation and others to come. So we must balance off our risks.

The Administration's Efforts with Regard to Women

Q: Mr. President, the Democratic platform in which you ran for election promises to work for equal rights for women, including equal pay, and to wipe out job opportunity discriminations. Now you have made efforts on behalf of others. What have you done for the women according to the promises of the platform?

The President: Well, I'm sure we haven't done enough. (Laughter) I must say I am a strong believer in equal pay for equal work, and I think that we ought to do better than we're doing, and I'm glad that you reminded me of it, Mrs. Craig. (Laughter)

Request from High School Children

Q: Mr. President, the boys and girls of the high school at Columbus, Ind., sent you a wire a week or so ago in which they reminded you that you had invited them to bring you any problems that they had. Their problem was that Joseph Turk, their Russian instructor - a very hard-to-find gentleman - was being taken off to be a clerk-typist in the Army. Has their request come to your attention and have you taken any action on it?

The President: No, it hasn't come to my attention, and we will give it to the responsible groups. I agree that the problem of bringing teachers in is a difficult one. But I think we ought to let the Defense Department make that judgment.

Reporter: Thank you, Mr. President.

THE PRESIDENT'S NEWS CONFERENCE OF

NOVEMBER 28, 1961

The President: Are there any questions?

QUESTIONS

The Situation in the Dominican Republic

Q: Mr. President, last week we had a show of force off the Dominican Republic. Under what circumstances would these ships and men actually have gone into action and is this an indication of policy in the hemisphere? ·Would U.S. forces be used to knock out any attempt by Castro, for instance, to overthrow an existing government?

The President: Well, the United States forces which remained in international waters were there because there was some feeling that steps might be
taken in the Dominican Republic which would end any hope that a democratic solution could be achieved. Because events in the Dominican Republic proceeded in
the way they did, United States forces have been gradually withdrawn.

It's our hope that, as a result of the conversations now going on in the
Dominican Republic, that we can make progress towards achieving the kind of
government which will permit the Dominican people to control their own destiny.

As to the broader questions, we would, of course, be concerned and have responsibilities as a member of the Organization of American States, if actions
were taken by one state against another state through the use of force, and we
would be most concerned about that whatever its source and particularly if its
source came from the one you describe.

The President's Travel Plans

*Q: Mr. President, do you plan a trip out of the country any time before the
first of the year?*

The President: We have not finalized any plans.

South Vietnamese Criticism of the U.S.

*Q: The Government-controlled press in South Viet-Nam is attacking the
United States now, apparently because we are asking for political reforms in
exchange for our military and economic assistance. I wonder if this has jeo-
pardized our effort to stop communism there, and if you could throw any light
on this situation for us?*

The President: Well, there have been stories in the press there that have
been critical of the United States and of course there have been stories in the
United States press which may in some cases bear a different relationship to
the Government than the press in Saigon does to its government but which nevertheless have suggested that the steps which are being taken within Viet-Nam to
counter the Communist threat have not been sufficient. We - of course, our
ambition is to permit the Vietnamese people to control their destiny, and we
are attempting to work with the Government and encourage steps which will increase the sense of commitment by the people of Viet-Nam to the struggle. These
steps are bound to be subject to discussion and controversy, and we are going
to continue to have our conversations with the Vietnamese Government.

The President's Address to the Russian People

*Q: Mr. President, what significance do you see in the fact that the Soviet
Government at this time permitted you to speak to the Russian people?*

The President: Well, I welcomed it. We had expressed, Mr. Salinger had -
I think other newspapermen in the United States had expressed their concern that
Mr. Khrushchev had been interviewed at some length by three or four American
newspapermen, that all his views were carried in full in the Western world and
particularly in the United States, but no similar opportunity had been given
to the President of the United States or any other American leaders and this
view was presented with vigor to Soviet representatives and I am delighted that
they decided to give us that opportunity.

*Q: Mr. President, when Mr. Khrushchev visited this country a couple of
years ago, he had quite a number of chances to speak to the American people on
virtually all of our radio, television, and newspapers. Would you welcome such*

an opportunity to do so personally in the Soviet Union to speak to the Russian people and see them?

The President: Well, I would think that Mr. Khrushchev came on invitation of the President of the United States and was a guest of the United States. I have not been given a similar invitation. I think that the important thing now is to attempt to work out a solution to the difficult problems which disturb our relations. The interview mentioned Germany and Berlin. There are also problems in southeast Asia, and that's the immediate task. And I think that probably they hold that view too in regard to any visit by a President of the United States that there are important problems that must be solved before such a visit would be rewarding to either side. No such invitation has as yet been extended.

Q: Mr. President, in your interview with the Izvestia reporter you said that what we objected to was the deprivation of a political choice, and I wonder if you could discuss with us how this criterion would apply to Finland where apparently the only anti-Soviet candidate and opponent to President Kekkonen has been pressured into retiring from the race.

The President: Well, I think the general thesis which I expressed on Saturday stands. We - what we desire is that the people of these countries will have a free choice. If they choose to follow under a condition of freedom, as I've said, with sufficient opportunity for alternative views to be presented, then we accept that. We would feel also, of course, that if they should choose the Communist system, then they should also be given the opportunity at another date to make another choice.

That is what we regard as freedom. That is not the view that has been held by the Soviet Union. And I would prefer to make that as a general statement rather than apply it to any particular country because some countries are having difficulties and I'm not sure that any statement that we might make at this time would be of assistance to them.

The President and Segregated Clubs

Q: Mr. President, you and your wife and other members of your family have declined to go to private clubs and to take part in other functions, even women's benefits at churches, where there was racial segregation. Now I wonder if you don't think it's simply fair that the President of the United States, members of his Cabinet, U.S. Ambassadors and other officers of this Government should decline to speak at and participate in functions where women newspaper reporters are barred?

The President: I feel that I have many responsibilities and the press has less and I would think that the press should deal with that problem and I'm sure that - I think it would be most appropriate if the members of the Press Club had a meeting and permitted you to come and present your views to them. (Laughter)

I will say that as we are expected, as President, to comment on everything, I will say that in my judgment when an official visit comes to speak to the Press Club, that all working reporters should be permitted in on a basis of equality. That is not a social occasion but a working occasion.

That happens to be my personal view and the members of the Press Club will have to decide it in the way they want. They are entitled to have any arrangement they would want in regards, I would think, to social occasions, but I would think that when there is an official visitor here as part of - the guest of the people of the United States and there's a meeting held, that all reporters should come on a basis of equality. But that - I am not a member of the

Press Club except honorary and therefore – but I give my view as an honorary member, not as President of the United States. (Laughter)

Relations Between NATO and the Warsaw Pact

Q: Mr. President, in your interview yesterday – published yesterday – you spoke of the possibility of a commitment to peace between NATO and the Warsaw Pact. Senator Mansfield early this month also suggested an exploratory meeting between the members of these two pacts to attempt to work out a better under-standing between them.

Are these two ideas, yours and Senator Mansfield's, in the same vein and do you envisage such a meeting?

The President: Well, as I stated, as we stated at the time of the visits of Chancellor Adenauer, we hoped that negotiations would take place in regard to Berlin and Germany, and of course, this is a question which would be re-lated to that. And at that time we would attempt to improve the relations be-tween the NATO and the Warsaw Pact countries.

I think there are some differences in the view expressed by Senator Mans-field and by me, but the purpose was the same – to provide a lessening of ten-sions between the two blocs and to improve their relations. I think that the details could best be worked out in negotiation, but we cannot have, of course, an increase in harmony between the two blocs until we've come to some negotiated and mutually satisfactory agreement in regard to Berlin and Germany. After we've done that, then such an agreement would be meaningful.

An International Administration on the Autobahn to Berlin

Q: Mr. President, could you tell us what you had in mind when you suggested in your interview with Mr. Adzhubei the creation of an international administra-tion on the Autobahn to Berlin?

The President: I would think that – what I'm anxious to do is to work out some system which will permit freedom of access for the people of West Berlin without constant pressures and without harassments which endanger their freedom and which increase the tensions between the countries.

One of the suggestions which have been considered is to provide some inter-national authority which will control traffic in the Autobahn and, therefore, guarantee its free movement. I think we would have to wait until negotiations began between the Soviet Union and the Western powers before any precise sug-gestions in regard to this kind of control might be put forward.

Q: May I ask a subordinate question, sir? Does this contemplate inter-national control under the United Nations, or something apart from the U.N.?

The President: The details, I would think, of what kind of an international authority might be arranged could be, I think, better a subject for the nego-tiations. There could be many different forms that it would take – four-power, U.N., or some other bodies – but it must be one, of course, which is acceptable to both sides. That would be difficult to achieve, but I believe, would be one of the chief points in any negotiations.

Budget Cut of the National Health Institutes by HEW

Q: Mr. President, Congressman John Fogarty has criticized as a devastating blow to major areas of medical research, the recent cut of $60 million by the Department of Health, Education, and Welfare from the budget of the National Institutes of Health.

Also, in the name of economy, the Atomic Energy Commission has announced curtailment of its reactor program.

Would you comment on this, and is any consideration being given to restoring these cuts?

The President: The difficulty - whenever we have a cut, well everyone wants economy and wants cuts. Whenever any cut is made, of course, there are always complaints about it. Now the fact of the matter is that we substantially increased over the Eisenhower budget the amount that we requested for the Department of HEW, including research - including support for the health institutes.

The House of Representatives increased our request and the Senate substantially increased it. Now the figure which Mr. Ribicoff cut to was, I believe, several million dollars above the figure that the House of Representatives themselves passed, and the fact of the matter is that the figure as it now stands in the area of HEW, cancer research and others is 25 percent now above what it was a year ago.

So that I think that we have funded these programs adequately. We would spend additional funds if we felt they could be usefully spent. And this matter has been very carefully examined.

And let me reiterate: the amount of money being spent is 25 percent above what was spent last year and it is above what was recommended by the House of Representatives itself, as well as being now above what we recommended in our budget, which was substantially above what President Eisenhower recommended in his budget.

Recent Personnel Changes

Q: Mr. President, could you discuss the recent personnel changes in your administration and the reasons behind them?

The President: The question was: would I discuss the recent personnel changes in our administration, and the reasons behind it. I think the first sentence of our announcement on Sunday, which said that we thought the changes would provide a better matching of the men with their tasks and responsibilities explains the change.

One of the problems, of course, is that our attention is focused today on - particularly on Western Europe, Berlin, Germany, the Common Market, and the Soviet and bloc tensions with the NATO Alliance and the United States.

We are, of course, also bearing heavy responsibilities and are extremely concerned with the course of events in South America, Africa, the Middle East and Asia.

Mr. Bowles has traveled a good deal in those areas before and after becoming Under Secretary. He is now going to devote his entire time to our problems and policies in those areas. I believe it's a much more effective use of his extremely - of his obvious talents to use him in this area, rather than using him in the area of day-to-day administration in the Department of State.

I regard this, as I've said, as an increased opportunity for Mr. Bowles, and I think it's vitally important to the United States. We do not want to become so concerned about the problems we face in Western Europe that we ignore the tremendous responsibilities and opportunities that are before the free world in these important sections of the world.

So that I'm encouraged by the changes and I'm grateful to Mr. Bowles for taking on this assignment. I think he can render a real service as he has in the past.

I'm also grateful to Governor Harriman for becoming, after holding probably as many important jobs as any American in our history, with the possible exception of John Quincy Adams, for now taking on the job of Assistant Secretary for the Far East.

Morale Among the Reservists

Q: Mr. President, there are reports that the morale among the Reservists who have been called up is bad. They claim they don't have - they say they have nothing to do; the equipment is inadequate. Do you care to comment?

The President: Well, I have seen the newspaper stories. There isn't any doubt that any newspaper can go out and interview men who've been called up. Their lives are disturbed. Many of them are older. They've all got jobs. For most of them it's a heavy sacrifice. And we are not at war.

And they go to camps which have perhaps been newly opened or where the equipment may not be immediately available. And they're bound to be unhappy. I've seen the stories in some cases where newspapers have reported that the Department of Defense is determined to keep these people in for more than a year.

Then when it was proved that that story was wholly wrong, they then write that the Pentagon has changed its mind and not going to keep them in more than a year and then sent their reporters around to examine and interview servicemen and build up the sense that Americans are not ready to serve their country.

Now let me make it very clear what the reason, that we called these men - the reason we called these men is that there is a direct clash of interest in a major area, which is Berlin and West Germany. There also is increased tension in Viet-Nam.

When we came into office, we did not feel that there was sufficient strength in our conventional forces. Of the 14 Army divisions, 3 were training divisions. And the United States has commitments all around the world.

Now, while we rely on our nuclear weapons, we also, as I've said, want to have a choice between humiliation and a holocaust. And therefore, we believe that calling these men up and their willingness to serve increased the chance of maintaining the peace.

There are countries where leaders have talked very strongly about standing firm in various areas, but do not have the military force to support that statement. We require it. The United States is the strongest power and the leader of the free world, and as such we must have the power to make our commitments good.

These men, who may be serving in a very cold and windy camp in Fort Lewis, in Washington, therefore, are rendering the same kind of service to our country that an airplane standing on a 15-minute alert at a SAC base in Omaha is rendering. We called them in, in order to prevent a war, not to fight a war.

And, if our efforts to hold the peace should fail, then, of course, they would be used in a more direct way. But their function today is to indicate that the United States is serious about its commitments; that it means to meet its commitments; that it wants to negotiate a peaceful settlement if it can, but it does not propose to surrender.

And therefore, I would hope that any serviceman who is sitting in a camp, however unsatisfactory it may be, and I know how unsatisfactory it is, will recognize that he is contributing to the security of his family in a most direct way.

And, in these days when weapons are so terrible, the important thing is to attempt to maintain the peace, and they're helping to do it.

And I think it's up to us to make sure that they do get the equipment. It is up to us to make sure that their training is useful. As I have said, we've sent the Inspector General out to Washington to look at the camp and to talk to the people involved.

But I do think it would be well for us all to recognize that in the first place, these men are not going to be kept in longer than a year. There has never been such a proposal in the Pentagon that I've ever heard of - newspaper reports to the contrary, notwithstanding. This has never been suggested.

Secondly, it is our hope to get these men out before their 12-month period.

Third, these men were called in at the request of the administration and with the approval of the Congress, which gave us the authorization to call them in. In my opinion they're rendering a valuable function. We are going to get them out as quickly as we can. But they are doing a service and I hope they recognize it and I hope that all of us who are in a position to communicate will explain to them and to their families how important their service is today.

Q: Mr. President, now the ──

The President: This chimpanzee who is flying in space took off at 10:08. He reports that everything is perfect and working well. (Laughter)

State of Western Readiness for Negotiations on Berlin

Q: Mr. President, now that you have met with Chancellor Adenauer and the British Prime Minister Macmillan has met with French President de Gaulle, will you give us your view, sir, of the present state of Western readiness for negotiations on Berlin?

The President: Well, there is one more step to be taken in that series of meetings, and that is the meeting between Chancellor Adenauer and General de Gaulle which is, was supposed to take place this week but has been delayed a week because of the Chancellor's cold, but which will take place before the meeting of the foreign ministers at the time of NATO. And at that time, then, we should be able more precisely to answer that question.

The President's Trip Abroad

Q: Could you clarify your rather mystifying remark about a possible trip abroad? Are you thinking of going to the NATO meeting in December?

The President: No, I'm not.

Q: Could you tell us anything more about it?

The President: I will as soon as we've made a decision about whether such a trip would be useful, but I'm not thinking about going to NATO. But I don't mean to be at all unresponsive, but the trip has not been - a trip has not been definitely arranged, and until it is, it would seem to me to be - and it depends on circumstances which may develop in the future and therefore it's really in about the status that I suggested.

Civil Defense Policy

Q: Mr. President, in attempts to clarify your civil defense policy, it's been reported that you favor community shelter, fallout shelters, over the private shelters. If this was so, could you give us some of your reasoning behind that move?

The President: Well, we have never thought that the Government could engage in the task of building shelters in each home because it would be a diversion of our resources and would vitally affect our deterrent strength which remains our best hope of avoiding a nuclear exchange. So that we have stated from the beginning and the decisions made last spring and summer in regard to the markings of available shelters emphasize the community structure.

We made some decisions in regard to Federal policy in relation to community shelters last Friday. We are now going to talk to some of the Governors who are directly concerned and involved in this matter because it requires cooperation between the Federal Government, the State, and the communities so that we will have a program and a budget to send to the Congress in January.

The emphasis will be on community shelters, and information will be made available to the individual as to what he could do within his own home. But the central responsibility, it seems to me, is for us to provide community shelters. It seems - it seemed the most effective use of our resources and to provide the best security for our people.

Financial Contributions to Extremist Groups

Q: Mr. President, there have been reports of sizable financial contributions to the sort of right-wing extremist groups that you criticized last week. Do you regard this as a danger to the elective process and will you press in the next session for some form of Federal financing of elections?

The President: Well, as you know we set up a committee to provide for Federal - at least to reconsider the whole problem of financing presidential elections. That was their only responsibility. There is a committee in the Senate which has examined other methods of financing other campaigns. As I understand it, what you're referring to is the contributions by some individuals or groups to right-wing movements, not so much candidates - is that correct.

Q: Yes.

The President: As long as they meet the requirements of the tax laws, I don't think that the Federal Government can interfere or should interfere with the right of any individual to take any position he wants. The only thing we should be concerned about is that it does not represent a diversion of funds which might be taxable to - for nontaxable purposes. But that is another question and I'm sure the Internal Revenue System examines that. But I would not want to interfere with the right of any individual to give his own finances or support to any movement that he chooses to do so, providng it comes within the laws, the present laws of the United States.

The U.S. and South Africa's Racial Policies

Q: Mr. President, the General Assembly last night voted to urge all nations to take separate and collective action to force South Africa to abandon its racial policies. What specific steps would you favor the U.S. taking to implement that resolution?

The President: I've not examined the language of the Assembly resolution so that I'm not able to answer that.

Legislative Priorities

Q: Sir, last year before the session of Congress began you listed domestic and foreign legislation that would be "must" for that session of Congress. Can you at this time list your priorities for legislation in the upcoming Congress?

The President: No, I think that the - I should do that in the State of the Union Address and we will. Quite obviously, we've touched on one of the matters which are of importance - civil defense. I talked previous to this about another matter which is medical care for the aged. But the general program I think should wait till January.

Trade Policy

Q: Sir, could you clarify one thing? There seem to be confusion and conflicting reports about whether you are going to press for a more liberal trade policy. Has the decision been made on that yet?

The President: A preliminary decision has been made in regard to the matter, yes, and will be announced in January. Once again there are some consultations which must be made and will be made with the members of Congress who have responsibility in the area in the month of December, and then we will go to the Congress in January with our program.

Q: Mr. President, Senator Goldwater has indicated his opposition to us becoming associated with the Common Market. Would you comment on that and perhaps sum up for us the possible effect the Common Market might have on the American economy?

The President: Yes, I don't know what the word "associated" means in the question. I don't know anyone - I have not heard it proposed that the United States should become a member of the Common Market or associated with the Common Market in the sense that the word is ordinarily used.

What we are concerned about is that we have the power to negotiate with the Common Market to protect our export industry. Now the Common Market will represent a tremendously important market for American production. It is one of our areas where we have concentrated most on in recent years and will - and represents a tremendous potential for us in the future, particularly when Great Britain joins it. But we don't - we want to, therefore, protect our export market.

We want to keep the ratio of exports to imports comparable to what it is today or perhaps even improve it, because if we're not able to export substantially more than we import, we're going to either have to cut off all assistance to countries abroad or begin to withdraw our troops home.

We spend over $3 billion a year in keeping our bases and our troops abroad. That represents a $3 billion drain or potentially gold drain upon us. The only reason we've been able to afford that, of course, has been that we've had a balance of trade in our favor of around $5 billion.

Now in addition we are concerned that American companies who are locked out of the Common Market because of their high tariffs will feel that the only way that they can get into the market will be through investing in Western Europe, and therefore we will have capital leaving, which will cost jobs. Every time an American firm invests in Europe and builds its company there, it hires European workers and not American workers.

Now we believe in the free flow of capital. We do not believe in capital exchange here. Therefore we have to have the ability to negotiate with the Common Market so that American goods can enter the market and we will not have American capital jumping the wall in order to compete.

So that this is a matter of great importance to the American workers and industry and to the American economy, and it is in that - because of that reason, as well as our desire to associate as closely as we can to Europe, which is going to be such an important power and force, that we are considering what our trade program will be. But if you use the word "associate" with the Common Market, or "join" the Common Market, that is not an accurate description of our policy.

The President's Advice on Closer Ties Between the Two Germanies

Q: Mr. President, do you favor, and did you urge on Chancellor Adenauer closer ties, particularly political ties between the two halves of Germany?

The President: No. In answer to your first question, the reason I answer it with some hesitation is the question of "ties". At the present time, for example, as you know, the East Germans and West Germans do negotiate in regard to trade. So that we have to decide - and those negotiations may continue and we will have a clearer idea of what form they will take if we get into negotiation.

Political ties could be defined in so many ways that I think that unless you would be prepared to define it more precisely, I think the wiser thing would be to wait till we got into negotiation with the Soviet Union and then to determine what these relationships would be.

I think my interview on Saturday indicated my general view of the Federal Republic and its actions in the future.

Trade Barriers and the Japanese Protest

Q: Mr. President, you have espoused more liberal trade barriers. Yet, the other day, you put machinery in motion that could result in a higher import duty on cotton textiles. Now I understand the Japanese have protested. How do you square your policy on lowering trade barriers with this sort of protectionist action?

The President: I square it in an attempt to achieve a balance which serves the interest of the United States and those countries which are involved around the world.

I will point out that the United States does sell cotton at a price which is vastly lower than an American manufacturer can buy it for. We sell it at the world price which represents a contribution by the United States to each pound or bale of cotton which is sold abroad, which permits a manufacturer in a country around the world to buy their cotton much lower than our manufacturers, which puts our manufacturers at a competitive disadvantage.

We do that for obvious reasons. But we have to try to balance off those burdens.

The President's Political Past

Q: Mr. President, a Republican Congressman making answer to your speech in Los Angeles in which you criticized extremist groups went back to 1949 and got a speech you made in Salem, Mass., in which you reviewed the loss of mainland China, and found in that what he considered inconsistencies. Would you care to comment on your view then and now?

The President: Yes. I always have felt that we did not make a determined enough effort in the case of China. Given the problems we now see, I think a more determined effort would have been advisable. I would think that in my speech in '49 I placed more emphasis on personalities than I would today.

And I would say that my view today is more in accordance with the facts than my view in '49. But my – I've always felt, and I think history will record, that the change of China from being a country friendly to us to a country which is unremittingly hostile affected very strongly the balance of power in the world. And while there were – there is still, of course, room for argument as to whether any United States actions would have changed the course of events there, I think a greater effort would have been wiser. I said it in '49, so it isn't totally hindsight.

Protection Against Fallout

Q: Mr. President, earlier you said that information would be made available to private citizens as to what they can do individually to protect against fallout. Do you have an opinion as to whether individuals should build private shelters or not?

The President: I stated that we are going to send out a booklet when it is ready. I hoped it would be ready by the end of November. The booklet will reflect the decisions we made in November, and I think it will tell them what the Federal policy will be; what we hope to do, and what each individual can do in his own home, which will provide greater assurances if an attack should come.

I want to emphasize that the best defense still remains the American deterrent.

But I do think that within each individual home that some steps can be taken which are not expensive, but which would, if a disaster should strike us, provide a greater security, though of course, there is no security against blast.

And there is bound to be, particularly as these new weapons increase in power, there are obvious limits to what any of us can do. But in answer to your question, the booklet which will be sent out, I hope shortly, will inform each individual what he can do within his own home as well as within his community.

Reporter: Thank you, Mr. President.

1962

THE PRESIDENT'S NEWS CONFERENCE OF

JANUARY 15, 1962

The President: I have just one announcement. I am sure you are all familiar with the story in this morning's paper of the documentation on the study of comparisons of those in our schools and universities and the kind of subjects which they study which was published by the National Science Foundation. This has been a matter of some concern to me for some time because one of the most critical problems facing this Nation is the inadequacy of the supply of scientific and technical manpower, to satisfy the expanding requirements of this country's research and development efforts in the near future. In 1951 our universities graduated 19,600 students in the physical sciences. In 1960 in spite of the substantial increase in our population, during the last 10 years, and in spite of the fact that the demand for people of skill in this field has tremendously increased with our efforts in defense and space, industrial research, and all of the rest, in 1960 the number had fallen from 19,600 to 17,100. In 1951 there were 22,500 studying in the biological sciences; in 1960 there were only 16,700. In the field of engineering, enrollment rose from 232,000 to 269,000 in the period 1951 to 1957. Since 1957 there has been a continual decline in enrollment. Last year the figure was down to 240,000.

This is a matter of growing concern. It is more than a matching of numerical supply to anticipate a demand, though this alone would be difficult. Because of the seriousness of this problem for the long-range future of the United States, I have asked my Science Advisory Committee, in cooperation with the Federal Council for Science and Technology, to review available studies and other pertinent information, and to report to me as quickly as possible on the specific measures that can be taken within and without the Government to develop the necessary and well qualified scientists and engineers and technicians to meet our society's complex needs - governmental, educational, and industrial.

In undertaking this task, the committee will draw on the advice and assistance of individuals and agencies, including the National Academy of Sciences, which will shortly begin at my request a new study of scientific and technical manpower utilization.

To all those who may be within the sound of my voice or who may follow your stories in the papers, I want to emphasize the great new and exciting field of the sciences and while we wish to emphasize always the liberal arts, I do believe that these figures indicate a need on the national level and also a great opportunity for talented young men and women. And I hope that their teachers, their school boards, and they themselves and their families will give this matter consideration in developing their careers.

QUESTIONS

The Berlin Question

Q: Mr. President, as you are aware, there has been nothing official on this, but there have been some unofficial reports stemming from Ambassador Thompson's first two exploratory conferences in Moscow. These reports are to the effect that the situation with Russia has not changed.

Could you tell us, sir, whether as a result of Mr. Thompson's two meetings in Moscow that you detect any evidence, new evidence, of a possible solution of our differences with Russia over Berlin?

The President: I think - it's my hope that these talks will continue, so that this matter will be subjected to the most thorough scrutiny and examination, to see whether such an arrangement is possible. Ambassador Thompson, I am hopeful, therefore, will meet with the Foreign Minister again and after these meetings have gone on for a reasonable period, we can make a much more concise judgment in answer to your question. But I think it would be premature today.

Q: Mr. President, in that connection, could you give us any idea of the length of a reasonable period of time?

The President: No, I think it would really depend upon what was happening during the negotiations. In other words, if progress were being made, or if there were evidence that progress could be made, of course, then the time would be different than it would be if there was no evidence of any meeting of minds. So I think the important thing now is to continue and I'm - Ambassador Thompson will.

The Indonesian Dutch Dispute

Q: Mr. President, the United States has made informal but strenuous efforts to reach a peaceful solution of the Indonesian Dutch dispute. Could you say, sir, if your hopes are in any way possible of fulfillment now, and if our efforts should fail, would we then turn to the United Nations?

The President: We do not have any more precise information than the news story with which you are familiar in regard to the statement of the Dutch. We have been extremely anxious that a peaceful accommodation be reached in this matter and have used our influence to bring that about. I am particularly glad that the Secretary General of the United Nations, Mr. U Thant, has been occupying himself with a good deal of energy to try to see if there is a possibility for a peaceful settlement.

I am hopeful that both parties will respond to his efforts, and that we can prevent an outbreak of hostilities between Indonesia and the Dutch. Great responsibility rests on both of these countries, and I am hopeful that they will give Mr. U Thant every cooperation because the alternative would not be happy for the world, nor, really, I think, in the long run, for the parties involved. A peaceful solution, of course, would be the best thing and that's what we're working for.

Trade Liberalization Program

Q: Mr. President, this is a question about your trade liberalization program. Some members of Congress from industrial areas are reporting privately that they are worried about the problems of their support of the program because some of their manufacturing constituents say that unless they are able

to get things, for example, like wool and cotton, at world market prices in-
stead of artificial prices, that they can't afford to go along with the idea
of reducing trade barriers. Can you give us your assessment of how serious
you think this problem is and do you see any possible encouragement to them
on it?

The President: Well, of course, there are two different - one is cotton,
which is in surplus here in the United States, and the other is wool, which we
import. In the case of cotton, as you know, we send out, export, about 6
million bales of cotton a year, and we import about 600,000 manufactured bales,
textiles. In fact, we export almost as much cotton, manufactured textiles, as
we import. So the export of cotton is a very important ingredient in our balance of payments.

I think the Japanese alone buy, I think, almost $240 or $250 million of
cotton. I believe, as I said before, that while some industries may not get
the same benefit out of this proposal as others will, that generally, it will
be very helpful to industry and very helpful to agriculture and most helpful to
the United States.

And I think that if the members of Congress begin to examine the figures
in their districts and in their States, and these figures are being prepared
which show where the balance of trade runs, then I think that we can get a
majority support for the legislation. A good deal of concern is expressed
about Japan, but we ran a half billion dollar balance of trade in our favor.
We sold Japan last year a half billion dollars more than they bought from us.
So that I believe the United States can compete.

As I said the other day, the fact is that the Common Market countries have
had an extraordinary economic growth, full employment and all the rest, and it
is to increase our employment and our opportunities that we are recommending
this. So in answer to your question, I believe that when the members of the
House and Senate have examined our proposal, examined its safeguards, examined
what it can do for employment, I am hopeful, in fact, I feel it very possible,
that we can secure a majority, even though it's a sophisticated matter and it
is difficult to explain quickly. But I think that when the educational job is
done, I think the country will understand that it is in our best interest.

American Troops in Vietnam

Q: Mr. President, are American troops now in combat in Vietnam?

The President: No.

Expansion of the Food-for-Peace Program

Q: Mr. President, Secretary Freeman has said that it's impossible to
expand the food-for-peace program and Mr. McGovern says it should be expanded.
Have you been able to resolve this difference?

The President: Well, I think it should be expanded as we can. I think
that Mr. Freeman's concern is with, first, the regular markets of trade, that
the food for peace should complement it and not cut across it, the obligations
we have to others who are also exporters of agricultural commodities, the
question of funds and finances, of how much - if we're talking about the
$2 billion a year, which we are now. I am hopeful that we can use our pro-
ductive power well in this field, but I think that the question of the balance, and I think that Mr. McGovern and Mr. Freeman in my judgment will be in
balance by the time they go before the Congress, because I think they both have

the same basic interests in using our food well and not having it wasted - in storage.

Bargaining Timetable in the Steel Industry

Q: What can you tell us about the administration's efforts to speed up the bargaining timetable in the steel industry, and what do you hope to accomplish by this?

The President: Well, I was hopeful, of course, from the beginning that an agreement would be reached in the steel industry, which would be, as I said in my letter to Mr. McDonald, which would be within the range of productivity and price stability, and which would come at a time, though I have not said this before, would come at a time which would prevent a repetition of what we saw in 1958 where there was a tremendous increase in inventory, in the first 6 months of the year which adversely affected the economy in the last half of the year, and also adversely affected employment in the steel mills themselves. So while they worked at high capacity for the first 6 months, there were a good many layoffs after the strike.

Now, if an agreement can be reached between the steel companies and the steel union, of course it would be well to have it come early, so that the country and the consumers of steel would be able to make their plans for the future without stockpiling.

Now this is a judgment for them. This is a free economy, and the Federal Government has no power unless there was a strike which affects the national emergency, but Secretary Goldberg is available for whatever good offices he may perform.

President's Comments on His First Year in Office

Q: Mr. President, after 1 year in the office of the Presidency, would you care to give us any of your comments about the first year and perhaps in particular the most rewarding and disappointing events that have come across your desk?

The President: Well, I would say the most disappointing event was our failure to get an agreement on the cessation of nuclear testing, because I think that that might have been a very important step in easing the tension and preventing a proliferation of the weapons, and also in making it more possible for us to have progress on disarmament and some of the other matters that divide us. The thing that I think is the most heartening is the fact that first I think there's a greater surge for unity in the Western nations, and in our relations with Latin America, and also I think it has become more obvious that people do desire to be free and independent. And while they may organize their societies in different ways, they do want to maintain a national sovereignty, which I would regard as a great source of strength to us. I've had other disappointments but those are important.

Coalition Government in Southeast Asia

Q: Mr. President, in the past it would seem that coalition governments lean toward Communist control. Are we then taking a chance in supporting a coalition type government in southeast Asia?

The President: We are taking a chance in all of southeast Asia, and we're taking a chance in other areas. Nobody can make any predictions for the future, really, on any matter in which there are powerful interests at stake. I think, however, that we have to consider what our alternatives are, and what the prospects for war are in that area if we fail in our present efforts and the geographic problems which have to be surmounted in such a military engagement, where there is no easy entrance by sea and where the geographic location is extremely a long way from us and very close to those who might become involved. So that there's no easy, sure answer for Laos, but it is my judgment that it is in the best interest of our country to work for a neutral and independent Laos. We are attempting to do that. And I can assure you that I recognize the risks that are involved. But I also think that we should consider the risks if we fail, and particularly of the possibility of escalation of a military struggle in a place of danger. So we're going to attempt to work out this matter in a way which permits us to try.

Checking Castroism

Q: Mr. President, the Inter-American foreign ministers are due to meet at Punta del Este next Monday. In advance of that meeting, could you tell us what kind of action you hope the meeting will take to check Castroism?

The President: Well, I think it is the consensus of the hemisphere that communism is a threat; that it's sustained and supported by alien forces; that it has no place in the Inter-American system; and that we are against dictatorships of the right and left. And now that the Dominican Republic is moving from a dictatorship of the right, we are hopeful that there will be – the voice of the hemisphere will speak against dictatorships of the left which are sustained and supported from outside the hemisphere. I think that we will get that consensus.

Control and Management of Farm Production

Q: Mr. President, the agricultural proposals now under preparation appear to involve a good deal of control of production and marketing by the Government. Following your long conference with Secretary Freeman, do you now hold the view that if the Government is to continue farm price support programs there must be control or management of production?

The President: Well, management – I think what we are attempting to do is to prevent the surpluses which we are able to produce because of the extraordinary productivity of our farms. I said the other day in the State of the Union Address that our per capita production has increased nearly 100 percent in the last 10 years, which is faster than our consumption is increasing, and as we have somewhat more difficulty maintaining some of our markets abroad, in my judgment we should attempt to provide with the support of the farmers and the Congress a reasonable balance which will protect their income. Otherwise, these surplusses will break the farmers' income, or they will be piled up so high in the sheds of the United States in storage that the whole program of trying to assist farmers will fall into discredit, and the farmer himself will be damaged. So what we are attempting to do – and this is extremely difficult because of the variety of opinions that are involved – is to try to work with the farmer and the Congress to try to bring about a balance between production for our domestic use, for our world use, for food for peace, and at the same time insure that the farmer's income will not be broken by surpluses, as it was to a substantial extent in the twenties. And that's our effort, and I think it's essential that we succeed if the public interest and the farmers are going to be protected.

Conduct of the Judicial System

Q: Mr. President, this has to do with the conduct of our judicial system. In the last several years at least two Federal judges have resigned from the bench to go back to practice law. Since Federal judges are appointed for life, would you care to comment on the possible impact of this type of resignation on the judicial system, and its effect upon the ethical standards of the community?

The President: I think that the reason that they are appointed for life is so that there cannot only be no actual improprieties, but no appearance of improprieties. And while I would not make any judgment in the two cases you mentioned, I don't think that anyone should accept a Federal judgeship unless they're prepared to fill it for life, because I think the maintenance of the integrity of the judiciary is so important. So I hope that all judges will stay to the end of their terms.

Algerian Problem

Q: Sir, last April, during the generals' revolt in Algeria, you made an offer, but it was not clear from here whether it was of support or offer of aid to General de Gaulle. If a similar instance should occur in the near future, would you make a similar offer to President de Gaulle of either support or aid?

The President: I don't think that you've described completely, precisely, the kind of message which I sent to General de Gaulle. And I think that probably proffer of assistance would not be a precise description of it. If we felt that - I would think it would be unwise to speculate about the future. But this was a matter which was handled by the French, and no request was made for assistance, and none was offered.

Kashmir

Q: Mr. President, in the case of Kashmir, India has failed to keep its promise to hold free elections and has resorted with impunity in attacking Goa on December 17th. Could you tell us what the United States could do to assure that a double standard of action does not arise in the United Nations?

The President: Well, there are several different questions. We are against a double standard of action in the United Nations, and I think we have attempted to make that clear, and that double standard goes to a whole variety of different things, not just the matters that you mentioned in your question.

Now, on the matter of Kashmir, we have been and are concerned that an accommodation or a solution be reached because both countries have numerous external and internal problems. And we have been assisting both countries to build a more viable economy and quite obviously everything that is put to arms as a result of their frictions, of course, takes it from the general effort, and we're going to continue our efforts.

Pending Appeals in the Office of Emergency Planning

Q: Mr. President, there are two appeals pending in the Office of Emergency Planning that relate to foreign trade. One seeks protection for the textile industry and the other seeks a reduction in import restrictions on residual oil. Could you tell us what progress is being made on these appeals and, in particular, if any recommendation has come to you?

The President: Well, we did make a recommendation about a month ago on residual oil which provided for some increase in the amount that could be imported in, I think most of it from Venezuela. In the matter of textiles, that is one of the subjects which was part of our seven-point proposal to the textile industry, that we would consider.

We have made some progress with the textile industry - the voluntary agreement, which was made by the Under Secretary, Mr. Ball, which is trying to bring about a happier distribution of textile production in a way that doesn't cause dumping. I think that that's been a help to the textile industry - the change we made in depreciation allowances. There are other matters we're now looking into, and this is one of them. But it is a fact that the importation of textiles this year, which had gone from about 4 to 7 percent from '58 to '60, was down for various reasons to 6 percent, so that the import situation was somewhat eased for the textile industry. But to answer your question, both of these matters are before us.

Destruction of the Berlin Wall

Q: Mr. President, criticism that we did not tear down the Berlin wall seems to be increasing rather than declining. Just about a week ago the Chairman of the Republican National Committee criticized your administration very strenuously. I don't recall that you've ever publicly discussed this particular phase of the question. Do you think it would be helpful for you to do so now?

The President: Well, I have discussed it. I stated that no one at that time in any position of responsibility - and I would use that term - either in the West Berlin-American contingent, in West Germany, France, or Great Britain, suggested that the United States or the other countries go in and tear down the wall.

The Soviet Union had had a *de facto* control for many years, really stretching back to the late forties in East Berlin. It had been turned over as a capital for East Germany a long time ago. And the United States has a very limited force surrounded by a great many divisions. We are going to find ourselves severely challenged to maintain what we have considered to be our basic rights - which is our presence in West Belin and the right of access to West Berlin, and the freedom of the people of West Berlin.

But in my judgment, I think that you could have had a very violent reaction which might have taken us down a very rocky road, and I think it was for that reason and because it was recognized by those people in positions of responsibility that no recommendation was made along the lines you've suggested at that time. Hindsight is --

Soviet Nuclear Tests in the Atmosphere

Q: It's been more than 4 months since the Soviets began their series of nuclear tests in the atmosphere, and I think you'd agree it would only be imprudent not to assume - to assume that they're not preparing further tests. Can you discuss what the overriding considerations are to cause us to give this potential enemy a gift of that length of time, and can you also tell us when we may expect a decision on your part in this matter of testing in the atmosphere?

The President: Well, as you know, we have tested underground, so that in talking about the gift of time, that matter should be taken into consideration. Secondly, of course, we were negotiating at the table in Geneva when the Soviet Union, after many months of preparation, began its tests.

I have announced that we are making our preparations to conduct atmospheric testing if it's considered to be in the public interest when those preparations are completed. So that it's wholly impossible for a free country like the United States, with a free press, to prepare in secret the extensive - make extensive preparations which would be necessary, at the same time we are conducting a very important and vital negotiation. So that the Soviet Union has that advantage. They have advantages as a dictatorship in this cold war struggle. But they have very serious disadvantages, and I think that we have to balance them one against the other.

Racial Segregation in Federally Assisted Housing

Q: Mr. President, during the election campaign you pledged that if elected you would issue an executive order prohibiting racial segregation in federally assisted housing. It's recently been reported that you have decided to postpone the issuance of such an order for some time. I wondered if you could give us your thinking on this timing question - why you want to put it off?

The President: Well, I think - I have stated that I would issue that order when I considered it to be in the public interest, and when I considered it to be make an important contribution to advancing the rights of our citizens. I will point out that this administration in the last 12 months made more progress in the field of civil rights on a whole variety of fronts than were made in the last 8 years. We have, for example, carried out a great many more suits in voting rights, the appointment of Federal employees, and judges, and their employees, and ending segregation in interstate travel and terminal facilities, the ICC's work, and the work being done in railroad and airports, and we have had - at least the communities involved made important progress in integrating in this field.

So we are proceeding ahead in a way which will maintain a consensus, and which will advance this cause. And I think a proper judgment can be made on this and all other matters relating to equality of rights at the end of this year, and at the end of our term. In my judgment we are going to make significant progress and I am fully conscious of the wording of the statement to which you refer, and plan to meet my responsibilities in regard to this matter.

Bond Issue of the U.N.

Q: Mr. President, would you care to comment on how the bond issue of the United Nations can tip the scale in favor of the United States?

The President: Can do what?

Q: Can tip the scale in favor of the United States.

The President: I think it can help us strengthen the United Nations, which I think is in the interest of the United States, and I think that if we do not have a bond issue, or a satisfactory substitute, and I have not heard of one, in my judgment the U.N. will go, sail, into very difficult weather in regard to its financing, and could be on the verge of bankruptcy. And I think this is a way, along with the decision which will be rendered by the Court in regard to the payment of their obligations - this is a way to spread the burden more equitably and insure the United Nations has adequate funds. Now, I look at what is happening in the Congo, where progress is being made towards the establishment of an independent Congo, and if Mr. Tshombe and the Prime Minister, based on their agreement at Kitona, can continue to make progress, we may have a real hope there.

So in my opinion, the United Nations justifies the effort we put into it substantially. We rely very heavily, as I said earlier today, on the Secretary General in regard to what is happening now in western New Guinea and Indonesia. So that I believe in it strongly, and I think that this is a way to strengthen it which tips the scale, I think, in the interest of peace, and those nations that wish to be free.

Women's Demonstration in Favor of Disarmament and Peace

Q: Mr. President, this afternoon 2,000 American women, many of them from distant places, demonstrated in a downpour in front of the White House in behalf of disarmament and peace. Do you consider this sort of demonstration useful and does it have an influence on you and other world leaders who are responsible for peace?

The President: Well, I think these women are extremely earnest and that they are as concerned as we all are at the possibility of a nuclear war. They talked this morning to Mr. Fisher, who is the Deputy Director of our disarmament agency. We stressed the effort we were going to put into the disarmament conference coming up in March. I saw the ladies myself. I recognized why they were there. There were a great number of them. It was in the rain. I understood what they were attempting to say, and therefore I considered that their message was received.

The Influence of the Military-Industrial Alliance in the Defense Spending Program

Q: Mr. President, almost precisely a year ago, President Eisenhower in his farewell address discussed the influence of the military-industrial alliance in the defense spending program. I wonder, sir, if, in your first year in office, you have developed similar concern for this problem?

The President: I think that President Eisenhower commented on a matter which deserves continuing attention by the President and also by the Secretary of Defense. There gets to be a great vested interest in expenditures because of the employment that is involved, and all the rest, and that's one of the struggles which he had and which we have, and I think his warning or his words were well taken.

Negotiations in the Common Market

Q: Mr. President, do you have any comment on the recent negotiations in the Common Market moving into the second phase, their negotiations with us on agricultural products?

The President: We have had a long negotiation, stretching back over 18 months, on the matter with the Common Market. We sent over Mr. Petersen and the Under Secretary of Agriculture, Mr. Murphy, in December. We sent them back again this week. The arrangement which has been developed in the last few days has improved our position. We always will have – and I believe that this is one of the arguments for the powers which I requested from the Congress – a difficult struggle with agricultural productivity rising in Europe, with the balance of agricultural trade. We are sending to the Common Market about a billion one hundred million and taking back about two hundred million from them – it's quite obvious that it's impossible for us to trade evenly with them on agriculture.

So, therefore, we have to trade across the board. Given the difficulties which the Common Market is now running into with agriculture, and which we will see more of when the British negotiations get advanced, I would think that this looks like the best arrangement that we could make and seems to be in the public interest and is, I think, on the whole, satisfactory.

Presidential Standards for Membership in Clubs

Q: Sir, there has been much to-do in the papers recently about memberships in various clubs affecting the members of your administration, having to do with the Cosmos Club and the Metropolitan Club, with which you are familiar.

Sir, do you have any particular standards of your own which you apply in your own case as to memberships in various clubs, as to whether they should be coeducational or biracial?

The President: I have said from the beginning that I thought this was a personal matter which involved not only the members of this Government, but involves everyone in the city and everyone in the country, and every individual must make his judgment in the way that he believes to be right. And I've stated that my application for the Cosmos Club was not being renewed.

Medicare Legislation

Q: Mr. President, you did not specifically mention doctors in your opening statement. If you get medicare legislation, where would you get the doctors, nurses, and hospitals to furnish the old people's needs?

The President: I was talking about scientists on this occasion, but as you know we have asked in the State of the Union Address for some assistance to medical schools and nursing schools. The fact of the matter is that our doctors are falling far behind the rate of increase in our population, and we are going to find it increasingly difficult to serve our people well. I don't think the solution should be to deny medical care to people, however. I think we can do much better than that, and I would suggest that the best remedy would be to assist us in the program we recommended to strengthen our medical schools so we can get the doctors we need.

Reporter: Thank you, Mr. President.

THE PRESIDENT'S NEWS CONFERENCE OF

JANUARY 24, 1962

The President: Good afternoon.

QUESTIONS

The Urban Affairs Bill

Q: Mr. President, the House Rules Committee, I understand, has just voted down your urban affairs bill. I wonder if in that view you plan to submit it again?

The President: Well, I will say this: It is my understanding that the House Rules Committee rejected by a vote of 9 to 6 the proposal which had come out, which we had sent up, and which had come out of the House Committee on Government Operations.

I am somewhat astonished at the Republican leadership, which opposed this bill. It is my understanding that all of the Republican members of the Rules Committee opposed the bill, I had gotten the impression 2 weeks ago, after reading the reports from the meeting in Oklahoma, that they shared our concern for more effective management and responsibility of the problems of two-thirds of our population who live in the cities. These cities are expanding. They face many problems - housing, transportation, and all the rest - which vitally affect our people.

This is a most valuable and important proposal, and for that reason, therefore, I am going to send it to the Congress as a reorganization plan, and give every member of the House and Senate an opportunity to give their views and work their will on this.

Limits on Public Statements of Military Figures

Q: Mr. President, could you discuss for us your general feelings about the limits which you feel should or should not be imposed on the public statements of military figures? Do you think that - what degree of review should be exercised over their public utterances?

The President: I must say I don't think that we could do better than to read the remarks of three distinguished military officers. General White's article in this week's Newsweek, Admiral Burke, a distinguished officer who is now retired, and General Lemnitzer, Chairman of the Joint Chiefs of Staff - all men of long experience, all men who understand the importance of the proper relationship between the military and the civilian. And I must say that after reading those three statements, I am strengthened in my conviction of the good judgment of Mr. Lovett's words when he said that this flag looks redder to the bulls outside than it does inside. I think that - I commend those three statements to the military and to the civilians, and I think they set a very proper guidance.

I'm glad this matter is being looked into by - particularly by a committee headed by Senator Stennis, who is an outstanding Senator. I am sure that it will be useful. But I do think that the relationship which has existed for so many years, which provides for civilian control and responsibility, and the coordination of speeches which interpret Government policy, so that the United States speaks with force and strength - I believe that we should continue this very valuable policy which has been carried out in my predecessor's administration, and the predecessor before, of giving guidance on speeches, so that particularly when they are given by high governmental officials - I understand 1200 speeches were submitted and given by the Defense Department, I think over 600 of them involved foreign policy matters, and were submitted to the Department of State. When I gave my State of the Union Address, I submitted that part dealing with foreign policy to the State Department for any comments, the part dealing with the Defense Department and national defense, to the Secretary of Defense for his comments. This is the way a government like ours, which is large and which deals with problems which are extremely important and sensitive, and which involve our relations around the world - this is the way we can coordinate and make effective expressions of our views. So that I am confident this hearing will be useful and it got off to a very good start with those three statements. In fact, the military seemed to me to appreciate the problem better than some civilians. (Laughter)

The Kashmir Dispute and Eugene Black

Q: Mr. President, there are persistent reports that you have proposed that Eugene Black of the World Bank lend his good offices to India and Pakistan to settle the Kashmir dispute. Could you say if this is correct, sir, and what your hopes for success might be, if so?

The President: Well, I asked Mr. Black if he would undertake to see if a solution was possible in this most difficult and delicate problem. It creates international tensions, of course, since we are assisting both of the countries. We want our assistance to be used in a way which is most effective for the people.

Obviously, peaceful relations between Pakistan and India are in the interests of world peace and the interests that we seek to promote. Mr. Black is widely regarded. He had a very successful period as negotiator on the Indus River matter and, therefore, he has generously consented, if it was decided by the parties involved that he could be helpful, to use his good offices, and I suggested that they consider this matter.

Robert Kennedy's Decision Not to Visit Moscow

Q: Mr. President, I wonder if you could tell us what considerations, other than a tight schedule went into your brother's decision not to visit Moscow on his trip?

The President: I thought his statement was as he described it.

Q: Was there any feeling, Mr. President, that high level talks would be useful until they had made some more conciliatory move on Berlin?

The President: No, I think the statement he gave was the reason.

The Trade Program

Q: Mr. President, there seems to be a feeling that you are in for a fight on your trade program. Could you say how you think this will develop, mostly along the economic lines, or sectional lines or political lines, or perhaps all three?

The President: It may be all three. I am hopeful that it will be certainly a bipartisan fight. I believe it will be. This matter received its first impetus from the report of Secretary Herter and Mr. Clayton. It - the general principles have been supported by people like Henry Cabot Lodge in his work with NATO and the Atlantic Council. It has been given a general support by President Eisenhower. So that I am hopeful that it will be a matter of bipartisan concern.

There will, of course, be sectional interests involved and there will be industrial interests involved, but I am hopeful about this because I think the facts, the necessities and our interests are so much on the side of our program that I believe that the Congress will respond.

The Strength of NATO

Q: Mr. President, are you and your military advisers completely satisfied with the makeup and strength of NATO at the present time?

The President: Well, I think we can improve NATO. I think that it's important that we add to the conventional strength of NATO. We've been emphasizing that. We, ourselves, have increased our contribution. I am hopeful that we can meet the targets which General Norstad stated as minimal if Western Europe is to be successfully defended and also if we are to have, as I have said, an alternative between nuclear holocaust and retreat. So I think it could be strengthened.

The Division of Powers

Q: Mr. President, in connection with the House Rules Committee vote, I wanted to ask you about an article that appeared this morning, and it was described as being based on an authorized interview with you. It included this sentence: "The President sees at the end of a year how nearly impossible it is to govern under the system of divided powers." Would you care to expand on that view?

The President: Yes. I haven't given any authorized interview - (laughter) - but if you want to know my views, of course there is a difficulty between a Congress and a President, an executive. We are coordinate branches. There are different views, different interests. Perspectives are different from one end of Pennsylvania Avenue to the other. I was 14 - I've been 14 times longer at one end of it than I have been at the other, so I appreciate the Congress' responsibilities.

I believe that on the particular issue that the Congress should speak its will because I believe it vitally important, particularly as these cities expand, they cross State lines. The mayors come to see us - and they've strongly supported this legislation. They move from department to department where their interests are assigned to different agencies under different conditions. This would be a very important step forward, and that's why I am going to follow a procedure of sending it to the Congress so that in this way we are bound to get a vote on it by the House and the Senate.

A Department of Urban Affairs and Housing

Q: Mr. President, if you are able to create a Department of Urban Affairs and Housing, there have been numerous reports that you would appoint Robert Weaver to this Cabinet position. Would you care to comment on these reports?

The President: Well, Mr. Weaver is the head of the Housing Agency and he was chosen for that position because he had long experience. I think he has done an outstanding job.

This would be the most important part of any new agency. If we did receive the authority, I would appoint Mr. Weaver to be the Secretary.

Ted Kennedy in Massachusetts

Q: Mr. President, your brother Teddy, in Massachusetts, seems to be running for something but none of us are very certain just what it is. Could you tell us if you have had an opportunity to discuss this with him and whether you can tell us the secret?

The President: Well, I think he's the man - he's the man who's running and he's the man to discuss it with.

American Air Bases in the Azores

Q: Mr. President, assuming the American air bases in the Portuguese Azores are vital to our security, could you explain to us if you expect the Government will have any difficulty negotiating leases - on those bases this year, especially in light of the report from Lisbon of our strained relations with Portugal?

The President: I think the Azores base is very important to us and to NATO and the negotiations will take place this year. We're hopeful that they will continue to permit us to use this base upon which 75 to 80 percent of our military air traffic to Europe depends, so that in these rather critical times in Europe that base is extremely important to us.

I'm hopeful that it will be possible for us to reach an agreement with the Portuguese for continued use of it. But that's a matter which will be negotiated between the countries.

The Price of Milk

Q: Mr. President, you said yesterday that more people ought to drink milk. None of the young marrieds I know of lay off it on account of radioactivity. They lay off it because they can hardly buy enough for children, and not themselves, on account of the price. Now, how is it that with the butter priced off the table and milk so high they can't buy it, we have surpluses that we buy up and give away?

The President: The price of milk has not - well, I don't have the latest figures here - in the last 12 months, overall consumer prices have not materially increased. Perhaps - so that I'm not sure that the whole explanation of the drop within the last 12 months, which has been quite sharp - in other words, the consumption has dropped by 1½ percent, while the population was going up 1½ percent, so that I don't feel, Mrs. Craig, even though I recognize that this is an important element, I don't believe it can be explained by price alone. We are attempting to make judgments as to what can be done to increase the consumption. I don't think that the dairy farmer, who averages about, I think, 82 cents an hour, is being overcompensated for his work. So that while price obviously is a factor, it is not the total explanation.

I was attempting to reassure on radioactive, and on the matter of - and also to see if we can stimulate it by example. Mr. Salinger drank it this morning - (laughter) - with no adverse effect.

Medical Care for the Aged

Q: Mr. President, do you have real prospects that your medical-care-for-the-aged bill will come out of committee finally for a vote up or down by Congress at this session?

The President: I have real hope that there will be a vote on the medical care for the aged this year, in the Congress, yes.

House Amendment to the Postal Rate Bill

Q: Mr. President, what is your view of the House amendment to the postal rate bill which would prohibit the Post Office from distributing mail labeled as Communist propaganda?

The President: Well, I think it does not give the Attorney General - I just had the language here - it doesn't give the Attorney General very clear guidance as to what he's supposed to label Communist and political propaganda. Is he supposed to label newspapers that may be received or speeches, or whatever they may be, so that the language is somewhat vague? In addition, I think we want to realize that this is a reciprocal matter. I think in the last 12 months, ending March 31, 1961, we sent - a total of 16 million pounds of mail of all types were sent to the Iron Curtain countries. A lot of it went to friends and relatives in Iron Curtain countries, food packages and all of the rest, and we were only receiving 2,300,000 pounds.

Now, there has been a drop in the amount of mail coming in from Communist countries in the last few months, really since last spring. If there is also an effort made by the Communists to deny us ability to send mail, it's going to present serious problems for a good many Americans who have been carrying on correspondence with friends and relatives. Now, I know that that's not the purpose. I think the Senate should examine the language very clearly and make sure that it's effective and is responsive to our national needs, and determine whether the rather generalized instructions to the Attorney General fall within the necessity of legal precision.

I think the American people are used to hearing all sides. I don't think that they are particularly impressed by a good deal of what I have seen of propaganda. We send a good deal of mail out and I want to be sure that our rights to send our mail and our views and our correspondence to all parts of the world are not interfered with. So that I think the Senate should look at it carefully.

The Military Censorship Issue

Q: Mr. President, in your comments on the statements about the military censorship issue, you make no reference to President Eisenhower's statement of yesterday. Would you care to comment on what he had to say?

The President: No. Everyone is giving their views. I've given mine. And my views are - I think I just gave them. President Eisenhower is entitled to hold his views and express them. And as I say, I thought Mr. Lovett and these other three military hit it so precisely that I strongly endorse what they said, and I'm filled with appreciation of the fact that three distinguished members of the military said it.

Security Risks in the State Department

Q: Mr. President, two well-known security risks have recently been put on a task force in the State Department to help reorganize the Office of Security.

The President: Well, now, who?

Q: William Arthur Wieland, a well-known man who for over a year the State-

The President: And who - now I think, Mrs. McClendon, I think that - would you give me the other name?

Q: Yes, sir - J. Clayton Miller.

The President: Right. Well, now, I think the term - I would say that the term you've used to describe them is a very strong term which I would think that you should be prepared to substantiate. I am familiar with Mr. Miller's record because I happened to look at it the other day. He has been cleared by the State Department. In my opinion, the duties which he is now carrying out, he is fit for. And I have done that after Mr. Rusk and I both looked at the matter, so therefore I cannot accept your description of him.

Q: Did you both look at Mr. William Arthur Wieland, too?

The President: I am familiar with Mr. Wieland. I'm also familiar with his duties at the present time, and in my opinion, Mr. Miller and Mr. Wieland, the duties they have been assigned to, they can carry out without detriment to the interests of the United States, and I hope without detriment to their characters by your question.

Radical Right Organizations

Q: Mr. President, considering that the one ingredient in all these radical right organizations seems to be anticommunism or possibly superpatriotism, would it be feasible or useful for you, or even for the Republican leaders, to appeal to these people to stop tilting at windmills and to make a common cause against the enemy? My question really is, do you think there is any merit in this idea?

The President: Well, I did attempt in my speech at Seattle, my speech in Los Angeles, and in other speeches to indicate what I consider to be the challenges that the United States faces, and I would hope that - there have been others who have done the same thing and I think we should keep that up. And I am hopeful that we can turn the energies of all patriotic Americans to the great problems that we face at home and abroad. The problems are extremely serious. I share their concern about the cause of freedom. But I do think that we ought to look at what the challenges are with some precision and not concern ourselves on occasions with matters such as character or integrity of the Chief Justice or other matters which are really not even in question.

Scholarship Aid for Reservists and National Guardsmen

Q: Mr. President, it has been reported that you have indicated an interest in the provision of some sort of scholarship aid, perhaps something similar to the GI bill, for the reservists and National Guardsmen that were recently called up. Could you give us a little clearer picture of your views? For example, would you favor something such as Senator Yarborough of Texas' cold war GI bill?

The President: Well now, on the general question of whether we should have a special scholarship program for reservists or draftees, this is a matter that is being considered. Senator Yarborough's bill was not in the administration's program on education this year. It involved a rather large sum of money, $350 million, at a time when we were making rather broad recommendations for our education. But whether there should be some special program of selected scholarships which would be available for competition is a matter which we are looking at, and which I hope to discuss with Senator Yarborough.

Strontium Levels in Milk

Q: Mr. President, as you have just emphasized, present strontium 90 levels in milk are certainly well within an acceptable range. But since milk is a major source of calcium and adequate calcium in the body apparently does help prevent deposits of strontium 90 in bone, it has been suggested that strontium removal plants, such as the one developed by the Government might be adopted by all the dairy industry to provide the Nation with a nutritious as well as a radiation-free source of calcium. Would you give us your views on this? What would you think of it?

The President: My information is that - and I think, as I stated yesterday, that this has not reached a point where any action such as you've suggested is necessary. Milk is safe and can be drunk with strong conviction that it's assisting health and not working against good health. Now, if the situation should ever change, we would inform the American people and take appropriate action. But for the present, the cow itself, along with other factors, makes our milk very safe and useful to drink.

Q: Yes, that is what I pointed out. The only thing is it has been suggested that many other foods are not as yet safe and do add to the strontium

burden in the body, and if one has a calcium-free source that is free of con-
tamination, this helps build up a resistance for these other things. It was
suggested from that point of view rather than because it is dangerous now or
even in the future. (Laughter)

The Electricians Union's Contract in New York

Q: Mr. President, in the face of your economic message urging both man-
agement and labor to moderate their policy regarding price and wage increases,
would you tell us how you feel about the electricians union's contract in New
York which calls for a 25-hour week?

The President: I stated, I think at the Steelworkers convention, before I
was elected, and I've stated since then, that I thought that the 40-hour week
was the - in view of the many obligations that we had upon us at home and
abroad, represented the national goal at this time. In addition, I've also
stated that I thought that labor-management contract should be settled within
the realm of productivity increases, so that there would be a beneficial effect
on price stability.

Now, this contract did not meet either one of those two standards, and
therefore I regretted it.

The Political and Economic Integration of Europe

Q: Mr. President, how do you feel or how does this Government feel about
the political as distinct from the economic integration of Western Europe?
President de Gaulle has seemed to stress confederation as distinct from federa-
tion, and the British don't seem to be very eager for a common parliament. What
is this Government's position?

The President: Well, we support the Treaty of Rome, and of course that
must be interpreted, and which is now a subject of negotiation between the Six,
and will also be a subject of negotiation with the British, particularly because of their Commonwealth obligations and so on. So we'll have to wait to
see how it evolves. But the general position of this administration, and the
previous one, was support of the Treaty of Rome, support of the integration of
Europe, because as Europe is strengthened we are strengthened. So that while
the details are matters, of course, of judgment for them, the general movement
we believe to be in the interests of the Atlantic Community.

Wider Trade Protection of Textiles

Q: Mr. President, more than one-third of the Senate and several influen-
tial members of the House have petitioned you today seeking wider trade protec-
tion on textiles. In view of their importance to your trade fight in Congress,
could you tell us how you plan to meet the request?

The President: Yes, I received a letter today from both, a good many members of the House and the Senate in regard to the negotiations which are going
to take place beginning next Monday, and they were anxious that in those negotiations, that we would be mindful of the desirability of maintaining a relationship between imports and national production. I believe last year's
imports of textiles were around 7 percent - that's 1960 - and they had gone
from 4 percent to 7 percent from 1957 to 1960, and then dropped to about 6 percent. I think that this was a request for us to be concerned about any agreement which might provide a substantial increase in textiles, and we are very
mindful of that, and we recognize the effect of all of this upon the trade bill
itself. So this is a matter of concern to us, too.

The Conference at Punta del Este

Q: Mr. President, could you tell us what the United States hopes will emerge from the present conference at Punta del Este?

The President: Well, I think that what we - I think - will see emerge is an implementation of the - really rather an effective statement of the concern that is felt by the people of Latin America and this country at the intrusion of communism into this - into our OAS family. And I'm confident that the negotiations that are now going on, and that the deliberations of the countries will be - will make their hostility to communism and totalitarianism very clear.

The Bill on Educational Television

Q: Mr. President, could you give us your views of the bill on educational television which is now pending in the House Rules Committee?

The President: I am sorry, I don't know enough about it to give you an informed opinion.

Government's Investigation of Racketeering

Q: Mr. President, in a very abbreviated interview this morning, the Attorney General said that the Government was looking into racketeering, the operations of racketeering, racketeers, in the stock exchange. Could you give us - could you comment upon this problem or give us any indication of the extent of it?

The President: I think I would rather have you go back to the Attorney General on it.

Fragmentation of the Communist Bloc

Q: Mr. President, in your speech out in Columbus, Ohio, you spoke of a fragmentation in the Communist bloc. Could you elaborate, tell us a little more about this trouble in the Red paradise?

The President: No, I did make a reference in my State of the Union to the closer integration of the free world at a time when that particular trend had not been the most noticeable trend in other parts of the world. But I think that until the pattern of the future is clearer and relationships are more precise, a good deal of our information must necessarily be surmised, and I don't really feel it would be useful at this time to explore it in more detail.

The President's Conservative Tendencies

Q: Mr. President, it has been suggested by columnists and others that over the course of the past year you have become more conservative, particularly that you recognize that the country may not be ready for the full Democratic platform. Could you comment on this assessment and tell us if you have changed your view of the role of your leadership?

The President: No, I consider the progress we made last year in implementing the platform was very beneficial: minimum wage, social security, depressed areas, and all the others, advances in the field of foreign aid authorization. We have sent up a good many more programs this year that were suggested in the platform. And I feel we're making, and going to make, progress toward carrying out the commitments of the country and the party. And we're staying at it.

Reporter: *Thank you, Mr. President.*

THE PRESIDENT'S NEWS CONFERENCE OF

JANUARY 31, 1962

The President: Good afternoon.

I want to - I take pleasure in welcoming the editor of Izvestia and Mrs. Adzhubei, to this Presidential press conference. He is, as I said, editor of a paper which carried our interview last November, and he's also a member of the Central Committee, and therefore combines two hazardous professions, of politics and journalism, and also Mrs. Adzhubei, who is the daughter of the Chairman. We're glad to have them here to observe an ancient American custom.

Secondly, I want to express my satisfaction, and I believe that of all Americans, at the action taken by the Organization of American States at the Punta del Este conference. Six resolutions, representing a six-point program, were passed by the conference early this morning. Not a single nation joined Cuba in voting against these resolutions. The 20 other nations of this conference joined in a vigorous declaration against Communist penetration of this hemisphere, in full support for the Alliance for Progress, and to expel Cuba from the Inter-American Defense Board. For the first time, the independent American states have declared with one voice that the concept of Marxist Leninism is incompatible with the inter-American system, and they have taken explicit steps to protect the hemisphere's ability to achieve progress with freedom.

Thirdly, I have an important announcement to make about the national stockpiling program. The purpose of this program over a period of several years has been to store for future use those strategic materials which might be essential to the Nation in the event of an emergency. After a review of this program, upon assuming the responsibilities of office, I was astonished to find that the total stockpile now amounts to some $7.7 billion worth of materials, an amount that exceeds our emergency requirements as presently determined by nearly $3.4 billion. In some cases the Government had acquired more than seven times the amount that could possibly be used. For example, the value of the aluminum in this stockpile exceeds the amounts we would need for 3 years in the event of war by $347 million. The excess supply of nickel is $103 million. This administration has taken steps to halt any new acquisitions to the stockpile with the exception of three items, still critically short, and on which we have spent less than $2 million. Unfortunately, the surplus of other materials is still growing, as the result of contracts negotiated prior to this administration's taking office.

It was apparent to me that this excessive storage of costly materials was a questionable burden on public funds and, in addition, a potential source of excessive and unconscionable profits. Last spring a detailed check was ordered, and our information to date has convinced me that a thorough investigation is warranted. The cloak of secrecy which surrounded this program may have been justified originally to conceal our shortages, but this is no longer the case, and secrecy now is only an invitation to mismanagement.

I have therefore discussed this matter with Senator Symington, chairman of the Senate stockpiling subcommittee. He agrees that the program should be completely explored, and without delay. I have assured him that we will make available to his subcommittee all the material we have already discovered and that the executive branch will cooperate fully with any investigation.

In the meantime, I have directed the various departments and agencies to accelerate their review of material requirements and I am appointing a commission to make a detailed review of our stockpiling policies, programs, and goals, in the light of changed defense strategy and improved technology. I am very much aware of the intricate and interrelated problems involved in this area, including the difficulties experienced by certain domestic mineral industries, the impact of world markets, and the heavy reliance of certain countries on producing one or more of these minerals. And I can say that we will take no action which will disrupt commodity prices.

All of these factors in a careful review of the program will be taken into account, but the full facts on this matter must be open to the public.

QUESTIONS

Prospects for Settlement of Issues of Concern to the U.S. and the USSR

Q: Mr. President, do these recent manifestations of cordiality between the United States and Russia - I am speaking specifically of your hospitality to Mr. Adzhubei, Mr. Salinger's conference in Paris with Mr. Kharlamov, Mr. Salinger's forthcoming visit to Moscow - do these evidences equate in any way with an increase of improvement in the prospects for settlement of such basic issues as Berlin?

The President: Well, of course, we would like to have a settlement of the basic issues which have divided the Soviet Union and the United States. The meetings - I think two meetings took place between Mr. Adzhubei and Mr. Salinger, and out of those meetings came an interview which I think was very useful in helping us to express the viewpoint of the United States on serious problems to the people of the Soviet Union.

The conversations in Paris last weekend were directed to the same question. Mr. Salinger's visit in response to an invitation that he's received, is also directed to improving communications. We hope that as communications improve, that the problems which cause tension and danger to the world will lessen. The negotiations on these matters, however, of policy, are matters which are being conducted in this case by Ambassador Thompson, who, I believe, has a meeting with Foreign Minister Gromyko, tomorrow, at the third meeting, so-called probes in regard to the matter of Berlin.

We're hopeful that these will bring a happy result. But I believe that any exchange of information, any exchange of views, any cooperation of any kind in these very hazardous times is very useful, so we're glad for them. And we are glad when they treat Americans as they do with courtesy when they visit Moscow.

Statements on Stockpiling

Q: Mr. President, in your statements on stockpiling, is there any implication of wrongdoing by an individual?

The President: I think that - no, I'm not making any implication. The only thing is I think that this is a large amount of money to be invested. I think the whole matter should be carefully looked into, contracts and all the rest, profits and so on. I would make no statement other than to say it's a matter which lends itself to a careful scrutiny by Senator Symington's committee and Senator Symington is most anxious to initiate such an investigation, which we both discussed last week and which we feel is overdue.

But we'll certainly wait, in answer to your question, on the investigation, before making any judgments.

U.S. Intentions at Punta del Este

Q: Mr. President, have you any reaction to the failure of some of our neighbors to the south - I am thinking of Argentina and Brazil - to go along with us all the way in our ambitions at Punta del Este?

The President: No. I think that I've indicated what I consider to be the most significant fact, which is on the basic question of the compatability of the Communist system with the inter-American system. I think there was a unanimity.

President's Urban Affairs Program

Q: Mr. President, some of the critics of your urban affairs plan charge that it's an invasion of States' and local rights. Would you comment on that, and would you also comment on it in a larger frame? For instance, what do you think of the argument that big government, so called, might not need to be so big if State and local governments were more efficient in fulfilling their duties?

The President: Well, in regard to the specific question on the - I don't believe that such a Cabinet position would interfere with the States. In my opinion it would supplement their efforts. There is a responsibility which the States have for various - and each city has - for certain important functions in the life of every citizen, but the Federal Government also has one.

There is a Department of Agriculture, which has contact with each individual farmer in the United States. That does not interfere with the county responsibility or the State responsibility.

Now, in the urban message I sent up yesterday, I pointed out that in our 10 leading cities, the citizens pay 35 percent of the income taxes paid in the United States. They have many serious problems which are increasing in time, particularly as our population increases by 3 million a year. I believe that these problems are entitled to a place at the Cabinet table.

Now, I'm interested in charges about big government - and I read these speeches, and then I receive a wire asking for the Federal Government to take over the operations of the New Haven Railroad. And we send a wire back to the States, after having put $35 million into maintaining that railroad: "What action are the States prepared to take?"

My experience usually is that these matters are put to the Federal Government by the request of cities, of States, or individual groups and it's not a question of the Federal Government anxious to extend its role, but rather that there is a need and no one responds to it and the National Government, therefore, must meet its responsibility. And I believe that with two-thirds of our people in the cities of the United States that they should be up alongside of the others in the Cabinet, so that we can deal more effectively with these programs.

The Situation in Laos

Q: Mr. President, there has been renewed fighting in Laos. Would you give us your evaluation of the situation there, whether or not this fighting would threaten a political settlement, and also the situation in South Viet-Nam?

The President: Yes, the - of course if the fighting - hostilities began, the hope of a settlement would be substantially diminished. There have been, as you know, a series of tentative agreements. There is still a disagreement over who shall hold particular cabinet positions. It is my understanding that there is scheduled to be a meeting at Luang Prabang on February 2 between those leaders of the various groups within Laos. It is my earnest hope that both sides will refrain from hostilities after a cease fire which has been in effect generally since last May, so that we can see if a peaceful solution can be reached. Because if hostilities begin, they bring reactions and counterreactions, and all of the work which has gone on in the negotiations of the last months could go up in smoke and fire. So that I'm hopeful that both sides will give the parties who are involved an opportunity to meet and continue and see if a solution can be reached, and I'm hopeful that both sides will work earnestly toward that goal.

The situation in Viet-Nam is one that's of great concern to us. There were, I think last week, nearly 500 incidents, deaths, ambushes and so on. It's extremely serious. The United States has increased its help to the government. I'm hopeful that the control commission will continue to examine that and come to some conclusions in regard to the Geneva accords.

We are anxious for a peace in that area, and we are assisting the government to maintain its position against this subterranean war.

Republican Efforts to Unseat Democrats

Q: Mr. President, a political question, sir. The Republicans are holding leadership conferences around the country, including one here in Washington today, with the purpose of upsetting the Democratic balance of power in congressional elections that are coming up. Would you care to comment on the task these Republican teachers have, and with what hope they might look toward success in the fall?

The President: No, I think that - I'm sure that I don't know who's giving the leadership direction but I'm sure that they'll have a varied program!

Reintroduction of Trade with Cuba

Q: Mr. President, as part of our effort to show our good faith as a result of the Punta del Este meeting, is there any possibility that this Government might reduce its trade with Cuba? Last year I understand we purchased from Cuba about $17 million worth of goods in excess of what we sold, largely in the field of tobacco. I was thinking of giving up cigars for the duration. Is that under consideration?

The President: Well, as you know, the trade which - the things we sell to Cuba have been foods and medicines, which I think the total amount, as I recall, was around $12 or $13 million. I think any decision in regard to trade would better wait until the Secretary returns and we've had a chance to discuss the matter with him.

The Lincoln Park Problem

Q: Mr. President, visitors who go out to visit Lincoln Park on East Capital Street are dismayed to find it a slum. Congress has authorized and the National Council of Negro Women will erect there a memorial stadium and a statue of the great woman educator, Mary Bethune. Now the transit company proposes to put an eight-lane freeway between the park and the Capitol, cutting it off. Could you inquire into that, and see if the freeway could be put further out beyond the park?

The President: Yes, I will. (Laughter)

You're very gentle today, Mrs. Craig.

The Purchase of United Nations' Bonds

Q: Mr. President, does the United States intend to precondition the purchase of the $100 million of United Nations bonds on support of the other $100 million by other countries, and, if so, would not such a precondition serve to raise a question of earnestness in the support of the U.N. by all nations?

The President: Yes, I think there's an obvious relationship between the amount that we purchase and the amount that other countries take. We stated that we would take - that we would consider taking $100 million worth of the bonds. It was our hope that other countries would take $100 million, I think the Canadians have indicated around $7 million, and the British $12 million, and I think the Scandinavian countries have given it careful consideration. I think Mr. Black, of the World Bank, has written to other governments, so that in answer to your question, there is a relationship obviously between what we could do and what others will do. I'm hopeful that both will meet their responsibilities in the matter.

Supervision Over the CIA

Q: Mr. President, in the debate just terminated in the Senate over the confirmation of John McCone as Director of the Central Intelligence Agency, a considerable body of opinion indicated that they were concerned about the supervision over CIA. Have you done anything in your administration to increase Executive supervision over CIA, and what is your view toward giving Congress a greater share over the supervision of CIA?

The President: Well, as you know, Congress does have groups that have a responsibility over CIA. They provide the budget, and they also provide - receive reports and confer and exercise supervision at the present time.

Secondly, I appointed General Taylor some months ago to be my representative in regard to matters affecting intelligence, and there are intergovernmental meetings in response to any activities that CIA might carry out with general supervision and it's a matter which has concerned me personally increasingly. So that those are the areas where there is control and I think it's up to all those who have control, as well as to Mr. McCone and the members of the CIA, to attempt to carry out their functions in a way which serves our interest, which I'm sure is their objective.

Visit to the USSR

Q: Mr. President, speaking of going to Moscow, could you tell us under what conditions you would accept an invitation to visit the Soviet Union?

The President: I would think that an invitation - and an acceptance of an invitation - would probably wait on the easing of the tensions which unfortunately surround our relationship. And so that, for the present, of course, until we have significant breakthroughs, that sort of journey would probably not be considered useful by either country. But we, of course, are always hopeful and we're making every effort that we can to bring an easing of tensions. And that's why Mr. Thompson is pursuing his course, and that's why we are making the other efforts that we're making.

Alliance for Progress Program

Q: Mr. President, could you tell us whether you expect any difficulty in Congress with your Alliance for Progress program by reason of the opposition of some of the bigger Latin American countries at the Punta del Este conference?

The President: I think that I could probably - the Congress, of course, has to make that judgment. In my opinion, the program is very essential; I think it was endorsed by 20 nations, the Alliance for Progress. This is a long struggle to improve the life of the people in this hemisphere. I think we must go ahead, and I'm confident that the Members of the Congress when they come back will feel the same way. So that what has happened recently, in my opinion, makes more desirable and essential the Alliance for Progress. That is where our efforts ought to be, and that's where we can serve the cause of freedom and I think the interhemisphere system best. So I'm hopeful that Congress will agree.

Government Supervision of the Television Networks

Q: Mr. President, two network chiefs recently have expressed fear of Government supervision of the television networks. The FCC has denied any such intention. Can you foresee circumstances under which FCC supervision of television programming might become necessary or useful?

The President: No. Do you mean of a different kind than now, a different relationship than that which now exists?

Q: Yes, over program content.

The President: No. I don't. I think, as you know, the FCC does have certain regulations with regard to the percentage used in public service. Mr. Minow has attempted to use not force, but to use encouragement in persuading the networks to put better children's programs, more public service programs. I don't know of anyone - and Mr. Minow has already denied considering changing the basic relationship which now exists.

Laos

Q: Mr. President, in connection with the situation in Laos, is Mr. Harriman in touch with his opposite Soviet number in order to get the cooperation of the Soviet Union in reducing the heavy infiltration of Viet-Nam units in Laos?

The President: Mr. Harriman, the Assistant Secretary, has indicated, as has the State Department, as have I, the great dangers in - to both sides in a resumption of hostilities. And we are making every effort to attempt to get an accord before this cease-fire, which appears to be strained somewhat, after many months, to try to get an accord before we have a breakdown of the cease-fire, and that is true of both sides.

Civil Rights Legislation

Q: Mr. President, last year the administration put forward no civil rights legislation. Now the administration has submitted a bill on literacy tests in voting and Secretary Goldberg has endorsed "in principle" an FEPC bill. Does this mean the administration has suddenly decided to go further on the legislative route in the civil rights field?

The President: I think that my State of the Union Address said that we would comment on the various bills, of which there are a great many that have been introduced. And that's what Secretary Goldberg did. In addition, I made specific reference to the question of voting, and literacy tests, and Senator Mansfield has indicated action would be on that bill. So it seems to me that we are where we said we would be in the State of the Union Address.

Floyd Patterson and Sonny Liston

Q: Mr. President, is there a small war imminent between Floyd Patterson and Sonny Liston?

The President: Well, that's a matter that you ought to talk to Mr. Patterson about. He hasn't confided fully in me.

Items Which Are Understockpiled

Q: Mr. President, in your statement on stockpiling policy, you referred to three items you felt were understockpiled. You didn't indicate what those were, and what considerations apply. Could you supply those for us?

The President: I think that this - as I say, the whole matter of stockpiling is a matter which would wait on Senator Symington. I did say that they involved, I think, the sum of about $2 million, so they're not significant, but they are in short enough supply so that we are continuing those purchases. But they are not of major proportions, though they are in this case significant.

The Belasco Theater

Q: Mr. President, they told us you took a cab ride or a limousine drive across from your house last night, at Lafayette Square, to inspect it. And in connection with that, you are familiar with the old Belasco Theater of Lafayette Square which now houses the United Services Organization home for the thousands of enlisted military people in the area. That theater as you know is going to be torn down. Does the Government and specifically you, as Commander in Chief, have any plans to place these people in a suitable area?

The President: The USO?

Q: Yes, sir.

The President: Well I'm sure we'll be delighted to cooperate with the USO in getting satisfactory facilities. Last night I was looking at the question of the building next to Blair House, whether that ought to come down, the court building, whether that ought to come down or trees should be planted there, and I thought that - in agreement with the Fine Arts Commission that trees should be planted there. (Laughter)

Collapse of Test Ban Negotiations with the Soviet Union

Q: Mr. President, what effect do you believe the most recent collapse of the nuclear test ban negotiations with the Soviet Union will have on the possibilities for success in the coming March 14 Geneva disarmament talks? And will this collapse have any effect on your decision, if any, to resume nuclear testing?

The President: Well, no progress was being made in developing a test ban which would have adequate inspection, and therefore we felt that it should be moved into the general disarmament conference, which begins on the 14th.

This failure, as I said somewhat earlier, represents the biggest disappointment of my first year in office, and continues to be a disappointment, because every action here as I say, breeds a response, and we have been anxious from the beginning to get an agreement which would prohibit tests with an adequate inspection. Now, we haven't been able to adjust that satisfactorily. Therefore it will put an additional burden and an additional opportunity before the Disarmament Commission. And of course our failure to get an agreement does increase the likelihood of various countries testing. That's one of the reasons why I was anxious that we get an agreement.

Possibility of Agreement with the USSR

Q: Mr. President, on this question of the changed atmosphere between the U.S. and the Soviet Union of late, just to set the record straight, is this so far entirely a matter of atmospheric or is there in any of the negotiating issues across the board any indication of the possibility of an agreement?

The President: I would say that on the question of Laos, that there has been evidence of a desire by the Soviet Union and the United States to come to the agreement along the lines suggested by Chairman Khrushchev and myself last June. On the question of Berlin and Germany, I don't think that significant progress as yet has been made. But I do think, as I've said, that the means of communication and the channels of communication should be kept very widely open, which has been a basic premise of ours for the last few months; which is the reason that Ambassador Thompson is working. Any way we can lessen the chance of danger, as I said at the beginning, we will explore. So that I think that attempts to separate the facts of the matter from what you would call atmosphere, though atmosphere can be very important in our lives, as we see every day.

Reduction of Oil Imports

Q: Sir, independent oil producers have urged you to take action quickly, even before completion of the Ellis study about June, to reduce oil imports. Now this week the independents are urging Congress to write into your trade program a provision reducing crude imports about 250,000 barrels daily and limiting them in the future to 14 percent of domestic crude oil production. Sir, do you think that the domestic producers will receive any relief from Executive action in the near future, and do you favor tightening of import controls on oil by such legislation as they propose?

The President: Well, in the first place, as you've suggested, this is a matter which is still being examined by Mr. Ellis' commission. In regard to legislation, I'm not familiar with this proposal; it's the first I've heard about it. There are, of course, obvious difficulties traditionally in attempting to write in quota restrictions on various commodities in any kind of trade legislation, because one begets another, and we can find ourselves with a whole series of limitations and exclusions which is the reason, I think, that Franklin Roosevelt originally came forward with the reciprocal trade program. But we are very much aware of the concern, the fact that in some of our States that the wells are down 10 or 11 days a month, and that this is a matter of serious concern to a good many Americans. I'll have to leave it at that at the present time because the study is not complete and I'd have to examine the legislation, other than my general comments on it.

The Urban Affairs Department and the Race Question

Q: Mr. President, to go back to the Urban Affairs Department, the Republicans say that you were playing politics last week when you said that you would like to have Mr. Robert Weaver, a distinguished Negro, to head that department. They also accuse you of injecting the race issue into this whole matter. Would you care to comment?

The President: No, I merely said in response to a question that it was quite obvious that Mr. Weaver is the very successful, able head of the - by far the largest division which would be placed in an urban department. It was well rumored that Mr. Weaver would be appointed to the Cabinet. In fact, it may have played some part in some decisions in regard to the matter, so I think it's much better to get it out in the open. Obviously, if the legislation had been passed, Mr. Weaver would have been appointed. It was well known on the Hill. The American people might as well know it.

Criticism of Mr. Salinger

Q: Mr. President, Congressman Alger of Texas, today criticized Mr. Salinger as a "young and inexperienced White House publicity man" - (laughter) - and questioned the advisability of having him visit the Soviet Union. I wonder if you have any comments.

The President: I know there are always some people who feel that Americans are always young and inexperienced, and foreigners are always able and tough and great negotiators. But I don't think that the United States would have acquired its present position of leadership in the free world if that view were correct.

Now he also, as I saw the press, said that Mr. Salinger's main job was to increase my standing in the Gallup poll. Having done that, he is now moving on - (laughter) - to improve our communications.

As I say, Mr. Salinger and Mr. Adzhubei are responsible for our interview, which I think was very helpful. And I think anything we can do - I don't think we should worry so much about Americans traveling abroad; I think they've acquitted themselves and so will Mr. Salinger. I'm sure that some people in the Soviet Union are concerned about Mr. Adzhubei's visits abroad. (Laughter)

A Tax Cut as an Anti-Recession Measure

Q: Mr. President, with regard to your authority to cut taxes as an anti-recession measure, a Democratic member of the House Ways and Means Committee said the other day that no such authority was necessary because a request would go through Congress faster than a declaration of war. What do you think of this and of the argument that this power might be used for political reasons as well as economic?

The President: Well, as you recall, in our proposal we harnessed it to a statistical base which was charted on the recessions which you have had since World War II and, therefore, would go off or be prepared to go off after we reached a certain peak of unemployment after a certain period of months. That is the purpose of it. So that it seemed to us it was a tool which would be most valuable.

As you know, Arthur Burns, who was Chairman of the Economic Advisers under President Eisenhower, has endorsed this proposal. It's been endorsed by people on all sides of the spectrum. There is nothing more costly, nothing more expensive than recurrent recessions. And if we can take action early enough, it was felt by economists and businessmen, the Council - for example, the CED and others, that this would be a way of easing the impact.

If you can tell me anything more expensive than the large deficits we ran as a result of the '58 and '60 recessions and the unemployment we had as a result of those recessions - I consider this to be soundly based.

Now, if we cannot get it, then we will have to consider the action that you've suggested. But I think it would be a very important standby tool. This

economy is a very - it fluctuates and moves - and we don't want to have a recovery in '62 and a lack of vigor in that recovery in '63 when early action
might maintain the economy and maintain employment. I hope this will be given
a long look, even though I realize the Ways and Means Committee has other priorities. But in my judgment, in the long run we have a good chance to have it
accepted.

Reporter: Thank you, Mr. President.

THE PRESIDENT'S NEWS CONFERENCE OF

FEBRUARY 7, 1962

The President: I have two announcements to make.

In the next days and weeks, there will be a good deal said and written about
two American policies, one in the field of disarmament, and the other in the
field of preparations which have already been announced, to be in a position to
test in the atmosphere if our national security indicates that it's desirable.

There is no inconsistency here in my judgment, because I think that we would
be deeply irresponsible not to follow both courses. We are making necessary
preparations for testing because of the wholly new situation created by the secretly prepared and massive series of 40 to 50 tests conducted by the Soviet Union last fall while active efforts for a test ban agreement were still going
forward.

This Soviet action took place in the face of a whole series of actions and
efforts on our side. In the last year we have made at least a dozen new moves
in a search for an agreement, and we have restated again and again our willingness to sign an effective treaty. We stated it before, during, and after the
Soviet tests. The Soviet tests not only ended the moratorium; they presented us
with grave questions as to the long range safety of avoiding all atmospheric
tests while the U.S.S.R. remains able to prepare in secret, and then test at
will.

We are amply strong for today and tomorrow, but we must consider the future,
too. These questions are still being reviewed. And there will be no testing
that is not clearly necessary, but I have ordered preparations because I shall
not hesitate to order the tests themselves if it is decided that they are necessary to maintain the effective deterrent strength of the United States.

Any other course would imply unilateral disarmament, and would serve no true
course of peace. But at the same time, and with equal energy, we shall go on
seeking a path towards a genuine and controlled disarmament. What this means
for atmospheric testing is methods of inspection and control which could protect
us against a repetition of prolonged secret preparations for a sudden series of
major tests. If and when effective agreements can be reached, no nation will be
more ready than ours to see all testing brought under control, and nuclear weapons as well. The fact that we must prudently meet our defense needs in the
meantime is only one more reason for working towards disarmament. So I repeat
that these two courses are consistent with each other. We must follow both at
once. It would be a great error to suppose that either of them makes the other
wrong or unnecessary.

I wholly disagree with those who would put all their faith in an arms race
and abandon their efforts for disarmament. But I equally disagree with those

who would allow us neglect of our defensive needs in the absence of effective agreements for controlled disarmament.

Secondly, I want to take this opportunity to express my pleasure at the Senate's action yesterday, retaining in the college aid bill the provision for 212,000 college scholarships. It is urgent that this provision be retained in the conference and not dropped out or compromised by another student loan program. A loan of $4,000 or $5,600 would enable many bright but needy students to receive 4 years of college, working his way for the balance. But one-half of all American families earn less than $5,600 a year, and they simply cannot take on that kind of debt. Colleges which are caught in financial squeezes themselves can afford to offer scholarships to only about 10 percent of their students. All American parents want their children to have an opportunity to go to college, but only a few are able to put aside the $7,000 which the average 4-year course now requires. The cost has nearly doubled since 1950 and, as I said in my message, this Nation as a result loses each year the talents of hundreds and thousands of our most talented high school graduates who cannot afford to postpone earning a living for 4 more years. This is a real national and individual loss, and I hope the Congress will keep the scholarships in the bill.

QUESTIONS

The Public School Bill

Q: Mr. President, in connection with your public school bill, two points: As I understand it, last year's piece of legislation is, for all intents and purposes, dead in the Rules Committee, and Mr. Powell has said he won't move unless urgently requested by you to do so. And now today, Cardinal Spellman said passage would bring an end to the parochial school system. Should your message be interpreted as that urging that Mr. Powell has talked about, and can the religious question be beaten?

The President: Well, as you know, when the Rules Committee, by a vote of eight to seven, tabled the bill last year, the procedures would now require a two-thirds vote of the Rules Committee to send it to the floor. I wish we could get a two-thirds vote. If we cannot, then another bill would have to come out of the House Education and Labor Committee, and I am hopeful that members of the Labor Committee - Education Committee - who did send the previous bill to the Rules Committee in the hope it would go to the floor - I'm hopeful that they will take action again. And because I think it is such an urgent matter, I will do everything I can to have the Congress take favorable action on this subject this year.

Now, in regard to the second part of the question, I took the oath to defend the Constitution. The position which I've taken on this matter I've taken after legal advice from the Attorney General, and from the counsel at the Department of HEW.

It is a - I said the maximum which I thought we could carry on under the United States Constitution, and as I take my oath to defend it, that would be my position, unless the Supreme Court decision should change the previous interpretation which had been made of that constitutional provision. So I am going to continue to take the position I now take, unless - based on constitutional grounds - unless there is a new judgment by the Supreme Court.

The Extent of the Battle in South Viet-Nam

Q: Mr. President, there seems to be some doubt, at least on the local level and in the region where this is going on, as to the right of the American people and the rest of the world to know the extent of the battle in South Viet-Nam. Could you tell us, sir, what the situation there is? How deeply are we involved in what seems to be a growing war and what are the rights of the people to know what our forces are doing?

The President: There is a war going on in South Viet-Nam. I think that last week there were over 500 killings, assassinations, bombings. The casualties are high. It's a - I said last week - a subterranean war, guerrilla war of increasing ferocity. The United States, since the end of the Geneva accord setting up the South Vietnamese Government as an independent government, has been assisting Viet-Nam economically to maintain its independence and viability and also had sent training groups out there, which have been expanded in recent weeks as the attacks on the government and the people of South Viet-Nam have increased.

We are out there on training and on transportation, and we are assisting in every way we properly can, the people of South Viet-Nam who with the greatest courage and under danger are attempting to maintain their freedom.

Now, this is an area where there is a good deal of danger and it's a matter of information. We don't want to have information which is of assistance to the enemy - and it's a matter which I think will have to be worked out with the Government of Viet-Nam, which bears the primary responsibility.

Muzzling of the Military at the Pentagon

Q: My question concerns the impasse which has arisen between Secretary Mc-Namara and the Senate subcommittee inquiring into the alleged muzzling of the military at the Pentagon. Do you support the Secretary, sir, in his refusal to identify the reviewers who have made specific changes in speeches, and have you any suggestion on how the impasse may be resolved?

The President: Well, I'd like to first review exactly what the Secretary of Defense has made available to the committee. He has made available every speech that was given; he has made available all the changes, in each speech, which was suggested by the 14 or 15 reviewers, two-thirds of whom are military officers, most of whom have had distinguished military records; he has made available the names of all of the reviewers. He has made - he has told the committee that he will make all of the reviewers available.

He has also informed the committee that he will send an explanation for every change and the arguments for it. What he has not done, and what he, in my opinion, should not do, is attempt to subject each of these men to a long interrogation as to, personally, the reasons for which they might have taken on this word or that word. The responsibility is Secretary McNamara's and he is going to accept that responsibility and, in my opinion, that is the only way that a department can function. If he is going to get honest and loyal support from those who work for him in carrying out his policies, then Secretary McNamara must accept the responsibility, and he does accept it.

And I think he has been extremely cooperative with the committee, and I don't think that Mr. McNamara or I, however, can agree to a harassment of individuals who are only carrying out the policies dictated by their superiors. And I think that Mr. McNamara has cooperated very fully and will continue to do so in the areas which I've named.

Q: Well, sir, would you recommend that he invoke Executive privilege, if necessary?

The President: If necessary, definitely.

U.S. Strength vs. Soviet Strength

Q: Mr. President, your statement that a wholly new situation has been created by the Soviet nuclear tests suggests, or might be interpreted to mean that they have made some breakthrough, perhaps even overtaken us in nuclear capability. Can you tell us what your estimate of our strength versus theirs is in the light of their tests?

The President: My statement today indicates our feeling about our relative position today and tomorrow, but this is a matter, of course, which is of continuing concern. These tests are very intensive. They have been in preparation for many months. And we - we could see a period go by possibly of another year or year and a half - secret preparations being made - and, suddenly, a new series of tests. And then extrapolations from those tests. And particularly when matters involving, for example, the anti-missile missile may be involved, you have to consider very carefully what the situation is going to be not today, not next year, but 3 years or 4 years from now. The United States went far along the road in an attempt to get an agreement, not only the previous administration, but this administration. As I've said before, it was obvious that these preparations had been going on for many months. Our preparations, which I have announced before, have taken many months since the Soviet tests. This is a long, drawn-out matter. And we cannot permit these tests to go on year after year, and at the same time expect that the security of the Western World is going to be protected. So I would say that my statement describes what I think is our present position, what our future risks are, and before any definite action is taken, any final decision is made, I will comment in detail to the American people for - the reasons for whatever decision we make.

Agreement with the British on the Use of Christmas Island

Q: Mr. President, in the circumstances which you have now described and with the preparations which you have ordered presumably going forward, have we now reached agreement with the British on the use of Christmas Island?

The President: A statement on that will be forthcoming very shortly, in the next 24 hours or 48 hours.

Criticism by Governor Rockefeller

Q: Mr. President, Governor Rockefeller had some harsh things to say about you last Thursday. It was in connection with your urban affairs proposal. I think he accused you of political fakery. I'm sure you know what he said. Would you want to comment on it?

The President: No. I was interested in the statement because, as you know, in 1956 and 1957, Governor Rockefeller recommended the exact proposal that we recommended. The only difference, and I was recently examining his recommendations to President Eisenhower, was that he recommended that civil defense be included, but as we have placed civil defense under the military, that really is the only significant change. So he must have, for one reason or another, changed his point of view on it.

The second reason he criticized me was because I, in response to a question, said Mr. Weaver was going to be appointed. Now, obviously, the Governor has forgotten that on March 12, 1953, when President Eisenhower sent up the proposal for the reorganization of the establishment of the Department of HEW, on the 13th it came from the White House that he was going to appoint Mrs. Hobby to be the Secretary. And the only reason that I was astonished that the Governor then forgot it was that he then became her deputy. (Laughter) And - so that it seems to me that the situation is not altogether dissimilar. However, I did read that - Mr. Reston's column in the Times, where Mr. Fulton Lewis had said that no one could get to the right of Barry Goldwater, but now I'm not so sure. (Laughter)

Disarmament and its Influenece on the Economy

Q: Mr. President, in the event the seemingly impossible task of a complete and checked to 100 percent disarmament could be arranged with the Soviets, some have speculated this would provide a very severe blow to our economy. Would you comment on that, sir?

The President: Well, the disarmament agency has made a study of that, and talked about some of the problems that might be forthcoming economically. But of course, we could never have a change comparable to the change we had in '45 when we went from a tremendously high expenditure, at a time when our gross national product was far less than it is today, into a terribly sharp drive, and had 3 very, very prosperous years of full employment, so that that would be the last reason, I think, that we would benefit. We can do so many more useful things from a social point of view with - if we had the funds that were available, so I don't think that's any argument against disarmament. The problem, of course, is to make sure our security is protected and that the inspection systems be adequate, and that's what's hung us up in the past.

Nuclear Tests

Q: Mr. President, could I ask you to amplify your statement on nuclear tests. Did you mean to suggest that any decision taken by this Government to resume atmospheric tests will be contingent upon further or future Soviet tests?

The President: No, it will be contingent upon our judgment as to the effects on our security of this series of tests, and the lessons and extrapolations that could be taken from them and what effect this might have on our security at a later date.

Disarmament

Q: Mr. President, last week in transmitting the report of the Disarmament and Arms Control Agency to Congress, you spoke not only of the hope but the expectation that significant progress toward workable disarmament would be made at Geneva. In the light of recent events, could you clarify this "expectation" part of it?

The President: Well, I put more stress on our hope and our earnest desire and our feeling that this arms race is - in the long run really doesn't provide really very great security for the human race or for all of those who are involved in it. And it's our hope, and I'm sure that we're going to make a major effort at this disarmament conference to see if we can call a halt, because nuclear weapons are spreading to other countries, and if we try to look at what the world is going to look like in 1970 or 1975, with all of the dangers that we will have with weapons of this size in the hands of a good many nations, we're going to make a major effort. I was merely attempting to indicate why I did not feel that our situation in these two areas was necessarily paradoxical.

George Romney's Criticism

Q: Mr. President, a businessman and politician named George Romney has accused your administration of not doing enough for business and your party of being dominated by labor unions. Would you take this opportunity to reply to those charges?

The President: No, I think that I'll just let Mr. Romney - I saw the program and the statement. I think that he said that neither this administration nor the previous one had done enough for business, and I think that we'll have to wait and see what - as Mr. Romney's positions evolve I think there may be a time for an appropriate comment - but I think it's still too early. (Laughter)

The John Birch Society and the Republican Party

Q: Mr. President, the Democratic organization has been criticized as unfairly attaching the John Birch Society to the Republican Party, sort of guilt by association. Do you believe that such far right radical groups properly belong in the Republican Party? (Laughter) And since General Walker is running as a Democrat in Texas, do you believe he properly belongs in the Democratic Party?

The President: That question must have taken some - work. I will say that President Eisenhower has been as vigorous in his denunciations of the John Birch Society as I have. I think that it certainly has no place in the Republican Party of President Eisenhower, and I'm sure that among the responsible heads of the Republican Party, it has no place in their party. I quite agree, it is totally alien, I think, to both parties.

Now, in regard to the second question, everybody is free to run, and the people will decide, in either party.

The Congo Airlift

Q: Mr. President, I understand that our Congo airlift has now surpassed the Berlin airlift of 1948. Could you tell me just what these supplies consist of and are we footing the bill entirely, or are the other U.N. nations also helping?

The President: Well, the cost of the airlift is being paid for by the United Nations, to which we contribute. One of the ways in which we had hoped to lessen our contribution, as I have said, or to make our contribution more effective, rather, was through the bond issue. But they've been carrying - since the United Nations has assumed a responsibility in the Congo, we have been carrying supplies into that area for many months. And in order to fulfill the purposes of the United Nations which I think extremely important to the Congo, and I think that the support we've given to the operations in the Congo in my opinion should be a source of satisfaction to us all.

Q: Mr. President, that U.N. bond issue proposal is meeting sharp criticism, at least vocally, on the Hill, one argument against it being that we are putting in more than our share, and another one that the interest rates are - there's a discrepancy. Mr. Stevenson, as you know, however, this morning, testified that it would be worth it if we just even had to give the $100 million to the U.N. Will you comment on the subject with your own thougths?

The President: Well, we have put a good many millions of dollars into support of the U.N., and we've done - we've put a lot of money in the support of a lot of operations which are designed to permit people to be free. I indicated we put a lot of money over the last 8 years into Laos. We have contributed a good deal in the effort in Viet-Nam. So that these efforts have all required expenditures of money. But we do it because we feel this is the only way that these countries can remain free. I think this bond issue represents a very sound investment for us. I am hopeful that other countries will match our effort.

The United States is carrying a heavy load, but not only in the United Nations; it's carrying a heavy load around the world. The United States is making a major effort, for example, in Berlin and Viet-Nam and in Latin America. The burdens that we carry are greater than any other free country. But I must say that if we did not carry them, in my opinion, the cause of freedom would collapse in a whole variety of ways. And, I'm hopeful as Western Europe is strengthened and the Common Market strengthened, that they will assume - not turn in, but rather out, and use the increased economic power of Western Europe to assist in maintaining the independence of these areas all around the globe, because we have been strained in our efforts to do so, although I think we ought to continue to do so, because the alternative will be a steady expansion of Communist power in all those areas, which I think would be far more expensive in the long run.

NATO as an Independent Nuclear Power

Q: Mr. President, you have just concluded talks with the Secretary General of NATO, Mr. Stikker, and also talks with General Norstad, the Supreme Commander of NATO. Could you tell us, sir, if and how far advanced are the plans to convert NATO into an independent nuclear power?

The President: I have no comment at this time. This is a matter, of course, coming from the proposal which was made by Secretary Herter and in which I stated again at Ottawa and which is a matter now of concern to the NATO Council. When the matter has proceeded to the point when decisions might be needed, then would be an appropriate time to discuss it.

Progress of the Space Program

Q: Mr. President, we have had several apparent setbacks and delays in our space field with the attempted moon shot, multiple satellite shot, and the postponement of the astronaut launching. What is your evaluation of our progress in space at this time? And have we changed our time table for landing a man on the moon?

The President: I think we - as I've said from the beginning, we've been behind. And of course, we continue to be behind. And we are running into the difficulties which come from starting late. We, however, are going to proceed. We're making a maximum effort, as you know, and the expenditures in our space program are enormous. And, to the best of my ability, the time schedule, at least I hope, has not been changed by the recent setbacks.

Stockpile Information

Q: Mr. President, stockpile information is no easier to come by than it was prior to your statement last week that a lot of this stuff ought to be declassified. Is there a disposition to hold this up for the Senate investigation or can you light a fire under some of these agencies?

The President: Well, I set up today a committee under Mr. McDermott, who is the head of the agency, with the Secretaries of Defense, State, Commerce, Labor, to look into the needs, our national needs, in the event of an emergency and also to consider the declassification of various matters.

I think all this will be completed by the time the hearings begin, and then I think the hearings will make the information very complete.

Completion of Studies on the Nuclear Test Question

Q: Mr. President, the nuclear test question has been under consideration for some months now. Could you give us some idea of the time schedule you perceive from here on with respect to completing the studies and making your decision?

The President: Well, we should know of - the studies and the examinations and the consideration by the Government should be, I would think, completed within the month.

Soviet Attitude on the Berlin Question

Q: Mr. President, there have been reports that Mr. Gromyko, in Moscow, has adopted such a negative attitude in his discussions on Berlin with Ambassador Thompson that the administration has decided that if the talks are to continue, that the Soviets will have to take the initiative in seeking the next meeting. Could you tell us whether this is true and could you discuss your outlook and reaction to these talks?

The President: No, we have not made very great progress in the talks. There has been a setting forth by each side of various positions. But I think the talks should continue and we are prepared to cooperate in continuing them - because the alternatives are not satisfactory - if we can possibly reach an accord. So we will continue to work even though the so-called probes have not produced any satisfactory common ground as yet.

The Banning of Nuclear Tests in the Atmosphere

Q: Mr. President, would the United States be willing, without further nuclear tests in the atmosphere, to sign a formal treaty with the Soviet Union banning such tests?

The President: Well, I've stated that our concern would be - we stated it before, since and, as I said, afterwards - that we would sign an agreement which provided for adequate inspections system - that's correct. But adequate inspection in regard to preparations, as well as testing. Because, otherwise -

Q: My question was hinged on further tests in the atmosphere.

The President: I understand that. We will support the passage of an effective treaty which provides for effective inspection, but we cannot take less in view of the fact of our experience of the past months, where it takes us many months to prepare for tests in the atmosphere. The Soviet Union could prepare in secret, and we would - unless we had adequate protection against a repetition of that incident. Any such test agreement obviously would be extremely vulnerable.

Christmas Island

Q: Mr. President, in connection with your forthcoming statement on Christmas Island, I understand that the United Nations Trusteeship Council, particularly Russia and India, will attempt or has attempted to prohibit all atmospheric testing in the Central and South Pacific. My question is: Is this true? If it is true, how much does it weigh in your decision to resume this testing?

The President: Well, I think that one of the reasons that Christmas Island becomes a matter of importance is because of our special trustee relationship with Eniwetok and because we are anxious to maintain the spirit as well as the letter of the trustee agreement. But in my opinion, that would not inhibit any action we might take in Christmas Island because the situation is entirely different legally and the responsibilities are entirely different, and that's also true of Johnston Island.

Steel Contract Negotiations

Q: Mr. President, with regard to the steel contract negotiations, you've said that you neither want a strike, itself, and you would like to get the contract settled soon enough to prevent the ill effects of anticipation of a strike. Do you have a date in mind by which time you think it should be settled, and how are you keeping in touch with the parties?

The President: Well, I don't have a date in mind, though I think the earlier the better because of the danger of stockpiling which will, in my opinion, produce later unemployment, if it is permitted to build up until June or July. Secretary Goldberg has been in contact with them, and I've indicated myself my strong feeling that the public interest and each of their private interests would be served by an early agreement.

Q: You have been in contact with them yourself, haven't you?

The President: Yes, I have, yes.

The Bond Issue

Q: Mr. President, just a minute ago you expressed the hope that because of our burdens the other nations would match our purchases in the bond issue. Several Senators yesterday were suggesting that we match their purchases. Would you be willing, the administration be willing, to turn this around so that -

The President: Well, I think we have to wait and see what the legislative prospects are. I think we ought to buy the $100 million worth. I think the other countries ought to buy $100 million worth of bonds. We are prepared to meet our responsibilities. I hope they will be. I think we should take an affirmative attitude towards the prospects of this and also to recognize how essential it is. Now, if this fails, then the U.N. will be, as Secretary Rusk said yesterday, in dire financial circumstances. It would obviously mean a complete - the emergency operation taking place in the Middle East and in the Congo would, of course, come to an end, unless we put in bilaterally a subsidy which would cause other countries to do a bilateral action of their own, and you would have chaos in the Congo and a defeat of any attempts to set up a stable and free government. I must say that I think to - that the promise there is of success against this disaster, which both administrations have been attempting to prevent, which is chaos and massive civil war and insurrections and all the rest in the Congo - I really feel we ought to go ahead on both sides. And I'm hopeful they will.

U.S. Proposal for an Inspection System

Q: Mr. President, on the test issue: if I understand what you've been saying correctly, you've introduced a new element into these negotiations - that is, inspection which would cover any possible secret preparations for tests. Is this in fact a new element that the United States is introducing and, if so, how might you meet that problem in an inspection system?

The President: I think this is a matter which should be discussed at the disarmament conference. But I think that any agreement - if we're not to have an agreement whereby some time would go by and then, when the Soviets have exhausted the information they have acquired from this series of tests, suddenly overnight begin another series of tests, meanwhile 2 years have gone by and many scientists and others who might have been working on this may have gone into other occupations.

This is a - I think it's a deadly business, this competition. And I don't say that much security comes out of it. But less security would certainly come out of it if we permitted them to make a decisive breakthrough in an area like an ICBM. So that we would have to have some assurances against a repetition of this summer's incident before we would feel that the treaty was a satisfactory one. But it is a matter which should be discussed, I think, in March at the disarmament conference.

Reporter: Thank you, Mr. President.

THE PRESIDENT'S NEWS CONFERENCE OF

FEBRUARY 14, 1962

The President: I have one statement.

There have been a number of questions directed to the White House and other governmental agencies about our release of Col. Rudolf Abel, and the freeing of Francis Cary Powers and Frederic Pryor from detention in the Soviet Union and East Germany, respectively.

Let me say first that I'm deeply pleased that the pilot, Mr. Powers, and the student, Mr. Pryor, have been released and reunited with their families. I shall be doubly pleased if their release turns out to be a sign of possible significant progress in the lessening of world tensions.

As for the whereabouts of Mr. Powers, I can state at this time only that he's in this country, that he has seen his father and mother, and that his wife is with him. He is undergoing important interviews by appropriate officials of this Government. Mr. Powers is cooperating voluntarily with the Government in these discussions. At the conclusion of these discussions, the information derived from these interviews will be made available to appropriate committees of the Congress, and Mr. Powers will be free to testify before the Congress, should the Congress so wish. Mr. Powers will be made available to the press at the earliest feasible moment.

Q: Mr. President, when Mr. Powers completes this interrogation and he's free to testify, what will his status be? Will the Government still have any claim on his services or will he be a free agent to go as he pleases?

The President: Well, he's a free agent, as I've said at the present time, to go as he pleases. He is cooperating voluntarily with the Government, and at the conclusion of the present discussions, he will be free to carry on whatever work he should choose.

Q: Mr. President, is it possible to say now how Powers was brought down in Russia, whether he was shot down or whether it was mechanical trouble?

The President: It would seem to me that this question and others relating to it really should wait until the interrogations have been completed, and until the Government has finished talking about all these matters with Mr. Powers. Then, as I say, he will be available, and will give whatever information would be in the national interest to give.

QUESTIONS

Prime Minister Macmillan's Statement on Nuclear Testing

Q: Mr. President, can you comment on Prime Minister Macmillan's statement yesterday that there will be no testing on Christmas Island before the opening of the Geneva conference, and have developments in the last week affected our plans?

The President: No, that statement of the Prime Minister of course is correct, and nothing in the events of the last week - if you're referring to the exchange of communications with Chairman Khrushchev which we had and the letter back, and now our letter back to him - that has not changed our plans. As I've stated, by the end of the month we will have concluded our analysis of our relative positions and we will be in a position to make a decision. But in any case, whichever way the decision would go, there would be no testing, as the Prime Minister said, on Christmas Island before that date.

Q: Mr. President, to refer to your letter to Premier Khrushchev this morning, without meaning to exclude other examples, could you give us one example of the kind of progress in the disarmament talks that might lead you to participate personally in a summit conference?

The President: If the discussions at Geneva indicated that genuine progress could be made which would provide for a responsible disarmament agreement, if it's going to be - truly meet the international needs, then of course, if we are moving ahead in that kind of area, and my presence at a meeting in Geneva would advance that cause, of course I would go. But our point is, in the letter, that what we want to do is try to make that progress in the negotiations. Then if we are making it and a meeting of heads of state would complete it or would materially advance it, then it would seem to me that every head of state would want to go.

Q: Mr. President, have you received any indication from the neutralist countries, particularly India, whether or not they would send foreign ministers or heads of state to the March 18th meeting?

The President: No. I don't know what the decision will be of the heads of the other governments to which Mr. Khrushchev addressed his letter.

Prospect of Rising Unemployment

Q: Mr. President, our Labor Department estimates that approximately 1.8 million persons holding jobs are replaced every year by machines. How urgent do you view this problem - automation?

The President: Well, it is a fact that we have to find, over a 10-year period, 25,000 new jobs every week to take care of those who are displaced by machines and those who are coming into the labor market, so that this places a major burden upon our economy and on our society, and it's one to which we will have to give a good deal of attention in the next decade. I regard it as a very serious problem. If our economy is moving forward, we can absorb this 1,800,000 even though in particular industries we may get special structural unemployment. We've seen that in steel, we've seen it in coal, we may see it in other industries. But if our economy is progressing as we hope it will, then we can absorb a good many of these men and women. But I regard it as the major domestic challenge, really, of the sixties, to maintain full employment at a time when automation, of course, is replacing men.

The Inclusion of Red China in Arms Negotiations

Q: Mr. President, do you agree with the view attributed to Ambassador Beam that any arms agreement the West reaches with Russia must ultimately include Red China to have real value?

The President: Yes, I would think there would have to be an agreement that would cover the world, if it is going to be valuable.

Q: Mr. President, you have indicated you would like some priority to the nuclear test ban at the meetings that open on March 14. Would the United States be willing to stand by the draft treaty of last April, that was laid before the Soviet Union then?

The President: Well, I've stated that we will – that it may be necessary to bring that treaty up to date. But basically we have indicated that we would sign an agreement which would have as its basis certainly the April proposal. There might be some new additions that could be made to it, but that is the basic thesis on which we've been acting since last April.

The Practice of Summitry

Q: Mr. President, in the past year you have had an experience with a whole variety of diplomacy and forms of diplomacy. Could you tell us what your thoughts are now on the practice of summitry?

The President: Well, my view is the same as it has been, and that is that a summit is not a place to carry on negotiations which involve details, and that a summit should be a place where perhaps agreements which have been achieved at a lower level could be finally, officially approved by the heads of government, or if there was a major crisis which threatened to involve us all in a war, there might be a need for a summit. But my general view would be that we should climb to the summit after careful preparation at the lower levels.

Nelson Rockefeller's Criticism

Q: Mr. President, Nelson Rockefeller on Sunday said that in his view the results of Punta del Este amounted to a diplomatic failure for the United States. Is there anything you would have to say on that?

The President: No. I disagree. I think that all of the countries of the hemisphere together made a finding that Cuba and the Communist system were not – should not be considered part of the inter-American system. And in my opinion that was a most important declaration, because it put the inter-American system squarely and unanimously against Communist infiltration. So that I do have a different view of the results, even though there's a division, of course, among countries as there is bound to be, as to the best methods of containing the expansion of communism. But on the general opposition to its expansion in this hemisphere, I think there was unanimity, and I regard that as most important.

The CIA Budget

Q: Mr. President, some Congressmen are again critical of the fact that they don't know how much they're voting for CIA or, due to the fact that the requests are hidden in other budgets, even when they're voting on CIA. Does this have any validity, do you think?

The President: The budget for the CIA is handled by the members of the Appropriations Committee of the House and Senate. It's bipartisan, and in- cludes members who are the most senior and the most experienced in the area. They are fully informed. Quite obviously, there are some limitations on what we're able to reveal in the national interest, but in my judgment the budgetary procedures which have been followed in the past have combined congressional responsibility and also protection of our vital interests.

The Censorship of Military Speeches

Q: This being Valentine's Day, sir, do you think it might be a good idea if you would call Senator Strom Thurmond of South Carolina down to the White House for a heart-to-heart talk - (laughter) - about the whole disagreement over the censorship of the military speeches and what he calls your defeatist foreign policy?

The President: Well, I think that that meeting should be probably prepared at a lower level - (laughter) - and then we could have a ——

U.S Involvement in Viet-Nam

Q: Mr. President, the Republican National Committee publication has said that you have been less than candid with the American people as to how deeply we are involved in Viet-Nam. Could you throw any more light on that?

The President: Yes, as you know, the United States for more than a decade has been assisting the government, the people of Viet-Nam, to maintain their independence. Way back on December 24, 1950, we signed a military assistance agreement with France and with Indochina which at that time included Viet-Nam, Laos, and Cambodia, We also signed in December of 1951 an agreement directly with Viet-Nam.

Now, in 1954, the Geneva agreements were signed and while we did not sign those agreements nevertheless Under Secretary Bedell Smith stated that he would view any renewal of the aggression in Viet-Nam in violation of the aforesaid agreements with grave concern, and as seriously threatening international peace and security. And at the time that the SEATO Pact was signed in 1954, Septem- ber 8, though Viet-Nam was not a signatory it was a protocol state, and there- fore this pact, which was approved by the Senate with only, I think, two against it, under article 4 stated that the United States recognized that ag- gression by means of armed attack against Viet-Nam would threaten our own peace and security. So since that time the United States has been assisting the Gov- ernment of Viet-Nam to maintain its independence. It has had a military train- ing mission there and it's also given extensive economic assistance.

As you know, during the last 2 years that war has increased. The Vice President visited there last spring. The war became more intense every month; in fact, every week. The attack on the government by the Communist forces with assistance from the north became of greater and greater concern to the Govern- ment of Viet-Nam and the Government of the United States. We sent - I sent General Taylor there to make a review of the situation. The President of Viet- Nam asked us for additional assistance. We issued, as you remember, a white paper which detailed the support which the Viet Minh in the north were giving to this Communist insurgent movement and we have increased our assistance there. And we are supplying logistic assistance, transportation assistance, training, and we have a number of Americans who are taking part in that effort.

We have discussed this matter - we discussed it with the leadership of the Republicans and Democrats when we met in early January and informed them of what we were doing in Viet-Nam. Mr. Rusk has discussed it with the House and

Senate Foreign Affairs Committee. Mr. McNamara has discussed it with the Armed Services Committee. The leadership on both sides, Republicans and the Democrats have been - we have explained to them our concern about what is happening there, and they have been responsive, I think, and evidenced their concern. So that there's a long history of our effort to prevent Viet-Nam from falling under control of the Communists. That is what we are now attempting to do, and as the war has increased in scope, our assistance has increased as a result of the requests of the government. So that I think we should - as it's a matter of great importance, a matter of great sensitivity - my view has always been that the headquarters of both of our parties should really attempt to leave these matters to be discussed by responsible leaders on both sides, and in my opinion, we have had a very strong bipartisan consensus up till now, and I'm hopeful that it will continue in regard to the actions that we're taking.

Q: Mr. President, do you feel that you have told the American people as much as can be told, because of the sensitivity of the subject? Is that right?

The President: I think I've just indicated what our role is. We have increased our assistance to the government - its logistics; we have not sent combat troops there, although the training missions that we have there have been instructed if they are fired upon to - they would of course, fire back, to protect themselves. But we have not sent combat troops in the generally understood sense of the word. We have increased our training mission, and we've increased our logistics support, and we are attempting to prevent a Communist takeover of Viet-Nam, which is in accordance with a policy which our Government has followed for the last - certainly since 1954, and even before then as I've indicated, and we are attempting to make all the information available that we can consistent with our security needs in the area. So that I feel that we are being as frank as we can be. I think what I have said to you is a description of our activity there.

The Kashmir Dispute

Q: Mr. President, a couple of weeks ago you told us of your hope of sending Mr. Eugene Black of the World Bank to India and Pakistan to see what could be done about the Kashmir dispute. Apparently Prime Minister Nehru doesn't like that approach, or feels it should be done another way. Do you have any present plan to try to move this issue off dead center through some other approach?

The President: No, the United States did make an effort in this regard. We are giving assistance to both countries. We would like to see the assistance used most effectively, and anything that increases the tension between them or causes our aid to be turned into military channels as a result of tensions with each other makes our aid less effective, and therefore we suggested Mr. Black might be able to fill a useful role. The decision was made by the Indian Government that that would not be appropriate at this time, and therefore - there is an election going on in India - I'm hopeful at the conclusion of the election that the two parties can make some progress in settling it among themselves, which is evidently what they prefer at this time.

The Attorney General's Visit to the USSR

Q: Mr. President, on the question - there have been persistent reports that the Attorney General is still going to visit the Soviet Union, before he returns from his trip abroad. Is there any such possibility?

The President: No, no.

The Renewal of U.S. Base Rights at Dhahran

Q: Mr. President, on the basis of your talks with King Saud, can you tell us what the prospects are on the renewal of our base rights at Dhahran?

The President: Well, we've never requested the renewal of our base rights. It's not a matter which is at issue between the two governments.

Q: You would expect it to lapse, then?

The President: Yes, we do, and we've made preparations for that, and that's what is the desire of both countries. So it has not been a subject, really, of discussion between us.

The Joint British-American Draft Agreement on Disarmament

Q: Mr. President, a few moments ago I believe you said that on the joint British-American draft agreement on disarmament, that it should be brought up to date. I wonder if you could expand on that a little. Are you speaking of an inspection of preparations, specifically, for testing?

The President: Well, I think that my statement last week indicated our concern about that matter but - and I think that the positions that we would take at the conference will be presented at that time. I don't mean to - I don't think anything particularly significant should be read into my response. We have stated that we will be ready to sign an agreement which provides for effective inspection and that is our position, and our position is based upon our proposal of last April. I'm not aware that there would be any significant change in that. If there is, it will be presented by the time the disarmament conference begins.

Unemployment

Q: Mr. President, going back to the question of unemployment, some 13,000 workers in one plant on Long Island are facing layoffs as a result of the Defense Department's decision to phase out one type of aircraft. Do you see any need for new steps to offset the economic impact of changing defense requirements such as cases as this?

The President: I think that the figures of the possible layoffs are not - are overstated in your question, because to the best of my information they would be substantially, very substantially, less than the figure that you gave, and that would be our - it is a matter of considerable concern, however, that anyone will be laid off at that particular factory, and we are concerned about it. In fact, I think that your publisher wrote me about the matter last week. We even heard from the Congressman and we are concerned about seeing if we can maintain employment at the highest possible level at that plant. The difficulty, of course, comes because the particular plane that they are manufacturing is not being continued and that presents us with a difficult decision in a number of areas. But we are very conscious of the problem that's faced at that plant and we are going to try to see if we can maintain employment as high as it's possible for us to do so, even though some cut, but of a much less figure than you mentioned, will perhaps inevitably come.

Increase in the Size of the House of Representatives

Q: Mr. President, would you approve a bill which would increase the size of the House by three members to solve a Massachusetts political problem?

The President: I would wait. It seems to me it's a decision which the House will have to make, and after the House has acted, the Senate has acted, and I see what the bill is, I'd make a judgment about whether it'd be approved or not.

The Red Chinese and a Nuclear Test Ban Agreement

Q: Mr. President, in the past it has been thought that the Russians might persuade the Red Chinese to agree to any nuclear test ban agreement that they might reach with the West. Now, it seems that the Russians' ability to persuade the Chinese to do very much is limited. How, then, do you see bringing the Red Chinese into any inspection and control system?

The President: Well it's obviously very difficult, but there is really no use in having an inspection system agreed upon between, say, the Soviet Union and the United States and some other countries and then have another country – large – carrying on intensive armaments preparation. Quite obviously, that would not protect our security. So this problem of bringing them in is a problem that must be considered before we would be able to have confidence in any disarmament agreement.

I quite recognize the hazards and the difficulties of attempting to bring them in. But if we are making progress – and we have a good deal of hurdles to overcome before we come to this particular question – it is a question which waits for us before the end of the road is reached. And it would be a very difficult one, but one that we certainly should have in mind as we start on this conference.

Exchange of Delegations Between the U.S. and the USSR

Q: Mr. President, last week the Capitol Hill paper, Roll Call, published an interview with the leaders of the Soviet parliament, in which they urged establishment of ties and exchange of delegations between the United States Congress and the Supreme Soviet of the U.S.S.R. What is your personal opinion about the desirability of such contacts?

The President: Well, I think that – I am very interested in any exchanges. I think the matter of whether the Congress should go is really a decision which the Congress themselves should reach. As far as my general interest, of course, I think that exchanges are very useful; but on the matter of the Congress itself, I think that it's a matter which the Congress can make a judgment on as to whether the national interest would be served by their going.

Status of the Monroe Doctrine

Q: Mr. President, in view of the avowed solidarity of Communist Cuba with the Soviet Union, what is the present status of the Monroe Doctrine?

The President: Well, in the first place, the – Mr. Salinger passed up a note saying that the OAS – the Organization of American States – has just excluded Cuba from its deliberations, which I think indicates the unanimity of the hemisphere in regard to this. We are attempting to carry out our policy through the Organization of American States, through the hemisphere. Quite obviously we have our own national interests to protect and our national security to protect, which we will do. And therefore, we attempt to accommodate the policies in a whole variety of ways, in order to serve the national interest.

Postponement of Colonel Glenn's Flight

Q: Sir, my question concerns the postponement of Colonel Glenn's flight today. This is the eighth time, I believe, that his flight has been postponed and among other things there's been a considerable ordeal on Colonel Glenn himself.

The President: That is correct.

Q: Do you think, sir, that it would have been better, that it would be better even now, to say, move up the date much deeper in the spring to a point where we would be more certain of the weather, instead of running the risk of repeated delays?

The President: Well, it is unfortunate. I know it strains Colonel Glenn. It has delayed our program. It puts burdens on all of those who must make these decisions as to whether the mission should go or not. I think it's been very unfortunate. But I have taken the position that the judgment of those on the spot should be final in regard to this mission, and I'll continue to take that judgment. I think that they would be reluctant to have it canceled for another 3 or 4 months because it would slow our whole space program down at a time when we're making a concentrated effort in space. But I am quite aware of the strain it's caused everyone, and it's been a source of regret to everyone, but I think we ought to stick with the present group who are making the judgment, and they are hopeful still of having this flight take place in the next few days. And I'm going to follow their judgment in the matter, even though we've had bad luck.

A Permanent Summer White House at Newport, R.I.

Q: Mr. President, what is your reaction to the proposal for a permanent summer White House at Newport, R.I.? Have you reached a decision on that?

The President: No. Mr. Udall - the proposal was made by, I think, Senator Pell and Senator Pastore, and it went to Mr. Udall, and I have not discussed the matter with him, and - though he is looking at the matter and is going to reply to them, I'm sure I will discuss it with him before a final decision is made.

Postal Rate Increases

Q: Mr. President, there has been a notable lack of activity in the Senate on postal rate increases. There is some indication this is tied to efforts to tie together rate increases with postal wage increases. Do you have any comment on this?

The President: I think we ought to move ahead on the postal rate increase bill. I am hopeful that the Senate will. The House met its responsibilities; I'm hopeful the Senate will. Then we can take up the question of pay increases. The administration has some recommendations in that area, but I think it would be a mistake to so intimately link them.

The Situation in Laos

Q: Mr. President, could you evaluate the situation in Laos in light of continuing Communist attacks at Nam Tha?

The President: I think it's - as I've said, the cease-fire is becoming increasingly frayed. It's my understanding that Souvanna Phouma has an audience with the King, and I'm hopeful that progress, which has been very slow in the last 30 days can be made in attempting to agree on a government. Obviously every day that goes by increases the dangers.

The Communist forces move forward. The government forces reinforce their people at the town. The town is very close to the Chinese border, so it's a very dangerous situation, because if the cease-fire should break down, we would have - be faced with the most serious decision. So I'm hopeful the cease-fire will continue to prevail, and that the various groups within the country will come to an agreement which will permit a neutral and independent Laos which has been the objective of our policy.

Censors in the Defense Department and the State Department

Q: Sir, you have already stated that it is our national policy to carry out the deletions that the censors were carrying out in the Defense Department, and State, and you said you did not want to divulge the names of these censors because they were carrying out your policy.

The President: No, that isn't what I said. I said - the names have been revealed in the military and in the State Department of those who have been involved in reviewing speeches.

Q: But you said you did not want to divulge the name of the specific censor who did the specific censoring.

The President: Yes, that is correct.

Q: My question, sir, now is: Would you tell us why it has to be national policy to delete from the speeches of admirals and generals such phrases as "emerge victorious," "victorious," "beat the Communists," and phrases like that?

The President: Well, those particular phrases I am not familiar with and, therefore, I don't know whether or not they were deleted. But I would say that if the - the purpose that I stated a month ago, and that is to make sure that governmental policy is - that the government speaks with one voice. Now, to give an example of the kind of thing that makes these reviews necessary, there was a speech which was brought to the White House, I think on January 23, which was to be given by Admiral Burke. We had a new administration. Admiral Burke, himself, sent the speech over because he wanted to be sure that anything he said which would be interpreted as being the policy of the new administration was in accordance with the new administration.

Admiral Burke was not aware that we were then carrying on negotiations for the release of the RB-47 pilots. So that it indicates how desirable it is. As I said, it also applies to me. I sent, as I said before, the State of the Union Address to both Defense and to the State Department so that they could see if there were any parts in it which they would want to comment on.

The Admiral Burke example, I think, indicates clearly how desirable it is to have speeches gone over by those who represent the Secretary of State or the Secretary of Defense. Now there's no doubt that on some occasions those reviews may have been unwise. After all, 1200 speeches came in, in one year, and I would not attempt at all to defend every change that's been made. But I do state that they are acting in good faith in every occasion, even though their judgment may not be as good as other people's may be.

Release of Military Reservists

Q: Mr. President, in the light of the apparent easing of tensions between the United States and the Soviet Union, particularly with respect to Berlin, can you say with any precision now when the military reservists might be released?

The President: No. The crisis continues and the reservists – the need for
reservists continues until there is an easing of the crisis or until we've been
able to replace them with other men. As you know, we are building two new permanent divisions which will be ready in August – one division – and September,
the other division. And, of course, that will then present us with an entirely
different situation in regard to their need. But until we have an easing of
the crisis in Berlin or these two new divisions, the need for the reservists,
of course, will continue.

Presidential Policy in the Cold War

*Q: Mr. President, a number of your rightwing critics say that your foreign
policy is based on a no-win policy in the cold war. Would you address yourself
to this charge?*

The President: Well, of course, every American whoever they may be, wants
the United States to be secure and at peace and they want the cause of freedom
around the world to prevail. Quite obviously that is our national objective.
And what we are anxious to do, of course, is protect our national security,
protect the freedom of the countries, permit what Thomas Jefferson called the
disease of liberty to be caught in areas which are now held by Communists, and
some areas where people are imprisoned. We want to do that, of course, without
having a nuclear war. Now, if someone thinks we should have a nuclear war in
order to win, I can inform them that there will not be winners in the next
nuclear war, if there is one, and this country and other countries will suffer
very heavy blows. So that we have to proceed with responsibility and with care
in an age where the human race can obliterate itself. The objective of this
administration, and I think the objective of the country, is to protect our
security, keep the peace, protect our vital interests, make it possible for
what we believe to be a system of government which is in accordance with the
basic aspirations of people everywhere to ultimately prevail. And that is our
objective and that's the one that we shall continue.

Reporter: Thank you, Mr. President.

THE PRESIDENT'S NEWS CONFERENCE OF

FEBRUARY 21, 1962

The President: I have one statement. It is increasingly clear that the
impact of Colonel Glenn's magnificent achievement yesterday goes far beyond our
own time and our own country. The success of this flight, the new knowledge it
will give us, and the new steps which can now be undertaken, will affect life
on this planet for many years to come.

This country has received more than 30 messages of congratulations from
other heads of state all over the world which recognize the global benefits of
this extraordinary accomplishment. And I want to express my thanks to them and
at the same time pay tribute to the international cooperation entailed in the
successful operation of the Mercury tracking network, and express particular
appreciation to those governments which participated in this international program by permitting the location of 18 such stations all around the world, including those in the Grand Canary Island, Nigeria, Zanzibar, Australia, Mexico,
Bermuda, and the Canton Island in the Pacific.

One of the messages that I received was from Chairman Khrushchev in the Soviet Union, suggesting that it would be beneficial to the advance of science if our countries could work together in the exploration of space. I am replying to his message today, and I regard it as most encouraging, this proposal for international cooperation in space exploration, including specifically Soviet-American cooperation, which I spelled out in my State of the Union Message of last year, and in my address to the United Nations. You may recall that last year in January of 1961 in the State of the Union Address, I said, "Specifically, I now invite all nations - including the Soviet Union - to join with us in developing a weather prediction program, in a new communications satellite program and in preparation for probing the distant planets of Mars and Venus, probes which may someday unlock the deepest secrets of the universe."

Previous to that, under the previous administration, many suggestions were made for international cooperation. On one occasion, the Vice President, then Senator Johnson, acting on behalf of President Eisenhower, presented a proposal to the United Nations for the peaceful uses of outer space.

We believe that when men reach beyond this planet they should leave their national differences behind them. All men will benefit, if we can invoke the wonders of science instead of its terrors. We look forward to visiting with Colonel Glenn on Friday and welcoming him to Washington next Monday.

It has been said that peace has her victories as well as war, and I think all of us can take pride and satisfaction in this victory of technology and the human spirit.

Q; Mr. President, can you tell us the nature of your actual response to Mr. Khrushchev on this proposal?

The President: We will indicate in the response our desire that space be explored peacefully and that we will be glad, in the United Nations and in any other forum, to discuss how this can best be done so that this new ocean which I referred to yesterday may be a peaceful one. I think it's particularly important now, before space becomes devoted to the uses of war. So we will be prepared to discuss this matter, as I say, at the United Nations, or bilaterally, or any other way in which this common cause can be advanced.

Mr. President, on the same subject, do you think it would be wise, or can you conceive of a situation where we would have Russian observers at a space shot by this country without United States observers being allowed to view up close the Russian shot?

The President: Well, as you know, today we permit observers from all countries, members of the press from all countries, to come and watch our shots, and this has been a very open procedure, and one of the reasons why I think we all take satisfaction is because we took our chances out in the open, and our delays, which were well publicized and which may have caused some satisfaction to those who were not our well-wishers - it seems to me we have a double pleasure when it goes well.

I do feel that, of course, if there's any cooperation it must be in the sense we are now discussing - it must be wholly bilateral, and I think that that, of course, would be one of the matters which we would discuss.

Q: Mr. President, pursuing this subject even further, do you have any indication beyond the rather nebulous but hopeful remarks of Mr. Khrushchev in his congratulatory message that they are really willing to get down to cases in cooperation in these areas?

One recalls that they did actually do something in this respect in the International Geophysical Year and I just wondered if between the time of the

State of the Union Message and now any other tangible developments have come up beyond or in addition to his statement yesterday.

The President: No, we have seen no evidence that we would be able to confidently expect in the last 12 months that this kind of cooperation would take place. But we, I might say, now have more chips on the table than we did some time ago. So perhaps the prospects are improving.

U.S. Receipt of Data from the Soviet Space Program

Q: Mr. President, can you say whether up to this day the international scientific community or American scientists have received any data from the Soviet space flights of Titov and Gagarin?

The President: You mean other than those we might have picked up ourselves?

Q: Yes, I mean through the international scientific community or any published works in the Soviet?

The President: Well, except for those that may have been published. I am not sure that we have. But before I give you a final answer perhaps I can ask Mr. Salinger and Mr. Hatcher to see if before the end of the press conference we could find out if there's been any more detailed information made available to us or to anyone else, so I'll come back to that.

Colonel Glenn's Achievements

Q: Mr. President, on a more local level, the Washington Daily News suggested today that since Colonel Glenn's achievements illustrate the ultimate in physical and scientific disipline, that all the schoolkids and all the surrounding schools in Maryland, Virginia, and Washington be let out to welcome him here Monday. Would you go along with that suggestion?

The President: We always follow the Washington Daily News - (laughter) - and I believe that that is being done. In this particular area, Washington, D.C., and perhaps those that may be nearby in Maryland and Virginia, we would be glad if they followed the example.

Situation in Laos and Vietnam

Q: Mr. President, there have been published reports to the effect that you have decided on a policy of disengagement in Laos after consultation with the Joint Chiefs of Staff. Could you clarify the situation as you see it in Laos and South Viet-Nam?

The President: No, I would say that our policy has been quite consistent since last April, when we agreed to the cease-fire, and we have, since that date, been attempting to organize a government and secure agreements from the parties who are involved internally and externally for a neutral and independent Laos. That is our objective, and we're continuing to work for it.

Many months have passed, but that remains the star by which we guide our course there, and therefore, it would be improper at this time to talk about disengagement. We are engaged in the task of attempting to build a neutral and independent Laos, and it is to that end that we are directing our effort. And it would be, as I say, not precise to state that on the advice of the Joint Chiefs or for any other reason we are withdrawing our interest before that task has been accomplished.

Chancellor Adenauer on the Berlin Question

Q: Mr. President, Chancellor Adenauer is reported to have said while talking with the parliamentary group of the CDU that possibly the time has come to break off the Thompson-Gromyko talks and throw the Berlin question into a Big Four foreign ministers conference. Do you have any comment on this?

The President: Well, I know that there was a newspaper report based on, supposedly, what the Chancellor said in a conversation, but I think there is some question as to whether that represented an accurate description of his views. I will say that that is not the impression that we have received, and, in fact, we have received an opposite impression, and that is that these probes, or these talks, while they have not been productive so far, nevertheless the subject is not exhausted, and we should continue. If, and I've said this from the beginning, there is some evidence that by raising them to a ministerial level that we would be more successful, then I think we ought to do it. But I do think that the conversations at this level now at least permit us to see whether there is any ground for a hopeful negotiation. I presume that what you mean by four powers would be the Soviet Union, the British, the French and ourselves. As you know, General de Gaulle has been unwilling to have a four-power foreign ministers conference, at least for France, until there is some evidence that such a conference might produce a useful result. So far the results have been comparatively minor, or minuscule.

Cease-Fire in Algeria

Q: Mr. President, recalling your own interest in Algeria as a Senator, have you any comment on the cease-fire agreement that apparently has now been reached between the rebels and the French Government?

The President: I'm hopeful that there is a cease-fire agreement, that it will permit an orderly and satisfactory solution, and we are, of course, most interested in the efforts that are being made to achieve that. I think that we should wait, as far as the United States is concerned, and watch the evolution with very concerned and friendly interest, which has been our policy for many months.

The Urban Affairs Proposal

Q: Mr. President, no doubt you are aware as to what Congress has done on the urban affairs proposal. Would you care to comment, sir, on what your next step would be regarding the plight of the cities, and also what the future might hold for Mr. Weaver?

The President: Well, I think there's going to be an urban department some time. There isn't going to be one now, but there's going to be sooner or later. You have too large a percentage of our population living in the city, 70 to 75 to 80 percent. They face many problems. The mayors of the country and others who are most concerned with them have supported this proposal. We're going to have an urban department. It may not come this year, but in my opinion it will become as necessary and inevitable as the Department of Agriculture or HEW. Now, the difficulty, of course, is that many of those who do not live in urban areas are opposed to it. But if we in this country began to adopt the system that everyone who lives in a city area voted against those things which were of assistance to the farmer, and everybody who comes from a rural area voted against those policies which provided a better life for people in the city, and everybody who lived outside the Tennessee Valley voted against the Tennessee Valley Authority, and everyone who lived in the East voted against the development in the Northwest, or the development of natural resources, this country would come to a grinding halt.

So I am hopeful that after a longer look is taken at this proposal, and it's analyzed on its merits, that in my judgment the Congress of the United States will support an urban program. I believe it's vitally important, and I regret that Congress did not see fit to adopt it. I don't think it is so much the administration's loss as it's a loss for the city and the country.

Now in regard to Dr. Weaver, he would have been admirably qualified as the head of the largest division which would have been included in the urban department. I see now that various people who opposed the urban department are now ready to support him for any Cabinet position he wishes, Defense, State, Treasury, or anything else. I consider him admirably qualified for this particular position because he's had long experience in it, and while I'm sure he is grateful for those good wishes for a Cabinet position where there is no vacancy, I think he feels that he would have been - that this country would have been better served to have voted for an urban department, and permitted him to continue his service in that capacity. Mr. Weaver will get along all right, but I think the question is, the people in the cities are the ones who have been defeated.

Soviet Planes in the Berlin Air Corridor

Q: Mr. President, Soviet planes are continuing to fly through the Berlin air corridor despite our objections. This comes at a time when the Soviets are increasingly critical about the alleged lack of progress in the Berlin talks in Moscow. Do you think this could be a pressure move by the Soviets to force us to come up with additional concessions in Moscow?

The President: I wouldn't attempt to draw any conclusions except to say that we've continued to fly the air routes into Berlin. And while those flights have not passed without some interference, I think the fact is that, of course, our rights in this area are being maintained. I'm hopeful that the Soviet Union and ourselves will be able, as I said from the beginning, to reach an accommodation, because obviously, any interference with these kinds of rights or rights which may be on the Autobahn, all these things carry with them hazards which none of us should welcome if we look to the possible end of the road.

So I would not make any judgment. I merely hope that it will be possible for them to desist.

In answer to Mr. Lisagor's questions, it says some exchange between the Soviet and U.S. scientists of informal nature, but only medical information. There was no technical information in regard to the exchanges which have taken place in space.

The Whereabouts of Gary Powers

Q: Mr. President, could you give us any information on the present whereabouts of U-2 pilot Powers and when he will be available for questioning by the press and Congress?

The President: There is, as you know, a board of inquiry which is examining whether Mr. Powers completed his contract. That board of inquiry is under the leadership of Judge Prettyman and represents outstanding citizens. Mr. Powers has been cooperating fully. He will be available for the Congress - this inquiry will be completed by the middle of next week - and he would then be available to the Congress and to the press. And I must say that there is so far no evidence that he did not comply with his contract, but I think we could make a more precise judgment at the next press conference, or a more final judgment, I would say.

Administrative Reforms in South Viet-Nam

Q: In your view, Mr. President, is the South Vietnamese Government now carrying out the administrative reforms and creating the political conditions in which our increased assistance can be most effective?

The Presdient: We're working with them to accomplish both of these objectives. And these objectives, I must say, are hard to carry out. This country's been in the struggle now for a number of years. It has not - it had not many skilled administrators when it got its independence in '54, and it had been at war for really, in a sense, with the Japanese occupation and the war with the French, for almost 15 years before that, so that it's a very difficult assignment. It is a fact, however, that the gross national product, agricultural production, health, education, all these things materially increased in the last 6 years. But I think it's a matter for which the Vietnamese Government must be concerned about. We're prepared to offer every assistance we can in making that Government a more effective instrument for the people.

Dependents of Servicemen Overseas

Q: Mr. President, concern has been voiced by church leaders that wives and children of servicemen cannot accompany them to Europe and live with them. They are worried about moral implications, breakup of homes. Since the logistic requirements are no longer so urgent, it seems, is there a chance that this order may be changed soon?

The President: Well, as you know, most of the servicemen in Europe have their - who are married - have their families with them. There may be some who do not. In addition, of course, we're concerned about the gold flow which comes because of our troop commitments to Europe. I've said before that we spend $3 billion a year in maintaining our military forces around the world, and our bases. So if we are able to cut that somewhat, we shall do so. But to be more specific, most of the servicemen now in Europe have their families with them. There are some who do not, and the purpose of it, of course, is to limit this drain.

Q: Mr. President, may I ask, was there not a memorandum on September 6 by the Defense Secretary forbidding the travel, though, for wives and children?

The President: We have attempted in recent weeks and months to limit the number of families going overseas, and the only reason for it has been that we are losing dollars and gold, and we have to attempt to bring it into balance, and this has been one of the ways which we've considered. We have left the families over there which were already there, but we're attempting to limit those that may go. This presents a hazard and a difficulty. But we're also very concerned about attempting to bring this flow into balance. And one of the ways is to try to cut that $3 billion to $2 billion or $1.9 billion, and one of the ways in which we can do this is to attempt to limit family travel even though quite rightly it does present burdens to those involved.

Fighter Escorts for Transports In and Out of Berlin

Q: Mr. President, I hope this isn't repetitious, but the United States Air Force has a great reputation in Western Europe for clearing the sky of interference. And it has been reported out of Germany that you are weighing a decision about giving fighter escorts to the transports in and our of Berlin. Would you want to comment on that?

The President: No. Every plane that has set out has completed its mission. Every plane that has set out to fly from West Germany to West Berlin has arrived.

Nuclear Testing

Q: Mr. President, in considering the conditions under which the United States might refrain from a resumption of nuclear testing, I wonder if you would comment on the following suggestion contained in a recent letter to the editor of the New York Times: "Let both sides be allowed to maintain preparations at the ready for immediate tests should the other side be detected setting off a surprise explosion."

The President: Well in the first place, that's part of the problem but not all of the problem. Part of the problem is the fact that the Soviet Union already had set off its tests, and - while the moratorium was in effect. And therefore we have to consider the effects upon our security of those tests. So that this suggestion does not meet the whole problem.

Secondly, it's more difficult for us to maintain ourselves at the ready to be prepared for tests. Some months have gone by since the Soviet tests. We have been making our preparations, as I have said. It takes many months, and we are concerned, that if we had another moratorium, that the Soviet Union would set a target date and be prepared and once again it would take us a period of time, perhaps not quite as long as this time, to carry out our own tests.

I would say the greater concern is the effect of the Soviet tests and the extrapolations which can be gained from them in making the judgment as to whether we should carry out our tests. But I did read the letter in the Times, and at least it is a suggestion which I considered and which others considered.

Foreign Student Opposition to the U.S.

Q: Mr. President, the Attorney General, your brother, has encountered evidence of a certain amount of hostility from student groups in various countries. Inasmuch as this has happened before with other American visitors in the past administration, have you given any thought to what it is about us that students in particular seem to resent? (Laughter)

The President: Well, one of the reasons that I was anxious to have the Attorney General make the trip was because of this very - rather curious factor, because you would feel that students, who are intellectually curious, would be attracted by a free society which gives that intellectual curiosity a chance to develop, rather than a totalitarian society. And therefore, as you know, in the Attorney General's schedule, on nearly every occasion he has spoken at colleges and universities, so I'm sure he will have some views of that. What has also interested me is the stereotype of the United States. It is a view of the United States almost 50 years old, and there is no doubt that it is a - Marxist oriented, and the - even in those cases where they may not be Communist.

There are many explanations for it. In the first place these were colonial areas. They were held under subjugation in many cases by Western powers. The road of revolt was in many cases because the Communists were most active. They dominated the thinking. And I don't think that the students have caught up with the tremendous changes which have taken place in the United States in the last 50 years, or with the fallacies in the Marxist system which have become obvious in the last 20 years.

In addition, I don't think we are able to emphasize those facets of American life which should be most attractive. I said yesterday that the University of California has more Nobel prize winners than the Soviet Union. They find in this country, and there are 40 or 50 of them, a climate which permits them to function most effectively. And all of the cultural efforts here, all of the intellectual efforts, all our great schools and universities, these are the part of the story we ought to tell.

I think the Attorney General attempted to communicate that, but of course, he is one voice. But he is attempting to - as you know, it's better to light a candle than curse the darkness. But I do agree with you that this is one of the most serious, and I think in many ways stimulating, problems we face - how to tell our story in a way that makes it new and exciting to young students and also have them examine objectively under the light of present circumstances the serious failures of the Marxist system, which can be told from the Wall to China. And I think that is our job, and I think the trip's been worthwhile for that purpose alone.

A Tax Reduction

Q: Mr. President, there has been considerable discussion regarding possible tax reduction. Would you tell us what the prospects are for an income tax cut within the next few years?

The President: Well, you were - I was set to answer that till you said "the next few years." I don't know what's going to be our economic situation in the next few years. Obviously, our present tax structure brings in, in good times, a tremendous revenue and if we do not have a recession and our present tax structure remains we would be in a position, obviously, where a tax reduction in a few years or in a period of time might be possible. The fact of the matter is that if we had not had the Berlin crisis, which required a $3.5 billion additional expenditure last summer at the time when we were considering our tax reform bill, it might have been possible to make changes in some of the categories. That was denied to us.

Therefore, for the present there is not a chance of a tax reduction. The key will be whether we can have continued prosperity, and I therefore urge again that the Congress consider very carefully the proposals that we've made which we hope can keep the economy moving ahead. I regard that as a problem which should engage our best efforts of both parties. And we sent up a number of proposals on which at least we have our ideas: capital expenditures, the income tax for a period of time if we begin to have a slump, retraining, youth employment, and all the rest. Now, if these aren't the proper means, I'd like to have other suggestions. But you can't look at '49 and '54 and '58 and '60, and say that nothing needs to be done. So I would hope that those who do not agree - and there seem to be some - with our suggestions, I think they're obligated to come forward with some of their own. And I can assure them we will look at them most carefully, because if we have another recession in '63 and '64, it will affect our gold problems, it will affect problem of unemployment, and all the rest. So I think it's a matter we all ought to be looking at and it's the kind of dialogue to which both of our parties ought to be addressing themselves, rather than some of the rather ancient arguments which it seems to me were settled in the days of Franklin Roosevelt.

Military Dependent's Travel

Q: Mr. President, in view of your remarks on the military dependents' travel, is it correct to believe, then, that such travel will not be resumed until the gold flow situation improves?

The President: I would prefer to talk to the - have you talk with the Defense Department who can perhaps give us more up-to-date information than I'm able to do today. And I can perhaps supplement that after the press conference with Mr. Salinger.

The Race in Space

Q: Mr. President, if we could go back to the space question, we have been talking about a race in space, for example a race between the United States and Russia to get to the moon. Suppose now we should get this international cooperation that you've been talking about. What form would it take? Would it go so far, for example, as a joint United States-Russia mission to the moon? Would it go that far? Or just how would it work?

The President: Well, I think it would be premature to attempt to suggest, because all we have now, so far, is an indication of interest, and we know from long experience that it's more difficult to transform these general expressions into specific agreements. So I think that we should wait until we see what response we get from the Soviets to our answer to Mr. Khrushchev and then decide what it is we can do. We are spending billions of dollars in space, and if it's possible to insure that space is peaceful and that it can be used for the benefit of everyone, then the United States must respond to any opportunity we have to insure that it's peaceful. But I can't give you an answer until we see whether the rain follows the warm wind in this case.

Set-Asides for Labor Surplus Areas in Selected
Civilian Agency Procurement Contracts

Q: Mr. President, Secretary Goldberg is understood to be considering a plan to permit 100 percent set-asides for labor surplus areas in selected civilian agency procurement contracts. If he indicates his approval of this plan, will you give yours in the form of an Executive order authorizing these increased set-asides?

The President: Well, I'd be very responsive to that, if we can do it. I think one of the great concerns - we have a rather limited amount of contracts, both defense and civilian, that go to areas of maximum unemployment. Partly that's because there aren't sufficient plants in those areas. But in answer to your question, if Mr. Goldberg suggests it, I would be inclined to approve it, though I'd like to - I'd first have to examine it in more detail than I have up to this time.

Reporter: Thank you, Mr. President.

THE PRESIDENT'S NEWS CONFERENCE OF

MARCH 7, 1962

The President: Thank you. I have two announcements.

I have today sent the following telegram to the chief executive officers of the major steel companies and to the president of the Steelworkers Union, and I quote:

"I appreciate your willingness to commence negotiations early and I share your regrets that the parties to the steel labor negotiations were unable to conclude a settlement in their negotiations of the past few weeks, despite earnestness and good will on both sides. The present temporary recess should enable both parties to reappraise their position. The best way to achieve a desirable settlement in the public interest is through free and responsible collective bargaining. An early labor settlement consistent with price stability in steel would be in the public interest, as well as in the interest of the parties themselves. The Nation as a whole I am sure shares my conviction that such an agreement would materially strengthen our economy and country. To this end I am requesting the parties to resume collective bargaining at an early date. I hope they will be able to meet together by next Wednesday, March 14."

The second announcement is that I want to comment on the tariff and trade agreements which have just been concluded at Geneva with the European Common Market, the United Kingdon, and 24 other countries following the largest and most complex negotiations in history. The specific details of the agreements we reached in the negotiations will be available this afternoon.

In summary, we obtained from the Common Market and other countries tariff reductions and commitments not to increase duties on $4.3 billion worth of annual exports. In return we granted similar concessions or gave up concessions previously accorded us on $2.9 billion of annual imports. These agreements were very satisfactory and very important. We obtained new concessions, both industrial and agricultural, on those very items which are most essential to the maintenance and expansion of our foreign trade, our export markets, and our effort to sell abroad to offset our balance of payments losses.

This was a good indication, moreover, that the United States and the Common Market will be able to work together and bargain together. Due to the limited bargaining authority we had under the present law, it was necessary to breach the peril points in a number of cases to avoid a complete breakdown in negotiations and to obtain worthwhile concessions for our own businessmen and farmers, but every effort was made to restrict such breaches to items that would not have significant impact upon the American economy.

These agreements, however, are as far as we can go until new legislation is enacted. The real opportunities offered us by the Common Market, and to the people of Europe, and the competitive challenge it presents to our enterprise system - all this is still ahead, and will always be beyond our reach, with all of the adverse effects it will have on our economy, unless a strong trade expansion act gives our negotiators the authority they need to speak for our country in these most important matters.

QUESTIONS

Geneva Negotiations

Q: Mr. President, in connection with your speech last week on nuclear test resumption and the forthcoming negotiations in Geneva, do you think the American public and the public of the world is justified in attaching to the Geneva negotiations any particular hope or expectation that these negotiations will be more fruitful than similar meetings with the Russians in the past?

The President: Well, I am sure they attach hope. Expectations is perhaps another matter. But hope should certainly be attached because these - this meeting is extremely important. I am not making optimistic predictions about its success, but I could make pessimistic predictions about its failure.

So that we go to the conference trying to get an accord. That is our interest. We believe it's in the best interest of the United States, the security interests of the United States as well as the security interests, really, of the entire world. So we just have to wait and see. But we're going there with a genuine effort because we believe it's most desirable to reach an agreement with the Soviet Union. Anyone who has read the history of the 20th century knows that increases of tensions, especially those which are worldwide, which engage great powers, are always dangerous, and when new and unprecedented weapons are thrown into this mix it makes anyone hopeful about Geneva, and the consequent easing of the tensions which would come from an accord.

Surplus Food to the USSR

Q: Mr. President, Mr. Khrushchev has recently stated in meetings in Moscow that his country is suffering quite a bit from a lack of food. Now, regardless of whether they ask or not, have you considered the possibility of loaning, selling, or giving the Soviet people any of our surplus food stocks?

The President: No, we do send food to Poland, as you know, and have sent a substantial quantity to Yugoslavia. There is no evidence that the Soviet Union has ever asked for it and my judgment is they do not want it. I think what Mr. Khrushchev addressed himself to was how they could improve domestic production. And therefore, in answer to your question, there has been no discussion of it, no consideration of it, and I do take some satisfaction from our difficulties which are overproduction under our free agricultural economy, even though it is a problem which has haunted good men.

Economic Recovery

Q: Mr. President, as you know, our rate of economic recovery has been very low indeed, and much less than anticipated. What further actions do you believe the administration should take now to speed up the slowdown in our recovery?

The President: Well, I think it's premature to suggest. I can't accept all the premise of your question. Mr. Goldberg, the Secretary of Labor, I believe this afternoon announced some figures, which said that the seasonal adjusted unemployment rate of 5.6 percent is the lowest level in 19 months and total employment which is 65,789,000 set a new alltime February record. And I think that we should wait till - let the winter go, and let's see what happens in February and March, then we can make a judgment as to whether there is a recovery.

You will recall that in August and September we had a leveling out, and then the economy took off again in October, November, and December. In addition, there's - I saw, as a matter of fact, reading the other day in the Wall Street Journal, that profits were up for companies - 22 percent, I think the highest in history. There's our price - in the last 12 months, prices only increased one-half of 1 percent, I think, which has only happened in this decade once, in 1955.

There's not an excessively high level of inventory buildup. I think that Mr. Heller, who has spoken on this matter, who I do not consider a natural optimist - I think he's been speaking what he believes. And therefore I think that this economy has more vitality in it than some of its premature mourners.

Francis Gary Powers

Q: Mr. President, now that you have seen all the available evidence in the Powers case, do you agree with Representative Vinson that Mr. Powers' U-2 was shot down at 68,000 feet by a ground launched rocket?

The President: Well, I think that the report of the CIA and the comments - the statements which Mr. Powers made, it seems to me, dealt with this matter. I have no other information beyond what you have seen in those two matters.

Q: Sir, I meant that Representative Vinson said the CIA believes that he was shot down by a rocket fired from the ground. I was wondering if you have any comment on that.

The President: I don't have any comment beyond what the CIA has said and what Mr. Powers himself has said.

Safeguards Against Secret Nuclear Testing

Q: Mr. President, could you define for us what might be acceptable at Geneva as a safeguard against secret preparations for testing, and specifically whether this would include an increase in onsite inspections?

The President: Well, I think that the American negotiators at Geneva will have some suggestions to make in that area, and as this conference is going to begin in a week, I believe it would be preferable to let them make their proposals at that time.

Summit Agreements

Q: Mr. President, you have said, and I think more than once, that heads of government should not go to the summit to negotiate agreements, but only to approve agreements negotiated at a lower level. Now it's being said and written that you are going to eat those words, and go to a summit without any agreement at a lower level. Has your position changed, sir?

The President: Well, I'm going to have a dinner for all of the people who've written it, and we'll see who eats what. (Laughter)

Let me state that I would go to the summit if - as you've stated - if some agreements had been made which could be climaxed most effectively by a summit meeting. I've also stated at an earlier press conference if I thought a trip to the summit might avert a war or if we were faced with an extremely dangerous situation, then I think it would be appropriate to go to the summit without prior agreements. But I think to go to the summit without having an understanding of what is going to be accomplished there, and some meeting of minds, I think disappoints rather than helps the cause, and that's why I've held the view that I do, and that's why I continue to hold it, and that's why I am looking forward to the spring.

U.S. Position on Nuclear Free Zones and Non-Nuclear Clubs

Q: Mr. President, since a number of governments have expressed their support for either nuclear free zones in different parts of the world or for a so-called non-nuclear club - among those governments, aside from the socialist communities, there is Brazil, Ireland, and Sweden - what are your feelings, sir, about those proposals, and what would be the position of the United States Government at the Geneva disarmament conference in this respect?

The President: Well, I think there are two or three different points in the question. I think the United States - I said at the United Nations that I thought it would be desirable to come to some agreement in regard to the transfer of nuclear weapons from one country to another. Now, when we get into ─ so that's one position which the United States has already taken and indicates its support of. Your other question was in regard to a nuclear free zone, and that, it seems to me, is a matter which must be examined. What else will be in the zone? What other forces will be in the zone? Where will this zone be? These are matters, I think, that could - will be discussed, I imagine, along with many other matters affecting armaments at Geneva and in other conversations.

But I think that we have to see what the language is, what the proposal is, what the effect of the situation is, before I could answer that question.

In addition, I'm not convinced that this makes a - is a total solution. If you have a missile that can carry a bomb 5,000 miles, does it really make that much - a significant difference, if you don't have a bomb stationed in this area but you have it 5,000 miles behind, which can cover that area?

So, therefore, I think it's a matter which should be discussed at the appropriate place.

Help to Underdeveloped Countries

Q; Mr. President, this morning before the Advertising Council you dwelt with some earnestness about the great burdens the United States is carrying. Are we safe in assuming this is another way of saying that you think some of our friends around the world should do more in the way of helping underdeveloped countries?

The President: Well, I'm hopeful they'll do more. I know that a good many Americans are concerned, as I said this morning, about the balance of payments, and as I have stated, the balance of payments problem of the United States could be settled overnight if we withdrew our security efforts around the world. It is the combination of the $3 billion that we spend keeping our defense forces overseas, combined with assistance we give in other ways, which provides for our dollar drain.

Now, those countries which are building up their reserves, I am hopeful will be willing and some of them have, France, for example, which has really spent a larger proportion of its national income for assistance to the former French community, really, than any country in the world. So, some countries are. But the United States bears a very heavy load, even in the consortiums that we go to, the United States loans frequently are soft, repayable in local currency and the loans of others may be at 3, 4, 5, 6 percent, so that this is a matter which involves us all.

Now, as Western Europe gets stronger and stronger, I'm hopeful that they will play a larger and larger role in this struggle in which we are involved. Because the United States - the reason our gold drain has been in the last 10 years, is due to this matter. The balance of trade has been in our favor every year, except one in the last 10 years.

It's been due also to investments abroad and some short-term capital movement. But if we were not making the great effort we've made, really since the Marshall plan, we would have a major convulsion because there would be a concentration of gold.

Now when we are carrying this heavy load, I would hope that the free countries would work together to attempt to assign this balance evenly.

We don't - we're ready to carry it, in the United States, to the maximum of our ability, but we carry it in Berlin and Saigon, and Latin America, and Africa, and the Middle East, and Pakistan, and India, and in a good many other countries, and this is a matter which should concern all free men.

News of South Viet-Nam

Q: Mr. President, there has been a scattering of very favorable news stories out of South Viet-Nam, but we don't have any overall coverage. I wondered if you could tell us how the subterranean war is going there, because the Pentagon won't put out anything; and also if you'd want to comment on the possibility of the use of tactical nuclear or antipersonnel weapons in that area?

The President: Well, I wouldn't really - I don't think you could make a judgment of the situation. It's very much up and down, as you know, from day to day, and week to week, so it's impossible to draw any long-range conclusions. And on the second matter, it's a - I'm not familiar with it, and it's a matter, really, I think, of the Defense Department, but it has not come to me. In any case, it's a matter, really, for the Vietnamese.

U.S. Payments to the U.N.

Q: Mr. President, to get back to Mr. Scherer's question about payments that other nations make. There have been some suggestions in Congress, as alternatives to your U.N. bonds purchase plan, that part of the United States outlay be in matching funds to what other nations buy or possibly to make a loan to the U.N. instead of purchasing bonds. Will you comment on these alternatives?

The President: Well, they're both before the Foreign Relations Committee. I felt that the plan we sent up represented the best interest of the United States and the U.N. and was financially sound. So I would like to stay with that. Now I think the Foreign Relations Committee has my recommendations and knows my views, and I think they're wholly competent - a very responsible committee - and I think they are wholly competent to make a judgment. I do hope that we can keep the U.N. moving, and they do depend upon a program of the kind I suggested. But I think the details I would much prefer to leave to them because it is now in their hands.

Discussion about Berlin and Southeast Asia at Geneva

Q: Mr. President, Secretary of State Rusk has said that it is entirely possible that at Geneva there will be discussions about Berlin and Southeast Asia. Would you favor such discussions at Geneva?

The President: I think that if these matters come up and if any progress can be made on them, of course I favor them. This is not the purpose of the disarmament conference, but anything that can ease relations or anything that could improve the situation in Berlin or in Southeast Asia, of course, ought to be talked about. I think that's quite obvious and we shouldn't miss any opportunity.

Peaceful Cooperation with the USSR in Outer Space

Q: Mr. President, could you give us any ideas of the areas in which we might explore peaceful cooperation with the Soviet Union in the exploration of outer space? What your specific thoughts might be?

The President: Well, I've written a letter today to Chairman Khrushchev, putting forward some proposals, and I think it will be released as soon as he has received it. But I do think it should wait till that. But we did make some suggestions in that letter.

U.S. Policy Toward a New Algerian Government

Q: *Mr. President, this is a twofold question: In the event that there is an Algerian, independent Algerian government established, do you contemplate recognizing it? And, second, should that government request or apply for economic and military aid, would you grant it?*

The President: Well, I think that this matter is so sensitive and coming to such a climax now, and being handled I think with skill, I believe on both sides, that I really think that it would be the wisest course to permit the situation to develop there before we begin to discuss what our actions would be at a later date. So that I think in the interest of the relations between the different parties involved that I will - but I will be glad to discuss that question as soon as a final solution has been reached.

U.S. Intentions Toward Okinawa

Q: *Mr. President, the Attorney General, when he was visiting in Japan, received many inquiries about U.S. intentions towards Okinawa, and I believe you had a Presidential body look into this question. Can you say now what the situation is there insofar as your intentions to give them more self-government?*

The President: As a matter of fact, the Attorney General said that it was really the matter which came up more in his conversations than any other matter, and is a matter of great concern to the Japanese. There was a very responsible committee went out and made some recommendations to us, which have been considered by the Joint Chiefs and others, and we are going to have some suggestions to make to the Japanese Government on this matter, though - in the next days - though quite obviously this is a very vital base. And from that base security is provided for a whole variety of countries in Asia. And so that we have to balance off the defense needs and also the legitimate interests of the people of Okinawa and of Japan. We are going to attempt to do the best we can, given those limitations, and make some suggestions very shortly.

Response of the Steel Companies and Unions to the President's View

Q: *Mr. President, have you any steps in mind to take, any moves to make, if the steel companies and unions do not respond to your view?*

The President: I'd put that with the - France, Algeria, in the sense that I think we ought to wait till we see what happens in the negotiations. These companies are free and the unions are free. All we can try to do is to indicate to them the public interest which is there. After all, the public interest is the sum of the private interests, or perhaps it's even sometimes a little more. In fact, it is a little more. But the Federal Government has no power in these negotiations, unless there was a strike which threatened the national health and safety, and that would be sometime late in the summer. So all we can do is attempt to persuade the parties to go around the bargaining table and point out to them how vitally the public interest is involved.

In the first place, this is a basic industry. We are in a period of recovery which we want to maintain. This is going to be regarded symbolically as a test of our ability to manage our economy in a competitive world. It will be looked on in Europe. I think the public interest is so involved, I think there's there's enough community of interest between the company and the union after their '59 experience that I am hopeful they can reach an accord, and I'm hopeful when they go back in March that they will do it. But we are limited by the Constitution and statutes and proprieties to the areas which I've discussed. But this - I hope they work it out, because it's in their interest as well as the public.

The Pace of the Congress

Q: Mr. President, the Congress has been in session for about 2 months now, and has not accomplished very much. Would you care to comment on how you feel about this present pace?

The President: Well, I must say that always in the first part of March we read about - that the Congress hasn't done much, and in fact last year at this time I think that not a single bill had been passed of any proportion - at the end of the year almost 30 bills. Now we have taken action in four or five areas. The higher education bill has passed both the House and Senate, and the conference hasn't met. I think the conference has come to a conclusion on the manpower retraining, the pension and welfare disclosures. The tax bill is about to come to the floor. I think that legislation is going to come really pouring out of these committees in the next month or 2 months. So I don't have any criticism at all of the pace of the Congress. The test would be whether the legislation which involves not only the well-being of a good many Americans, such as medical care for the aged, but also those pieces of legislation which will help us fight the next economic turn down - whether those pieces of legislation will be passed. And I'm hopeful that the Congress will consider those very carefully or their alternates. But I must say I think you cannot - I think the Congress is moving ahead. I think in some ways it's further ahead than last year, and I think we're going to get a good deal of legislation from the Congress this year.

The Prospects for Disarmament

Q: Mr. President, I know you don't want to prejudice your position in advance of Geneva, but I want to ask you this: Prospects for disarmament and/or a nuclear test ban treaty are indeed pretty dim. What happens if those prospects don't brighten? Do we continue testing? Do the Russians continue testing, escalating the nuclear arms race, ad infinitum?

The President: I suppose that is certainly the danger, and the reason why we are attempting to get an agreement on the cessation of nuclear tests. The reason why I said I thought it would be perfectly proper for us to discuss Berlin and Germany or South Asia is because these matters directly influence the progress of armaments. Without the Korean War - after all, our budget went from $14 billion up to what it is now, and we ourselves have had to spend a good deal more because of Berlin and South Asia, so that I do think there is a direct relation between these political questions and armaments and disarmament. But if we fail to get an agreement on testing, then of course, as I've said, we test. And I presume that others will test. And I regard that as a very risky, in the long run, procedure for the future of the human race.

On the other hand, if we do not test and others test, that has a risk. And I made the determination that that would be the greater risk. Now we're going to try here before the end of April, and we'll also continue trying after the tests begin, if we're unable to get agreement before then. Because I'd much prefer a test agreement than to continue this kind of competition.

The B-70

Q: Mr. President, strong forces in Congress are talking about legislative action to direct you to spend procurement funds for the B-70. I wondered if you could give us your thinking on the B-70 substantive issue, and on the power of Congress to direct you to spend money in such a way.

The President: Well, on the substantive issue, as you know, we put in funds to develop three different prototypes of the B-70. And the - it was proposed by the Air Force that they would have 140 B-70's which would cost $10 billion, which would be ready by 1970 or '71, and that is a large sum of money, and we have a good many manned aircraft. We have over 640 B-52's as well as an extensive missile armory, which is coming in; Polaris we have now, Minuteman we will have, Titan we have now, Atlas we have now. So the question really is whether we should put that large sum of money into manned bombers which will be available in '70 and '71. That's the first point.

The second point is that, according to those who have studied it in the Defense Department, we really can't spend the money now. A good many of the e-quipment - much of the equipment which would go into a B-70, some of it, first, hasn't been developed yet, and we really won't have our major flights in the B-70 till '63 and '64. Now if it's decided in '63 and '64 that we have a strategic need for the B-70, we should then go ahead with it. But to get the money today, when we haven't developed the prototype, seems to me to be - or at least it seemed to Secretary McNamara, who has given it a good deal of study, and to General Lemnitzer, and, I think, to Admiral Anderson and the other members of the Joint Chiefs - Decker - with the exception of the Air Force, it does seem to me to be a - not the most judicious action.

Now, the Congress has a great authority and responsibility. They know a good deal about it. So I think that this is a matter which I hope we can talk about - the Appropriations Committee, the Armed Services Committee of both the House and the Senate, and we can get a better judgment as to what the language will be at the end. But I hope we take a cold look at when this force will be ready, what position it's in today, whether we are prepared to go ahead with production, and what will be the use of this particular force in 1970 or '71 with all of the progress that's being made in missiles, ground-to-air missiles against planes, and in view of the fact that we are going to spend over a billion dollars equipping our present force of B-52's with Skybolts, which will extend their life and their effectiveness. But in the final analysis, this is a matter on which I have relied very heavily on Secretary McNamara, in whom I have the greatest confidence.

The Attorney General's Overseas Trip

Q: Mr. President, the pictures of the Attorney General's overseas trip showed him saying that he was there as the representative of the United States Government. Now, outside of speaking to students, will you tell us what his mission really was and what he achieved?

The President: Well, I, his mission was to - as I said at the previous press conference, his particular mission and interest was to try to talk to students and to intellectuals and others who are among the future leaders of these countries and whom we have not always enjoyed, for reasons which have not always been precise to us, the happiest relations. So I think that that stimulated his visit. He is an official of the United States Government, and I think that those who are in official positions were anxious to talk with him and discuss their problems. The fact of the matter is that five other Cabinet officers went to Japan last fall. I don't know whether you - and a good many

Cabinet officers, Mr. Goldberg, Mr. Hodges, have been to Africa. I think that people who hold positions of importance in the American Government ought to travel, and they learn. I call on them for advice as members of the Cabinet, or the Security Council, and, in addition, they tell these people that we have a very vital, moving country here. And I think his trip was very worthwhile.

Brazilian Seizure of an American-Owned Telephone Company

Q: Mr. President, against the background of the Brazilian seizure of an American-owned telephone company, Congressman Adair, and I believe Senator Long, and others, have introduced legislation which would, in effect, cut off assistance from the United States to nations where American assets have been expropriated without compensation. Would you comment on the desirability of that, and also on the impact of that seizure on America's - on the American public's support of the Alliance for Progress program?

The President: Well, now, as you know, the telephone company was seized by the governor of a province who has not always been identified particularly as a friend of the United States and we have been attempting to work out an equitable solution with the Brazilian Government. Nobody has ever questioned the right of any government to seize property, providing the compensation is fair. The United States is involved with the Brazilian Government in attempting to adjust this matter. I can think of nothing more unwise than to attempt to pass a resolution at this time which puts us in a position not of disagreement with a governor of a state, who is not particularly our friend, but, instead, really, with the whole Brazilian nation, which is vital and which is a key and with which we must have the closest relations. So that we want this matter settled. It is in our interest and in the interest of Brazil.

Private capital is necessary in Latin America. There isn't enough public capital to do the job. And, therefore, we are working on it and the Brazilian Government has been responsive in attempting to work out a satisfactory solution. President Goulart is coming here in April, and we will be discussing many matters which involve our relations. And I must say that if you look at the map and realize the vitality of Brazil, I think that we ought to keep a sense of proportion. We don't want to make the work of those who dislike us easy by reacting to things which happen in a way which strengthens them and weakens the influence of the United States.

The Preservation of Indiana Dunes

Q: Mr. President, you have suggested that the Indiana Dunes, a natural area comparable to that on Cape Cod between Nauset and North Truro, be reserved to the Nation as a national park. It is now in danger of being destroyed by the erection of a steel mill and an artificial harbor. Do you think there is any chance of Federal action to save this area for the Nation?

The President: Well, we made our recommendation and we'll follow and see what the Congress does with it. It's highly controversial. But we expressed what we thought was in the best interests, with the large number of people who live in that immediate area. And we'll continue to watch it through the Congress.

Reporter: Thank you, Mr. President.

THE PRESIDENT'S NEWS CONFERENCE OF

MARCH 14, 1962

The President: I have a letter which we are releasing which is to Secretary Rusk, and I will read the most significant paragraph in regard to the opening of the disarmament conference and American policy there.

It says:

"My earnest hope is that no effort will be spared to define areas of agreement on all of the three important levels to which Prime Minister Macmillan and I referred in our joint letter of February 7 to Premier Khrushchev.

"Building upon the principles already agreed, I hope that you will quickly be able to report agreement on an outline defining the over-all shape of a program for general and complete disarmament in a peaceful world. I have submitted such an outline on behalf of the United States to the United Nations General Assembly last September, but an outline is not enough. You should seek as well, as areas of agreement emerge, a definition in specific terms of measures set forth in the outline. The objective should be to define in treaty terms the widest area of agreement that can be implemented at the earliest possible moment while still continuing your maximum efforts to achieve agreement on those other aspects which present more difficulty. As a third specific objective you should seek to isolate and identify initial measures of disarmament which could, if put into effect without delay, materially improve international security and the prospects for further disarmament progress. In this category you should seek as a matter of highest priority agreement on a safeguarded nuclear test ban. At this juncture in history, no single measure in the field of disarmament would be more productive of concrete benefit in the alleviation of tensions and the enhancement of prospects for greater progress.

"Please convey on my behalf and on behalf of the people of the United States to the representatives of the nations assembled our deep and abiding support of the deliberations on which you are about to embark. I pledge anew my proposal and continuing interest in this work."

QUESTIONS

The Democratic Candidate for Senator from Massachusetts

Q: Mr. President, we had the announcement this morning of a new Democratic candidate for the Senate in Massachusetts, a young man I believe you are familiar with. I wonder, first, if you could tell us whether or not you advised him for or against his decision, and whether you approve it; and two, aware of his stated preference that you not get involved in his campaign and your strong endorsement last week of Senator Smathers of Florida, what the guideline is for your participation in party contests of this nature?

The President: Yes. Well, in part, I am aware of the campaign. I think that my brother stated, and I think Mr. Salinger stated earlier today, that he was running, seeking the Democratic nomination. This is a judgment for the people of Massachusetts. I will not take part in that campaign, except I will go to vote in the primary in September. But my brother is carrying this campaign on his own and will conduct it in that way.

Now, in regard to Senator Smathers, Senator Smathers is an incumbent Senator, and I would - and I think that - I was hoping he would get elected.

Congressman Fascell is the incumbent Congressman. Both, as a matter of fact, have been active in the Democratic Party and were active in my campaign. I was delighted to endorse them. But Teddy is running, as he stated, on his own.

President's Visit to Mexico

Q: Mr. President, about the first of the year while you were in Palm Beach over the Christmas holiday, Mr. Salinger announced that you had accepted an invitation to visit Mexico, but left the date open, and it was our understanding then that you would go in the first half of the year, possibly in the late spring. I wonder what the status of that trip is? Do you still intend to go to Mexico by, say, some time in June?

The President: I still expect to go in the first half of the year; that's correct. The trip is on, yes.

Request for Foreign Aid Funds

Q: Mr. President, some of the economy experts on the Hill have indicated they are going to take the axe to your request for foreign aid funds. Could you tell us what any sizeable cut might mean to your plans and program?

The President: Well, I know foreign aid - it's always open season on it. But I must say, if anybody will look at a map, as I tried to say in the message, of our obligations in Europe and in NATO, the assistance which we have committed ourselves to, and the importance of the countries - countries like Greece, Turkey, Iran, Pakistan - the importance of India being able to maintain a viable economy, our commitments to Thailand, Viet Nam, the Republic of China, South Korea, Africa itself, and now, with the great commitments to Latin America and the Alliance for Progress, it seems to me that it would be extremely unwise not to give us the resources to assist these countries to maintain their independence.

We spend $51 billion-odd on defense alone as well as other billions for the Atomic Energy Commission's work and so forth. Here are these countries which are right in the line of fire, which are dependent upon us for assistance, and we are unwilling, in other words, to give them the help? In Latin America, these countries which are trying, with staggering problems in some of these countries, with mass unemployment, or an average income of $100, no schools in many cases, turn to us for help. India, with an average income of $60, the fight at a crucial stage; in fact, those who seem to, on some occasions, to want to put the axe to foreign aid hardest are the ones that make the most vigorous speeches against communism and call for a policy of victory.

In my opinion the fight is being fought in these towns and cities and states all around the world. And I believe this program is just as important as our national defense. Over half of it is directly tied to arms assistance, which means that it represents an additional appropriation, in a sense, for the Pentagon. And I would think it would be the most unwise act possible to cut our assistance program.

I am more conscious of that than I ever was, sitting where I do. We bear great responsibilities, and if anyone feels that these countries are unimportant, or that it doesn't make any difference if Latin America is taken over, or if significant countries are, by Communists, and if they're not interested in this fight, then they should cut it.

But I am interested. I think we should carry it on. It's been supported by people in both parties. It is a bipartisan issue and I'm hopeful that the Congress will recognize how vital this program is to our security.

State of the Economy

Q: Mr. President, a domestic question, please. You conferred earlier this week with labor leaders. They left the White House saying that in their opinion our economy was dragging in its forward thrust. Later, published reports said that you had agreed with them. Would you comment, please?

The President: No. I stated to them that, of course, we were not as happy about January, that the figures in January were not as high as we hoped they would be. The preliminary estimates we've got now for February indicate that February is much better. My position, I said to them, is the same that I expressed at the press conference a week ago. I think we should wait. We do have confidence in this economy. The problem, of course, that concerns them is that there may be increases in productivity which - and there may be increases in capital investment and consumer spending and all of the rest, but you still have these large pools of unemployed in places like Detroit, Pittsburg, or Gary, where you have technological changes.

You have steel now where there is 85 percent capacity which is the highest that we have had for a long time and yet you have, according to Mr. McDonald, that day nearly 125,000 people out of work in the steel industry. So that this is a serious national problem, unemployment during a period of prosperity which - or relative prosperity.

Now I think that we have sent up a number of programs which I believe will be of help. Manpower retraining, which has now been passed, I think will be of help. And youth employment opportunities, I'm hopeful action will be taken on that. I think our trade program itself would be very helpful. I think that the programs I've suggested for stimulating the economy - for example, I think it would be certainly in our national interest to pass the bill providing for permanent national standards for the payment of unemployment compensation, so that those who are affected will be benefited.

I'm hopeful that they'll pass the so-called Clark bill, public works bill, and also give us additional powers to fight a recession if it comes again.

These are some of the proposals which we have suggested and which they support and we may come forward with others as the year goes on if our economy does not show sufficient vitality. But it is a problem and a matter of concern to them as well as to us.

Summit Conference in Geneva

Q; Mr. President, you have said that you would go to a summit conference at Geneva to ratify agreements, and you also said that you might go to help resolve disagreements. Under what circumstances would you not go to a summit conference at Geneva this spring?

The President: Well, I am not sure that the description you have given of my position is precisely the one that I've given. I stated that I would go there to ratify an agreement, that I would go there if we were on the brink of a war or a serious international crisis, where my presence would make a significant difference. I would add a third one: I would go if I thought it was in our national interest.

Now, that's really - we'll have to make a judgment whether any of those three conditions have been met before I would go. I am not - I do not intend to go unless there is - a situation develops which I believe would make such a trip fruitful and rewarding. And my position, it seems to me, is constant, and we will have to wait to see whether events make such a trip useful.

Committing Troops to Viet-Nam

Q: Mr. President, will you go to Congress for approval before committing combat troops in Viet-Nam or elsewhere?

The President: Well, if - coming back to the phrase, if you mean would I go to the Congress before committing combat troops, as you know, there are a good many Americans who are now there who have not, as I said before in a press conference, fallen under the description which is generally used in using the phrase "combat troops." I have described what their mission is and what instructions they're operating under. If there is a basic change in that situation in Viet-Nam which calls for a constitutional decision, of course I would go to the Congress.

In the meanwhile, I have consulted with the leaders of Congress and those who bear particular positions of responsibility in the matter.

Nuclear Test Ban Treaty

Q: Mr. President, there is a school of thought which believes that we should include in any nuclear test ban treaty a provision which would permit us to conclude our scheduled April tests. This is based on authoritative reports that the Soviets in their recent nuclear tests have sufficient data to develop an anti-missile weapon, and that we vitally need our own atmospheric tests to catch up with them. Would you care to comment on this matter?

The President: Well, in the first place, I've not seen authoritative reports which state as a result of their recent tests they have developed an anti-missile system.

Q: Data, Mr. President.

The President: Data? Well, data, everything contributes to the development of data. We're carrying on a Nike-Zeus test ourselves which will contribute data. That's the first point. The second point, I'm not aware that our tests will contribute data. But I am not convinced, nor have I known of anyone else, that they would provide a breakthrough in this very complicated area of the anti-missile. I think Mr. McNamara has expressed some views on the difficulties of developing an anti-missile system. And the third point is that if the position of the United States stays as it is, we would prefer to secure a test ban treaty. We believe that to be not only in the interest of the peace and the world but also in the interest of the United States. In our opinion, our security position would be strengthened if there were no more atmospheric tests because - and we believe that if the others are going to test then we have to test. But we would prefer to have no test. Therefore, I prefer an effective treaty.

Freeing Cuba from Communism

Q: Mr. President, many Latin Americans are wondering whether the recent expulsion of Cuba from the OAS and the trade restrictions by the United States will help free Cuba of communism. Could you tell us what positive action the United States could take to make Cuba less dependent upon the Communist bloc?

The President: Well, we are attempting to work with the hemisphere to isolate the expansion of communism in the hemisphere. And that has occupied a good deal of our attention and it was the purpose of the meeting at Punta del Este. And I believe that that purpose was achieved in that the nations of the hemisphere unanimously, with the exception of Cuba, went on record as considering communism alien to the hemisphere.

Now, we have also carried out certain trade actions indicating our position in regard to Cuba, and we are continuing to consider what can usefully be done to expand freedom in this hemisphere.

Inspections of Nuclear Tests

Q: Mr. President, there have been reports that some Western officials at the disarmament meeting at Geneva have expressed doubt that any system of inspection and control, no matter how rigid or comprehensive, could possibly either prevent or detect secret preparations for nuclear weapons tests in an area as large as the Soviet Union. Would you give us your view on that?

The President: Obviously, I think that we could develop a system which would predict, or which would detect, significant results with an effective inspection system. Preparations - of course, there is no guarantee, because preparations are another matter, there is no guarantee that any inspection system can be worked out that can predict all inspections. But I think that we could work out a system that would detect a series of tests. And that would be most useful. We could also, and will suggest, some proposals to at least make it more difficult to prepare - make preparations. But I've never suggested that we could develop a foolproof system on preparations. And I don't regard that as significant, as being able to detect the tests themselves, because once - preparations are only important if they lead to tests. Once the tests come, then if the system is satisfactory, we receive a notification and could take action ourselves. There would be a time loss, but it would not be as - the important thing is to have some ability to detect preparations and also a very effective ability to detect the tests themselves.

Federal Insurance Against Property Loss

Q: Mr. President, I believe as a Senator about 6 years ago you were a co-sponsor of legislation passed by Congress entitled The Federal Flood Insurance Act of 1956, setting up a program of Federal insurance and coinsurance against property loss by floods and other damage, water damages. That program never got off the ground because of lack of appropriations. In view of the devastating northeaster on the East Coast last week, and the importance of some kind of insurance against water damage, which is not provided by the insurance companies in the rebuilding of these areas, would you consider requesting appropriations to get this flooded Federal insurance program under way again?

The President: Yes. Well, I know that your - why this has become a matter of - living - (laughter) - and I must say that I think your experience indicates the desirability of legislation. The legislation is still on the books - the authorization - the Senate passed the appropriation, but the House did not. So I would support it if - in fact, I will take another look at it and see whether we should recommend a supplemental appropriation in regard to the matter. But I do think the bill was useful and I think the experiences in the recent storm generally along the coast would indicate the desirability of the bill and the appropriation.

The USSR and the Berlin Air Corridors

Q: Mr. President, the Russians have been playing a very dangerous game in the Berlin air corridors, dropping tinfoil fragments and so on. Does this Government contemplate any countermeasures to discourage them from carrying their harassment further?

The President: Well, obviously, the harassment makes it more difficult to reach accord on Berlin and has been the subject of very vigorous representations by Secretary Rusk and by Lord Home at Geneva. And, obviously, it makes it, as I've said, more - it presents additional hazards in securing a satisfactory accord.

If the Soviet Union desired to see this matter settled peacefully, it would seem to me that all sides, both sides, should bend every effort during these days, particularly during the time of the Geneva disarmament conference, to avoid incidents that are liable to lead to actions and counteractions which can only intensify the danger. But we are waiting to see what effect the representations of the two Secretaries have had on the Soviet Union in regard to the chaff, which is a particularly dangerous kind of action.

Unemployment

Q: Sir, during your 1960 campaign, when you spoke of getting the country moving again, a lot of States and a lot of voters interpreted this to mean jobs for themselves. And now, recently, States such as Ohio, Michigan, and Pennsylvania have been complaining that some of their defense contracts have been going elsewhere and the ones they had under the previous administration, that is, the level has not stayed even as good as it was. Do you have any comment on this situation?

The President: No, I would have to - in my opinion, I don't think that in any of those three cases, even though this matter of contracts is a matter of continuing concern - defense contracts - we have a particularly difficult problem in Detroit, which has been the subject of a recent discussion. I don't think that the contracts in any of those three States - and I'd have to check it - are less than they were before.

The question is whether the distribution of the contracts is as equitable as it can be. The Defense Department, when manpower policy No. 4 was repealed in 1953, was given express indications by the Congress that they were not, except for the set-aside portion of the contract, that they were not supposed to attempt to steer contracts into areas where there might be unemployment.

I supported Defense manpower policy No. 4, but since that time the Defense Department has not been able to take that into consideration.

On the other hand, equity dictates that these contracts be assigned in areas which are not only efficient but where there is a work force which can be effectively used. But I will say that we have been considering the problem. Governor Lawrence discussed the problem of Scranton with me when he came to see me. We were talking about the problem of Detroit. My judgment is, and I would have to recheck it, that probably in these States the contracts are equal to or greater than they were the year before. But there is a concentration of contracts in a relatively few States which is historic, and I am concerned that in the case, as I say, of Detroit and two or three others where there's high unemployment, we do try to get some work to them, and it's a matter now which we are discussing.

Exporting Wheat to Communist China

Q: Mr. President, there have been reports that the United States Government has been considering an application to export from $75 million to $100 million worth of wheat per year to Communist China over the next 3 years. Could you say if there is any bona fide request from the Chinese for such an export of wheat, and if so what do you think about it?

The President: No, I've heard of no requests from them for the wheat. There have been two companies in the United States which have put in a request for a license to - one was the International Trading Company, I believe, of Seattle, and one other company - which have put in requests for the right to export wheat to China. But there is no information that they are working on an assignment or as an agent, and the United States Government has no information that the Chinese Communists have requested us for wheat.

Funds for the B-70

Q: Mr. President, if Congress should pass legislation directing you to spend additional funds for the B-70, would you feel bound by any such direction?

The President: I think that we should wait until the Congress has acted and the Appropriations Committees have acted and then we can make a much better judgment as to what the final situation will be. But it's a matter which I am confident that - I'm very hopeful can be adjusted satisfactorily. And I think we ought to wait on action.

Inspection Against Clandestine Nuclear Tests

Q: I wonder if we could be quite clear about what seemed to be an emendation of your statement of last month about the necessity for inspection against clandestine preparation for nuclear tests. Then you seemed to lay great emphasis upon the necessity for inspection against preparations. I understood you to say just now that you thought that the detection of tests themselves was more important than the inspection against preparations.

The President: That's correct. I said that because quite obviously you could prepare for years and have no tests. So the tests themselves, which carry out the results of the inspection, of course are a matter of particular significance because you could be preparing indefinitely. That is not to say that preparations are not important. We are going to make proposals in regard to inspection of preparations. I merely attempted to balance off two important matters and give you what I considered to be the one with the greater weight.

Latin America and Submission of Reforms to Alliance for Progress Centers

Q: Mr. President, much of the criticism of the Alliance for Progress centers on the charge that the Latin American countries are slow in submitting development plans for their countries and in effecting the reforms that are a precondition of getting that aid. I think only three countries have submitted plans, and three countries have made no attempt at reforms. I'm curious as to whether the Government has considered setting a cutoff date for reforms, or perhaps cutting off aid to countries which don't effect tax reforms and land reforms, as a way of making this program more popular.

The President: Well, I think we should have some sense of perspective about the Alliance for Progress. It was, after all, only - the organization took place only 7 months ago. This is a whole new communal effort. I attempted to describe yesterday some of the things which have been done during that 7-month period. Some of these countries have made great efforts, with great difficulties, to carry out the kinds of reform which would make our assistance most useful. Some other countries are in the process. But there - every one of these issues must be fought out within each country because if it were easy it would have been done long ago. So I do think that we should not - having set our hand to a program which I believe has great potential, we should attempt to work as closely as possible with each one of the governments in assisting them. It requires in many cases personnel which they do not have; it requires experience and technical training which they do not have. The problem of the Marshall plan was rebuilding; here it's a case of building, in many cases. So this is an extremely difficult task. There are a good many local pressures which make this fight harder. In many cases countries must put in fiscal reforms which cause - which have a deflationary impact, with all the political hazards that they produce. In some of these countries they are carrying out these reforms and these reforms - as I say, each one of them hurts some group in that country at the beginning. And, therefore, they're very difficult. And yet they have to carry them out when they're hanging, in some of these cases, with Communist minorities who are exploiting every discontent. So that while I feel we should be very positive in our efforts in this community effort, I do think we should have some understanding of how complicated this task is and give this child a chance to build some strength before we psychoanalyze him.

Dairy Price Support Program

Q: The House Agriculture Committee last week, sir, rejected your temporary dairy price support program, and there are indications they will make some substantial changes in the rest of the farm bill. If the Congress does not approve a bill that carries most of your recommendations, do you foresee some cutoff or specific time when you would recommend the ending of the existing programs?

The President: Well, as you know, the decision of the House majority of the Agricultural Committee, and which I thought was unfortunate, meant that the dairy farmers would not have till December to adjust themselves to the production standards which the agricultural bill set. Instead they must adjust themselves, unless there's some change made in that decision, by April, which will, I would say, would have a great - it would produce a harsh effect on the dairy farmers. And I would hope that the Agricultural Committee of the House would reverse that decision. It - I must say I found it to be inexplicable, because it's - we are asking them and putting burdens on them and restraining them, and to compel them to do it in as brief a time as this, I think produces unnecessary hardship.

Defense Contracts

Q: Mr. President, I wonder if you could clarify a little further your position on defense contracts? At one of your recent press conferences you discussed this in relation to areas of unemployment, and this seems to have become an issue in the California gubernatorial campaign. Former Vice President Nixon takes the position that you are injecting politics in the allocation of defense contracts, and Governor Brown takes the opposite position. I wonder if you could clear it up?

The President: What action is it of mine that has injected politics into the -

Q: I think at your last press conference you discussed this.

The President: No. I was asked a question with regard to a matter that was before Secretary Goldberg, and I think the reporter who asked me specifically said nondefense expenditures. Now, the fact of the matter is that defense expenditures in California are higher than they were under the previous administration for both defense and space, and in fact, as you know, in California the contracts amount to a - traditionally and historically since World War II, to a high percentage. So I was responding to a question which was asked in regard to nondefense expenditures and a suggestion of Mr. Goldberg's that perhaps we could use these contracts in nondefense areas, in areas of high unemployment. So that I didn't really see that that was a fuse sufficient to light off Mr. Nixon. (Laughter)

Health Care for the Aged

Q: Mr. President, this week you accepted an invitation to address a mammoth rally in behalf of health care for the aged in Madison Square Garden in May, I believe. Is this part of an all-out administration effort to obtain a vote on this issue during this session of Congress?

The President: That is correct.

Q: Then it is not true that the administration leaders will hold off for another year?

The President: Oh, no, this plan will come to a vote, in my opinion, definitely in the United States Senate, and I am hopeful in the House, before the end of this session.

Reporter: Thank you, Mr. President.

THE PRESIDENT'S NEWS CONFERENCE OF

MARCH 21, 1962

The President: I have one announcement. I've received this morning Chairman Khruschev's reply to my letter of March 7 on outer space cooperation.[1] I am gratified that this reply indicates that there are a number of areas of common interest. The next step clearly is for the United States representative on the U.N. Outer Space Committee, Ambassador Francis Plimpton, to meet in New York with the Soviet representative to make arrangements for an early discussion of the specific ideas of the Soviet Union and the United States. I have designated Dr. Hugh Dryden, Deputy Administrator of the National Aeronautics and Space Administration, to take the lead for the United States at this time in subsequent technical talks with Soviet representatives.

The United States is deeply committed to making all possible efforts to carry forward the exploration and use of space in a spirit of cooperation and for the benefit of all mankind. I am hopeful that there will be in this area prospects for practical cooperation.

QUESTIONS

The Russian Position on Onsite Inspections

Q: Mr. President, in Geneva in the talks that are going on now, the Russians have expressed the feeling that any onsite inspection in connection with an atomic test ban treaty would be an invitation to espionage and even be insulting. The British, on the other hand, have spoken in the last 24 hours of settling for an absolute minimum of verification.

I wondered what you consider an acceptable minimum of verification. In other words, would the United States accept any sort of inspection system that did not embrace the right of international inspection teams to be on Soviet soil as well as U.S. soil?

The President: Well, I think it's so much better to permit the Secretary of State, Arthur Dean, and Mr. Foster, who are carrying the lead for the United States, to conduct the negotiations. We have - it's possible to pick up a number of disturbances from the observation posts outside the Soviet Union. But, of course, the great difficulty is that you cannot distinguish by seismic means alone, at this range, between an earthquake and a possible nuclear explosion. And it is for that reason that we have felt that there must be onsite inspection and the ability to make that determination if a suspicious event should occur. It does seem to be a very basic difference between the Soviet Union and the United States because they have suggested that they would not be prepared, even if the devices were located off the territory of the Soviet Union, they would not be prepared to permit an inspection team to come on to make the precise determination as to the location and kind of disturbance which had taken place. So there is a disagreement between the Soviet Union and ourselves. I think that on the details of the discussion in the negotiations, we have sent very able men to represent us and I think they will represent the interests of the United States in this matter.

The U.S. and the U.N.

Q: Mr. President, Senator Jackson says that this administration and the last have been putting too much stock in the United Nations and that a strong Atlantic Community offers the best avenue to peace. What is your view on this?

The President: I see nothing contradictory in a strong Atlantic Community and the United Nations. Nor is there anything contradictory in a strong Organization of American States and the United Nations. In fact, the United Nations, when it was written in 1945, gave room for these regional organizations, of which there are a great many and of which the United States is a member. I support the United Nations very strongly and I think the American people do, not because its power is unlimited and not because we commit our policy to the United Nations so much as because we believe that it serves the interests of the United States and the interests of the United States are in an association of free people working together to maintain the peace.

Now, I would be very unhappy if the United Nations were weakened or eliminated. You would have a great increase in the chances of a direct concentration in some place like the Congo between the great powers. It might involve the United States directly and perhaps the Soviet Union on the other side. The United Nations serves as a means of channeling these matters, on which we disagree so basically, in a peaceful way. But that doesn't suggest that we have to choose between the Atlantic Community and the United Nations. We believe in the Atlantic Community; we are committed to strengthening it. We are attempting, for example, to do that in a number of ways - and in fact, our association is constantly growing more intimate. And we also support the United Nations. Senator Jackson is a very valuable Senator who's done very effective work and anything he says deserves a good deal of attention. I do want to point out that on this matter, certainly, there's no disagreement between us.

Discussions at Geneva

Q: There have been reports from Geneva, sir, that for all practical purposes the discussions there are deadlocked, not only in the field of disarmament but on such other topics as discussions with the Soviets concerning Berlin. Do you subscribe to that, sir, or do you think there is additional hope for further talks?

The President: Oh, I think the talks should go on. The conference has only been in session for - I'm not prepared to abandon it in any degree, and I think it would be a mistake for us to feel that its prospects are finished.

Criticism of the U.N. Bond Proposal

Q: Mr. President, in connection with your remarks about the United Nations, we have recently read criticism of the U.N. bond issue proposal and about the bill that has come out of the Senate Foreign Relations Committee. Would you comment on these matters, too, please?

The President: Well, there has been an alternate suggestion put forward for meeting the financial crisis of the United Nations. I think most people are aware that the United Nations faces a very serious financial crisis - that unless it receives assistance by one means or another, that the operation in the Congo, upon which so much depends, will end and we will have a very difficult and perhaps chaotic situation which will, I think, be far more costly to us in the long run and far more hazardous. So we have to come to their assistance.

The second problem, of course, is that we have been meeting our assessments and we've been paying over 50 percent of the special assessments which were developed as a result of the Congo operation and as a result of the operation in the Middle East to keep the peace. Now, it seemed to us, and to the General Assembly - and I think this is an important point - it may be possible to suggest other plans but this is the one that the General Assembly has adopted.

The General Assembly puts forward this proposal which will make it compulsory in the future, and this will be particularly true when the World Court renders its opinion, and our judgment is they'll render an opinion that these special operations must be paid as regular assessments, otherwise the country involved will lose its voting power.

Now, this is the plan the United Nations has adopted and we have committed ourselves and we hope the Congress will support this effort. We said we would buy $100 million worth of bonds. The Foreign Relations Committee stated we would buy $25 million worth of bonds and up to $100 million if the other countries met their quota.

Now, so far over $50 million has been pledged by other countries. Senator Aiken and Senator Hickenlooper - Senator Hickenlooper was a member, I think, of a delegation to the U.N., Senator Aiken has been a long time supporter. This is not a hostility to the U.N. on their part. They feel that this plan is preferable. But in my judgment it would mean that the United Nations would be faced with attempting to pay back $100 million in 3 years. I don't think that there is any evidence that they can do it. It would have to be submitted to the General Assembly to be voted upon after they voted upon a different plan. The smaller nations definitely could not contribute to it, and in my judgment it would be back in our lap at the end of 3 years.

Now, the General Assembly has moved. We are moving on a plan which I think offers a hope of success. As I say, already a number of countries have met their responsibility. We hope they'll go higher to the $100 million. I think we ought to go ahead and I'm hopeful the Senate and the House will, because in my judgment failure to go ahead in this ground is going to mean a collapse of this special effort, and then what's going to happen in the Congo and the Middle East? I think it would be a great mistake, and I'm hopeful that the Senate will consider it very carefully.

In my judgment, every survey shows that 80 to 85 percent of the American people realize the importance of the United Nations. And this is vital to the life of the United Nations, this issue.

Q: Mr. President, on the bond issue again, when you sent your message up to Congress you said that the proceeds of the bond issue would be used to

liquidate the debts of the United Nations for the Congo and Middle East opera-
tions. And a few days later when Mr. Rusk went up, he said that the proceeds
would be used to pay for these two operations for 18 months beginning next
July 1st. The Senate Foreign Relations Committee was not able to get this
straightened out in testimony. I wonder if you could state what the ———

The President: Well, I don't - I think - I'm not familiar with - I'm not
aware that there is a disagreement between the statement that I made and Mr.
Rusk made. I'd have to check his testimony and my statement to see if there
was a disagreement. But there is a debt, and there will be need for funds.
And therefore it seems to me that in a sense both positions are in accordance
with the - both Mr. Rusk's statement and my statement are not exclusive. We're
going - this goes to meet the debts, and to maintain these special operations
for the next 18 months.

The President and the Cuban Operation

Q: Mr. President, there seems to be some continuing difference of opinion
between yourself and Mr. Nixon, and I wondered if, in view of yesterday's state-
ment, you feel that the CIA should have briefed you about the Cuban operation
during the 1960 campaign?

The President: I thought that yesterday's statements by the White House
and by Mr. Dulles were very clear, and I think that closes the matter as far
as I'm concerned.

The Use of Outer Space

Q: Sir, about this agreement that the U.N. Committee is now working on to
get peaceful uses for outer space for the United States and other nations - it
has been mentioned several times that this agreement would be patterned after
the Antarctic Agreement, and, if so, would this not mean that we would give up
any future scientific or territorial gains and would have to submit to inspec-
tion by foreign nations? And how would you separate your peaceful uses from
your military uses, because wouldn't all of these scientific gains go together?

The President: Well, it's hard to - I would say that this is a - I had not
heard this comparison. I'm not sure that there is a precise comparison between
the Antarctic and outer space. I do think that this is a matter that will be
negotiated. I think that the interests of our country will be protected in
that negotiation. I can assure you, in fact, they will be. But we are anxious
to assure, if possible, that outer space is used peacefully in order to protect
the interests of the United States. So I think we should go into the negotiations and see if it's possible for us to cooperate, because there's not much
security, as space continues to be more and more under the hazard of being used
for military purposes.

The President's Medical Care Plan

Q: Mr. President, the critics of your medical care plan have charged that
this will be the opening wedge for socialized medicine in this country. Would
you care to comment on that, sir?

The President: Well, it is an old argument, when a case is lost, to argue
that it is all right here, but what is it going to mean for the future. Under
that argument, there would not have been any progress on any social legislation
in this country. That was the argument that was used aginst the Social Security Act in the thirties. It was the argument used against the minimum wage, it

is the argument used against any agricultural program. It is the oldest argument in the world. The fact of the matter is, this is a useful program, it is developed for a special purpose, and, in my judgment, it's going to be adopted. I believe it has a good chance this year, if not, in the future, and it's in the economic as well as the social interests of the people of our country. But to say, "I am against it because in a future date somebody else may do something" doesn't seem to me to be a rational argument, and it was the kind of argument which was successfully defeated on many occasions during the administration of Franklin Roosevelt.

The Trial of Prisoners in Cuba as War Criminals

Q: Mr. President, what is your reaction to the news that the 1200 prisoners from the Bay of Pigs are going to be tried as war criminals in Cuba? Specifically, do you feel there's anything this Government can do for them?

The President: We would - have been attempting - as you know, the Red Cross has been attempting to secure an entrance into Cuba to see about the feeding of the prisoners. Of course, it is a matter of great national as well as personal distress.

The United States' Food Surplus

Q: Many people not farm experts are perplexed by the continuing food paradox - a million starving even outside Communist countries, while we're up to our necks in surplus. And they wonder why we can't go far beyond extending Public Law 480, church distribution, and so forth, and really make tremendous amounts of surpluses that we can't seem to get rid of available to the hungry. Would you discuss economic or other factors preventing this?

The President: Well, we are putting a good many hundreds of millions - in fact, billions - into this program. I think the - there isn't any doubt that we could produce more food. We could produce, really, more of almost everything in the United States. There is a limit to what the United States is able to maintain. We spend, as you know, billions of dollars each year on our agricultural program. It isn't as if this - the limitation, in answer to your question, is really a financial one. How much can the United States afford to put into its agricultural program? We're putting in $6 billion; we're giving away, as I say, hundreds of millions, indeed some billions of dollars worth of food, in an unprecedented effort. I agree we should always try to do more. But in answer to your question, the reason is only the limitation of available funds. This food has to be bought, and it has to be appropriated for, and it has to come out of the taxpayers of the United States. We do an awful lot, not only on this program of food but also on foreign aid. In fact - and have done it for a great many years. And I think we should. But I think that - I would certainly contrast the record of the United States in this regard to other countries, even those with a surplus of agricultural abundance, and what we've been able to do through private agencies and through the Federal Government.

The Senate Foreign Relations Committee's Plan on the Bond Issue

Q: Sir, a clarification on your comments on the bond issue. Do you find the Senate Foreign Relations Committee plan an acceptable one?

The President: Yes, I do. I do.

The Price of Stock in the Proposed Communications Satellite

Q: Mr. President, the Attorney General has suggested that the price of stock in the proposed communications satellite corporation be reduced from $1,000 to $100. Has any thought been given to reducing this price to $1 so all the taxpayers could get in on the ground floor?

The President: I think that the - of course the limitation is that there may be quite a long period of time before there is any return on this invest- ment. We attempted in the program we set up to balance off the need for large investments by - which only a few companies can make, and also to permit it to have a broader distribution than just a few large companies. We're attempting to make an adjustment. As you know, a good many companies are unwilling to in- vest in the satellite, because it would require a good many years before they would get a return. And I don't know - I would have to examine whether it's in the public interest to lower the price. I don't think that the return would be, to the American people, in dollars and cents, except as part perhaps of a participation in a great new effort. I'm not sure the dollar and cents return would be comparable to what they might be able to get in other areas, at least for a great many years.

Soviet Recognition of the Algerian Government

Q: Mr. President, the Soviet Union has recognized the Algerian Government before it has formally taken place. Would you say what you think about this, and what the United States might possibly do towards recognition and at what time?

The President: Well, as you correctly say, there is a cease-fire now in effect in Algeria. A government has not been established. There is still - in the field of foreign policy France still bears responsibility. A government will be developed and at that time the United States will take the proper ac- tion. I think that this matter, as I've said from the beginning, is a very sensitive and difficult matter that's been handled with great skill by Presi- dent de Gaulle. It's been handled by those on the Algerian side with a de- sire to - not to destroy but rather to build, and I think the United States should take a similar attitude rather than attempting for political purposes to exploit a situation. I think we should wait until the proper moment and the proper moment finally will come.

A Buildup of Cuban Military Strength

*Q: Mr. President, there are reports from Guantanamo Bay of a buildup in Cuban military strength in the fortifications outside the American naval **base** there. Do you consider this a threat to the base, and do you have any plans for increasing the base's defenses?*

The President: Well, we're always concerned about the defense of American territory wherever it may be and would take whatever proper steps were neces- sary. We have no information that there's a, if that is your suggestion, that some attack on Guantanamo is about to take place. We see no evidence of that.

Porter Hardy's Subcommittee and the State Department

Q: Mr. President, Congressman Porter Hardy's subcommittee has been having some troubles getting hold of some records from the State Department, and they have contended that lawyers at the State Department are barring them from these records which deal with the foreign aid in Cambodia, which was used in a Rus- sian-sponsored hospital. Now I realize this took place before your adminis- tration took power, but there is the contention by the committee that the State

Department at the present time is withholding the records. I wonder if they have consulted you on this, and if you have given the State Department any instructions?

The President: I'm generally familiar. My understanding is that they have turned over the cables to the committee, but they have not - they have agreed, I think, and this may be subject to change afterwards, my understanding is that they have agreed to turn over the names that might be involved in an executive session. But we cannot run the executive branch of the Government if every Foreign Service officer, or everyone else who is acting in good faith - and if there's evidence that it is not in good faith, then we ought to bring that right out and he ought to be, he ought to have some action taken. But if he's acting in good faith, then how can we expect honest reporting from them? Or how can we expect that they're going to - if they feel that this might be, 6 months or a year from now, be used against them in some hearing, about which they can only presume?

The responsibility is on us to carry out the foreign policy of the United States with the cooperation of the Congress. And we don't - I'm sure the Congress would not want us to be inhibited in getting our information upon which our judgments must be reached. We desire to cooperate with Congressman Hardy. I believe he said he was going to - he's seen me on one occasion about another matter last year. I think I saw somewhere or heard some place that he is planning to discuss this directly with me. And I'll discuss it, and I'm hopeful that we can work this out as other matters have been worked out, in a spirit of comity. But I do think there are important issues at stake.

A Zonal Disarmament Plan

Q: Mr. President, Dr. Hans Bethe has commented favorably on a zonal disarmament inspection plan that has been put forward by Professor Louis Sohn of Harvard University. The plan would operate on a random sampling basis, and would supposedly satisfy the United States desires by opening up territory to verification on a sampling basis, while at the same time pleasing the Russians by not opening up their entire territory to what they say they fear would be espionage. I wonder if you would comment on whether parts of this proposal offer constructive possibilities?

The President: Well, I think one of the suggestions in the matter of preparations which have been discussed, which we all recognize is a rather difficult matter, of determining if preparations are being made for testing, was this. I'm not sure that the genesis was the same as the one you've suggested, but it had been suggested that a sampling system might be used.

But I think once again this is a matter which I think should come forward in the proper way at Geneva. But I am familiar with the - a proposal which is either the same or similar.

Demonstrations by Mobilized Reservists at Military Camps

Q: Mr. President, at some of our military camps there have been demonstrations by mobilized reservists, including in one case an attempted hunger strike. I wonder if you couldn't comment on these demonstrations, and couldn't you give the reservists some notion of when they might be released?

The President: Well, I understand the feeling of any reservist, particularly those who may have fulfilled their duty and then they are called back. And they see others going along in normal life, and therefore they feel: how long are we going to be kept?

We have stated that we are, as you know, building two new divisions which will replace these reservists, and which will come into effect — I think the dates are August and September.

Now, on the question of releasing the reservists, we will release them on the first possible date consistent with our national security. They were called up because of the crisis in Berlin, and because of the threats in Southeast Asia. And I do not think that anyone can possibly read the papers and come to the conclusion that these threats do not continue. There is no evidence that we are going to quickly reach a settlement in either one of these areas.

These reservists are doing a very important job. In my judgment, the fact they were called up and the fact they responded has strengthened the foreign policy of the United States measurably since last July and August.

Now, secondly, there is always inequity in life. Some men are killed in a war and some men are wounded, and some men never leave the country, and some men are stationed in the Antarctic and some are stationed in San Francisco. It's very hard in military or in personal life to assure complete equality. Life is unfair. But I do hope that in many ways — some people are sick and others are well — but I do hope that these people recognize that they are fulfilling a valuable function, and that they will feel, however humdrum it is, and however much their life is disturbed and the years have been yanked out of it, they will have the satisfaction afterwards of feeling that they contributed importantly to the security of their families and their country at a significant time.

Talks Between the U.S. and the USSR

Q: Mr. President, could you tell us whether the reports you've received on the talks between Secretary Rusk and Mr. Gromyko in the last day or two on the Berlin problem have produced even a glimmer of a possibility of a modus vivendi of some sort?

The President: I would think it would be wiser to let the talks continue, which they are, and then to make a judgment as to our prospects when these talks have reached a more final stage, which they have not as yet.

Congressional Support for the Administration's Domestic Program

Q: Would you care, sir, to evaluate for us the quality of congressional support the administration's domestic program is getting at the present time? I ask this because in some circles there is a belief that certain congressional leaders in your party are more prone to negotiate the terms of surrender even before they start fighting for your program.

The President: Well, I read the same — (laughter) — I think that we've secured — I think they blame the leadership and they blame me and they blame the Congress, and I think we've secured the passage of important legislation already: one we signed the other day, the pension and welfare bill; the one the week before, the manpower training. We have, I hope, passed good bills in the House and Senate on higher education. I hope that the conference will not give us the worst features of both but, rather, the best features of both, the House and Senate bill.

We are moving ahead in the committees in other areas. So I think we can make a much fairer judgment on the quality of the Congress and the Executive as the session goes into the summer, than we can today. But I have had complete cooperation from Senator Mansfield and Senator Humphrey — the leader and the whip — from Speaker McCormack, from Congressmen Albert and Hale Boggs, and from George Smathers. So I must say that they've been very faithful and I think they're doing the best they can.

You have to remember that this House of Representatives is somewhat evenly balanced. We only won the Rules Committee fight at the beginning of this session, at the time Mr. Rayburn put his enormous prestige on the line, by only six votes. These are not easy matters. We are very critical, frequently, of failure of other countries to take needed action, but we have to realize it's a hard fight even in our own country.

Settlement of the B-70 Question

Q: Mr. President, I understand that an exchange of letters at the summit has settled the question of the B-70, or the RS-70. Can you tell us who won what and from whom?

The President: Well, I think that if you took the powers of the Executive and the powers of the Congress and pushed each to its logical, or at least its possible conclusion - not its logical but its possible conclusion - you would have, in a Government of divided powers, you would have a somewhat chaotic situation. If they refused to appropriate the salary of members of the Government, if we took actions which failed to consider the responsibilities of the Congress - in a country where the constitution gives divided responsibilities we have to attempt to adjust the strong feelings on both sides.

In my opinion, there was no winner and no loser except, I think, the relations between the Congress and I think the public interest.

Guantanamo Bay

Q: Mr. President, you used the words "American territory" in relation to Guantanamo Bay. Is that not subject to an incorrect inference of the true position of that bay?

The President: My answer was an attempt to not particularly select one area or another. It's the legal definition of Guantanamo, maybe not precisely, though I would have to look that up. I would say it's an area which the United States, under a treaty with Spain, at the turn of the century, was given rights to maintain and to hold, and whether it's - it may be, as I say, incorrect legally to call it a territory, and I would not want to launch a new description of Guantanamo, and I may be very well subject to correction - only that it's an area which is under the responsibility now of the United States. That may be a more precise term.

Resumption of Nuclear Tests in the Atmosphere

Q: Mr. President, in explaining the need to resume nuclear tests in the atmosphere, you said we're spending huge sums on some military programs, including hardened missile sites, and that we can't be certain how much of these preparations might turn out to be useless when we know more about thermonuclear explosions. In the wake of increased missile accuracy and warhead yields and the fact that the Russians can build very large bombs, can you tell us, as Commander in Chief, why we're expanding what would appear to be an increasingly vulnerable land-based missile system, rather than putting our efforts in mobile land-based systems, or directing more of our deterrent to sea where they cannot be zeroed in?

The President: Well, I think that - as you know, the Secretary of Defense, and those who have particular technical competence, made a judgment that the present arrangements were more satisfactory than the so-called mobile Minuteman. That is filled with difficulties, too; transporting always - 24 hours a day - around the railroads of the United States, missiles to be fired at any moment, is not - offers - has a debit side too. So that in balance this was felt to be the most satisfactory device. And, in addition, as you know, we have the alert, those that are in the air, and we also have Polaris. So that the - I think the reason is a desire not to commit all of our resources to any one particular weapons system. But I do think a judgment was made that the efficiency of the mobile, at the present time, was not sufficiently demonstrated over the hardened site to warrant a program in that regard, particularly as we develop more successfully devices for interpreting a possible missile attack. So that we have a warning system which would be sufficient to get our Minuteman off the hardened base. But I think the more they looked at the trains going through America, the less desirable it seemed.

U.S. Offer to Withdraw a Demand for Control Posts for Nuclear Test Bans

Q: Mr. President, did I understand you to say that we had offered to withdraw our demand for control posts for nuclear test bans inside the Soviet Union?

The President: No.

Q: And they had refused?

The President: No. What I said was that those who advocated a system for attempting to - and there are those - to carry on an inspection system by having devices located off the territory of the Soviet Union, I think would also agree that you cannot make a successful distinction by this means between an earthquake and an underground nuclear explosion. And that therefore there has to be even under this system, which is not the one the United States is now - has put forward - even under this system you would have to have an inspection in order to make that distinction. So that the - and the Soviet Union has rejected that kind of inspection. So that I was merely attempting to indicate that those who advocated that policy did not have a policy which gave any assurances of success and which the Soviet Union has already in effect - has rejected.

Reporter: Thank you, Mr. President.

[1]See item 96 of the *Public Papers of the President.*

THE PRESIDENT'S NEWS CONFERENCE OF

MARCH 29, 1962

The President: I have several announcements to make.

It is with extreme regret that I announce the retirement of Associate Justice of the Supreme Court Charles Evans Whittaker, effective April 1. Justice Whittaker, a member of the Supreme Court for nearly 5 years, of the Federal Judiciary for nearly 8 years, is retiring at the direction of his physician for reasons of disability. I know that the bench and the bar of the entire Nation join me in commending Mr. Justice Whittaker for his devoted service to his country during a critical period in its history.

Next, I want to take this opportunity to stress again the importance of the tax bill now before the House of Representatives. An attempt is being made in that House to defeat this bill by sending it back to committee, and if it is killed we will have lost a most valuable opportunity to find jobs for the college and high school graduates who will be seeking those jobs in June of this year. We will lose our best hope of modernizing our machinery and our equipment, and giving our industry an inducement to set up their investment so that they can compete on more equal terms with foreign investors and producers.

We will be abandoning an effort to close all foreign tax havens that drain our jobs and dollars away from our shores. And we will be permitting $630 million a year in taxes due from stockholders and bondholders to go uncollected, even though these taxes are on the books. Even though one-third of these people are paying their taxes in good faith, yet because of the difficulty of collecting them, nearly $630 million due to the Treasury does not come in each year, which means that those wage earners, the small businessmen, and others who have their taxes withheld from their salaries and their paychecks must pay more.

We need this bill, finally, to help close off our loss of gold and our balance of payments. To make that less, we must modernize our equipment and our businesses so that they can compete, and we must close the loopholes which permit and encourage industry to invest overseas. I hope that every member of the House of Representatives who believes in spreading the tax burden fairly, who wants to improve our balance of payments position, who wants this country to grow in new equipment and new jobs, will support this bill as the best means of achieving these goals today. And I find great difficulty in understanding the position of any political party which makes it a matter of party objective to defeat this bill at this most important time.

Third, I have a statement which Mr. Hatcher will have for you on the problems of nuclear test inspection.

Let me just say in summary that after hearing Mr. Rusk's report of the work that's been done in Geneva, of his excellent work, I am convinced that the problem of inspection has now emerged clearly as the central obstacle to an effective test ban treaty. We cannot accept any agreement that does not provide for an effective international process that will tell the world whether the treaty is being observed. The Soviet Government so far flatly rejects any such inspection of any shape or kind. This is the issue that has been made clear in Geneva. We remain earnestly determined to work for an effective treaty, and we remain ready to conclude such a treaty at the earliest possible time.

Q: Mr. President, is the situation such in regard to nuclear testing that there is no longer any doubt, that there are no further reservations that we will resume testing at the end of this month?

The President: No, we are going to continue to work. The position remains the same as it did in our speech of March 2. We desire an effective treaty but, as I have stated, what is preventing the passage of an effective treaty or its acceptance is the refusal to permit any inspection on the territory of the Soviet Union.

While it's possible for us to pick up by seismic means an explosion underground, we cannot make a distinction by seismic means between an earthquake, of which there may be three or four hundred a year, from the Soviet Union and a nuclear explosion, without an actual inspection. And that is the issue upon which the conference is now divided and we are going to continue to work to see if we can get a treaty which will permit inspection.

QUESTIONS

Agreement on a Steel Contract

Q: Mr. President, what's your reaction to the apparent general agreement between both parties on a steel contract?

The President: The steel contract, of course, has not been agreed to. It's necessary on Saturday for the executive committee, which has been called together by President McDonald, to meet to consider any agreement and that meeting must be followed by the wage policy committee of the Steelworkers Union, which is composed of representatives, I think 230 of them, of the rank and file. They must consider the matter, too.

At the end of those considerations, and after these bodies have made their judgments, we can make a determination whether an agreement will be reached.

Let me say that both the union and the company have worked long and hard. I have been most impressed by their willingness to consider this contract ahead of time, by their desire to meet their responsibilities to the country here and abroad, and I commend them both, and I am hopeful that in the next few days we will have an agreement. But the agreement must depend upon the approval of the responsible parties in the company and in the union.

Events in Argentina

Q: Would you give us your assessment, sir, of the recent events in Argentina and their possible impact upon the Alliance for Progress?

The President: Well, I think the events there are still uncertain enough, and the reports are still not clear enough and I think, therefore, it would be unwise, lacking that kind of precise information, for us to make comments at this time on events in another country.

Rules on Carpetbagging

Q: Mr. President, have you accepted the rules on carpetbagging that were laid down last week for California?

The President: Well, I thought that the thing just sort of worked out - I thought it was handled very satisfactorily from my point of view on each side.[1] (Laughter)

Q: Mr. President, you once told us you had an opinion as to whether Mr. Nixon should enter the race for the California governorship, but you never did tell us what that was. Could you tell us about it?

The President: Well, I think I said at the time I'd be glad to confide it to him and he has not as yet spoken to me about it. I'll be glad to go back to California and talk to him about it. (Laughter)

Q: Mr. President, Mr. Nixon in his book has indicated that he feels he won three of the four debates. In view of this, do you think that future debates are advisable?

The President: Well, I would think that they would be - they'd be part of the '64 campaign. I've already indicated I'll be glad to debate, even if I did, as the Vice President suggested, lose three out of the four. (Laughter)

The Soviet Union and Berlin

Q: Mr. President, one of the several mysteries about Soviet foreign policy seems to be the fact that despite 3½ years of threats since November 1958, Mr. Khrushchev has not actually forced a complete showdown on Berlin. In the light of what information Mr. Rusk has brought to you, have you any inkling as to why he has followed this line of what might be called casual urgency, and do you feel that there is any hope involved in it?

The President: No, I don't - I would not want an impression to be created that we in any way underestimate the urgency and the immediacy of the problem. This is a matter of vital concern to both countries. I think that both sides must realize that any effort to push this thing beyond a certain point could result in a great damage to the vital interests of both countries and would lead to all sorts of hazards. So I think that we continue to talk because we are anxious to see if it's possible to prevent a situation arising where excessive action might be taken by either side to advance its own interest which could lead to a response which, as I say, has a good deal of potential danger in it.

So in answer to your question, Mr. Morgan, I would say the situation is a very difficult one. I think that it is a matter of importance to both sides, and, therefore, I think both sides have proceeded with a good deal of care, because they realize it is so important and therefore could bring about, we hope, a very happy solution, though none has been forthcoming, but could, if miscalculations were made or mistakes made by anyone, could bring about a very unhappy one. So that we proceed with care and we welcome the care with which others may proceed.

The Situation in Laos

Q: There appears to be a situation of deadlock in Laos, Mr. President, with the Royal Laos Government not going ahead in the formation of a government of national union. Do you anticipate any review or reevaluation of our policy towards the Royal coalition government?

The President: Well, we belive strongly as the best way of protecting interests of Laos and the interests of Southeast Asia, that we should have a neutral and independent Laos under a government led by Souvanna Phouma. That's our policy and I think that opposition to that policy is somewhat unwise. The alternatives are not very bright. And if the cease-fire should end, I think it would present the people of Laos with a good deal of danger. I think we should reach a solution based on the government, the coalition government, under Souvanna Phouma, and I hope that the Royal Laotian Government will support that position. I think it represents, it seems to me, great hazards to them not to.

Mr. Rusk's Talks with Mr. Gromyko

Q: Mr. President, did the Secretary of State tell you anything regarding his talks with Mr. Gromyko in Geneva that would indicate that the climate for a possible summit this year might be better than it has been in recent weeks?

The President: Well, I think I've explained my position on the summit. I don't think I can add to it. The matter of a summit has not been discussed by the Secretary since he's been back, with me.

The President's Talk with President Eisenhower

Q: Mr. President, can you tell us any more about your talk with General Eisenhower last Saturday?

The President: No, we had a very useful talk, and I think, as Mr. Salinger said, we discussed some of the problems the United States faces around the world and also I attempted to tell him more or less what our status was in each of those particular crisis areas.

Differences Between Castro and the Leaders of the Cuban Communist Party

Q: Mr. President, there seems to be some growing differences between Fidel Castro and leaders of the Communist Party in Cuba. Could you comment on this and what it may portend for American foreign policy toward Cuba?

The President: No, I think the situation is unclear there, and while it is true that revolutions frequently devour their children, it's still not clear enough for us to make any judgment as to the power struggle that may be going on there.

The Supreme Court Reapportionment Decision

Q: Mr. President, would you comment on the Supreme Court reapportionment decision, and say whether there is anything the Federal Government could do to support it?

The President: I think, as you know, when the matter was before the Supreme Court the administration made clear its endorsement of the principles implicit in the Court decision, as a friend of the Court, and I don't think it's probably appropriate to comment on the merits of a specific case in litigation, but I think our position on the general principle was quite clear. Quite obviously, the right to fair representation and to have each vote count equally is, it seems to me, basic to the successful operation of a democracy.

I would hope that through the normal political processes, these changes to insure equality of voting, equality of representation, would be brought about by the responsible groups involved, in the States, and in the National Government.

Now, in the case that was involved here, for many years it was impossible for the people involved to secure adequate relief through the normal political processes. The inequity was built in and therefore there was no chance for a political response to the inequity. The position of the Government, the Federal Government, the administration, as I say, was made clear by Solicitor Cox. And I would hope now the Court having taken a position, I would hope that those responsible in the various States - and this is a matter not confined merely to Tennessee, but it is true of Massachusetts and other States - I would hope that because of the change in population areas that every State would reexamine this problem and attempt to insure equality of voting rights. There's no sense of a Senator's representing 5,000,000 people sitting next to a Senator representing 10,000 people, and then when no relief comes, to say the Court is taking action where it should not. It's the responsibility of the political groups to respond to the need, but if no relief is forthcoming, then of course it would seem to the administration that the judicial branch must meet a responsibility.

A Successor to Justice Whittaker

Q: Mr. President, what about a successor to Justice Whittaker? This will be the first opportunity, the first occasion you have had to appoint a Supreme Court Justice. Do you have any general thoughts on the process you would follow in selecting one, and is Secretary Ribicoff one of those whom you would consider?

The President: We will have - what I am announcing today is the resignation of Justice Whittaker. I think it would be appropriate to announce his successor on another occasion, and his successor will be announced shortly.

Q: In that connection, will there be any general principle you would follow? Would you consult the Bar Association, or how would you go about the process of selecting a successor?

The President: I would think that we could - when the time comes that we make the selection, I think it would be appropriate to respond in any way that anyone would like to ask me the reason for the selection.

Visit of the President of Brazil

Q: Could you comment on the visit here of the President of Brazil next week?

The President: We welcome him. Brazil is a vital country in Latin America, the largest, and we are therefore extremely anxious to have the President visit us.

The Steel Question

Q: Mr. President, a two-part question on steel: Although the contract is not yet buttoned up, in view of what you now know about the proposed agreement, do you see any justification for an increase in the steel industry's prices this year? The second part: If the steel industry gets the multimillion dollar tax saving envisioned in the investment press, and also the faster writeoffs that Mr. Dillon plans to grant this spring, should the steel producers reduce their prices?

The President: I think that on the question of the steel, until the contract is signed I think it would not be appropriate to make any comment in response to your question or in response in detail to the potential agreement, itself. I think that the company and the union have carried on their negotiations. I think we should permit that process to be completed before we make any statement. And that won't be done, if it is done, until this weekend.

On Balancing the Budget

Q: Mr. President, in view of economic conditions and in view of the message that you sent to Congress last - or the request that you sent to Congress last Monday, for a public works bill appropriation of $600 million, two things about the budget: one, do you expect that it will balance next year, and two, do you feel that it should balance next year?

The President: I think we can make a better judgment on the budget prospects after we have gone through, really, I would think, not only the March figures but also the April buying, and it's been our hope that the budget would balance. If business recovers in the way that we have hoped it would, the budget would be in balance. In regard to the proposal we sent up, what we are concerned about is that even though unemployment has dropped and even though there is a recovery, an increase of, I think, nearly $45 billion in the Gross National Product since last year at this time, an increase in wages for our manufacturing workers of nearly 6 percent in the last 12 months, an average of almost $4.80 a week, even though consumer resources are almost $20 billion higher than they were a year ago, all these things give us hope that this recovery will be sustained. And we can get a better - and if that is sustained then the budget will be in balance. The problem, of course, is that even in a period of recovery there are these islands of unemployment which have been left behind for many years as a result of successive recessions and technological changes. And these people, with some of them the unemployment may average 10, 13, 15 percent in places like sections of northern Minnesota, Pennsylvania, West Virginia, eastern Kentucky, southern Illinois, and so on, I think we ought to help these people. In addition, this would benefit construction workers, and their rate of unemployment is twice that of manufacturing, so I'm hopeful Congress will pass this bill.

The Possibility of an Attack on the Mainland by Formosa

Q: Mr. President, this morning Generalissimo Chiang Kai-shek is reported to have said that an invasion of the mainland may come at any time. Under our treaty arrangements with the Republic of Formosa, consultation is required with this Government. Could you tell us whether in fact there have been such consultations under that treaty, and what the view of this administration is toward this problem?

The President: I have not seen the General's statement. There has not been consultation under the treaty of the kind envisioned in the treaty.

U.S. Initiative in a Nuclear War

Q: Mr. President, could you elaborate on the idea attributed to you in a magazine article that there may be circumstances under which we would have to take the initiative in a nuclear war?

The President: Yes. I think Mr. Salinger's statement made it very clear that this was intended to be merely a restatement of a traditional position where if a vital area - and I think the area that Mr. Salinger used was West Europe - were being overrun by conventional forces, that the United States would take means, available means, to defend Western Europe. It was not intended to suggest, as Mr. Salinger said, that this meant that the United States would take aggressive action on its own part, or would launch an attack, a so-called preventive attack on its part. That's not our policy nor the policy of previous administrations. The article read in context makes it clear that we're talking about if there was an attack of overwhelming proportions by conventional forces in an area such as Europe, we would meet our treaty commitments.

The President's Attitude on His Office

Q: Mr. President, your brother, Ted, recently on television said that after seeing the cares of office on you, that he wasn't sure he'd ever be interested in being the President. I wonder if you could tell us whether if you had it to do over again, you would work for the presidency and whether you can recommend the job to others.

The President: Well, the answer is - to the first is "yes" and the second is "no." I don't recommend it to others - (laughter) - at least for a while.

Support Prices for Dairy Farmers

Q: Mr. President, Secretary Freeman tomorrow is going to reduce support prices for dairy farmers. This is the same thing that Ezra Benson did 8 years ago, to correct a surplus situation. Now, does this mean that the administration's farm program is the same as the Republican's when the going gets rough?

The President: No, it isn't at all. As you know, the administration requested agreement by the Congress to permit us to maintain support prices at the present levels till next December, in the hope that in the meanwhile it would be possible for us to work out general legislation which would assist the dairy industry to meet the present problem of overproduction and underconsumption. The agricultural committees of the House and Senate, with the Republican members unanimously voting and joined by some Democrats, voted against giving us this permission.

The law compels the Secretary of Agriculture, therefore, unless agriculture is in short supply - dairy products or milk is in short supply, to reduce the support price, so that he is compelled by statute to take this action.

Now, we have as you know a great surplus of butter and of milk and this has been a matter of concern for some months. I think it would have been far more satisfactory, however, in fairness to the dairy farmers who will be adversely affected, if we had been given consent to carry on our present support price to December. And I think in the meanwhile we could have taken actions, legislative and administrative, which would have given them some relief from the present burden which will be thrust upon them.

I wish the agricultural committee had not taken the position it did, and I wish they would reconsider it.

U.S. Policy on Formosa

Q: Mr. President, could you restate our policy on the Chiang Kai-shek situation? Is it merely to support the Nationalist Chinese on Taiwan, or would we help them in an effort to recapture the Communist mainland?

The President: I think that - I'm not aware of the statement that's been made. We have not been consulted about, as I stated, in the way that the agreement would call for, and therefore, I would think that there'd be no use in explorations of potential situations. Quite obviously, there's the desire that - of the people of Formosa - that they be returned, but we have to consider all the responsibilities and problems which all of us bear. And I've not heard that any new proposal is now under consideration.

The Reapportionment Decision

Q: Mr. President, again on the court decision. It's been suggested that it might be well for the President of the United States to provide some special leadership and direction as a followup to the apportionment decision. How does that strike you?

The President: Well, I think it's incumbent upon all of those of us who hold office in the States and in the National Government to take every action that we can to have this matter settled by the responsible political groups. And in my earlier statement, I urged these States and State legislatures to carefully reconsider this problem. As I say, those who object to the court taking the action they are taking, it seems to me, are not on very solid ground when they also do not support actions in the States to bring redress. So that I think all of us, in the States, the National Government, the Congress ought to consider the matter very carefully.

The Trade Expansion Bill

Q: Mr. President, supporters of your trade expansion bill feel that you have misjudged the implications of your decision to raise the carpet and glass tariffs. Do you acknowledge the danger of Common Market retaliation, and renewed efforts by every protectionist industry and union to demand further restrictions on imports?

The President: No, I don't see the logic of that. I've stated in our first bill, in the bill that we sent up, and I stated at the time, that we would attempt to provide protection to those companies which might be adversely affected. In the new legislation, it gives us a number of means by which that protection can be effectively granted. In this case, there have been seven cases by the Tariff Commission which have come to my desk as President. In the case of three of them, I believe, they were by split decision, four of them were unanimous, two were accepted by me, and two were rejected. Now, in this case there has been unemployment and loss of jobs which have assumed serious proportions in the carpet industry and in the glass industry. I recognize that this places a burden on foreign producers. But in the cases which we're now talking about, our unemployment is substantially greater than theirs, their balance of payments situation is substantially better than ours - in the case of Belgium, they've been adding gold rather than losing it, their unemployment rate is half of ours. We have therefore, with reluctance, determined that the situation in these two industries is sufficiently serious so that they must be given some protection of the kind which is provided under present law.

Now, I know this will be a disappointment to those involved abroad, but we have very serious problems in the United States. We are losing gold, we have high unemployment in some industries, and therefore I considered that on balance this protection should be granted.

Now that doesn't, in my opinion, mean that we shouldn't have effective trade legislation. The purpose of the trade legislation is going to be stimulating employment on both sides. But there are areas where, which I hope under the new bill, we'll be able to give protection to the workers through the various provisions which are suggested, which are far broader and far more effective than the ones under the present law.

Spy Satellites

Q: Mr. President, there are now a number of Midas and Samos spy satellites circling the earth. Do you think the perfection of these satellites will eventually give the United States the type of surveillance over the U.S.S.R. which will make inspection effective?

The President: No, I don't envision that situation.

Majority Will in a Free Election

Q: Mr. President, as a general proposition, what do you think of the denial of the will of the majority as expressed in the free election, even though this majority may want to promote a nondemocratic form of government?

The President: Is this a - have special application to a situation?

Q: As a general proposition?

The President: Well, I would think that - I would have to - I have stated, in answer to your question, in a general way in - I think in my interview with Mr. Adzhubei[2] where I commented on what the position of the United States is in regard to free elections and the choice of the people. And providing the free choice continues, of course, they must make their judgment. But I'd prefer to keep it - I'll be glad to talk to you about it sometime as an academic question.

Underground Nuclear Testing

Q: Mr. President, on nuclear testing, last winter from Palm Beach there was a comment that underground testing didn't particularly advance the art of weapons. Why, then, is it necessary - this may be a naive question - but why is it necessary, then, to insist on inspections which will detect every last underground test?

The President: I don't think our inspection system says that. I think there should be, however, a potential. And I'm not sure that we can - the view which was - which you state that I had - I think the underground tests potentially could be more rewarding than they may have been in the past, number one. We don't say they should investigate every test. There is a - I think we could - we have said we would settle for a limited number of inspections, but I don't think that we could. As we are an open society, obviously we could not test; they could test. And unless we have at least the right to, on occasions, examine whether tests are being carried out, I would think that we were not being responsive to the security of the United States. They could carry on their underground tests, then carry them, and suddenly begin as they did their atmospheric tests, in breach of the treaty, in breach, certainly, of the understanding of the moratorium last summer. So that I think we have to have some inspection.

Federal Aid for the Construction of State Hospitals

Q: Mr. President, there are a number of bills before Congress urging Federal aid for construction of new State hospitals for the treatment of narcotic addicts. Would you indicate your attitude toward such legislation?

The President: There is legislation which has been ——

Q: It proposes ——

The President: —— building the hospital in New York?

Q: —— building of new State hospitals for treatment of narcotics addicts.

The President: Yes. Well, I would certainly support a sufficient number of hospital beds to provide effective treatment for addicts. And if our hospitals in Texas and Kentucky, our two hospitals are not sufficient, I will certainly support others. And I know there's been a good deal of interest in the hospital in New York, which is now being examined.

[1]As reported in the New York Times, Richard M. Nixon, a candidate for Governor of California, was asked how he liked having the President and Attorney General Robert F. Kennedy in the State. Mr. Nixon is said to have referred to the President and his brother as carpetbaggers. The White House Press Secretary replied at a news conference in Palm Springs: "I don't know anybody in the United States, no matter in what State he resides, who considers the President of the United States a carpetbagger, wherever he is."

THE PRESIDENT'S NEWS CONFERENCE OF

APRIL 11, 1962

The President: I have several announcements to make.

Simultaneous and identical actions of United States Steel and other leading steel corporations increasing steel prices by some $6 a ton constitute a wholly unjustifiable and irresponsible defiance of the public interest.   In this serious hour in our Nation's history, when we are confronted with grave crises in Berlin and Southeast Asia, when we are devoting our energies to economic recovery and stability, when we are asking reservists to leave their homes and families for months on end and servicemen to risk their lives - and four were killed in the last 2 days in Viet-Nam - and asking union members to hold down their wage requests at a time when restraint and sacrifice are being asked of every citizen, the American people will find it hard, as I do, to accept a situation in which a tiny handful of steel executives whose pursuit of private power and profit exceeds their sense of public responsibility can show such utter contempt for the interests of 185 million Americans.

If this rise in the cost of steel is imitated by the rest of the industry, instead of rescinded, it would increase the cost of homes, autos, appliances, and most other items for every American family.   It would increase the cost of machinery and tools to every American businessman and farmer.   It would seriously handicap our efforts to prevent an inflationary spiral from eating up the pensions of our older citizens, and our new gains in purchasing powers.

It would add, Secretary McNamara informed me this morning, an estimated $1 billion to the cost of our defenses, at a time when every dollar is needed for national security and other purposes.   It would make it more difficult for American goods to compete in foreign markets, more difficult to withstand competition from foreign imports, and thus more difficult to improve our balance of payments position, and stem the flow of gold.   And it is necessary to stem it for our national security, if we're going to pay for our security commitments abroad.   And it would surely handicap our efforts to induce other industries and unions to adopt responsible price and wage policies.

The facts of the matter are that there is no justification for an increase in steel prices.   The recent settlement between the industry and the union, which does not even take place until July 1st, was widely acknowledged to be noninflationary, and the whole purpose and effect of this administration's role, which both parties understood, was to achieve an agreement which would make unnecessary any increase in prices.   Steel output per man is rising so fast that labor costs per ton of steel can actually be expected to decline in the next 12 months.   And in fact, the Acting Commissioner of the Bureau of Labor Statistics informed me this morning that, and I quote, "employment costs per unit of steel output in 1961 were essentially the same as they were in 1958."

The cost of the major raw materials, steel scrap and coal, has also been declining, and for an industry which has been generally operating at less than two-thirds of capacity, its profit rate has been normal and can be expected to rise sharply this year in view of the reduction in idle capacity.   Their lot has been easier than that of one hundred thousand steel workers thrown out of work in the last 3 years.   The industry's cash dividends have exceeded $600 million in each of the last 5 years, and earnings in the first quarter of this year were estimated in the February 28th Wall Street Journal to be among the highest in history.

In short, at a time when they could be exploring how more efficiency and better prices could be obtained, reducing prices in this industry in recognition of lower costs, their unusually good labor contract, their foreign competition and their increase in production and profits which are coming this year, a few gigantic corporations have decided to increase prices in ruthless disregard of their public responsibilities.

The Steelworkers Union can be proud that it abided by its responsibilities in this agreement, and this Government also has responsibilities which we intend to meet. The Department of Justice and the Federal Trade Commission are examining the significance of this action in a free, competitive economy. The Department of Defense and other agencies are reviewing its impact on their policies of procurement. And I am informed that steps are under way by those members of the Congress who plan appropriate inquiries into how these price decisions are so quickly made and reached and what legislative safeguards may be needed to protect the public interest.

Price and wage decisions in this country, except for a very limited restriction in the case of monopolies and national emergency strikes, are and ought to be freely and privately made. But the American people have a right to expect, in return for that freedom, a higher sense of business responsibility for the welfare of their country than has been shown in the last 2 days.

Some time ago I asked each American to consider what he would do for his country and I asked the steel companies. In the last 24 hours we had their answer.

I've got one other statement here. Mr. Hatcher is going to release a statement in regard to the release of the Guards. Let me say in summary that Secretary McNamara and I have carefully reviewed our progress in achieving permanent increases in our military strength. We have concluded that the rate of progress of this effort is such that if there is no serious deterioration in the international situation between now and August, we shall be able in that month to release all those who were called involuntarily. Our continuing strength after this release will be much increased over what it was a year ago.

Just as an example, the number of our combat-ready Army divisions in active service after the release will be 16, as against 11 a year ago. The release is not the result of any marked change in the international situation, which continues to have many dangers and tensions. It is the result, rather, of our successful buildup of permanent instead of emergency strength.

The units we release will remain available, in a new and heightened state of combat readiness if a new crisis should arise requiring their further service. I know that I speak for all of our countrymen in expressing our appreciation to all those who've served under the adverse conditions of living in camps and being taken away from their families. And their service and the willingness of the great, great majority of all of them to do this uncomplainingly, I think, should be an inspiration to every American.

And lastly, last Saturday I issued an Executive order creating a Board of Inquiry to inquire into the issues involved in the current labor dispute in the west coast maritime industry. The Board of Inquiry filed its written report with me today. In its unanimous report, the Board stated:

"The current strike, if continued, will affect approximately 130 cargo and passenger ships, including those which constitute the principal mode of transportation of passengers and vital cargo to and from the State of Hawaii."

Other reports I have received clearly manifest that a continuation of this strike imperils the national health and safety.

I have therefore instructed the Attorney General to seek an injunction against this strike under the national emergency provisions of the Labor-Management Relations Act of 1947. While an injunction will restore the west coast maritime industry to full operation and return the strike members to work for 80 days, it should not, and I hope will not, interfere in any way with efforts towards full settlement.

I call upon the parties to make that effort, to achieve that settlement quickly. However, the public interest does not permit further delay in applying for an injunction. Consequently, I have made the decision to direct the Attorney General to apply for an appropriate order.

QUESTIONS

The Steel Situation

Q: Mr. President, the unusually strong language which you used in discussing the steel situation would indicate that you might be considering some pretty strong action. Are you thinking in terms of requesting or reviving the need for wage-price controls?

The President: I think that my statement states what the situation is today. This is a free country. In all the conversations which were held by members of this administration and myself with the leaders of the steel union and the companies, it was always very obvious that they could proceed with freedom to do what they thought was best within the limitations of law. But I did very clearly emphasize on every occasion that my only interest was in trying to secure an agreement which would not provide an increase in prices, because I thought that price stability in steel would have the most far-reaching consequences for industrial and economic stability and for our position abroad, and price instability would have the most far-reaching consequences in making our lot much more difficult.

When the agreement was signed, and the agreement was a moderate one and within the range of productivity increases, as I've said, actually, there will be reduction in cost per unit during the next year - I thought, I was hopeful, we'd achieved our goal. Now the actions that will be taken will be - are being now considered by the administration. The Department of Justice is particularly anxious, in view of the very speedy action of the companies who have entirely different economic problems facing them than did United States Steel - the speed with which they moved, it seems to me, to require an examination of our present laws, and whether they're being obeyed, by the Federal Trade Commission and particularly the Department of Justice. I'm very interested in the respective investigations what will be conducted in the House and Senate, and whether we shall need additional legislation, which I would come to very reluctantly. But I must say the last 24 hours indicates that those with great power are not always concerned about the national interest.

Q: In your conversation with Mr. Blough yesterday, did you make a direct request that this price increase be either deferred or rescinded?

The President: I was informed about the price increase after the announcement had gone out to the papers. I told Mr. Blough of my very keen disappointment and what I thought would be the most unfortunate effects of it. And of course we were hopeful that other companies who, as I've said, have a different situation in regard to profits and all of the rest than U.S. Steel, they're all - have a somewhat different economic situation.

I was hopeful particularly in view of the statement in the paper by the president of Bethlehem in which he stated - though now he says he's misquoted - that there should be no price increase, and we are investigating that statement. I was hopeful that the others would not follow the example, that therefore the pressures of the competitive marketplace would bring United States Steel back to their original prices. But the parade began. But it came to me after the decision was made. There was no prior consultation or information given to the administration.

Dependents Going Overseas

Q: Mr. President, now that General Clay is coming home from Berlin, don't you think that the service wives have borne the brunt of our gold shortage long enough, and should be permitted to join their soldier husbands in Europe? After all, you can almost say that service couples have had to bear a cross of gold alone, and in a very lonely way. And spring is here and everyone knows that the GI's - (laughter) - get into much less trouble and do their jobs better if their wives and kids are with them.

The President: I agree. And, we're very sympathetic. We are trying to make an analysis of how important this saving is to our general problem. As I've said, it costs us $3 billion to maintain our forces and bases overseas. That money must be earned by a surplus of exports over imports. And that's - I've asked Secretary McNamara to try to reduce that in the next 12 to 18 months by $1,100,000,000, in order to try to bring this gold flow into balance. And that means taking a third out of the Defense Department without reducing its strength. So that's why these women are bearing hardships - and these families. And that's why I contrasted such unhappiness to the last 24 hours, because the fact of the matter is, if we're not able to compete, this results in a larger increase of imports from foreign markets, and therefore lowers our dollar values - and those wives are going to have to stay home.

SAC's False Alarm

Q: Mr. President, when the Strategic Air Command had a false alarm for a few moments last fall, were you notified? And if not, do you think you should have been? And have you made arrangements to be, if there are any cases in the future?

The President: That story, in my opinion, was overstated. There was a breach in the communications between the base at Thule and at - and our Continental Command. As you know, we were in a 15-minute alert. This lasted for a few seconds. General Power alerted those forces which were on a standby basis. There are constant drills. It was not that we were, as I saw in some papers - primarily those in Europe - a few seconds from war, because the fact of the matter is it would have taken many, many - several hours before they could have taken off and begun to fly, and we were always in control. So that I thought General Power took the right action before anything was done which would in any way have threatened the security of the United States. Of course, the communication would have come immediately. But there is always this problem of being on the alert.

Decision to Increase Steel Prices

Q: Mr. President, if I could get back to steel for a minute, you mentioned an investigation into the suddenness of the decision to increase prices. Did you - is the position of the administration that it believed it had the assurance of the steel industry at the time of the recent labor agreement that it would not increase prices?

The President: We did not ask either side to give us any assurance, because there is a very proper limitation to the power of the Government in this free economy. All we did in our meetings was to emphasize how important it was that there be price stability, and we stressed that our whole purpose in attempting to persuade the union to begin to bargain early and to make an agreement which would not affect prices, of course, was for the purpose of maintaining price stability. That was the thread that ran through every discussion which I had or Secretary Goldberg had. We never at any time asked for a commitment in regard to the terms, precise terms, of the agreement from either Mr. McDonald or Mr. Blough, representing the steel company, because in our opinion that is - would be passing over the line of propriety. But I don't think that there was any question that our great interest in attempting to secure the kind of settlement that was finally secured was to maintain price stability, which we regard as very essential at this particular time. That agreement provided for price stability - up to yesterday.

Significance of General Clay's Return

Q: Mr. President, could you interpret for us the significance of General Clay's return? Does it mean that the administration now believes that the Berlin crisis is negotiable?

The President: No, no. When he came with us, as you know, he was the responsible officer in the Continental Can Company. And he said he would take a leave of absence to January. And then in January we asked him to stay further. But he has said for several months now that he really felt that his obligation was to return. We have - he's recommended very highly the responsible Americans who are there. When he comes back tomorrow I'm going to ask him, and I'm sure he will respond, to continue to act as consultant to me on the matter of Berlin; to make periodic visits and to be available to return there at any time that we should conclude that his presence would be valuable. So that we have - I notice Mayor Brandt said that General Clay might be more helpful to the cause here than he would be even there. And I think what the Mayor meant was that his experience there and his work in the last 7 months would be very valuable to the administration. So his service continues and the problem of Berlin continues.

Steel Price Increase and the Cost of Living

Q: In your statement on the steel industry, sir, you mentioned a number of instances which would indicate that the cost of living will go up for many people if this price increase were to remain effective. In your opinion, does that give the steelworkers the right to try to obtain some kind of a price - or a wage increase to catch up?

The President: No. Rather interestingly, the last contract was signed on Saturday with Great Lakes, so that the steel union is bound for a year, and of course, I'm sure would have felt like going much further if the matter had worked out as we had all hoped. But they've made their agreement and I'm sure they are going to stick with it. It does not provide for the sort of action you've suggested.

Q: Still on steel, Senator Gore advocated today legislation to regulate steel prices somewhat in the manner that public utility prices are regulated and his argument seemed to be that the steel industry had sacrificed some of the privileges of the free market because it wasn't really setting its prices on a supply and demand, but what he called administered prices. Your statement earlier, and your remarks since, indicate a general agreement with that kind of approach. Is that correct?

The President: No, I don't think that I'd stated that. I'd have to look
and see what Senator Gore has suggested, and I'm not familiar with it. What I
said was that we should examine what can be done to try to minimize the impact
on the public interest of these decisions, but though we had, of course, always
hoped that those involved would recognize that. I would say that what must disturb Senator Gore and Congressman Celler and others - Senator Kefauver - will be
the suddenness by which every company in the last few hours, one by one as the
morning went by, came in with their almost, if not identical, almost identical
price increases, which isn't really the way we expect the competitive private
enterprise system to always work.

The U.S. Position in the Dispute Between the Netherlands and Indonesia

*Q: Mr. President, would you clarify, please, the United States position in
the New Guinea dispute between the Netherlands and Indonesia? Recently there
have been reports of displeasure from the Netherlands that proposals put forward by the United States were not fair to the Netherlands.*

The President: Well, I agree, I think everybody is displeased, really, with
our role, because our role is an attempt - Ambassador Bunker's role has been,
under the direction of U Thant, to try to see if we can bring some adjustment
to prevent a military action which would be harmful to the interests of both
countries, with which we desire to be friendly. So I suppose it's hard to think
of any proposal that we could make which would be welcome on both sides.

I'm hopeful that if we can be useful, we'll continue to try to be. If both
sides feel that we cannot be, then perhaps others can take on this assignment,
or perhaps it can be done bilaterally. But I - Ambassador Bunker is a diplomat
of long experience and great skill, and our only interest is to see if we can
have a peaceful solution which we think is in the long-range interest of the
free world, of our allies - with whom we're allied - the Dutch and the Indone-
sians, whom we would like to see stay free. So that the role of the mediator
is not a happy one, and we're prepared to have everybody mad, if it makes some
progress.

Direct Procurement of Steel

*Q: Mr. President, in connection with the steel situation again, is there
not action that could be taken by the executive branch in connection with direct
procurement of steel under the administration of the Agency for International
Aid - I mean the aid agency. For example I think the Government buys about
a million tons of steel. Now, could not the Government decide that only steel -
that steel should be purchased only at the price, say, of yesterday, rather than
today?*

The President: That matter was considered, as a matter of fact, in a conversation between the Secretary of Defense and myself last evening. But at
that time we were not aware that nearly the entire industry was about to come
in, and therefore the amount of choice we have is somewhat limited.

*Q: Sir, too, on this thing, in the case of identical bids which the Govern-
ment is sometimes confronted with, they decide to choose the smaller business
unit rather than the larger.*

The President: I'm hopeful that there will be those who will not participate in this parade and will meet the principle of the private enterprise competitive system in which every one tries to sell at the lowest price commensur-
ate with their interests. And I'm hopeful that there will be some who will

decide that they shouldn't go in the wake of U.S. Steel. But we have to wait and see on that, because they're coming in very fast.

Q: Mr. President, 2 years ago, after the settlement, I believe steel prices were not raised.

The President: That is right.

Q: Do you think there was an element of political discrimination in the behavior of the industry this year?

The President: I would not - and if there was, it doesn't really - if it was - if that was the purpose, that is comparatively unimportant to the damage that - the country is the one that suffers. If they do it in order to spite me, it really isn't so important.

Q: Mr. President, to carry a previous question just one step further, as a result of the emphasis that you placed on holding the price line, did any word or impression come to you from the negotiations that there would be no price increase under the type of agreement that was signed?

The President: I will say that in our conversations that we asked no commitments in regard to the details of the agreement or in regard to any policies which the union or the company - our central thrust was that price stability was necessary and that the way to do it was to have a responsible agreement, which we got.

Now, at no time did anyone suggest that if such an agreement was gained that it would be still necessary to put up prices. That word did not come until last night.

Cuban Release of Prisoners

Q: Mr. President, there has been a price increase in Cuba as well. Mr. Castro has increased the price that he's put on human life in the release or tentative release of the prisoners captured in the abortive invasion attempt last year. Would you comment on this, please?

The President: Well, I think that all of us had hoped that the day when men were put on the block had long ago passed from this hemisphere. And it had from every country, until very recently in Cuba. I think Mr. Castro knows that the United States Government cannot engage in a negotiation like that, and he knows very well that the families cannot raise these millions of dollars. It's rather interesting, so what he has done really in effect is sentence them to 30 years in prison. It's rather interesting that Castro himself, when he engaged in an operation under a dictator whom we've been harshly critical of - that he was let out of prison after an open trial in 15 months. He regards for his own countrymen - not the countrymen who from his point of view may have been wrong, but who fought in the open, and who took their chances, and were young men - he regards the appropriate treatment for them and for thousands of other Cubans to be this long prison sentence of 30 years which, in my opinion, is why Mr. Castro is increasingly isolated in the company of free men.

Tax Benefits to Industry

Q: Mr. President, the steel industry is one of a half dozen which has been expecting tax benefits this summer through revision of the depreciation schedules. Does this price hike affect the administration's action in this field?

The President: Well, it affects our budget. Secretary Dillon and I discussed it this morning. Of course, all this matter is being very carefully looked into now.

Nonintervention Between Communist and Capitalist Blocs

Q: The Presidents of Mexico and of Brazil announced a principle of adherence to nonintervention between the Communist and the capitalist blocs. Does this accord with what President Goulart told you when he was here in Washington?

The President: Yes. I haven't seen the joint statement, but I'm sure it does. I think we are bound together through the Organization of American States, and it's difficult to comment on a joint statement that I've not read, but I think President Goulart says the same in Mexico as he does in Washington.

The Legion of Merit to a Japanese Officer

Q: Mr. President, General Lemnitzer has recently conferred our Legion of Merit on a Japanese officer who apparently planned the Pearl Harbor attack. Can you think of any particular reason for this award?

The President: Yes. The reason given was that he had been a distinguished officer of the Japanese Air Force; that his relations with the United States had been extremely cooperative. He was acting as a military officer. And I - I think that this kind of - the days of the war are over, and I thought that it was appropriate. He's a distinguished flyer, and while we all regret Pearl Harbor and everything else - but we are in a new era in our relations with Japan, fortunately.

American Deaths in Viet-Nam

Q: Sir, what are you going to do about the American soldiers getting killed in Viet-Nam?

The President: Well, I'm extremely concerned about American soldiers who are in a great many areas in hazard. We are attempting to help Viet-Nam maintain its independence and not fall under the domination of the Communists. The Government has stated that it needs our assistance in doing it. It's very - and it presents a very hazardous operation, in the same sense that World War II, World War I, Korea - a good many thousands and hundreds of thousands of Americans died. So that these four sergeants are in that long roll. But we cannot desist in Viet-Nam. And I think that it is the fact that these men, operating very far from home, very far indeed from Saigon, under great danger - and there are many others - the fact of their contributions, as well as the Wisconsin and Texas National Guard, it is in that setting that I look at the present actions.

Reporter: Thank you, Mr. President.

THE PRESIDENT'S NEWS CONFERENCE OF

APRIL 18, 1962

The President: I have several announcements to make.

The United States has today tabled at Geneva an outline of basic provisions of a treaty on general and complete disarmament in a peaceful world. It provides a blueprint of our position on general and complete disarmament as well as elaboration of the nature, sequence, and timing of specific disarmament

measures. This outline of a treaty represents the most comprehensive and specific series of proposals the United States or any other country has ever made on
disarmament. In addition to stating the objectives and principles which should
govern agreements for disarmament, the document calls for the grouping of individual measures in three balanced and safeguarded stages. We are hopeful
through the give and take of the conference table this plan will have a constructive influence upon the negotiations now in progress. I want to stress
that with this plan the United States is making a major effort to achieve a
breakthrough on disarmament negotiations. We believe that the nations represented at Geneva have a heavy responsibility to lay the foundations for a genuinely secure and peaceful world starting through a reduction in arms.

Secondly, I believe it would be appropriate to say a few words to follow up
last week's events concerning steel prices.

First, let me make it clear that this administration harbors no ill will
against any individual, and industry, corporation, or segment of the American
economy. Our goals of economic growth and price stability are dependent upon
the success of both corporations, business, and labor and there can be no room
on either side in this country at this time for any feelings of hostility or
vindictiveness.

When a mistake has been retracted and the public interest preserved, nothing
is to be gained from further public recriminations.

Secondly, while our chief concern last week was to prevent an inflationary
spiral, we were not then and are not now unmindful of the steel industry's needs
for profits, modernization, and investment capital. I believe, in fact, that
this administration and the leaders of steel and other American industries are
in basic agreement on far more objectives than we are in disagreement.

We agree on the necessity of increased investment in modern plant and equipment. We agree on the necessity of improving our industry's ability to compete
with the products of other nations. We agree on the necessity of achieving an
economic recovery and growth that will make the fullest possible use of idle
capacity. We agree on the necessity of preventing an inflationary spiral that
will lead to harmful restrictions on credit and consumption. And we agree on
the necessity of preserving the Nation's confidence in free, private, collective
bargaining and price decisions, holding the role of Government to the minimum
level needed to protect the public interest.

In the pursuit of these objectives, we have fostered a responsible wage
policy aimed at holding increases within the confines of productivity gains.
We have encouraged monetary policies aimed at making borrowed capital available at reasonable cost; preparing a new transportation policy aimed at providing increased freedom of competition at lower costs; proposed a new trade
expansion bill to gain for our industries increased access to foreign markets;
proposed an 8 percent income tax credit to reward investment in new equipment
and machinery; and proceeded to modernize administratively Treasury Department's
guidelines on the depreciable lives of capital assets; and, finally, taken a
host of other legislative and administrative actions to foster the kind of
economic recovery which would improve both profits and incentives to invest.

I believe that the anticipated profits this year for industry in general -
and steel in particular - indicate that these policies are meeting with some
measure of success. And it is a fact that the last quarter of last year, and
I think the first quarter of this year, will be the highest profits in the history of this country, and the highest number of people working, and the highest productivity. So that while there are serious economic problems facing us,
nevertheless I believe that progress is being made and can be made and must be
made in the future.

Third, the vast majority, as I stated, of our reservists have responded to the call of service in accordance with our best traditions. Unfortunately, the widespread publicity given to the complaints of a small minority have subjected many of these men to unaccustomed pressures. Upon learning that a private first class faced a court-martial for writing a letter critical of my actions, I contacted the Secretary of the Army who has the difficult task of maintaining proper discipline, and he agreed with me that such offenses are more misguided than criminal in intent. Therefore, I have asked the Army to cancel the trial of Pfc. Larry D. Chidester at Fort Lewis, Wash., and in the same spirit of the Easter Week I have directed the Army to remit the balance of the sentence of Pfc. Bernis G. Owen, at Fort Polk, La.

Next, we are releasing today the reports submitted by the Presidential Commission on Campaign Costs.[1] I want to express my profound gratitude to this group made up of very experienced men representing those who've been active as students and as participants in the political process, fundraisers, in both parties, who've come forward with a unanimous report which is now being examined by the administration, and will be the basis of legislative recommendations sent to the Congress which I think can provide a significant advancement of the public interest in this very vital field.

And lastly, I am happy to announce that Mrs. Eisenhower has agreed to serve as honorary cochairman, with Mrs. Kennedy, of the National Cultural Center. The National Cultural Center, begun in the administration of President Eisenhower, is the most significant cultural undertaking in the history of Washington and is of enormous importance to the cultural life of our Nation as a whole.

I am gratified that Mrs. Eisenhower will be part of this undertaking which we hope to bring to success in the coming months.

QUESTIONS

The Grand Jury Investigation in New York

Q: Mr. President, how does the change in the situation between last week and this affect the grand jury investigation in New York? There have been reports it will be soft-pedaled. Are these true or are the potential monopoly aspects still such as to warrant pressing the investigation?

The President: Well, the grand jury has been called in order to investigate a possible violation of the law and this is a matter now before the grand jury. And of course in accordance with the procedures provided this matter will be brought to a - continue to see if such a violation occurred.

Resumption of Atmospheric Testing

Q: Mr. President, does there remain any considerable doubt on your part as to the necessity for resuming atmospheric testing shortly, and if and when you do resume testing, do you intend to announce it in advance?

The President: Well, I think the situation is the same as it was on March 2. The United States desires to achieve a responsible agreement to prevent future tests, providing for an effective inspection system. We stand ready now to conclude that test.

The response we received and that Prime Minister Macmillan received to his letter last week, would indicate that the chances of securing that agreement now for an effective inspection have - seem to be very negative; and if we do not get that agreement, then of course we shall proceed, as I stated on March 2.

In regard to any announcements to be made, they will be appropriately made at the time.

Aid to France's Nuclear Force

Q: Mr. President, there are reports that some of your top military advisers are urging the United States to help France with the development of its nuclear striking force. Have you given this problem any consideration, and what do you think about it, sir?

The President: Well, I think that the policy of the United States, of course, continues to be that of being very reluctant to see the proliferation of nuclear weapons. We are attempting to, in our disarmament offers that we've made we are attempting, and in my speech last September before the United Nations I said that I thought it would be regrettable if nuclear weapons proliferated, or spread. So that our policy continues on that basis, and will continue unless we feel that security requirements suggest a change.

Victory in the Steel Situation

Q: Mr. President, there has been considerable speculation that the victory you have won in the steel situation will be of great assistance for the passage of your legislative program in Congress. Would you care to comment on that, sir?

The President: Well, I hope it's of assistance in passing the tax credit, which is intended to provide, combined with price stability, a means for our industry to modernize itself, and in fact to encourage it. I'm hopeful - in my opinion if the rise in prices have been permitted to stand, it would be extremely difficult to secure the passage of this legislation. I think that the line that has been held provides a much better atmosphere, and I think that if this legislation is passed it will materially help the steel companies and industry in general. And I'm very strongly in support of it.

As far as the rest of the program, I think that that part of the program which is involved with the economy, I think will be helped by the fact that we've been able to maintain at this time a stable price level.

Revival of the Federal Flood Insurance Act of 1956

Q: Mr. President, you said several weeks ago that you would take another look to see if you should request a supplemental appropriation this year to revive the Federal Flood Insurance Act of 1956. Have you reached any decision on that?

The President: There is a meeting, as you know, of some of the Governors who were involved. It either has been in the last few hours or is today, and they're meeting with some of our Government officials. This is one of the matters being considered by the Governors and by the Federal Government.

The Ban on Uniting Dependents with Servicemen

Q: Mr. President, Mr. Rockefeller told me last night that he thought it was terrible that service wives, of which his daughter Mary is one, cannot join their husbands abroad. So now we have not only cold and lonely hearts but also politics injected into this situation. And I'm wondering if now that steel prices aren't going up, the ban on service couples getting together might be lifted. It's been more than 7 months.

The President: Yes, I understand, and I think I attempted in the last press conference to respond to the question. I stated we have a very serious problem involved in gold, that as I said last time, we're asking the Secretary of Defense to reduce our overseas expenditures by a billion dollars, and the responsibility falls very heavily upon him and upon all of us. We do not desire - obviously, it's against our national social interest to separate these families and we have done it to the extent that we have done it only because of a very serious crisis. Now, we - that crisis - at least that situation in regard to gold continues and Secretary McNamara is continuing to analyze the best way to provide for the saving of a billion dollars.

Q: Yes, I realize that, and I know that the gold situation is very serious, and I am wondering if you directed Secretary Dillon to look into the serious situation of American companies setting up plants abroad so often to escape American tax dollars or to take advantage of the cheaper labor abroad.

The President: As you know, in the bill which passed the House of Representatives, there is a section which deals with the problem of companies established abroad in order to evade taxes, and that's a matter now before the Senate. And it is an attempt to discourage that drain on our - on the dollar and gold by tax policies, and so we are attempting to meet it in a whole variety of ways.

Wage and Price Increases

Q: Mr. President, two questions in the wake of last week's developments. First, assuming that a price increase in steel would eventually be necessary and justified, do you have any thoughts as to how this price increase should be reached? And secondly, if some major labor union made excessive demands for wage increases, would you move as sharply against that union as you did last week against steel?

The President: Well, to take the second part first, we had worked very closely with the steel union in an attempt to persuade them that it was in their interest to meet the standards set by the Council of Economic Advisers, and it was done. And that is why this matter came into particularly sharp focus last week.

Now, as far as the first part, I think that my original statement discussed our general views on it. This is a free economy. These matters are reached by the process of competition and collective bargaining. What we are attempting to do is to try to have them consider the public interest, which after all is their **interest - the problems involving price stability, national security,** and all the rest. They're very much interrelated, and this is particularly true in the basic industries. But the - our power is that - if the industry is competitive, prices are reached through the normal process of competition, and collective bargaining agreements are reached in the normal way. But we would like both labor and management to be very conscious of the public stake at this time, and that's what we are attempting to bring forth. We hope they'll - be conscious of it.

Q: Mr. President, I asked the first question specifically because the Wall Street Journal and some other spokesmen of business have accused you directly of having set the price in steel.

The President: Well, I'm aware of the accusations. What we attempted to do was project before the steel companies the public interest. And it was a combination of the public interest placed upon the table in front of them, and competition which I think brought the price down, by the fact that several companies refused to increase prices, and therefore competition worked its will. We want to be sure that competition is an active force in our economy. But I would not accept the view of the Wall Street Journal in regard to at least my feeling of the description of my actions or of the public interest.

Q: Mr. President, Chairman Miller and other Republican leaders have focused a good deal of criticism on the nocturnal activities of the FBI. Could you shed any light on that, sir?

The President: No, they were attempting to - reporters have called up a good many people in the middle of the night themselves - (laughter). And I - all we were attempting to do was to find out so that we could decide about the grand jury meeting, whether the reports in regard to the quotations which said one thing, and then there was a statement that they were misquoted, and then the next day there was a clarification. We wanted to get the facts on this.

Now, both the reporters were cooperative; I didn't realize they would be woken up at the time they were. The decision was made early in the evening, and I suppose making the connection, the FBI followed ahead, and I - and as I say, all the reporters, except that of the Wall Street Journal were most cooperative, But the intention was not to disturb the reporters. The intention was to get the information as quickly as possible so we could determine what action we would take before the grand jury, and as always the FBI carried out is responsibilities immediately.

School Desegregation

Q: Mr. President, would you care to comment on developments in New Orleans where the Archbishop excommunicated three people for hindering school desegregation?

The President: No, the action of the Archbishop related to private acts and private individuals, which did not involve public acts or public policy, so that carrying out the spirit of the Constitution which provides a separation between church and state, I think it would be inappropriate for me to comment on that.

Assurances from the Steel Industry

Q: Mr. President, last week you stated that the administration had not asked for assurances from the steel industry that prices would be kept where they were when the contracts were ratified. I wonder if you can tell us whether you received such assurances, either directly or indirectly, and I am prompted to ask because the day the contracts were ratified you stated that the settlement was noninflationary.

The President: That's correct - that's correct. I think we responded to this last week, when I stated that I did not ask, for the reasons which I gave, the steel companies to give a commitment that they would not increase prices. But I stated at the time that it was very clear that our whole effort was to secure a noninflationary settlement.

Q: But my question, Mr. President, was directed as to whether such assurances were given to you, regardless of ——

The President: No, I said last week - I said they were not. If you read last week's interview, you will see that they were not asked and they were not given.

Q: And not given, is that right?

The President: That's correct. On the other hand, during the conversations which were held, it was made very clear the purpose of our attempting to persuade the steel union not to accept an inflationary settlement. And no statement was made during any of those conversations that a price increase would immediately follow the wage accord, particularly if that wage accord were noninflationary. So that while no request was made for a commitment, on the other hand no statement was made which would have indicated to us that if the union cooperated and accepted a very low increase, that on the other hand there would then still be an automatic price increase.

Q: Mr. President, you agree that it's important for the steel companies to modernize their plants. Does the Government have any ideas about helping steel to do this, that is, aside from the 8 percent tax credit?

The President: And also the rewriting of schedule F, the depreciation allowances, and already a study has been on for some weeks. We've already done that in the textile industry and we are now analyzing steel and certain other basic industries in order to improve their depreciation position.

Secondly, I do want to say that in regard to profits that the last quarter, and as I said the first quarter, were the highest profits in the history of the United States and, therefore, I feel that while some particular companies and some industries may have special problems that the overall profit situation is not unsatisfactory.

Soviet Proposal for a Test Ban

Q: Mr. President, Mr. Tsarapkin, Soviet delegate to the disarmament conference in Geneva, told representatives of the Women's Strike For Peace that Russia would negotiate a nuclear test ban treaty with the United States if the United States would close down just one of its missile bases overseas as a gesture of good faith. When the women reported to Ambassador Dean he suggested they refer the proposal to you. Would you give us your view, sir?

The President: Well, I've never heard that proposal made by the Soviet Union. In other words, they would agree, as suggested - well, now, I don't think you can read the letter of the Chairman to the Prime Minister and get that impression. There's no - I - we have never heard that they would agree to an effective test ban, an inspection system, if we would close down one base, and my judgment is that there's no evidence for believing they would.

Q: Well, this - they told this to these private people.

The President: Well, at the conference at Geneva - and I'm sure that if there's - Mr. Dean will be glad to ask if that is so. But my judgment would be based on all the conversations which have gone on for many weeks and, in fact, the 3 years of negotiations. There is no evidence that they would do this. It's a lot different from saying we'll agree to negotiate about it if such an action is taken. They are now negotiating about it. We've been negotiating about it for 3 years. We were negotiating last August when they began testing. So I think that it indicates the long gap, as I said before, between an agreement to negotiate and negotiating an agreement.

Q: Sir, I would like to ask you if the reports from Geneva on the radio this morning about the U.S. disarmament proposal are correct, and that is that the U.S. proposes to scrap all armies and weapons and have a U.N. police force. I could not find out if this was the draft, because the drafts have not been made public to the American people or to all members of Congress yet.

The President: Yes, they're being made public today, Mrs. McClendon, and the description you have given is not an accurate one of our proposal.

Q: *You say it is not inaccurate?*

The President: Not — not an accurate one of our proposal.

Q: *Would you tell us what it is?*

The President: Well, Mrs. McClendon, the treaty will be made available to the members of the press today and will describe the various stages upon which we propose that disarmament might be taken, what actions we will take during these various stages, what protections are given to the security of the United States, and I think that when you have read the entire treaty you will realize that my response — the description you have given is not — at least is not comprehensive.

U.S. Proposals on Berlin

Q: *Mr. President, over the weekend, as you know, there has been somewhat of a flap over some proposals which the United States might make to the Soviets on Berlin. Could you tell us in this connection, sir, whether you would think it desirable to give the East Germans a technical voice in any international authority which might control access to West Berlin, provided it is part of an arrangement which guarantees our existing rights?*

The President: Well, I would have to examine that language again that you've just submitted to me. (Laughter) The question really is the status, the position, the authority of the East German regime in regard to any access authority. That really is one of the — that has been a basic issue since these discussions started. So that I could not attempt to respond to your question unless we had definitions of the technical commission, its power, the status of the East German regime in that authority, whether it was held by the Four Powers, what were the means by which the Four Powers exercised their rights — these are all the questions which are the subjects of negotiations between the Soviet Union and ourselves. This matter, however, certainly is one of the points which are now under discussion with the Soviet Union, how we can reconcile the problem of access, and maintain our position there. But I think as the Department of State has said, the government in West Germany has been kept informed and the proposals that we have talked about before, that we're talking about now, are in the general channel of previous proposals that have been discussed with the Soviet Union.

Price Controls

Q: *Mr. President, some of your critics feel that you set prices or have gone into the field of price control by Executive fiat in the steel situation, and further that this sets a precedent which you have to follow in future situations. Do you feel that you have set a precedent, that as these situations arise you would again have to invoke this sort of power?*

The President: I think the steel — I've stated I think in our statement what I believe to be the general policy of this administration in regard to prices and wages. Everyone is quite aware of what the powers are of the Government, and the limitation on those powers, and what the presumptions are — that collective bargaining will be free and that the competitive system, the competition within industry, will maintain prices at a reasonable level. I've attempted to state the public interest involved in all these negotiations and we will have to try to continue, as we have in the past, to bring these matters before labor and management in an attempt to provide the kinds of agreement which will maintain price stability. We're going to attempt to do that. But I have not suggested that our power - that we have powers to set or that those powers would be desirable to set prices or to set wages. But we can attempt, it seems to me, to bring before the parties in the most effective way possible, the public interest that is involved, and must be involved, particularly in these basic industries, when competition, our balance of payments all involve our national security and our military forces abroad. The interrelationship makes the public interest mandatory in these matters, and it's our responsibility to present it to those involved, which is what we tried to do in steel.

Negotiations with the Aerospace and Missile Aircraft Industries

Q: In that connection, Mr. President, the next major round of negotiations appears to be with the aerospace and missile-aircraft industry, with the two unions, the machinists and auto workers, already asserting that they want wage increases considerably above the formula laid down by the Council of Economic Advisers. And they point out that the Government is really a major party to these negotiations since they have the contracts. Would you assert the public interest in these negotiations?

The President: I think the public interest is very definitely involved, but I - in asserting the public interest we have always recognized the proper limitations of that - of the power of the Government to enforce any collective bargaining agreement. We do not have that power. That power has not been given to us. But we will certainly attempt to describe to the people involved, particularly in a program which is so important to the national security, we will attempt to describe the public interest, which, after all, is their interest as well as that of **the** Nation. Now, whether these parties will be responsive, as the steel union was, and as, on Friday, the steel companies were, of course, is a matter that will be seen in the future.

Our Status as Spokesman in the Berlin Talks

Q: Following up the question on Berlin, sir, our negotiations with the Russians have been carried out in behalf of the other occupying powers as well. In view of the flurry he referred to over the weekend and in view of the definite French reservations, would you tell us a little bit about how we stand as, in effect, the spokesman for the Four Powers at this moment?

The President: Well, I think that Mr. Von Eckhart, speaking for the West Germans, made a statement that they had been in consultation with us, and that they had confidence in our efforts. The French have had reservations from the beginning in regard to these probes, and we are continuing these probes in order to determine whether there's an effective basis for high negotiations. And we shall continue. The United States - this is a very dangerous area, involving vital interests of both sides, which could - even though at this present time the temperature has been lowered - could blow up anytime. And I don't think that we are meeting our responsibilities to our own people if we do not make every effort, in addition to strengthening ourselves militarily, and indicating a determination to protect our vital interests, to see if an accord can be reached. Because we - obviously it would be in the international interest if this particular area which is so susceptible to pressure because of its geographical position could be - an agreement could be reached. So we're going to continue to do it. Now before any agreement is finally signed, if we ever get that far, of course, the French and the British and the West Germans would all be very much participants. But the stage we're at now is to see whether such an agreement can be reached.

Q: Can we take it, sir, that as of this moment, the West Germans as the party most directly affected support these proposals that we are putting forward?

The President: I think that the West Germans are – should really speak for themselves. But I have no reason to believe that the West German Government does not support the efforts we are making to determine whether an accord can be reached. But as far as their own position on each particular matter, I think they would – should state that.

Resumption of Nuclear Testing

Q: Mr. President, in view of what you have called the very negative prospects for obtaining an effective nuclear test ban agreement with Russia, have you now set a specific date for the United States to resume testing in the atmosphere?

The President: I think that the time was described in the March 2d speech.

Profit Sharing

Q: Mr. President, there has been a good deal said recently, and I think you have addressed yourself to the fact that ——

The President: But in answer to your question, there's not a specific day been set, no.

Q: —— that labor's gain should be tied to productivity and that their wage increases would be. Not much has been said as to whether the investor should also share in this productivity, and apparently they didn't in the recent steel negotiations.

The President: Oh, the productivity. No, the owners of steel stocks have shared very much in the last 10 years. I don't think there's any question. I think there has been a split of – six times in the United States Steel stock since 1948-49, and they've been paid a very good dividend, and they have very strong equity. And what is true of U.S. Steel is true in even greater extent in other steel companies, and, as I've said, in industry in general. So that I think the shareholders – and the shareholders will do very well. For example, one of the problems is to increase the cost of steel at a time when you are only using 60, or 65, or 70 percent of your capacity. If you could – there would have been perhaps about a $260 or $270 million present capacity increase in profits of the steel companies, but if you could get the capacity of steel up to 85 or 90 percent, you would have had – you would have a $500 million increase in their profits at present prices. So the real problem in the steel industry is unused capacity. But in answer to your question, the shareholders have participated in increased productivity.

Reporter: Thank you, Mr. President.

[1]"Financing Presidential Campaigns, Report of the President's Commission on Campaign Costs," dated April 1962 (Government Printing Office, 1962, 36 pp.).

THE PRESIDENT'S NEWS CONFERENCE OF

MAY 9, 1962

The President: Good afternoon.

I have one announcement, a statement. Because mail received at the White House and by Members of the Senate indicates that a great number of people have been badly misinformed concerning one feature of the pending tax bill, I want to take this opportunity to set the record straight on our proposal to collect taxes which are due on dividends and interest.

The paid advertisements and circulars financed by the savings and loan associations, who have made great profits in recent years and paid very little in taxes - I think something like $5½ billion, while paying $70 million in taxes - by banks and others, have led many people to believe (1) that this is a new tax or a tax increase; (2) that it will take money unjustly from honest taxpayers; (3) that it will create a mountain of red tape costing more than it will bring in; and (4) that it will harm the elderly, the widows and orphans, or others in low income.

Not a single one of these charges is true. This bill simply proposes to collect taxes on dividends and interest income in the same fashion that it has been collected on our wages and salaries for the past 19 years. This is not a new tax. It has been on the books for years.

Those recipients of dividends and interest who already pay their taxes will not be affected in any way. Those whose income is too low to be subject to tax will not be affected, for they can exempt themselves from withholding by a simple statement. The only ones affected will be those individuals who are not now paying the taxes they owe on this income, either through neglect or for some other reason.

This is tax evasion, tax evasion of $800 million a year which must be made up by other taxpayers who pay their taxes. And it should be remembered that about 80 percent of dividend income goes to fewer than 7 percent of the taxpayers whose income exceeds $10,000 a year. In short, defeat of this provision will not help older people with small incomes who would be either exempt from it or could file each quarter for a prompt income by filling out a simple slip at the Post Office or bank, as is done every year by those who are involved in withholding. It will help - the defeat of this bill - only those whose evasion of present taxes is costing every honest taxpayer dearly.

More enforcement, more education, more electronic brains cannot do the job, but withholding, as we have seen for the past 20 years, will treat all taxpayers fairly. And this country has prided itself on being willing to bear its heavy burdens honestly, and here is $800 million in taxes which have been on the books for years which is not now being paid and which must be made up by every other taxpayer, particularly those who find themselves, their wages, withheld on wages and salary.

So I am hopeful that those who oppose this bill, particularly savings and loan banks, who have benefited so greatly, who have not been paying their taxes of almost any **kind**, and who wish to defeat the bill because it does place a just burden on them, and who wish to defeat it by misinforming so many millions of people - I hope they'll start to send out the correct record.

QUESTIONS

Newspaper Strikes

Q: Mr. President, the newspapers in Detroit and Minneapolis have been closed by a series of strikes for about a month now. The unions, or some of the unions involved, have been taking turns in calling these strikes one at a time in shutting down the newspapers or keeping them shut. I wonder whether you would comment on these strike tactics and whether this blackout on news in these two major cities affects the general welfare and the public interest of the country to a point of being a matter of national concern in your frame of reference?

The President: Well, as to the last part, there's nothing in a strike of this kind that involves national emergency legislation, but of course, any newspaper strike is unfortunate because it affects not only the people involved on the paper, but it affects the whole community, the distribution of news, and business. It's my understanding that on these strikes Federal mediators have been involved in attempting to be of assistance. And this matter was brought up to me this morning and I discussed it with the Secretary of Labor, Mr. Goldberg, who said he would be glad to be of any use that he could, if the parties felt that he could be helpful. I'm hopeful that a speedy solution can be reached.

It seems to me, as I've said on several occasions recently, these responsibilities must be borne by the parties. These aren't matters which can be settled by Government edict, or that should be. But I am hopeful that these and other matters can be settled, and Secretary Goldberg would be glad to be helpful, and the Federal Mediation is already on the scene and has been for some time.

The Press

Q: Mr. President, perhaps in this connection you would comment for us on the press in general, as you see it from the Presidency. Perhaps, its treatment of your administration, treatment of the issues of the day?

The President: Well, I am reading more and enjoying it less - (laughter) - and so on, but I have not complained nor do I plan to make any general complaints. I read and talk to myself about it, but I don't plan to issue any general statement on the press. I think that they are doing their task, as a critical branch, the fourth estate. And I am attempting to do mine. And we are going to live together for a period, and then go our separate ways. (Laughter)

Election Results

Q: Mr. President, have you any comment on yesterday's election results, insofar as they affect your administration - the primaries?

The President: I am pleased at the result of the last few days, in Florida and Texas.

Q: You have in the past endorsed some candidates in primaries, where there was opposition.

The President: I endorsed Congressman Fascell and Senator Smathers, at the dinner in Miami.[1] I think those are the only fights which I took an active part in, in the primaries.

Q: I was thinking of Hale Boggs, too, but that's not important.

The President: Well, it is to Congressman Boggs! (Laughter)

Q: I meant it was not important to quibble about.

The President: Yes, that's right, I understand.

Q: But, does the administration have a favorite in Texas between Connally and Yarborough?

The President: I don't know whether "endorse" is the proper word. I spoke as highly of Congressman Boggs as I could, because my opinion of him is that high. But in the case of Texas, I was pleased that both candidates who had been attacked for their connection with the administration did very well. But they're electing a Governor in Texas. This is a decision for the people of Texas, and I am sure they would resent any outside interference and an attempt to talk from Washington about who should be Governor of Texas. They are very qualified to make a judgment, and I'm sure that they will make one which suits them.

Negotiations with the Soviet Union on Berlin

Q: Mr. President, my problem concerns the negotiations with the Soviet Union over Berlin. Chancellor Adenauer, as you know, has been critical in recent days over both the proposal for a 13-nation access control organization, and also toward the idea of the exploratory talks in themselves. Do you contemplate any change in signals in view of the Chancellor's objections?

The President: No, I don't think, at least from what I can gather - it's not easy. I don't think that that would be a correct interpretation of the German Government's position as of this time, as my understanding is that they are interested and support our exploratory talks on the access authority. What has concerned them is the makeup of the access authority, and this has been - since this matter was brought out into the public some weeks ago, before the Athens meeting, this has been the subject of a discussion between the two governments. So I place that in one category. The access authority, itself, which has been before us, really as a suggestion for many months, is not in controversy. It is the organization of the access authority, the relative power and position of the various members of it which has been the subject of some exchanges, which is quite natural.

It's not easy. The United States is attempting to carry on negotiations for several powers and all of them have different ideas how it ought to be done. And we have to attempt to coordinate it, and at the same time present a position which has some hope of working out in a peaceful way. So I put that as one area.

Now, on the talks themselves we have never had any statement from the German Government, or Chancellor Adenauer, that these talks should not continue. These talks are going to continue. As I understand the Chancellor's statement - and I think it is worth reading his entire speech in order to understand exactly what he means, and not fragments - he's not very optimistic about these talks. In fact, he quoted Secretary Rusk as saying that he did not believe that these talks - given the positions of the two parties - that these talks would produce a fruitful result. And maybe they won't. We have never said that they would, and we have never expressed high optimism about them. One of the members of the Foreign Office today said that they support the talks, but that the Chancellor was concerned that there was undue optimism. We have never been unduly optimistic. But we believe that there should be a continuation of these talks.

Everything that was said at Athens, everything that's been said before, everything I have heard in the last 2 days - the German Government supports the position that we should continue the exploratory talks. And I believe we should. No country has done more than the United States in the last 12 months to strengthen our military forces in order to protect our commitments. But we hope, in calling up 160,000 men, adding billions of dollars to our defense budget, which was not done by many other countries who speak with vigor now - I would feel that the purpose of it, we hope, is not to fight a nuclear war but to establish an environment which permits us to have a useful exchange. As Winston Churchill said, "It is better to jaw, jaw than to war, war," and we shall continue to jaw, jaw, and see if we can produce a useful result. We may fail, but in my opinion the effort is worth it when we're dealing with such dangerous matters, and when we've seen the history of this century, when statesmen, and leaders, and others have brought about failure and brought about war as a result. So we're going to see what we can do.

U.S. Policy in Laos

Q: Mr. President, last February at a news conference you told us that the cease-fire was becoming frayed in Laos and in the event that it was broken, it could lead to a very serious decision. I wonder, Mr. President, now that the cease-fire has been broken, and if efforts should fail to reestablish it, would it cause a reexamination on the part of the United States towards its policy there?

The President: Well, we *are* concerned about the break in the cease-fire. And, as you know, the State Department, the Acting Secretary of State - the Assistant Secretary of State today met with Ambassador Dobrynin - this afternoon. We've already indicated to one of the cochairmen of the British Government our great concern about it. Our Ambassador in Moscow met with the Foreign Secretary of the Soviet Union, Mr. Gromyko. We do believe, and have said from the beginning, that the negotiations should move much more quickly than they have. The longer this rather frayed cease-fire continues, the more chance we will have of the kind of incidents we've had in the past few days. That's why we were hopeful, after the meetings at Geneva last summer and fall, that the negotiations between the parties involved would take place last fall, and we could organize a government, rather than trying to continue to hold lines which in some cases are exposed and which are subject to this kind of pressure.

So that has been our view. The longer it goes on, and the longer there is not an agreement on a government, the longer some groups stand out from these kinds of conversations, then the more hazardous the situation becomes.

On the particular incident, however, it's a clear breach of the cease-fire. We have indicated it and we hope that the Soviet Union, which is committed to a policy based on the statement at Vienna, in regard to Laos - we are hopeful that we can bring about a restoration of the cease-fire. But we've got to use the time to try to move ahead in our political negotiations. Now, I agree it's a very hazardous course, but introducing American forces which is the other one - let's not think there is some great third course - that also is a hazardous course, and we want to attempt to see if we can work out a peaceful solution, which has been our object for many months. I believe that these negotiations should take place quickly. This is not a satisfactory situation today.

The Construction Industry in California

Q: Mr. President, on another labor-management issue, there's a matter of some concern in northern California. The construction industry there may face a general shutdown because of the dispute between employers and the labor unions. The employers association appealed to the administration for help some time ago, and there has been a strike spreading during this time. Have you personally concerned yourself with this?

The President: I'm not aware of the appeal. In what way was the appeal made? The Federal mediators are there. In what way was it suggested?

Q: It was an appeal they addressed to the White House, sir, and it has gone as far as the Secretary of Labor, I believe.

The President: What is the suggestion that they want? What do they want us to do?

Q: They simply want some form of help, from the administration.

The President: Well, what - do they want us to settle it?

Q: I don't know.

The President: I want to point out that as I said to the Chamber of Commerce, and as President Wagner of the Chamber of Commerce said, labor and management should settle these matters by themselves. We cannot settle labor matters in disputes across the country, unless they involve those areas where there may be a great national basic industry. But we cannot go from city to city, unless we are going to change the whole pattern of labor-management relations, and you get in, then, to wage and price setting, which we are opposed to. So that we are attempting to set down general guidelines in as effective a manner as we can, which we hope will govern these negotiations. I would hope that they would have an effect upon the construction industry, and its employees, as well as upon other industries. And I know that the Mediation Service is involved in this. I know that the Secretary of Labor in this case also is glad to be of assistance in providing his good offices. But this is a free society, and these gentlemen finally have to make their agreement themselves.

Now, if a shutdown occurs which involves the health and safety, then of course it involves the National Government. But I have the impression that there is a great desire on every side to settle these matters without the United States Government. And we want to give them a fair opportunity to do that.

Questioning of the President and Thoughts on World Peace

Q: Mr. President, back to your relations with newsmen. According to a poll released this morning, a large percentage of our people, or the people who were polled, believe that the newsmen attending, and news ladies, do not ask you really important questions. I want to know what you think of that and at the risk of repetition, one of the questions they seemed to think was most important: Did you have any ideas towards any new steps to ease tension and promote world peace?

The President: Well, we are attempting in two areas, which are both critical areas. One, I said we're continuing our conversations in Berlin. We have attempted in the last 2 or 3 days to indicate our concern about the matter in Laos. We are participating in Geneva in the disarmament talks. We have put forward the most far-reaching plan of any administration or the American Government ever, in regard to disarmament. We have labored for a long time - even to the point of - it's well known to us - to get an agreement on a cessation of nuclear tests. We are attempting to - lacking an accord, we have maintained our military forces so that through that means we can, as I've said, set an environment for parleys. And we have supported the United Nations in the Congo and elsewhere, which we regard as a very valuable arm in this struggle for peace. We are prepared to go any distance in order to maintain the peace providing it does not involve the breaking of any commitments of the United States or involve any diminishment of the basic national security of the country.

Q: Do you think we've overlooked any important questions, sir?

The President: I'm sure we have —

Q: — I meant the newsmen asking you.

The President: — in the sense that we are trying, for example, to strengthen the Alliance for Progress. We've - I exchanged correspondence with Mr. Khrushchev about 2 months ago about our willingness to provide for the cooperation in space. We have supported resolutions at the United Nations which I believe in, in regard to the peaceful uses of outer space. We have thrown our space program open. It's been maintained chiefly under civilian control and therefore peaceful control. And we are attempting, on every level, cultural exchanges and all the rest to see if it's possible in these two different worlds to let them live together without destroying each other.

But I think we always have to do more and we shall continue to do so. But it really requires a response in order to have peace, and so far we have not been able to evoke a response of sufficient force.

Guidelines for Wage Increases

Q: Mr. President, on the question of the administration's guidelines for wage increases, Mr. Reuther, in his report to the United Auto Workers, said that he disagreed at least in part with the guidelines. He said that the principle of tying increases to productivity should be applied only after certain catch-up wage increases. Now, just before you made your speech up there, he issued a statement indicating that he agreed with the administration. Has the administration been in touch with Mr. Reuther and has there been a meeting of minds on this?

The President: Well, we've been in touch with Mr. Reuther, yes. As I say, I went up there yesterday, and I did see his statement. And I thought it was a fine statement that he made, in which he indicated his general agreement with what we are attempting to do.

President's View of Businessmen

Q: Mr. President, at the time of your controversy with the steel industry, you were quoted as making a rather harsh statement about businessmen. I am sure you know which statement I have in mind.

The President: Yes. You wouldn't want to identify it, would you? (Laughter)

Q: Would you tell us about it, Mr. President?

The President: Would I want to comment on it?

Q: Yes.

The President: Oh, well, the statement which I have seen repeated, as it was repeated in one daily paper, is inaccurate. It quotes my father as having expressed himself strongly to me, and in this I quoted what he said and indicated that he had not been, as he had not been on many other occasions, wholly wrong.

Now, the only thing that was wrong with the statement was that, as it appeared in a daily paper, it indicated that he was critical of the business community - I think the phrase was "all businessmen." That's obviously in error, because he was a businessman himself. He was critical of the steel men. He'd worked for a steel company himself. He was involved when he was a member of the Roosevelt administration in the 1937 strike. He formed an opinion which he imparted to me, and which I found appropriate that evening. (Laughter) But he confined it, and I would confine it. Obviously these generalizations as repeated are inaccurate and unfair, and he has been a businessman and the business system has been very generous to him. But I felt at that time that we had not been treated altogether with frankness, and therefore I thought that his view had merit. But that's past, that's past. Now we're working together, I hope.

Reverse Freedom Rides

Q: Mr. President, do you have any comment on the so-called reverse freedom rides, whereby some southern segregationists are attempting to send Negroes north?

The President: Yes. Well, I think it is a rather cheap exercise in - you know, in this country people are moving every day by the thousands. Twenty-five percent of our population live in different States in the last decade than they did. There are hundreds and thousands of people coming from one State to another. So that this, rather, exercise in publicity to indicate, if I - this man, it seems to me, really doesn't merit very much comment. I think he's - we have difficulties in every area. We have people who are out of work in every area. There are people who are inadequately housed in every area. And we ought to do better in every area. But it seems to me, as I said the other day, there is no city, traditionally, that has enjoyed a happier reputation than New Orleans. And that reputation, in my opinion, based on my visit there Friday, is highly deserved. And I would not let one man possibly blacken it.

Vice-President Johnson and the 1964 Ticket

Q: Mr. President, there have been rumors in print in and out of Texas that Vice President Johnson might be dropped from the Democratic ticket in 1964. I'd like to ask if you have any reason whatever to believe that either end of the Democratic ticket will be different in 1964?

The President: Well, I don't know about what they will do with me, but I am sure that the Vice President will be on the ticket if he chooses to run. We were fortunate to have him before - and would again - and I don't know where such a rumor would start. He's invaluable. He fulfills a great many responsibilities as Vice President. He participates in all of the major deliberations. He's been in the Congress for years. He is invaluable. So of course he will be, if he chooses to be, part of the ticket.

The Use of Outer Space

Q: Mr. President, it has been the stated policy, as you said earlier, for this Government to restrict outer space for peaceful objectives only. Will not the proposed H-bomb explosion 500 miles up jeopardize this policy and objective?

The President: No, I don't think so. I don't think so. I know there's been disturbance about the Van Allen belt, but Van Allen says it's not going to affect the belt, and it's his! (Laughter)

But it is a matter which we are - I've read the protests and it is a matter which we are looking into to see whether there is scientific merit that this will cause some difficulty to the Van Allen belt in a way which will adversely affect scientific discovery. And this is being taken into very careful consideration at the present time. So that I want you to know that whatever our decision is, in regard to the Van Allen belt, it will be done only after very careful scientific deliberation, which is now taking place - during this past week - and will go on for a period. In regard, generally, what we are attempting to do is to find out the effects of such an explosion on our security, and we do not believe that this will adversely affect the security of any person not living in the United States.

Railroad Pay Raise

Q: Mr. President, a special emergency panel has recommended a 10.2 cent an hour pay raise for about 500,000 railroad employees, which is estimated to cost about $100 million a year. You have observed that the Board said it would be noninflationary. Do you believe it would be noninflationary?

The President: Well, I would - the Board stated it would be noninflationary, and I stated it was my judgment that they should negotiate a noninflationary statement, a settlement. Now the railroads have objected to the arrangement by saying it's too much, the railway unions too little.

I am hopeful that the parties will negotiate, and we would, of course, be glad to be of any technical assistance we could, if we are asked, in order to determine the extent of - what effect it would have on the cost of living. But it was a good board. They made a very flat statement in regard to it, and I think that what is now incumbent on both parties is to see if they can reach what I would consider a noninflationary agreement.

A Uniform Patent Policy

Q: Mr. President, there have been various congressional and executive studies in an effort to develop a uniform patent policy covering inventions made under Government contracts, and we're wondering if you intend to submit any legislation to spell out a uniform Government patent policy?

The President: Well, it's a difficult problem, because you have to balance off the gains on the one hand and at the same time the incentives to companies to spend their own funds in order to develop patents which would give them a return in other years. So that we have some differences in the Space Agency problem, the Department of Defense, and perhaps another agency of the Government. But it is a matter which is being reviewed now by those agencies which are most involved. And if we have any changes to make at the conclusion of that, then I will send recommendations to the Hill.

The International Access Authority

Q: Mr. President, more fundamental, perhaps, than the numbers game that is being played between Bonn and Washington over the international access authority and how many members it ought to have, there seems to be a sense of insecurity in Bonn at the moment and in Germany, generally, about the degree to which this administration will support the basic position of no recognition of East Germany, no degree of recognition at all. I wonder if you could define that point just a little bit. How far are we prepared to go?

The President: Well, we've never suggested that the access authority - which was a proposal which could have easily been rejected and alternate language suggested in accordance with the normal exchanges between governments, which is the reason we sent it – it was never suggested that that constituted a *de facto,* or *de jure* recognition of the East German regime, which we have not supported, because we have supported the concept of the reunification of Germany.

We, after all – the East German Government, or regime, and the West German Government were participants in the same room at the 1959 Geneva conference. They didn't sit at the table, but they sat in chairs just behind the table. Now, what did that constitute? After all, the East German regime controls over 90 today – supervises over 90 percent of the traffic into Berlin, and there are these exchanges in regard to that traffic. What does that constitute? I don't think it constitutes recognition. And it doesn't by either *de facto* or *de jure.*

We participate in the Laos convention in Geneva with the Chinese Communists in an attempt to work out an accord in Geneva on Laos. We don't recognize them either way.

So that what we're attempting to do is to work out a solution which will provide more security for the people of West Berlin. Because when the difficult times come, it is the United States that carries the major burden and is looked to to take the major actions which will sustain the freedom of the city. So that I think we have some rights to at least explore the possibilities of finding a better solution than we now have.

But in answer to your question, we did not believe and do not believe the proposals that we made constitute a kind of recognition. For example, among the 13 of the proposals there was a West Berlin, which is not a separate government, and there was an East Berlin, which is not a separate government. So that it was an authority, which might be compared to the Port of New York and not a government, a governmental group, or a group of governments. But this sort of necessity to debate this matter for a month makes it very difficult to carry on any negotiations with the Soviet Union because all of our proposals are on the table and fought out in public even before they become our official position. So that it seems to me the best thing to do would be to – if anybody has any objection, to tell us – and we have said from the beginning that in our efforts to reach an accord, we certainly recognize the necessity of maintaining unanimity in the alliance.

I don't know whether this is the best way to carry on these negotiations if these matters are going to become so publicly debated. If this isn't the best solution, perhaps some other way should be done, and we'll be glad to hear that suggestion. But we carry the major military burden, we enforce, and have the major military buildup – 160,000 Americans called up since last July – and it is not difficult to make suggestions and say, oh, well, you shouldn't do this or that, and at the same time some countries do not play as active a role as we've been willing to play in an attempt to work this out.

Q: In that connection, sir, I wonder do you have any theory or any information as to the reason for the agitation, the degree of agitation?

The President: No, I think a lot of it – I must say I read his Monday's speech in which he stated – Chancellor Adenauer – that the most important result of Athens can be summarized in one sentence: the unity of the free West. If you think back to the ministers' meeting of NATO in 1961, unless my memory fails me, it was in December – this was Chancellor Adenauer – "there the unity of the free people of the West did not look good. And the unity of the free people of the West, I am convinced, is the best asset of freedom."

But he said this: "The whole political future in the East of Germany finally depends on the unity of the West. And I believe we can be very satisfied with the way this NATO conference went."

So I think that some of this is speculation which does not serve the cause. Mr. Drew Middleton in the *Times* made a very strong article on the work Secretaries McNamara and Rusk had done. He said that they had witnessed "a striking demonstration both of the United States reasons for leading the West and its ability to do so." So I think we had pretty good unity as of Saturday or Sunday, and I hope we will this Saturday or Sunday.

The Literacy Test Bill

Q: Would you care to comment on the voting in the Senate today on the cloture petition on the literacy test bill, and whether you think this is possible as a piece of legislation this year?

The President: Well, there were two votes. One was on the motion to table, and that got a rather large vote against tabling. If that vote indicates that the members are for it, that would be very encouraging - I think it was 63 to 33 or 34. On **the** motion, however, for cloture, which would permit us to have a vote on this matter, then the members voted differently.

As I understand it, Senator Mansfield is trying again Monday, but if we don't succeed, if the Senate doesn't succeed - if the country doesn't succeed in getting the vote by Monday, cloture, then of course there's no use saying you're for it, because it won't ever come up. And I must say I find it extremely difficult to understand how anybody can - though I respect Senator Cooper, and I know his concern is constitutional, and I respect the others who have various things - but I must say this involves the right to vote. And I've seen these cases of people with college degrees who were denied being put on the register because they supposedly can't pass the literacy test. It doesn't make any sense. So I'm hopeful the Senate will vote, and there'll be another chance on Monday.

Reporter: Thank you, Mr. President.

[1]See Item 77, of the *Public Papers of the President.*

THE PRESIDENT'S NEWS CONFERENCE OF

MAY 17, 1962

The President: Good afternoon. Any questions?

QUESTIONS

The Billie Sol Estes Affair

Q: Mr. President, with the word "scandal" again in the wind in Washington, would you care to comment on the Billie Sol Estes affair and tell us if you believe that Secretary Freeman has handled the case properly?

The President: Well, as you know, the Billie Sol Estes case came to public attention when the United States Government indicted him on April 5. We requested a bail of $500,000 which was not granted - it's down to $100,000 - and since that time we have been conducting a very thorough investigation with nearly 75 members of the FBI involved in this investigation. These affairs are most complicated. Billie Sol Estes dealt through almost 23 companies.

In addition, we have taken immediate action against all of those Federal employees, of whom there have been four in the Department of Agriculture, who have been involved in improprieties. The investigation is continuing and will continue. The Department of Justice, Internal Revenue, Senator McClellan in the Senate, Congressman Fountain in the House - all of them are involved in attempting to determine whether any Federal employee or member of Congress were involved in any improper action. I can assure you that if any members of the executive branch are involved, any improprieties shown, they will be immediately taken action against - immediately disciplined appropriately.

Now in regard to Secretary Freeman, I've stated already my high regard for him. Secretary Freeman I think has had a matchless reputation. He worked his way through the University of Minnesota; he was a football player, graduated Phi Beta Kappa. He had most of his jaw shot off at Bougainville as a captain in the Marines; he was Governor of Minnesota for three terms. He's the head of this Department, has over 100,000 employees, and it's been a most challenging job, and I have the greatest confidence in the integrity of Secretary Freeman.

I point out again that the matter of Billie Sol Estes came to public attention in the way that it was because the United States Government, this administration, indicted him.

Q: Mr. President, in the same vein, a little more philosophically. This sort of thing, a scandal where one or more Federal employees are involved for private gain with people on the outside, this sort of thing seems to recur administration after administration; it doesn't seem to follow any political pattern. How do you propose, or do you have any ideas on how to prevent this or wipe it out?

The President: Well, I agree that we have over two million employees, you've got a good many people that take advantage or attempt to influence them, seek private gain. As a result of congressional intercession, or as a result of special favors in the administration, a good many of the decisions that these men make involve large sums of money, contracts, and all the rest - pressures are put upon them. Some succumb. Most do not. What we attempt to do is to provide for procedures whereby any improprieties will be immediately detected. We attempt to establish the highest ethical standards which are possible. We take immediate action when an impropriety is revealed, and we attempt to maintain the morale and discipline of the United States Government.

Improprieties occur in a good many different kinds of life, whether it's labor, management, Government. Not all people are able to withstand these pressures. But we intend that the personnel of the United States Government will meet the highest ethical standards possible, and when they do not, action will be taken. My experience is that the great, great majority of them do. They are not paid very highly in most cases. They are dealing with matters of vital concern, and I think on the whole they do a good job. When they don't, it is most unfortunate and most regrettable because all of us want the Federal service to be of the highest possible standards.

A New Head of HEW

Q: Mr. President, there have been published reports that you have made up your mind to appoint Dr. Weaver as head of the Health, Education, and Welfare Department, when a vacancy occurs. Can you give us your comment on that?

The President: I have made no decision because, of course, no vacancy has occurred. When it does, I will announce a successor - if one does - immedi ately.

Differences Between Paris and Washington

Q: Mr. President, General de Gaulle, a couple of days ago at a news con-ference, made some points which seemed to underline the differences between Paris and Washington. He spoke of his determination to proceed with his nuclear deterrent in order not to rely upon the United States in that respect. He also spoke of the confederation rather than a more intimate political unity in Europe, and discounted the efforts of the United States in the Berlin negotia-tions, which I think he said was trying to square the circle. Some people be-lieve that these differences between France and the United States are more fun damental and pose a greater danger to the Western alliance than those between Bonn and Washington, which have been more publicized.

I was wondering if you would care to address yourself to the question of difficulties between France and the United States, and more particularly wheth-er you believe, a year having elapsed since your meeting with General de Gaulle, that it would be worth while for you and the General to get together again.

The President: Well, on two of those - one of those three matters, of course, is a matter which involves completely the European: this question of the federation versus confederation. That is a matter which the Europeans must decide. Our interest in Europe is only that we believe that the freedom of Europe and the defense of Europe are bound up with the freedom and defense of the United States. Therefore, we have made large expenditures in men and money, we have committed ourselves, we have participated as a very active member of NATO. The nuclear deterrent of the United States, I think, has helped defend Europe for a great many years. But as to what the relationship should be be-tween the countries of Europe, that is a matter of course, primarily for them.

On the matter of Berlin, it is a matter of the greatest concern to us. We wish to have some voice in events there because if the moment of truth comes, it is the United States which is expected to take the very vigorous action which could involve our security as well as that of Western Europe. And to use an old familiar American expression, we wish to be in on the take-off of these matters.

I've already commented on why I think it desirable to continue these conver-sations with the Soviet Union over Berlin. It's a vital matter which involves the interest of both; it's highly charged. I see only advantage in carrying on a conversation. Before any conclusions are reached, of course, we would attempt to have an agreement among our allies.

Now, the third matter is more from a philosophical stand. We do not believe in a series of national deterrents. We believe that the NATO deterrent, to which the United States has committed itself so heavily, provides very adequate protection. Once you begin, nation after nation, beginning to develop its own deterrent, or rather feeling it's necessary as an element of its independence to develop its own deterrent, it seems to me that you are moving into an in-creasingly dangerous situation.

First France, and then another country and then another, until a very solid and, I think, effective defense alliance may be somewhat weakened. That, how-ever, is a decision for the French. If they choose to go ahead, of course they will go ahead, and General de Gaulle has announced they are going ahead. We do not agree, but he cannot blame us if we do not agree anymore than we blame him if he does not agree with us.

Now, as to the long-range future of Europe. This is a matter, as I have said, of debate inside France and inside Europe. But I will say, speaking personally, that however difficult becomes this dialog with General de Gaulle over what I would call the Atlantic Community and the respective roles of each country within it, I would think it would be a far more difficult situation if General de Gaulle were not as stalwart in his defense of the West. We do not look for those who agree with us, but those who defend their country and who are committed to the defense of the West. I believe General de Gaulle is. So we will get along. I'm not sure that we would get any greater agreement if we meet. There is a limit to the advantages of these kinds of dialog, but we will continue, at least, to maintain a contact which I hope will not be acrimonious - certainly in this case.

The Laotian Situation

Q: Mr. President, could you bring us up to date on the Laotian situation since the dispatch of our troops to Thailand? Specifically, do you feel that we have increased the chances of our getting caught in a shooting war in Southeast Asia?

The President: We are continuing to hope that there will be a national - government of national union, which has been our policy, as you know, for a year. We are going into Thailand at the decision of the Thai Government. Our own decision provides for the defense of Thailand. The latest information indicates no further breach of the cease-fire. We also have indications that the three princes will engage in conversation shortly. I hope they will produce a government. That is our objective. As I have already indicated, the great hazard is of a shooting war in Asia - in the jungles of Asia - and it is our object to bring about a diplomatic solution which will make the changes of such a war far less likely.

Q: Mr. President, in light of your answer to this question, sir, could you give us any idea how long the American troops will be needed in Thailand?

The President: I cannot at this time.

Q: Have you any idea under what conditions they might return?

The President: I cannot at this time. They have only been in there for a very short while, and we can't tell when they will come out. It will depend a good deal on what conditions are in Thailand and the neighboring countries.

Q: Mr. President, could you tell us, please, what you would consider the restoration of an effective cease-fire? Would this involve the withdrawal of the Communist forces to their position before the attack on Nam Tha, or more or less acquiescence which would permit the talks to go forward on the government?

The President: Well, naturally, we would prefer as great a withdrawal to the line that was in effect a week or so ago as we could get. I would think, however, that the peace along the line which now may exist, of course, is essential.

Q: Mr. President, would you review for us the considerations that you had in mind last weekend when you took this rather swift action to move more American troops into Thailand?

The President: Yes. We're concerned about the breach of the cease-fire, the sign of deterioration in Laos, which brought Communist forces to the border of Thailand up in the - near the Mekong River section of - not too far from Nam Tha, and we did not know whether this was an indication of a general breach of the cease-fire which, of course, would immediately imperil Thailand. So that in our desire to stabilize the situation we got in touch with the government, which was already in touch with us, and worked out the proposed course of action.

Railroads and Unions

Q: Mr. President, the railroads and five operating unions broke off talks today. There has already been a Presidential commission report on this dispute, so the next step may be up to you. Can you tell us if you have any action in mind, and when you might act?

The President: Well, I think we are keeping very close contact with it. They have the recommendation of the Board, and Secretary Goldberg is watching it very carefully. If there is anything that we can do appropriately, we will do it.

France's Creation of a Defense Community Apart from NATO

Q: Mr. President, President de Gaulle seems intent on creating a defense community apart from NATO. If he continues in this way, do you think there is any danger of reviving an isolationist sentiment in this country?

The President: Well, I think it would be quite a long time before members of Europe, all of them, would feel in a position to defend themselves without the presence of the United States. The United States does not maintain nearly 300,000 troops and spend over a billion dollars - in dollars, and therefore in gold - in Europe becuase it chooses to do so against the wishes of those who are present. We have been asked to come and asked to stay. If we were not asked to stay, then we would take, I think, a different view of it. But I have not heard anyone suggest that the United States today withdraw from Europe or that it relax its guarantees which consist of all kinds of defense procedures.

Now the day may come when Western Europe may feel that it can maintain its own security. Of course it would relieve the United States of a very heavy burden. But that day has not come. We want Western Europe to be independent and free. We want to prevent the outbreak of a war. We want no one to be in any doubt about the intentions of the United States. You've obviously seen on two occasions, when war broke out in Europe, there was some question of what the ultimate attitudes of the United States would be. NATO does not leave that in question. NATO guarantees. So this is the important defense for Europe and important defense for us and every evidence I have is that the Europeans wish that to continue. Now, the day may come when their power is such that they can proceed on their defense without the United States, and no one in the United States that I know of wishes to stay a moment longer than our presence is desired or desirable.

Eisenhower's Suggestion on the Estes Case

Q: Mr. President, former President Eisenhower in connection with the Estes case has suggested that all of the investigative agencies, in contrast to his own administration, are under one political party. He suggested the possibility that you might wish to follow the precedent of President Coolidge and invite some Republicans in to lay before them some of the information on the Estes case, that they might not know of. Do you regard this as a good idea?

The President: Well, I have great regard for Senator McClellan, who I do not believe approaches any matter such as this on a partisan basis, and his committee is made up of Republicans and Democrats. All the information which we have will be made available to that committee, and all of the reports of the

FBI. As I've stated before, this matter came to public attention because this administration indicted Mr. Estes before a State agency in Texas or any place else moved. In the case of some of the recent matters, to which reference was made, they were not brought out by the administration in power, but brought out by congressional investigating committees. We did not have any evidence by either Republican or Democrats of a major concern about the possibility that Mr. Estes would be involved in so many operations which had such little basis. So that I can assure you that the information which is collected will be turned over to the congressional committees involved, to the Republicans and Democratic counsels of each committee, and that Senator McClellan will, I'm sure, Congressman Fountain in the House, and all the others will meet their responsibilities very fully, as we are attempting to meet ours.

Progress in School Desegregation

Q: Mr. President, today is the 8th anniversary of the Supreme Court school desegregation decision. Do you feel that progress in this area has been rapid enough?

The President: Well, I think we can always hope that more progress can be made in the area of civil rights, or equal opportunity, whether it's in employment or education or housing or anything else. There is a good deal left undone, and while progress has been made I think we can always improve equality of opportunity in the United States.

An ICBM Warning System in the South

Q: Mr. President, why is it that we have no intercontinental ballistic missile warning system to the south of us in the Gulf or South America, in view of some of the recent reports that the Russians have said that they might come at us from the south?

The President: Because our early warning system, as you know, was first developed for airplanes, which were coming from the north. Then it was converted to missiles, and it is being completed for missiles in the north. The flight to the south is an extremely long trip, which does not permit the kind of accuracy which a northern flight would permit, and as we develop Minutemen and other missiles which can take off with very little notice, the advantages of a long trip with relative inaccuracy will be far less to the Soviets. Their hope, in other words, of knocking out our ability to strike them after they might have struck us, of course, is far less to the south. But my judgment is that as time goes on, such a system will be developed.

Status of the Stock Market

Q: Mr. President, the stock market slump lately seems to indicate a lack of investor confidence in the economic outlook. Do you have any comment on the behavior of the market?

The President: No. I think that – I would not attempt to figure its ups and downs. As you remember, it took a very sharp slump in 1956 just before we had an extremely good year the next year. At that time, I think in 1957, the value of the stock compared to the earnings was about 12 to 1. At the time of the high year it was around 22 to 1. But every indication we have indicates that this is going to be a record year in profits, wages, productivity. The new figures which I think have been announced this afternoon call for a construction at an annual rate of 1.5 million housing units, which is the highest we've had for three years, so we believe that the United States economy should have confidence. But the question of the relationship between stock prices and earnings is a matter for those who are in that business.

Eisenhower's Criticism of Legislation

Q: Mr. President, would you care to answer former President Eisenhower's charge that many bills you support would put too much power in the Presidency, and that's the real threat to liberty in this country?

The President: Well, he gave - I don't want to get into a political discussion with President Eisenhower. I think he gave five examples. One was our farm bill. Let me make it very clear that one of the problems in agriculture, of course, has been the tremendous increase in commodities which must be stored. And one of the problems in the Estes case is this very one.

The fact of the matter is there was in 1953 about $2.5 million of surpluses that had to be stored. Now it's $9 billion, for which we pay $1 billion a year. Mr. Estes went into the grain storage business way back in 1959. In fact, of the $7 million which the Federal Government has paid to him for storage, about $5 million of it was paid prior to January 1961.

Now we're going to have an agricultural bill before the Congress in the next 2 or 3 weeks, and I think the American people should understand very clearly that if the bill we propose is defeated, we will then go back automatically by statute to the Benson program, which provides no effective controls on production, a support price which will increase by large amounts the amount of materials that we have to store away, and the burden to the taxpayer.

This could involve billions of dollars over the next 4 or 5 years. Unless we can bring into balance supply and demand more effectively than we've done - and we have done it in cotton and tobacco - unless we can do that in grain, you're going to have not $9 billion to be stored away, but 10, 11, 12, 13 or 14. We spend $6 billion as a budget item for the Government every year on agriculture. It will go up 7, 8, 9, so I think that we have to have an effective balance of supply and demand or otherwise you will have these situations where grain storages are bursting at the seams. And you have the kind of pressures which we have been witnessing in recent months.

I think that the best hope represents this legislation. And, let me make it very clear, if this bill is defeated it will cost the taxpayers of the United States $4 billion more in the next 4 years for agricultural appropriations as well as storage. So this represents, in my opinion, a chance to do something for the farmer that's effective for the consumer and also for the taxpayer. And those who oppose it are committing us to an expenditure of at least 4 or 5 billion dollars over a very short period of time as well as taking our storage problem up to 11, 12, 13 billion dollars. I think it would be a great, great mistake. And I think this represents our best chance to do something about the kind of situation which resulted in Mr. Estes' manipulations.

The 1963 Budget

Q: Mr. President, we have unofficial estimates that the 1963 budget will be from 4 to 7 billion dollars. Have you any report from your officials as to what it will be?

The President: No, we don't. It depends, of course, upon the state of the economy. As I've said from the beginning, if the economy reaches the level that we had hoped it would, and if the Congress takes action on postal legislation, and if it meets its responsibilities as I hope it will in the field of agriculture, our budget should be within balance.

Now, if the economy falls, if the Congress takes no action on postal rates, and if it defeats our efforts in farm legislation, then there will be a very different problem which we will have to face up to. But I do want to point out that one of the most important steps we can take in the general public interest is the support of the legislation. Because people who vote against it, feeling that we don't want any new legislation on the books have to realize that there is permanent legislation on the books which then goes into effect, which is known as part - which was identified with Mr. Benson, which did not bring prosperity to the farmer or well-being to the Federal budget.

A Nuclear Test Ban

Q: Mr. President, Ambassador Dean indicated this week that after we finish our tests, and the Russians finish their tests, that perhaps there would be a very good atmosphere to achieve a nuclear test ban. Do you share this view, and also do we have any reason to believe that this might be true?

The President: Well, I think we have to wait until the situation develops, where our tests are concluded. I understand there seems to be evidence the Soviets may test, and we will then have to see what the situation is.

Relations with West Germany

Q: Following up last week's discussion on misunderstandings between ourselves and the West Germans, sir, you've talked to the West German Ambassador. So has Mr. Rusk, and in addition Mr. Dowling has been to see the Chancellor. Can you tell us, sir, are our relations with the West Germans back on the track or moving in that direction now?

The President: Yes, I think they are. We are now waiting, as the result of the conferences in Athens and as a result of our suggestions directly to the German Government and the Chancellor, for their comments and any proposals they might make on the access authority which was the matter of most immediate concern. We shall hear from that - from them shortly.

Wage Decision by the Amalgamated Clothing Workers

Q: Mr. President, in the light of your insistence on price and wage stability, what is your reaction to the decision of the Amalgamated Clothing Workers yesterday to demand a 35-hour week from employers?

The President: I believe we should have a 40-hour week. I've said that from the beginning.

Possibility of Europe Becoming a Third Force

Q: Mr. President, your earlier answer on the European problem about the possiblity of Europe some day being able to defend itself suggests a good possibility that Europe might some day become what some people call a third force. Do you think that this could happen and still be in the interest of the whole Atlantic Community, or would this so disrupt the Atlantic Community that it would be a detriment?

The President: I think it would be most regrettable to attempt to break what has been built by so many men of good will in every country, the Atlantic Community. There is a - when you talk about third force, of course, it has a number of meanings. But my judgment is that the security of the West is best tied to a continuation of the Atlantic Community and its expression through NATO. Within NATO, of course, there will be the European Community, which will form a very effective, I hope, and strong and vital force for the stability of the West, and we've supported that. Every administration, including this one, has supported the building of the European Economic Community even though it may not be, in every case, in our economic interest, because we believe it builds a stronger Europe. That's why we support the admission of Great Britain. So there is no difference of opinion between Europeans on this matter and ourselves. What I would regret would be any effort which would attempt to divide Europe from the United States and perhaps Canada, because I believe that the oceans should unite rather than divide. I do not anticipate that that will come. I think the mutual dependence is so obvious. But I do suggest that if that day should come, we would not want to give anyone the impression that we were in Europe in order to impose ourselves, but really rather to meet our common obligations. We have been accepted in Europe on that spirit, and we will stay in Europe as long as the desire is there for us to stay. And I've seen no serious evidence that anyone desires us to leave, because I think they realize that that would affect adversely the security of Europe and the balance of power.

Favoritism or Negligence in Administration Appointments

Q: Mr. President, it seems uncontradicted that Mr. Estes was around town spreading quite a little bit of money around trying to be helpful, and I wonder if you have run across any indications that there was any favoritism or negligence resulting from this in the appointment of the man to the National Cotton Advisory Committee initially, or in the cotton allotment pools at a later stage, or the grain storage pattern generally?

The President: Well, these are all matters being investigated. I think Secretary Freeman has already suggested that he has not been able to determine such favoritism. But I believe that we should wait until these investigations are completed. I am not informed about all the details of all transactions. All I know is as of today it does not appear that Mr. Estes was given, as Secretary Freeman has said, but I don't take anything for granted in this matter. That's why we have 76 FBI agents working on it, and, as I have said, the Department of Agriculture has assigned a penalty against him of nearly $600,000. We have carried out - I'm sorry - our bail was not accepted at a half a million dollars - and this Government is staying right on Mr. Estes' tail.

Legal Basis for Our Sending Troops to Thailand

Q: Mr. President, what was the legal basis for our sending troops to Thailand? Was it a bilateral arrangement that we have with the Thai Government, or was it a SEATO arrangement?

The President: No, the actual legal basis was to put us in a position to fulfill our obligations under the SEATO treaty.

Q: Well, Mr. President, are the other members of the SEATO treaty organization doing the same?

The President: They have been asked to do so, and there has been indication of a favorable response from several of them. This is a decision for them. But we have responded and met our obligations.

The Massachusetts Primary and Administration Aid

Q: Mr. President, speaking of Presidential power, there have been some reports from Massachusetts of the use of administration aid and comfort to the senatorial campaign. I wonder if you've laid down any line as to what should be the role of yourself and your associates in this primary contest?

The President: Well, I've already commented on that. I'm not becoming involved in this campaign. I don't know what you're referring to, but I'm very sympathetic. I'd like to comfort my brother, if that's what you mean, but I'm not involving myself in this campaign.

Q: What about your associates, sir?

The President: Well, what are you referring to? What actully are you referring to?

Q: I mean, is there a rule as to whether they should go up to the State or not?

The President: No member of the White House staff is planning to go to the convention, nor will be, to the best of my knowledge, in Massachusetts between now and the convention.

Possible Attacks on Laos and Thailand

Q: Mr. President, back on the subject of Southeast Asia, has there been any indication that the Pathet Lao intended to march against Thailand or against the capitals of Laos and, second, under what conditions would the United States send its troops into Laos?

The President: In answer to your first question, I don't know what their intentions may be. I am hopeful their intentions will be to maintain the cease-fire. Obviously, as I've said, the breach of the cease-fire in the case of Nam Tha was a blow to the concept of the cease-fire. That is what initiated our action in the case of Thailand. On the second matter, we have to wait and see. I think it's very important that the princes form a government of national union for the preservation of their own country.

Problems Involved in **Influence** in Government

Q: Mr. President, in the light of the situation to which Mr. Smith alluded and the occurrence of the Estes situation, do you plan any steps to notify or to tell people in your service and in the departments to remind them of the problems involved in influence and so on in the Government? Do you plan any stepped up ——

The President: We have, as you know, at the beginning of the administration, set down what we regarded as ethical standards for the members of the administration. I think the fact that action has been taken, in each of the cases where any impropriety occurred, immediately, I think is the best evidence that we do not wish to have anyone who serves even indirectly or can be suspected of serving two masters. So that I think it's very clear that wherever this occurs we will take immediate action.

Reporter: Thank you, Mr. President.

THE PRESIDENT'S NEWS CONFERENCE OF

MAY 23, 1962

The President: Good afternoon. Are there any questions?

QUESTIONS

Legislation on the Payment of Medical Bills

Q: Mr. President, assuming that the King-Anderson bill passes, as you have predicted, do you then envision, perhaps next year or the year after, going to Congress again and asking for a plan which would provide similar coverage to pay doctor bills?

The President: No, that is not planned. I notice that legislation was criticized one day for going too far in limiting the relationship between doctors and their patients, and on another day, the next day I believe, certain members opposed to the King-Anderson bill attacked it for not including doctors. This bill includes provisions for payment of hospital bills, nursing care, out-patient care. It does not attempt to interfere in any way with the relationship between the doctor and the patient, and we have no plans to provide such legislation.

The Refugee Problem in Hong Kong

Q: Has the administration any plans for dealing with the refugee problem in Hong Kong?

The President: Well, I notice in the press this afternoon that some effort now seems to be, at least is reported to be, made by the Chinese Communists to stop the flow of refugees. We are, of course, providing food for about a half a million refugees in Hong Kong, and have been for some years. The British have been doing an extraordinary job in finding employment, feeding the people who are there. There are several thousand refugees in Hong Kong and surrounding areas who have been cleared by our consular people for admission to the United States, and under the authority of Congress, which has been granted in similar cases, we are attempting to expedite their admission to the United States, under the power given to the Attorney General by the legislation - the same legislation which has permitted us to bring in Hungarian refugees and Cuban refugees.

It should be pointed out, however, that this does not get at the basic problem, which is that of a tremendous country, 650 million people, where the food supply is inadequate, and it swamps and dwarfs, obviously, Hong Kong and any effort we could make in regard to admission. But at least we are helping to feed those who are there, though the primary responsibility has been very ably borne by the British, and we are attempting to bring in some refugees who have been cleared for admission to the United States.

Q: Would you consider it in the national interest, sir, to make an offer of American surplus grains as a Food for Peace Program to mainland China, to Communist China, at this time?

The President: Well, there's been no indication of any expression of interest or desire by the Chinese Communists to receive any food from us, as I said at the beginning, and we would certainly have to have some idea as to whether the food was needed and under what conditions it might be distributed. Up to the present we have no such indications.

The Situation in Thailand

Q: There are published reports today, sir, that the Army group which originally remained in Thailand is not equipped with live ammunition. There seems to be some discontent among the troops over this. Would you discuss the situation?

The President: Well, the ammunition is there. They haven't had – of course this is a friendly country – they haven't had ammunition clips in their guns, in their barracks, at all times. But the ammunition is available in case they were forced to move into a military area, or where military action might be taken of course the ammunition would be given. But it's not customary, in this country or in a friendly country like Thailand, these troops are not under attack – for ammunition to be inside the guns. But the ammunition is there, and it's quite adequate for any situation that might come, and further ammunition will be stored in appropriate places. It's merely a question whether all guns are loaded at all times in a friendly country, and unless there is sharp control, of course, by the military commanders, practice firing and all the rest. Until that is organized well, the ammunition is naturally under control.

The American Medical Association and Medical Care

Q: Mr. President, could you tell us what you thought of the American Medical Association's reply on Monday night to your proposal – your speech on Sunday – about medical care? And also could you tell us what sort of reaction you have had so far in the White House to the two television speeches, yours on Sunday[1] and the American Medical Association's?

The President: Well, I read the statement and I gathered they were opposed to it. (Laughter) What I thought was remarkable was that the language used was so similar to the language which the AMA used when it opposed and successfully defeated the proposal which President Eisenhower sent up a number of years ago, to provide for reinsurance of private health schemes. That was a proposal – I was on the committee, as a matter of fact, that heard it and supported the legislation – and the AMA led the fight against it and defeated it. In addition, the AMA was one of the chief opponents of the social security system in the thirties. The words, "a cruel hoax" were used against the social security system at that time as they are used today.

The statement – the description of our bill I did not recognize. Now I think that the American people know quite well what this problem is. There isn't anyone in the United States who will not have or has not already had a case of a parent who is sick for a long period of time, with the burden falling very heavily upon either them, or their savings, or upon their children.

There isn't any doubt that we take care, in this country, of those who have no resources. They are treated. We take care of those who are well enough off to pay for all of their bills. What this bill would particularly help are those who have some savings and who nevertheless find themselves hard hit, or their children who have some savings and find themselves faced with these large bills which in the short space of 1, 2, 3, and 4 months can run up into several thousands of dollars. So that I feel that the AMA may not support this bill, but I think the American people will, and I think more and more doctors are supporting it. And I think it's extremely important legislation.

Now, in regard to the mail, I would say that the mail we've gotten as a result of the speech is about evenly divided. But I will point out that I'm not as convinced - I was just looking at the White House mail. I got last week 28 letters on Laos, which is an extremely important problem, of which 14 disagreed with our policy and I think 6 supported it and others were undecided. I got 440 letters on a tax - the cancellation of a tax exemption for a mercy foundation, so-called, in a State in the United States, which is of not, I wouldn't think, great national significance - about 20 times as much mail on it. So that mail, unfortunately, is not true as an indicator of the feelings of the people.

In my judgment, if this matter comes to the floor of the Senate, it will pass this year. If it comes to the floor of the House, it will pass. And it will serve just as effectively as the social security bill has served us since the 1930's. Those who are opposed to social security should oppose this, but those who believe that social security has served this country well should support this because it is in that tradition.

Hong Kong Refugees

Q: Sir, do you feel there is anything besides hunger, besides this great flood of refugees going into Hong Kong? There have been reports that some of these refugees have exit visas from China. Is there anything more here that meets the eye?

The President: As I understand it, the British have accepted those who are political refugees; those who are not they have been forced to turn back because Hong Kong is so crowded. I read reports that they do not seem to be suffering from acute malnutrition, but there isn't any doubt that there is a food crisis. The distribution of food, the structure of the economy and the state in some of these areas in China have broken down, and many people desire to leave. If they could leave, I think many more would.

Q: Do you feel that the Chinese Government has perhaps become more oppressive and that this is a cause rather than hunger?

The President: I think it would be difficult to make an informed judgment as to all the motivations of those who are leaving but it's certainly a combination of those factors.

The Billie Sol Estes Case

Q: Mr. President, in connection with the Billie Sol Estes case, there appears to be a possibility that a Federal official was murdered in this case. In view of that, do you think that Secretary Freeman was altogether justified in saying, as he did, that this case had been ballooned out of proportion?

The President: Well, I think we should wait until the FBI has completed its investigation of the matter. I couldn't - Mr. Freeman is not - I don't think the Texas local officials made a judgment in regard to the case which has been accepted until recently. Now the FBI and the local authorities are reexamining the case and we'll get a much better idea when the examination is completed.

The President and de Gaulle

Q: Mr. President, apart from your statements last week in the press conference and your speech that evening on the future of the Atlantic alliance, [2] *are you making your views clear to President de Gaulle and Chancellor Adenauer before they meet on June 2?*

The President: Well, I think the views of all the parties are well known to each other. I don't plan any further communication on the matter.

Medicare Compromise

Q: Mr. President, would you accept a medicare compromise that did not include social security financing?

The President: Social security is the heart of the financing, the heart of the legislation. That isn't a compromise. That'd be - just be giving up on the bill, and we don't plan to do that.

Misunderstanding with West Germany

Q: Mr. President, are you satisfied that our misunderstanding with West Germany over the Berlin proposals have now been straightened out, and that discussions will be resumed with the Soviet Union with the full support of the West German Government?

The President: I think the misunderstandings have been straightened out. As far as the positions of the parties, that we must wait on until we analyze the German proposal, which has just been received, as you know, within the last 24 hours. That will be analyzed and a proper response will be made to the West German Government. As far as the talks, as I have said, they will continue.

Help for the Stock Market

Q: Mr. President, do you plan to take any action to help the stock market, if it gets any worse?

The President: Well, I think the economy, which is moving steadily forward, is the best stimulant to the stock market - the most natural one. The figures we have for April are encouraging. Car sales, increased retail sales, and all the rest indicate that the economy has a good deal of strength, so that I believe that the stock market will move in accordance with the movement of the economy, as a general rule.

Now, there have been many, at least four, occasions since the end of the Second War when the stock market has dropped at the time the economy was rising. I think last week we talked about this. I gave an example of 1956, when the stock market went down at the time when the economy was steadily rising. The economy is rising, unemployment is down, the prospects in this month are good and, therefore, I think that the stock market will follow the economy.

As I said before, the stock market was very high. If when you're talking about valuation of 22 times earnings or dividends, that's a very high sale and twice as much as it was, for example, in 1957. But as far as the long haul for the stock market, I think it will keep in line with the economy. I think that the prospects for the economy for this year, as I've said, are good.

Policy in Southeast Asia

Q: Mr. President, is our true commitment to Southeast Asia similar in principle to the one we have in Western Europe, that is, are we ready to deny Communist force throughout Southeast Asia?

The President: Well, our treaty relationships with Laos and Viet-Nam and Cambodia are somewhat different than our NATO relationship. As you know, they were covered by SEATO, and they were protocol states by SEATO. Thailand itself, is, of course, a signatory, which is in a comparable way the same as NATO.

Q: My question, sir, is this: would we pull our forces out once the Laos Government is formed, or would we feel we had to stay there until we were sure that Communist force would not exert itself in that area?

The President: Well, we'll have to make a judgment of what the situation is in those areas. I quite agree that when you put troops in they become difficult to take out, unless the situation is stable, so that I've not ever said that the troop movement in Thailand - its end could be predicted. But we are staying there and then we will make a judgment as to how long they should stay, based on the events, as we have in Europe.

Removal of Grain from Billie Sol Estes' Warehouses

Q: Mr. President, the Agriculture Department has given only one reason for withdrawing its grain from the warehouses of Billie Sol Estes in Texas, this being that it is in the public interest. They have declined further comment. In view of the fact that the Department has previously said that there was nothing wrong with the warehouses or the operations, could you comment, sir, on how it would be in the public interest to remove the grain when the creditors are depending on this income to help settle their bills?

The President: Well, we are not, as you know, removing the grain immediately. We are removing it - moving it into the normal channels of trade over a period of time. If we moved it out immediately it would cost the Government about $2 million. We're moving it out, with more speed out of this terminal than we would out of others because of all the circumstances surrounding the case. But we are going to move it out, but it's over a period of time and it will not be moved from one terminal to another terminal, but instead will be moved into the normal channels of trade in a way which will not cost the United States Government anything. But I think it's appropriate that under reasonable conditions the grain is moved away from that terminal.

White House Conference on National Economic Issues

Q: Mr. President, would you care to evaluate the White House Conference on National Economic Issues that has just concluded? Do you feel there is a value in having this mass ventilation of ideas between labor and ——

The President: Yes, I do. The meeting, of course, had two phases. One was of public speeches. I wished in the public speeches that we could have discussed what I feel are some of the newer problems that the economy faces and which labor-management faces. I understand that in the private meetings that there was a much more - there was a willingness to forget some of the old basic arguments between labor and management and consider some of the new challenges. But I think that this is only the first of what I hope will be a series.

I believe that there really isn't much sense in having a long argument about the union shop or about industry-wide bargaining. Those arguments are well known, the positions are hard, and are taken clearly on both sides. As I said, in my opening, what I would like to hear them talk about is how the Government, labor, and management can function so as to provide for a steadily increasing economy, what we can do about the flow of gold, how we can prevent periodic recessions at every 2 or 3 years, how we can maintain full employment as other free countries have, what's the proper relationship between government and business and labor, what should be our budget policies, our debt policies. These are all matters which concern us today and about which we must do something. I would like to have their views on it. Not so much their views on questions which have been debated, about which we're fully informed of the point of interest of each of the parties, but rather these new, and as I've said, rather sophisticated and technical questions.

It's my understanding that in the private meetings there was discussion heading in this direction. I hope, therefore, we will have another conference quite soon so that we can continue to talk about these things. I will be very appreciative to the business advisory committee, which is now looking into giving us some suggestions on the flow of gold, and the CED's committee, which is going to study the economy of several European countries. I have asked our Council of Economic Advisers to consider particularly the case of France, which has had rather extraordinary economic vitality, so that I hope we can begin to focus our attention on these matters in the next few months.

Food Shipments to Brazil and Maritime Union Strikes

Q: Mr. President, last weekend in New York you made it quite clear that you were anxious to help Brazil with emergency food shipments, and about the same time one of the maritime unions began picketing the ship which was to carry that food to Brazil. I wondered if you had any feeling of disappointment in that, or whether you had any fatherly advice on union leaders?

The President: I understand that the ship is now being moved to the dock to load and is going to Brazil, that this matter has been settled.

Cooperation Between the U.S. and the USSR on Weather Information

Q: Mr. President, Dr. Harry Wexler of the United States Weather Bureau and his counterpart in the Soviet Union jointly have presented a plan to be approved by the Economic and Social Commission of the United Nations for studying world weather by earth satellites. Do you view this as an optimistic sign that the United States and Russia may ultimately cooperate both on space and on earth?

The President: We felt the first place to start was on weather, and I think that any progress we can make on that would be very welcome. I must say that we strongly support any cooperative effort we could make on weather, predictions of storms, and all of the rest, and I hope it will lead to other areas of cooperation in space.

Growth Rate of Western Europe

Q: Mr. President, on this matter of the growth rate of Western Europe, you have several times pointed out that it is twice ours. What relationship do you think this has with deficit financing?

The President: Well, that's what I think we ought to be - one of the matters we ought to be talking about. Their budgetary system, as opposed to ours, is somewhat different and that's one of the matters which I've asked the Council of Economic Advisers to look at; it's one of the matters which the CED should look at. I'm not sure that our budget keeping is as modern as the economy demands.

In addition, I think we ought to look at our tax structure, which of course we're doing, as part of the overall tax reform we're going to send up next year. Does our tax system stimulate the economy or does it serve as a drag on the economy because of the way it hits the structure at a time when the economy is moving out of a recession into a period of prosperity?

The 1958 and '60 experience and perhaps the experience this winter all indicate that these are matters which should be very carefully looked at. In other words, I don't think we should be satisfied with the way we are operating our economy as long as we are not going at full blast, as they are.

Now, the question is, how much of this, as I've said, is due to the Common Market, how much of it's due to a different stage of economic growth, and how much of its due to different economic planning, different relationships between the various segments of the economy? These are all matters which I believe all of us in government, management, labor, and the public ought to be looking at, to see if there's something that we can learn that's to our advantage.

What we don't always realize is that while the economy may be in a - the budget may be in a deficit overall for a fiscal year, that deficit may be concentrated in the first few months. Then as the year goes on the taxes begin to come in and you then begin to get a surplus which, of course, has a brake effect on the economy. In addition, the cash budget as opposed to the administrative budget has an entirely different impact on the economy. So that all these are the kinds of questions which I would like to see us - by "us" I mean all of us who are concerned - talk about and not merely concentrate our attention on these rather old slogans and fights which shed heat but not too much light on the matters which are directly before us.

Federal Government Action Against Cigarette Smoking

Q: *Mr. President, there is another health problem that seems to be causing growing concern here and abroad and I think this has largely been provoked by a series of independent scientific investigations, which have concluded that cigarette smoking and certain types of cancer and heart disease have a causal connection. I have two questions: do you and your health advisers agree or disagree with these findings, and secondly, what if anything should or can the Federal Government do in the circumstances?*

The President: That matter is sensitive enough and the stock market is in sufficient difficulty (laughter) without my giving you an answer which is not based on complete information, which I don't have and, therefore, perhaps we could - I'd be glad to respond to that question in more detail next week.

Stock Pile Investigations and the Billies Sol Estes Defraud

Q: *Sir, from your knowledge of the stock pile investigation which Senator Symington is developing for public consumption, I was wondering if you think the amount of money lost to the Government there will in time dwarf the Billie Sol Estes defraud?*

The President: Well, as we have said, there is no evidence that the Billie Sol Estes fraud has cost the United States Government any money.

Q: *Yes, I realize that ——*

The President: There have been improprieties - but let me, if I may, finish - the amount of money in this case, as came out yesterday, which revealed that because of an intervention by certain public officials that it cost the Government $650 million and the company made a $5 million windfall, of course, when you compare the amounts of money, this is obviously a greater loss to the Government. But I would not attempt to make a judgment of either case and its ultimate effects until these investigations are completed, both Senator Symington's and the FBI's.

British Difficulties in Common Market Negotiations and U.S. Relations with the Market

Q: Mr. President, the British appear to be facing difficulties in their negotiations with the Common Market group regarding safeguards for their trade with the Commonwealth nations. In the possible event that the British did not affiliate with the European Economic Community, would that cause us to reappraise our plan to cooperate with the Common Market?

The President: No. Of course, we're going to cooperate with the Common Market. The Common Market is in existence. We believe that it will contribute to the political stability of Europe as well as its economic well-being if Great Britain should become a member. So we have supported the admission of Great Britain. If Great Britain does not join, of course - which we believe would be unfortunate - the Common Market, the six, would still exist, and we would deal with the six and with Great Britain. But we think that the interests of Europe, the interests of the free world, of the Atlantic Community, would be best served by Great Britain being a member.

President's Willingness to Meet Former President Eisenhower in a Televised Discussion of Domestic Issues

Q: Sir, would you be willing to participate with former President Eisenhower in a TV discussion of a domestic issues before the country in the elections this fall?

The President: Well, I would have to wait and see. Neither one of us are candidates this fall. (Laughter) There will be many candidates. I've already stated that I would debate, if I were a candidate in 1964, against whoever I was running against. I haven't heard any suggestion that we debate this time. We'd have to wait and see what the situation was. President Eisenhower and I are both appearing on a program this week on the necessity for the passage of an effective trade bill in cooperation, and I think that that is, in this case, a constructive relationship in the national interest. What next fall will bring we will have to wait and see.

Implications of the Government Pay Raise

Q: Mr. President, do you feel that the Government pay raise you proposed is inflationary? How does that square with your ——

The President: Not the proposal we sent. No, it is not inflationary. It fits within the guidelines.[4]

Q: Mr. President, as you know, the Indonesian Government has accepted the Bunker proposal. In the meantime, the Netherlands has not. In the meanwhile, guerrilla warfare activities are increasing in that area. What do you think is the prospect of future negotiations?

The President: Well, as you know the United States has been working very hard, with the help of Ambassador Bunker, to attempt to work out a solution which would make the kind of military action which is now taking place unnecessary. We have not had success. I believe that Ambassador Bunker is discussing this matter now with responsible officials of the United Nations to see what further action could usefully be taken. But I hope that the proposals of

Ambassador Bunker would be considered very carefully by both sides, because we would be very concerned if the situation in that section of the world disintegrated or degenerated into a complete military conflict between these two countries. So we're - Ambassador Bunker is in New York today on that very matter.

Reporter: Thank you, Mr. President.

[1]See Item 202 of the *Public Papers of the President.*

[2]See Items 198, 199 of the *Public Papers of the President.*

[3]In a statement released in New York City on May 19 the President announced an increase in emergency food shipments to drought-stricken Northeast Brazil.

THE PRESIDENT'S NEWS CONFERENCE OF

JUNE 7, 1962

The President: Good afternoon. I have a brief preliminary statement. I would like to say a few words about our economic outlook and program.

I think most financial experts have realized for some time that an overpriced market could not hold up once investors recognized that inflation was ending. Price-earning ratios which averaged on Dow-Jones 23 to 1 could not be justified unless there was heavy inflation in prospect. And we have been working to prevent inflation, which gives a very misleading and spurious picture of economic health. We must not permit the effects of this adjustment, however, to hamper the growth rate of our economy, with which we have, as you know, not been fully satisfied. While our recovery from last year's recession has been a good one, production, profits, and employment are at alltime highs, and the prospects for continued economic expansion remain favorable. In view of corporate and consumer cash on hand, we should take every appropriate step to make certain that recovery is stronger and longer than before and is not cut short by a new recession.

Taxation: In the first place, our tax structure as presently weighted exerts too heavy a drain on a prospering economy, compared, for example, to the net drain in competing Common Market nations. If the United States were now working at full employment and full capacity, this would produce a budget surplus at present taxation rates of about $8 billion this year. It indicates what a heavy tax structure we have, and it also indicates the effects that this heavy tax structure has on an economy moving out of a recession period.

We saw that after the '58 recession, we've seen it after the '60 recession in the last months. We have proposed, therefore, the following:

One: A $1,300 million tax credit of 8 percent on new investment in machinery and equipment, which will increase the typical rate of potential profits on modern plant expansion in this country to the same extent, for example, as a 20 point reduction in corporate income taxes, from 52 to 32 percent on the profits to be realized from a new 10-year asset. The tax bill containing this stimulus and offsetting revenue measures has been before the Congress for well over a year. And I am hopeful, particularly, that it can be passed very shortly, because one of the areas of concern in the economy has been the slowness of plant investment, and I think that if we can settle this matter of the tax credit quickly. I think it can have a most stimulating effect on new plant investment this year.

Two: Administrative revision of the Internal Revenue guidelines on the economic life of depreciable assets, to make them more realistic and flexible in terms of actual replacement practices. These revisions to be issued within the next month will also make over $1 billion in added cash reserves available for additional business investment and, thus, these two actions combined, which we hope will be taken in the next 30 days, constitute in effect a tax cut for American business of over $2.5 billion.

Three: A comprehensive tax reform bill which in no way overlaps the pending tax credit and loophole-closing bill offered a year ago will be offered for action by the next Congress, making effective as of January 1 of next year an across the board reduction in personal and corporate income tax rates which will not be wholly offset by other reforms - in other words, a net tax reduction.

Four: I have asked the Congress to provide standby tax reduction authority to make certain as recommended by the eminent Commission on Money and Credit, that this tool could be used instantly and effectively should a new recession threaten to engulf us. The House Ways and Means Committee has been busy with other important measures, but there is surely more cause now than ever before for making such authority available.

Five: I have asked the Congress to repeal the 10-percent transportation tax on train and bus travel, resulting in a tax saving of $90 million a year, and to reduce it to 5 percent on airlines. Action on this tax package will provide our economy with all the stimulus and safeguards now deemed necessary, and I hope such action will be forthcoming.

Mention should be made also of other measures already pending before the Congress which would be of immediate help to our economic expansion and our unemployed workers. A bill to help youth employment - and one out of every four of our boys and girls out of school under 20 are unemployed - a bill to help youth employment has been pending before the Rules Committee since March 29. I hope action can be taken on it.

A bill to authorize Federal, State, and local public works this year in areas of heavy unemployment and to provide standby authority for the future has already passed the Senate. Inasmuch as last year's temporary unemployment compensation program has benefited no additional unemployment since April 1, a pending bill to extend that program for 1 year should be passed by the Congress before they go home. Every week thousands of people find their unemployment compensation exhausting, must go on public assistance, and this should be a matter of great concern to all of us.

Improvements in our welfare program to help those at the bottom of the economic ladder passed the House on March 15. Other pending bills - the trade bill, the pay reform bill, and others - will all have a beneficial effect on our economy once they are enacted by Congress. There is no need for this country to stand helplessly by and watch a recovery run out of gas. We have a program to boost it and I hope that all those who are concerned about their stocks or their profits or their jobs will help us get action on this program.

I have full confidence in the basic strength and economic potential of this country and the free world. We in the United States, business, labor, and the government, all of us working together, rather than at cross purposes, must rise to our responsibilities to maintain the forward thrust of our economy. The economic productivity and potential of the United States is the heart of our strength. Unemployment last month declined. Consumer income has been rising rapidly. New homes are being built at a remarkable rate. And this administration intends to do its full share of the task required to realize our full economic potential.

Q: Mr. President, I take it from your statement that you have no intention of recommending a tax cut to take effect before the next year. Would you confirm that? And also tell us if you can envision any circumstances which would require tax reduction before next year?

The President: I think my statement goes into the various tax proposals that we make in some detail. Of course, this is our best judgment at this time. Of course, if new circumstances brought a new situation, then we would have to make other judgments. But this is our judgment and we believe that this is the most responsible and effective line to take. And I think that if we get action in all the areas which I have described - and they are all very possible - that we can provide a good sustaining lift to the economy.

Q: Mr. President, in the same subject, can you discuss any thinking on rates or how far the reduction will go that you intend to propose in January? And second, sir, if you don't get some of these provisions or proposals which you regard as quite vital, are you think in terms of asking Congress to return in the fall if they don't pass them, say, by mid-September?

The President: Well, I think the tax - the proposed tax bill you are talking about for next January, the work on it should be completed later in the summer. So at that time I think we could discuss it in more detail.

On the other matter, I would - already it has passed the House. The depreciation we can do by administrative action, and we are going to do that, and, as I say, that amounts to over $1 billion. That will be completed in the next 30 days. It has already been done in the textile industry. But the whole job will be completed in the next 30 days.

The other bill, the tax credit, has passed the House. It is now in the Senate Finance Committee. It can be of most valuable assistance in the area where our economy has had the most difficulty, and that is on the question of plant investment. So that if you could put these two together, as I said, it amounts to $2,500 million, and I think would be of great assistance to the economy. So I am very hopeful that the Senate will act on this legislation. If they do not, of course we will have to take a look at the situation. But this bill was proposed last year, and a year now has gone by, and now we are going through other months. I think the very fact that some companies are uncertain as to whether they are going to get the tax credit does have a depressing effect upon their investment plans.

QUESTIONS

Meeting with President de Gaulle

Q: Mr. President, there is a report, unofficial report, from Paris this afternoon that a meeting between you and General de Gaulle is in the process of being arranged. Is this correct?

The President: No, I haven't heard that. No.

Aid to Communist Countries

Q: Mr. President, why do you think the Senate voted so sharply yesterday to tie your hands on sending aid to Communist countries, especially in defiance of pleas from the White House on the point? And do you think anything can be done to rectify the situation beyond the amendment put in today on food?

The President: Well, the amendment that was put in today on food will be very helpful, because the primary assistance that we have been giving, for example, to Poland, has been through food. In addition, it permits the private organizations to continue to function.

In Yugoslavia we have been giving aid in food; there was some limited development assistance which would not be possible under the Senate amendment. There has been a good deal, of course, of frustration about these programs. They have been under attack for many years and we've carried this aid program since the Marshall Plan days, and I suppose people do get tired. But our adversaries are not tired. The desire of people to remain independent - the Polish people want to be independent, they are not Communist by choice but by hard circumstances forced upon them, and I think that we should continue to hold out some hope for them. We are not prepared to take military action to free them, quite obviously, and we did not undertake anything like that during the Hungary revolt, but I do think that we should not slam the door in their face. So that I am glad that the Senate went as far as it went today.

Yugoslavia has been more complicated, and I know that the programs of assistance have been under attack, but the primary assistance now is foodstuffs and it has been quite limited. But Yugoslavia is not a member of the Warsaw bloc. The break between Yugoslavia and the Soviet Union in the late forties probably did more to maintain the independence of Greece, when that border was closed, than any other single action. And those who were associated with that effort know how close it was in Greece, and I think there is an advantage in encouraging national independence. We may not approve of the government of Yugoslavia, or they may not approve of our government, but at least they have maintained an independent status in regard to joining the Warsaw bloc, or in regard to their dependence upon Moscow. Now, that might change. In that case, of course, our policy could change. But I do think that flexibility is necessary. No one has any idea what the circumstances will be in the next 12 months. We might find it necessary or desirable to give some assistance to a country which was following an independent policy; we might find the language of yesterday denying us that flexibility. I am glad the Senate went back as far as it did. I do think that they should give us the right to give assistance when we deem it in the national interest. I remember this fight was made under President Eisenhower and I supported his efforts at that time to maintain this flexibility - on two occasions - and I am glad at least we have had given some flexibility by the action of the Senate today.

Items on the Tax Bill

Q: Mr. President, in your introductory statement, you didn't mention two items which are in this year's tax bill, the withholding on dividends and interest, and the payments on earnings of American firms overseas before those earnings are repatriated. Are you prepared to relinquish this request now or to postpone it until next year?

The President: No, the major one of course, which is the withholding, is not a new tax. That tax is on the books today and has been for many years. All we are now talking about is a more effective way of collecting a tax. So that is not a new tax.

Now, the other tax of course is the tax on so-called tax havens, and on dividend - and on money, which would put those companies on a basis comparable to American companies. This has been tied to making it less attractive to American capital to leave this country. That is the purpose of that amendment and I am hopeful that it will pass, in as close a form as it is possible to what it was when we introduced it, because the gold flow concerns us all.

But those taxes, in my opinion, represent responsible actions. But what I was talking about is the stimulus that will be given by the total tax package - putting all this together to the American business, plus the depreciation, of course, which represents, as I say, a clear gain for business.

Reorganization of the Aid Program

Q: Mr. President, in connection with the aid fight in the Senate yesterday, there continue to be reports that you are dissatisfied with the reorganization of the aid program administratively. Could you discuss that?

The President: Well, no, that is not correct. I am concerned about the progress we are making in the Alliance for Progress. I think the aid agency has made important gains. I think the long-range authorization which was given to us by the Congress last year has been most helpful, and I think we benefited from it in our programs. It permitted us to associate in consortiums which I think have produced much better economic planning. The matter, of course, of primary concern to me is the Alliance for Progress. We are engaged in a tremendous new joint venture. All these countries are faced with very difficult economic problems - balance of payments problems, great dependence on one or two commodities, raw materials which suffer in price fluctuations, and all such internal difficulties as we've seen in the case of two or three countries in the last month. So that we are not dealing with a situation even as stable as it was in Europe at the end of World War II when we began the Marshall plan. So that this matter continues to be of concern to me, that the Alliance move forward.

But I would say that generally I think that the aid agency is improved over what the situation was before the Congress gave us the additional tools.

John Bailey's Statement about Governor Rockefeller

Q: Mr. President, last Friday, John Bailey, the Democratic National Chairman, made a speech in which he accused Governor Rockefeller of racial prejudice toward Negroes. I wonder if you felt even in an election year this was a justified statement.

The President: No, I don't think - I haven't seen any evidence that Mr. Rockefeller is prejudiced in any way towards any racial group. I am glad to make that statement, and I am sure that some of the statements the Congressman - the Chairman of the Republican Committee - has made about me will be, I am sure, similarly repudiated by leading Republicans. (Laughter) I have been waiting for it for about a year and a half!

Legislation in Congress

Q: Mr. President, you have given Congress an awful lot to chew in this session and some of them are getting a little impatient, this being a campaign year. Do you think that the Congress ought to stick around, at least until Labor Day or later, nonetheless, to get through the bulk of this program, or do you propose to give them some top priority list and say, that is it?

The President: Well, I'm sure we'll probably have to come to a priority, as you say. Time is coming on, it is election year, and the Congress wants to get home. These programs are important, however. Going down the list: medical care for the aged, youth employment, aid for higher education, the trade bill, the tax bill, there's a good many of very great importance so that the normal authorizations and appropriations - the legislation which I named here - it's hard to pick a list. But obviously, we're going to have to, because we've only got a limited time left.

The Inter-American Proposal

Q: Mr. President, can you give us your first impression on the Inter-American Center proposal which was presented to you today?

The President: Well, I listened to the presentation. I'm going to have a meeting with the Department of Commerce to listen to it in more detail and then, with the Senators and Congressmen who are involved, see if we can come to some decision about it.

Nuclear Equipment for France

Q: Mr. President, there have been persistent reports that either the American Government or Britain intends to offer nuclear information or equipment to France in order to get better terms for Britain to enter the Common Market or to improve relations with General de Gaulle. I think the latest version is that General Gavin is to come to Washington with an alleged recommendation that American nuclear equipment be provided. What do you think of this concept?

The President: I think these matters are not related. Secondly, General Gavin, I think, has already issued a statement in regard to his position. He had planned to come to Washington. I think he was going to address a commencement audience in New England next week, and that was the purpose for which he was coming back. But I don't think the matters are related, and - either in the minds of the French or in the minds of the United States.

American and British Aid to Egypt

Q: Mr. President, this is a question about American and British aid to Egypt. In Cairo in March I was told that you and President Nasser had engaged in a rather extensive correspondence, not all of which has been made public. And I wondered if he told you anything in that, that you can tell us, about his Middle East activities or gave any assurances that would make him more eligible for aid now than he used to be?

The President: No, I don't know about that. We haven't had any extensive correspondence, and as you know, most of the assistance we have been giving Egypt has been in foodstuffs. We continue to attempt to have good relations with the U.A.R., but I have received no information or assurances from President Nasser in regard to any future policy decisions which he might make.

Meeting with Spanish Republicans in Caracas

Q: Mr. President, did you meet with some Spanish Republicans in Caracas in December of 1961? And did you tell them that you would work to overthrow the Franco Government in Spain?

The President: The answer to both questions is no.

The Economy, Unemployment, and a Balanced Budget

Q: Mr. President, do you believe that the economy will reach the 4 percent unemployment target that you have set for mid-1963, with a balanced budget in the fiscal year?

The President: Obviously we are going to have to wait and make a judgment as to whether we are going to reach 4 percent. We are down to substantially lower, of course, than it has been – unemployment, but still not satisfactory. And I think it would be impossible to make a precise judgment today about whether we are going to reach that figure.

Medical Care Legislation

Q: Mr. President, could you clarify the situation on medical care legislation? The opponents of the administration measure, the Anderson-King bill, which is tied to social security, say that the passage of that law or that measure would cause the repeal of the Kerr-Mills law, which now affects protection for certain needy. Are these the facts?

The President: No, the fact – in fact, the argument against passing the Anderson-King – one of the arguments has been that there are some people who were not involved and covered by Social Security. But they would still be covered by present law. They'd still be covered by the Kerr-Mills bill. It doesn't seem to me that that is a substantial argument against covering nearly 14 million other people who are entitled and – who are covered by Social Security. In addition, it may be possible to take other measures, to provide additional assistance for those who were not covered by Social Security. Many States, as you know, of course, have not passed the Kerr-Mills. I don't think that the State that the A.M.A. spokesman comes from – Dr. Annis – has passed the Kerr-Mills bill, enabling legislation on the State level.

I think that we ought to pass the King-Anderson bill, medical care for the aged under Social Security. And I think the argument that we shouldn't do it because we're not going to be able to include everybody under it seems to me to be wholly misleading. We can include 14 million people, and we can continue the legislation we have on the books for the others, and in addition we can take additional special steps for them, which I would support.

Comments by the Mexican Ambassador to the OAS

Q: Mr. President, yesterday, the Mexican Ambassador to the Organization of American States made some statements which could be regarded as offensive to some of your appointees, to this country and to its residents. Normally, when an official spokesman for a country makes such a comment it could be construed as a deliberate way of withdrawing an invitation for a visit, which has been extended to you. Could you comment?

The President: No, I have seen – no, as far as I know, and I am sure I know, the invitation by the Mexican Government stands, and I am sure that this is a matter which the Mexican Government themselves can deal with more effectively than I could. The OAS is an international body, and that speech – statements are made in debate, and I think this is really a matter between the representative and his own government rather than between this government and the Ambassador.

Republican Criticism of White House Authority

Q: Mr. President, Republicans in Congress put out a statement of policy today, which among other things, says this: a stable dollar is not likely to result if control of the Federal Reserve System rests in the White House. This is taken to be an attack on your proposal that the President have authority to appoint his own Federal Reserve Chairman. How important is this to you?

The President: First, the point of the matter is that what we have proposed is with the strong support of the Chairman of the Federal Reserve, that the term of the Chairman be the same as with the President, which was the original intention of the legislation when it was first passed. But it has no effect upon me, if that is what they are thinking of, which I presume they are, because the matter of the Chairman's position comes up in 1963. So that I have no - if I were anxious to get control of the Federal Reserve, the matter comes up in 1963. What we are talking about is for other Presidents in other days. And it is a reform which the Chairman of the Federal Reserve, the Commission on Money and Credit, and many others have thought would be very helpful in the liaison between the President and the Federal Reserve.

We, after all, are very closely associated in our responsibilities, though the Federal Reserve is independent and reports to the Congress. So that it has no application to me, and it is like a good many other things that are said. They are not wholly based on fact, but they sound rather good when those speeches are made.

Our GNP and the Possibility of a Balanced Budget

Q: Mr. President, do your economic counselors still believe that the gross national product will reach $570 billion this year and do they also believe that you can balance the Federal budget in the fiscal year?

The President: They are - I would think they are not as convinced as they were that we will be up to $570 billion. But we will, I think, have a good chance, if we carry out the steps I recommended, of being close to $570 billion.

As I say, we had the best month, almost in our history in autos; houses are up, actually consumer goods are moving very fast. The one area which is causing concern in the economy has been plant investment, which has not been as high as they originally hoped it would be in January.

Now, if we can, by the various tax measures I have discussed, and by other steps which may become useful as time goes on, give sufficient demand so that business can go into new plant investment or be persuaded to, encouraged to, then we can made this a very good year. It's going to be, we hope, a good year anyway, but I don't think we can get to $570 billion unless plant investment steps up beyond the projected 8 percent. And quite obviously, the sharp decline in the market is not - certainly is bound to make it somewhat more difficult, though it is - I believe there is very strong - there is very good vitality in the economy and I think it can be substantially boosted by the steps I've recommended.

Range of the Net Tax Cut

Q: Mr. President, in connection with your January tax proposal, for next January, without going into rates can you give us any idea of the range of the net tax cut that you are thinking of, in total amount?

The President: No, I think it would be better to wait until the program is completed.

Cigarette Smoking and Killer Diseases

Q: Mr. President, can you comment on the Public Health Service announce-
ment of a special panel of experts to study whether there is a link between
cigarette smoking and certain killer diseases? And can you tell us whether
the study will be a matter of months or years, or just what the ——

The President: Well, I think the statement that the Surgeon General issued
this morning, I think, gives the position of the Surgeon General, which I have
supported, and is in direct response to the question which you asked 2 weeks
ago, and now that the survey will take some months - it will go into 1963, but
I think that that announcement is in response to your question. You've been
answered.

Funds for Fallout Detection and Surveillance and Monitoring Systems

Q: Mr. President, the National Advisory Committee on Radiation has report-
ed that there are serious gaps in our fallout detection and surveillance and
monitoring system. And they have recommended a very substantial increase in
spending over the next 7 years that will amount to almost half a billion dol-
lars. Can you give us your reaction to this, and whether or not it is being
seriously considered, or whether you feel that we should increase our funds
by that much?

The President: I couldn't make a judgment on that yet. I think that we
ought to do more than we're doing but we have not determined on our program as
yet.

Mr. Nixon's Prospects in California

Q: Mr. President, could you tell us how you size up Mr. Nixon's showing in
California, and give us any inkling of your own political plans this fall?

The President: No, the primaries are difficult - (laughter) - and I think
that he emerged from a tough one, which I congratulate him for. Now, as far
as my plans, I will be active in the fall, but we haven't fixed a definite
schedule.

Republican Criticism of Leadership in Foreign Affairs

Q: Mr. President, that Republican statement you mentioned earlier, called
the "Declaration of Party Principles," charges, among lots of other things,
bankruptcy in leadership in foreign affairs and incompetence of the New Fron-
tier destroying confidence. Would you care to comment upon that sir?

The President: It isn't true, but - no.

U.S. Backing for a Coalition Government in Laos

Q: Mr. President, the three princes of Laos are getting together at last
in the formation of a coalition government. Assuming that such a government
should be agreed upon, to what extent would the United States go in backing
it up economically, and to what extent would we expect them to preserve a neu-
tral policy?

The President: Well, the first talks were encouraging. If it worked out
and we had a neutral and independent Laos, we would of course support it with
every proper means, and we would hope it would be able to maintain its position
of being neutral and independent.

Reporter: Thank you, Mr. President.

The President: I have one more. (Laughter)

The President and Mayor Wagner

Q: Mr. President, there seems to be a serious disagreement between you and Mayor Wagner of New York about the reelection of Congressman Buckley. Do you feel this is a serious split and are you doing anything to heal this split either between you and the mayor, or the split in the New York party?

The President: Mr. Smith was right, as usual! (Laughter)

No, we have a different opinion about it, and we've made our views known, and I am continuing to hold mine and I am sure he does. I am for Congressman Buckley and he's for someone else, and that's the way it's going to be, I guess.

THE PRESIDENT'S NEWS CONFERENCE OF

JUNE 14, 1962

The President: I have one opening statement.

The welfare and economy of the American public would be seriously damaged by the strike now being threatened by the flight engineers union against three major airlines, TWA, Pan American, and Eastern. This action would create and have a significant impact upon our economy, and we have made every effort during the past months to bring about a happy solution.

This dispute stems from the recommendations made last year by the special commission I established that flight crews on jet aircraft be reduced from four men to three men. No one has questioned either the wisdom or the necessity of that recommendation.

The commission also recommended that all presently employed flight engineers are to be given prior job rights on the three-man crews and that any changes made in the transition would in no way prejudice their representational rights. The companies agreed to pay all costs of training the flight engineers to enable them to serve on three-man crews.

The Air Line Pilots Association, in a related dispute involving Pan American Airways, agreed that arbitration was the responsible means of settling this matter, and the airline companies in this dispute have accepted my request made in accordance with the applicable provisions of the Railway Labor Act that all issues be voluntarily submitted to the final and binding judgment of a three-man arbitration panel composed of outstanding public, labor, and management leaders.

But the flight engineers union has ignored this request. They are threatening to strike for still more job and representational security for wage increases of more than 20 percent over a 3-year period, for reduction in working hours - from 85 hours a month to 75 hours a month - and other demands.

Eighteen hundred men are threatening a strike which would cause the immediate layoff of some 60,000 employees, the immobilization of 40 percent of the Nation's airline service, and the loss of over $1 million a day from international flights, which our balance of payments cannot afford.

We have been, under the Railway Labor Act procedures, seeking a settlement for 17 months, but the flight engineers have not accepted the decision of the National Mediation Board. They have rejected the report of the special Presidential commission on jet crews. They have refused to accept the careful recommendations of the three Presidential emergency boards. They have failed to cooperate with the long and thoughtful mediation efforts offered by the National Mediation Board, the Secretary of Labor, and the Special Mediation Panel. And this morning they rejected my request to submit these issues to arbitration.

A strike could have, as I have said, a significant impact on our economy at this time. I strongly urge the flight engineers to meet their public responsibilities, to reconsider their action, and to either submit this case to arbitration or agree with the carriers on some other means of settling this dispute without any interruption of operation.

Q: Mr. President, should the flight engineers not meet your request, would you then be prepared to go to Congress with a request for emergency seizure powers?

The President: We would have to wait until - I am hopeful that the flight engineers will heed my request and submit this matter, as I have said, to arbitration, or find some other satisfactory method of settling it peaceably. We have been working, as I have said, for more than a year, because of the responsibilities placed upon us by the Railway Labor Act which covers the airlines. And I am very hopeful that the engineers will reconsider this matter. If they do not, of course, we then will have to consider what would be the proper action.

QUESTIONS

Administration's Role in Wage and Price Discussions

Q: Mr. President, following up your recent statements on the economy, particularly your speech at Yale the other day and the Solicitor General's yesterday, is it the Government's intention to play an active role in major labor and industry wage and price discussions and, if so, how would this role be played?

The President: No, I think that - I have not read the speech of the Solicitor. My speech at Yale, I think, was quite clear. It dealt mainly, chiefly, with another subject, which was that we should attempt to engage in a dialog on the very intricate questions which are involved in the management of a very complicated economy such as ours, in order to maintain full employment and keep our economy moving.

As far as the - we have attempted to indicate, of course, through the Council of Economic Advisers and by other means, our concern that we follow policies - particularly in those basic industries which affect our competitive position overseas - that we follow policies that permit us to continue to compete, and to continue to keep our economy moving. But these - this is a free economy in the final analysis and we have to attempt to work out the solutions on a voluntary basis.

Weapons for India

Q: Mr. President, India is reported leaning toward the purchase of MIG aircraft from the Soviet Union, and the equipment to manufacture such aircraft in their country. Does the United States have any alternative plan or offer to such an arrangement, and what effect might this have on the tensions within the area?

The President: This is a matter which is being considered in this Government, and also being considered with other governments. It is a matter on - Ambassador Galbraith is returning to India at the end of the week and will, I am sure, be reporting to us on the situation as well as giving our views.

It would seem to me that we should keep it at that level at the present time.

Mr. Khrushchev's Remark Regarding the U.S. Threat

Q: Mr. President, in a note to the Japanese Government today, Soviet Premier Khrushchev said that it is a criminal act that "a certain element is trying to prepare for a surprise attack on us, by trying to attain the upper hand in the application of nuclear weapons." Would you address yourself to that remark?

The President: No, I haven't seen that statement. We are not preparing, if he is referring to us and I don't know who else he might be referring to, but the United States is not, quite obviously - it has not been our policy, we made it clear what our policy is, which is to build for our own security. The United States has gone to great lengths, as far as nuclear weapons, to secure effective means of control over their testing. The world knows the history of how this present series of tests began, and our great reluctance to commence them. And we have been engaged for many, many months in Geneva in the test ban discussions and also in the disarmament conference to secure some effective means of bringing an end to the arms race, including the nuclear arms race, and also bringing world tensions under control.

We are seeking to do so in Berlin; we've been seeking to do so in Southeast Asia. And I'm confident that if there is good will on both sides, that there can be a lessening of tensions. But there has to be good will on both sides.

Overpopulation and Poverty

Q: Mr. President, this is a question about a recent report called "Does Overpopulation Mean Poverty?" It recommended expanded Government research on fertility control and expanded technical assistance to underdeveloped countries seeking to solve problems of overpopulation. What is your attitude toward those recommendations?

The President: I haven't seen those recommendations. I've said from the beginning that these were matters which every country must decide for itself. This is not a matter - as it goes to basic national feelings, personal feelings. This is a matter which each individual, each family, each country must determine. It cannot be determined by the actions of another country.

The Effect of Deficits

Q: Mr. President, in your Yale speech you spoke of deficits as not being necessarily inflationary or harmful. As you know, the attitude about deficits among the American people is largely an unfavorable one. I wonder in light of that if you can elaborate on why you think that deficits may not be bad or harmful.

The President: Well, it depends. As I tried to say at Yale, the key word is "necessarily." I think there has been a feeling that deficits bring inflation with them. And I attempted to make the point at Yale that we had had surpluses in the 3 years after the war, rather large budget surpluses, and still had very sharp inflation; that we had had deficits in 1958 and in 1962, and that there had been a stable price level. The largest deficit was in 1958, $12-1/2 billion. The point I am trying to make is that what we must be concerned about is trying to maintain the vitality of our economy. And that the administrative budget, which is the budget people talk about, is not wholly revealing of the amount of money that the Government takes in. If the administrative budget were balanced, the Federal Government would be taking in about $4 billion more than it was spending. On the cash budget side - these are all rather complicated subjects because of the trust funds and all the rest - that has a deflationary impact on our economy.

Now, we have to realize that we had a recession in 1958 and a recession in 1960. We do not want to run through in this country, which is the - on which so much depends, which is the source of strength for the free world - we do not want to run into periods of recurrent recession. One of the ways that has been considered to avoid this is by following a budget policy which is related to the economy and not related to what I called rather formal traditional positions which may not be applicable to the present time. And I thought the experience of Europe, which has had a decade of unequalled progress, partly because they have managed their economy with some skill, partly because they are in a different period of growth, partly because of the Common Market, that it had some lessons for us. These are the matters, I said at Yale, that we should be talking about: how we can manage our economy, what should be our budget policy? And the automatic response that a deficit necessarily produces inflation is not necessarily true.

The President's Efforts Regarding Business

Q: Mr. President, a lot of people seem to feel that the idea of a Democratic administration trying to win the confidence of business is something like the Republicans trying to win the confidence of labor unions. Do you feel, sir, you are making headway in your efforts? Have you seen anything to indicate that business is coming around to your point of view on the economy and that the confidence you asked for is being restored in the market place?

The President: Well, as I said, what is necessary is not really whether some businessmen may be Republicans - most businessmen are Republicans, have been traditionally, have voted Republican in every presidential election. But that is not the important point - whether there is political agreement.

The important point is that they recognize and the Government recognizes, and every group recognizes, the necessity, as I have said, of attempting to work out economic policies which will maintain our economy at an adequate rate of growth. That is the great problem for us. They feel, as I said, that they would be happier if there were a Republican in the White House, but there was a Republican in the White House in 1958 and we had a recession, and there was in 1960. So I think that what we have to realize is, is that I could be away from the scene, which might make them happy, and that they might have a Republican in the White House, but the economic problems would still be there. So that what I hope is that we can address ourselves to those and not to a political matter because, after all, the presidential race isn't until 1964 and at that time it would seem to me to be the appropriate time to argue politics.

Right now we should be concerning ourselves with the real problems of our country, which are of great interest to me economically - which are to them, which are to labor, which are to all American people.

Q: Mr. President, there is a feeling in some quarters that big business is using the stock market slump as a means of forcing you to come to terms with business. One reputable columnist, after talking to businessmen, obviously, reported this week their attitude is now, we have you where we want you. Have you seen any reflection of this attitude?

The President: I can't believe I'm where business - big business, wants me. (Laughter) I read that column in the St. Louis Post-Dispatch, as a matter of fact, and I found that Mr. Childs made the point that some, as I believe his phrase was, rich men were quoted as having said what you have said. I cannot believe that anybody thinks that in order to take some political - gain some political benefit, it would be a source of pleasure to them to see the stock market go down or see the economy have difficulties. I don't believe that anyone who looks at our problems at home and abroad could possibly take that partisan an attitude. So I don't accept that view. I know that when things don't go well they like to blame the Presidents, and that's one of the things which Presidents are paid for. But I think what we want to be concerned about, as I have said before, is not a personal dialog as much as it is a dialog on the problem of what tax policies, what budget policies, fiscal policies we should pursue. Because if it were merely a matter of the party, or of personalities, we would not have had our experience that we had in the late fifties. So that shows there's something more substantive here. And this is what concerns, I think, all of us - or should.

Review of Far Eastern Policies

Q: Mr. President, Senator Mansfield a few days ago suggested a review of Far Eastern policies because he said they seem to him either marking time or, at worst, on a collision course. Do you think such a review is necessary?

The President: Well, we've been reviewing it. As you know, we've been attempting in the case of Laos to work out a policy which would prevent either one of those situations. Whether we shall be successful or not, only time will tell.

I know that we have put large sums of money, and the situation there is still hazardous. What is true there of course is true all around the world. This is a period of great tension and change. But if the United States had not played a part in Southeast Asia for many years, I think the whole map of Southeast Asia would be different. I am delighted - as you know, I have the highest regard for Senator Mansfield, and I think we should constantly review, and I think as he suggested, we should make judgments between what is essential to our interest and what is marginal. We have been attempting with great difficulty to carry out a policy in Laos which would permit a neutral and independent government there. In Senator Mansfield's speech he used the examples of Burma and Cambodia. Those were the examples that were also used at the Vienna meeting by Chairman Khrushchev and myself in which we stated the kind of government that we both said we hoped would emerge in Laos. That is the commitment that was made by the Soviet Union and by the United States.

Now we've moved to a different plateau and we are going to see whether that commitment can be maintained. But on the other hand, if - and I am sure Senator Mansfield - and I know Senator Mansfield does not think we should withdraw, because a withdrawal in the case of Viet-Nam and in the case of Thailand might mean a collapse of the entire area.

Limits on the Foreign Aid Bill

Q: Mr. President, the Senate passed a number of restrictive amendments on the foreign aid bill besides that limiting aid to Yugoslavia and Poland. Do you think this reflected a growing disenchantment in the Senate on the whole question of foreign aid, and do you think such actions as that contemplated by India in purchasing jets from the Soviet Union has anything to do with that disenchantment?

The President: Oh, well, it's a - we've carried it a long time - and Senator Mansfield's speech showed it's a - the world is still with us, and still uncertain, and all of our effort and all of our sacrifice has not produced the new world. But it is not going to.

What we are attempting to do is to maintain our position. There have been a good many changes in the Communist bloc in the last 10 years, and some of those have been - should encourage friends of freedom. So what we want to do is maintain our position and that of our associated nations with us in this effort, and not to desist in 1962 because the race is not over and we have not been completely - we have not come to home port. We are still at sea. Now, I think we ought to stay there and continue to do the best we can.

There was, as has been revealed in the press, Mr. Kennan - Ambassador Kennan - who has been very realistic in this appraisal of our relations with Yugoslavia, is extremely disturbed about what has happened. He feels, and the story quoted him in the paper as saying, that this has been a great gift to the Kremlin at this particular time. And Mr. Cabot, our Ambassador to Poland - both of these men are long experienced, Mr. Kennan probably the longest experienced, almost, of any American, in his studies of the Soviet Union - both of them regard this action as a major setback and as a great asset to Moscow. I don't think we should do those favors to them if we can help it.

Q: Mr. President, in this same connection, you have had a great deal of trouble with the Democrats on other parts of your legislative program. Have you arrived at any new formula for persuading them to come along?

The President: Oh, I think the Democrats - except for a few Democrats who have habitually voted with the Republicans - the Democrats have done pretty well today, for example, on the debt limitation. Every year during, I think, President Eisenhower's administration, except 1953, he had to ask for a change in the debt limit. Every time I voted for it, to give him that power. Today on the final roll call on a measure which instead of giving us our request of 308 would have rolled it back to 285 billion, which would, of course, have meant that every defense expenditure - space, agriculture, veterans, and every other commitment of the Government - would have been in great difficulty and would have been, of course, extremely difficult for us to maintain our - meet our obligations. Every Republican in the House except nine voted against us. Now it passed, however, because the Democrates met their responsibility. They did in the House on the tax bill; they have on the trade bill. I think that we do expect, however, that all these matters will not be made matters of party loyalty and we have to get some support from the Republican side, and on occasions in the Senate we certainly have gotten it.

We now have a farm bill upcoming next week. That farm bill can save $1 billion a year to the taxpayers of this country; over a period of 4 years, $4 billion. Now this is a vote which is in the best interests of American agriculture and is in the best interests of the country, and is in the best interests of the economy of the United States. I hope that this will not be made, as it's indicated, a party issue on which every Republican will then vote against us and we will find ourselves with a very close vote on a matter which has the first chance of bringing some order out of what is a very chaotic situation.

If we fail and our farm bill is defeated, we go back to the program which is in permanent legislation, the Benson program, which has brought us great so-called - which has brought us tremendous surpluses and expenditures of over $6-1/2 billion by the Government every year.

So there is a very good chance, and I think that we have a right to expect that on these matters of great national import, that at least we will receive some help from across the aisle, because on other occasions many of us voted to give assistance to the President of the United States when he was a member of the opposite party.

On the question of aid to the Poland-Yugoslavia matter, I voted twice to give President Eisenhower the flexibility he felt he needed in order to conduct foreign policy. He bears a great responsibility and the Congress does also, but I thought that he should have that power, if the situation required it. I would hope that those who are on the opposite side would also, at a time particularly when there are so many things which are encouraging in the world to us, would be willing to sustain us in giving us a similar power.

Q: Mr. President, on the farm bill: you have said, and others in the administration have said repeatedly, that the present programs, because of their expense, cannot go on indefinitely. If Congress should refuse to enact your current program, would you feel required to request the Congress to repeal the existing price support program without controls?

The President: Well, the choice, it seems to me, is very clearly - the satisfactory provision is the one that we have suggested. Now, if we fail there, of course, then we have, as you have said, the permanent legislation in which we have price supports and no controls, which of course will pile our surpluses up bigger and, I think, depress our farm income. We would then have to consider what appropriate legislation would be asked for. But the bill we have sent is the one we need. We don't want a bill which has no support for the farmers; we don't want to go to the Congress and say, "Now that you have refused to permit us to have a balance between supply and demand of the kind you have in tobacco and cotton, now we are going to pull out and have no support for the farmers." So that this is the best solution - the one we have before the House next week, and which has already passed the Senate.

Hong Kong Refugee Problem

Q: Mr. President, in regard to the Hong Kong refugee problem, yesterday the Colonial Secretary said that food and clothing relief would not resolve the colony's problems, nor would immigration, but that Hong Kong would welcome the assistance of other governments in building hospitals, schools, and clinics, and so forth. Is the administration considering this type of assistance?

The President: Well, we have contributed very heavily, as you know, toward food. I am not aware that any request has been made for additional assistance, but we would certainly be prepared to consider it, and we - along with other governments.

Proposals for a Senior Service Corps

Q: Mr. President, proposals for a Senior Service Corps, patterned after the Peace Corps, for the older members of our population have been discussed by your Council on Aging at its first meeting. How do you view this?

The President: I think - at the Council on Aging that's one of these things they're looking at, and I think they're going to make a report to me very shortly. And I think that they'll give us some recommendations on it.

Latin America and the Alliance for Progress

Q: Mr. President, do you feel the Latin American countries are making the contribution that they should within the problems they face on the Alliance for Progress?

The President: Some countries are making a major effort, in some countries the effort is slower. As you know, in nearly every country they're dealing with staggering problems, including exchange problems, which are partly induced by the decline in the price of the raw materials they're getting, so that Latin America faces - in many of the countries, they're making a real effort. They face great problems, and I'm hopeful that the United States will be persistent in supporting the Alliance for Progress and not expect that suddenly the problems of Latin America, which have been with us and with them for so many years, can suddenly be solved overnight merely by, within a period of a few months. It's going to take a long time, but at least in some countries they are making progress towards it.

An Exchange of Letters Between Kennedy and Khrushchev

Q: Mr. President, in reference to your exchange of letters with Chairman Khrushchev on Laos,[1] with both of you suggesting that this might lead to settlement of other international problems, could you comment on two aspects of that: one, is the Laotian formula in any way applicable to divided Berlin, or divided Germany, and secondly, if it is not, is there still a hope perhaps that this might be a step toward another summit meeting for settling outstanding problems?

The President: No, I don't see the parallel. The situation is different in Berlin than it is in Laos, quite obviously. Obviously if we can solve by peaceful means and not only get an agreement, but make it work, and both parties demonstrate a sincere commitment to a solution of what has been a difficult problem over a period of time, then it would encourage us to believe that there has been a change in atmosphere, and that other problems also could be subjected to reason and solution. That is why I regard the Laos matter as so important. We have to wait now and see whether we can make this agreement, which has been signed, make it work. If we can, then it will be encouraging step forward to more amicable relations between the Soviet Union and the United States, and we can discuss other problems. There is nothing on a summit as yet.

Renegotiation of the Panama Canal Treaty

Q: Mr. President, President Chiari of Panama said at his press conference this morning that the binational commission which will be set up to consider points of difference between Panama and the United States would have the power to consider renegotiation of the Panama Canal treaty. I was wondering if this was your attitude also or what your attitude is towards this interpretation of your talks?

The President: Well, I haven't seen - I would rather not comment on the statement until I have seen President Chiari's statement in toto. I think the communique[2] describes quite clearly the responsibilities of the commission, and it is going to get to work right away. I would have to look at his statement and read it in detail before I could tell about his interpretation.

Status of the Space Program

Q: Mr. President, about a year ago you sent to the Congress a greatly expanded space program, and I was wondering if you could give us your own assessment of how we stand technologically, how you think the American people as a whole have responded to the space effort, and when you plan any major realignment such as a bigger military role.

The President: Such as a what?

Q: Such as a bigger role for the military in space.

The President: Starting at the end, the military have an important and significant role, though the primary responsibility is held by NASA and is primarily peace, and I think that that proportion of that mix should continue. I think the American people have supported the effort in space, realizing its significance, and also that it involves a great many possibilities in the future which are still almost unknown to us and just coming over the horizon. As far as we are, I don't think that the United States is first yet in space, but I think a major effort is being made which will produce important results in the coming months and years.

Duties on Carpets and Glass

Q: Mr. President, in view of the Common Market retaliation, would you perhaps be prepared to concede that it was an error to raise the duties recently on carpets and glass?

The President: No.

Q: Do you have any intention of rescinding it or will it stand?

The President: No, it is going to stand. Carpets and glass were a unanimous recommendation of the Tariff Commission. They were very hard hit. We were quite aware of the fact that actions would be taken by the Europeans. If we had had passage of the Trade Act, we could have then offered an alternate package which I think would have prevented retaliation. Retaliation is not the most satisfactory device, but as you know, we were limited under present law, and, therefore, not able to be as forthcoming as we might have hoped. But there was a particularly drastic situation facing us in carpets and glass, and the Tariff Commission found unanimously that relief should be granted and we went ahead and granted it, and I would not change it.

Pressure for a Positive Vote on the Debt Limit

Q: Mr. President, I wonder if you think the Congressmen yesterday were justified who said that there had been pressure put on them to get them to vote for the rise in the debt limit and that this pressure had come from the Defense Department to people in districts with large defense contracts; who were told that these defense contracts under negotiation might not be completed if they did not vote for the debt limit?

The President: Well, I think - I'm sure - I hope that it was explained to every one what the effect would be if we did not - if we had to have a stretch-out - were not able to pay our bills. And that would have been the situation. I recall very clearly in the fall of 1957, in my own State of Massachusetts, when there was a stretchout and the contractors and others had to assume the - pay their own bills. It not only had a very drastic effect on them, but according to Brookings Institution and a good many other studies it was one of the factors which helped lead to the 1958 recession. This would have taken, in effect, in a period of 4 months, $2 billion out of our economy at a time

when we need money flowing into our economy. So they were only being informed
of what was a fact, which was that we could not pay the bills in some of these
areas if we were not given the kind of flexibility which had been requested of
the Congress. It's the same flexibility, as I have said, that President Eisenhower requested and which he received, and which we have now received.

A Tax Reduction Plan

*Q: Mr. President, while most of business certainly doesn't oppose your in-
come tax reduction plan, many businessmen have said if you really want to give
business and the economy a shot in the arm, that you should give them a better
break on depreciation, tax writeoffs, and so forth. Now I know that a new
schedule is coming out, I think within the month, but in addition to that, do
you contemplate anything in this area that will help?*

The President: We are going to, as I said before, by the 6th of July come
forward with the quicker depreciation writeoffs under schedule F for $1,200
million. That could have been done any time in the last 15 to 20 years. We
have been working on it now for a year. That is going to be important.

In addition, under the tax bill itself, it provides very important assistance to business if we are able to secure its passage by the Senate. And,
of course, the third provision of the tax bill is the standby tax authorities
in case unemployment begins to move up, which will permit us to have a temporary tax reduction in many brackets. All those I regard as very important.

Reporter: Thank you, Mr. President.

[1]Item 239 of the *Public Papers of the President*.
[2]Item 242 of the *Public Papers of the President*.

THE PRESIDENT'S NEWS CONFERENCE OF

JUNE 27, 1962

The President: Good afternoon. I have two statements.

The situation in the area of the Taiwan Strait is a matter of serious concern to this Government. Very large movements of Chinese Communist forces into
this area have taken place. The purpose of these moves is not clear. It seems
important in these circumstances that the position of the United States Government be clearly understood.

Our basic position has always been that we are opposed to the use of force
in this area. In the earlier years President Eisenhower made repeated efforts
to secure the agreement of Communist China to the mutual renuciation of the use
of force in the Taiwan area, and our support for this policy continues.

One possibility is that there might be aggressive action against the offshore islands of Matsu and Quemoy. In that event the policy of this country
will be that established 7 years ago under the Formosa Resolution. The United
States will take the action necessary to assure the defense of Formosa and the
Pescadores. In the last crisis in the Taiwan area in 1958, President Eisenhower made it clear that the United States would not remain inactive in the
face of any aggressive action aginst the offshore islands which might threaten
Formosa.

In my own discussion of this issue in the campaign of 1960, I made it quite clear that I was in agreement with President Eisenhower's position on this matter. I stated this position very plainly, for example, on October 16, 1960: "The position of the administration has been that we would defend Quemoy and Matsu if there were an attack which was part of an attack on Formosa and the Pescadores. I don't want the Chinese Communists to be under any misapprehension. I support the administration's policy towards Quemoy and Matsu over the last 5 years."

Under this policy sustained continuously by the United States Government since 1954, it is clear that any threat to the offshore islands must be judged in relation to its wider meaning for the safety of Formosa and the peace of the area.

Exactly what action would be necessary in the event of any such act of force would depend on the situation as it developed. But there must be no doubt that our policy, specifically including our readiness to take necessary action in the face of force, remains just what it has been on this matter since 1955. It is important to have it understood that on this point the United States speaks with one voice. But I repeat that the purposes of the United States in this area are peaceful and defensive. As Secretary Dulles said in 1955, "The Treaty arrangements which we have with the Republic of China make it quite clear that it is in our mutual contemplation that force shall not be used. The whole character of that Treaty is defensive."

This continues to be the character of our whole policy in this area now.

Secondly, I want to emphasize once again how deeply I am convinced that the passage this year of the trade expansion bill, on which one House will vote tomorrow, is vital to the future of this country. To recommit this bill back to the committee is to defeat it. To extend it for 1 year is to defeat the purpose, because we have exhausted the powers given under the previous - under the present - law. All its bargaining authority has been used up, and it will mean that we will fall back and behind at a time when the Common Market in Europe is moving ahead. This is no time to penalize our industry and agriculture by denying them markets. If we cannot make new trade bargains with the Common Market in the coming year, our export surplus will decline, more plants will move to Europe, and the flow of gold away from these shores will become more intensified.

It is for these reasons that this bill has enjoyed bipartisan endorsement from the very beginning, and I am confident that the members of both parties will support this bill in the national interest tomorrow.

QUESTIONS

Supreme Court's Decision on Prayer in Schools

Q: Mr. President, in the furor over the Supreme Court's decision on prayer in the schools, some members of Congress have been introducing legislation for constitutional amendments specifically to sanction prayer or religious exercise in the schools. Can you give us your opinion of the decision itself and of these moves of the Congress to circumvent it?

The President: I haven't seen the measures in the Congress and you would have to make a determination of what the language was and what effect it would have on the first amendment. The Supreme Court has made its judgment, and a good many people obviously will disagree with it. Others will agree with it.

But I think that it is important for us if we are going to maintain our constitutional principle that we support the Supreme Court decisions even when
we may not agree with them.

In addition, we have in this case a very easy remedy and that is to pray
ourselves. And I would think that it would be a welcome reminder to every
American family that we can pray a good deal more at home, we can attend our
churches with a good deal more fidelity, and we can make the true meaning of
prayer much more important in the lives of all of our children. That power is
very much open to us. And I would hope that as a result of this decision that
all American parents will intensify their efforts at home, and the rest of us
will support the Constitution and the responsibility of the Supreme Court in
interpreting it, which is theirs, and given to them by the Constitution.

Bill to Aid Higher Education

Q: Mr. President, in a somewhat related field, there seems to be an im-
passe in a conference committee on a bill to aid higher education over a 5-year
period, that $1-1/2 billion bill. There are some administration figures who
have been advocating the House bill which provides across the board grants for
all types of colleges, including church-related colleges, as opposed to the
Senate version which provides loans only for church-related colleges, and I
wonder what your position is. Which of these two versions do you prefer?

The President: Well, as you know, the administration sent up a program
which is somewhat different from the bills that are in the Congress now, which
provided loans to all schools. As you know, based on the brief on which I
relied last year in my comments on the question of aid to nonpublic schools,
secondary schools, I stated at that time that the brief indicated, and my own
analysis indicated, and that of the Department of HEW, that there was not a
comparable constitutional question on aid to higher education, to non-State
colleges or universities.

In my opinion there are very clear limitations based on the Supreme Court
decisions on aid to nonpublic schools in the secondary field. But in those
fields the attendance is compulsory, it is universal. There is particular
tradition connected with our public school system which has placed it in a
special place in the traditional and constitutional life of our country. This
is not true of higher education. So I did not feel, based on that, that there
was a constitutional question, a public policy matter. And I am hopeful that
the Congress will report our legislation which will assist schools of higher
learning and also that some arrangement will be made on scholarships, and that
all schools will be treated as they are in research grants and other ways -
will be treated in the same fashion.

Our Attitude on Chinese Nationalists Returning to the Mainland

Q: In connection with your China statement, would you say, sir, what the
position of the United States would be toward a return to the mainland by
Chinese Nationalist forces? There have been reports recently, from Taiwan,
that the time may be approaching for such a move.

The President: Well, it seems to me that the statement indicates the view
that I wish to express today. I think the statement at the conclusion emphasized the defensive nature of our arrangement there. That was true in 1955.
General Eisenhower made that clear, I think, in his letter to Senator Green
in 1958. I have made it clear today that our arrangements in this area are
defensive.

American Troops in Europe

Q: Mr.President, in your television interview about a month ago now, explaining your new trade expansion bill, I was impressed with your emphasis on the need for the European nations to take over more of their own defense. My questions are two: Does this mean that you would like to see a gradual withdrawal of U.S. troops from Europe; and, two, are you also considering sending men to Europe on shortened tours of, say, 1 year, without their families?

The President: Well, I would hope that we could withdraw or lessen the number of forces at some time but certainly not under present conditions until we have had a clear indication of what the future is going to be in Berlin. Quite the reverse, as you know, we have in the last 12 months strengthened our forces in Berlin and we have expressed our hope that other members of NATO would strengthen theirs. The United States has six divisions in Western Germany. Other members of NATO have substantially less, with the exception of the West German Government itself, and I would hope that they strengthen their forces. They represent a large geographic area with ever-increasing wealth. The United States cannot sustain this burden of maintaining the atomic deterrent, maintaining the sea strength we do, our ground commitments all around the globe, and still maintain such a large force in Western Germany. But we shall continue to do so as long as we feel it contributes to the security of Western Europe and the maintenance of our commitments.

Now, in regard to your second question, that is not a matter which is before us at the present time. At the present time we are planning to continue the tours of duty that we have on the books.

Reduction of Our Commitment to Quemoy and Matsu

Q: Mr. President, in your campaign for the Presidency, in connection with the offshore islands, you suggested in advance of any violent attack in the area that might be construed as an attack upon Formosa and the Pescadores that we might reduce our commitment to Quemoy and Matsu, that this was not the appropriate place to draw the line because the islands were strategically indefensible and unnecessary. What is your view now?

The President: I think that my statement represents the view of the United States Government, and the view of the United States Government is regulated by the resolution which was passed in - by the Congress in 1954, and which has been interpreted by President Eisenhower and again by me.

President Eisenhower, as you know, had some views about what should be the extent of the commitment of the Chinese Nationalist forces to these islands and, as a matter of fact, sent Admiral Radford out in the mid-fifties to discuss it. I also made some statements. My views on the matter in 1954 when the treaty came up are well known. But the fact of the matter is I also said in the fall of 1960 that there should be no withdrawal from these islands under the point of a gun, and that the matter of these islands - that the President must make a judgment based on the resolution of the Congress, that the action he will take will depend upon his judgment as to the effect of any action which the Chinese Communists might take on Formosa and the Pescadores.

Now, that is what my statement says. We stand in the traditional policy which has been true since 1954.

Support for the President's Legislative Program

Q: Mr. President, speaking generally about your legislative program, do you feel that it has had the proper degree of support from the Democratic majorities in the House and Senate?

The President: No, we haven't gotten the legislative program. I don't think we ought to go home until we get a good deal more of it by. I think that is the wishes of the majority. We should realize that some Democrats have voted with the Republicans for 25 years, really since 1938, and that makes it very difficult to secure the enactment of any controversial legislation. You can water bills down and get them by, or you can have bills which have no particularly controversy to them and get them by. But important legislation, medical care for the aged and these other bills, farm programs, they are controversial, they involve great interests, and they are much more difficult.

Now, if you recall in January 1961 when we had a very basic issue before the Congress, which was whether the administration and the National Democratic Pary would have the power to put its program on the floor of the House, the fight over the rules with Speaker Rayburn coming to the well of the House and making this a matter of his own personal prestige, we won that by five votes.

That indicated how close the balance was in the House of Representatives. Some Democrats vote with the Republicans, and have for a good many years. So that we have a very difficult time, on a controversial piece of legislation, securing a working majority. That is why this election in November is an important one, because if we can gain some more seats, we will have a workable majority, and if we don't, then of course we will not. So that I am concerned about what progress we make. There is no sense in the Congress going home without taking action on a whole variety of steps which will strengthen our country and our economy.

Now, on the farm bill, where we got defeated, as you know, by a close vote, there were powerful interests against it. In the first place, there was the unanimous opposition, with the exception of one Congressman, of the Republicans. And in addition there was the opposition of those who store surpluses. They like to have additional surpluses built up. There are 9 billion of them now, but they want more because they make money out of it. Then there are those who want cheap feed, and they want - the more surpluses there are, the cheaper the feed is. So that those who feed livestock, they did not want it. Then there are other parts of the country who want to plant corn, and who figure that if there are restraints on production they won't be able to plant it. So there are powerful interests that build up, and to try to get a program under control is very difficult. The fact of the matter is if we secured passage of that bill, it would have meant a saving of $1 billion, and that means that if we do not get a bill this year, it will cost $7-1/2 billion in the next budget, instead of $6-1/2 billion for agriculture. In addition, the farm income will drop, as it dropped in the fifties, because the surpluses will pile up. We will try to buy them under the support price, which is compulsory - the permanent bill - the surpluses will pile up, the farmers' income will go down, and no one will benefit.

So I think it is a great mistake.

Now, what is interesting, if I may conclude, is that there was support indicated, after our bill was defeated, for the emergency feed grain bill. The Republicans indicated they would support it. Yet last year when that bill was up, all but four or five voted against it. Now, it is hard to get bills by, that put restraints, but these are the kinds of bills, the tax bill and others, that a complicated economy such as ours much have passed.

They may not be of great emotional public issues, but we have got to pass them or otherwise we will begin to lose control of the management of our economy and of our governmental finances.

So that I think the Democrats have to do better and I hope some Republicans would support us. We supported President Eisenhower in important matters, and I would hope some Republicans will support us on the trade bill, which is vital, and on other measures as the summer goes on.

Secretary Rusk's Trip to Europe

Q: Mr. President, Secretary Rusk has just about completed his rounds of the Western European capitals. I wonder if you can give us an evaluation of this trip, with particular reference to whether this Government has now accepted France's determination to build its own nuclear power, and whether we will seek to coordinate and integrate that power into the NATO system?

The President: We have always accepted its determination to do so. What we have not agreed to is to participate in the development of a national deterrent. We believe that is inimical to the community interest of the Atlantic Alliance, that it encourages other countries to do the same.

Now, France has determined to do so, she is going to do it. But I think that for the United States to associate with that effort, to associate with the concept of additional independent national nuclear deterrents, to play our part in its development, would be a mistake, both from the point of view of the United States, of the Atlantic Community, and of peace, because other countries will be compelled to do the same. And in my judgment, the NATO Alliance and the steps we have taken to implement the NATO Alliance give adequate security to Europe and the United States. I think we should stay with that. Now, the French do not agree, and they are going ahead. We accept that. But we do not agree with it.

Edward Kennedy's Candidacy

Q: Mr. President, going back to the fall election, there has been considerable criticism of the candidacy of your brother, Ted, for Senator from Massachusetts. Among your most vigorous supporters it is said that there are going to be too many Kennedys in Washington and that Ted has not demonstrated a capacity for this. Would you comment and tell us whether you think this might be an issue in the fall?

The President: Well, I don't know whether they - I would characterize them as my most vigorous supporters, but I would say that there has been criticism. But as Ted, my **brother**, pointed out, there are nine members of my family. It is a big family. They are all interested in public life. So public life is centered - at least the great issues - in the United States Capital. Now, the people of Massachusetts are going to decide that. He had a very vigorously contested convention. He is going to have a primary in September. He will have a very vigorous fight in November. And I would think the people of Massachusetts could make a judgment as to his qualifications and as to whether there are too many Kennedys.

Now, as far as my own judgment, aside from the fraternal relations, I did put him in charge of managing my campaign in '58 in Massachusetts. But more important, he was in charge of our western campaign in the preconvention period which was a very intensive campaign, where we secured the support of a good many delegates, and in charge of our campaign in the West in the campaign itself, so that I have confidence in his ability. The people of Massachusetts must make the judgment, however.

Ransom for Castro Held Prisoners

Q: The organization of a committee to raise $62 million to ransom the invasion prisoners held by Castro was announced yesterday. One of its members is your sister-in-law, Mrs. Radziwill. Do you approve of public subscription to ransom these prisoners? And don't you think this money would contribute a great deal towards easing Castro's economic difficulties?

The President: Well, I am not informed about it. She is a good citizen and is free to make a judgment and anyone who wishes to contribute certainly is free to do so. And I certainly sympathize with the basic desire, which is to get a good many hundreds of young men out of prison whose only interest was in freeing their country. So I am certainly not critical of any efforts that are being made in this field.

Campaigning by Congress

Q: Mr. President, some members of your own party have a feeling that it might be a good idea to get Congress out of town and get them out to campaigning. On the other hand, you have outlined today quite a program remaining, and I wonder if you had any specific date in mind when you would like to see them go?

The President: No, I think that is up to them. It is much easier in many ways for me, and for other Presidents, I think, who felt the same way, when Congress is not in town - (laughter) - but it seems to me that we cannot all leave town. We ought to all stay here. I think Congress is determined to try to bring up a program which is useful: higher education; we've got medical care coming up next week; we've got the trade bill. I think that we've got a number of things left to do and I am confident the Congress will stay and try to do them.

Chiang Kai-shek's Desire to Return to the Mainland

Q: Mr. President, in December 1954, following the signing of the Mutual Security Treaty with Nationalist China, there was an exchange of letters between the United States and Nationalist China under which Nationalist China pledged itself not to take forceful action against the mainland without the consent of the United States. Do you think it is within the spirit of that exchange of letters that Chiang Kai-shek should be making statements proclaiming his intention of regaining a foothold on the mainland?

The President: No, I think that that letter still governs. We would regard the agreement which was part of the '54 action, that no such action as you mention would take place without the agreement of the United States, and I have indicated that our interest in this area is defensive, and we would like to have a renunciation of the use of force. Does that explain it?

Withdrawal of Forces from Berlin

Q: Mr. President, you mentioned Berlin in connection with the presence of our sizable forces in Europe. Have you thought of any reduction or withdrawal of those forces with respect to having a written agreement on Berlin, or would lessening of tension suffice?

The President: No, it would be a strategic and tactical judgment as to the use of our resources which would include, of course, men and financial resources, and the assessment of what effort the other countries were making.

For example, and this is only for example, we would have to make a judgment as to whether a conventional force of sufficient size could be developed in Europe to maintain itself without the use of atomic weapons, short of an all-out attack by the Soviet Union. This would require a different force level than it would if we decided to use weapons under different conditions. These are all part of the matter which we must consider. We must also see what the Europeans themselves are doing about conventional forces. And we also must take into account our dollar - our balance of payments problems. As you know, it costs about $750 million to keep our forces in Germany. That is balanced off by German purchases here. But it costs us $325 million to keep them in France, and that is not balanced off - $200 million-odd in Britain - $100 million in Italy. We have to make a judgment of what is in the best security interests of the United States.

But let me just make it clear that a good deal of what we are now talking about is in a sense academic. We plan to keep the six divisions in Europe for the forseeable future.

Eisenhower on Defense Spending

Q: Mr. President, General Eisenhower said the other night that he felt the current present administration was spending too much money on defense. He also said that he felt the administration was floundering in the face of various problems. Would you care to comment on those two points?

The President: No, I think, I would be glad - I think we are spending a good deal of money on defense, and I don't enjoy it. But on the other hand, I think we live in a very dangerous world, and I believe that being strong helps maintain the peace. I must say on the one hand that we seem to be under attack by some Republicans for not doing enough to stand up to the Communists, and on the other hand by those who say we are spending too much on defense. There should be some coordination of policy, because it seems to me that otherwise it may appear that the Grand Old Party may be floundering. (Laughter)

Business and the Administration

Q: Mr. President, a poll of about 30,000 businessmen by the Research Institute of America came up today with a vote of 2 to 1 in favor of your legislation, including the tax credit and the trade bill. Yet at the same time a substantial majority considers the administration hostile to business. What does this apparent inconsistency suggest to you?

The President: Well, I think that it suggests that most businessmen, number one, are Republicans, and, number two, that they realize what is in the best interests of business and the country, and that is the trade bill and the tax credit.

I am glad to have that poll even though it did not result in a resounding vote of confidence for the administration. I think the fact that businessmen so strongly support these two pieces of legislation which have been somewhat - which have been attacked by a few, or relatively few, who have mounted a very effective attack - I thought this was a poll which every member of the Congress should look at carefully. I think the businessmen are right. Both of these pieces of legislation are useful. I think the administration is, also. But more importantly is the fact they are supporting two important bills which I hope will pass, and which will be in the interest of the American economy, this year.

The President's Mexican Trip

Q: Mr. President, I wonder if you could tell us something about your plans for your Mexican trip and any comments you have relating that to the general Latin American situation?

The President: I think it is important. Mexico is extremely important. I am following where President Roosevelt and every other President since then have gone to pay a visit. We have been honored by visits from the Presidents of Mexico. We are neighbors. There are a good many problems that we have in common, as well as opportunities. And, in addition, we are anxious - I am anxious - to discuss not only the bilateral relations but also what we together can do to strengthen the democratic fabric in all of Latin America.

Tax Reduction

Q: Mr. President, 4 weeks ago you said that you had no plans to propose tax reduction at that time, at the moment, but that in new conditions you might think about it again. In the past month, the economic situation has not gotten markedly better, and the stock market has gotten worse. What do you think of tax reduction now?

The President: I think if we decide it is needed we will propose it, though I do point out that we do have one bill which would give us standby powers on tax reduction which I think would be very useful. It doesn't seem as if we are going to get action on that, but that is a tax reduction bill which would give us powers to move if the economy turned down. It has taken us nearly 18 months and we haven't finally gotten a judgment on our tax credit bill, which indicates the length of time it can take moving through the ordinary procedures of the Congress. That is why the standby power is important.

However, we will continue to watch the economy. There are good signs in the economy and there are signs which are not so good, so we will continue to watch it very carefully and make a judgment.

Nuclear Tests and Nuclear Fallout

Q: Mr. President, the recently released report of the National Advisory Committee on Radiation has pointed out that in the event the fallout contamination from weapons testing should exceed acceptable limits only you have the authority to halt testing and order countermeasures. The report also points out that responsibility for action against other nuclear hazards has not been clearly assigned. Under what circumstances would you halt nuclear tests or order countermeasures to protect against these hazards, and are you considering assigning responsibility for countermeasures against all nuclear hazards to a special agency?

The President: Well, as of today, the situation is such that our interests are served by testing. In addition, as you know, the iodine content has increased recently. The hazard is not present and will not be present, from our tests. Quite obviously, if tests are carried on for a long period of time all over the world this will become an increasingly serious problem. It is not today, however, and there is no health hazard here in this country nor will there be from our tests.

The President's Opinion on Prayer in Schools

Q: Mr. President, aside from your constitutional responsibilties, as an individual American Citizen do you personally approve or disapprove of the Supreme Court decision outlawing prayer in public schools?

The President: I think my answer was responsive to that question.

Mr. Rostow on American Foreign Policy

Q: Mr. President, did you ask Walt Whitman Rostow to draw up this paper on foreign policy and defense policy, or did he just undertake it on his own to interpret the policies of the Government?

The President: To interpret the policy – he was acting as the successor to Mr. George McGhee and fulfilling his function of policy planning and one of the functions of the policy planning staff is to plan policy. (Laughter) And that is what he is attempting to do.

Now, the fact of the matter is that we have in the National Security Council voluminous papers from the fifties which are the general guide of policy lines in the United States. But there have been a good many changes since the 1950's. In the first place, we discussed one of them today, the French atomic rearmament, the question of the Sino-Soviet relations. There are a great many problems, Castro and all the rest.

We are examining to see – guerrilla warfare, anti-insurgency – what should be our military policy in it, what should be our force levels. These are matters which the State Department and the Department of Defense are examining and will come through to the National Security Council to see whether there should be any changes in the policies that were laid down in the 1950's. So Mr. Rostow is fulfilling his function. I have not studied the paper; the Secretary of State has it. But Mr. Rostow is acting under instructions and acting very responsibly.

Q: Mr. President, what are your views on the present situation in Laos?

The President: Well, I am concerned that the agreement which came into effect in June among the three princes, that it shall be successfully implemented, and that the Geneva accords agreed to last summer shall be amplified at the coming Geneva conference. Laos continues to be a matter of great concern to us. We have never suggested that there was a final, easy answer to Laos. On the other hand, there is a cease-fire, there is a government; they are meeting in Geneva. We will continue to cooperate in every way we can. It is a situation which is as uncertain and full of hazard, which life is in much of the world, and we will continue to support the concept of an independent and neutral Laos, to which Mr. Khrushchev has also given his personal commitment.

Reporter: Thank you, Mr. President.

THE PRESIDENT'S NEWS CONFERENCE OF

JULY 5, 1962

The President: Good afternoon. I have two statements on two bills now before the Congress.

I want to express my very strong support for the foreign aid bill which the House leadership now expects to bring to the House of Representatives next week. Our foreign aid programs have made great demands on our people, and still do, but they are vital to our security and are carefully designed to re-spond to the national interests of the United States, as well as the mainten-ance of the peace and security of the free world.

Three facts should be kept in mind. Almost half of the money authorized in the foreign aid bill is for military assistance, or supporting funds for the defense of countries directly threatened by aggression or subversion. More than 80 percent of the money committed to economic assistance is in the form of loans, not grants, and these loans will have to meet our aid criteria and be repaid in dollars.

More than 80 percent of the money appropriated for the foreign aid program will be spent here in the United States on goods and services supplied by Amer-ican businesses and American workers, under new and tighter procedures which are being developed. Most importantly we simply cannot stand aside in the face of the needs of developing countries. In Latin America, for example, it is more urgent than ever that the Alliance for Progress should go forward. Here is an area with an income per capita one-eighth of our own. In some of these countries they are overwhelmingly dependent on a single export commodity, and they have to sell at wholesale and buy at retail. It is estimated that Latin America has 50 million underprivileged adults, and 11 million children of school age who are not in school. The stirrings of revolution can be felt in this hemisphere. It will either be peaceful or violent. We want it to be peaceful. But we have to do our part with our sister republics in assuring that. This is a bipartisan bill, supported by my predecessors since 1945, and I hope we can get favorable action this year.

The second matter is to urge strong support for the Senate effort which is now going forward under the leadership of Senator Anderson to pass a medical care for the aged bill, under Social Security. The bill which is now coming before the Senate is a strong bill. It meets the problems of those who have not been covered by Social Security. It provides participation by the Blue Cross, by private insurance companies. It is an effective bill, and I think could mean a good deal to our older citizens and their children who must sus-tain them. I hope the Senate will act and then the House.

QUESTIONS

A Tax Cut

Q: Mr. President, there seems to be growing sentiment in various sectors, both labor and business, for a tax cut this year. Have your discussions with Secretary Dillon this week opened the door at all to such action in 1962?

The President: No. We are continuing to watch the economy. We have, as you know, planned a tax cut and tax reform to come next year. We, of course, would prefer to maintain that schedule. We are continuing, however, to watch the basic indicators of the economy, and if we feel that the situation in the economy warrants a tax cut, then, of course, we would recommend it. At the present time we are maintaining our previous schedule. But I think the recom-mendations of the Chamber of Commerce, which is, of course, intimately in touch with the business community, and also the recommendations of the AFL-CIO, in regard to the need for tax cuts, should be very seriously considered by the Executive, as it is by me, and by the Congress, because representing as they do business and labor, giving their recommendations in favor of a tax cut, we have to take that judgment into very careful balance, which we are.

A Declaration of Interdependence and the Atlantic Alliance

Q: Mr. President, regarding your proposal for a declaration of interdependence and a concrete Atlantic alliance, can you give us any particulars on how these goals can be achieved? I am thinking in terms of how long a period of time may be involved and whether eventually this would be based on alliances or some form of political union.

The President: As I said yesterday,[1] the first task is for Europe, in its own way and according to its own decisions, to complete its organization. When a decision is reached in regard to Great Britain's joining, which we hope this summer, then, of course, this work will move ahead at a more accelerated pace. What I was attempting to suggest yesterday was that any view in Europe or any stories which might appear that we regard this strong and increasingly united Europe as a rival, were not true. We regard it as a partner. We regard it as a source of strength.

It is true that when this united Europe develops, that, of course, its relationship with us will be different than it has been in the past. The NATO alliance of a series of independent countries placed special responsibilities upon the United States which we were glad to assume, but which - of course, the relationship would be different between a single powerful Europe or a union of powerful European states and the United States. We would have to work together on economic matters.

As you know, we have been carrying great burdens in many parts of the world, the dollar has - military, economic, political - and I am hopeful that when Europe has completed its work, that Europe and the United States can then attempt to complete and harmonize its relationship in a way that will benefit not merely the United States and Europe but also, as I said yesterday, would look outward. We do not want this to be a rich man's club while the rest of the world gets poorer. We want the benefits of this kind of union to be shared. The first task is Europe's, then it will be the United States'.

Relations with the USSR

Q: Mr. President, today you named a new Soviet Ambassador. No doubt you have talked in general terms or will talk in those terms with him about his mission. I wondered if you could discuss briefly in a general way your feelings about the relations with the Soviet Union since you have taken office and what you expect in the months ahead.

The President: Well, in the case of our new Ambassador, Mr. Kohler, I have worked very intimately with him for the last year and a half, because he has been the head of the so-called task force on Berlin and has participated in all the ambassadorial meetings. So that he goes to the Soviet Union with complete knowledge of the Government's policy and also my complete confidence.

We've continued to attempt to work for an adjustment of those major tensions which disturb the relationship between the United States and the Soviet Union and between the free world and the Communist world. We have not always been as successful as we had hoped, but we are continuing. We're continuing the discussions over Berlin. We are now in conference in Geneva on Laos, where we are hopeful that a satisfactory treaty can be reached. We are going to be back in conference on July 16 on disarmament with the Soviet Union, so that we are continuing to see if it is possible to reach an accommodation for the peaceful use of space. In a whole variety of ways we are attempting to lessen the chance of conflict with the Soviet Union and maintain our own security and the peace of the free world. That is the object of our policy.

It cannot be accomplished quickly. It will require, I think, some time to come. But that is the object of our policy and we are going to attempt to continue to live in peace with all countries, and particularly those countries whose military potential is such that any great conflict would involve the future of both of our countries, and of the race. And Ambassador Kohler will attempt to carry out this policy which I have stated, necessarily, in a most general way.

The Atlantic Partnership and Deterrence to Aggression

Q: Mr. President, you say that the Atlantic partnership would be an advance on what we now have. How would it better achieve those things you claimed for it yesterday in Philadelphia? That is, a greater deterrent to aggression; a banishment of war and coercion; and some of the other things?

The President: Well, this will represent an extremely powerful body of people and productive power - the North Atlantic, North America, and Europe having nearly four or five hundred million people, having a productive power which is enormous, and steadily increasing. This represents a very vital source of strength.

My concern is that the relationship between Europe, using it in the single sense, and the United States, be intimate. We have been dealing, as I have said, with a great many countries which are smaller than the United States. Now we are going to have not one country but one great organization, if the effort is successful in Europe. And, I'm hopeful that we can reach accommodations on the economic relations, of trade, and also the problem of currencies and all the rest; on the problem of military policy; and then that we can emphasize, which I suggested yesterday, that we look outward.

We do not want a Europe, as I have said, and a United States to be a core of an increasingly disintegrating world. And therefore we're concerned with the admission of the raw materials of Latin America to Europe; we're concerned about the Pacific community - the Philippines, Japan, and the others - and we are concerned that Europe and the United States play their proper role in assisting the underdeveloped world.

There are statements of general policy. They must wait, therefore, for precise implementation while Europe completes its work. But I wanted to indicate yesterday how much we favored this, and we do regard it as a source of strength and satisfaction and not as a rival. Europe does not want to be dependent upon the United States and we do not want that relationship, and I think we meet as equals when this work is completed.

The Sugar Act and Conflicts of Interest

Q: Mr. President, two questions based on the passage of the sugar act and the foreign lobbying attending it. First, what do you think about the exercise by the House Agriculture Committee of what is essentially the power to make foreign policy by allocating quotas? And secondly, on the lobbying itself, do you believe there is involved the kind of double standard here? The Executive is controlled by very strict rules on conflict of interest. Do you think something similar to this should be expected of Congressmen?

The President: Well, as you know, the bill that we sent up to the Congress did not provide for this allocation of quotas. The final bill which was passed by the Congress, which I have not yet signed, plus the amendments made today - in the legislation before the Senate today - I think provide for an improvement over the situation as it was in the original House bill. Now, the second - though it is not everything that the administration wished for.

The second question is this matter of lobbying. I don't think it's a double standard. These men are all private people, they're not Government people, so that I wouldn't say it's a double standard. But I think it is an unfortunate situation when men are paid large fees by foreign governments to secure quotas and where, in some cases, there are contingency fees. For every ton of sugar they get allocated to their country, they secure a payment of so much. Well, now, that is not satisfactory.

I understand that appropriate committees of the Congress may look into the matter. And I think the fact that so much publicity has been given to this may serve as a deterrent. As you know, the bill which has passed the House and Senate, combined with today's bill, provides for a gradual phasing down of these quotas and we will have less of it. And I think we ought to have less of it.

The Atlantic Partnership as a Political Unit

Q: Mr. President, I think Mr. Shoemaker's question included a question about whether this Atlantic partnership would be a political unit. Could you elaborate on that?

The President: No, I would think that in a sense we have a political union - it depends on how you define "political." We have in NATO alliance the obligations to accept it under the NATO alliance. The North Atlantic Council, OECD, DAG, and all the other organizations which have been set up represent political commitments. And of course these political commitments will, perhaps, take a different form as Europe changes its form, and I hope a more intimate one. But as I've said, the first task is Europe's, and it will not be accomplished overnight any more than, of course, the length of time which elapsed between the Declaration and our own Constitution.

Impressions of Martin Luther King

Q: Mr. President, what do you think of the propriety of the Reverend Martin Luther King intervening privately with the Chairman of the Home Loan Bank Board in a controversial case pending before that agency?

The President: Yes. I understood that this is a matter which you brought to the attention of the White House and it's now being looked at to see whether there were any - what the actions were. As far as I know, so far, there is no illegal action. But our examination of the matter is not completed.

Latin American Assistance in the Cuban Situation

Q: Mr. President, without regard to your statement in Mexico, do you consider that progress has been made in enlisting the cooperation of the Latin American countries in handling the Cuban situation? And with specific regard to Mexico, do you feel that anything that occurred there has weakened your position, or ours, or the Organization's in any way?

The President: Well, the answer to the last part, I would say no. In answer to the former part, as you know, the action taken at Punta del Este indicated, I think, a general recognition that Marxism-Leninism was incompatible with this hemispheric system.

340

Fallout Shelter Program

Q: Mr. President, the Armed Services Committee has not scheduled any hearings on your request for $460 million for a big fallout shelter program, and apparently it has had no prodding from you. My question is, do you expect to renew your appeal for this program?

The President: No, I have talked to the responsible officials involved. I hope the hearings are held. I hope they can be held this month. I hope we'll secure the money we requested. As you know, within the last 10 days I've sent up a supplemental appropriation request for around $35 million for the distribution of food throughout the country, which would be available in case of an attack. These matters have some rhythm. When the skies are clear, no one is interested. Suddenly, then, when the clouds come - after all, we have no insurance that they will not come - then everyone wants to find out why more hasn't been done about it. I think we ought to take the action recommended by the administration. It may be that there does not seem to appear to be a need as of today, but that does not mean that there may not be need for it at a later date. Then everyone will wonder why wasn't more done. I think the time to do it is now.

Under the program which we started some months ago, nearly 60 million shelters have been identified. We want to have food in them and other necessities, and I'm hopeful that the Congress will implement the program we have sent up.

Invitations to Industrialized Countries to Build Plants in the U.S.

Q: Mr. President, the United States has reportedly invited Japan and other industrialized countries to invest in the building of plants in this country. Would you explain the thinking behind that, sir, and does it imply also that we are discouraging U.S. investment overseas in plants?

The President: As you know, United States investment overseas has been very heavy. In fact, it has been one of the matters which of course affects our balance of payments. Over the long run it does not; over the immediate run it does. We are anxious to have others invest in the United States, and particularly to invest in those areas where there may be higher unemployment. So this program is being operated through the Department of Commerce.

We've also attempted to speed up the number of tourists who come here. We want investment to come here. All of these will affect our balance of payments and affect our employment. We don't want our capital merely to be invested outside of the United States. We want foreign capital matching to come here. And that's the purpose of this program.

Equal Time Requirements for Candidates

Q: Mr. President, there are proposals to suspend the equal time requirements to permit major candidates for House and Senate and Governor to debate this year. Do you favor this?

The President: Yes, I'd like to see the legislation, but I think the purpose as you've described it - I would favor it, yes.

Conflict Between the Port and Lake Michigan Area

Q: Mr. President, this morning Governor Welsh of Indiana visited you about the conflict between the Port and the Lake Michigan Lake Shore area. He has referred us to you about your comments on that. Did you give him any encouragement on it?

The President: No. He explained the concern of Indiana - the effect on the jobs. As you know, there is an opposition to this proposal based on the effect it will have on the national park there. The Budget Bureau is having an analysis made tomorrow, which I think Governor Welsh and the representatives will attend. There also will be a White House representative there to hear that discussion, and then we'll make a report or recommendation to the Congress, shortly.

The Democrats and Business

Q: Sir, the Democrats of Michigan are hoping to invite you to a $1,000 a plate brunch for a select group of businessmen, with the understanding, which is rather interesting, that if the list is complete, of about 40 men, the list will then be sent to the White House. Whereupon you are to write them invitations for a meeting to discuss the Government's relations with business. Would you care to comment on that idea, and whether this is something that might - or what this might do to the idea that the Democrats are not the party of business?

The President: Well, I think, let me say I haven't heard of this brunch - (laugher) - so we have no plan. We are having luncheons to which businessmen and others will be invited. That doesn't cost any amount of money. I would think the problem of political parties raising funds is a difficult one. I'm not familiar with this one. I don't think that I'll be able to participate in it. But I'm very concerned about the problem which both parties have, of the difficulty of raising funds to carry on campaigns.

Now, the last part, I agree that the Democratic Party is not the party of business. There are an awful lot of businessmen who have supported the Democratic Party. I think its base is very broad traditionally. It includes wide spectrums of the American public and does not confine itself to merely one section.

Segregation in Federal Housing

Q: Mr. President, I believe you've been in office about 17 months and still haven't signed that order against racial segregation in federally financed housing. Could you tell us when you do plan to sign that?

The President: I will announce it when we think it would be a useful and appropriate time.

Q: You will sign it before the end of your term?

The President: I have said already I will meet any commitments of that kind that I've made. I will point out that we have carried on a great many activities in the field of civil rights, Executive actions, including actions by the Department of Justice and others, and I will take action as it appears that they will accomplish the result which we want to accomplish, which is providing equal opportunities.

The President's Views on Tensions with the USSR

Q: Mr. President, you indicated that one of your prime interests is the lessening of tensions with the Soviet Union. I believe Mr. Khrushchev and Radio Moscow indicated in the last few days that they think Mr. McNamara's Ann Arbor speech enunciating a counterforce doctrine was an aggressive policy. Do you see any conflict between the two?

The President: I think Mr. McNamara's speech was an attempt to explain why the United States opposed the idea of expanding national deterrents. He was devoting himself to that. That was his purpose, to try to explain and put theory behind the practice of American policy which is to discourage the expansion of national deterrents as inimical to the cause of peace. So that I regarded it in that sense as constructive and, if read from that point of view, I would hope that others would regard it so.

Plans for Filling the Post of Secretary of HEW

Q: Mr. President, the name of Robert Weaver has frequently been mentioned as a possible successor to Secretary Ribicoff, who has announced he will resign in a week or so as Secretary of Health, Education, and Welfare. Can you tell us what your plans are to fill that post?

The President: No, not until the Secretary resigns.

A Tax Cut and Deficit Spending

Q: Mr. President, two related questions on the economy. Could you spell out a little bit the formula that you will use to make the decision, whether you will ask a tax cut this year or not? And secondly, did Mr. Heller's observations in Europe as to the remarkable status of their prosperity draw you in any way further toward being convinced that deficit spending is a good idea in terms of our own problem?

The President: No, well, I think I explained in a previous address at New Haven about my view that the budget should be - of course, at times when there is a strong inflationary pressure in the economy, we should pursue a different budgetary policy than we do at a time when the economy is sluggish, because if the economy remains sluggish you have a deficit anyway. Witness the '58 deficit of $12 billion because of a drop in earning power and a drop therefore in tax revenues. In addition, as the International Bank at Basel pointed out, there will be at times when you'll want to run a deficit budget policy and a higher interest rate policy in order to protect your gold. So that these fine judgments have to be made.

Now as to the first part of your question, we will look at the indicators, the basic indicators which have had some sort of historical significance in previous years as indicating a prognosis for the economy. In addition, we are going to come out next week with the tax depreciation schedule, which is now at the printers. We are hopeful we will get action on our tax credit bill. We are hopeful we will get action on the public works bill, and some of the other programs which we have talked about, tax power - set-aside tax power. All these could affect our judgment as to whether we should go to Congress this year. But the basic question will be to try to make an analysis as to the health of the economy over the next months, and whether '63 is the appropriate time, or now.

Progress on the Berlin Question

Q: Mr. President, Premier Khrushchev said yesterday that in his view there had been some progress in settling the Berlin problem, and in a speech later on in the day he said the time for decision seem to be at hand. Do you agree?

The President: Well, I think we should continue to examine whether we can reach an accord on a matter in which we have powerful interests, and on which we do not see alike. So it is a very difficult negotiation. Mr. Dobrynin and the Secretary spoke just before the Secretary's visit. I am sure they will be meeting shortly again.

Solution to the Chamizal Zone in El Paso

Q: Mr. President, in line with your communique in Mexico, I wonder if you think there will be a solution soon to the Chamizal Zone in El Paso? And if you think this will mean a dividing up of the property between the two countries? Or what are your personal views about it?

The President: As you know, there have been long negotiations about the Chamizal. This territory was awarded to Mexico in the arbitration award of 1911, but the United States did not accept it. Since then, as a result of the United States failure to accept the arbitration, Mexico has been unwilling to take any other matter into arbitration, which has, of course, therefore - lessened the harmony between the two countries. We are anxious to see if this matter could be disposed of. The difficulty is that since 1911 there have been schools, a lot of people have moved in there, and you have a different situation in the area involved than you did in 1911 because of the interests which have built up there. That's what's made it so difficult to solve. But what we indicated was our strong desire to reach an accord on this matter, which we're going to attempt to do, taking into account the problem which is now there in El Paso and the interests of the people involved, and the interests of the Mexican Government. But it is a matter that we cannot afford to continue to treat with some indifference, because the United States failed after agreeing to arbitration, then backed down and did not accept the award.

Eisenhower's Comments on the Republican Party

Q: Sir, this is somewhat related to an earlier question. The other day General Eisenhower described the Republican Party as the party of business. Now do you consider this fair or accurate as to the Republican Party or the business community?

The President: Well, I think that - as I say, I dislike disagreeing with President Eisenhower, and so I won't in this case. (Laughter)

Increasing the Quality of the Congress

Q: Mr. President, last week I believe you indicated that you'd like to have a somewhat better Congress, and you hinted that you would campaign this fall for that purpose. Does that mean, perchance, that you might campaign only for those Democrats who have supported the major part of your programs, or will you campaign for all Democrats who want you?

The President: Well, I suppose you have answered the question. Those who want me to campaign for them are people who have generally supported the major part of the programs. So I don't think we are going to have a problem.

The Medicare Bill

Q: Mr. President, concerning the medicare bill, would you elaborate on why you don't favor inclusion of doctors' fees? Is it a matter of legislative strategy or of philosophy?

The President: I think that the doctors are very strong against being included. They feel that this would involve the Government in the doctor-patient relationship. Therefore we have concentrated our efforts in attempting to assist people to pay their bills, hospital bills, and, quite obviously, if they find that eased, they will be in a better position to work out their relationship with their doctors. It is because we have not included doctors that I have found it very diffiuclt to understand why the American Medical Association

has found this legislation so unsatisfactory. It does not involve them directly. It involves the payment of hospital bills. And in view of the fact that
the Federal Government participates in the construction of hospitals through
the Hill-Burton Act, from which doctors benefit in their practice, I found
the AMA's extreme hostility to this bill somewhat incomprehensible.

A NATO or European Nuclear Force

*Q: There have been a great many dope stories on the matter of a NATO or
European nuclear force and America's attitude towards it, so much so that some
of us, at least, are a little hazy as to what the real situation is. Can you
give us an up-to-the-minute statement on America's attitude towards the building of such a force, and how far we would go to help them build it, including
also whether we favor a truly independent European nuclear force, that is, one
not subject to United States veto?*

The President: Well, the United States Government feels that the present
arrangement under NATO gives full and sufficient guarantees for the integrity
of Europe. It places special responsibilities upon the United States, but I
think the United States in the last 17 years has indicated its determination
to meet its commitments, and to implement its responsibilities. But of course,
as time passes, Europeans become increasingly concerned, particularly as the
Soviet Union has developed not only atomic power but also missiles, which puts
Europe directly under the gun, as well as the United States.

Therefore, stronger pressures have arisen in Europe for a European nuclear
force not as dependent upon the United States as the present one. What we
have suggested is that this is a matter that Europe should consider carefully,
that we would, of course, be responsive to any alternate arrangement they wish
to make. We would examine it. We recognize their problem. But we think it's
a matter in which Europe should come forward with some suggestions, and not
for the United States to attempt to impose its views, particularly as we regard the present arrangement as a secure one for Europe. But if Europe does
not agree with that, and she may not - particularly as she develops this additional union - then we'd be prepared to discuss an alternate arrangement. But
so far no such proposal has come forward.

Meeting with Governor Brown

*Q: Mr. President, Governor Brown is coming here to see you this afternoon.
I wonder if you have any advice for him in the contest with Mr. Nixon and what
your overall view might be of the campaign in California, with eight new seats,
and all?*

The President: No, I saw Mrs. Brown here. I don't know whether this has
helped give her any advice. I would not advise Governor Brown. I think this
is a matter for the people of California. He seems to be doing very well. He
was running far behind in the beginning, in polls. And now he is leading in
the polls by substantially more than I led at the end of the election. So I
will be glad to - I want to see Governor Brown on matters which involve the
interest of California. But on how he should conduct the campaign and all the
rest, he's a much better judge of that than I am. I think he carried California by a million votes the last time he ran, or very close to it. So I think
he knows more about California and how to run than I do.

*Q: Mr. President, if you will support Democratic candidates who ask for
your help, does that include the primaries as well as the election? And what
is your view of the man you are going to finally end up supporting in Massachusetts?*

The President: No, I am not planning to get involved in any more primaries any place.

Reporter: Thank you, Mr. President.

[1]Item 278 of the *Public Papers of the President*.

THE PRESIDENT'S NEWS CONFERENCE OF

JULY 23, 1962

The President: Good afternoon.

I understand that part of today's press conference is being relayed by the Telstar communications satellite to viewers across the Atlantic, and this is another indication of the extraordinary world in which we live. This satellite must be high enough to carry messages from both sides of the world, which is, of course, a very essential requirement for peace; and I think this understanding which will inevitably come from the speedier communications is bound to increase the well-being and security of all people here and those across the oceans. So we are glad to participate in this operation developed by private industry, launched by Government, in admirable cooperation.

QUESTIONS

Soviet Intentions on Berlin

Q: Mr. President, again there are reports that the Soviet Union is preparing to sign an early and separate peace treaty with East Germany. These reports come at a time when the Soviet attitude on Berlin seems to harden and at a time when Mr. Rusk's talks with Gromyko have reached a standstill. Can you tell us what you know of Soviet intentions and how you view the present prospects for a Berlin settlement?

The President: We have made no progress recently on a Berlin settlement. Mr. Rusk, of course, will be seeing Mr. Gromyko again before he leaves Geneva, and in fact would stay in Geneva if a useful purpose could be served. There has been a strong difference of opinion in regard to Berlin, its viability and its guarantees, and we have not been able to reach an accord on our very different and vigorously held positions. So that I cannot report progress; and it is, of course, of concern to us all because, as I said from the beginning, when the vital interests of great countries are involved, in one area on which there are very varying views, it's a source of concern and some danger to us all.

(At this point transmission to Europe via Telstar began.)

We hope that an accord can be reached. We continue to try to reach one. But we've not made progress recently forward.

Agreement on a Test Ban

Q: Mr. President, the Russians appear to insist on being the last ones to conduct nuclear tests because we were the first. Would you see any basis for hope that there could be an agreement on a test ban reached after they finished their next series of tests?

The President: Well, the tests that we carried out were due to the breach of the moratorium by the Soviet Union last fall. We will have to make an analysis of their tests and see whether they present a further risk to our security. In this constant pursuit, everyone desiring to be last, of course, increases the danger for the human race. We are very reluctant to test. We will not test again unless we are forced to because our security is threatened and because as a result of new Soviet tests we find ourselves unable to meet our commitments to our own people and those who are allied with us. We will, therefore, have to wait. I'm sorry the Soviet Union is testing. They tested – they broke the agreement and tested last fall. We tested in response. Now they carry out another series of tests and the world plunges deeper into uncertainty.

Accomplishments of the Congress

Q: Mr. President, as a result of some of the congressional action on measures you've submitted to them, including the vote on the medicare plan in the Senate, some Republicans on the Hill have suggested that perhaps this Congress could not accomplish anything further, that it might be best to adjourn and go home. Would you go along with that view, sir?

The President: Well, that would be a disastrous course of action. There are still most important measures, which I recognize a good many Republicans oppose, the trade bill, the youth employment and opportunities bill, aid for higher education, the U.N. bond issue – these are merely some of the bills which are still before the Congress and on which the Congress should act before it goes home. The tax reform, the farm bill – Congress has no farm bill, and we would be reduced to relying on the 1958 act if the Congress doesn't act this year. Now I recognize that the Congressmen who said that the Congress should go home oppose our action in all these areas. But I believe this Congress should stay here and take action on them, and I think it will. But I think we have in that one statement a very clear indication of what the issue is going to be this fall, those who are opposed to action on all these fronts and those who feel that there should be action. The choice, of course, will belong to the American people.

Hearings on a Proposed Tax Cut

Q: Mr. President, was the decision of the Ways and Means Committee to open hearings on the tax cut, proposed tax cut, taken at your recommendation?

The President: No, I had a consultation with Chairman Mills. I'm not sure that the description of the purposes of the hearing are exactly the ones that – as I understand it they're looking at the economy and getting recommendations from various groups. I discussed it with Chairman Mills and it was his decision and that of the Committee but I thought it was useful.

The Gold Drain

Q: Mr. President, several times recently you expressed concern about the gold drain. Why does the United States, of all of the major nations in the world, permit foreign holders of its currency to exchange it for gold, and while this practice continues, even if we achieved a balance of international payments, would we be able to stop the drain of gold?

The President: If the United States refused to cash in dollars for gold, then everyone would go to the gold standard and the United States, which is the reserve currency of the whole free world - we would all be dependent upon the available supply of gold, which is quite limited.

Obviously, it isn't enough to finance the great movements of trade today and it would be the most backward step that the United States has taken since the end of the Second World War. We have substantially improved our position this quarter, the second quarter over the first quarter. Our loss is down to almost a third of what it was in the first quarter. Our loss, based on the first and second quarter of this year, is about half of what it was last year, and about a third of what it was the year before. We hope that we can bring our balance of payments into balance by the end of next year.

We are not going to devalue. There is no possible use in the United States devaluing. Every other currency in a sense is tied to the dollar; if we devalued, all other currencies would devalue and so that those who speculate against the dollar are going to lose. The United States will not devalue its dollar. The fact of the matter is the United States can balance its balance of payments any day it wants if it wishes to withdraw its support of our defense expenditures overseas and our foreign aid.

(Telstar's transmission of the conference ended at this point.)

Now, these have been undertaken, and we have put over $50 billion into Europe alone since 1945. We are not requesting them to do anything but to meet their responsibilities for their own defense, as we are helping to meet them. We spend $1.5 billion in the defense of Europe and the NATO commitments. Thirty percent of the infra structure of NATO is paid for by the United States. We don't object to that. We are not going to devalue. We are going to be able, we think, to bring our balance of payments into balance by the end of next year, and I feel that those who hold dollars abroad have a very good investment and - we have over $16.5 billion here in the United States; we have over $50 billion held by American citizens in investments overseas. This country is a very solvent country. So that I feel it requires a cooperative effort by all those involved in order to maintain this free currency, the dollar, upon which so much of Western prosperity is built.

I have confidence in it, and I think that if others examine the wealth of this country and its determination to bring its balance of payments into order, which it will do, I think that they will feel that the dollar is a good investment and as good as gold.

Evaluation of the Economy

Q: Mr. President, a great many people are giving their opinion of the domestic economy. Could you give us your evaluation at this time?

The President: No. I think that - as you know, there are some indications which are very good and some indications which are disappointing. I've said from the beginning that I think we can probably get a better look at what prospective actions the Congress and the Executive should take when we get the July figures. We can make a better determination then as to whether we are in a plateau, or whether this is a period which would require more vigorous Executive action. Some of the profit reports which came out last weekend showed that some of our major companies are making the highest profits in their history. In fact, as you know, General Motors, RCA, and others were far beyond - 50 to 75 percent above last year. There are encouraging indications - auto sales, consumer purchases have held up. Investment is down. Housing has been down. They've been, as I say, a mixed bag, and I think we can get a better look at where we're moving when we get the July figures in early August.

Arthur Dean's Statements at Geneva

Q: Mr. President, there's been some confusion over what Arthur Dean did or did not say at Geneva a week ago. I wonder if you can clarify for us whether he was suggesting that it might be possible to enforce a nuclear test ban without going into the Soviet Union?

The President: That's not the position of the United States at this time. As you know, there has been additional information gathered as a result of our underground tests, in the ability to detect an underground test at a range, and to distinguish between an underground test and an earthquake. This material which has just come through the Defense Department is being studied by the Disarmament Agency, the State Department, and the Defense, and whatever information we have will be made available to the disarmament conference at Geneva very shortly. The national governmental considerations of this information should be concluded by the end of this week. It is information which is in a sense encouraging as to our ability to distinguish. But whether we can do - the range at which we can do it, the sharpness of the distinction, what kind of instruments would be required, what would be the role of inspectors themselves - those will have to wait until our conclusions in the next few days.

Aid to the Third World from Europe

Q: Mr. President, I think you welcomed the President of Ecuador to Washington today, and you mentioned a moment ago the expense of this Government in the defense of Europe. I wondered if you feel that countries such as Ecuador and others are getting enough help from Europe in their economic and social development programs?

The President: Well, what concerns me is not only this question of whether sufficient aid has been given. As you know, actually there hasn't been aid in the sense that we understand it. There've been some long-term loans, but at reasonably high rates of interest. What has concerned us most about Latin America has been the fact that these countries are nearly all of them dependent upon very few commodities. Ecuador itself is dependent really on the export of three commodities; these prices have been dropping. They are dependent upon the European market, and we are concerned that the Common Market will be open and not take restrictive steps against the importations from Latin America, which would increase greatly their already very, very serious problems. So that what we are most concerned about now is not the question of aid, but rather that Europe will be open to the commodities of Latin America - the bananas, the cocoa, the coffee, and the others upon which these countries depend. Otherwise, their foreign exchanges are going to drop out of sight and you're going to have more and more desperate internal situations. So we're asking Europe to make the Common Market, as I've said from the beginning, an increasingly open institution which radiates prosperity, and not a closed shop with particular ties to former colonial possessions in Africa. But this is, of course, a matter we must negotiate with the Western Europeans, and I'm sure that Monsieur Monnet and others who have been so instrumental in developing the Common Market, share this view of an expanding free world economy.

Military Aid

Q: Mr. President, some have criticized the administration for withholding aid from the military dictatorship which has taken over Peru, and at the same time asking Congress for permission to give aid at your discretion to Communist dictatorships such as Yugoslavia and Poland. Do you feel free to discuss with us reasons for this distinction?

The President: Well, at the present time the President of Peru is imprisoned. President Prado, who was a guest of this Government a short while ago, and who was a guest of Franklin D. Roosevelt during World War II, is in prison. We are anxious to see a return to constitutional forms in Peru, and therefore until we know what is going to happen in Peru, we are prudent in making our judgments as to what we shall do.

We think it's in our national interest, and I think the aid we're giving in the other areas is in our national interest, because we feel that this hemisphere can only be secure and free with democratic governments. We wish that were true behind the Iron Curtain, and it is to encourage a trend in that direction that we have given some assistance in the past, and advocate it now.

The Congo Situation

Q: Mr. President, the Congo appears to be receding rather than progressing towards integration.

The President: That is correct.

Q: Do you have thoughts on this and what might possibly be done?

The President: Yes, we have been very concerned about the Congo because we have been unable to reach an accord between the Katanga and the Government of the Congo and all - and time is not running in favor of the Adoula Government. It has very little funds. The great resources of the Congo are in the Katanga. Mr. Tshombe and Mr. Adoula have been unable to get together. This is very, very serious. The Union Miniere, the company which controls these vast resources in the Katanga, pays its taxes just to the Katanga, not to the central government. It leaves Mr. Adoula without resources. It has weakened his position and I think that those who are sympathetic to the Katanga's effort are liable to find complete chaos in the rest of the Congo. So that I support the United Nations effort there to encourage the integration of those areas on a reasonable and responsible basis. The United States stands very strongly behind that policy and I'm hopeful that under the leadership of U Thant we can make that policy effective, with the support of Mr. Adoula and Mr. Tshombe, who will come to see that together this country can be viable, and separate it will be chaotic.

Martin Luther King's Comments on the President

Q: Mr. President, Dr. Martin Luther King said yesterday that you could do more in the area of moral persuasion by occasionally speaking out against segregation and counseling the Nation on the moral aspects of this problem. Would you comment on this, sir?

The President: I made it very clear that I'm for every American citizen having his Constitutional rights, and the United States Government under this administration has taken a whole variety of very effective steps to improve the equal opportunities for all Americans, and will continue to do so.

Russian Peace Treaty with East Germany

Q: Mr. President, in the absence of any agreement on Berlin, could you discuss with us what the consequences might be were the Russians to go ahead now and sign a separate peace treaty with East Germany?

The President: Well, I would rather not look into that clouded crystal ball because, of course, our rights to Berlin are based upon World War II and the agreements coming out of World War II, and are not subject to unilateral abrogation. But I think I'd rather talk about what we can do to work out an equitable solution rather than to talk about what might happen under these conditions. At the present time we are still talking with the Soviet Union, still negotiating, and I think that we ought to continue on that track as long as we possibly can before we consider where we are going to go on other roads.

Q: Mr. President, are you making any progress toward a direct telephone line to Mr. Khrushchev for use in case of emergency?

The President: I have not done that, no. We have communications with the Soviet Union. I think the problem is not at the present time communications. The problem is that there is a difference of viewpoint. We understand each other, but we differ.

Q: In that same connection, sir, could you tell us anything about your talk with Ambassador Dobrynin and whether or not this was the beginning of perhaps a series of direct consultations between you and the Ambassador?

The President: Yes. I hope to see Ambassador Dobrynin periodically. Mr. Khrushchev is seeing our Ambassador fairly frequently. And I think that it's useful in order to indicate our viewpoint. I've said for a long time that any study of history, particularly of this century, shows the dangers of governments getting out of touch with each other and misunderstanding each other. Therefore, I want to be sure that we have the closest understanding of our position and of their position. These meetings, I think, help indicate what we believe and also they are very helpful to me in hearing an exposition of the Soviet viewpoint. So I will continue to see him.

Republican Sentiment in the Middle West

Q: Mr. President, according to Dr. Gallup's latest poll, there's been a sharp rise in pro-Republican sentiment in the Middle West and a parallel or opposite drop in your popularity stock of about 10 points. Do you have any explanation of your own for this phenomenon, if it is one, and does it bother you with the administration facing now a mid-term election?

The President: Well, I think it said I dropped personally from 79 percent to 69 percent. I think that if I were still 79 percent after a very intense congressional session I would feel that I had not met my responsibilities. The American people are rather evenly divided on a great many issues and as I make my views clearer on these issues, of course, some people increasingly are not going to approve of me. So I dropped to 69 percent, and will probably drop some more. I don't think there is any doubt of that.

President Eisenhower, I think, in the November election of 1954 was down to 58 percent. But he survived, and I suppose I will.

Now, as to the congressional drop, I thought it was abnormal in the winter, before the Congress began. I think what the American people have to understand is that the Republican Party, by and large, with very few exceptions, has opposed every measure that we have put forward, whether it's agriculture, whether it's in medical care, whether it's in public works, whether it's in mass transit, whether it's in urban affairs. And they have been joined by some Democrats who for a great many years have opposed a good many Democratic programs.

Now this grouping has cost us - we lost medicare, a change of 2 votes would have won it, and in the House a change of 10 votes would have passed our farm bill. And that's why this election in November is a very important one. If the American people are against these programs, then of course they'll vote Republican, and we will have a state of where the President believes one thing and the Congress another for 2 years, and we'll have inaction. There are those who believe that is what we should have. I do not. That is why I think the choice is very clear, in other words. November 1962 presents the American people with a very clear choice between the Republican Party which is opposed to all of these measures, as it opposed the great measures of the 1930's, and the Democratic Party - the mass of the Democratic Party - the administration, two-thirds or three-fourths of the Democratic Party, which supports these measures. Fortunately, the American people will have a choice. And they will choose, as I have said, either to put anchor down or to sail. So we'll see in November.

Q: Mr. President, do you plan any reprisals against the Democrats who haven't supported you?

The President: No, I think that most of the Democrats who have not supported me are in areas where - are in one party areas. And what I am going to do is attempt to elect, to help elect, Democrats, though I've never overstated what a President can do in these matters. I'm going to help elect Democrats who support this program. The areas I will be campaigning in are seats where there will be a very clear choice between Republicans who oppose these actions and Democrats who support them. That's where I am going to go.

The President's Labor Message

Q: In view of the increase in strikes and other major labor disputes, could you tell us, sir, why you have not yet sent up a labor message, and when you intend to do so?

The President: I don't think there has been an increase in strikes.

Q: I think the figures show they are up this year over last year.

The President: Well, these figures are still very limited in the amount of strikes. There was a serious one out in California in the construction trade that went on for some length of time. But we are attempting to use the powers which have been given to us, and also particularly the Mediation and Conciliation Service, and the Secretary of Labor, and myself to attempt to bring about peaceful solutions. We will continue to do that. If I thought there were any congressional power that would assist us, then I would ask for that, but I'm not aware of any strike which we've had this year, which would have been settled more amicably and more responsibly by an additional grant of power by the Congress.

The Question of a NATO Commander

Q: Mr. President, there are reports that President de Gaulle is irritated over your swift appointment of Gen. Lyman Lemnitzer to be Commander in Chief of U.S. Forces in Europe upon the retirement of General Norstad on November 1. Would you please tell us if you have received the same reports, and also give us your opinion on whether the next Supreme Allied Commander of NATO should necessarily be an American?

The President: General Norstad informed me in May when he was here that he wished to retire this fall. After that, during the Secretary of State's visit, and by other means, we discussed this matter with other governments, including the French Government, to find out whether they wished - if it was in their view satisfactory to have an American appointed. Now we were informed that they accepted the appointment of an American, and supported it. Then when General Norstad came this time to see me, it was arranged that his resignation would become effective October 1, and we then sent in the name of General Lemnitzer, who is our senior military officer, and a distinguished one.

So that I am not aware that there was haste in the matter of naming an American or nominating an American which is after all the responsibility of the North Atlantic Council. And quite obviously if the North Atlantic Council asked us to nominate an officer, I would nominate our senior officer, General Lemnitzer, who is very adequately equipped to deal with these matters.

Now, I've seen some stories that might suggest a contrary view, but the fact of the matter is General Lemnitzer could have retired in October and there would have been a vacancy as Chairman of the Joint Chiefs of Staff. Therefore, when I nominated him to be the Commander of American Forces in Europe and also indicated that if we were invited by the North Atlantic Council to nominate an American, that he would be our nominee. I did it with complete freedom, because I felt that after working with General Lemnitzer for a year and a half, he was the best officer for that position at this time.

Now, I am sorry that General Norstad is leaving. He did an extraordinary work, and he was particularly - I found his judgment to be particularly reliable during this last spring, and I think every one in Europe shares the same feeling of confidence. I think that they'll develop the same confidence in General Lemnitzer. So I'm not sure that the stories are wholly accurate.

Economic Policy

Q: Mr. President, in your January economic report you said that if demand falls short of current expectations a more expansionary policy will be pursued. Actually, sir, as you know, demand has fallen substantially short of your target for the past 6 months. I wonder if you can tell us what the factors are that have caused you to postpone taking action to stimulate the economy.

The President: I think I made that rather clear, that we are waiting until the end of July, the July figures. The expansionary policy which we've talked about is in the area of a tax cut, which is a matter, of course, which must go through the Congress. And I think the Congress, as well as the administration, would want to be convinced that this remedy, which is not an easy one and which can be very controversial, that this remedy is the most desirable at this time. And I think that as long as the figures are as mixed as they are, as long as there are such strong differences of opinion among people who are well informed about where the economy is going, I think that it's wiser to wait for the July figures to see if that will give us a clearer picture. Because we may be in a plateau which may carry through 5 or 6 months to January of next year, when we've proposed a tax cut anyway, or we may be in a different period. But there are all kinds of figures and many of them are contradictory.

As I said, the profit figures for the first half in some industries are extraordinary. The consumer purchasing power is held up. What has been particularly disappointing has been investment, and we have to consider whether a tax cut, and if so, what kind of a tax cut, would stimulate investment, if that becomes our need. This matter is so complicated, must go through so many different committees of the Congress, and will be subject to the most careful scrutiny, that we want to be convinced that the course of action we're advocating is essential before we advocate it.

Gunnar Myrdal's Comments on U.S. Society

Q: Mr. President, the other day Gunnar Myrdal, the Swedish economist, said in Stockholm, after a return from a visit to the United States, that he regard- ed it as inexcusable for so rich a country as ours to have so many slums, to have inadequate schools, and lacking a variety of social services. And he des- cribed our economy as stagnant and he traced the roots of this alleged stag- nancy to the Eisenhower administration. Would you care to comment on this es- timate of our situation?

The President: Well, I think it is regrettable that we have not been able to develop an economic formula which maintains the growth of our economy. If we were moving ahead at full blast today, of course you would have full employ- ment. Also, he made the point that a stagnant economy falls heaviest on the Negroes, who, of course, are the first out of work and the last reemployed. I think he felt that the emphasis upon the traditional budget had served us ill. I have been exploring that question somewhat myself.

The Electoral Goal in November

Q: Mr. President, on the political front, what is your goal in November, given the fact that despite the big Democratic majority currently, you're having a lot of trouble? Does that mean your goal is to increase the House Democrats, say by 20, and the Senate by some number?

The President: Well, as you know, we lost 20 seats in 1960. As I've said before, the rules fight, which I regarded as a very important one in January 1961, we won by only 5 votes, with 19 Republicans. Now, we don't get any Re- publicans any more for any measure – with the exception of the trade bill, and even there the leadership opposed us – but fortunately I think a good many Re- publicans realized that this was not a party issue, but a national issue. And I hope that they feel the same way in the Senate, because I regard it as such, and the bill has equal sponsorship from the Republican and Democratic sides. So we put that and the aid bill outside of the political dialog, fortunately.

But I would like to see us win even a few seats. I am not as ambitious as your figures would indicate, because history is so much against us. If we can hold our own, if we can win 5 seats or 10 seats, it would change the whole opinion in the House, and in the Senate, because we lose by 5 votes. There really isn't a measure before us that I don't think we couldn't pass with a change of 5. That was the farm bill and the same is true in the Senate on med- icare, a change of 1 or 2 seats in the Senate. So we're not required to do any more than hold our own and gain between 5 and 10 seats. Now that, of course, is going to be an extremely difficult job and has been done, I believe, since the Civil War only twice – in this century, of course, only once.

Telstar Transmissions

Q: Mr. President, now that the U.S. image is being transmitted instantane- ously overseas by Telstar, do you think the U.S. networks should make a greater effort to do something about the "vast wasteland"?

The President: I'm going to leave Mr. Minow to argue the wasteland issue.

Democratic Vote on the Medicare Bill

Q: Mr. President, the other day after the medicare vote, you said that a handful of Democrats voted against you. There were 21. This prompts two questions: wasn't it a pretty big handful, and won't this tend to inhibit you in setting this forth as an issue?

The President: No. Two-thirds of the Democrats voted for it, a third of the Democrats voted against it. About six-sevenths of seven-eighths of the Republicans voted against it. So that this combination of almost total Republican opposition with a third of the Democrats defeated us by 52 to 48.

Now the issue in November, every seat that is being contested betweeen Republicans and Democrats, really, I would say, in 80 percent or 90 percent of the cases, would be between those who oppose medicare and those who are for it. So that there isn't any doubt that there is in a party as large as the Democratic Party those who do not support a good many of the programs. The alliances may change but, of course, we lose a third or a fourth, and we have since 1938. But the fact of the matter is this administration is for medicare and two-thirds of the Democrats are for medicare and seven-eighths of the Republicans are against it. And that seems to me to be the issue.

Reporter: Thank you, Mr. President.

THE PRESIDENT'S NEWS CONFERENCE OF

AUGUST 1, 1962

The President: Good afternoon. I have several announcements.

Recent events in this country and abroad concerning the effects of a new sedative called thalidomide emphasize again the urgency of providing additional protection to American consumers from harmful or worthless drug products. The United States has the best and the most effective food and drug law of any country in the world, and the alert work of our Food and Drug Administration, and particularly Dr. Frances Kelsey, prevented this particular drug from being distributed commercially in this country. Nevertheless, the drug was given to many patients on an investigational basis. We are reviewing what steps can be taken administratively to make this stage in the future less dangerous. We have recommended a 25 percent increase in the Food and Drug Administration staff, the largest single increase in the agency's history, and the full amount was voted today by the conferees of the Congress.

And it is clear that to prevent even more serious disasters from occurring in this country in the future, additional legislative safeguards are necessary. The bill reported by the Senate Judiciary Committee on July 19, while embodying many of the recommendations contained in the message of March of this year,[1] does not go far enough, as Senator Kefauver and others have pointed out in their supplementary review on the committee report. I hope the members of Congress will adopt those more careful provisions contained in the administration bill introduced by Congressman Oren Harris, of Arkansas, in the House. The administration bill, for example, unlike the Senate judiciary bill, will allow for immediate removal from the market of a new drug where there is an immediate hazard to public health which cannot be done now, and contains with it many other very essential safeguards which I hope the Congress will act on this year.

Secondly, we are completing a careful review of the technical problems associated with an effective test ban treaty. This review was stimulated by important new technical assessments. These assessments give promise that we can work towards an internationally supervised system of detection and verification for underground testing which will be simpler and more economical than the system which was contained in the treaty which we tabled in Geneva in April 1961. I must emphasize that these new assessments do not affect the requirement that any system must include provision for on-site inspection of unidentified underground events. It may be that we shall not need as many as we've needed in the past, but we find no justification for the Soviet claim that a test ban treaty can be effective without on-site inspection. We have been conducting a most careful and intensive review of our whole position with the object of bringing it squarely in line with the technical realities. I must express the hope that the Soviet Government, too, will reexamine its position on this matter of inspection.

In the past it has accepted the principle, and if it would return to this earlier position we, for our part, will be able to engage in an attempt to reach an agreement on the number of on-site inspections which is essential. Ambassador Arthur Dean has been participating in these deliberations and will be returning to Geneva promptly. He will be prepared for intensive technical and political discussions of these problems.

And finally, I want to express my very strong hope that the House of Representatives will give approval to the U.N. bond proposal. The U.N. is engaged at this very time in two very important negotiations, one involving the Congo, the other involving the future of West Iran. And it is daily proving its effectiveness in maintaining the peace and stability of much of the world.

This would be a most unfortunate time if we withdrew our support from it. And I'm therefore hopeful that the House will follow the Senate's example and give us the power to participate in this U.N. bond program which I believe to be essential for its survival, just as I believe that the survival of the United Nations is essential for the peace of the world.

QUESTIONS

The Problem of Thalidomide

Q: Mr. President, in connection with your opening statement in this period of anguish over the use of this drug, with women asking for abortions, there's apparently been some difficulty in running down all of the remaining stocks of thalidomide still in this country. Is there anything short of what you told us or is there anything additional that the Government can do without legislation to run down these remaining supplies of this drug and take it into custody?

The President: No. The Food and Drug Administration has had nearly 200 people working on this and every doctor, every hospital, every nurse has been notified. Every woman in this country, I think, must be aware that it is most important that they check their medicine cabinet, and that they do not take this drug, that they turn it in. Every citizen, of course, should be aware of the hazards. And I'm sure they are.

Now, what we have to concern ourselves about is the, first, appreciation to Dr. Kelsey who spared us this terrible human tragedy which has been visited on families in Germany, and to provide both administrative and legislative safeguards to lessen the chance of such action coming in this country again.

Also, I think, to see if we can assist our other countries in providing effective safeguards for their own citizens, because the interrelationship between them and us is very intimate.

International Nuclear Controls Stations

Q: Mr. President, has the new information we've turned up - from our underground tests - affected our position on the need for international controls stations on Soviet territory, and have we any indication that the Russians are now disposed to negotiate or modify their position?

The President: No, I think that our position, which Mr. Dean will elaborate, has been that the national control posts should be internationally monitored or supervised. That's the first point.

The second point: we have no information in regard to the Soviet position. What we've been attempting to do is to bring our own position in line with new scientific data which became available to us in late June. We are completing that with a final meeting before Mr. Dean goes back this afternoon. But the general position will be developed by Mr. Dean, but at least I've outlined it.

British Decision to Terminate the Agreement on Thor Missiles

Q: Mr. President, the British announced earlier today the decision to terminate the agreement on the Thor missile bases. Two questions: Were you given advance notice of this decision? And secondly, what will be the effect, militarily and psychologically?

The President: We were given advance notice. Mr. Watkinson, Mr. Thorneycroft's predecessor, had discussions with Mr. McNamara, and Mr. Thorneycroft informed us of the statement he was going to make in Parliament today.

Secondly, it should have no adverse effect, psychologically. Our ability to meet our commitments to the defense of Western Europe in the conventional and in the nuclear field remains unchanged by this announcement, and the United States commitment remains unchanged.

Developments in Southeast Asia

Q: Mr. President, in the last 10 days there have been a series of developments beginning with the agreement on Laos, and yesterday ending with the announcement of an agreement on Indonesian-Dutch settlement on New Guinea. There was also the Malaya and Britain announcement that a Malaysia Federation will be formed. Will you comment on these developments and the effect it has on that area and what danger spots you perceive?

The President: Well, the agreement, of course, on West Irain has to be approved by the two governments involved, although we are very much indebted to Ambassador Bunker and to those who participated on behalf of the two countries in the negotiations here, and, of course, to the Secretary General of the United Nations, U Thant.

We are also hopeful that the full significance of the Geneva accord on Laos will be recognized by all the countries that were signatories, and that there will be withdrawal of foreign troops, that Laos will not be used as a springboard, and that the ICC will be effective and be given full powers. This will be determined, of course, for the future.

As to the general situation there, we are still concerned about the implementation of the accord, and also about the situation in Viet-Nam. We have made two - we have a chance for two significant - three significant steps now as you described them. If we could get an agreement satisfactorily between Mr. Adoula and Mr. Tshombe in the Congo, this would be an important summer, though we still have very significant problems that still involve our relations with other countries coming up. But at least there is progress in those areas.

Report on Events in Albany Ga.

Q: Mr. President, it was, I believe, on July 11th that you asked the Attorney General to prepare a report for you on events in Albany, Ga. If you have received this report, will you tell us what it says, and if the Federal Government can or contemplates action to preserve Negro rights in Albany?

The President: We have been - I have been in constant touch with the Attorney General and have received more or less daily reports, and he's been in daily touch with the authorities in Albany in an attempt to provide a solution. There is - what is involved here is partly local laws and partly those laws which involve the National Government, particularly as they might involve public facilities, and some of these matters are in the court.

Let me say that I find it wholly inexplicable why the City Council of Albany will not sit down with the citizens of Albany, who may be Negroes, and attempt to secure them, in a peaceful way, their rights. The United States Government is involved in sitting down at Geneva with the Soviet Union. I can't understand why the government of Albany, City Council of Albany, cannot do the same for American citizens.

We are going to attempt, as we have in the past, to try to provide a satisfactory solution and protection of the constitutional rights of the people of Albany, and will continue to do so. And the situation today is completely unsatisfactory from that point of view.

Extending the Timing of Additional Nuclear Testing

Q: Mr. President, have you reached a decision yet as to the extent and timing of additional nuclear testing required by this Government?

The President: No, as you know, we are repairing the pad at Johnston Island, and we will make a judgment in regard to those three tests when the pad is completed. That will of course conclude - if we go ahead with those tests - that will conclude this series of tests.

Q: Excuse me, sir. Did you say three tests?

The President: I believe there were three that are still to be done.

The Tax Cut

Q: Mr. President, the Gallup poll published today shows that some 72 percent of those polled are opposed to a tax cut if it means the Government will go further into debt. Can you tell us what factor this will be in your decisions about the tax cut?

The President: Well, as I have said before, we are going to wait until we get the July figures, which will be available in this first 10 days, after the first 10 days of August. In addition, we'll make a judgment as to whether those figures indicate we're in a plateau or whether we are in more serious economic difficulty. And the figures, of course, today on unemployment, which are the lowest they've been for the last 18 months, are somewhat encouraging, but we can make a more final judgment in early August. Then we will discuss that matter with the appropriate members of the responsible committees.

Now, that question was asked in a particular way. You might get a different answer if you'd asked the question differently. If you said, "Do you believe in a tax cut as a means of preventing a recession at some future date, and unemployment which will bring potentially a larger deficit and a further increase in the debt?" I think you might have gotten a different percentage, and particularly if the 1958 experience had been recalled, where there was no tax cut and there was the largest peacetime deficit in history because of a drop in income levels. All this must be taken into consideration as well as the views of the members of the House and Senate, the schedule of the House and Senate. For example, the Senate Finance Committee will not even conclude its hearings on the trade bill until the first of September, and then have to go into executive session. We recommended a tax bill last year which has just been reported out yesterday from the Senate Finance Committee, 18 months after we recommended it. So that it does require very careful judgments, not only of the economic factors, but also of the legislative situation.

The President's Health

Q: Mr. President, it's been a long time since we've had a definitive report on your health from the best possible source. How is your aching back?

The President: Well, it depends on the weather, political and otherwise. It is very good, though, today.

The Financial Status of Ambassadors

Q: Mr. President, there are reports or indications that Ambassador Gavin is resigning, at least in part because of the financial burden of maintaining his post in Paris. Does this indicate that your Palm Beach agreement with Congressman Rooney is not working, or do you feel that Ambassadors now have adequate representation allowance?

The President: No, I think Representative Rooney has done everything he said he would do, but I think the situation still squeezes, because Ambassador Gavin has some family, some children to educate. And while he has received sufficient funds to keep his nose above the water, he has not been given funds which would permit him to meet his family responsibilities in a proper way. So that we are going to have to - I hope to have another talk with Congressman Rooney and see if we can be somewhat more generous. The fact of the matter is we are far more stringent with our Ambassador to Paris than I believe the French Ambassador to the United States is treated. And the same is true with London and some of our other major posts. So I think that while Congressman Rooney has met the requests we made, I think we might have to change the request.

The Economy

Q: Mr. President, Senator Goldwater says that if the economy continues to move sideways, then the economy will become an issue in this year's political campaign. Are you willing to match the record of your administration in the economic field with that of the last administration?

The President: Well, I don't think the record of the last administration, particularly from '57 on, was satisfactory. I'm not satisfied with our record. And I don't think that any American ought to be. Now if we wanted to compare the economic statistics, the day that I assumed office and today, you'd find that the gross national product was up 10 percent, that - in a whole variety of areas the improvement is between 10 and 15 percent. Even profits have gone from an annual average of about $40 billion to $50 billion, and the Standard and Poor level of stock prices is about 5 points above what it was at the time that I took office. But that still is not sufficient.

We have to provide a greater rate of growth because of our increase in population, and even though our gross national product may have gone from around $500 billion to $550 or $555 billion on an annual basis this year, it still - there is still a gap between what we are doing and what we could do, based on our manpower and on our plant capacity.

So that Senator Goldwater - I would be glad to compare statistics, but where I think we disagree is that there are some things we think we should do about it. I think if we could get the standby tax bill, which would meet the problem which I responded to in an earlier question, that we could then apply that tax reduction if the economy, for example, began to drag in the fall or the winter of 1963.

The problem is now that if we go by this session without a tax reduction then recommend one in January - if you go through the usual procedures the bill will not come to the floor of the Senate possibly until late summer, and by then we would have gone through nearly a year more. So I support that bill. It's my understanding that the Senator in question does not.

In addition, I support the public works bill, the youth employment, youth opportunities bill, manpower retraining, additional funds, and so on. So I think that we have suggested some areas where action would help us meet the problem that I am very conscious of, which is that as a country since 1957 we have not been fulfilling our capacity. But if we want to just compare statistics we will be glad to compare them to the recession which was in effect when I took office.

Indian Purchase of Soviet Jets

Q: Mr. President, you said some time ago that Ambassador Galbraith was taking up with the Indian Government the question of the purchase of Soviet jets. Has he had any success in dissuading Mr. Nehru from making such a purchase?

The President: Well, he has talked to Mr. Nehru some time ago, some weeks ago. I don't believe he has had a recent conversation with him. Since that time, a mission has gone to London to look at Lightnings. I understand a mission has gone to Moscow to look at Migs. The Indian Government itself will make its final judgment as a sovereign power. Mr. Galbraith only attempted to suggest some of the factors which were of interest to us as a friend of India.

Nuclear Control Posts

Q: Mr. President, in your intial statement on nuclear testing, you said that it was perhaps possible to rely on fewer control posts. Does this mean that we formally plan an offer reducing the number that we've suggested or will you wait to talk about numbers only after the Soviets first accept the principle of on-site inspection?

The President: We first have to have an acceptance of the principle. Then as the scientific information is made available, a conclusion could be reached as to what would be the appropriate number of on-site inspections. In addition, because of the new scientific information, we believe that we can provide a more immediate worldwide system of control posts, at substantially less cost than the former proposals that we made, less in number but more effective in determining seismic explosion, or movement. So that we believe that this system, the new data, can provide a more effective control than we've ever had before, but it does not provide a substitute for on-site inspection because there will still be a good number of events which may occur in the Soviet Union for example, and we will not be able to detect without inspection whether these are earthquake or seismic events.

The Communications Satellite Bill

Q: Mr. President, Senate opponents of the administration's communications satellite bill contend that some provisions of this bill would infringe on your authority in the foreign affairs field. How do you feel about that?

The President: I don't agree with that. This bill was carefully drafted. We've had a number of conferences about the matter. We believe that it is the most effective way of providing for the development of a communications satellite. The responsibilities of the Federal Government are very well reserved, both in the membership of the Board, the powers of the Federal Communications Commission, the power of the State Department, the general Executive powers of the Presidency, so I must say that I think the bill is the best way to do it. The Senate itself must reach a judgment as to whether they agree.

On-Site Inspections and Control Posts

Q: For clarification, sir, if I understood you correctly, you said originally that research would now permit a reduction in the number of on-site inspections and would also permit an internationally monitored system of control posts. Does this mean, sir, that we could now forego the international control posts?

The President: No, I think the language I used was carefully chosen and is precise. Mr. Dean can develop our thoughts in more detail, but the phrase I used is the one that describes our position on that matter - internationally monitored supervised national control posts.

Q: In place of our previous proposal, sir?

The President: Well, I think that Mr. Dean can describe our proposal, but I've described it in general phraseology as I have our general position, which will be filled in by Mr. Dean at Geneva.

The Nuclear Test Ban and Production of Delivery Vehicles

Q: Mr. President, there has been some criticism by some disarmament specialists, among them Dr. Louis Sohn of Harvard, who is consultant to the Arms Control and Disarmament Agency, that far too much time and effort have been spent in trying to negotiate a nuclear test ban and too little attention has been given to the more basic problem of limiting and controlling production of delivery vehicles. Would you give us your view?

The President: We are now involved, as you know, at Geneva, on this question of general and complete disarmament. The Soviet Union has stated that it will not permit inspection of what may be left over. We can inspect what they destroy but not what they retain. As Mr. Lovett said this morning, in a particular image that we can count the bodies but not the births. So that's our particular problem, and until we are able to get an inspection of what is in production we cannot get an agreement on general and complete disarmament. But it is to secure that agreement that we're now at Geneva.

Q: Mr. President, we're getting ready to negotiate on this disarmament at Geneva and why, can you tell us, was this proposal of the United States made there not presented first to the American people fully and to the Congress rather than just to a few individuals, not even to the leaders of both House and Senate or both parties before it was made at Geneva? Won't it be much harder to vote down a treaty that results from this negotiation later on? And wouldn't it have been better for the American people to have debated this first before the proposal was made internationally?

The President: There're a number of facts in your question which I am not sure I agree with. In the first place, there has been testimony before the Joint Committee on Atomic Energy, making available to the Joint Committee the information which was secured scientifically in late June. In addition, that information, all that we had, was published in early July.

Now, we are not proposing to reach any agreement that will not be submitted to the United States Senate in accordance with our traditional procedures. I am describing our position. All the technical information which we have will be made available, so that I think that we are acting in accordance with our traditional position.

The point is that the information in regard to our improved ability to detect seismic events, this only became scientifically available to the United States really in late June. So we are attempting to get this information out as widely as possible. We will discuss it fully at Geneva. We'll make it available to the Joint Committee. Mr. Foster, our disarmament administrator, has discussed it with various members of the Congress. We've met about it in the National Security Council. We are proceeding in an orderly way and I can assure you that we are as concerned about the security of the United States − the people who are involved in this discussion − as anyone could possibly be. We're also anxious to get a treaty if we can get it. And we feel that we have struck a very appropriate balance between these two facts.

Q: Sir, wasn't it true that Mr. Foster didn't go before the Joint Committee on Atomic Energy until after the proposals had been made public in Geneva?

The President: Not the proposals, because the proposals − the first discussion of any proposals we may make were made by me this afternoon. What was made public was the new scientific information as to our ability to detect an earthquake or a nuclear event below ground, what the difference of materials might be, alluvial, granite, and all the rest. That is the only information which has been made public, because we are attempting, therefore, to bring our policy position up to date with our new scientific information. But we are not talking about − we have made available fully the scientific information through Mr. Dean and we are discussing what effect this might have on our policy. And the Members of Congress and the country will be kept fully informed about it. I quite share with you that they are entitled and must know because obviously any treaty that we would sign would require the support of two-thirds of the Senate, and therefore they are going to be kept step by step in touch with us.

Reduction of the Flow of Gold Abroad

Q: Mr. President, can you tell us any recent steps that have been taken to reduce the flow of gold abroad?

The President: Any recent steps? A good many recent steps have been taken involving negotiations between the Under Secretary of the Treasury, Mr. Roosa, and the foreign banks. In addition, as you know, I made a comment about the efforts which Secretary McNamara was making to lessen our balance of payments for our military from $3 billion to $1.6 billion and we hope, in a year, to a billion a year, our loss there. We are tying our aid more and more, and we will bring it this year, the loss in dollars in aid, from $1.3 billion to $800 million, and we are - in the tax bill we are providing additional provisions in the tax bill which will make it less attractive to take dollars abroad. And this is a matter under very constant concern and, as I said before, we hope by the end of next year to bring our balance of payments into balance.

I think we discussed last week why drastic remedies of the type of devaluation would be self-defeating, and would not be employed by this Government. I think that if we proceed on the basis that we are, that by the end of next year, if our exports maintain their present rise and our wage-price structure remains the same as it is now, relative to Europe, that we can bring this into balance.

American Strategy on Nuclear Engagement

Q: Mr. President, after the resignation of General Norstad was announced, there have been many speculations in Europe that there may occur a complete change in American strategy going as far as to a nuclear engagement. Could you comment on that?

The President: I can't understand possibly how anyone could come to that conclusion. General Norstad requested that he be permitted to resign. He'd held the position for a great many years. The Chairman of our Joint Chiefs, General Lemnitzer - there may be those who for their own reasons wish to put this story out, but there is no evidence for it. General Lemnitzer will carry on the policies of the United States Government the same way as General Norstad has done. So those rumors are wholly unfounded, wholly untrue, and the slightest check by those who transmit them through Europe would demonstrate that they are unfounded. I can assure you we are continuing our defense of Europe. And I've said before, we cannot maintain the defense of Europe without also maintaining our nuclear strength on which this adminstration has spent a good deal of additional funds. So I can assure you that the stories are untrue, though I have some idea of where they come from and why.

Developments in Peru

Q: Mr. President, can you tell us if you consider the developments in Peru encouraging toward the point of our recognizing the new government there? And also, is there any comment you'd like to make on the discussion of your policy toward Peru?

The President: We are encouraged by the release of President Prado. We are encouraged by the fact that civil liberties have been restored. We've been encouraged by the assurances of the junta that free elections would be carried out in a period of time, and we are anxious that some clear assurances be given that there will be - that they will abide by the results of these elections.

We had relations with President Prado's government. When that government was overthrown and the President imprisoned, it was quite natural that we would reexamine our relations. That reexamination is going on and we have been encouraged by those signs which I've named and we hope that there will be other evidences that there will be a return to constitutional free government, which is the object of the Alliance for Progress.

Discovery of Fallout in Utah Milk

Q: Mr. President, with regard to the fallout which has been discovered in milk in Utah, has your administration planned any precautionary steps, and specifically, will there be more air bursts in Nevada?

The President: Any radioactive materials that come from the tests in Nevada have been dissipated, or if they have not completely been dissipated, will be very immediately.

Now, secondly, I am not aware of any futher test - in fact, there are not any further tests in Nevada.

Progress of the Alliance for Progress

Q: Mr. President, although there are not going to be any celebrations on this first anniversary of the Alianza para el Progreso, do you feel satisfied or pleased with the rate of progress so far obtained by the Alianza, by the Alliance for Progress?

The President: Measured by all that has to be done, I think we have to do much better, but that is the point of Ambassador Moscoso's determination to mark the day rather than celebrate it.

The President's Opinion on Pharmaceuticals

Q: Mr. President, is it correct to infer from your earlier remarks on drugs that you would like to see reversed the present situation whereby pharmaceutical houses are able to distribute drugs on an experimental basis through doctors without Federal approval?

The President: I would like to see - I think that we can administratively improve the control of the Food and Drug Administration, of the distribution of drugs during this period. So, in answer to your question, while the worst - I would say that generally I am in favor of a great degree of Federal supervision.

Now I want to say, on the other hand, that of course we've had remarkable medical progress from these drugs. There is - the fact is that this drug was tested on animals, and at least for a year, my information is there were no signs of deformity. Very recently, in a test there was. But we cannot always get a clear indication from animals. These tests may show up as being wholly safe, and after very careful work these may be distributed with due warnings, and there may be hazards in them. But I think we have to improve, which we can administratively, this phase of our procedures.

But I do want to say that all of our advances, I suppose, require some risk. In this case, however, fortunately, due to the very fine work of a doctor, we were spared a good deal of disaster which, as I've said, the Germans have experienced. But in answer to your question, I think we ought to be tougher on this phase of it.

Reporter: Thank you, Mr. President.

[1]Item 93 of the *Public Papers of the President.*

THE PRESIDENT'S NEWS CONFERENCE OF

AUGUST 22, 1962

The President: Good afternoon. I have several announcements to make.

First, two of our nuclear powered submarines have completed an historic rendezvous under the polar ice pack, and then surfaced together through a small opening in the ice at the North Pole. The submarines - the U.S.S. Skate from the Atlantic Fleet and the U.S.S. Sea Dragon from the Pacific Fleet - are now on their way back to the United States. This is the first time that two of our submarines have worked together in this manner under the Arctic ice pack and I want to congratulate all those who were involved in this exceptional technical feat.

Secondly, this Congress in the next weeks has an opportunity to write what I think will be a very impressive record, for there are many bills of great importance now pending before the Congress. I want to take this opportunity to stress five particularly important measures which will be acted upon very shortly:

First, the farm bill, which the Senate passed today, gives us an opportunity to bring some sense and reason and control into an area which has been marked by excesses and chaos in recent years. It extends for another year our presently successful feed grain program while repealing the 1958 Benson feed grain approach, and gives us our new wheat program essentially as we originally requested it, and it contains other important steps toward a wiser use of our land resources and rural area development.

Secondly, the drug bill, which has been tightened in the Senate Judiciary Committee, much along the lines that I requested, will give us every safeguard to protect our American citizens.

And third, a constitutional amendment to outlaw the poll tax in Federal elections will be taken by the House of Representatives on Monday, where a two-thirds vote is essential if we are to finally eliminate this outmoded and arbitrary bar to voting. American citizens should not have to pay to vote.

Fourth, the trade expansion bill, the most important measure to be considered by many a Congress, must pass the Senate with bipartisan support as it did the House and without restrictive amendments that will make it impossible for us to bargain for our factories and our farms into the Common Market.

Fifth, and finally, the U.N. bond issue, as I have said many times, poses a test of this Nation's good faith in supporting the peacekeeping efforts of the U.N. and opposing those who try to starve it to death. This bill has had overwhelming bipartisan support in the Senate and in the House Foreign Affairs Committee. But this is one of the issues that is not Democratic or Republican, but is American. This bill will help the U.N. and it will help the United States. It will save us money in the long run and will help keep the peace, which is most important. I'm confident it will be approved by all thoughtful members of both parties in the House.

QUESTIONS

Russian Abandonment of Commandant's Office in Berlin

Q: Mr. President, Russia has announced the abolition of its commandant's office in Berlin. I wonder if you can give us your appraisal of the meaning and importance of this action and what you think the Western Powers should do as a result of this action.

The President: Well, I believe the Department of State has already issued a statement and in that statement they indicated we're going to be consulting with the British and the French who also bear a responsibility. I think our statement indicated, certainly our view, that the Soviet action cannot unila-terally affect our rights, which are quadripartite in Berlin. This will be the central theme of our response.

Foreign Aid to Countries Doing Business with the Soviet Bloc

Q: Mr. President, I wondered, could you tell us your general feeling about countries which receive aid from the United States and still do business with the Communist bloc nations? Specifically, do you think a country receiving aid from us has a moral right to engage in business deals for military or econ-omic purposes with the Communist bloc countries?

The President: Well, I think that nearly every country that I know of en-gages in economic deals with the Communist bloc. There are other countries which we have for a long period of time assisted which have also received – which we assisted economically – which have received assistance of various kinds from the Communist bloc. So that I don't think it's a moral issue. I think we have to make a judgment as to what serves our interest, whether the country is attempting to maintain its freedom, whether the country is pursuing policies which are not inimical to the long-range interests of the United States.

We make that independent judgment on each occasion. I know that I can judge the countries that you are thinking of, and I would say that at least in one country, which I assume you are thinking of, we have felt that the assist-ance which we have given them has helped maintain a very significant country – if you're thinking of the question of India. While the matter of military assistance has not been settled as I understand it in India, most of their assistance in the past having come from the British, it is an extremely large country, 450 million, extremely important; it is free, it is non-Communist. It has indicated it is going to attempt to maintain its freedom, and therefore I think it's in our interest to support it because if it ever passed behind the Iron Curtain, if the present efforts to maintain democracy should fail, then I would think the cause of freedom would have been very adversely affected not only in Asia but all through the underdeveloped world.

The Race in Space

Q: Mr. President, the Soviet Union's latest exploit, the launching of two men within 24 hours, seems to have caused a good deal of pessimism in the Uni-ted States. You hear people say that we're now a poor second to Russia. How do you size up the situation, Mr. President, for the present and the future?

The President: We are second to the Soviet Union in long-range boosters. I have said from the beginning – we started late, we've been behind. It's a tremendous job to build a booster of the size that the Soviet Union is talking about, and also have it much larger size, which we are presently engaged in the Saturn program. So we are behind and we're going to be behind for a while. But I believe that before the end of this decade is out, the United States will be ahead. But it's costing us a tremendous amount of money. We're presently making a tremendous effort in research and development. But we just might as well realize that when we started late, last year as you know, we made a decision to go to the moon, with bipartisan support. And it's going to take us quite a while to catch up with a very advanced program which the Soviets are directing and there's no indication the Soviets are going to quit.

So there they started with a lead and they determined to maintain it. We've started late, and we are trying to not only - we're trying to overtake them, and I think by the end of the decade we will, but we're in for some further periods when we are going to be behind. And anybody who attempts to suggest that we're not behind misleads the American people.

We're well behind, but we're making a tremendous effort. We increased after I took office, after 4 months, we increased the budget for space by 50 percent over that of my predecessor. The fact of the matter is that this year we submitted a space budget which was greater than the combined eight space budgets of the previous 8 years. So this country is making a vast effort which is going to be much bigger next year and the years to come and represents a very heavy burden upon us all. But we might as well recognize that we're behind now and we're going to be for a while. But what we've got to do is concentrate our efforts. And I think we're doing that, but we can always do better.

Q: Mr. President, in that same area, would you agree with Senator Cannon and others who believe that the space program not only should be expanded, but should be militarized in something like a Manhattan District crash program?

The President: Well, now, we are spending, for military purposes in space, three times what we were in 1960, about $1,500 million. The two - at least at present - the two important points that should be kept in mind are, one, the ability to build a large booster which can put a larger satellite into the atmosphere. That is being done. NASA is doing that, although there has been, of course, under the Titan III contract, a booster program for the military.

In addition, the guidance, navigation, etc., that's extremely important. That we are making a major effort in. So that I recognize that there are those who oppose this program and then suddenly a month later say we ought to suddenly go ahead on a different basis.

The fact of the matter is that 40 percent of the R and D funds in this country are being spent for space. And that's a tremendous amount of money and a tremendous concentration of our scientific effort.

I'm not saying that we can't always do better, but I think the American people ought to understand the billions of dollars we're talking about, which I believe a month ago was mentioned as a great boondoggle. I think it's important, vital, and is a great interrelationship between space, military, and the peaceful use of space. But we're concentrating on the peaceful use of space which will also help us protect our security if that becomes essential.

Thurgood Marshall's Nomination

Q: Mr. President, it's been almost a year since you nominated Thurgood Marshall for the Federal Bench. Senator Keating of New York charges that the subcommittee hearing this nomination is delaying it by ridiculous and unlawyerlike questions. Do you share the Senator's view of the holdup on this confirmation?

The President: I think it has been much too much delayed. I am confident, in fact I am sure, that the Senate will not adjourn, and I've been given those assurances, that the Senate will not adjourn without action being taken by the United States Senate on the Thurgood Marshall appointment. When it does come for a vote, and it will, it is my judgment the Senate will confirm him overwhelmingly.

In regard to Senator Keating, I do think it's interesting to point out that there were seven Circuit Court vacancies during the previous administration which the Senators from New York had something to say about the appointments to those, and Thurgood Marshall was not nominated on any of those occasions.

The President's Letter to Chancellor Adenauer

Q: Mr. President, could you say anything about the letter which you have written to Chancellor Adenauer, which was delivered yesterday? There is a certain difficulty here for us because so often in the exchange of these letters, the word of it first comes out in Bonn, and it necessarily reflects the German point of view, and we're somewhat at a disadvantage to present the point of view of our own Government.

The President: No, I wrote Chancellor Adenauer a letter. It was a general statement of our policy and of our interest in satisfactory relations with the West German people, and also an attempt to respond to some of the rumors which had been discussed at a previous press conference in regard to possible changes in strategic policy or tactical policies by the United States in Western Europe. Those are the matters we dealt with, and I think that it would be - I don't think it's customary to release a letter from the sender to the receiver. I don't know whether the letter is going to be released, but I think it is in the hands of the receiver.

Military Significance of the Soviet Space Shot

Q: Mr. President, would you say what military significance, if any, you see in the recent Soviet double orbiting, and also in view of the fact that we're spending about twice as much money for civilian space activity as for military activity, do you expect any possible change in this ratio?

The President: We're considering in the Defense Department whether there are further steps that might be taken to protect our security. But I want to emphasize that the distinction which is made by some, and perhaps suggested by your question, doesn't seem to me to be wholly applicable. The important things at the present time, as I said, are the size of the booster and the size of satellite, and the navigational control. Now, those are carried on by both the Defense Department and by NASA. But of course the information is interrelated; and also whatever skills we acquire in those three areas are interrelated and serve many purposes.

Q: Mr. President, do you see any military significance?

The President: Well, of course, we're not quite clear as to what the military significance will be, because at the present time it is possible to send a missile from one country to another with a warhead, and with a great degree of accuracy. But it's very possible that there will develop military significance. And it is for that reason that the military program is being carried on - $1.5 billion. And there is also of course the benefits we get from the civilian space program, upon which we're spending many billions of dollars, in these three areas which can tie in, if necessary, into the military field.

The Possibility of Talks with Khrushchev

Q: Mr. President, it's been well over a year now since you met Chairman Khrushchev at Vienna. The Berlin affair seems to be blowing up towards a cold winter of some sort. There are rumors that he may come to the U.N. this fall. If in fact he did, do you think it would be useful about that time for you to have another talk with him?

The President: Well, I think it would be unwise to attempt to make a judgment. I don't know whether he's coming. We've received no information about it. Of course, if he did come, he would be - I would hope I would have a chance to talk with him. But I haven't heard that he is coming and we have no information to that effect. But I hope to see - whatever heads of government that come in the fall for the U.N. session I would hope to see.

Travels Around the Country

Q: There have been reports, sir, that you are considering some more non-political journeys around the country, specifically this time to the urban centers such as Chicago, Cleveland, and Philadelphia, to deal with urban renewal problems. Can you comment on these reports?

The President: Well, we haven't made any judgment about it, though the matter has been considered. I thought the trip, the nonpolitical trip, of last weekend was useful. In addition, in early September we have the anniversary of the Housing Act, but we haven't made any judgment as to whether it should be appropriately celebrated by such a trip.

Racial Representation in the Administration

Q: Mr. President, at the present time there are 97 ambassadors, of which 2 are Negroes. In view of the fact that this is the same number of the previous administration and you've made significant strides in the domestic field as far as rights are concerned, how do you feel about the fact that it is only 2 percent and do you think this should be changed?

The President: Yes, I think we should, definitely. Definitely we should, not only in the higher ambassadorial level but all through the Department as well as the AID agency. I quite agree we have to do better.

The Gubernatorial Election in New York

Q: Mr. President, after your conference with Mayor Wagner last week, there were reports that you had agreed to endorse Robert Morgenthau as the Democratic gubernatorial nominee in New York. This, presumably, is an election of some considerable importance to you. Could you tell us, do you have a preference for this election and who he might be?

The President: No, and I wouldn't take any position on the matter until the Democratic convention meets in mid-September. I think the choice ought to be made there.

Control of the Business Community

Q: Mr. President, referring to the recent disclosures by Wright Patman, do you think that the Ford or Rockefeller Foundation or any other tax-exempt foundation should be able to control the ownership of a large segment of the business community by owning manufacturing plants and retail establishments and such?

The President: Well, Mr. Patman made several points. Of course, he was critical of some foundations which are being used as tax dodges or for the purposes which you suggested. Other foundations, certainly the two that you named, of course, that's not true. I think his only point there was the rather enormous amount of money contained in both foundations and, therefore, the effect that this might have upon the economy. But I was most particularly interested in the first point, which is whether some foundations are being used as a tax dodge or as a method of avoiding taxes and all the rest. And I think that what we are now examining is whether this is a question of tighter administration by the Internal Revenue, which Mr. Caplin is looking into, or whether we need new legislation.

On the other hand, I think it fairness to point out that this is an extraordinary development, these foundations, and have done a tremendous job in wide ranges in a most efficient way. So I think we want to be fair, but we want to be sure to catch those who are penalizing the others.

Use of U.N. Bonds

Q: Sir, I wonder if you could tell us whether or not the $100 million in U.N. bonds which you want the Congress to vote, if you can guarantee that that will not be used for military action against the Katanga - in Katanga - with a repetition of some of the atrocities that have been verified by such eye witnesses as the reporter Smith Hempstone and others.

The President: Well, the purpose of the loan, as you know, is to prevent the United Nations from collapsing, which it will economically unless we're able to secure this special fund, which will come partly from the United States and partly from the other countries. The long-range financing of the United Nations we put on a sounder basis, we hope, as a result of the decision of the Court, the World Court.

Now, on the question of the Katanga, I have supported the effort of the U.N. to prevent a complete chaos and dissolution in the Congo which, in my opinion, would lead to the setting up of a radical, possibly undemocratic government in the Congo. So that I feel the most important step now that can be taken by Mr. Adoula, Mr. Tshombe, joining together in a constitutional arrangement which will provide for an accord in the Congo.

But I can just assure you that if the U.N. is denied funds, it will mean the collapse of peaceful efforts not only in the Congo but in many parts of the world. The recent agreement over West Irian was carried on under the auspices of U Thant. I would think that this money is vitally important, and I cannot accept such an immediate identification as your question suggests between this fund and atrocities.

The Stockpiling Investigation

Q: Mr. President, some months ago from this platform you announced the stockpiling investigation. It's now well along. What do you think of the case that the committee has made out against Mr. Humphrey?

The President: I thought that everyone should read Senator Engle's speech. I thought it was clear and indicated that this matter should be looked into further.

Omission of the 1962 Tax Bill

Q: Mr. President, was there any significance in your omission of the 1962 tax bill in your list of desirable legislation? Does it mean that ———

The President: Oh, no, no. I was just thinking really of the bills coming up in the next 7 days. I was not attempting to set out a program for the Congress, which I did suggest in my speech a week ago.[1] I'm just talking about the bills which will be before the Congress within the next week.

Q: Is that coming up now?

The President: But the tax bill, if it comes up next week in the Senate, definitely, of course, is one of our priority items.

But I mentioned the trade bill, because it seems to be - it's in a very important stage now, being considered by the committee. What concerns me most about the trade bill is we'll get a trade bill, but we may get a bill so limited, which is so circumscribed on negotiating power that we will have the shadow of a bill and not the substance. And to attempt to protect our markets abroad, which in this last few months we've had a tremendous balance - export balance over imports. If we fail to get the power that we need it will be a very bad blow to us all. So that's the reason I separated that from the tax bill, which I'm hopeful will pass also.

Q: Do you think the withholding is an important part of the tax bill?

The President: Very desirable. I think, as you know, they have an alternate language suggested by Senator Byrd, which will bring in some money. I don't think it's as effective as the withholding, however, and I'm sorry that the Senate has not, or at least the Senate committee did not accept withholding. Sooner or later we will. I'm confident if we don't do it in this session we're going to, because it is quite logical that those who receive money should pay their taxes in the same way that people that receive wages find their taxes withheld.

The Missile Strike

Q: Sir, are you going to take any further action to end the missile strike at Huntsville?

The President: As you know, the National Labor Relations Board is involved with an injunction there, the Missile Committee - Mr. Goldberg is involved. I am very hopeful those men will go back to work. I think it is a great mistake for them personally, and also it is a great loss to the country. The strike should be ended definitely. They all should return.

The President and Edward Kennedy's Candidacy

Q: Mr. President, the National Committee for an Effective Congress in a recent statement said that the candidacy of Edward M. Kennedy for the Senate in Massachusetts has hurt you personally politically, and has hurt the Democratic Party nationally. Now the suggestion is that you could have headed off your brother's candidacy if you had wished. Do you have any comment on this?

The President: Well, I think the people of Massachusetts can make a more effective judgment for a more effective Congress than even this committee. And I think they will.

Economic Myths and Realities

Q: Mr. President, 2 months ago you invited the Nation to join a great debate on economic myths and realities in pursuit of fresh ideas and fresh thinking. Could you tell us, first, if you're satisfied with the response and, second, if you have any plans or proposals for uplifting that debate?

The President: No. I think we can always - we need a good deal more light on it, this matter.

I think that the Joint Economic Committee hearings have been very useful. The discussions by not only Americans but by Europeans of our fiscal and monetary policies have been very beneficial. I think that there's a good deal more consideration being given to them now than there has been in the past. We can do a lot more about it. I intend to continue to discuss what the proper mix should be under certain economic conditions. But it's quite a long struggle to try to change the thinking which has been driven into us for so many years. The concept - I talked to a distinguished banker the other day, who was one of those who most strongly believed that the fiscal deficit of 1962 was going to bring inflation in the winter and spring of 1962. Now he agrees that of course that didn't happen. So we've got to attempt to make more successful judgments and try to determine what should be both our interest rate policy and also our debt policy in times of economic slowdown.

Former President Hoover's Suggestion

Q: Mr. President, what do you think of former President Hoover's suggestion that a council of free nations be formed to supplement the United Nations and to act when Communist obstruction prevents the U.N. from acting?

The President: Well, we've been attempting to do that, of course, through the OAS, NATO, SEATO, and SENTO, and I think that we could certainly consider means of improving those agencies. I think one of the problems which we now have is how to improve the NATO, the North Atlantic Treaty Council, OECD, and all the rest, and how we can improve the functioning of the OAS.

It isn't really a question of a new organization as much as breathing new life and a community spirit into the organizations that we have. But I thought President Hoover's speech was worthy of a good deal of thought by us.

Communist Troops and Supplies in Cuba

Q: Mr. President, do you have any information or indication that Communist-bloc troops or new supplies of any kind have been landed in Cuba recently?

The President: Yes, new supplies definitely, in large quantities. Troops? We do not have information, but an increased number of technicians.

Q: What is the significance of this, in your opinion?

The President: Well, we are examining it now.

Q: Do you think it is aimed at any other Central American country?

The President: No, there is no evidence of that. And we're not talking about - as far as the numbers - we're not talking about the kind of entrants in numbers which would provide support for the sort of operation you suggested. What we are talking about are supplies and technicians of a rather intensive quantity in recent weeks.

Request for Peace Corps Assistance by the Acoma Indians

Q: Mr. President, the Acoma Indians of New Mexico recently asked the Government to send Peace Corps technicians to their reservation. They were turned down. In view of the extensive efforts being made abroad, why can't we extend this kind of service to Indian groups within our own borders that are every bit as depressed as some of the foreign groups that we're helping?

The President: Well, I am not familiar with that. I think - the Peace
Corps was set up to be sent abroad. Mr. Shriver and others have suggested
setting up a Peace Corps at home and we have now been looking into that. But
I haven't heard of this proposal. Whether we should particularly do it with
the Indians I think is worth looking at.

The Fall Campaign

*Q: Mr. President, can you tell us how much time you expect to be devoting
to the campaign this fall?*

The President: No, I can't, but I will be devoting some of my time in October and in late September.

Results in the Recent Congressional Races

*Q: Mr. President, speaking of non-political matters, as you were a minute
ago, the recent defeat of Congressman Frazier in Tennessee and the very
close call of Congressman Loser have been blamed by some of the labor groups on
their opposition to your bill on medicare through the higher social security
taxes. Are you pleased with these results? Do you agree with that analysis
and do you think you'll use this issue a little bit more in the other races?*

The President: I've always said that I thought health care for the aged
would be a very important issue this fall, and that the American people would
make a judgment. I think that that will certainly be one of the factors they
will take into consideration in deciding which members they will support. I
think this bill is essential, very valuable, very important, very responsible,
and I think it will be an important issue in the fall. And I think it's been
proven already to be.

Travel to Europe and U.S. Dependents

*Q: Mr. President, I understand that airlines between the United States and
Europe are already heavily booked for U.S. tourist travel to Europe as soon as
the lower fares go into effect in the fall. My questions are two:*

*First, are you concerned about this heavy spending and what it's going to
do to our gold reserves for the last quarter of the year; and, two, do you
think that service families will be happy to be separated from their military
husband-fathers who are again being sent to Europe, this time for a 6-month
tour, starting in October, when they read of other Americans free spending in
Europe while they are being kept home to save the gold drain?*

The President: I think it is very difficult for a good many of them to
understand the difference between the burdens and obligations put on those in
the public service and the freedom which is available to those in private life.
We lose a billion dollars a year in our balance of payments between what we
spend abroad as tourists and what we spend - what tourists spend here. But
Americans move freely and I think we have to do the best we can to bring our
balance of payments into balance.

We're asking the servicemen to accept this sacrifice. We've not attempted
to limit Americans going abroad, and I don't think that it would be desirable.
We're trying to emphasize the freedom of goods to move, people to move, and
all the rest, capital to move, and we are hopeful, however, as I've said before, that by the end of 1963 we'll have brought our balance of payments into
sufficient balance to permit Amrican troops greater freedoms than they now have
in this regard.

Supplies Going to Cuba

Q: Mr. President, you spoke of the increased supplies going to Cuba. What countries are they going there from?

The President: Oh, the bloc.

Stockpiling Investigation and Profits of the Hanna Nickel Company

Q: Mr. President, would you comment on George Humphrey's charge that the stockpiling investigation is a stab at the back of President Eisenhower, and also do you think that the profits made by his Hanna Nickel Company are the unconscionable profits that you referred to back in January?

The President: Well, they are extremely large profits with very little risk to the company - extremely large profits. Now of course, the Hanna Company, itself, was investigated, not Mr. Humphrey as a responsible official of the Hanna Company, so I don't really see how - I can quite understand the desire of some witnesses to identify themselves with President Eisenhower or to limit the investigation by charging that it's an attack on President Eisenhower, but I think the Congress ought to do its job.

There are billions and billions involved in this stockpiling and I think it's important that the American people know how much was paid and who made the money out of it and that's what's being done in this case. And there'll be other cases coming up after the Hanna case, because there are other very large profits involved by a good many other people.

The Nomination of Governor Almond

Q: Mr. President, 4 months ago you nominated former Governor Almond of Virginia to the U.S. Court of Customs and Patent Appeals. Since that time the Senate Judiciary Committee has done nothing whatever towards his confirmation. I wonder if you will comment on that situation, and also if you will say whether you plan to make a recess appointment if the Senate fails to act?

The President: Well, I don't quite understand why the Senate is failing to act. Governor Almond is a distinguished Governor of Virginia. It was my understanding when his name was sent up there that there was no objection by the Senators involved. I regret very much that the Senate isn't acting. I hope it will before the Senate has ended. I will make a judgment on what we do if it doesn't act at that time. But I'm still hopeful that the Senate will act because I think Governor Almond would be a very good judge.

The Economic Survey in Indonesia

Q: As a result of your agreement with President Sukarno, Mr. President, you have sent an economic survey team to Indonesia known as the Humphrey mission. Would you comment on the content or recommendations of the Humphrey report?

The President: No. I think we better wait until the matter has been examined by the Government.

Reporter: Thank you, Mr. President.

[1]Item 328 of the *Public Papers of the President*

THE PRESIDENT'S NEWS CONFERENCE OF

AUGUST 29, 1962

The President: Good afternoon. I have several announcements to make.

I regret to announce that Associate Justice Frankfurter has retired from regular active service on the Supreme Court. He has served in the Court for 23 years, and for many years before that had an illustrious career as a lawyer and teacher. During his service on the Court, the direction of the law has been channeled by many important decisions which he has rendered. He has always been a vital force in directing those decisions. Few judges have made as significant and lasting impression upon the law. Few persons have made so important a contribution to our legal traditions and literature. Now regard for his health has compelled him to take a less active part in the Court's labors, and we shall miss him.

To the vacancy created by Justice Frankfurter's retirement, I intend to appoint Secretary Goldberg. Secretary Goldberg will bring to the Court a wealth of experience gained from the active practice of law for over 30 years. He has had an enviable record of accomplishment at the bar and his character, temperament, and ability superbly qualify him for service on the Court. I believe that his scholarly approach to the law, combined with his deep understanding of our economic and political systems, will make him a valuable member of the Supreme Court. His place as an adviser and as head of the Department of Labor will be difficult to fill, but I am confident that he will find an equally wide opportunity for public service in his new position.

In Geneva this morning the Soviet representative proposed that agreement should be reached on a cutoff time for all nuclear weapon tests and that this date should be set as of January 1, 1963. I'm happy to say that the United States Government regards this as a reasonable target date and would like to join with all interested parties in a maximum effort to conclude effective agreements which can enter force on next New Year's Day. To accomplish this purpose the governments involved must accelerate their negotiations looking toward an agreed treaty.

For our part in the United States, such an agreed treaty must be presented to the Senate for consent to ratification. We therefore have no time to lose. The world will welcome an agreement that a way should be found to stop all nuclear testing at the end of this year. But I must point out again that in order to end testing, we must have workable international agreements, gentlemen's agreements and moratoria do not provide the type of guarantees that are necessary. They do not give assurance against an abrupt renewal of testing by unilateral action. This is the lesson of the Soviet Government's tragic decision to renew testing just a year ago. Nor can such informal arrangements give any assurance against secret underground testing. That is why we must have a definite agreement with reasonable and adequate assurance. The United States cannot be a party to any renewal of false hopes which the Soviet Government shattered last September. The two treaties now before the Geneva conference have been prepared with care to meet the technical necessities of an effective test ban. If the Soviet Government will accept a serious and formal agreement in either form, a real downward turn in the arms race is possible. The United States Government for its part will spare no effort to this end.

Finally, I am very happy to announce and express great pleasure that the Schola Cantorum of the University of Arkansas won first prize for a 40-voice choral group at the Arezzo International Polyphonic Group contest in Italy. This is the first time this contest has ever been won by an American group.

They were sent by private citizens. The prize of 300,000 lira was presented by President Segni and Prime Minister Fanfani. We are inviting them to the White House at the Rose Garden at 12 noon, September 4, and we are very proud of them.

QUESTIONS

Meat and Grain Prices

Q: Mr. President, how do you feel about the prospects of the National Farmers Organization holding meat and grain off the market until processors promise to pay higher prices? Do you think, for example, the farmers have the same rights as an industrial union to strike and thus deprive consumers of their product?

The President: Well, there's no evidence that they are planning to deprive consumers of their products. What they would like to do is get a higher price for their products and it is a fact, of course, that farm income is low. Last year it was $2 billion above the figure of 1960, the highest it has been in 9 years, but farmers are very - particularly those that live on small farms, work a very hard day, and are paid a relatively low wage.

This kind of an effort has been tried, in the twenties and the thirties and other occasions, and it's not been successful because there are so many farmers. They are so separated that it's not been possible to have them together present a bargaining position, and it is because of that that the Federal Government has entered into the matter. So I could not speculate on what their success will be.

Campaigning in the South

Q: Mr. President, we were told the other day that Wilkes Thrasher of Chattanooga had been in to see you and that you were inclined to support his candidacy for Congress from Tennessee. Today we had an announcement that he is on the American delegation that's going down to observe, or help Trinidad celebrate its independence. I was wondering if this constitutes your idea of support or whether you have any plans, perhaps, to do a little political or nonpolitical campaigning in the South?

The President: No, this does not constitute the action which I would hope to take to support his candidacy, this visit this weekend. This is a nonpolitical trip of his. As far as coming to Tennessee, I've no plans as yet and in fact, I haven't worked out my schedule for any State. But I support his candidacy.

Consultations with Khrushchev

Q: Mr. President, the United States has been urging four-power consultations in order to reduce tensions in Berlin. In this connection there have been reports of a foreign ministers meeting in advance of the General Assembly and also there has been speculation that you may personally meet with Mr. Khrushchev at the U.N. Would you give us your views on this, please?

The President: Yes. On the first matter there will be a meeting of the foreign ministers before the meeting of the General Assembly. It's been agreed to in prinicple; the time and location has not been set.

On the second matter, I think I responded last week to the question of Mr. Khrushchev's coming. We have no information and I've nothing really to add to what I said last week on this matter.

Secret Nuclear Tests

Q: Mr. President, some time ago you spoke about the problem of dealing with preparations of nuclear tests which can be carried on in a secret society to our disadvantage, as you pointed out. Can you tell us what has happened to this problem in these current negotiations?

The President: We have indicated that if we could get an across the board agreement which would include a cessation of atmospheric tests and underground tests with adequate inspection for the underground tests, that we would feel that our security would be advanced, and we would accept that.

If there is only an atmospheric test ban which does not require inspection, of course, then other underground tests would continue. Quite obviously, the first agreement is the most desirable one. If we can't get that because of the Soviet Union's reluctance to permit us to have an effective inspection system, then we would like to get the second, because that would have an effect on the arms race and it would also have an effect, of course, on the problem of radiation. In that case, of course, underground testing would be permitted and we believe that that would give us sufficient assurance against the kind of event which happened last September.

Pornographic Material in the Mails

Q: Mr. President, a recent decision of the Supreme Court said that the Postmaster General does not have the authority to keep pornographic material out of the United States mails except in a limited way, and the most dreadful stuff is coming into our homes into the hands of our children, brought by the United States mails. Now, have you or will you talk with the Attorney General and the Postmaster General as to how this can be remedied?

The President: Well, the statutes on the distribution of pornographic literature are well, I am sure, known. There's always been a problem, of course, of what is pornography and what is not. And the courts have made judgments in regard to several well-known books recently which some people regard as pornographic and others regard as great literature. I would not make the judgment today.

I think it is a problem, not only in the mails but on the magazines, and it's a matter of concern for parents. I don't think that the Post Office can be expected to do anything but carry out the laws, nor can the Attorney General, and the laws, which are interpreted by the courts, are quite clear.

The Berlin Situation

Q: Mr. President, in connection with Berlin, there have been reports that the Soviets are interested in holding a four-power meeting, that is, a meeting of the four occupying powers in Berlin, to discuss the Berlin situation. Have you seen any indications of this?

The President: No, I'm not familiar with any proposal by the Soviet Union to discuss - perhaps you'd repeat exactly what it is ——

Q: There have been indications or there have been reports that the Soviets are interested in a four-power meeting.

The President: No, I have seen nothing about that. I've seen no recent proposal by the Soviet Union that there should be a four-power conference in Berlin to discuss the future of Berlin. We've had no indication that the Soviet Union has made that proposal.

Edward Kennedy in Massachusetts

Q: Sir, your brother is campaigning for the Senate on a slogan that he can do more for the State of Massachusetts. Does this imply that if he were elected, he would have more advantages as a Senator than other Members of the Senate?

The President: No. I think what he assumes is - as a matter of fact, I believe that the slogan is very similar to the one that I used in 1952, and we worked very hard for Massachusetts. I think he thinks that he can work very hard for Massachusetts and do more for it than the other candidates. I don't read any more into it than that. And I'm sure other candidates feel that they can do more. Only the people of Massachusetts, fortunately, can make the judgment, not the Republican press.

Decision on the Foreign Aid Bill

Q: Mr. President, the decision of the House leaders to put off consideration of your foreign aid bill until September 19 is being interpreted as a sign that it is weak and in some danger of losing. Is this your attitude?

The President: I know the hazard in committee, but that has happened before. There are two primaries next week and we have the problem of the U.N. bonds, so it's really a scheduling matter, not a question of attempting to delay its coming up. I would say I can imagine nothing more shortsighted than to cut the heart out of this program, as some people wish to do. I was looking at some figures today which showed that the Soviet Union had given in economic and military assistance to one country, Indonesia, over $300 million in the last 12 months. They are giving, as we all know, substantial military and economic assistance to Cuba, as well as many other countries. Now, here are these countries, particularly those in Latin America, which have many economic, serious economic problems, those countries in Africa which are newly emerging, those countries along the Soviet Union border beginning with Greece, Turkey, Iran, Pakistan, India, Thailand, and others, South Viet-nam, many of them are hard pressed, South Korea, the Republic of China - they depend upon the United States to assist them in maintaining their freedom. Now we have an appropriation for defense, an appropriation for the Atomic Energy Commission. It seems to me to be the height of folly to appropriate these large sums of money for military organization, and let these very vital countries pass into the Communist bloc. I find it very ironical that those who make the strongest speeches against the Communist movements are the ones who want to cut this program the hardest, which is the most valuable weapon immediately that we have on the front lines against the Communist advance. This is a position which I've held, which President Eisenhower holds, and President Truman before him. I can assure any member of the Congress, or any citizen sitting here, this is a very vital program, and I would hope that it would be approached from a bipartisan point of view as it has in the past. This is completely removed from the Democratic-Republican dialog. We would not have been successful last year without help of Republican members in the House and Senate, and I'm sure that a good many of them are going to help again, because this is in the vital interests of the United States.

Inspection Against Nuclear Preparation

Q: Mr. President, could we make quite sure of the import of your remarks on inspection against preparation, because in a news conference last February you said that this would be necessary for even a ban on atmosphere tests. Were you saying just now that we do not believe that this kind of inspection against preparation is necessary?

The President: What I am suggesting is if the test agreement covered only the atmosphere, that there would be under such an agreement possible – quite obviously – a continuation of tests underground and there would be other steps which we could take under those conditions which would keep our preparations, if there was a sudden breach of the kind we had last year, which would keep our preparations in a position to protect our interests.

Mr. Justice Frankfurter

Q: Mr. President, was it when you called on Mr. Justice Frankfurter about 2 weeks ago at this home that he informed you of his intention to retire ——

The President: No.

Q: —— and could you also shed some light on when you decided to appoint Secretary Goldberg?

The President: Yes. I received a letter from the Justice. He did not discuss it with me nor did I with him. I received a letter from him yesterday and I wrote him last night, and I will release both of these letters right after this news conference. I decided after I received the Justice's letter that I would appoint Secretary Goldberg, last night, and discussed it with him on that occasion.

Senator Capehart's Allegation about Cuba

Q: Mr. President, Senator Capehart of Indiana in a speech the other day said that the Communists are sending troops into Cuba, not technicians, as you told us last week. Capehart, according to the UPI, also called for United States invasion of Cuba to stop the flow of troops and supplies. Would you comment, sir?

The President: We've no evidence of troops. And I must say that I know that this matter is of great concern to Americans and many others. The United States has obligations all around the world, including West Berlin and other areas, which are very sensitive, and, therefore, I think that in considering what appropriate action we should take, we have to consider the totality of our obligations, and also the responsibilities which we bear in so many different parts of the world.

In response to your specific question, we do not have information that troops have come into Cuba, number one. Number two, the main thrust, of course, is assistance because of the mismanagement of the Cuban economy which has brought widespread dissatisfaction, economic slowdown, agricultural failures, which have been so typical of the Communist regimes in so many parts of the world. So that I think the situation was critical enough that they needed to be bolstered up.

However, we are continuing to watch what happens in Cuba with the closest attention and will respond to - will be glad to announce any new information, if it should come, immediately.

Q: Mr. President, did you answer my question, or Capehart's suggestion that we invade Cuba? What was that answer?

The President: I'm not for invading Cuba at this time. No, I don't - the words do not have some secondary meaning. I think it would be a mistake to invade Cuba, because I think it would lead to - that it should be very - an action like that, which could be very casually suggested, could lead to very serious consequences for many people.

Soviet Involvement in Berlin

Q: Mr. President, the Soviets, as you well know, are continuing to use armored cars to transport their military personnel into West Berlin. Some persons on the scene have expressed the view that unless we object to this, it will give the Soviets additional rights in West Berlin which they have not had in the past and correspondingly reduce our rights in West Berlin. What could you tell us ——

The President: I don't hold that view at all. I don't agree with that. In my opinion, it doesn't have that effect at all.

A Guarantee for Cambodia's Neutrality

Q: Mr. President, Prince Sihanouk of Cambodia has proposed that the 14 nations involved in the Laos conference be reconvened in order to guarantee Cambodia's neutrality. How feasible is such a proposal?

The President: We are examining his proposal, and we've had conversations with officials of that government. We of course strongly support Cambodia's independence, neutrality, and the sanctity of its borders, and we would of course be glad to take any step which would advance the maintenance of those rights to which Cambodia as a sovereign power is entitled. So we are attempting to consider what step will most usefully advance the objectives which Prince Sihanouk wrote us about.

The question of the conference, and whether this would advance it, is a matter which is being considered, but his interests as expressed in the letter are our interests, and in my opinion should be the interests of other free nations.

Troops in Cuba

Q: Mr. President, I wonder if a distinction could be made with respect to the troops in Cuba. Some of us were told at the State Department the other day that there is Russian military personnel in Cuba, that these are military technicians, and are the people who are probably going to operate missiles, similar to the Nike missiles. Is this in accord ——

The President: I don't know who told you that at the State Department, that they're going to operate Nike missiles, because that information we do not have at this time. There certainly are technicians there. They may be military technicians. We don't have complete information about what's going on in Cuba, but in the sense that troops - the word "troops" is generally used, they've had a military advisory commission there for a long period of time, so there may be additional military advisory personnel there or technicians. But on the question of troops, as it's generally understood, we do not have evidence that there are Russian troops there. There is an expanded advisory and technical mission.

Q: Are there no antiaircraft missiles shipped into Cuba?

The President: We have no information as yet. That doesn't mean that there haven't been, but all I'm saying is that we have no such information as yet.

Violation of a Nuclear Test Ban Treaty

Q: Mr. President, William C. Foster, head of the Arms Control and Disarmament Agency, has said that even if an East-West nuclear test ban treaty with adequate safeguards were negotiated, there's no assurance that it will not be violated. In view of this, and the rising levels of fallout, would there be then much of a risk in signing a treaty to ban all tests in the atmosphere, in the air, outer space, and water, and undertaking then a voluntary moratorium on underground testing?

The President: Yes, there would be a great risk, because we've been through the moratorium route. I would hope we could sign the atmospheric test, which does not require inspection. The underground tests to do require inspection to determine if there's been cheating. We went that road before for 3 years, and we found while we were negotiating, the Soviet Union had been preparing for many months to test so we couldn't accept that again.

NATO Ships as Transports of Soviet Goods to Cuba

Q: Mr. President, this morning's newspapers carried reports out of Moscow to the effect that traffic from the Soviet Union to Cuba has increased so substantially that they're using ships from NATO countries to deliver some of these goods. Is this a matter you think the United States should take up with the NATO countries?

The President: Yes, definitely, definitely, and I should think that those who are associated with us would consider this matter very carefully, and consider what steps they could take to discourage it.

Q: We have up to now not asked our NATO partners?

The President: We've been in consultation with them about the matter.

Use of U.N. Bonds

Q: Sir, I wondered if you've had time this last week to figure out some means whereby we might insist that if we give money to the U.N. by bonds, buying bonds or through a contingency fund, that there's some way that we could make them guarantee that the money we give them would not be used in military action against Katanga, and also be used by troops that commit atrocities.

The President: Well, I thought we went over this road last week, but I'm glad to go over it again.

Q: You said that you had not immediately agreed with the part about atrocities, and I thought maybe this last week you might have had time to reconsider.

The President: Yes, I have thought about it, and I would say that I'd just like - I know the interest some have in Katanga, which I have always found to be interesting, but I will say that the situation in the Congo is very critical. And it's not only the matter of the Congo, of Katanga, but also the situation in the rest of the Congo, which has no funds except those that have been supplied by the United Nations and by the United States, in very limited amounts of trade, and if we are unsuccessful or if the Congolese are unsuccessful - in bringing about a union on a satisfactory basis between the Katanga and the Congo - the remainder of the Congo - you are liable to find a very critical situation in the rest of the Congo, which would be very dangerous to the free world. So I would hope that those who have enlisted on one side or another would consider the general interest of a united Congo in a peaceful non-Communist Africa, which I believe very much at issue.

Now, in regard to the U.N. bonds, I strongly support it and I think that the cause of the United States as well as the free world would be advanced if the bonds were passed and the United Nations kept going. I don't want to see the United Nations go bankrupt and all of its peacekeeping machinery go into the ash can.

The Monroe Doctrine

Q: Sir, would you tell us what the Monroe Doctrine means to you today in the light of world conditions and in Cuba?

The President: The Monroe Doctrine means what it has meant since President Monroe and John Quincy Adams enunciated it, and that is that we would oppose a foreign power extending its power to the Western Hemisphere. And that's why we oppose what is being - what's happening in Cuba today. That's why we have cut off our trade. That's why we worked in the OAS and in other ways to isolate the Communist menace in Cuba. That's why we'll continue to give a good deal of our effort and attention to it.

The Nuclear Test Ban and U.S. Security

Q: Mr. President, on the question of nuclear tests, can you explain how the security of the United States can be adequately protected by an agreement on our part 4 months hence to sign a test treaty, ban treaty, while the Soviet Union is in the middle of an extensive series of tests? Does this mean that you have determined that in this series they cannot catch up or overtake us?

The President: We do not believe that they could make sufficient progress in this series of tests to adversely affect our security, number one; and number two, if we do not get an agreement, and I would say the chances are not - I'm not sanguine about the chances of an agreement - if we do not get an agreement, the danger to the United States will be greatly increased as more and more countries develop an atomic capacity and present us with an increasing danger as the decade goes on. So in answer to your question, I believe that the quicker we can get a test agreement the better off we will be.

Q: Mr. President, did you once say that you would make a determination at the end of any Russian series as to whether there would be a need for another American series?

The President: I tried to respond that in our judgment our security would be assisted by an effective agreement if we could secure it by January 1st, or by any other date, because I consider the constant development of new and more dangerous weapons by not only the United States and the Soviet Union, but by other powers, and particularly the very strong possibility that proliferation will mark this decade if we don't get an agreement, as a matter of maximum peril to the United States, as well as the free world; and, therefore, if we can get an agreement it's in our interest and in our security.

Those who oppose an agreement should consider what our security will look like at the end of this decade if we do not have the agreement and we have the possibility of 10 or 15 countries having these weapons, and when one goes off, it may mean they all go off. So this administration will leave no stone unturned to get an agreement, if we can get it, and provide for our security on the basis which I enunciated in my original statement.

Censorship of International Telecasting and Broadcasting

Q: Mr. President, a memorandum from the FCC has been reported sent to the White House relating to censorship of international telecasting and broadcasting. Would you care to comment upon your attitude towards such censorship?

The President: I'm not familiar with it. No, I haven't seen such a memorandum.

Q: What is your attitude toward such a proposal?

The President: I'd like to see the memorandum. Then I can give you a much more responsive answer.

Use of DDT and Other Pesticides

Q: Mr. President, there appears to be growing concern among scientists as to the possibility of dangerous long-range side effects from the widespread use of DDT and other pesticides. Have you considered asking the Department of Agriculture or the Public Health Service to take a closer look at this?

The President: Yes, and I know that they already are. I think particularly, of course, since Miss Carson's book,[1] but they are examining the matter.

Talks with Governor Brown

Q: Mr. President, a day after you left California last week, the proposed debate between our Governor and Mr. Nixon blew sky high, and it's been suggested since in public speculation that you advised our Governor to avoid this kind of confrontation. As the reigning champion in this field, I wondered if you would like to tell us whether or not you did discuss this with Governor Brown and also if maybe the time has come when you would tell us what you once suggested you would have advised Mr. Nixon.

The President: No, but I will say I never did discuss the format with Governor Brown. I understand that Governor Brown is suggesting the format which was used in the '60 campaign, which was used the other night in Boston and which I think is very satisfactory. But they have to work out those details. Now I think that the best - in answer to your last, I will be glad to tell you in November.

The Extent of Participation in the Nuclear Test Ban

Q: Sir, would you explain how an agreement to be signed only by the currently existing nuclear powers could prevent the arising of other nuclear powers?

The President: Quite obviously, if other powers went ahead with testing, of course, then the agreement would cease to have very much effectiveness.

It is our hope that the signing by the major nuclear powers today will arrest the spread and not make it essential. But it is only a hope.

Reporter: Thank you, Mr. President.

[1]Rachel Carson, Silent Spring (Boston: Houghton Mifflin Co., 1962).

THE PRESIDENT'S NEWS CONFERENCE OF

SEPTEMBER 13, 1962

The President: I have a preliminary statement.

There has been a great deal of talk on the situation in Cuba in recent days both in the Communist camp and in our own, and I would like to take this opportunity to set the matter in perspective.

In the first place, it is Mr. Castro and his supporters who are in trouble. In the last year his regime has been increasingly isolated from this hemishere. His name no longer inspires the same fear or following in other Latin American countries. He has been condemned by the OAS, excluded from the Inter-American Defense Board, and kept out of the Free Trade Association. By his own monumental economic mismanagement, supplemented by our refusal to trade with him, his economy has crumbled, and his pledges for political freedom. His industries are stagnating, his harvests are declining, his own followers are beginning to see that their revolution has been betrayed.

So it is not surprising that in a frantic effort to bolster his regime he should try to arouse the Cuban people by charges of an imminent American invasion, and commit himself still further to a Soviet takeover in the hope of preventing his own collapse.

Ever since communism moved into Cuba in 1958, Soviet technical and military personnel have moved steadily onto the island in increasing numbers at the invitation of the Cuban Government.

Now that movement has been increased. It is under our most careful surveillance. But I will repeat the conclusion that I reported last week: that these new shipments do not constitute a serious threat to any other part of this hemisphere.

If the United States ever should find it necessary to take military action against communism in Cuba, all of Castro's Communist-supplied weapons and technicians would not change the result or significantly extend the time required to achieve that result.

However, unilateral military intervention on the part of the United States cannot currently be either required or justified, and it is regrettable that loose talk about such action in this country might serve to give a thin color of legitimacy to the Communist pretense that such a threat exists. But let me make this clear once again: If at any time the Communist buildup in Cuba were to endanger or interfere with our security in any way, including our base at Guantanamo, our passage to the Panama Canal, our missile and space activities at Cape Canaveral, or the lives of American citizens in this country, or if Cuba should ever attempt to export its aggressive purposes by force or by threat of force against any nation in this hemisphere, or become an offensive military base of significant capacity for the Soviet Union, then this country will do whatever must be done to protect its own security and that of its allies.

We shall be alert, too, and fully capable of dealing swiftly with any such development. As President and Commander in Chief I have full authority now to take such action, and I have asked the Congress to authorize me to call up reserve forces should this or any other crisis make it necessary.

In the meantime, we intend to do everything within our power to prevent such a threat from coming into existence.

Our friends in Latin America must realize the consequences such developments hold out for their own peace and freedom, and we shall be making further proposals to them. Our friends in NATO must realize the implications of their ships engaging in the Cuban trade.

We shall continue to work with Cuban refugee leaders who are dedicated as we are to that nation's future return to freedom. We shall continue to keep the American people and the Congress fully informed. We shall increase our surveillance of the whole Caribbean area. We shall neither initiate nor permit aggression in this hemisphere.

With this in mind, while I recognize that rash talk is cheap, particularly on the part of those who do not have the responsibility, I would hope that the future record will show that the only people talking about a war or an invasion at this time are the Communist spokesmen in Moscow and Havana, and that the American people defending as we do so much of the free world, will in this nuclear age, as they have in the past, keep both their nerve and their head.

Q: Mr. President, coupling this statement with the one of last week, at what point do you determine that the buildup in Cuba has lost its defensive character and become offensive? Would it take an overt act?

The President: I think if you read last week's statement[1] and the statement today, I made it quite clear, particularly in last week's statement, when we talked about the presence of offensive military missile capacity or development of military bases and other indications which I gave last week, all those would, of course, indicate a change in the nature of the threat.

Q: Well, Mr. President, in this same line, have you set for yourself any rule or set of conditions at which you will determine the existence of an offensive rather than a defensive force in Cuba, and, in that same connection, in your reading of the Monroe Doctrine, how do you define "intervention"? Will it require force to contravene the Monroe Doctrine or does the presence of a foreign power in any force, but not using that force in this hemisphere, amount to contravention of the Doctrine?

The President: Well, I have indicated that if Cuba should possess a capacity to carry out offensive actions against the United States, that the United States would act. I've also indicated that the United States would not permit Cuba to export its power by force in the hemisphere. The United States will make appropriate military judgments after consultation with the Joint Chiefs of Staff and others, after carefully analyzing whatever new information comes in, as to whether that point has been reached where an offensive threat does exist. And at that time the country and the Congress will be so notified.

QUESTIONS

Export of U-2 Aircraft

Q: Would you state, sir, whether or not the United States has given export licenses for the export of U-2 aircraft to other nations, other than Nationalist China? And if so, what is our policy?

The President: No, we have not. These export licenses were given, as you know, in July of 1960, and were sold to the Nationalist Chinese Government. And we have no plans to see any further ones or grant any other export licenses.

Soviet Announcement on Berlin

Q: Mr. President, would you comment, please, on the Soviet announcement that they apparently will shelve discussion on Berlin until after our elections in November?

The President: I thought that the leaders of both political parties in the Congress indicated very clearly that on this matter of Berlin there was not a political division within the United States, and that our position in Berlin, which carries over a long commitment, stretching back through many years, several administrations, would not be affected by whatever the results may be in the November election.

The Alliance for Progress and Latin American Problems

Q: Mr. President, could you tell us why the Alliance for Progress has not made more progress in the past year on Latin American problems, in your judgment?

The President: Well, the Alliance for Progress is a tremendous effort which is, by the united effort of the free countries of Latin America and the United States, to attempt to bring about an increase in the standard of living and the opportunities for the people of Latin America.

Latin America has been neglected for many, many years. I would hope that a good many Americans who are particularly concerned about Cuba today would also take a very careful look at the very low standard of living of much of Latin America, the bad housing, the unemployment, the bad health of so many of the people there. We are engaged in a monumental task in attempting to increase the standard of living of the people of Latin America, and we have available for that purpose a good deal less money than we had available for the rebuilding of Europe, which had a highly developed labor force, great technical skills, and which required only an infusion to provide an increase over the prewar standard of living.

Here we do not have the technical skills. We do not have the planning staffs. We have, in a sense, neglected Latin America, so that we are engaged in a tremendous operation with insufficient resources. And I think we are moving ahead since Punta del Este. But there's an awful lot of business left unfinished and will be for some time. You cannot remake the face of Latin America overnight and provide better opportunity.

In addition, I'm very anxious that the countries of Western Europe, particularly the Common Market, will concern themselves with Latin America. Latin America depends on its export markets to Europe in order to maintain its economy.

Latin America has had a flight of capital in recent months which has been serious. In addition, the price of its primary products has also dropped in recent months. So that even the assistance we have given has not been enough to keep Latin America even, and particularly when its population increase amounts to almost 3 percent. So we're faced with staggering problems in Latin America and I hope that in our concentration on the particular problems which I discussed at the opening, we will extend our view and realize that what's at stake here is the freedom of a good many countries which are in very dire straits today.

Joel Broyhill's Comments

Q: What did you think, sir, of the rather harsh things that Republican Congressman Joel Broyhill in nearby Virginia had to say about you and your Press Secretary because Mr. Salinger gave a party last night for his Democratic opponent?

The President: Well, I can see why he would be quite critical of that, but I will say that I've never read so much about a Congressman who's in the paper as I do about that Congressman and see less legislative results. (Laughter)

The President's Answer to Dr. King

Q: Mr. President, Martin Luther King had telegraphed you asking for Federal action against anti-Negro terrorism in the South, and at least one Negro organization has threatened to picket you with the allegation that the Federal Government has not done enough. Could you tell us whether you have answered Dr. King, and give us the thought that you gave him, and whether you can say that or not, can you give us a comment on the problem?

The President: We are in contact with Dr. King and others who have communicated to us about it. I don't know any more outrageous action which I have seen occur in this country for a good many months or years than the burning of a church - two churches - because of the effort made by Negroes to be registered to vote.

The United States Constitution provides for freedom to vote, and this country must permit every man and woman to exercise their franchise. To shoot, as we saw in the case of Mississippi, two young people who were involved in an effort to register people, to burn churches as a reprisal, with all of the provisions of the United States Constitution - at least the basic provision of the Constitution guaranteeing freedom of worship - I consider both cowardly as well as outrageous. The United States now has a number of FBI agents in there, and as soon as we are able to find out who did it, we'll arrest them and we'll bring them before a jury, and I'm sure that they'll be appropriately dealt with.

But let me say that nothing, I think - and I'm sure this is the view of the people of the States - the right to vote is very basic. If we're going to neglect that right, then all of our talk about freedom is hollow, and therefore we shall give every protection that we can to anybody seeking to vote. I hope everybody will register in this country. I hope they will vote. I commend those who are making the effort to register every citizen. They deserve the protection of the United States Government, the protection of the State, the protection of local communities, and we shall do everything we possibly can to make sure that that protection is assured and if it requires extra legislation and extra force, we shall do that.

The Chicago Northwestern Railway Strike

Q: Sir, in connection with the Chicago Northwestern Railway strike, how long do you believe such a major transportation tieup can be allowed to run on before the public interest requires Presidential intervention or congressional action?

The President: Well, as you know, we exhausted the procedures of the Railway Labor Act in that case. The only provision which is available to us would be the Taft-Hartley under a finding that the national interest and security was affected, so that we would have to make that legal judgment. It's my understanding that representatives of both of these parties have been meeting with Mr. Wirtz during the last few days, and that some progress has been made.

I think it's very important that the parties come to an agreement immediately because there are great interests of nine States affected: a good many farm crops, which should be coming to harvest, which are in the field - and public welfare suggests that these two important groups come to a conclusion, I would hope, over the weekend.

I am hopeful of it, and, as I say, the latest report I had today was that progress had been made. So I'm hopeful that both sides will make the sufficient concessions, if that's the word, to permit an agreement, because the public interest suggests an agreement is due.

The Continuance of Atmospheric Tests

Q: Mr. President, it was generally understood that the current test series would be over by now and it now appears that the atmosphere tests may continue on into November. Can you tell us why this decision was made to continue?

The President: Well, there're two reasons. One is that, as you know, because of the blowup in the pad at Johnston Island and because of the earlier failures of the communications system in the missile, we are not able to carry out these tests which were the most - among the most important, if not the most important, of our series. So we're going to finish those.

In addition, as a result of the earlier tests of this Dominick series, there were certain things learned which we would like to prove out. So that we have agreed to a limited number of tests including the Dominick series. And also we have taken some steps to prevent a repetition of the incident which caused an increase in the number of electrons in the atmosphere, by lowering the altitude and the yield so that lunar flights will not be further endangered.

The Cuban Situation

Q: Mr. President, can you tell us whether you discussed the Cuban situation with General Eisenhower on Monday, and, if you did, whether there was an agreement between U.S. party leaders that it shouldn't be an issue in this fall's campaign?

The President: We discussed all problems, and, of course, that was one of them, but I didn't request any such agreement from him.

The National Automobile Show

Q: Mr. President, in connection with your plans for next month, do you think you will find time to visit the National Automobile Show in Detroit?

The President: I'm hopeful I will. Yes, I think I might.

Soviet Criticism on Cuba

Q: Mr. President, in the recent Soviet statement on Cuba, the Russians implied that perhaps the main reason the United States is so exercised about Cuba now is because of our election coming up. I'd like to ask you if you agree with this premise, and, more pointedly, do you think that the Republicans are going to make political hay out of Cuba?

The President: Well, I would not want to comment on the extent of the Soviet knowledge of our pre-elective process, nor would I suggest that the concern over Cuba is due to the fact that Cuba is close to the United States territory and that Cuba is obviously tying itself closer to the communist bloc. The arrival of these weapons and technicians has caused increasing alarm by not only the Members of Congress but also by the administration and by the American people. I would think that it's part of our serious problems in which we are engaged in a tense concentration in many parts of the world at a dangerous time and it's quite natural that this action would bring a good deal of concern. I would not suggest that those who are concerned about it are motivated by political purposes or that the Soviet judgment that they are is accurate.

H.R. 10

Q: Mr. President, in view of your intention to try to close some tax loopholes next year, do you find either the House or the Senate version of H.R. 10 acceptable this year?

The President: Well, I want to wait until the conference, and of course the Senate version is much more acceptable than the House version, but even the Senate version requires some careful analysis and I'm sure - I think it would be more useful to wait until after the conference and then make a judgment as to whether we should go ahead with this bill or whether we should wait until the general reform of next year.

The Implied Soviet Threat on Cuba

Q: Mr. President, the same Soviet statement which was mentioned earlier implied that the Soviet Union might intervene militarily on the side of Cuba in the event the United States was forced to take military action. Would this implied threat be a major factor in any decision you might be called upon to make?

The President: No, the United States will take whatever action the situation, as I described it, would require. As far as the threat, the United States has been living with threats for a good many years and in a good many parts of the world. But the United States will not take any action that the situation does not require and will take whatever action the situation does require along the grounds which I indicated in my opening statement.

Peaceful Uses of Space

Q: Mr. President, in the area of peaceful uses of space, you've said that we shall be first, but if we refrain from competing with Russia for warlike space vehicles, as Mr. Gilpatric has said, doesn't this almost condemn us to a second place finish in the military field?

The President: No. As I said last week, in the first place we're spending $1,500 million a year on our military space program.[2] What is key for the success both of peaceful exploration of space as well as the military mastery of space are large boosters, effective control of the capsule, the ability to rendezvous, and all of the rest, so that there is an obvious usefulness if the situation should require - military usefulness for our efforts, peaceful efforts, in space.

There is no sense - in addition, as you know, very recently we determined to go ahead with the Titan III, which gives the United States Air Force a very strong weapon if that should become necessary. So that the work that NASA is doing on Saturn, the work the Air Force is doing on Titan, the work that's being done on the Apollo program and Gemini and the others, all have a national security factor as well as a peaceful factor.

Q: Mr. President, could you say a little more about what Mr. Gilpatric meant by allowing the Russians to go first with hydrogen weapons in space?

The President: I'm not aware that we're intending the Russians to go first with hydrogen weapons.

Q: He said we wouldn't go until they did.

The President: Well, I think the United States is attempting, and with this administration as you know, is making a very massive effort in space. As I said, we are spending three times what we spent last year in space, and more in this year's budget than the 8 previous years, so that this is a tremendous effort, $5-1/2 billion as well as the money that we're spending for the military use of space.

As I say, the size of the booster, the capsule, and the control all would have, if the situation required it, a military use. We hope it does not; we hope that space will be used for peaceful purposes. That is the policy of the United States Government. But we should be prepared if it does not. In addition, as I've said from the beginning, both the Soviet Union and the United States both have a capacity today to send a missile to each other's country with a nuclear warhead on it. So that we must keep some perspective as to where the danger may lie. But the United States, in the effort it's making both in the peaceful program and the military program, all of this will increase our security if the Soviet Union should attempt to use space for military purposes.

Robert Frost's Visit with Khrushchev

Q: Mr. President, Robert Frost, the poet, recently came back from a trip to Russia and said he had a message from Premier Khrushchev for you. I think the American people would like to know what that message was, and what message he might have taken over from you to Premier Khrushchev. Would you tell us what that was?

The President: No, he didn't take a message, except the message of his own personality and poetry, to Russia and to Mr. Khrushchev, and his character. I have not received his message, though I hope to see him shortly, and if I do, I will if it's - I'm sure I'll be glad to communicate it to you and to the American people.

Latin American Role in the Cuban Situation

Q: Mr. President, you mentioned in your opening statement that proposals might be made to the Latin American countries. Could you give us some idea of your philosophy of what the Latin American countries' role should be in this Cuban situation?

The President: No, I think it would be more appropriate - as you know, Mr. Rusk plans to meet with them this month at the time the General Assembly opens, and I think it would be more appropriate for they and he to meet and confer on the matter, and at that time we will have some suggestions.

U.S.-USSR Cooperative Ventures in Space

Q: Mr. President, have you received any response from the Soviet Union to indicate that they are, in fact, considering cooperative ventures with the United States in space, other than those negotiated earlier in satellite weather research by the late Dr. Harry Wexler? If not, are you still hopeful that such cooperation is likely in the near future?

The President: No. As you know, Dr. Dryden had some conversations in Geneva in regard to the matter, and some progress was made, but it's limited in its scope and we would hope more could be done. And more, perhaps, could be done if the atmosphere between the two countries should be improved.

The President's Authority in the Cuban Affair

Q: Mr. President, you said in your opening statement that you now had full authority to act in the Cuban affair. In view of this, do you think there's any virtue in the Senate or the Congress passing the resolution saying you have that authority?

The President: No. I think the Members of Congress would, speaking as they do with a particular responsibility - I think it would be useful, if they desired to do so, for them to express their view. And as I've seen the resolutions which have been discussed - a resolution which I think Senator Mansfield introduced and which Chairman Vinson introduced in the House - and I would think that - I'd be very glad to have those resolutions passed if that should be the desire of the Congress.

The President's Request for Reserve Mobilization Powers

Q: Mr. President, will you tell us some of your thinking on your request for special reserve mobilization powers? The international situation has led you twice to request such special legislation. You could call a million reservists if you declared a national emergency. Why don't you do that?

The President: Well, I think there're several stages of a possible crisis. The call of a national emergency, I would say, is near the final step of a crisis. But there may be increased threats which would require us to call some reservists, particularly in the air, maybe at sea, possibly on the ground. Last year, when we called the reservists, the two divisions, the Wisconsin and Texas Divisions, we also laid plans for making two more divisions permanent, which came into effect this summer - August and September - so that those two divisions served a purpose of giving us this reserve during the period of the crisis at that time, and at the end of it we had two permanent divisions.

We have, as you know, of course, increased our Army strength from 11 to 16 divisions in the last year and a half. Now, if we need - of course, if we're in a national emergency, where the United States is threatened with very serious military action, of course there would be no hesitancy in declaring it. But we might be in a situation where the declaration of a national emergency might not be the most appropriate step, and in that case we would use the power granted to us by the Congress.

Q: Mr. President, in that connection, your request for only 150,000 reservists would seem to not enforce the opinion expressed because it seem no stage at all.

The President: Well, I think that ———

Q: You said that you've strengthened the Armed Forces.

The President: That's correct. Then we have 150,000 more that we could call. They could be in very critical areas. As I have said, the air and the sea are two, and, of course, there could be Guard divisions called. If the United States were obliged to reinforce its forces any place, the ability to call up needed men would make an appreciable difference. Now, as I say, we always have the final weapon, or nearly final weapon, of a national emergency and the power to call a million men. But the Joint Chiefs of Staff and the Secretary of Defense felt that this intermediate step could be very useful during the period when Congress is out of session.

The Aerospace Dispute

Q: This question concerns the aerospace dispute. As you know, the auto-workers and the machinists unions have accepted the Presidential board's recommendation, and recommendations, sir, which I believe you have also found acceptable as a basis for settlement. The four leading aerospace manufacturers, especially Lockheed, have rejected the basic union shop recommendation. Now the unions feel they are being forced into a strike posture, as a result of the company's attitude. Could you tell us something of your opinion and your reaction to the situation and what the equities in this area are?

The President: Well, in the first place, most major industrial companies or industries in the United States have accepted the union shop many years ago - the steel industry, the auto industry, the aluminum companies, other basic industries. The union shop is part of collective bargaining, and particularly under the terms suggested by Dr. Taylor - a two-thirds vote - people do not have to join the union to get the job. After they've come to work, if it's an opinion of a large majority of the members, then they would join the union. This, as I say, has been acceptable for many years to many companies which are even larger than the ones that are involved. That's the first point.

Now the second point is that the total package, it seems to me, should be considered as a package. The economic proposals made are not excessive. They come well within the guidelines suggested by the Council of Economic Advisers. The unions are accepting a financial settlement which is not particularly generous in relation to certain other unions in recent years. They feel that the total package, however, is acceptable. I would hope the companies would accept it, because if a strike comes, in view of the fact that the recommendation of the fact-finding board headed by Dr. Taylor, who also was given a comparable assignment by President Eisenhower in the steel strike case - which indicates his own high reputation and that of the panel - I would hope that the companies would accept it, because if there is a strike, the responsibility would be very clear, I think, to the American people for such an action. I would hope there wouldn't be a strike, that business would go on, that the companies would accept the report.

The Upcoming Elections

Q: Mr. President, do you favor the election of every Democratic candidate for Congress? How many seats do you feel you need in the Senate and the House to get a Congress that will put across your legislative program?

The President: Well, I would be glad to go through the names with you. I've said from the beginning that I would probably be supporting any Congressman who was interested in my support. I think there are probably some Democrats who might not be particularly anxious for my support and, therefore, my endorsement would not be required across the board. Those Congressmen who are interested in my supporting them are usually people who hold the same general view of the necessity for this country making progress that I do.

Now, secondly, this Congress is ending. I think that it is somewhat like Lazarus. It has revived. It's moving and we are going to see the session end, in my opinion, with the passage of a good trade bill, with a tax bill which will come out of the conference, I hope a higher education bill, and a good many other bills which 2 months ago seemed to be in the deep freeze. So I think that we're making progress.

What I think is important is because these votes – and we will get a farm bill, I hope – because these votes are so close, because their program is opposed by the opposition party, almost across the board, and because some Democrats join, I would hope that we could hold the number of seats we have and perhaps pick some up, even though I recognize that it's going to be a very intensely fought election.

The President's Trip to Houston

Q: Sir, when you went to Houston the other day you didn't take along Congressman Casey whose district you went to, and you also didn't take along Senator Yarborough from Texas. I wonder why you did this and I also wonder if you were motivated in leaving Casey at home because he had opposed you on some issues.

The President: Well, you say I didn't take Senator Yarborough, and he said I have been in close concert so, of course, the reason was not that which you have suggested. We did not take any Congressman or Senator along to Florida though we visited it. We didn't take any Congressman or Senator along to Alabama because this was a program trip.

Q: One was already there, wasn't he?

The President: Oh, yes, and we invited all the Congressmen and Senators who were in the districts to come with us on the trip. For example, Senator Long from Missouri, came with us to the McDonnell plant. We would have been glad to have anyone come. But we invited the members of the Space Committees of the House and Senate, the ranking Democrat and Republican. We also brought Congressman Thomas along, who is Chairman of the Appropriations Committee for the space program. And that was the total invitation because this was a nonpolitical trip.

Reporter: Thank you, Mr. President.

[1] Item 352 (14, 17), *Public Papers of the President.*

[2] See Item 340 (5), *Public Papers of the President.*

THE PRESIDENT'S SPECIAL NEWS CONFERENCE WITH

BUSINESS EDITORS AND PUBLISHERS

SEPTEMBER 26, 1962

The President: Mr. Secretary.

You gentlemen look very well after having been talked at all day. But we want you to know how much we appreciate your coming to Washington and giving the members of the administration who are concerned with those matters which are of particular interest to you, and to us, a chance to explain our policies and also, I hope, and from all I've heard, the exchange has been back and forth, so that I think the Government will benefit.

This is an artificial city, a governmental city, and well removed by design from a good many of the influences and pressures of ordinary life which you deal with on every occasion. So that it's very advantageous to us to have you come to Washington and tell us about some of your thoughts on us, which we read about with great interest, and also have a chance to talk to you.

I wanted to just sum up more or less what our view was of the economy, where it is now and where we're falling short, and what our target should be in the coming months. In the first place, I think that while we're all proud of the accomplishments of our economic system, and it has been an extraordinarily effective system in serving the needs of our people over a long period of time, we also do have a responsibility to look with candor at our shortcomings in order to attempt to develop courses of action which will make our system even more effective.

We all know that in spite of impressive economic advances during the last months, the last year and some months, there are several areas across a broad economic front that must still give us serious concern.

First, we have a rate of unemployment which is unacceptably high.

Two, we have significant industrial capacity which is not fully utilized, the steel industry being the most obvious example.

Three, we have persistent economic distress in certain regions. This is an old problem that's been with us for a great many years. But we still have the serious structural unemployment in the coal regions, steel - eastern Kentucky, West Virginia, Pennsylvania, southern Illinois, parts of Indiana, and eastern Ohio. And we still have a shrinking but troublesome deficit in our international balance of payment. And we still have a rate of economic growth which has lagged behind that of other major industrial nations.

These problems affect us all and none of us can escape responsibility for trying to meet them. We have attempted in the past 20 months to set forth policies and carry out programs which would provide a sound and solid basis for economic progress at home and abroad.

For the first time since the war I believe the American economy has moved forward simultaneously towards a number of major economic goals: full employment, though as I say we still have some to go; faster growth, at the same time avoiding inflation; and moving a long way towards a balance of payments equilibrium and also keeping a free competitive market and their functioning in operation.

Your copies of the summary of the 1961-62 economic expansion policies give you the particulars of what our economic growth rate has been since January 1961. I want to say, however, that with the problems that we still have, I think all of us in Government and in business should be thinking of what additional steps we could take which would be of assistance in maintaining an economic growth rate which will absorb the increase in our population and also those who are technologically dislocated.

We have to do that at home while at the same time maintaining a competitive position abroad, particularly with our European neighbors which will permit us to compete in their markets on a satisfactory basis in order to protect our balance of payments position.

So that, therefore, while we want to maintain a steady growth of the economy here at home, we also want to maintain the strictures that we can against inflation here at home which would deprive us of an increasingly advantageous economic position - particularly a position which has developed in the last 3 years in our ability to get our goods into Western Europe on a satisfactory basis.

This balance is very fine because, quite obviously, if we have an increase in costs, which are excessive in the United States, it could throw our hopes – upon which we are building so much of the success in our trade bill – it could cause us a drop in our exports and an increase in our imports, another critical period for our balance of payments, and therefore for the dollar, with all that that could mean to the United States at home and abroad.

I want to indicate, therefore, how complicated I think our task is. But there is so much slack in our economy that I think we should be able to take steps, and I'm hopeful our tax policies next year will provide an additional stimulus to the economy without threatening us with inflation.

And it seems to me that the fiscal – the monetary – procedures which we have available could effectively prevent any new inflationary pressure which might come because of a particular fiscal policy which we might follow.

I would like to say one word about the competitive market system because I think there seems to be, on occasion, some question among businessmen as to the views of those of us in Washington on this matter. Our experience during the present expansion has also demonstrated our ability to achieve impressive economic gains without shrinking the area of market freedom. I regard the preservation and strengthening of the free market as a cardinal objective of this or any administration's policies.

It is well to remind ourselves from time to time of the benefits we derive from the maintenance of a free market system. The system rests on freedom of consumer choice, the profit motive, and vigorous competition for the buyer's dollar. By relying on these spontaneous economic forces, we secure these benefits:

(a) Our system tends automatically to produce the kinds of goods that consumers want in the relative quantities in which people want them.

(b) The system tends automatically to minimize waste. If one producer is making a product inefficiently, another will see an opportunity for profit by making the product at a lower cost.

(c) The system encourages innovation and technological change. High profits are the reward of the innovator, but competitors will soon adopt the new techniques, thus forcing the innovator to continue to push ahead.

The free market is a decentralized regulator of our economic system. The free market is not only a more efficient decision maker than even the wisest central planning body, but even more important, the free market keeps economic power widely dispersed. It thus is a vital underpinning of our democratic system.

Price and wage controls paralyze the operation of the free market, and that is why we have opposed them. Likewise, unnecessary Government regulation undermines the efficiency of the market. That is why, in my transportation message to Congress last April[1], I urged that Government controls be curtailed, and the scope for competition broadened in the important transportation sector of our economy. A market, of course, is not a fact of nature. It is a creation of man and, as such, we have no guarantee that it will work effectively and impartially if we pay no attention to it.

We must encourage and protect the availability of full information, safeguard competition, and extend freedom of opportunity to individuals and businesses to participate fully in the economy in accordance with their desires and their abilities. The full benefits of the market system can only be felt when all of our people and all of our resources are used as wisely and effectively as possible.

It is, of course, natural that we will disagree as to how these goals can be implemented on occasion. Such controversies are essential to the democratic system, and also essential to democratic progress. I think it's important, however, that the controversy be based as soundly as possible on facts and on the most detailed information, that this information be made available as widely as possible in order to make sure that the businessmen of the country play as significant a role as their responsibility warrants.

As editors and publishers of the Nation's business magazines, you have a responsibility to bring to your readers accurate information concerning the activities of the Federal Government in those areas in which you are particularly concerned. I hope that this conference has helped to clarify the substance and rationale of Federal Government programs and policies, and that it will be helpful to you in your task of reporting on these activities to your readers who depend so much upon the information you provide them.

I'll be glad to answer any questions that anyone might have.

QUESTIONS

Administration Sensitivity to the Business World

Q: Mr. President, do you believe that your administration is unduly sensitive to the alleged hostility of the buisness world?

The President: Well, we're unduly and alleged, I would say. (Laughter) I would think that we are sensitive naturally to hostility, if that were the appropriate description, by any segment of the economy. This system of ours really depends upon comity, upon cooperation, if it is going to function. Therefore, hostility from the business section, labor, agriculture, East or West, North or South, would make it much more difficult for us. So I would be sensitive to hostility from the business community.

I recognize that there is a political difference between this administration and most businessmen. I'm not really concerned about that political difference, because I think that it's traditional and, quite honestly, no Democratic administration has banked heavily on the amount of support it would get politically from the business community. What I'm concerned about is, however, in all these very intimate interrelations - whether it's the dollar, whether it's the new trade bill, all the rest, transportation - that we have as close an understanding as possible. A good many of the proposals that we may make to improve the state of the American economy require congressional action. We want to try to make sure to the extent that it's possible that we secure the support where we can of the business community.

In my judgment, we had a good deal of misunderstanding with the business community which did not serve the public interest this year on our tax bill. We really didn't get the kind of support that the investments credit, in my opinion, would warrant as a stimulus to our economy. The whole fight against the withholding, the impression that was widely created that this was a new tax, rather than a method of collecting a tax which had been in effect for many years - and now, as I look forward to an intensive study of taxes this fall by us, and presentation to the Congress, I would like to describe the relation between business and the Government as one of cooperation, and one of amity, and one that disregards the alternate Novembers, when we may be divided politically, and instead work on the common task of making this economy move ahead.

Significance of the Free Market

Q: Mr. President, you spoke a moment ago of the significance of the free market. May I ask how that statement jibes with what we heard from Mr. Ball[2] this morning, who told us that we have just concluded our first international global commodity price support operation, or how that statement jibes with our current agricultural program?

The President: Well, I think that if we talk about the first, we are at-tempting to get an agreement on coffee because if we don't get an agreement on coffee we're going to find an increasingly dangerous situation in the coffee producing countries, and one which would threaten investments, private invest-ments, from abroad, in those countries, and would threaten, in my opinion, the security of the entire hemisphere.

I must say that I was looking yesterday at some figures on what the drop in coffee prices has done to a country with which we have the closest relations, Colombia. And all the aid that we have given Colombia has, of course, not amounted to the amount that Colombia has lost in foreign exchange due to the drop in the price of coffee.

So I think we have to be concerned with the problem of our primary pro-ducers, whose prices have been declining in the last 3 years and who are faced with very serious instabilities in their own countries. So that while we would like to have what we might call a completely free competitive market, I think in these cases the national interest is served by the international agreement.

Now in agriculture we have - of course, a good deal of our agriculture is in the free market. The problems that we have particularly, of course, are in wheat, in the feed grains, and, of course, in cotton, tobacco, peanuts, the so-called basics.

There it has been felt that a withdrawal of governmental support would pre-cipitate a decline in prices which would be of such an extraordinary range that it would bring an economic collapse in the Middle West which would adversely affect the entire economy. The Purdue University study of the effect of a drop in or withdrawal of the Government from the support business has indicated the very serious effects this would have on the entire economy. On the other hand, of course, we pay a very large bill. We have been attempting in this Congress, with some success, but not total success, to provide that those who receive the supports will not plant an unlimited amount.

We have had, as I say, some success. But I think that those members of the business community who feel that the solution is a total withdrawal of the Gov-ernment's support program, I don't think we're going to see that in the very near future and, number two, I'm not sure that it would serve our long-range interests. But there are, of course, obvious limitations.

The transportation industry is regulated. There are, of course, limita-tions on the free market. But basically this is a free market economy, and the fact of the matter is, it is the freest market economy of any industrialized society in the world today, and I think we can take some satisfaction in that. It's the freest in the world.

The Tariff Classification Act

Q: Mr. President, you mentioned business cooperation. The administra-tion's target date for you to proclaim the Tariff Classification Act is January 1st. Would you give consideration to postponing that about 45 days so that Government and the import trade can get a chance to study that 2 inch volume of our new tariff?

The President: I will give that consideration, definitely.

Problem of Inflation

Q: Mr. President, in connection with the problem of inflation, would you agree that the fact that the excessive supply was greater than the effective demand was a greater factor in keeping the prices stable than any Government action?

The President: Yes, I think that's fair, though I think we made a contribution which was unacknowledged and comparatively unsung last spring.

But I would think that - I would think your thesis is right. I think that as everything has a good and bad side, the good side is the stability of the price level. Unfortunately, it comes from an excess, to a degree of excess of supply. And this is also true of the fact we have wage stability.

The manufacturing wage rate - because we have unemployment - the manufacturing wage rate increase in the United States in 1960-61 was a 2.8 percent increase in annual rate and in 1961-62 was 2.4 percent, which is the lowest it's been since 1947. The reason has been the one that you in part stated.

The hourly earnings in June 1961-62, of the United States show about a 3.0, while Belgium, for example, was 7.7. In fact, we had less than any country except Canada. Germany, for example, was 12.9 percent. As you know, that has been true since 1959. That's why I say our competitive position has improved but the reasons for it in both the wage rates and in commodities owe a good deal to the reasons you suggested.

The "Union Shop"

Q: Mr. President, business leaders in the aerospace industry feel very strongly that you have demonstrated your alleged anti-business attitude in forcing a union shop on them. An IAM official has indicated that he is not particularly pleased with this approach to a union shop. In view of its significance for all industries, would you comment on this?

The President: Yes. As you know, we set up a committee headed by Dr. Taylor because we - most of these missile companies, aerospace companies are really very much dependent upon the Government. The Government is their major purchaser. Therefore, any contract or any increase would, of course, be paid for in good measure by the Government.

Number one, any interference with production would be paid for by the American people because all these programs are vital. So that I set up a committee which was acceptable to both labor and management which was headed by Dr. Taylor from Pennsylvania, who had performed a similar function for President Eisenhower in the steel case in November of 1959, and included on it an arbitrator for Bethlehem. And it was a panel which, as I say, was acceptable. They made the report.

This was not done by the United States Government. As part of the report was the exceptions to the union shop. The fact is the wage section of the report was not as generous as the unions felt that they must have. On the other hand, the union shop was unacceptable to some of the companies. But as I said the other day at a press conference, the union shop in major industries has been accepted for a great many years - automobiles, steel, aluminum. This is not something new or radical. We've had that, as I say, in our basic industries. I can't think of any of them, really of our basic industries, that have not had the union shop.

So I don't think that this is asking very much. And as I say, it's not my report. It is Dr. Taylor's report. Now you can have an economic struggle out there on the coast in these industries, and you can have a strike, and then where are we all going to be on missiles and planes and all the rest?

So this was an attempt to work out an equitable solution. Obviously, neither side is very happy with it. The unions feel the wage section is too limited, and the companies don't like the union shop section. But I think that probably it's as equitable a solution as you would get from a long economic struggle.

And I think our experience in the steel industry, where you had a 6-month strike and then finally settled on terms you probably could have settled on 6 months before, indicates that if we can prevent the strikes, particularly in the vital industries, it's in the public's interest.

The Wilderness Bill

Q: Mr. President, what is the status of the wilderness bill?

The President: Well, unfortunately, it's quite far out, in the sense that the bill is unsatisfactory and not very satisfactory in the House. It is in the Senate. And I hope we can get a good bill. I think many of us who travel around the United States know what an asset this is, and I hoped the bill would pass in a form similar to that in which we originally discussed it. I think if I may say so, this bill is an example of some of the problems which we have here in dealing with the business community. This is a bill which conservationists and others feel strongly is in the national interest. It does, possibly, cut across the interests of mineral producers or lumbermen and others, and they, therefore, may feel that the very sponsorship of such legislation is antibusiness. But it isn't. It's an attempt to protect the public interest. And it's quite natural that those who may be adversely affected may suffer. But that doesn't warrant the general labeling of antibusiness. As a matter of fact, a good many businessmen who complain about the antitrust actions of the Federal Government, this administration or others, if they would see the letters that come in from businessmen demanding that we take such action they would realize how difficult it is to keep all businessmen, or indeed, all everybody else, happy.

Reporting in the Aerospace Field

Q: In the last few months it has become increasingly difficult to report in the aerospace field. There is, however, a DOD order outlining the mechanics of working with the press. Yet the order is secret. How can we get copies of it?

The President: Arthur Sylvester - I'll ask him about it.

Q: I asked him Tuesday.

The President: What did he say? You are with which magazine?

Q: Western Aerospace.

The President: Fine. I will talk to him, without success, I'm sure.

The Two-Price System in Cotton

Q: A couple of weeks ago, Mr. President, you said you'd recommend to the Department of Agriculture that it prepare legislation to eliminate the inequity of the two-price system in cotton. Did you have in mind the substitution of a one-price system?

The President: Well, I think that we will, in January, present a program which will eliminate the inequities. I think it would be better for the Agriculture Department to finish its analysis of the various alternatives, but it definitely will be presented. Now there isn't any doubt that when it is presented, it's going to make some people unhappy. It will make the textile manufacturers happy. It will perhaps make some other people less happy. Otherwise, it would have been done long ago. There's no magic to this. It means a struggle, but I think the struggle is worth while, because I think it is really foolish to pile on this extra burden on the manufacturer, and then at the same time try to hang it on another way on the importation of textiles.

Q: Did you have in mind removing the inequity of the one-price system at one step, just eliminate it, or would it be a phased proposal?

The President: Well, I would prefer to wait until we get it through the Department of Agriculture, but we will have it in January.

H.R. 10

Q: Mr. President, what are your views on H.R. 10, the self-employed pension bill?

The President: I am going to take a good look at it after the Senate has acted, which may be today. It does represent a budget loss, as you know, of $100 million or $125 million, depending on which figures you use. In addition, it would be ideally more suited to a reform bill and I think would be part of any reform bill which we would be presenting next January, so that we have to weigh the factor of the loss versus the factor that it did pass the House unanimously and has widespread support. I expect that it will pass very generously in the Senate if it hasn't already done so, and then will come to us. And then we will have to take action.

It is – the principle has equity to it. The problem is that it does represent additional loss of revenue this year, and there are other groups who have a claim which is equal but which we have suspended in action because of budget losses, and so we really have to decide whether this is the fair way to do it this year for this group or whether it should be part of a package in January.

Perhaps we can have about two more questions. I know you are tired.

Crude Oil Import Program

Q: Mr. President, several weeks ago the Director of the Office of Emergency Planning presented to you a study on the crude oil import control program. Have you anything to say at this point particularly as to when there might be a decision, or what direction the decision might take?

The President: The report was not wholly accepted by me, so that I don't expect any announcement will be made about the matter at the present time.

Competition with the Communists

Q: Mr. President, in time of a hot war, we are asked to sacrifice time and money and lives. Do you believe that this country can win over the Communists in the long run without greater sacrifices?

The President: Yes, I think that the United States or the free world is going to be successful. And now, the question of sacrifices – I think the United States will do whatever must be done to provide for that success. What is difficult is the operation of a free society and who sacrifices.

Talking about one of our problems, which is gold, we have been attempting to cut down, as you know, the amount of money we lose from the expenditures abroad for the maintenance of our national defense, from $3 billion to about $1.5 billion. There have been suggestions that there be even further cuts. We also have been cutting the $1.3 billion loss we incur in our AID program down to $800 million. To do that, of course, we have to give up a good many projects which are very important. We have the Buy American, and in the case of Viet-Nam it requires them to buy products in the United States, which they could buy next door substantially cheaper. We do that in order to protect our gold balance. At the same time we lose net a billion dollars a year from tourists abroad. Our tourists spend a billion dollars more than their tourists, and therefore that is spent particularly in Western Europe, which already have dollar surpluses.

We also invest abroad about two and a half billion dollars. No other country would permit that kind of movement of capital. But we do it as a free society. I indicate this only because at the time when we're talking about writing a tax bill, which would deal with loopholes, and which would put American businessmen in a position of equity with American companies who might be investing abroad and selling here in the United States the products they make abroad, a good many businessmen felt that was unfair and was perhaps antibusiness. But it isn't at all. We just have to attempt to balance what is the national interest between cutting down on the number of troops we have abroad or cutting down the very vital programs abroad as opposed to losing a billion dollars on tourists or two and a half billion dollars here, and other funds other places.

I mention that example because I think it indicates quite clearly the complexities of the alternatives which we have, to us as a Nation, and though you may have a private interest in an expenditure abroad, it also affects the public interest, because each of those expenditures has some effect upon the supply of the United States gold at Fort Knox, and its movement.

So in answer to your question, I've some feeling that a good many of the calls for sacrifice are very genuine. But the difficulty is, without a central authority of a kind repugnant to us, it's difficult to make these sacrifices equitable. And that is where we get into a difference of view. But in answer to your question, I think the job can be done, and I think the United States, as one of a number of countries, can do it.

Delegate: Thank you, Mr. President.

[1]Item 129 of the *Public Papers of the President.*

[2]George W. Ball, Under Secretary of State.

THE PRESIDENT'S NEWS CONFERENCE OF

NOVEMBER 20, 1962

The President: I have several statements.

I have today been informed by Chairman Khrushchev that all of the IL-28 bombers now in Cuba will be withdrawn in 30 days. He also agrees that these planes can be observed and counted as they leave. Inasmuch as this goes a long way towards reducing the danger which faced this hemisphere 4 weeks ago,

I have this afternoon instructed the Secretary of Defense to lift our naval quarantine.

In view of this action, I want to take this opportunity to bring the American people up to date on the Cuban crisis and to review the progress made thus far in fulfilling the understandings between Soviet Chairman Khrushchev and myself as set forth in our letters of October 27 and 28. Chairman Khrushchev, it will be recalled, agreed to remove from Cuba all weapons systems capable of offensive use, to halt the further introduction of such weapons into Cuba, and to permit appropriate United Nations observation and supervision to insure the carrying out and continuation of these commitments. We on our part agreed that once these adequate arrangements for verification had been established we would remove our naval quarantine and give assurances against an invasion of Cuba.

The evidence to date indicates that all known offensive missile sites in Cuba have been dismantled. The missiles and their associated equipment have been loaded on Soviet ships. And our inspection at sea of these departing ships has confirmed that the number of missiles reported by the Soviet Union as having been brought into Cuba, which closely corresponded to our own information, has now been removed. In addition, the Soviet Government has stated that all nuclear weapons have been withdrawn from Cuba and no offensive weapons will be reintroduced.

Nevertheless, important parts of the understanding of October 27th and 28th remain to be carried out. The Cuban Government has not yet permitted the United Nations to verify whether all offensive weapons have been removed, and no lasting safeguards have yet been established against the future introduction of offensive weapons back into Cuba.

Consequently, if the Western Hemisphere is to continue to be protected against offensive weapons, this government has no choice but to pursue its own means of checking on military activities in Cuba. The importance of our continued vigilance is underlined by our identification in recent days of a number of Soviet ground combat units in Cuba, although we are informed that these and other Soviet units were associated with the protection of offensive weapons systems, and will also be withdrawn in due course.

I repeat, we would like nothing better than adequate international arrangements for the task of inspection and verification in Cuba, and we are prepared to continue our efforts to achieve such arrangements. Until that is done, difficult problems remain. As for our part, if all offensive weapons systems are removed from Cuba and kept out of the hemisphere in the future, under adequate verification and safeguards, and if Cuba is not used for the export of aggressive Communist purposes, there will be peace in the Caribbean. And as I said in September, "We shall neither initiate nor permit aggression in this hemisphere."

We will not, of course, abandon the political, economic, and other efforts of this hemisphere to halt subversion from Cuba nor our purpose and hope that the Cuban people shall some day be truly free. But these policies are very different from any intent to launch a military invasion of the island.

In short, the record of recent weeks shows real progress and we are hopeful that further progress can be made. The completion of the commitment on both sides and the achievement of a peaceful solution to the Cuban crisis might well open the door to the solution of other outstanding problems.

May I add this final thought in this week of Thanksgiving: there is much for which we can be grateful as we look back to where we stood only 4 weeks ago - the unity of this hemisphere, the support of our allies, and the calm determination of the American people. These qualities may be tested many more times in this decade, but we have increased reason to be confident that those qualities will continue to serve the cause of freedom with distinction in the years to come.

Secondly, I would also like to announce that I have today signed an Executive order[1] directing Federal departments and agencies to take every proper and legal action to prevent discrimination in the sale or lease of housing facilities owned or operated by the Federal Government; housing constructed or sold as a result of loans or grants to be made by the Federal Government or by loans to be insured or guaranteed by the Federal Government; and housing to be made available through the development or redevelopment of property under Federal slum clearance or urban renewal programs.

With regard to existing housing facilities constructed or purchased as a result of direct loans or grants from the Federal Government, or under Federal guarantees, or as a result of the urban renewal program, I have directed the Housing Agency and other appropriate agencies to use their good offices to promote and encourage the abandonment of discriminatory practices that may now exist.

In order to assist the departments and agencies in implementing this policy, and to coordinate their efforts, I have established the President's Committee on Equal Opportunity in Housing. It is neither proper nor equitable that Americans should be denied the benefits of housing owned by the Federal Government or financed through the Federal assistance on the basis of their race, color, creed, or national origin.

Our national policy is equal opportunity for all and the Federal Government will continue to take such legal and proper steps as it may to achieve the realization of this goal.

And finally, over the last weekend, the Chinese have made great advances in northwestern India. Now they have offered some kind of cease-fire proposal and we are in touch with the Inidan Government to determine their assessment of it. In order to better assess Indian needs, we are sending a team to New Delhi, headed by Assistant Secretary Averell Harriman, including Assistant Secretary of Defense Paul Nitze and other representatives of the Defense Department and State Department. It will leave tomorrow.

In providing military assistance to India, we are mindful of our alliance with Pakistan. All of our aid to India is for the purpose of defeating Chinese Communist subversion. Chinese incursions into the subcontinent are a threat to Pakistan as well as India, and both have a common interest in opposing it.

We have urged this point in both governments. Our help to India in no way diminishes or qualifies our commitment to Pakistan and we have made this clear to both governments as well.

QUESTIONS

The No-Invasion Pledge

Q: Mr. President, with respect to your no-invasion pledge, there has been considerable discussion and speculation in the press as to the exact scope of this pledge. I believe that Chairman Khrushchev, in his letter of the 28th, made the assumption, or the implication, or the statement, that no attack would be made on Castro, not only by the United States, but any other country in the Western Hemisphere. It appeared to be an implication that possibly you would be willing to guarantee Castro against any and all enemies anywhere. Now I realize that in your letter there was nothing of that sort and you've touched on this today, but I'm wondering if you can be a bit more specific on the scope of your no-invasion pledge.

The President: I think that today's statement describes very clearly what the policy is of the Government in regard to no-invasion. I think if you re-read the statement you will see the position of the Government on that matter.

Q: Mr. President, in speaking of "adequate verification," does this mean that we insist upon onsite inspection? Would we be satisfied with anything less than actual, on-the-spot inspection in Cuba?

The President: Well, we have thought that to provide adequate inspection, it should be onsite. As you know, Mr. Castro has not agreed to that, so we have had to use our own resources to implement the decision of the Organization of American States that the hemisphere should continue to keep itself informed about the development of weapons systems in Cuba.

The Indian Situation

Q: Mr. President, in connection with your statement on India, would you say if you foresee any need for direct U.S. participation in the border difficulties there in the way of manpower? Will we have to send troops there?

The President: There's been no indication of that. I think we can get a more precise idea of what the Indians need to protect their territorial integrity when Governor Harriman returns, and also, I understand a similar mission may be being sent from London. And I think by the end of the week we ought to have a clearer idea of what the cease-fire offer means, what the military pressures are in India, and what assistance they would like to receive from us, but as of today I've heard nothing about American troops being requested.

Q: Does that include trainers and advisers?

The President: No, I think - we can't tell precisely what the Indians require, and that's why this mission is going tomorrow, composed of representatives of State and Defense.

Communication with Khrushchev

Q: Mr. President, apparently you've established quite a free-flowing channel of communications with Chairman Khrushchev. I wonder if you could comment any on this, perhaps telling us how many messages you've exchanged, some of the tenor of those, and if this will be a pattern for the future?

The President: We've exchanged several messages in an attempt to try to work out the details of the withdrawal of the IL-28's and also a system of verification, in an attempt to fill in, in detail, the assurances given in the letters of late October. So that's what the corresponsdence has been about.

I think that's been very clearly stated. And as I say, today a message was received, several hours ago, indicating that the IL-28's would be taken out. The main burden of the negotiation, however, has been borne by Mr. McCloy and Governor Stevenson in their conversations, but I have continued to indicate how we defined offensive weapons, which has been the subject of the negotiations between Mr. McCloy and Mr. Stevenson on the one hand, and the Russians on the other.

In addition, the question of adequate verification has been a subject of the correspondence and a subject of the negotiations.

Q: Mr. President, in the various exchanges of the past 3 weeks, either be-tween yourself and Chairman Khrushchev or at the United Nations, have any is-sues been touched on besides that of Cuba, and could you say how the events of these past 3 weeks might affect such an issue as Berlin or disarmament or nu-clear testing?

The President: No. I instructed the negotiators to confine themselves to the matter of Cuba completely, and therefore no other matters were discussed. Disarmament, any matters affecting Western Europe, relations between the Warsaw pact countries and NATO, all the rest - none of these matters was to be in any way referred to or negotiated about until we had made progress and come to some sort of a solution on Cuba. So that has been all we have done diplomatically with the Soviet Union in the last month.

Now, if we're successful in Cuba, as I said, we would be hopeful that some of the other areas of tension could be relaxed. Obviously when you make pro-gress in any area, then you have hopes that you can continue it. But up till now we have confined ourselves to Cuba, and we'll continue to do so until we feel the situation has reached a satisfactory state.

Suppression of the News

Q: Mr. President, your administration, like others, is being criticized for its handling of information. The point is being made that reporters are being hampered in carrying out their role as the link between Government and the American people, that we're not keeping the American people well informed, as a result of Government policies. LeRoy Collins, former Governor of Florida, now head of the National Association of Broadcasters, has accused both the De-fense Department and the State Department of news suppression in the Cuban crisis. Would you care to comment on your general feeling about that, Mr. President?

The President: Well, it is true that when we learned the matter on Tuesday morning until we made the announcement on the quarantine on Monday afternoon, that this matter was kept in the highest levels of Government. We didn't make any public statement about it. And I returned to Washington that Saturday morning because I had a campaign trip that was going to take until Sunday even-ing, and I had to come back, and we did not want to indicate to the Soviet Union or to Cuba or anyone else who might be our adversaries, the extent of our information until we had determined what our policy would be, and until we had consulted with our allies and members of OAS and NATO. So for those very good reasons, I believe, this matter was kept by the Government until Monday night. There is - at least one newspaper learned about some of the details on Sunday evening and did not print it for reasons of public interest.

I have no apologies for that. I don't think that there's any doubt it would have been a great mistake and possibly a disaster if this news had drib-bled out when we were unsure of the extent of the Soviet buildup in Cuba, and when we were unsure of our response, and when we had not consulted with any of our allies, who might themselves have been involved in great difficulties as a result of our action.

During the week, then, from Monday till Sunday, when we received Mr. Khru-shchev's first message about the withdrawal, we attempted to have the Govern-ment speak with one voice. There were obvious restraints on newspapermen. They were not permitted, for example, to go to Guantanamo because obviously that might be an area which might be under attack.

Since that Sunday we have tried to, or at least intend to attempt to lift any restraints in the news. And I'm really - as a reader of a good many papers, it seems to me that the papers more or less reflected quite accurately the state of our negotiations with the Soviet Union.

They have, in a sense, been suspended because we've been arguing about this question of IL-28's, so there hasn't been any real progress that we could point to or any hard information that we could put out until today, which we're now doing.

Now, if the procedures which have been set up, which are really to protect the interest and security of the United States, are being used in a way inimical to the free flow of news, then we'll change those procedures.[2]

Effect of the Election Results

Q: Sir, in another area, could you give us your analysis of the election results and your analysis as to what effect this may have on your program in Congress next year?

The President: Well, I think we'll probably be in a position somewhat comparable to what we were in for the last 2 years. We did better than we had hoped in the election, but we still did not pick up seats, and we lost and won a number of votes by very close margins, particularly in the House.

It really will depend on whether we can maintain a good deal of unity in the Democratic Party and also whether we receive some assistance from some Republicans. If the Republicans vote unanimously against us and we lose 40-odd Democrats - about one-fifth of our number - then we will have difficulty. If we get the kind of Republican support that we got at the beginning of last year in the rules fight, then we can put some of these important programs through. So I think we have to wait until they come back before we can make a judgment, and we may be about in the position we were in the last 2 years.

Plans for Christmas

Q: Mr. President, the people of Florida are hoping that you and your family will again spend Christmas with them. Can you tell us what your present plans are, sir?

The President: My father and mother are going to Florida in December, and my wife and children hope to go there for Christmas, and if my situation here permits, I will go for Christmas. If the question is a result of some stories that the tourist business in Florida is off because of our difficulties, I hope it will not be too dangerous in Florida this year. (Laughter)

Housing Order

Q: Mr. President, with regard to your housing order, could you explain, first, why you've taken so long to sign the order; second, does it become effective tomorrow morning for loans and guarantees and everything, that quickly?

The President: Yes, that's correct.

Q: And, third, what assessment have you made of the possible economic impact of it?

The President: Well, I said that I would issue it at the time when I thought it was in the public interest, and now is the time.

Secondly, it will become effective immediately. Thirdly, I don't think that its immediate effect - there may be some adverse reaction, but I think that we will be able to proceed in the development of our housing industry, which is important to our economy. I know one builder the other day in part of New York said that he would be very much against the housing order because it would hurt his development, and he was reminded that there was a more stringent law in effect in New York at the time. So that I think some of the fears have been exaggerated. In any case, it's sound, public, constitutional policy and we've done it.

The Possibility of a No-Invasion Pledge

Q: Mr. President, another question on Cuba. Is it your position, sir, that you will issue a formal no-invasion pledge only after satisfactory arrangements have been made for verification and after adequate arrangements have been made to make sure that such weapons are not reintroduced once more?

The President: Quite obviously, as I said in my statements, serious problems remain as to verification and reassurance, and, therefore, this matter of our negotiations really are not - have not been completed and until they're completed, of course, I suppose we're not going to be fully satisfied that there will be peace in the Caribbean.

In regard to my feelings about what remains to be done, and on the matter of invasion, I think my statement is the best expression of our views.

Q: Mr. President, what would we accept as a guarantee, as a safeguard against reintroduction? Can that be achieved by anything short of continuous aerial reconnaissance?

The President: Well, I think that what we would like to have is the kind of inspection on the ground which would make any other means of obtaining information unnecessary.

Q: A continuing inspection after the settlement ——

The President: Inspection which would provide us with assurances that there are not on the island weapons capable of offensive action against the United States or neighboring countries and that they will not be reintroduced. Obviously, that is our goal. If we do not achieve that goal, then we have to use other resources to assure ourselves that weapons are not there, or that they're not being reintroduced.

Khrushchev on Capitalism

Q: Mr. President, the other day Khrushchev stated that Communists could learn something even from capitalists, and he even had a few kind words to say about profit incentives. Do you read any great amount of significance into this?

The President: No, I don't. No. Except human nature is the same on both sides, fortunately, on both sides of the Iron Curtain, which is why I'm optimistic about the ultimate outcome of this struggle.

U.S. Relationship with the U.N.

Q: Sir, would you please clear up for us our relationship with the United Nations? If we wanted to invade Cuba, if we wanted to take unilateral action in any way, could we do so without the approval of the United Nations?

The President: Well, I don't think a question - you have to really give me a much more detailed hypothetical question before I could consider answering it, and even under those conditions it might not be wise. Obviously, the United States - let's use a hypothetical case, which is always better - the United States has the means as a sovereign power to defend itself. And of course exercises that power, has in the past, and would in the future. We would hope to exercise it in a way consistent with our treaty obligations, including the United Nations Charter. But we, of course, keep to ourselves and hold to ourselves under the United States Constitution and under the laws of international law, the right to defend our security. On our own, if necessary - though we, as I say, hope to always move in concert with our allies, but on our own if that situation was necessary to protect our survival or integrity or other vital interests.

Information Policies

Q: Mr. President, with regard to the information policies, much of the controversy has centered on two specific orders: there's the Sylvester directive at the Pentagon which is for policing the contacts of the press with individuals in the Pentagon. And there's another order by Manning in the State Department which deals with the same general area. There's been quite a lot of criticism where some of the veteran correspondents have contended that this could cut down on the contacts, the normal flow of news, and also could cut down on controversy, I wonder if you have thought in terms of revising this, modifying it, or changing it?

The President: As I said, we would modify it or change it if it turned out that it has the result that you suggest. As it is, we are tonight suggesting that there be lifted the 12 points that we made to the press in regard to voluntary restraints on the movement of troops and so on. That will be lifted tonight. There will be a change, I think, in the State Department policy directive, because the need there is somewhat different from what it is in the Defense Department. In the Defense Department we are dealing not only with the problem of movement of troops, but also with the question of the very sensitive intelligence, and the methods by which that intelligence is received, and I don't think that, as yet, it's been demonstrated that this has restricted the flow of essential news out of the Pentagon. Now if it does, we'll change it. But I haven't been convinced of that as yet.

Brazil's Urge for a Ban on Nuclear Arms

Q: Mr. President, Brazil has urged that a ban be declared on nuclear arms and delivery vehicles not only in Cuba, but in the rest of South America. Do you support this proposal and would you favor extending a similar ban on other areas, such as the Middle East, where Senator Javits has said that the continuing buildup of Soviet arms in Egypt, Syria, and other Arab states may provoke the next East-West crisis?

The President: Well, we're interested in the Brazilian proposal, which is under discussion at the United Nations. We're interested in it, and a similar proposal has been made for Africa. We would be interested in that, too.

The question comes down to the willingness of the countries of Latin America to accept the Brazilian proposal, and the development of an adequate inspection system. That's the issue.

Alger Hiss' TV Appearance

Q: Mr. President, how did you feel about the appearance of Alger Hiss on a television program on the career of Richard Nixon?

The President: I didn't see the program, but I thought Mr. Hagerty and Mr. Minow expressed a view with which I'm in sympathy.

An Income Tax Cut

Q: Mr. President, are you going to ask Congress for a $10 billion income tax cut in January, as recommended by your Labor-Management Policy Committee?

The President: The question of the tax cut is going to be discussed in the administration in the next 10 days, and we'll have recommendations to make the first part of January. Until then, I'll have to withhold, until we finally decide what we are going to do - the amounts, and where the cut will come.

Relations Between the USSR and Red China

Q: Mr. President, would you give us your estimate as to the current relations between Communist China and Communist Russia, particularly in relationship to the events in Cuba and in India?

The President: No, I don't think that any comment that I might make would necessarily be accurate, because there's a variety of opinions in regard to the matters which may be in dispute. And in addition I think that it's a matter which we should study. There's no assurances that it means it is helpful to us or harmful, as yet, but I think we have to wait. I said the other day that I thought this was a rather climactic period, and I think that we can perhaps tell in the next months what is going on in the world beyond this hemisphere with more precision. As of tonight it would be just estimates, and I think it would be a mistake to indulge those right now.

Q: Mr. President, you said you will change this procedure at the Defense Department when it's been demonstrated that the present is too restrictive ——

The President: That the public interest isn't being met, that's correct.

Q: How are you going to find out? The present situation is that the officers and others down there are reluctant to have any contacts with newspapermen because of not only the time they spend with the newspapermen, but the time in writing of the reports.

The President: Well, I'll bring that to Mr. Sylvester's attention, but I do - I'm not sure that we're suggesting that - in the first place, this rule has been in effect in the CIA for many years. Are we suggesting that any member of the Defense Department should speak on any subject to any newspaperman and the newspaperman should print it or not print it as he sees fit without any effort to attempt to limit the printing of news which may deal with the collection or the methods of collection of intelligence information?

Q: No, sir. It was just a question of - there are many areas other than the movement of troops and so forth.

The President: And intelligence. And in those areas which are not involved there, I would be delighted to talk to Mr. Sylvester and with representatives of the press and see if we can get this straightened out so that there is free flow of news to which the press is entitled, and which I think ought to be in the press, and on which any administration really must depend as a check to its own actions.

So I can assure you that our only interest has been, first, during this period of crisis and over a longer period to try to - not to have coming out of the Pentagon information which is highly sensitive, particularly in the intelligence areas, which I can assure you in my own not too distant experience has been extremely inimical to the interests of the United States. Now that is our only interest.

Beyond that, I think it ought to pour out. And as far as I'm concerned, I'll be glad to discuss with Mr. Sylvester and Mr. Manning. Now, as I've said, Mr. Manning is going to attempt, now that we passed at least a phase of this crisis, he will, I think, attempt to improve his order and improve the flow of information.

I will say, as an example that information has not necessarily been cut off, is the fact that Governor Stevenson sent a message on his conversation with U Thant - reporting U Thant's 2-day visit to Cuba - it was finally distributed in the Department of State by 8 a.m. By 10, before the Secretary of State had seen it, it was on a wire and one of the wire services had it completely, including some of the quotes from it, and it caused Governor Stevenson some pain. So that I think information has been flowing out, but if it isn't we'll get it out, so I can assure you that we'll work on it.

Q: I mean in the area other than national security.

The President: That is correct.

A Climactic Period

Q: Mr. President, when you speak of this as a climactic period, can you sketch in what you think some of the ultimate possibilities are?

The President: No, I don't think we can, but I do think if 5 years ago we had looked at the world, I don't think we would have made a judgment that it would have moved quite the way it has moved, that China and India would be involved in a very serious struggle which may lead to a full-scale war if it hasn't already, and that relations in many parts of the world would be as changing as they are.

I think this is a very climactic period.

Reporter: Thank you, Mr. President.

[1]Executive Order 11063 (27 F.R. 11527).

[2]Earlier, on October 24, the White House had released a memorandum to editors and radio and television news directors listing 12 categories of military information vital to the national security concerning which no further releases would be issued by the Department of Defense. The memorandum requested that during the tense international situation all news media exercise caution and discretion in the publication of such information which possibly might come into their possession from other sources.

THE PRESIDENT'S NEWS CONFERENCE OF

DECEMBER 12, 1962

The President: Good afternoon.

On behalf of the American people, I wish to express my gratitude to the French Government for its decision to lend the Mona Lisa of Leonardo da Vinci for exhibition in the United States. This incomparable masterpiece, the work of one of the greatest figures of the greatest Western age of creativity, will come to this country as a reminder of the friendship that exists between

France and the United States. It will come also as a reminder of the universal nature of art. At the National Gallery in Washington, beginning January 8, the Mona Lisa will be exhibited with the special care so great a work of art merits.

Mrs. Kennedy and I particularly want to thank President de Gaulle for his generous gesture in making possible this historic loan, and Mr. Andre Malraux, the distinguished French Minister of Cultural Affairs, for his good offices in the matter.

And now to turn to the more physical side: For the past 2½ years the American Athletic Union and other amateur athletic groups organized as federations, have engaged in a dispute which now threatens proper representation for the United States in international competition. This includes the Pan American games at Sao Paulo and the 1964 Olympic games in Tokyo. A number of efforts have been made to resolve the differences between the AAU and the federations. This administration has made and is making its good offices possible in every way. Ultimately the Attorney General was called in to attempt to further settle these differences.

After this final effort last month, it appeared that these organizations had agreed to put aside their differences long enough to permit the United States and its athletes to compete in international competition, and particularly in the Olympics of 1964.

Now, however, even that coalition has been tangled by a whole group of conflicting interpretations. The governing bodies of these groups apparently put their own interests before the interests of our athletes, our traditions of sport, and our country. The time has come for these groups to put the national interest first. Their continued bickering is grossly unfair. There is no winner, but there are many losers - thousands of American amateur athletes, the American athletic community, and the traditions of American sportsmanship. On behalf of the country and on behalf of sport, I call on these organizations to submit their differences to an arbitration panel immediately. If we do not, we will not have an Olympic team in 1964. It is my earnest hope that these groups will quickly abandon their concern with victory for themselves at the conference table and focus on their more proper concern, victory for sportsmanship.

QUESTIONS

Khrushchev's Speech on Cuba

Q: Mr. President, in his speech today Khrushchev said, among other things, that he was holding the United States to its pledge against invading Cuba or was ready to take measures of his own. What is your reaction to the speech and what is the situation now regarding a no-invasion pledge? Would we ever make one such a formal declaration without first obtaining on-site inspections?

The President: Well, I haven't had a chance to analyze the speech with the care with which such a speech obviously should be studied. Number two, Governor Stevenson and Mr. McCloy are now up in New York, and have been for some weeks, discussing this matter of our future position toward Cuba and the Soviet Union's position toward Cuba, the question of weapons, inspection, aerial observance, invasion.

At present, I would say that our situation was best described in the statement that I made at our last press conference. I am hopeful that the negotiations that are now going on in New York will come to some conclusion in the not too distant future. But pending that, I would say that we are going to stay with what I said 2 weeks ago. In the meanwhile we will maintain - take every step that's necessary to make sure that these missiles are not reintroduced into Cuba or that offensive weapons are not reintroduced. And we are taking those means daily.

Governor Stevenson and Cuba

Q: Mr. President, in connection with Governor Stevenson and Cuba and some of the recent reports on the position taken by the Governor in the National Security Council, against this background, can you tell us, sir, whether prior to your announced decision on October 22, that Governor Stevenson took at any time a position that was contrary or counter to the final decision as you announced it?

The President: Well, as I said before, I would not attempt to describe, verify, or in any way discuss the position that any member of the National Security Council has taken. The National Security Council is an advisory body to the President; in the final analysis, the President of the United States must make the decision. And it is his decision. It's not the decision of the National Security Council or any collective decision. That was my view and my statement on Cuba a year ago, and it's my view on Cuba and the policies we followed recently this year.

I don't really think that there's much advantage to various press speculations on various positions which the members of the National Security Council took on the days from Tuesday to the next Sunday. Quite frankly, those positions frequently changed as members of the Council examined the alternatives and the possible repercussions of various courses of action. And it is my view that when the final consensus was reached and when I finally made a judgment - and the judgment was not really completed in its ultimate sense until the Sunday morning - that every member of the Executive Committee of the National Security Council supported the policy we finally adopted.

I would say, after having read various statements of the past 10 days, that any historian - and I think this matter should be left to historians - who walks through this mine field of charges and countercharges, should proceed with some care.

Q: Do you agree with Ambassador Stevenson, that the authors of this article acted irresponsibly?

The President: I've never attempted to characterize members of the press. I think that they have to meet their responsibilities. I've had some criticisms with various points which have been made, and I wouldn't attempt to characterize writers of this article or any other.

Q: Do you plan any inquiry to learn who it was that breached the security of the National Security Council?

The President: Yes, well, I've satisfied myself that these matters have never, as you know, never can be or very seldom are ever really determined with precision. It's my judgment that this statement or interpretation of Governor Stevenson's position did not come from a member of the National Security Council. I satisfied myself on that. I never heard anyone characterize Governor Stevenson's position in that way and I am satisfied, myself, that no one did.

Now, there are other people that might have. But that's a matter for the reporters and it's a matter that, as I say, I think can be much better left to history when the whole record will be spread out in great detail.

Q: You don't know, then, who leaked it?

The President: No, I don't know who, and I think it's unfortunate if any-body discusses any matter that comes before the National Security Council be-cause I think it lessens its effectiveness. But I have satisfied myself that the remark did not come from a member of the National Security Council.

The Role of Britain in Atomic Defense

Q: Sir, if it becomes necessary to cancel the Skybolt missile program be-cause of missile operational inability, what role can Britain play in our mu-tual atomic defenses?

The President: Well, I think it will play a significant role as a nuclear power, and the problem with the Skybolt is that it is the most sophisticated weapon imaginable. To fire a missile from a plane moving at high speed to hit a target 1,000 miles away requires the most advanced engineering, and of course it has been, really, in a sense the kind of engineering that's been beyond us.

We've put a half a billion dollars into it already. To complete the system might cost another - and to buy the missiles that we would want might require $2.5 billion. The five tests have not been successful, so that there really is the question of how much it is worth to the British and ourselves to put in that kind of money when we have competing claims for our available funds.

On the other hand, the British have a very important equity in the matter. It was to discuss that equity that Mr. McNamara went to Great Britain. I'm sure that it will be a matter which will be discussed with the Prime Minister in Nassau, and the United States, which is reviewing its budget, will take no fin-al decision until these conferences have been completed.

The Tax Cut

Q: Mr. President, has the opposition expressed by Chairman Wilbur Mills of the Ways and Means Committee changed the administration's position on tax cuts that it has proposed for the next year?

The President: Well, I think that Mr. Mills' interview should be read in entirety. And if you read the entire article, it does not suggest that the administration, under some circumstances, and Mr. Mills may be so far apart. In fact, I'm going to see Congressman Mills today.

I'll be talking about the matter somewhat further on Friday night at the New York Economic Club, and will make detailed proposals.

We intend to go ahead with our program. And then, of course, it will be up to the Ways and Means Committee and the Congress to make a judgment as to whether they will accept it. What I think should be of concern to us all is not the question of the immediate business prospects for the next 3 or 4 months, but, really, the general trend of our industrial growth, our employment lag, over the last 5 or 6 years.

And really we should consider not only our own economic situation but that of Western Europe. I think that Mr. Jacobsson, of the International Monetary Fund, made a speech in 1959 or 1960 saying that the great period of the infla-tionary thrust might be coming to an end and what should concern the Western capital countries was really deflation.

And I'm hopeful that as we have a chance to explore this matter with the Congress that they will give it very close attention. Quite obviously Mr. Mills will have a very decisive voice in the final decision, but we hope to adjust our viewpoints so that we can get some action on this program next year.

The President's Official Papers

Q: Mr. President, your speaking of historians induces me to ask you this: most former Presidents have put their official papers in libraries in their home States where they are not readily available to scholars and historians who come here to work with the Library of Congress and other agencies here. Have you decided where to put yours and would you consider putting it in Washington?

The President: Yes, I am going to put it in Cambridge, Mass. (Laughter)

Let me say I know that we have a library now in Independence, Hyde Park, Mr. Hoover's library at Stanford, Mr. Eisenhower's library at Abilene. There are advantages and disadvantages. In some ways it helps stimulate scholarship in those areas; in addition, through scientific means of reproduction, microfilms, and all of the rest, it's possible to make documents available generally here in Washington, and through the Archives, the Library of Congress, and at the libraries. The number of scholars who deal with these subjects in detail, it seems to me, will find it possible in a central place to get the kind of documents that they need. So that while there is a problem, as you suggest, I think that we can, and this will certainly be increased as time goes on, we will find it possible to so reproduce the key documents that they will be commonly available, I would hope, in Washington. There are a great many other advantages to a library – if you've gone to Franklin Roosevelt's library and to Harry Truman's library. It offers a good deal of stimulus to the study of American history, besides being a place where you can keep for a long time documents. There are many other things of interest which I think are rather advantageous to have spread around the country, particularly as it stimulates the study of the Presidency.

The Need for More Scientists

Q: Speaking of scholars, Mr. President, you and Dr. Wiesner have been putting heavy stress on the need for more scientists in this country.

The President: Yes, that's right. They are just releasing their report on the shortage of engineers.

Q: I wonder what your reaction is to a program in some of the New York City schools, where scientists from private industry, I believe at General Sarnoff's suggestion, are going into classrooms and giving lectures and demonstrations with the object of encouraging scientific careers?

The President: I think it would be useful, because I think motivation is one of the problems. In addition, lack of funds is the problem to which the committee just addressed itself. We're going to have a big shortage of engineers, mathematicians, scientists, a good many of these men who would have the potential cannot afford the doctorate studies. It will require an investment by the Federal Government. But the kind of program which provides motivation you've talked about will be very useful.

Negro Conference on Foreign Policy

Q: Mr. President, 3 weeks ago, six distinguished Negro leaders convened a conference on foreign policy in the Negro community at Arden House. They passed a number of resolutions and they also passed resolutions to confer with you. Have you received the resolutions, and if so, do you have any comment? And number two, do you intend to meet with the six Negro leaders?

The President: Yes, I'm supposed to meet with them. I am not familiar with all of the resolutions. I remember one of them with regard to the question of Ambassadors in the foreign service, and a good many other places. And I am meeting with them.

Shipping to Cuba

Q: Mr. President, can you tell us what's being done to curb Western and other shipping to Cuba, the measures that are being taken, if any, curbing shipping by Western nations, and other unaligned countries shipping material into Cuba. There's a great deal of shipping en route there now, according to the information we get.

The President: Yes. As you know, the shipping of any kinds of goods of the kind that would be used as offensive weapons, of course, action would be taken by the United States. Regular shipping, the United States has attempted to use its influence with members of NATO and others to discourage shipping. Some countries have responded and the United States is preparing other regulations which will affect shipping which should be available within the next 2 weeks.

Project Rover

Q: Mr. President, after your trip to Los Alamos Laboratory, New Mexico, is it your intention to ask for more money to speed up Project Rover, or for nuclear propulsion in space?

The President: We're going to let these tests go on, of the reactor. These tests should be completed by July. If they are successful, then we will put more money into the program, which would involve the Nerva and Rift, both the engine and the regular machine. We will wait until July, however, to see if these tests are successful.

It should be understood that the nuclear rocket, even under the most favorable circumstances, would not play a role in any first lunar landing. This will not come into play until 1970 or '71. It would be useful for further trips to the moon or trips to Mars. But we have a good many areas competing for our available space dollars, and we have to try to channel it into those programs which will bring us a result, first, on our moon landing, and then to consider Mars.

Prisoners in Cuba

Q: Mr. President, I wonder if you could bring us up to date on what is being done to get the prisoners out of Cuba, and whether you think it's in the national interest to give food and medicine to Cuba to get these men back?

The President: Well, this is being done by the private committee of the —

Q: But is that in the national interest? Do you favor that, sir?

The President: It is being handled by a private committee composed of the families of the prisoners, and a committee of which Gen. Lucius Clay and others are members, and I'm very sympathetic to their efforts.

The Tax Program

Q: You stated, sir, that you were going ahead and present your tax program to the Congress. Two questions about that program, in view of Mr. Mills' statements and the talk there has been about tax reduction: do you still plan, in your program, to ask for a reduction that would be retroactive to January 1, 1963; and will this program be in two parts, a program of quick tax reduction and a program of long-term reform?

The President: I think it would be better to wait until the first of the year before we get the precise details.   But there would be, in our proposals, tax cuts involving 1963.

Progress in Viet-Nam

Q: Mr. President, it was just a year ago that you ordered stepped-up aid to Viet-Nam. There seems to be a good deal of discouragement about the progress. Can you give us your assessment?

The President: Well, we are putting in a major effort in Viet-Nam.   As you know, we have about 10 or 11 times as many men there as we had a year ago. We've had a number of casualties.   We put in an awful lot of equipment.   We are going ahead with the strategic hamlet proposal.   In some phases, the military program has been quite successful.   There is great difficulty, however, in fighting a guerrilla war.   You need 10 to 1 or 11 to 1, especially in terrain as difficult as South Viet-Nam.

So we don't see the end of the tunnel, but I must say I don't think it is darker than it was a year ago, and in some ways lighter.

"Offensive Weapons" in Cuba

Q: Mr. President, could you define for us the term "offensive weapons" in the context of the Cuban situation, and are you satisfied that such weapons no longer are in Cuba?

The President: I would refer you back to the exchange of letters between Mr. Khrushchev and myself for our definition of offensive weapons.

On the second part of your question, it is our best judgment that the missiles have been removed from Cuba, and the planes.   Now, these things are never 100 percent, and it is for that reason that we are insisting on verification, or if we can't get the kind of international inspection we will continue to use our own method of verification, which we believe gives us assurance against a reintroduction of these weapons into Cuba.   And I think that the methods we are using to determine the status of military activity in Cuba are very effective, and are being used frequently.

I think we have the President of Chile.   We are very glad to welcome him here on his first visit to the United States.

And he told me that he had a press conference yesterday and that the press in America were far gentler than they were in Chile.   (Applause)

We don't want to give him the wrong impression, so I'll call on Mr. Chalmers Roberts.   (Laughter)

Direct Communication with the Kremlin

Mr. Roberts: Mr. President, the administration proposed in Geneva today some sort of direct communication between the White House and the Kremlin, either a telephone or teletype. Could you tell us what was in your mind in proposing this and how it is related to the Cuban affair, and the fact of the delay?

The President: There was a delay, as you know, in the communications back and forth, in the Cuban affair.   In some degree I think that on one or two occasions it was necessary to rely on open broadcasts of messages, rather than sending them through the coding procedure which took a number of hours.   What was happening was that when we finally concluded our day and sent the message to the Soviets, they were just waking up, and when they finished their day and prepared their messages for us, we were just waking up. So that it was taking time. The coding procedures were slow. In a nuclear age speed is very desirable. So we are hoping that out of this present conversation we can get instantaneous communication or at least relatively instantaneous communication.

Q: Were you speaking, sir, of teletype or telephone? You once told us you didn't think a telephone was very useful.

The President: I think that that's probably true. I'm not convinced that telephoning would have speeded, or that conversation on the telephone between Mr. Khrushchev and myself would have speeded a solution of the Cuban crisis. Teletype I think might have made it a safer situation. A phone might be the solution but teletype certainly seems to have some advantages, yes.

Q: Mr. Khrushchev's speech today is considered a major policy declaration. It seems to be moderate in tone. I was wondering if you found any encouragement in that tone.

The President: No, as I say, I've only had a general description and it seemed to be directed really more to the members of the bloc, but I haven't really concluded an analysis of it.

Effect of Brazilian Economic Problems

Q: Mr. President, Brazil has not fully carried out the anti-inflation measures which she pledged herself to carry out last year when she got large new loans and rescheduling of old loans. And now she is in very deep economic trouble. What effect do you think this has upon the other nations in Latin America who are trying to meet the demands of the Alliance for Progress program, and what is the possible effect upon members of Congress in their attitude towards aid and the Alliance?

The President: Well, I think the situation is most painful to the Brazilians, themselves, with inflation of 50 percent - which is almost unprecedented over any period of time without causing the most severe dislocations - 50 percent inflation increase in the cost of living within a year. So that I think that this is a matter which the Brazilians must deal with. There is nothing, really, that the United States can do that can possibly benefit the people of Brazil if you have a situation which is so unstable as the fiscal and monetary situation within Brazil.

So this is of concern to the Government. It must be and it certainly is of concern to us. I understand that the Finance Minister of Brazil will be coming to Washington in January. Our Ambassador to Brazil has just been back for consultations which we discussed this matter with them, and I think that the Brazilian Government is aware of the strong concern that we have for this inflation which eats up our aid and which, of course, contributes to a flight of capital and, therefore, diminishes rather than increases the stability of the state.

Satire on the Presidency

Q: Mr. President, it's been a long time since a President and his family have been subjected to such a heavy barrage of teasing and fun-poking and satire. There have been books on "Backstairs at the White House," and cartoon books with clever sayings, and photo albums with balloons and the rest, and now a smash hit record.

Can you tell us whether you read and listen to these things, and whether they produce annoyment or enjoyment?

The President: Annoyment? No. Yes, I have read them and listened to them and actually I listened to Mr. Meader's record, but I thought it sounded more like Teddy than it did me - (laughter) - so he's annoyed.

Discussions with the President of Chile

Q: We understand there will be a communique concerning your discussions with the President of Chile, but meanwhile we are wondering if these discussions, in your judgment, have accelerated or will accelerate the Alliance for Progress in that country and in Latin America generally.

The President: I think it definitely will accelerate it.

Q: Mr. President, this also has to do with the Alliance for Progress. A-side from the good intentions expressed by various governments in Latin America, how much real advance has been made in the area of economic, social, and political reform, and number two, is there any procedure by which those reforms can be evaluated here or in the OAS?

The President: Well, as you know, there is a procedure under the Alliance for Progress, the so-called wise men, who have been analyzing and approving the various steps that we take under the Alliance for Progress, without attempting to be in any way exclusive. I know that a good many reforms have been made in Venezuela, Colombia. In fact, in Chile we have been discussing, and the President has described some of the agrarian and tax reforms that Chile is now undertaking, which give us greater promise for the future. So that I think, even though as I said in my toast yesterday, the problems of Latin America are staggering, lack of resources and the overdependence on one or two commodities, these governments in many cases are making a very determined effort under staggering difficulties. We had a visit from the President of Honduras the other day. Fifty-six percent of the people of Honduras are illiterate. These are terribly difficult problems. So that I don't think we should be impatient with failure, but we should not desist because we've not solved all the problems overnight.

In the case of Chile, as the President has pointed out, they depend, as many other Latin American countries do, on one or two commodities for their foreign exchange. The prices of these commodities in the case of nearly every country of Latin America have dropped in the last 3 or 4 years. The price of raw material exports of Colombia, as I pointed out in another press conference, has dropped more than our aid has given them. Brazil depended on coffee and coffee has dropped, though we hope the coffee agreement will make some difference.

So that I am disturbed, but I think we ought to realize that we are dealing with the most staggering problems.

Q: If I may follow up on that, sir, recently the OAS sent down a task force to Latin America, and they came up with a report that there wasn't sufficient participation by labor and other groups of that sort in the planning areas of the various governments, and that seemed to be an objective of the Alliance for Progress. Is there any way by which that process could be speeded up?

The President: I think the strengthening of the labor movement would be really one of the most desirable things we can do. Otherwise, the labor movement is going to be disaffected and go to the radical left. This is a problem Mr. Moscoso was dealing with all the time, and I am glad to be reminded of this particular point.

DECEMBER 12, 1962

The Flow of News to Reporters

Q: Sir, I wonder if, as a matter of policy, you would tell us if you favor important Government stories going to a restricted few reporters who may be specially called in for this, or if, as a matter of policy, you would let the people of your administration know that you think news should flow freely to all reporters at the same time?

The President: I think - yes, I will let them know, and I think it ought to. I'm not aware that the privileged few - I think that obviously some of the weekly magazines do different kinds of stories than the daily reporters, but I don't think there should be a discrimination because of size or sex or any other reason. (Laughter)

Criticism of the John Birch Society

Q: Mr. President, in some of our major cities, John Birch or rightwing-type groups have been organizing boycotts against stores which carry imports from Iron Curtain, so-called Iron Curtain countries, and in some cases intimidating the stores. The State Department suggests that this is contrary to our policy of encouraging nonstrategic trade with those countries. I wonder if you share that view about those boycotts?

The President: Yes. I don't really think that - I think that it harasses merchants and I don't think it really carries on much of an effective fight against the spread of communism. If they really want to do something about the spread of communism, they will assist the Alliance for Progress, for one thing, or they will encourage their children to join the Peace Corps, or they will do a good many other things which are very greatly - they will be generous to students who come to the United States to study, and show them something of America. Those are the things that really make a difference. Not going down and because some merchant happens to have Polish hams in his shop, saying he is unpatriotic, doesn't seem to me to be a great contribution in the fight against communism.

Life Article on the Security Council

Q: Mr. President, there was a very specific denial from your office about the authenticity of the second article to appear in relation to what went on or what didn't go on in the Security Council. I am referring to the Life magazine article. There has been a good deal of speculation which has arisen as a result of a failure to say whether or not the first article which created all the furor was authentic.

The President: I want to say now the White House statement dealt with only two points in the second article. One was whether the White House had in any way authorized or suggested the article in the Saturday Evening Post, and, number two, whether the White House had made members of the National Security Council available. Both of those were untrue. The White House had nothing to do with the determination to write the article or with its preparation. And that was what we addressed ourselves to. I will not get into a discussion of the various positions of the members of the National Security Council. Governor Stevenson has already made a reference to his position.

The fact of the matter is that Governor Stevenson renders very distinguished service, as I have said. I nominated him for the Presidency in 1956. I would not have supported him for the Presidency if I had not believed that he would be an effective and responsible President. He has done an excellent job at the United Nations.

I am surprised that anyone would possibly think that it would be in the interest of the country, or the administration, or the White House, that any lessening of his influence would be provided.

The reporters who happened to be - the Presidency is not a very good place to make new friends. I'm going to keep my old friends. But I am responsible for many things under the Constitution, but not for what they write. That's their responsibility and that is the way we will continue it.

Administration Priorities

Q: Mr. President, Congress has appropriated and you have approved a $10 million expenditure for the construction of an aquarium here in Washington. It has been noted that the dependent and needy children in Junior Village, who are urgently in need of additional housing, have not been similarly favored. Would you comment on this unusual order of priority?

The President: Well, I think that one of the unfortunate things, and I think the Congress should bear responsibility in part for it, is that we have inadequate expenditures for the needs of the people of the District, particularly the younger people, for our schools, our teachers are overburdened, recreational facilities are inadequate, and we're dealing with a very difficult situation right here in the District of Columbia.

Now, some people make a judgment that that's an indication that there is something wrong with the District and the way to deal with it is just to squeeze the District harder. I don't think the Congress has appropriated sufficient funds for the interests of the District, particularly of the younger people in the District, and this is the center of the capital of a leading country of the free world and it will be to our disgrace if we have any situation develop in the City of Washington, this rather beautiful city in some ways, which is not a credit to all of our people. So I think that there may be need for an aquarium, there may be need for a good many buildings, but in my opinion the resource of youth here should be more adequately developed.

Reporter: Thank you, Mr. President.

1963

THE PRESIDENT'S NEWS CONFERENCE OF

JANUARY 24, 1963

The President: Good afternoon. I have an opening statement.

It would be well to remind all concerned of the hard and fast realities of this Nation's relationship with Europe - realities of danger, power, and purpose which are too deeply rooted in history and necessity to be either obscured or altered in the long run by personal or even national differences. The reality of danger is that all free men and nations live under the constant threat of the Communist advance. Although presently in some disarray, the Communist apparatus controls more than a billion people, and it daily confronts Europe and the United States with hundreds of missiles, scores of divisions, and the purposes of domination.

The reality of power is that the resources essential to defense against this danger are concentrated overwhelmingly in the nations of the Atlantic Alliance. In unity this alliance has ample strength to hold back the expansion of communism until such time as it loses its force and momentum. Acting alone neither the United States nor Europe could be certain of success and survival. The reality of purpose, therefore, is that that which serves to unite us is right, and what tends to divide us is wrong. The people and Government of the United States over the three past administrations have built their policy on these realities. The same policy has been followed by the people and governments of Europe. If we are to be worthy of our historic trust, we must continue on both sides of the Atlantic to work together in trust.

QUESTIONS

The Bay of Pigs Invasion

Q: Mr. President, as you may be aware, there seems to be some conflict on the part of history involving the Bay of Pigs invasion. As you know, the Attorney General says that no United States air support was contemplated, so therefore there was none to be withdrawn. Yet today, editor Jack Gore of the Fort Lauderdale, Fla., News says that to a group of editors who visited you on May 10, 1961, you told them that air cover was available, but you had decided not to use it.

Mr. Gore says you told these editors that one reason for your decision was that Ambassador Stevenson had complained that any such action would make a liar out of him in the U.N. Now also today, a Mr. Manuel Penobos, who has been rather vocal for the last day or two, a member of Brigade 2506, says that the United States military instructors of that brigade promised the men that they could expect air cover. Now, out of this welter of seemingly different stories, I wonder if you can set us straight on what the real situation was?

The President: Yes. There was not United States air cover planned, so that the first part of the statement attributed to the Attorney General, of course, is correct. Obviously if you're going to have United States air cover, you might as well have a complete United States commitment, which would have meant a full-fledged invasion by the United States. That was not the policy of the United States in April 1961.

What was talked about was the question of an air strike on Monday morning by planes which were flown by pilots, B-26 planes which were flown by pilots based not in the United States, not American planes.

That strike, as the Attorney General's interview in the U.S. News and World Report described it, was postponed until Monday afternoon. I think that the members of the brigade were under the impression that the planes which were available, which were the B-26 planes, would give them protection on the beach. That did not work out. That was one of the failures. The jets, the training jets, which were used against them were very effective and, therefore, we were not - the brigade was not able to maintain air supremacy on the beach.

So I think that the confusion comes from the use of the word "air cover," not to talk about the United States air cover as opposed to air cover which was attached to the brigade, some of which flew from various parts of this continent, not from the United States. So I think that will make it clear. As I've said from the beginning, the operation was a failure and the responsibility rests with the White House.

We engaged in intensive analysis of the reasons for the failure afterwards, headed by General Taylor, who is now Chairman of the Joint Chiefs of Staff. In the Congress the Senate Foreign Relations Committee conducted an investigation, and it seemed to me that the conduct of operations in October 1962 indicated that a good many lessons had been learned.

As to the recollection of the editor, there was no such conversation of the kind, at least that has been read to me. The problem of air cover and one of the reasons that the invasion failed may have well been discussed, but only in the terms that I have described, because what I have described are the facts.

The Nuclear Test Ban Treaty

Q: Mr. President, Mr. Gromyko has said that France must sign any nuclear test ban treaty if it is to be meaningful. In view of that, are you still encouraged by the prospects for such a treaty? And also can you tell us what this Government's position now is on whether Communist China should also be a signatory to the treaty?

The President: Well, I think the first problem is to attempt to negotiate the details of the treaty while these conversations are now going on with the Soviet Union, the British, and the United States. Then, if we are successful, if we work out a treaty which we believe gives us assurances, which we believe can provide for an end of testing and security for the countreis involved, the Senate of the United States accepts it under the constitutional provisions. Then I would hope that other countries would be willing to sign it. If other countries signed it, then, of course, great progress would be made. If other countries did not sign it and began to test, then we would have to make a judgment - and I'm sure that this would be written into the treaty - we would have to make a judgment as to whether this destroyed the treaty, the purpose of the treaty, and that therefore, the treaty was at an end. But I think we ought to go at it one step at a time.

The first step is to see whether the British and the Americans can work out an effective test ban treaty with the Soviet Union. Once that's done, then I think we can move on to these other questions.

Soviet Military Buildup in Cuba

Q: Mr. President, there are new reports of a Soviet military buildup in Cuba. I wonder if there's any truth to this report and if it might pose a threat to our intelligence operation there, our surveillance.

The President: No, we have been conducting continued surveillance. The best information we have is that one ship has arrived since the October crisis, which may have arms on it, and possibly military cargo. But there has not been a military buildup, in that sense, of equipment coming in from outside of Cuba. There's no evidence that this ship carried any offensive weapons.

Now, on Cuba itself, there are still - we think that probably about 4,500 Soviet technicians who were connected with the offensive weapons were withdrawn after the late October agreement. We figure there are still approximately 16 or 17 thousand Russians there, that the Soviets are continuing to operate the SAM sites and other technical pieces of equipment, and there are some organized units, the same organized units we've described before, which are still on the territory of Cuba. They are exercising, building some barracks. That is the kind of activity which is going on. There is no influx of military equipment, other than the ship. And, as I say, our scrutiny of Cuba is daily.

Foreign Aid and the Most-Favored-Nation Clause

Q: Mr. President, do you have any plans to go to the Congress to ask for a revision of the foreign aid treatment to Yugoslavia and Poland, an alteration of the most-favored-nation clause?

The President: Yes, I would hope that the Congress would reconsider the action it took last year in connection with the trade bill. We are in a very changing period in the world, in fact in all parts of the world, behind the Iron Curtain and indeed on this side of the Iron Curtain. To take legislative action which denies us an opportunity to exploit or to develop whatever differences in attitude or in tempo which may take place behind the Iron Curtain seems to me to be unwise. Once the Congress takes its action, that legislation exists for 2, 5, or 10 years. The situation during that period of time may change.

Now, I believe that we would be better off if we had - if the President, whoever he was, was given the option of extending the most-favored-nation treatment to Poland and Yugoslavia. The trade really is better in this case than aid, and we could then make a determination, based on the situation in both of those countries, whether the most-favored-nation privileges should be granted.

I'm not suggesting that in every case they should be. I'm not suggesting that in some cases they shouldn't be removed. But I do think that it should be a weapon in the arsenal of the President, with the President reporting to the Congress, the Congress maintaining close scrutiny, and not merely to make a judgment today on events when events may entirely change in the next 12 months. So I will recommend it to the Congress.

Voting Rights for Puerto Ricans

Q: Going back to the Caribbean, sir, would you favor letting the residents of Puerto Rico vote in presidential elections, even though they retained their commonwealth status, and thus pay no Federal income taxes?

The President: I hadn't heard that that was a proposal. The proposal that I heard might be put before the voters of Puerto Rico in regard to a commonwealth status did not include the right to vote in presidential elections. If they're going to vote in presidential elections, you raise a question of whether you should be a State, and take on the burdens and the privileges of statehood, so that I'm not prepared to say today that we should extend that particular privilege to Puerto Rico. Puerto Rico has seemed well satisfied with the present arrangement, which gives them a very advantageous position for their own economic and political development.

Onsite Nuclear Inspections

Q: In connection with the test ban talks, sir, your science advisers have said that the main issue now is the number of onsite inspections. Do you see any room for compromise between the 3 Mr. Khrushchev has offered and the 8 to 10 that you feel is adequate?

The President: I think that Mr. Foster is conducting the negotiations, and would be able to conduct them better probably if he developed the American position as time goes on, rather than attempting to develop it here at this time, when the negotiations are still in process. There is not only the question of the onsite inspections, but the location and the number of the automatic devices, and all this has to be meshed in, kinds of inspection, how free the inspectors will be, these are all questions which really ought to be negotiated at the table.

Q: Could you tell us, sir, in your own mind you must have seen some hope in the original letter.

The President: Yes, the fact that the principle of onsite inspection was accepted was very important, and that's the reason that we are participating in these negotiations at the top level to see if we can make a breakthrough here, because I think a breakthrough would be most important. There was an earlier reference by Mr. Lisagor to other countries beginning to test. This might have far-reaching repercussions and therefore we're very interested in keeping them going, to have them be successful. But I think Mr. Foster should determine the American position as time goes on.

Winston Churchill as U.S. Citizen

Q: Mr. President, a joint resolution has been offered in Congress to make Sir Winston Churchill an honorary citizen of the United States. I think it has been sponsored by Senators Young and Randolph, and by Mrs. Bolton. I know you took a stand on this as a Senator, but you've never been asked about this as President. What is your sentiment, your judgment about honoring the old guy this way?

The President: Well, it isn't essential as far as indicating our regard for him, but I would be delighted if the Congress passed a resolution, whether it's honorary citizenship or an expression of esteem. Some way or other it would be appropriate perhaps to remind Sir Winston Churchill of our regard for him. But it's written very large in any case. This would be a gracious act at this time.

A Democratic Convention in the South

Q: Mr. President, it has been 34 years since Houston. How do you feel about the Democrats going south again for a national convention, namely Florida?

The President: I think it would be fine, but I think it is really a question, once again, that is a negotiation which is extremely intense, being conducted by the National Committee, and involves the amount of — the South is prosperous and perhaps they would be able to compete successfully with Chicago,

Philadelphia, and some of the other areas. Geographically, I think it would be very good.

Limitation on Terms for Congressmen

Q: Mr. President, you have said that you are in favor of the two-term limit to the office of the Presidency. How do you feel about former President Eisenhower's suggestion that the terms of Congressmen also be limited?

The President: It's the sort of proposal which I may advance in a post-presidential period, but not right now. (Laughter)

New York and Cleveland Newspaper Strikes

Q: Mr. President, do you have any comment you care to make on the New York and Cleveland newspaper strikes?

The President: Yes, I wish that strike could come to an end. It doesn't come under the Taft-Hartley because it's not a national emergency, but it is a hardship on the men involved, and it affects adversely the prosperity of the city, and it affects the abilities of the people, particularly because New York is such a center. I hope it's going to be possible to compromise it. This sort of struggle to see who can stand the pressure the longest may be of interest to one side or the other, but it's hard on those involved, and I would hope that reason would motivate both sides and that they would reach the compromise which ultimately they're going to reach anyway. So I'm hopeful that the two sides will make a judgment that free collective bargaining must be responsible if it's going to be really free.

The Polaris Missile

Q: Mr. President, this has no relation to Skybolt, but are we not putting too many eggs in the Polaris basket if we're going to give Polaris missiles to the north and south of Europe, and doesn't the land mass of Russia and the position of the seas - doesn't that make it very hard to maneuver this Polaris to really hit at the heartland installations in Soviet Russia?

The President: Well, as you know, we also maintain the Minuteman, which does have a wide range, and Titans, and we still have bombers and still have planes based on Europe itself. If you look at the total arsenal, it's a very, very large one, and I think it gives very, very adequate assurances for the protection of Europe and the United States. We don't rely only on Polaris, even though Polaris is a very, very good weapon.

Liberalization of Immigration Laws

Q: Mr. President, when you were Senator, you were very active in efforts to liberalize our immigration laws. Have you any plans to advance this ambition of yours now?

The President: Yes. We are going to make some proposals in regard to redistributing particularly the unused quotas.

Q: Could you expand on that at all now?

The President: No. As you know, there is a total quota limitation on those permitted to come into the United States. Some of the countries do not use the quota. We have had some suggestions over a period of years as to how these unused quotas could be redistributed. That's the area that we're interested in now.

The Tax Bill

Q: Mr. President, on the tax bill, in your mind how much interdependence is there between the size of the revisions and the size of reductions?

The President: Could you expand that?

Q: Well, Congress seems to be more interested in reducing taxes than in making reforms.

The President: In reforms versus – right. Well, as you know, our proposal was for a $13 billion cut, more or less, and a $3 billion reform. Congressman Mills has been particularly interested in the reform, not only because it secures back some of the revenue, because there are inequities in the present tax law, but also there are some reforms which will stimulate growth and steer income or investment into areas which better serve the national purpose. So I consider both very important. I think it's essential we get a bill by this year, that we begin this tax reduction this year, if we're going to maintain or develop or stimulate our economic growth. The Congress will have to make the judgment whether both reform and revision, reduction, can be done this year. I would hope that they could be. In the final analysis, it's going to be their judgment, however.

Q: Mr. President, would you accept a revision and a tax cut which did not embody these reforms either this year or in some agreement?

The President: Well, I think it would be too early to make a judgment. I would think it would be unwise to carry out our total tax reduction package, which would then be $13-1/2 billion, unless we picked up revenue some other place, or reduced the amount of the cuts. So my judgment is that the package is the best approach. I'm hopeful that Congress will hold on to both. I put as the first priority, however, action this year, so we'll just have to wait and see whether both can be done this year. In any case we should be able to make progress, come what may, on the first step of the three-stage reduction, and I think it's physically possible to do both the reform and the revision this year and I think that is Chairman Mills' idea too.

Thanksgiving Day Riots in Washington, D.C.

Q: Mr. President, most of our racial dramas have been played in the deep South, but recently there was one here in the Nation's Capital, commonly referred to as the Thanksgiving Day riots in the D.C. Stadium, in which a large group of Negroes attacked a smaller group of whites. Since you last met with us, a citizens' committee has investigated the matter and issued a report referring to this lawlessness and mass misbehavior and criticizing the lack of discipline in the schools, classrooms, and so forth. I wonder, Mr. President, as President and as first citizen of the District of Columbia, if you could comment on the riot itself and the report; whether you think it's a fair report?

The President: Well, I think that there was a bad situation after that game. There have been riots connected with a lot of sports events, but this had a force to it which was worse than most. One of the purposes of our separate budget was to try to highlight the need for additional funds for schools, for housing, for changes in the environment, for assistance to young people who are neglected, orphans or who are with one parent or another. I think that what we ought to do is realize that the riot of that day highlighted a very bad situation in the District of Columbia, that a good many of our young people are neglected, that they are not counseled and they are not – the District doesn't pay as much attention to them, that the funds are inadequate and Congress has probably limited the appropriations too greatly, that the Executive has not paid enough attention to it.

We have appointed Mr. Horsky, who has been acquainted with this problem for years, to work in the White House on this problem of the District of Columbia, so that I'm hopeful that we will, in the next 12 months be able, together with the Congress, to do something to ease the situation in the District. It's up, of course, to the families involved, the schools involved, but I'm sympathetic to both the families and the schools because they deal with a very strange situation here in the District. A good many changes have taken place, and there is social unrest, and it ought to concern us all.

I might not have agreed with all parts of the report, but if the report serves to turn the attention of the Congress and the Executive and the District and the people who live here on the problems of the District, instead of always looking at our wide boulevards, I think it would be very useful.

Pressure on Civil Service Employees

Q: Mr. President, have you looking into reports by some civil service employees that they are subjected to pressure to buy $100 tickets to the Gala, and what do you think of this practice?

The President: Yes, I'm not aware of anyone who was pressured. I haven't received any report. It would be unfortunate. I can only say that anyone who bought a ticket or didn't buy a ticket are on the same basis.

The U.S. and the Economic Community

Q: Mr. President, in the event that Great Britain is shut out of the Common Market, how would that be likely to influence the United States plan to associate itself with the Economic Community? And how will it, in general, affect American interests?

The President: Well, we don't plan to associate ourselves with the Community. We plan to negotiate with the Community in order to provide for the admission of American goods as we had planned to negotiate with countries which are not members of the Common Market. We have strongly supported Britain's admission to the Common Market, however, because we think it helps build a united Europe, which, working to equal partnership with the United States, will provide security for Europe, for the United States, and together Europe and the United States – we can concern ourselves with the very pressing problems which affect so much of the world and Latin America, Africa, and Asia.

The United States concerns itself particularly, as distinguished Europeans – Dr. Adenauer, Mr. Schuman, Mr. de Gasperi, and others – in building a strong, vital, and vigorous Europe. Now that is coming about. I would be reluctant to see Europe and the United States, now that Europe is a strong and vital force, to go in separate directions because this battle is not yet won. In Latin America alone, we face critical problems in this decade. If Latin America is unable to trade with Europe and with the Common Market, we face very, very great economic problems which we cannot solve alone in Latin America. So our invitation to Europe is to unite, to be strong, and to join with us as an equal partner in meeting the problems of other parts of the world in the same way that some years ago the United States helped Europe build its strength.

Now, that's our hope. That has been the object of the American policy for 15 years. That's been the object of the policy of great Europeans who helped bring about a reconciliation some years ago between France and Germany. We've seen the recent manifestation of that reconciliation.

But there are problems throughout the globe that should occupy our attention, and the United States does not have the resources to meet them alone. We hope Europe and the United States together can do it on the basis of equality. That is why we have supported the admission of Britain to the Common Market.

In the final analysis this must be a judgment of the countries in Europe, the six. What kind of a Europe do they want? Do they want one looking out or looking in? What do they see as the balance of forces in the world today?

Now Europe is relatively secure. The day may come when Europe will not need the United States and its guarantees. I don't think that day has come yet, but it may come, and we would welcome that. We have no desire to stay in Europe except to participate in the defense of Europe. Once Europe is secure and feels itself secure, then the United States has 400,000 troops there and we would, of course, want to bring them home.

We do not desire to influence or dominate. What we desire to do is to see Euorpe and the United States together engaged in the struggle in other parts of the world. We cannot possibly survive if Europe and the United States are rich and prosperous and isolated. Now, we're asking that Europe together, united, join in this great effort, and I am hopeful they will, because after all that has been in the object of the policy of, as I have said, a great many Europeans for a great many years. And now, when success is in sight, we don't want to see this great partnership dissolve.

The Withdrawal of Some U.S. Missile Bases

Q: Mr. President, the Foreign Ministers of Turkey and Italy have announced that some of our missile bases are being withdrawn from their countries. Since these missile bases have often been the target of Soviet wrath, is there any expectation or possibility that there might be return concessions now for those?

The President: No. We are going to put Polaris submarines in there, a much more modern weapon, in the Mediterranean. We feel that provides a more adequate security. The British are phasing out the Thor missile, a missile which came into existence after the Jupiter, and in favor of the Polaris also. So I think we are going to be in a stronger position.

Relations with Argentina

Q: Mr. President, the Foreign Minister of Argentina, as you know, is in the United States this week, and it seems to be one of those refreshing cases where we've found a very loyal friend in a very major country down there. I wonder if there is anything you can say about that relationship in view of your discussions with the gentleman here this week?

The President: The relationship has been good. As you know, the Argentine sent destroyers and air units to the assistance of the United States at the time of the quarantine, which we were very grateful for. There is an International Monetary Fund group down there in Argentina now considering the Argentine's economic problems. We are watching that very closely and we're analyzing - when that study is completed - what we can most usefully do to be of assistance to the Argentine.

Need for a New Manned Strategic Bomber

Q: Mr. President, in your long-range defense planning, do you foresee a need for a manned strategic bomber after the current B-52's and B-47's are worn out?

The President: Yes, there may be - yes, there may be a need. That plan will last through 1970. We are securing, as you know, three B-70's. We have no further plans to develop at this time, but there may be a good many struggles in the globe in the late sixties or early seventies which are not subject to solution by missiles, but which may be more limited war, and where manned bombers may be very useful.

Establishment of a President's Conference of Governors

Q: Mr. President, in view of the expanded powers and functions of the Federal Government, have you thought of establishing a President's Conference of Governors to discuss your mutual plans and problems?

The President: No. As you know, there is a Governors' Conference that does take resolutions, and we are in liaison with them. As a matter of fact, I met with about 12 or 13 Governors last Saturday morning. But there is not a formal conference under way. But the liaison is very immediate. And, as you know, the United States budget today would be balanced if it were not for the assistance that the United States Government is giving to hard pressed States and local communities.

Mr. McNamara and the Republican Presidential Candidacy in 1968

Q: Mr. President, there have been published reports that some high placed Republican people have been making overtures to your Secretary of Defense for him to be their 1968 candidate for President. Mr. President, if you thought that Mr. McNamara were seriously considering these overtures, would you continue him in your Cabinet?

The President: I have too high a regard for him to launch his candidacy right now. (Laughter)

Desegregation at the University of Mississippi

Q: According to unofficial estimates, the Federal Government has already spent more than $4 million on the enforcement of the desegregation orders at the University of Mississippi. To this point, do you consider that effort worth it? And would you consider it to be an effort that had failed if, for some reason, Mr. Meredith had to leave the university during this winter?

The President: Well, it's not only $4 million but, of course, two people were killed and a good many were wounded, and it's had wide repercussions and some of them have been unfortunate. However, if the United States Government had failed to exert its influence to protect Mr. Meredith and Mr. Meredith had been denied admission by force, or if he had suffered physical attack, that would have been far more expensive.

This country, of course, cannot survive if the United States Government and the executive branch do not carry out the decisions of the court. It might be a decision in this case which some people may not agree with. The next time it might be another matter, and this Government would unravel very fast. So there's no question in my mind that the United States executive branch had to take the action that it did.

I would be sorry if Mr. Meredith leaves. College is difficult enough under any conditions. He's been subjected to a good deal of harassment and anyone who has gone through his experience in college would find it difficult to continue. I hope he continues. If he doesn't, that is a loss not only to Mr. Meredith but I think the University of Mississippi.

The French Nuclear Deterrent

Q: Mr. President, the theory was put forward in Europe this week that France must have its own separate nuclear deterrent because the Europeans cannot be sure that the United States 5 or 10 years from now would defend Europe with as much determination as we acted with during the Cuban crisis, whereas the Europeans could be sure that the French would. How do you answer such reasons?

The President: Well, actually, wasn't it put more directly than that, that what happened at Cuba proved that the United States might not defend Europe? That is a peculiar logic. If we had not acted in Cuba, that would have proved we would defend Europe? I don't think it would. So that once you accept that as the thesis, whatever we did in Cuba can be used to prove a point. Now the point is that since the Soviet Union developed its own nuclear capacity there is a balance, in a sense, between these two forces and neither will use it, and, therefore, Europe cannot rely on the United States.

Now, there may be reasons for a country to wish a nuclear force of its own, and France has put forward its reasons. But in my judgment, it's inaccurate and not really in the Alliance interest to justify it on the grounds that the United States would fail to defend Europe by whatever means are necessary.

I think the United States over the last 15 years has given - and in fact before that, the last 20 years - has given evidence that its commitments are good. Some in some parts of Europe may not believe that commitment, but I think that Chairman Khrushchev does and I think he's right.

In addition, once you begin to say that the United States will not come to the assistance of "X," can't someone say that perhaps France will not come to the assistance of Germany, and then everyone decides they must rely upon their own deterrent, and pretty soon you have as many deterrents as you have countries.

I think if France wishes to develop its own deterrent, that that's its judgment. It's done so. I have never had the slightest doubt that General de Gaulle would respond to the needs of the alliance. He responded when we were in difficulty in Cuba. I would hope that our confidence in him would be matched by his confidence in us.

Reporter: Thank you, Mr. President.

THE PRESIDENT'S NEWS CONFERENCE OF

FEBRUARY 7, 1963

The President: Good afternoon. I have one announcement to make.

I am pleased to announce that I intend to reappoint Mr. William McChesney Martin, Jr., as Chairman of the Board of Governors of the Federal Reserve System, and Mr. C. Canby Balderston as Vice Chairman for another term when their present terms expire in a few weeks.

Mr. Martin has been a member and Chairman of the Board since 1951. Previously he had served the Government with distinction as Chairman and President of the Export-Import Bank, Assistant Secretary of the Treasury, and United States Director of the International Bank for Reconstruction and Development. As Chairman of the Board of Governors, Mr. Martin has cooperated effectively in the economic policies of this administration and I look forward to a constructive working relationship in the years ahead.

As you know, the Federal Reserve System is a fully independent agency of the United States Government, but it is essential that there exist a relationship of mutual confidence and cooperation between the Federal Reserve, the economic agencies of the administration, including especially the Secretary of the Treasury, and the President.

Mr. Martin has my full confidence, and I look forward to continuing to work with him and his colleagues on the Board in the interests of a strong United States economy.

QUESTIONS

The Cuban Threat

Q: Mr. President, in your view, do you believe that the Cuban threat, militarily, has increased, decreased, or stayed on status quo since the removal of the offensive weapons?

The President: Well, there has been, since the removal of the offensive weapons, a reduction of 4500 people, we estimate. So to that degree the threat has diminished. And, of course, it is substantially different from the kind of threat we faced in October when there were offensive missiles and planes present. There still is a body of Soviet military equipment and technicians which I think is of serious concern to this Government and the hemisphere. But there has not been an addition since the removal of the weapons, there has not been an addition and there has been the subtraction of that number of personnel.

The Blockage of British Admission to the EEC and the
French Nuclear Deterrent

Q: Mr. President, since your last news conference, General de Gaulle has blocked the admission of Britain to the Common Market. De Gaulle has also indicate: that he wants an independent nuclear deterrent. Some people feel that these are fatal blows to Western allied unity. What do you think?

The President: Yes, he has, of course, been committed to an independent nuclear deterrent for a long time. We are concerned at the failure of the British to secure admission to the Common Market. We have supported the unification of Europe, economically and politically. There have been some references, I know, in some parts of the European press, that the United States does not seek to deal equally with Europe as an equal partner.

I think anyone who would bother to fairly analyze American policy in the last 15 years would come to a reverse conclusion. We put over $50 billion worth of assistance in rebuilding Europe. We supported strongly the Common Market, Euratom, and the other efforts to provide for a more unified Europe, which provides for a stronger Europe, which permits Europe to speak with a stronger voice, to accept greater responsibilities and greater burdens, as well as to take advantage of greater opportunities.

So we believe in a steadily increasing and growing Europe, a powerful Europe. We felt Britain would be an effective member of that Europe. And it was our hope, and still is our hope, that that powerful Europe, joined with the power of the North American Continent, would provide a source of strength in this decade which would permit the balance of power to be maintained with us, and which would inevitably provide for an attraction to the underdeveloped world.

I think it would be a disaster if we should divide. The forces in the world hostile to us are powerful. We went through a very difficult and dangerous experience this fall in Cuba. I have seen no real evidence that the policy of the Communist world towards us is basically changed. They still do not wish us well. We are not, as I said at the last press conference, in the harbor. We are still in very stormy seas and I really think it would be a mistake for us to be divided at this time when unity is essential.

Now, the United States is prepared to make every effort to provide Western Europe with the strong voice, to join with Western Europe, to cooperate with it to work out mechanisms that permit Europe to speak with the power and the authority that Europe is entitled to.

What we would regard as a most serious blow would be, however, a division between the Atlantic, the division between the United States and Europe, the inability of Europe and the United States to coordinate their policies to deal with this great challenge. There is the danger to Europe and the danger to us. And that must not take place. If it does, it will have the most serious repercussions for the security of us and for Western Europe.

The Role of the Secretary of State

Q: Mr. President, at a time when the Secretary of State and his department have been coming in for some criticism, Senator Jackson's subcommittee on national security policy has said the Secretary should play a larger role in national security affairs. What do you think the Secretary of State's role should be? And do you think your view and his are the same on this matter?

The President: Yes, my view and his are the same. The Secretary of State is the principal adviser to the President in the field of foreign policy. He is also the chief administrative officer of the Department of State which includes many responsibilities but whose central responsibility, of course, is to carry out the day-to-day business, as well as to set down the larger - and advise the President on the development of larger policies affecting our security.

Mr. Rusk and I are in very close communion on this matter. We are in agreement, and I have the highest confidence in him, and I'm sure that - but I do think that Senator Jackson's suggestions deserve very careful study. One of our great problems is we deal with the whole world, and the Department of State is involved, the Treasury may be involved, Agriculture may be involved, Defense may be involved, and the intelligence community involved. The coordination of that in an effective way which finally comes to the White House is one of the complicated tasks of administering our Government in these days.

Soviet Military Personnel in Cuba

Q: Mr. President, what, if anything, do you propose to do about the continued presence in Cuba of the Soviet military personnel? Are you just going to let them stay there?

The President: Well, as you know, we've been carrying out a good many policies in the last 4 months, since October. We were able to effect the withdrawal of the missiles. We were able to effect the withdrawal of the planes. There has been a reduction of 4,500 in the number of personnel. That was done by the United States being willing to move through a very dangerous period and the loss of an American soldier.

The continued presence of Soviet military personnel is of concern to us. I think the actions the United States has taken over the last 4 months indicate that we do not view the threat lightly.

Q: Mr. President, Defense Secretary McNamara apparently failed to convince some Republicans that all offensive weapons are withdrawn from Cuba. What more, if anything, do you believe the administration can do to convince some of the critics?

The President: Well, I don't know what more we can do. Mr. McNamara went to great length. As he pointed out, he exposed a good deal of information, and also he went further than under ordinary conditions we would have liked to have gone in telling our story.

Now, he has asked, and I endorse, and Mr. McCone has asked, that if anybody has any information in regard to the presence of offensive weapons systems or, indeed, the presence of any military force or weapons on the island of Cuba, I think they should make it available to General Carroll, who's in charge of intelligence for the Defense Department - if they would turn the information over.

Now, we get hundreds of reports every month, and we try to check them out. A good many of them are just rumors or reports, and even some of the Members of Congress who've come forward either refuse to say where they've heard the information or provide us with reports which do not have substance to them.

Now I cannot carry out the policy of the United States Government on the question if obviously there were offensive missiles found in Cuba contrary to Mr. Khrushchev's pledge. It would raise the greatest risks in October. But to take the United States into that path, to persuade our allies to come with us, to hazard our allies as well as the security of the free world, as well as the peace of the free world, we have to move with hard intelligence. We have to know what we're talking about. We cannot base the issue of war and peace on a rumor or report, which is not substantiated, or which some member of Congress refuses to tell us where he heard it.

This issue involves very definitely war and peace. And when you talk about the presence of offensive weapons there, if they are there, I think the Soviet Union is aware and Cuba is aware that we would be back where we were in October but in a far more concentrated way.

Now, if you're talking about that, and talking about the kinds of actions which would come from that, it seems to me we ought to know what we are talking about. Now it may be that there are hidden away some missiles. Nobody can prove, in the finite sense, that they're not there, or they might be brought in. But they're going to have to be erected, and we continue complete surveillance. They have to be moved. They have to be put onto pads. They have to be prepared to fire. And quite obviously, if the Soviet Union did that, it would indicate that they were prepared to take the chance of another great encounter between us, with all the dangers.

Now, they had these missiles on the pads and they withdrew them, so the United States is not powerless in the area of Cuba, but I do think we should keep our heads and attempt to use the best information we have. We've got, I think, as Secretary McNamara demonstrated - we're taking the greatest pains to try to be accurate, but we have to deal with facts as we know them, and not merely rumors and speculation.

Now, as I say, these things may all come about and we may find ourselves again with the Soviet Union toe to toe, but we ought to know what we have in our hands before we bring the United States, and ask our allies to come with us, to the brink again.

Q: *Mr. President, what is the administration's position now about the on-site inspections that you were insisting upon in October? Is that now a dead letter?*

The President: Yes, that's right. Cuba did not agree to on-site inspection unless there was inspection of the United States, which we did not agree to, and part of that was the question of the no-invasion pledge, and the rest. So that there has been no on-site inspection and I don't expect to get any. And I don't expect that Cuba will agree to the kind of on-site inspection that would give us more assurances than we have at the present time through photography.

Q: *Mr. President, because we depend so much on photo reconnaissance, what would be our position if the President of Cuba should forbid that and perhaps take a protest to the United Nations about what you call our daily scrutiny over their territory?*

The President: I would think we would deal with that situation when it comes up. This is a substitute, in a sense, for the kind of on-site inspection which we hope to get and which was proposed by the Secretary General of the United Nations at the time of the October crisis. The United States cannot, given the history of last fall, where deception was used against us, we could not be expected to merely trust to words in regard to a potential buildup. So we may have to face that situation, but if we do, we'll face it.

The New York and Cleveland Newspaper Strikes

Q: *Mr. President, the New York newspaper - and Cleveland - strikes do not fall at the present time under the Taft-Hartley law, and the impact of the New York strike can be seen by the fact that New York's economy is off 8 percent in department store sales. Do you feel that there should be some sort of legislation to bring strikes of this nature which affect the economy within the Taft-Hartley law, or do you see a larger role for the Government in these types of strikes?*

The President: Well, it's hard to have a strike under the Taft-Hartley law or under any language. You mean, really, that the Government would be involving itself in hundreds of strikes, because a good many strikes which do not affect the national health and safety can affect local prosperity, so that you would find the Government heavily involved in dozens of strikes.

I must say that I think that I believe strongly in free, collective bargaining, but that free, collective bargaining must be responsible, and it must have some concern, it seems to me, for the welfare of all who may be directly and indirectly involved. I am not sure that that sense of responsibility has been particularly vigorously displayed in the New York case, this trial by force. It may end up with two or three papers closing down, and the strike going on through the winter.

It would seem to me that reasonable men - there should be some understanding of the issues involved, and I don't think in my opinion that the bargaining there has been particularly responsible.

Withdrawal of Soviets from Cuba

Q: *Mr. President, Mr. Khrushchev apparently gave you some reason to believe last October that the Soviet military personnel were going to be withdrawn from Cuba. That hasn't happened. And my question is: Is there any official dialogue going on now to find out why the Russians are still there?*

The President: Well, as I say, there has been this reduction which we already described. In addition, as Mr. McNamara described yesterday, a picture of some evidence of some equipment being moved out. This is a continuing matter which is being discussed, obviously, with the Soviet Government, and we would expect that we would have clearer information as to the prospects as these days go on. But it has not been completed, and quite obviously in that sense is unfinished business.

Q: Mr. President, what chances do you think or do you believe there are of eliminating communism in Cuba within your term?

The President: I couldn't make any predicition about the elimination. I am quite obviously hopeful that it can be eliminated, but we have to wait and see what happens. There are a lot of unpleasant situations in the world today. China is one. It's unfortunate that communism was permitted to come into Cuba. It has been a problem in the last 5 years. We don't know what's going to happen internally. There's no obviously easy solution as to how the Communist movement will be removed. One way, of course, would be by the Cubans themselves, though that's very difficult, given the police setup. The other way would be by external action. But that's war and we should not regard that as a cheap or easy way to accomplish what we wish.

We live with a lot of dangerous situations all over the world. Berlin is one. There are many others. And we live with a good deal of hazard all around the world and have for 15 years. I cannot set down any time in which I can clearly see the end to the Castro regime. I believe it's going to come, but I couldn't possibly give a time limit. I think that those who do, sometimes mislead. I remember a good deal of talk in the early fifties about liberation, how Eastern Europe was going to be liberated. And then we had Hungary, and Poland, and East Germany, and no action was taken.

The reason the action wasn't taken was because they felt strongly that if they did take action it would bring on another war. So it's quite easy to discuss these things and say one thing or another ought to be done. But when they start talking about how, and when, they start talking about Americans invading Cuba and killing thousands of Cubans and Americans. With all the hazards around the world, that's a very serious decision, and I notice that that's not approached directly by a good many who have discussed the problem.

General de Gaulle on Nuclear Power and the European Situation

Q: Mr. President, General de Gaulle has indicated that it was the Nassau Pact which made him declare for an independent nuclear force. Yet, there are reports that as long ago as June of 1961 he told you in Paris that he had his own plans for organizing Europe, once there was no European crisis. Now do you feel it was the Nassau Pact or the easing of the Berlin crisis by the Cuban showdown that caused him finally to declare publicly for this?

The President: Well, as you know, the independent nuclear force he has been committed to for a number of years. There have been a number of explanations and reasons given, some contradictory, as to why he finally made - why he took the action that he did.

If you will re-read the Nassau Pact, we did give assistance to the British, the Polaris. The British did commit their forces to NATO. We did agree to make a similar offer, because there may have been technical reasons why the French were unable to accept the same kind of offer, and we did open the dialogue with General de Gaulle as to what progress we could make in this field. And we also agreed to a multilateral force. The whole emphasis of Nassau was on strengthening NATO and on the NATO commitment. So General de Gaulle has indicated that he is not an admirer of NATO. In my opinion, NATO is what keeps the Atlantic and Europe together.

Now what he said in Paris, he said he would have some suggestions for reorganizing NATO. Therefore, your quotation was not quite in the context in which he used it, and he obviously sees Europe as strong and France as occupying a particular position. And the question really is whether we are going to be partners or whether there will be sufficient division between us that the Soviet Union can exploit.

But I must say that the whole purpose at Nassau was to meet our obligations to the British, Skybolt having failed, and also to contribute together to the strengthening of NATO and therefore, those who object to that, it seems to me, in a sense, really object to NATO. And those who object to NATO, object to this tie between us which has protected the security of Europe and the United States for 15 years and can still, in this decade, if given support which it needs on both sides of the Atlantic.

Q: Could we pursue this a little bit further? Some thoughtful observers are saying that in view of the United States difficulty with General de Gaulle, and in a slightly lesser and slightly different way with the Diefenbaker government in Canada, that one of our basic problems with our allies is in convincing them of the sincerity of our desire for partnership, and that, therefore, we've got to seek some new kind of relationship with our allies to demonstrate that we really are interested in partnership.

Do you agree with this, and if you do, would you think it would involve some kind of a formula in which they would actually participate in the control of nuclear weapons, and the kicker is, could this formula be sold to the United States Congress?

The President: The Nassau agreement, as you know, did attempt, by its emphasis on the contributions which we would commonly make to the multinational force, and our support of the multilateral force, was an effort to deal with this problem of providing the Europeans who lacked a nuclear capacity a greater voice in the management of the weapons, and in the political direction of the weapons, and in its control.

We thought it was unwise to provide for - encourage the development of national deterrents. The Germans, in their '54 statement, took themselves out of the national deterrent and indicated that they would not develop it. I must say that it seems to me we should attempt to build on what we started at Nassau, in the multilateral force, to give those who do not have a deterrent, who do not wish to develop it for economic or political reasons, a larger voice and control in nuclear weapons.

To be successful and do something more than merely provide a facade, a different facade, of United States control, will require a good deal of negotiation and imagination and effort by both of us. When we have come to a conclusion, or during a conclusion, we will continue to consult with the Congress which has special responsibilities. We are conscious of our obligations under the McMahon act and, therefore, it will be very sensitive and difficult but I think a possible operation for us to carry out in the coming months. The purpose of it is the one you described, to prevent the Alliance from dissolving on this very difficult and sensitive question of control of nuclear weapons, which is tied up with sovereignty.

The Nassau agreement was an effort to meet that. Now, it is important to realize that a good many Europeans hold this view of the support of the multilateral force, and also there's been great evidence of strong support for NATO, a support which I'm hopeful will be indicated not only by words, but by actions in the coming months.

The Dock Worker's Strike

Q: Mr. President, do you consider the settlements reached in the dock work-ers' strike, which is generally pegged at 5 percent, within your wage-price guidelines, and would you consider a comparable settlement in the upcoming steel negotiations?

The President: Well, I wouldn't attempt to get into steel right now, thank you. (Laughter)

Cuba as a Military Threat to the U.S.

Q: Mr. President, to go back to Cuba, you have said that the presence of Russian forces on the island are a matter of concern. I would like to ask this question, sir: Do you think that Cuba is a serious military threat to the United States?

The President: I think we ought to keep a sense of proportion about the size of the force we're talking about. We are talking about four groups, 1100 to 1200 men each. Those are the organized military units. That's about 6,000 men. Obviously, those forces cannot be used to invade another country. They may be used to maintain some sort of control within Cuba, but obviously are not a force that can be used externally. And in addition, Cuba cannot possibly - it lacks any amphibious equipment, and quite obviously our power in that area is overwhelming.

I think the big dangers to Latin America, if I may say so, are the very dif-ficult, and in some cases desperate, conditions in the countries themselves, un-related to Cuba. Illiteracy, or bad housing, or maldistribution of wealth, or political or social instability - these are all problems we find, a diminishing exchange, balance of payments difficulty, drop in the price of their raw mater-ials upon which their income depends. These are all problems that I think are staggering, to which we ought to be devoting our attention.

Now, I think Castro has been discredited in the past months substantially, as everyone of our surveys in USIA show. One of the reasons has been the mis-sile business and also the presence of Russian forces which, in a sense, seem to be police units. So that what I think we should concern ourselves with, quite obviously, is Cuba, but Cuba as a center of propaganda and possibly sub-version, the training of agents - these are the things which we must watch about Cuba. But in the larger sense, it is the desperate and in some cases internal problems in Latin America, themselves unrelated to Fidel Castro whose image is greatly tarnished over a year ago, which caused me the concern and why I regard Latin America as the most critical area in the world today and why I would hope that Western Europe and the United States would not be so preoccupied with our disputes, which historically may not seem justified, when we have a very, very critical problem which should concern us both in Latin America.

Q: Now that I have your answer, I think the answer is that you do not think that it is a great military threat, but rather a threat in these areas that you speak of?

The President: The military threat would come if there was a reintroduction of the offensive weapons. But the kind of forces we are talking about, which are 6,000, do not represent a military threat. Cuba is a threat for the rea-sons that I have given, but it is a threat - I don't want to give the whole an-swer again - but it is a threat for the reason I have tried to explain to you.

Q: Mr. President, according to the recent remarks of Secretary Rusk, he said Mr. Khrushchev indicated that Soviet troops would be removed from Cuba in due course. Do you feel you have a commitment from Mr. Khrushchev in this regard, and what do you take "due course" to mean?

The President: That's what we are going to try to find out. That was the statement that was made. As I say, that's why I think in the coming days and weeks we may have a clearer idea as to whether that means this winter or not. And that's a matter of great interest to us.

Q: Do you feel you have a commitment, sir, from Mr. Khrushchev?

The President: I have read a statement of Mr. Khrushchev's that these forces would be removed in due course or due time. The time was not stated and, therefore, we're trying to get a more satisfactory definition.

The Zero Tariff Authority

Q: Mr. President, because Britain did not get into the Common Market, the zero tariff authority in the Trade Expansion Act is virtually meaningless now. At the time you proposed it, you said this was vital authority, to get our exports into Europe. Do you propose or do you plan to ask Congress to restore the authority, or if not, do you support the Douglas, Javits, and Reuss bills that are in to do that now?

The President: No, we hadn't planned to ask the Congress, because we do have the power, under the trade expansion bill, to reduce all other tariffs by 50 percent, which is a substantial authority. We lack the zero authority.

On the other hand, it's going to take some months before these negotiations move ahead. It's possible there may be some reconsideration of the British application. I would be responsive and in favor of legislation of the kind that you described. It is not essential, but it would be valuable, and if the Congress shows any disposition to favor it, I would support it.

Management of the News

Q: Mr. President, ever since Mr. Sylvester talked about what is called "managing the news," there's been a lot of confusion on the subject.[1] Do you feel the administration has a responsibility to engage in a sort of information program, educating people in the fact that under certain circumstances this practice has some ethical validity, and if this is not done, how will the public know when it's getting factual information and when not?

The President: I think it gets a good deal of factual information. The problem of the Federal Government, the National Government, what information it puts out, and I think we're trying to give the information, on the matter of Cuba we've been trying to be accurate. And there's also, it seems to me, the information of the press to make a judgment as to whether information that is coming out is accurate, not only by the National Government, but by others, and to subject that to careful scrutiny as they do our information.

Now, I remember a story the other day in one of our prominent papers which had a report of a Congressman about the presence of missiles - no supporting evidence, no willingness to give us the source of his information. We are not, after all, a foreign power.

And on page 10 was the statement of the Secretary of Defense, giving very clear details. That was page 10 and the other was page 1. So it's a responsibility of ours and, it seems to me, also the press. I would think a good many Americans, after the last 3 weeks of headlines, have the impression that there are offensive weapons in Cuba. Now it is our judgment, based on the best intelligence that we can get, that there are not offensive weapons in Cuba. I think it is important that the American people have an understanding and not compel, because of these various rumors and speculations, compel the Secretary of Defense to go on television for 2 hours to try to get the truth to the American people and, in the course of it, have to give a good deal of information which we are rather reluctant to give about our intelligence gathering facilities.

Q: Mr. President, do you feel that it is possible that the defensive weapons now going into Cuba, or there now, could be used for offensive purposes? For example, could not a defensive missile be used, launched from a PT boat or some other vessel? And if you do find this to be true, do you feel that any action would be requird?

The President: The range of the missiles on the Komar, the 12 Komars, is, I believe, 18 miles. So we would not regard that as a weapon which would be used in an attack on the United States. If there is going to be that kind of an attack on the United States, then you're going to have an attack from places other than Cuba, and you're going to have them with much larger weapons than a Komar torpedo boat can carry. Then you are talking about the willingness of the Soviet Union to begin a major war. Now if the Soviet Union is prepared to begin a major war, which will result in hundreds of millions of casualties by the time it is finished, then, of course, we all face a situation which is extremely grave.

I do not believe that that's what the Soviet Union wants, because I think they have other interests. I think they wish to seize power, but I don't think they wish to do so by a war. I therefore doubt if a Komar torpedo boat is going to attack the United States very soon. Now, it's possible - it's possible - everything is possible. And after our experience last fall, we operate on the assumption while hoping for the best, we expect the worst. It's very possible that the worst will come and we should prepare for it. That's why we continue our daily surveillance. It is possible, conceivable.

We cannot prove that there is not a missle in a cave or that the Soviet Union isn't going to ship next week. We prepare for that. But we will find them when they do and when they do, the Soviet Union and Cuba and the United States must all be aware that this will produce the greatest crisis which the world has faced in its history.

So I think that the Soviet Union will proceed with caution and care, and I think we should.

Reporter: Mr. President, thank you.

[1]Arthur Sylvester, Assistant Secretary of Defense (Public Affairs). See 1962 volume, this series, Items 410 [8], 515 [7, 14, 19].

THE PRESIDENT'S NEWS CONFERENCE OF

FEBRUARY 14, 1963

The President: Good afternoon. I have a preliminary statement.

I have sent to the Congress today a special message on legislative measures affecting our Nation's youth, stressing in particular the administration's bill to promote youth employment opportunities. This measure, which I hope will be among the first to be considered by both Houses, is urgently needed. A number of young people in the potential labor market age group will increase in this decade nearly 15 times as fast as it did in the 1950's. Seven and one-half million students are expected to drop out of school during the sixties, without a high school education, entering the labor market unprepared for anything much other than unskilled labor, and there are fewer of these jobs all the time. Young men and women no longer in school constitute already 18 percent of our total unemployment, although they comprise only 7 percent of the labor force. These figures reflect a serious national problem. Idle youth on our city streets create a host of problems.

The youth employment opportunities act will give many thousands of currently unemployed young people a chance to find employment, to be paid for their services, and to acquire skills and work experience. It will give them a solid start in their work in life.

<u>QUESTIONS</u>

The President's Tax Plan

Q: Mr. President, when you submitted your tax plan in the 1964 budget with its 11.9 deficit, you anticipated a certain amount of resistance to it. Walter Heller, however, says that some of this opposition comes from what he calls the basic puritan ethic of the American people. Do you think the time has come to abandon or at least update this puritan ethic he speaks of?

The President: No, I think that people are concerned about the size of the debt, and I am, and I think they're concerned about the deficit. But what I am most concerned about is the prospect of another recession.

Now, a recession is what would give us a massive deficit. I have already pointed out that in 1958 President Eisenhower thought he was going to have a half billion dollar surplus. At the end of the 1958 recession he had a $12½ billion deficit, the largest peace-time deficit in the history of this country.

We had another recession in 1960, which also increased our deficit. Now we have had an increase since the winter of 1961 in our economy. I am anxious, however, not to see a slide into another recession. In 1958, a recession, in 1960, a recession; the large deficit will come if we move into another recession.

And, in my judgment, the best argument and the one which was most effective as far as I was concerned was that the reduction in taxes was an effort to release sufficient purchasing power and was an effort to stimulate investment so that any downturn in business would be lessened in its impact and could be possibly postponed.

Now, if we don't have the tax cut, it substantially, in my opinion, increases the chance of a recession, which will increase unemployment, which will increase the size of our deficit. So that's what it comes down to. And I think that with the record we have had in the last 5 years of over 5 percent unemployment, two recessions, I think the important thing for us to do is prevent another one. Therefore, I think the tax cut should be looked at not as a method of making life easier, because if that were the only issue I think we would all be willing to pay our taxes to keep our economy going. But the tax cut argument rests with the desire to stimulate the economy and prevent a recession which will cost us the most - domestically, internationally - on our budget and on our balance of payments.

U.S. Policy Toward Europe

Q: Mr. President, in connection with the review of U.S. policy toward Europe, I wonder if you're even thinking about cutting down on the number of troops in Europe or adopting any measures of economic or political reprisal against President de Gaulle?

The President: No. In answer to your second question, definitely not.

In answer to the first question, as you know we have withdrawn over a period of some months some logistic forces, but we've kept our combat troops constant and, in addition, their equipment has been improved. We still have our six divisions and plan to maintain them until there is a desire on the part of the Europeans that they be withdrawn, and we've had no indications from any country in Europe that there is such a desire. If there was, of course, we would respond to it. They are there to help defend Europe and the West, not because we desire to keep them there for any purpose immediately of our own.

Resistance to Tax Reform and Tax Cuts

Q: Mr. President, back on taxes, I realize it's too quick to make precise reading on the fate of your tax reform and tax cut bill in the Congress, but there seems to be unusual resistance, not only to the tax reform, but several Senators and Congressmen are telling reporters that their constituents show a resistance to tax cuts. And then today, the administration received another setback in the defeat of the attempt to increase the size of the Senate Finance Committee.

Taking all these things together, could you give an assessment of how you think the bill is going to do; and, secondly, could you say whether you think it may be necessary for you to carry the problem to the people directly in a series of speeches or something of that kind?

The President: Well, I think it's a hard fight. The tax reform cuts across some of the most dearly held rights of any of our citizens. Some of them have been written into law, partly as a balance to rather high tax rates - in fact, very high tax rates. It's hard to get them changed.

Tax reform is, of course, a wonderful principle, but when you begin to write it in detail, it becomes less attractive. But we are talking about a $13.5 billion tax cut, with about 3 billion, 2 or 3 hundred million which would be recouped by the reform. In addition, we would find ourselves with a better balanced tax system and one which would be more effective for the economy. If we're not able to get the tax reform which we had suggested, there probably would be adjustments made in the overall reductions.

But I must say I recommend this because I think it's in the best interests of the economy of the country. In 1954 there was a tax reduction. Within a year the economy had been sufficiently stimulated that there were higher revenues at the lower tax rates than there had been the year before.

We have a tax system that was written, in a sense, during wartime to restrain growth. Now if you continue it, this country will inevitably move into a downturn and I would think our experience of '58 and '60 indicates that something has to be done. And in my opinion, the most effective thing that can be done at this time is our tax program.

Now, those who are opposed to the tax program should consider what the alternative is. And I think it's a restricted economic growth, higher unemployment. If we fail to do something about unemployment and begin to move into a downturn, higher unemployment, there'll be increased pressures for a 35-hour week as a method of increasing employment, and I think it would be far more costly in the long run to the Government and to the economy to defeat our bill. I think it ought to be approached the way.

What alternative does anyone have for increasing and maintaining economic growth in view of the large deficit of 1958 and in view of two recessions, in 1958 and 1960? Our plan to prevent a recession this year and the years to come is our tax bill and I think the Congress, I hope the Congress will adopt it. And I think the country, those who oppose it, should consider very carefully whay they will have as far as economic growth for this country if it is defeated.

Now we can take it to the people, as I am today, and on other occasions, and do the best we can.

Franklin D. Roosevelt, Jr.

Q: Mr. President, a number of Republicans have questioned the qualifications of Franklin D. Roosevelt, Jr., to be Under Secretary of Commerce. Would you like to answer them?

The President: Yes. They questioned the qualifications of his father to be President, and I think that Mr. Roosevelt - I am hopeful will be confirmed. I wouldn't have sent him up there unless I felt that he would be a good Under Secretary. I served with him in the Congress, and I am for him strongly. I hope the Senate confirms him.

Interdependence and Partnership with Europe

Q: Mr. President, there has been a great deal of talk between Europe and here about interdependence and about partnership. Is this Government at the stage of making the decision in fact to share command and control of nuclear forces with our European allies?

The President: We are, as you know, putting forward and have suggested a multilateral force as well as a multinational force, which will, I think, substantially increase the influence that the Europeans have in the atomic field. It is a very difficult area because the weapons have to be fired in 5 minutes, and who is going to be delegated on behalf of Europe to make this judgment? If the word comes to Europe or comes any place that we're about to experience an attack, you might have to make an instantaneous judgment. Somebody has to be delegated with that authority. If it isn't the President of the United States, in the case of the strategic force, it will have to be the President of France or the Prime Minister of Great Britain, or someone else. And that is an enormous responsibility. The United States has carried that responsibility for a good many years, because we have placed a major effort in developing a strategic force. I said in my State of the Union address that we put as much money into our strategic force as all of Europe does for all of its weapons.

Now, it's quite natural that Western Europe would want a greater voice. We are trying to provide that greater voice through a multilateral force. But it's a very complicated negotiation because, as I say, in the final analysis, someone has to be delegated who will carry the responsibility for the alliance. We hope, through the multilateral system, through the multinational system, that we can provide Europe with a more authoritative position, a greater reassurance that these weapons will be used with care for the defense of Europe. I am hopeful that the negotiations which will be carried out by Mr. Merchant will have that effect, but I think we deal, because of the time problem which I just mentioned, we deal with a very difficult problem.

Q: If I may just follow up, would you expect to have the U.S. position clarified and nailed down before the NATO ministers meeting in Ottawa in the spring?

The President: Yes, that's right. Mr. Merchant will be going ahead in about 10 days and begin discussions in Europe of a more detailed kind.

I just want to point out that because of the enormity of the weapon and because of the circumstances under which it might be fired, there is no answer which will provide reassurance under the most extreme conditions for everyone. We feel, however, that with what we now have and what we are ready to propose, carrying out the Nassau proposal, that additional assurances can be given which we believe will - which we hope will satisfy the Europeans. Now, if it doesn't, then we will be prepared to consider any other proposals that might be put forward. But in the case, for example, of France, we are not talking in that case of a European nuclear force. We are talking about a French nuclear force. So that to make it a European force would require substantial political developments in Europe. That time might come and if it does, we would be glad to consider joining with them or cooperating with them in any system which they might wish to develop.

A Berlin Settlement

Q: Mr. President, there are reports from London that the United States and the Soviet Union are about to resume discussions on a Berlin settlement. What could you tell us about that?

The President No, no conclusion has been reached on that. As you know, we have had a series of talks over the last 2 years, which have not been promising enough to lead to negotiations, and we have had - no decision has yet been reached by the alliance as to whether exploratory talks will be resumed, or whether the conditions would be such that they would have some hope of advancing the common interest. So in answer to your question, this matter has not been determined.

Major Problems of the Atlantic Alliance

Q: Mr. President, what do you consider the major problems and their priorities right now within the Atlantic alliance, in view of General de Gaulle's veto?

The President: Well, there's the military problem which we have just discussed, and also the economic problem. Those are the two, and they're both important and I would not rate a priority. Economic problems, maintaining trade, maintaining a cohesive economy between the Western Europeans and ourselves, providing for development of orderly markets, and perhaps most important, providing some better opportunity for the underdeveloped countries which supply the raw materials, who have seen their commodity prices drop in the last 3 years and the cost of the goods they buy go up. So I would say those are the problems that are immediately before the Community.

General Norstad's Suggestion Regarding NATO

Q: Mr. President, on the NATO matter, I wonder if you could comment on General Norstad's suggestion that an executive committee be established within the NATO Council, which would have the power to decide perhaps by a majority vote rather than a unanimous one on the use of nuclear weapons.

The President: Yes, I think that we ought to consider that. As you know, General de Gaulle has not been prepared to discuss a multinational force. If he was, we would be prepared to discuss General Norstad's proposal. General Norstad's proposal, however, might not reach the needs of those countries which are not nuclear powers. But if the European countries chose to delegate their authority to General de Gaulle or to Prime Minister Macmillan, we would certainly be prepared to discuss General Norstad's proposal.

But we are talking about - when we talk about Europe, we have to realize there are a good many countries of Europe, some of which are nuclear and some of which are non-nuclear. The question always is whether the arrangements between the nuclear powers will meet the genuine needs of the non-nuclear powers, or whether they're going to have to go the national deterrent route, which we believe will be both expensive and dangerous.

The Cuban Threat to the American Republics

Q: Mr. President, the Special Security Committee of the Organization of American States has reported that the present military situation in Cuba now constitutes a much more serious threat to the peace and security of the American Republics than it did when this committee was authorized at Punta del Este last January, a year ago. In view of that, I wonder if there is anything you have in mind that these American Republics could and should be doing at this time to meet that threat in a collective way?

The President: I think the part of the report which is most significant is the emphasis they put on subversion in the continent, the movement of men and perhaps money against the constituted governments. That is a matter which the United States Government is giving its greatest attention to this winter, the question of the lessening not only of the subversion that may come from Cuba but from other parts of the hemisphere. And I consider that our primary mission for the hemisphere this winter.

Cuban Shipping Orders

Q: Mr. President, before the Cuban shipping orders were issued, there was quite a discussion about our pleas to our allies to have their shipping companies not let themselves be used as vessels to carry goods from Soviet Russia to Cuba. But when your shipping orders came out, there was no mention of penalty or policy on that. Will you tell us why?

The President: There has been a substantial reduction. I think the number of free world ships going into Cuba in January was about 12. So that our order has just gone out.[1] There has been about a 90-percent drop in free world trade in the last 2 years to Cuba. Free world trade in Cuba - that is, Latin America, Western Europe, and ourselves - was 800 million 2 years ago. It is down to about 90 million. I think it is going to be reduced further. Our proposals have just gone into effect but there has been a substantial reduction in free world shipping to Cuba in the month of January. As I said, it amounted to only 12 and is steadily declining.

U.S. Prestige Abroad

Q: Mr. President, last weekend, the Republican leadership turned upon the administration an argument that you very effectively used in the 1960 campaign that the prestige of the United States abroad had fallen. You were able to substantiate those charges by citing polls taken by the Eisenhower administration. What do you think of these charges and are polls now being taken?

The President: USIA takes surveys on the standing of what they think of the United States, or what they may think of the President, or what they may think of us technically, and all the rest in different groups.

One of the reasons I was able to speak with some confidence of the reduction of Castro's standing was that other governments in the hemisphere have

taken studies, surveys, and have made them available to us. I think that we
have difficulties because, of course, as Winston Churchill said, "the history
of any alliance is the history of mutual recrimination among the various people." So there are bound to be difficulties.

But I think that the United States is known to be a defender of freedom and
is known to carry major burdens around the world. Now, we have to wait and see
both what our prestige is abroad and at home, when we get clearer ideas, I
think, in the next 2 years.

Governor Nelson Rockefeller

*Q: Mr. President, Governor Rockefeller has been attacking you more and more
vehemently, giving rise to the suspicion that he wants to be the Republican candidate next year. Is he the man that you think you'll be running against?*

The President: No, but I do think - I've felt the same suspicion. But
whether he will be successful or not, I think only time will tell. That's a
judgment that the Republicans will have to make. I think that all these discussions of our policies and criticisms can be very useful, but I feel that we
should put forward some alternative proposals - that's number 1. Number 2,
whenever the United States has a disagreement with a foreign country, I think
it's a mistake always to assume that the United States is wrong, and that by being disagreeable to the United States it's always possible to compel the United
States to succumb. One of the results of that has been that the United States
is paying the major bill all around the world for a good many activities that
serve the interests of others besides ourselves. So that I think that we have
to realize that we are going to have disagreements. They go to the heart of
the alliance and the purposes of the alliance. They all involve the security
of the United States. Those questions which involve disagreements on the atom,
which were mentioned earlier, are very important questions. There are bound to
be differences of opinion. And there should be, because as I say, they involve
life and death. So that we're not involved in an empty argument about nothing.

Now, in addition, these arguments come more frequently when the danger,
outside danger, decreases. There isn't as much of an overt Soviet military
threat to Berlin now as there was some months ago. Whatever success we may
have had in reducing that threat, of course we pay for it by increased problems
within the alliance. But if the threat comes again, the alliance will join
together. But I think we just have to make up our minds that we have paid an
enormous bill in the last 15 years, amounting to billions of dollars. We pay
today, the United States, six divisions in Western Germany; the other countries
have one or two or three. We pay a large share of foreign assistance. Other
countries pay much less. Our bases overseas, about which there has been some
argument, they are there to serve to protect Western Europe. We don't mind
paying for them, but we would like to at least have it recognized that the primary beneficiary may be those who are closest to the Soviets. So I expect
there're going to be these disagreements. But that's because we're moving into different periods, and it's partly because some of the outside military dangers which so threatened us just a short while ago have become lessened. They
may come up again, but for the period now we're enjoying the luxury of internal
dissention.

Soviet Nationals in Cuba

*Q: Mr. President, most of the Cuban dialogue has been confined to military
personnel and military operations. Does the Government have any information on
the nationals of the Soviet bloc who may be in Cuba to train the Cubans in sa-
botage and subversion and political penetration of Latin American countries?*

The President: Well, I am sure that among the technicians or military people there, or paramilitary, there are those who are participating in that kind of training. And that's why we are anxious to stop the flow in and out of those who may be the beneficiaries of those studies.

Q: *Do we have any idea of the number or any idea how we can stop them?*

The President: Well, the problem is to get the cooperation of other Latin American countries in limiting the flow in and out, at schools, colleges, which also includes political indoctrination. I think there were 1200 students from Latin America that went into Cuba last year. I'm sure a good many of them were politically indoctrinated; some of them obviously were given training in more direct forms of political action.

I don't think we should regard, however, the Communist threat as primarily based on Cuba, the Communist threat to the hemisphere. There's a good deal - there is local Communist action unrelated to Cuba which continues and which feeds on the hardships of the people there, northeast Brazil, and other places. So that Cuba is important, but even if we are able to stop this kind of traffic, we will still deal with the native Communist movement.

The Multinational Nuclear Force

Q: *Mr. President, could you elaborate a little on an earlier statement you made in connection with the control of the multi-national nuclear force? You seemed to stress the time element of 5 minutes, perhaps, to make a decision. Isn't this force essentially to be a submarine or seaborne force, and isn't one of the beauties of this kind of a force that you don't have to come to a quick decision?*

The President: Yes, but there is still the need for relatively quick time, so that I think you are still dealing - you may not be dealing in every case with 5 minutes, but you're dealing with - very difficult to hold a vote of all the members of NATO, take a majority vote, on firing these missiles. What we hope to do is to indicate guidelines for any action which a commander might take which will give assurance to the Western Europeans. Our feeling is very strong that they have that assurance now. The presence of 400,000 American troops and their families in Western Europe, people who we would not permit to be overrun, I think is a testament to our determination to honor our commitments. In addition, the very obvious fact that Western Europe is essentially the security of the United States.

The loss of Western Europe would be destructive to the interests of the United States. So we feel that there is no question that these weapons would be used to protect the security of Western Europe. General de Gaulle has said that monopoly always serves those who benefit from it. I don't think that we alone benefit from it. I think Western Europe benefits from the enormous efforts which Americans have made. However, if these two factors, the presence of our troops and our security guarantees, are not good enough, we hope to be able to work out devices which will give a stronger participation to the Europeans and, therefore, strengthen their sense of participation and their common sense of allegiance to the NATO cause which we share.

I must say, in looking at the dangers we face, I put dangers in other areas to be higher than the prospect of a military attack on Western Europe. But Western Europe is the one that lives under the gun, and we are going to do everything we can to work out devices which will increase their sense of security.

Payment of Farm Aid to Cuba and the Publication of Communist Propoganda through the U.N.

Q: Mr. President, you were speaking a few moments ago about paying bills. I wonder if there is anything that you believe we could or should do to stop paying for farm aid to Cuba and the publication of pro-Communist propaganda through the United Nations, as we've recently learned we may be doing?

The President: Well, we are not going to put any money into the program in Cuba. There aren't any United States dollars that will go into that program. Now on the book, as I understand, the book was published a year ago. There was a book written by an American group and it was balanced off by a book written by a Communist. The Soviet Union are members of the United Nations. It's difficult to prevent their participating in some of these programs unless you broke the United Nations and the bloc withdrew. So you are going to have some cases of the kind described. We try to minimize them, but quite obviously, they are members, they pay, they receive. But I don't think the book, which I understand came out a year ago - it doesn't seem to me that - I think we are going to survive the book.

The U.S. and its European Allies

Q: Mr. President, to get back to our problems of our allies, it would seem like, in a way, that President de Gaulle's intention to develop France's own nuclear capability and his recent pact with Chancellor Adenauer would meet in perhaps a rather perverse way, and certainly not as you envisaged it, our desire to begin withdrawing from Europe and having Western Europe assume more of its own defense. I'd like you to comment on that.

And, also, I understand that the Department of Defense is studying a new proposal whereby servicemen will go overseas for 1 year without their families, both to Europe and all over the world. Would you comment on that, too, please?

The President: Yes. I don't think that certainly the speeches in the German Parliament last week or speeches subsequent to the Franco-German treaty indicated that the Germans felt that their security could be guaranteed without the presence of the United States. If they felt that, then our purpose in being in Europe would be ended, and of course we would want to withdraw our forces. But as long as Western Europe does not feel that their security can be guaranteed without the presence of the United States, the United States will stay, and we hope that we will be able to work in cooperation on other matters. Now we'll have to wait and see. We are attempting to develop means of cutting our dollar losses. As I said, a year ago they were $3 billion a year - our balance of payments losses - because of our security commitments overseas. We're trying to cut them. But we will announce it if we're going to go into a plan such as you suggested.

The Business Community and the Tax Bill

Q: Mr. President, can you tell us, on taxes, again, are you satisfied with the support that you've gotten from the business community on the tax bill, so far?

The President: Well, as you know, the Chamber of Commerce wants a tax cut, but they want it in the higher income areas, and, in addition, they're opposed to the reforms we suggested, because some of them remove loopholes which means, of course, others have to pay. But I think at least they do support a tax cut. I think out of the Committee on Ways and Means we are going to get a bill for a tax reduction which will be a good bill. I think the more people look at the alternative, I think the more general support we'll get.

Withdrawal of Troops from Europe

Q: Mr. President, back on the subject of American troops in Europe, the Pentagon on Monday and Tuesday knocked down stories that there were plans to withdraw some American troops from Europe. On Wednesday, it announced that 15,000 had already been pulled out. What I'd like to know, sir, is why was this withdrawal done secretly, and also if you could expand some on your plans with respect to the shape of the American forces in Europe.

The President: Well, to the best of my knowledge – I'm not familiar with the events you described – it was not intended to be secret. It's been going on for some months. It's a lessening of the number of logistic forces there, particularly those that were built up during the summer of 1961, subsequent to the Vienna meeting. But we have not at all lessened the number of our combat troops. As I said, the United States has six divisions with the best supporting equipment of any of the divisions on the Western front, according to the NATO studies. Our forces are more equipped to fight, can fight quicker, with better equipment, for a longer period, than any other forces on the Western front. That will continue to be true. Some countries – France has only a division and a half in West Germany and it's quite close to the French border. Ours are further ahead, and ours can fight for quite a number of days. So that we are keeping our strength in Western Europe. The fact is we are stronger than we were a year ago.

It was not intended in any way to be a private withdrawal, which is impossible.

Q: Mr. President, you spoke of dangers in other areas. Do you consider dangers developing in Southeast Asia as a result of the proposed formation of Malaysia? This is Britain relinquishing her colonial ties.

The President: That is correct. We have supported the Malaysia Confederation, and it's under pressure from several areas. But I'm hopeful it will sustain itself, because it's the best hope of security for that very vital part of the world.

Reporter: Thank you, Mr. President.

[1]A White House release dated February 6 announced that steps had been taken to assure that U.S. Government financed cargoes were not shipped from the United States on foreign flag vessels engaging in trade with Cuba. The release stated that Government agencies concerned had been directed not to permit shipment of any such cargoes on vessels that had called at a Cuban port since January 1, 1963, unless the owner of such ship gave satisfactory assurances that no ship under his control would thenceforth be employed in the Cuban trade.

THE PRESIDENT'S NEWS CONFERENCE OF

FEBRUARY 21, 1963

The President: Good afternoon.

I have sent to the Congress today a message on the needs of our 17½ million senior citizens. The number of people in this country age 65 and over increases by 1,000 every day, as science prolongs the life span. But it is not enough for a great nation merely to add to the years of life. Our object also must be to add new life to those years. I have recommended a reduction in the taxes of older citizens by nearly $800 million, an increase in social security and old-age assistance protection, and new efforts in employment, housing, education, recreation, and community service.

My most important recommendation is a revised hospital insurance program for senior citizens under social security. Only 10 to 15 percent of the health costs of senior citizens today are reimbursed by private insurance. Hospital costs have quadrupled since the war, and now average more than $35 a day. And since a great many retired workers have little more than $70 a month on social security, prospects of the usual two or three bouts in the hospital after age 65 confronts them with an impossible choice. They either have to ask their children or grandchildren to undergo financial hardship or accept poverty and charity themselves, or suffer their illness in silence. I think this Nation can do better than that. Social security has shown for 28 years that it is a logical first line of defense in this field.

The revised bill would give every individual the option of selecting the kind of hospital insurance protection that will be most consistent with his budget and health outlook, to be administered without any interference with medical practices, much as Blue Cross is administered today.

It would include a special provision for those who do not have social se-curity coverage. I feel very deeply that this legislation should be enacted this year if we are to fulfill our responsibilities as a great free society.

There is one other statement I wish to make. The New York newspaper strike is now in its 75th day. The situation has long since passed the point of pub-lic toleration. The essence of free collective bargaining in this country is a sense of responsibility and restraint by both sides, not merely an effort by one side or the other to break those who sit across the bargaining table from them.

It is clear in the case of the New York newspaper strike that the Local of the International Typographical Union and its president, Bertram Powers, inso-far as anyone can understand his position, are attempting to impose a settle-ment which could shut down several newspapers in New York and throw thousands out of work. Collective bargaining has failed. The most intensive mediation has failed. This situation which is bad for the union movement all over the country, bad for the newspaper managements and bad for the New York citizens, more than five million of them, who are newspaper readers.

In my view, one solution to this prolonged strike, if no immediate progress is made, would be for the striking printers, companies, and other involved unions, to submit their differences to independent determination of some kind. I cannot see any other alternative which at present would bring about a solu-tion to this critical labor dispute which has already had a vital effect on the economic life of this great city of New York.

QUESTIONS

Attacks on U.S. Shipping by Cuba-Based Planes

Q: Mr. President, could you elaborate on what is meant by "all necessary action" to prevent attacks on our shipping by Cuba-based planes?[1]

The President: Yes. I have asked the Department of Defense to make any necessary revisions in standing orders so as to insure that action will be taken against any vessel or aircraft which executes an attack against a vessel or aircraft of the United States over international waters in the Caribbean.

Q: Mr. President, in the same vein, taking your announcement about the message from the Russians on removal of some of their troops and this incident involving the fishing boat which has produced some very loud reaction in Congress, including Speaker McCormack saying it is an act of aggression, Senator Russell advocating a "hot pursuit" policy, these two things together, how does it affect the net situation with Cuba? Are we better off or worse?

The President: Better off or worse than when? Yesterday?

Q: Than before the Russian message was received or before this fishing boat incident.

The President: I don't know whether these two incidents can be - these two matters can be that clearly linked. I think that we are very interested in seeing the withdrawal of Soviet troops from Cuba and we'll be watching the progress that's made in that area over the next 3 weeks.

I don't think we know the full reasons behind this attack on this vessel, whether it was a deliberate decision by the Cuban Government or a decision by the pilots involved. In any case, I think we made it very clear what our response will be and we would hope that this response would make any future attacks such as this unlikely.

Q: Mr. President, does the fact that the note of protest was sent to the Cuban Government mean that the United States Government holds the Cubans accountable for the use of Mig's instead of the Russians?

The President: Yes. These planes came from Cuba and flew under a Cuban flag and, therefore, unless the Soviet Union should claim that they were flying them, we would hold the Cubans responsible.

U.S. Prestige Abroad

Q: Mr. President, the USIA is keeping secret so far the prestige polls about United States prestige abroad, which you referred to last week. Do you think that is justified or might you direct them to release those polls?

The President: No, I don't - there are only - there are some polls which would probably be not in our interest to release. They really go to the polls which may have been taken which involve the personalities of other countries, policies of other countries, which might provide some diplomatic embarrassment. There is no poll involving the standing of the United States or the standing of any political figure in the United States that would be embarrassing to release.

We are, I think, going to have a - USIA is going to have a conversation with Congressman Moss, and also with the ranking minority member, and go over the polls. If it seems to be - these polls will be available to any Member of Congress. Most of them could be released at any time.

There are several which would be unwise to release, but which do not involve the prestige of the United States. So that I think that at periodic intervals we will be able to release really all polls unless they involve directly the interests of the United States. I would not think that any poll dealing with the prestige of the United States would involve such an interest, so we would be glad to release those at periodic intervals.

Soviet Weapons in Cuba

Q: Mr. President, today's incident has caused some people in Congress again to say that the rocket-firing proves that the Soviet weapons in Cuba are not defensive. Will this incident cause the administration to reevaluate its definition between offensive and nonoffensive weapons?

The President: Yes. I think we made that very clear. When we are talking about offensive weapons, we are talking about weapons which have the capacity to carry great damage in the United States, bombers, particularly missiles. A Mig, with its rather limited range, is not regarded ordinarily as an offensive weapon, and the attack which took place on this vessel, which was lying in the water and which did not, as I understand, carry any flag, was relatively - it was 40 miles or so off the coast of Cuba. I don't think that that changes our definition.

The President's Hospital Plan

Q: Mr. President, the hospital plan that you just discussed, of course, failed of passage in the 87th Congress. What do you think its chances of passage are in this current session of Congress; and also, how willing are you to enter some sort of compromise with those Republicans who are in favor of a hospital plan to help its passage?

The President: There were five Republicans last year who joined with Senator Anderson, and they have introduced a bill which is comparable to the Anderson bill of last year. I would hope that it would be possible for the Members of the Congress, regardless of party, to support the program. Now, it failed. A change of one Senator would have passed it last year. I would hope that this year it could pass the Senate. It has the problem of coming out of the Ways and Means Committee.

I think it has a good chance this year, and I would hope that Members on both sides would support it. I think it's a vital piece of legislation. As I say, the people who really have the most to win in this matter are not only those who are over 65, but also their children who support them, and who must also educate their children at the same time. If an adult is sick for a prolonged period of time, and I know very few people who have not had some experience with this, they have some understanding how quickly these bills can mount up. So I think we might get the bill by this year.

Adam Clayton Powell

Q: Mr. President, Congressman Adam Clayton Powell has been in the news quite a bit recently. Much of the publicity has been evoked by an attack on him by Senator Williams of Delaware on the floor of the Senate. There have also been published reports that his activities are embarrassing to the White House. Number 1, since you are a former Member of the Senate, what do you think of the propriety of Senator Williams' attack on Mr. Powell; number 2, are the activities of Mr. Powell embarrassing to the White House; and number 3, as President of the United States, what is your assessment of him as a Congressman and as a Negro leader?

The President: I would not comment on the dispute between Senator Williams and Congressman Powell. Congressman Powell has proved in his life that he is well able to take care of himself. (Laughter)

Number 2, I have not been embarrassed by Congressman Powell.

Number 3, I would not attempt to rank Congressmen. What I am most interested in is the passage of legislation which is of benefit to the people. I
thought last year that committee did a good job, in the House Education and
Labor Committee, in passing out bills which were very useful - minimum wage,
the education bill. I would hope we would have the same kind of record this
year.

I think that is the best answer to any attacks. And I hope the chairman
holds that same view.

Attacks on U.S. Shipping

*Q: Mr. President, would it be possible to say, in the event of future
attacks upon our shipping in the Caribbean, whether we would turn to the
doctrine of hot pursuit?*

The President: I would prefer to leave our status as I have described it,
and to make judgments as they come along. We've made it very clear now that
the United States will take action against any vessel or plane which attacks
our planes or vessels. But the details of those standing engagements, I think,
can wait on events. But there will be an initial response. How far the pursuit would go, and all the rest, is a matter which I think the Secretary of
Defense, the Joint Chiefs of Staff, the Secretary of State, we all might consider as the situation develops, and as we see whether today's action was an
isolated incident, the result of a pilot decision, or was a deliberate decision
by the Cuban Government which forecasts other attacks. I would think when we
have got a clearer pattern, then we could make a judgment on whether hot pursuit should be carried out to the shores of Cuba.

Managing the News

*Q: Mr. President, the practice of managed news is attributed to your ad-
ministration. Mr. Salinger says he has never had it defined. Would you give
us your definition, and tell us why you find it necessary to practice it?*

The President: You are charging us with something, Mrs. Craig,[2] and then
you are asking me to define what it is you are charging me with. I think that
you might - let me just say we've had very limited success in managing the
news, if that's what we have been trying to do. Perhaps you would tell us what
it is that you object to in our treatment of the news.

Q: Are you asking me, sir?

The President: Yes.

*Q: Well, I don't believe in managed news at all. I thought we ought to
get everything we want.*

The President: Well, I think that you should, too, Mrs. Craig. I am for
that. (Laughter)

Air Support to India

*Q: Mr. President, spokesmen for the Indian Government said today India
will ask the United States, Britain, Australia, and Canada to provide air defenses in the event that they are attacked by Chinese Communist aircraft.
Would you tell us how you feel about this air support to India, and under what
circumstances we would give it?*

The President: Yes. Well, there was an original request made in November,
and then the British Government and the United States Government have sent a
mission out at the present time to explore this matter of air security with the

Indian Government. The mission has not completed its task or made recommendations. We are anxious to help India maintain itsef against an attack, if such an attack should come again, and I think it's a matter which we ought to explore with the Indians in the next 4 or 5 weeks. India is a key area of Asia - 500,000,000 people. It was attacked without warning after trying to follow a policy of friendship with countries on its border. We will find ourselves, I think, severely - the balance of power in the world would be very adversely affected if India should lose its freedom. So we will be responsive to India, when we have a clearer idea of what the challenge is and what their desires are, and what our capabilities are. But we don't have that now and won't have it until the joint mission comes back.

Policy on a 35-Hour Week

Q: Mr. President, does the fact that Secretary Wirtz, just a few days ago, informed the AFL-CIO Executive Council that the administration would not object to a negotiated 35-hour week represent a change in policy?

The President: Well, I have only seen the newspaper report because Mr. Wirtz has been on an island in Florida, and so I haven't had a chance to talk with him. I think he made it clear that we were opposed to a change in the 40-hour week by statute.

I would be very reluctant to see any change by negotiation of the 40-hour week to a 35-hour week if it was going to substantially increase the cost, the labor cost, per unit of production, if it was going to make it more difficult for us to compete abroad, if it was going to launch an inflationary spiral of wages and prices in the United States. So I would prefer to wait until I have a chance to see Mr. Wirtz's statement in detail. My own position is opposed to the 35-hour week.

The Nuclear Test Agreement

Q: Mr. President, just before Senator Humphrey left Geneva, he said that unless a nuclear test agreement were in final stages of preparation by April, that mankind might lose forever this unique opportunity for agreement. Do you think that April should be more or less the deadline month which will determine whether the Soviets ever intend to agree to this?

The President: No, I don't think April 1st in the sense of sort of an ultimatum. I would hope that we would have progress by April 1st, but that's 5 weeks away. There are a good many detailed matters to be settled. I would think by springtime we should know whether the Soviet Union is willing to make those arrangements which can provide for a satisfactory test. But I wouldn't put down the date and say by this date we will know finally.

We've been on this business for 15 years. I must say that a good many people are opposed to this effort which is being directed by Mr. Foster in Geneva, and quite obviously it's a matter which we should approach with a good deal of care. But the alternative, if we fail, of increasing the number of nuclear powers around the world over the next 5, 10, 15, or 20 years, that alternative which I think is so dangerous keeps me committed to the effort of trying to get a test ban treaty. I think it's what motivates Mr. Foster and others who have been involved in this for many months. There are, of course, critical areas which must be very carefully defined. But I think people who attack the effort should keep in mind always that the alternative is the spread of these weapons to governments which may be irresponsible, or which by accident may initiate a general nuclear conflagration. So we are going to keep at it if not by April 1st, beyond April 1st.

The New York Printers' Strike

Q: Mr. President, as I understand it, the New York printers are very firmly opposed to arbitration as you suggested. Do you see the need of legislation in strikes like the New York and Cleveland strikes, in the public interest?

The President: No, I haven't suggested - I tried to use a different phrase rather than arbitration, because of the traditional position of the printers against arbitration. But I did suggest a third party might be able to play a bridging role.

I don't think that today we ought to consider compulsory arbitration. As I have said before, this is a matter which involves a community, a city; it's not a national issue, it doesn't affect the national health and safety. And I think the best solution is for the union to demonstrate a sense of responsibility and not merely try to carry this to its final ultimate of cracking the publishers, because if they do it they will close down some papers and I think will hurt their employment possibilities themselves.

I think the best thing now is to see if we can get a third party in who can move perhaps a step beyond mediation but still perhaps not to the final step of arbitration which, as you say, historically they have been unwilling to accept.

The President's Tax Program

Q: Mr. President, there is obviously quite a strong opposition in Congress and in some segments of the country to your tax program. Yet you've made it quite plain that you consider the economic stimulus of that program to be very important to the economic future. Well, now, in the event that the program is cut down to the point where that stimulus would not be forthcoming, what alternatives are there, or in preparation, and would these include a large increase in public spending?

The President: Well, I would think that we have a number of programs which we've sent up since the first of the year - retraining and youth unemployment and all of the rest - which will be of help, but I think the most useful thing can be the kind of tax cut that we've suggested.

I quite agree that it ought to be large enough to do the job, and I think that the expenditures which we're now making, plus the proposed tax cut, plus the revisions, I think will give us a stimulus to prevent the kind of downturn I talked about last week.

My judgment is we're going to get the tax cut. There isn't any doubt that the NAM want a tax cut of a certain kind, the AFL-CIO want another one, and CED want a different kind, some economists want another kind, but at least there is a consensus there should be a tax cut.

There is a majority support, in my opinion, among those who are closest to the economy who understand it the most, there should be a tax cut.

What they are arguing about is who should get the cut and how it should be divided, but I think the Ways and Means Committee and the Senate Finance Committee can deal with that task. I believe we're going to get a tax cut because I think the argument is overwhelming in favor of it, and those who oppose it would have to take the responsibility for any deterioration in the economy which might come about over the next months - or rather years, because the prospects still look good for the economy now - but would have to take the responsibility. And I would think that they would be reluctant to take that responsibility in view of the pattern of the economy in the late fifties.

Difficulties with Haiti

Q: Mr. President, do you have any comment on our recurring difficulties with Haiti?

The President: No, but it is a very critical situation in Haiti.

Russian Troops and Weapons in Cuba

Q: Mr. President, now that the Soviets apparently have agreed to remove some of their troops from Cuba, do you feel that you should press for the removal of the remainder of the Russian troops in view of the fact that if they leave without their weapons, that these weapons will fall into the hands of the Cubans themselves?

The President: Yes. Well, I would think that - we have indicated very clearly that we would find it difficult to accept with equanimity a situation which continued Soviet troop presence in Cuba. I think we have made that very clear. Now there has been, as I have said, a series of withdrawals of missiles, planes, and some men. We have to wait and see now in the coming months, and we will continue to work on the matter as we have over the last 4 months.

Restrictions on Imports of Wool Textiles

Q: Mr. President, you met with New England and Western Senators about a month ago and promised them an answer on their request that you impose further restrictions on imports of wool textiles. Have you reached that decision?

The President: Well, we have discussed the problem of wool imports increasing from about 17 percent up to 21 or 22 percent, and then the danger of going to 25 percent. This is a matter of concern.

On the other hand, the countries which are exporting to the United States are very anxious to maintain this market. I get periodic meetings from chicken growers who are anxious for us to provide a free flow of chickens into Western Europe, and from other Members of Congress who are anxious for us to prevent a free flow of textiles into the United States, others who wish us not to limit the importation of oil, and others who wish us to encourage the exports of various other things into the market.

It's quite difficult to get a balance, but that's what we're attempting to do. Governor Herter is working on it. We are attempting in this rather varied economy, with interest, some of which wish to encourage exports, some of which wish to diminish imports, we are attempting to get a fair balance. Quite obviously we cannot have it all our way, just exports without accepting some imports. Woolens, however, are a particularly sensitive problem. This administration had conversations last year about woolens which have made us anxious to see if we can limit. We are in touch with the various governments. It's rather a difficult time now, however, because of the British not getting into the Common Market, which has made them more sensitive about their export markets.

In addition, we have some difficulties with the Japanese over cotton textiles. So that so far we have not been successful, but it is a matter which Governor Herter is talking about a good deal.

Washington, Moscow and Troop Withdrawals

Q: Mr. President, some French newspapers seem to be convinced that there is a quid pro quo arrangement between Washington and Moscow on removal of troops and other matters. Could you indicate what sort of diplomatic leverage this Government has used to bring about the troop withdrawal?

The President: Yes. I think on November 6th, in a letter to Mr. Khrushchev, I indicated that the continued presence of troops, as well as the bombers, was a matter of great concern to us. And he wrote back, as I said before, in November, saying that in due course or in due time that he planned to remove those troops which were necessary to the defense of the offensive weapons.

We have been back to him on this matter several times, most recently by Mr. Rusk and Mr. Dobrynin, and Saturday Mr. Dobrynin gave the message which has been already announced. So that we've kept at it, indicating that we believe it creates tension in the Caribbean and also makes it more difficult for us to adjust our other problems between the Soviet Union and the United States as long as this is being used as a military base by the Soviet Union.

Q: Mr. President, would you please give us a picture of the current economic condition of Cuba and how much of an achilles' heel it might present currently to the Castro regime?

The President: Well, I think they've had a bad economic situation. It's costing at least $1 million a day for the Soviet Union to sustain the economy. The sugar crop has not been very good, even though the world price of sugar is up. They have other economic difficulties. It is not in my opinion an ornament of the Communist system. And those in Latin America who may have been attracted at the beginning by whatever *elan* that Mr. Castro had I should think would be disillusioned by the economic deterioration which has taken place in the island, and which is obscured to some degree by Soviet subsidies.

Q: Mr. President, you indicated in answer to a previous question that you have told Mr. Khrushchev that it would be difficult to solve other problems until we have the Cuban problem settled. I wonder if you could tell us what other problems may be solved after the Cuban problem?

The President: Well, we've got a good many matters which are of concern to us. I didn't put it quite that way. But there are a good many matters involving disarmament and all the rest, matters which we're now in conversation with, and quite obviously what happens in Cuba affects our ability to work out equitable arrangements with them. You can go all around the world, and the Soviet Union and the United States are in discussion or in disagreement, beginning with Laos, and all the way through Europe, Latin America, and other places, in space and on the ground and underground.

Q: Would you think Berlin would be a problem that could be settled, and if so, perhaps how?

The President: I don't know whether an equitable solution can be worked out in Berlin. We don't know. That's a matter which has been considered, and as you know, we've had over the past 2 years exploratory talks to see whether serious negotiations could be undertaken. But we have never found that these talks have indicated that there was a basis for an accord about Berlin.

At the present time this question of further exploratory talks has come up, and we are now considering whether there is a satisfactory basis for negotiations. I make a distinction between the talks and negotiations, but we've not been able to reach any understanding with the Soviet Union on some of the basic principles which we believe - accepted by them - which we believe essential for the maintenance of the viability of the city.

The Nassau Pact and NATO

Q: Mr. President, can you tell us how the Nassau Pact jibes with the new reports that are making the rounds now about a surface fleet of NATO nuclear weapons? And can you tell us whether there is any difference in the difficulty it might be for you to get permission from the Congress to share either the warheads or the nuclear-propelled shipping?

The President: Well, the principle of the Nassau accord would carry whether it was a submarine or a surface ship. There are technical advantages and disadvantages to both. The surface fleet could be probably more easily multi-nation manned; it would come sooner. It would not involve a balance of payments loss for the countries which would be involved, as the ships could be built there as well as here. So this is a matter which Mr. Merchant will be discussing with them.

Q: But, Mr. President, I mean on the matter of getting permission from the Congress, would not the Congress have to approve American warheads——

The President: I think the Congress should approve any arrangement which is made, which is as important as this, whether it's a submarine or whether it's a surface ship. In my judgment this matter should be submitted to the Congress, to the Senate, and we would plan to do so, because regardless of any legislative limitations, I think it's an important matter which the Congress should have a chance to give its views on.

Q: Mr. President, what basis do you have for your belief that a test ban treaty would inhibit the proliferation of nuclear weapons, and if you got a test ban treaty, how would this be used in the case of France?

The President: Well, in my judgment, the major argument for the test ban treaty is the limiting effect it might have on proliferation. Quite obviously, if it did not have that effect, then the treaty would be abrogated, and any treaty would so state that either side would have the right to abrogate the treaty if proliferation resulted.

Now, on the question of France, France has been recognized as a nuclear power by the Soviet Union. It would be up to the Soviet Union to make a judgment as to what action they would take on the treaty, if France continued to test. This is a matter which we will have to discuss with the Soviet Union. In addition, we are concerned about other countries testing, so that we would have to - the Soviet Union and the United States and Great Britain would have to make a judgment as to the position of France, after consultation with France, and would also make a judgment as to what action we might take if other countries tested. There is no guarantee, if we sign a nuclear test ban, that it will end proliferation. It is, however, our feeling that the Soviet Union would not accept a test ban unless they shared our view that proliferation was undesirable. And it might be a weight in the scale against proliferation, and I so regard it.

Now we are quite far apart on the details of a test ban treaty. Even if we get the test ban treaty, it may not have the desired effect, but in my opinion it's very much worthwhile making the effort and we will continue to do so.

Cuban Air Attack

Q: Mr. President, in view of the action of the Cuban Mig's in firing on this two-man shrimp boat, is the Government making an inquiry as to the possibility that this may have been the fate of the Sulphur Queen, *the industrial tanker which left Beaumont on the 2nd of February and has not been heard from since the 3rd of February?*

The President: We've no information that that is the reason. Certainly, we would examine it, but we have no information.

Q: Mr. President, Secretary McNamara, I believe, has testified that we have intelligence that in Russia they have hidden missiles in hard stands underground. Have you explored the possibility that perhaps we might have those in similar sites in Cuba that would not show up in the aerial reconnaissance?

The President: I think Secretary McNamara, himself, stated that he felt beyond a reasonable doubt that that situation did not exist.

Q: Mr. President, the Defense Department announcement on the incident in the Florida Straits said simply that the Mig's fired near the shrimp boats.

The President: That is correct.

Q: And you used the term "attack." Did these Mig's attack the boat and miss or did they harass the boat?

The President: That's a - I don't think we have the answer to that question. I think the shots came within - what? 40 yards of the boat? I would think, if you are on the boat, that is regarded as an attack, and whether they were trying to hit the boat or whether they were merely attempting to target practice - all these things, I think, we will have to look at in the next day or so.

Reporter: Thank you, Mr. President.

[1]Shortly before the news conference the Press Secretary to the President had read the following statement to the reporters:
"A strong protest has been sent forward through diplomatic channels against an air attack by Cuban aircraft on an unarmed American fishing vessel. The United States Government will expect a full explanation from Cuba. Orders have been given to the armed forces to take all necessary action against any repetition of such an attack."

[2]Mrs. May Craig, Portland (Maine) Press Herald.

THE PRESIDENT'S NEWS CONFERENCE OF

MARCH 6, 1963

The President: Good morning.

Important steps are being taken in the Congress this week with respect to three major parts of the administration's program and I want to take this opportunity to stress their importance to every American family.

First, hearings are being completed in both Houses on the youth employment opportunities bill, and I hope this measure can be enacted before the Easter recess. One million of our youths are out of school and out of work, creating an explosive social situation in nearly every community. This bill would put their hands to work, and minds, in our parks and forests, manning our hospitals and juvenile centers, and developing skills and work experience which will help them in later life.

Secondly, hearings have been completed in the House on our bill to train more physicians and dentists, to expand our medical colleges, and to provide loans to deserving students. With our population increasing every year, with the number of doctors and dentists in relation to that population increase deteriorating, it really seems a waste of our most valuable resources, which are our skills, to turn deserving young men and women away from our medical schools because they can't afford to go. We need them and we need their talents, and I hope this bill will pass.

Third, hearings begin in the Senate this week on our bills to combat mental illness and mental retardation. Almost every American family at some stage will experience or has experienced a case of mental affliction, and we have to offer something more than crowded custodial care in our State institutions. Our task is to prevent these conditions. Our next is to treat them more effectively and sympathetically, in the patients' own community. I hope the Congress will act on this bill.

QUESTIONS

A Tax Cut Possibility

Q: Mr. President, is it fair to assume from the language you used before the American Bankers symposium that, if necessary, if all else fails in Congress you would accept a $13½ billion tax cut without any reforms at all?

The President: No, that isn't what I said. The program which we have sent up is the fairest and most equitable program, and the most fiscally responsible program. It provides for a combination of tax reduction and tax reform, and I think that a good many of the reforms make more equitable the tax reductions, make more equitable the burdens which the great mass of our taxpayers carry.

So that I think that the best program is the one we sent up which provides for a $13½ billion in tax reduction and $3½ billion revenue in tax reform. I think that's the best combination. What we will do will depend of course on what kind of a bill the Congress enacts, but my judgment is that they will enact a tax reduction bill which will include important elements of the reforms that we sent up.

Possibility of CIA Involvement at the Bay of Pigs

Q: Mr. President, can you say whether the four Americans who died in the Bay of Pigs invasion were employees of the Government or the CIA?

The President: Well, I would say that there are a good many Americans in the last 15 years who've served their country in good many different ways, a good many abroad. Some of them have lost their lives. The United States Government has not felt that it was helpful to our interest and particularly in the struggle against this armed doctrine with which we are in struggle all around the world to go into great detail.

Let me say just this about these four men: They were serving their country. The flight that cost them their lives was a volunteer flight and that while because of the nature of their work it has not been a matter of public record, as it might be in the case of soldiers or sailors, I can say that they were serving their country.

And, as I say, their work was volunteer.

Soviet Underground Tests

Q: Mr. President, on Monday Adrian Fisher of the Disarmament Agency said that even if the Russians were able to test underground indefinitely this would not alter the strategic military balance between the United States and the Soviet Union. He said this was the executive assessment. Given that assessment, can you tell us what considerations then would prevent accepting a test ban on the terms set by Russia?

The President: I don't think, if I may say so - in my opinion that is not what is the administration's position. We have suggested that we would not accept a test ban which would permit indefinite underground testing by the Soviet Union. We would not accept a test ban which did not give us every assurance that we could detect a series of tests underground. That's the administration's position. We wouldn't submit a treaty which did not provide that assurance to the United States Senate. Nor would the Senate approve it.

Q: You believe that the present insistence on seven will have to be maintained - is that correct?

The President: I believe that we will insist upon a test ban treaty which gives us assurance that if any country conducted a series of clandestine underground tests that that series would be detected.

Now we have not only the problem of the number of inspections, but the kinds of inspections, the circumstances under which the inspections would be carried out, so that we have a good deal of distance to go in securing an agreement with the Soviet Union. We've not been able to make any real progress on the question of the numbers, but I want to emphasize that this is only one phase of it. We have to also discuss what the area would be, in each test, what would be the conditions under which the inspectors would move in and out.

I want to say that we have made substantial progress, as a result of a good deal of work by the United States Government in recent years, in improving our detection capabilities. We have been able to determine that there are a substantially less number of earthquakes in the Soviet Union than we had formerly imagined. We have also been able to make far more discriminating our judgments from a long distance of what would be perhaps an atomic test and what would be an earthquake. But we have not been able to make those discriminations so effective that we can do without onsite inspections and without a sufficient number to prevent a series of tests being carried out which would be undetected. I can assure you that no agreement will be accepted which would permit any such conditions.

Republican Assessments of Budget Cuts

Q: Mr. President, the Republicans in Congress are saying they can cut your budget all the way from $5 billion to $15 billion. Do you think there is any room for substantial cuts in the budget?

The President: Well, the Congress can make a judgment on that, but I think we reduced the requests of the three services by $13 billion, and we cut out the program such as Skybolt and we decided not to go ahead with the installation of Nike-Zeus. There are many very hard decisions made in reaching the figure that we reached.

Now, this idea that there are three services and therefore you can save $3 billion by cutting $1 billion out of each and at the same time when a good many members make speeches which are very militant, which would suggest that the solution to our problems can be best obtained by war actions or warlike actions, it doesn't seem to me that we ought to be cutting our defenses at this time.

Now, in addition to that, it's been suggested that we cut school lunches, that we cut aid to dependent children. I want to see these in more detail. I think we have been generalized enough. Are you going to cut these kinds of programs which are essential to a better life for our people? Are we going to be permanently second-best in space? Because if you cut the space programs substantially, that's what you are writing into law, and I thought the United States made a commitment that we were not going to be second permanently. And we are not going to be second in the field of national security. The fact of the matter is the Congress last year appropriated half a billion dollars more than we had requested for national security. Now they are talking about cutting it $3 billion or $5 billion.

I don't think that the struggle is over. So I would be opposed to those kinds of cuts, and my judgment is that we sent up a hard budget. The fact of the matter is that the nondefense, nonspace expenditures were held even, though in the previous years for the last 10 years or so they increased by nearly 7 percent.

I think we made a hard budget. Now you may be able to cut some of it. But I think that I want to know where they're going to cut it and whose life is going to be adversely affected by those cuts.

Russian Troops in Cuba

Q: Mr. President, three related questions: Do you have any accurate information on the number of Russian troops that have been removed from Cuba? Are you satisfied with the rate of troop removal? And was there in the Russian aide memoire any suggestion or provision for verification of troop removal?

The President: No, the answer to your question would really be no to all of them. (Laughter)

U.S. Policies in Europe

Q: Mr. President, your policies in Europe seem to be encountering great difficulties. Cuba continues to be a problem. At home unemployment is high. The school bill seems far off. There seems to be more concern in the country for a budget deficit than for a tax cut. In view of all these things there is some impression and talk in the towns and country that your administration seems to have lost its momentum and to be slowing down and moving on the defensive. I wonder if you could comment on this feeling in the country?

The President: Yes. I've read that. There is a rhythm to personal and national and international life and it flows and ebbs. And I would say that we are still - we have a good many difficulties at home and abroad. And the Congress has not acted yet on the programs we've sent forward so that we are still in the gestation period in those areas. Some of our difficulties in Europe have come because the military threat to Europe is less than it has been in the past. In other words, whatever successes we may have had in reducing that military threat to Europe have brought with it in its wake other problems. And that is quite natural and inevitable. I prefer these problems to the other problems.

I think that in the summer of 1961 - and of course this all may come again - we were calling up reserves in preparation for what might be a collision of major proportions between the Soviet Union and the United States in Berlin. I would say our present difficulties in Europe, while annoying in a sense, or burdensome, are not nearly as dangerous as they were then. As far as Cuba, it continues to be a problem. On the other hand there are advances in the solidarity of the hemisphere. I think we've made it clear that we will not permit Cuba to be an offensive military threat. I think that we are making some progress in other areas so that if you ask me whether this was the "winter of our discontent" I would say no. If you would ask me whether we were doing quite as well this winter as perhaps we were doing in the fall, I might say no, too.

Federal Judgeships in the South

Q: Mr. President, yesterday Governor Rockefeller charged that you had been appointing "segregationist judges" to the Federal bench in the South. Private-ly, some NAACP officials have said before that that they, too, had been crit-ical of some of the judgeship appointments that you had made in the South, and that that had blunted a certain amount the aggressive stand that the executive branch had taken against segregation and race problems in the South. Will you comment on that?

The President: No. I think that some of the judges may not have ruled as I would have ruled in their cases. In those cases there is always a possibil-ity for an appeal. On the whole, I believe - and this is not true just of this administration, but the previous administration - I think that the men that have been appointed to judgeships in the South, sharing perhaps as they do the general outlook of the South, have done a remarkable job in fulfilling their oath of office.

So I would not generalize. There may be cases where this is not true, and that is unfortunate. But I would say that on the whole it has been an extra-ordinary and very creditable record and I would say that of Federal judges gen-erally that I have seen in the last - certainly in the last 10 years.

The Withholding of Information on the Cuban Situation

Q: Mr. President, of late some of your congressional critics have started to charge that your administration has been deliberately withholding important information on the Cuban situation. Among the claims that have been made is that your Central Intelligence chief, John McCone, actually knew before Octo-ber 14th that the Soviets had planted offensive missiles in Cuba. Is there anything that you can say on this?

The President: No. I've seen charges of all kinds. One day a distin-guished Republican charges that it is all the CIA's fault, and the next it is the Defense Department's fault, and the next day the CIA is being made a scapegoat by another distinguished leader. So that we could not possibly answer these charges, which come so fast and so furiously. Mr. Arends[1] said the other day that the testimony by the Air Force before the committee indica-ted that we knew all about this October 10th, even though General LeMay[2] made it very clear in the same testimony that the Air Force didn't have such infor-mation. So we are not in a position to answer these.

I think in hindsight, I suppose we could have always, perhaps, picked up these missile bases a few days earlier, but not very many days earlier, be-cause the missiles didn't come in, at least in hindsight it now appears, until some time around the middle of September. The installations began at a later date. They were very fast, and I think the photography on the same areas, if we had known that missiles were going in, 10 days before might not have picked up anything. The week before might have picked up something. Even the pic-tures taken October 14th were only obvious to the most sophisticated expert. And it was not until the pictures taken really the 16th and 17th that you had pictures that would be generally acceptable. So this was a very clandestine and fast operation. So I feel that the intelligence services did a very good job. And when you think that the job was done, the missiles were discovered, the missiles were removed, the bombers were discovered, the bombers were re-moved, I don't think that anybody should feel that anything but a good job was done. I think we can always improve and particularly with the advantage of hindsight. But I am satisfied with Mr. McCone, with the intelligence community and the Defense Department, and the job they did in those days particularly taken in totality.

The President's Visit to Costa Rica

Q: Mr. President, as you prepare for your visit to Costa Rica this month, there seems to be a position there among the Central American countries in Panama that the United States should take a more active leadership in attacking the problem of Cuba. I wonder if you could give us some of your thoughts about how you think this project should move along that you might find it possible to discuss with your colleagues there in San Jose?

The President: Well one of the matters, of course, that is of interest to us is the question of the movement of people in and out who might be trained by the Communists in Cuba for guerrilla work or subversion in other parts of the hemisphere. This is an action which must be taken by each of the countries in Latin America. We are making proposals to them bilaterally. There has been an OAS Committee which has reported on the need for control. Now it's up to the Latin American countries, I would hope in common consultation as well as individually, to take those steps which will control the movement of people in and out. So we'll know who they are, why they're going, what happens to them when they get there, and when they're coming out, and what happens to them when they come out. This is the kind of thing which each country finally has to do itself because it is part of the element of sovereignty that the control of movement is within the country of citizenship, but we are bringing this to the attention of the Latin American countries as perhaps one of the most important things we can do this winter. In addition there have been other things which have been done on trade, diplomatic recognition, and all the rest. But I think we've indicated very clearly that what we feel is the wisest policy is the isolation of communism in this hemisphere. We would hope that the countries of Latin America with us will participate actively in that program.

Canada and the U.S.

Q: Mr. President, recognizing the interdependence of Canada and the United States and of course conscious that the current anti-American flareup is about defense, are there any attempts being made to ease the irritations that are chronic, such as wheat surplus policy or the trade balance between the two countries?

The President: Well, on the wheat we're in constant communication with the Canadians and other wheat producers, that our disposal under P.L. 480 would not disturb their normal markets. In the question of trade balances, we were able to be of some assistance to Canada during its difficulties some months ago, on the Canadian dollar, with other countries, and I would hope that the United States and Canada would be able to - having been joined together by nature - would be able to cooperate.

The Relationship of Interhandel and the Firm of I.G. Farben

Q: Mr. President, for 20 years the Justice Department has assured Congress that it had evidence showing that Interhandel was a cover for the German firm of I.G. Farben, and therefore the seizure of General Aniline and Film in this country during World War II was justified.

Now in the past few days there has been an agreement between Justice and Interhandel on the division of the proceeds from the sale of General Aniline. Has Justice Department discovered that its facts are wrong, or has there been, or is this the result of pressure from the Swiss Government.

The President: No, I would say that the agreement is an equitable agreement. It could have gone on 10 years more in the courts, and it has been now 15 or 20 years. The lawyers have enjoyed it, but I don't think that there is anything else - I don't think we would get a better arrangement if we continued the litigation for another 10 years. We feel that the arrangement which has been worked out will return the assets to those who have a claim to them, and I think the division of resources is fair.

So that I think it was the best solution.

Transference of the Chamizal to Mexico

Q: Mr. President, reports from Texas seem to indicate that the United States is ready to transfer the Chamizal to Mexico. If this is true, could you give us some idea of the timetable expected?

The President: No, but there have been negotiations on Chamizal for a good many years, and they were stepped up following the visit to Mexico. We are close, I would hope, to an agreement, and I think that the next week should tell us whether we can get an accord. The advantage of course of the Chamizal is that if we can get a solution, is that it will wipe out a black mark in the record of the United States where we refused to accept an arbitration claim 40 years ago and as a result we have never been able to get the Mexicans to agree to any arbitration with us. So I am very anxious to see it settled, and we have made pretty good progress on it. There are still some questions that have to be settled but the prognosis I would think was hopeful, and I would think we would know in the next few weeks.

The NATO Nuclear Force

Q: Mr. President, I have a two-prong question on the NATO nuclear force. First, can you tell us how goes the Merchant[3] mission? And secondly, the lack of enthusiasm, if we can believe the press, reflects a certain amount of public opinion in Europe as to the Polaris-armed surface force because of its alleged greater vulnerability as compared to the atomic submarine. Why haven't the proposals for a conventionally powered submarine force been put forth, a proposal which would not apparently annoy Congress as much as an atomic submarine and would cost only about half as much as the atomic submarine?

The President: There are some people who are opposed in Europe to the multilateral concept because of national reasons. Now if we had come forward with a proposal for submarines, those submarines would have to be built in the United States. They would be quite expensive; they would take at least 2 years or so longer than this program would; there would be elements of control by the United States inevitably because of various technical reasons, and that system would have been under attack.

Now I think that if anyone will examine that argument between surface and submarine they will feel there's a good deal of merit to the surface argument. In the first place, the submarine is a very difficult weapon system to operate. It's not easy to find merchant ships at sea. It took us more than 2 days to find the recent Venezuelan ship in the Caribbean. They are not easy to find. It took us longer to find the Portuguese ship some months ago. The ocean is a large ocean.

Now we are going to be part of that multilateral force. Can you imagine a situation where the Soviets could discover every one of these ships and mark them and then attack them, destroying the American flag and the Americans aboard and not expect that that would not launch a general conflagration which would include Polaris, Minuteman, and every other weapon which might be involved? That they could isolate this force which the United States was part of and expect that they could attack the surface ships successfully without any of these ships firing a missile and not initiate the use of all the nuclear weapons?

I just don't think that the logic is on the side. This way the ships can be built there; the force can be built more quickly; there is not a balance of payments drain; it's much easier to operate from the surface if you are going to have a multilateral force.

Now, number two, how goes the Merchant mission? In the first place we have indicated that we would keep our commitments to Europe, and we have indicated that our atomic strength is sufficient to defend Europe and the United States and our other interests. There has been concern however in Europe about what might happen over a long period. So, in an attempt to meet that concern without providing for the ultimate distribution of nuclear weapons to every national entity which would increase the danger and increase the expense and not increase the security, this concept of a multilateral force was put forward. We are responding to European suggestions. And it may be that when the proposal is examined in detail they may not feel that it provides sufficient additional security to warrant the additional expenditures of money and may decide that the present arrangement is satisfactory. That, we, of course, would accept. But if they are interested in the multilateral force, if they feel the multilateral force does provide extra security, the United States wants to be responsive. We take the lead in this matter because we are the nuclear power and have had the nuclear experience. It may take some months of negotiation to determine whether such a force can come into being, but if there is a desire for it we are responsive to it. And that is why Ambassador Merchant is going because we feel this is a way of maintaining the close ties between Europe and the United States.

So I think that if we decide in the final analysis, or Europe decides that this isn't what they want, we would be glad to hear any other proposals and we would feel that the exploration itself has been interesting and useful, because if we had refused to cooperate, then the burden really would have been on us.

Amendment to the Foreign Assistance Act

Q: Mr. President, Congressman Leonard Farbstein has announced that he will introduce an amendment to the Foreign Assistance Act which would give the President the right to deny aid to any nation that discriminates against American citizens because of race, creed, or color. How do you view this and would you exercise this mandate?

The President: Well, I would like to take a look at his language, and find out under what conditions it would give us this power, before I could comment on the amendment.

The Shipping of Soviet Oil to Cuba

Q: Mr. President, former Ambassador Guillermo Belt, the Ambassador from Cuba to the United States in the old days, said in a lecture at Georgetown Visitation Convent last Sunday that Castro would not be able to survive 2 weeks if he was denied Soviet oil. I wonder if there isn't something that you can do about this, or maybe bring greater pressure on some of our allies who are shipping Soviet oil in their ships to Cuba?

The President: Yes, but those are not our figures. There isn't any doubt that over a long period of time that denial of oil would make a difference. To deny the oil would require, of course, a blockade, and a blockade is an act of war, and you should be prepared to go for it. I think we indicated last October that in periods where we considered the United States was in danger, we were prepared to go as far as was needed to remove that danger, and we would, of course, be willing always to do so again, if we felt there was a situation which carried with it that kind of danger to the United States.

But you should not be under any impression that a blockade is not an act of war, because when a ship refuses to stop, and you then sink the ship, there is usually a military response by the country involved. We are attempting to persuade NATO and other countries not to ship into Cuba, but the primary source of shipments into Cuba are bloc ships, and at this time we do not believe that war in the Caribbean is to the national advantage.

Significant Changes in the Soviet Union

Q: Mr. President, it is 10 years now since the death of Stalin, and it's a fact ironically noted much more in the Western World than the Communist world. Could you give us your appraisal, sir, of the significance of the changes in the Soviet Union in terms of the future, of the East-West relations in this period of time?

The President: No, I think that it would take at least a half hour program on a national network, and I couldn't comment on that. (Laughter)

The Resumption of Friendly Relations with Cuba

Q: Mr. President, yesterday U.N. Secretary General U Thant received a letter from the Cuban Foreign Minister in which Roa hinted that the Cubans might like to discuss the resumption of friendly relations with us. I wonder if you think that this might be possible, and if so, what conditions would have to be met first?

The President: Well, I understand the **note** had some reference to it from Havana but the note actually delivered at the U.N. did not have any such references. We have said on many occasions that we regard the **communization** of Cuba and the attempt to subvert the hemisphere as matters which are not negotiable. I don't see any evidence that there is in prospect a normalization of relations between Cuba and the United States.

U.S. Relations with Venezuela

Q: The length of your joint communique with the President of Venezuela, you say "The President of the United States pledges the full support of his country to the Republic of Venezuela," et cetera. Could you tell us something about the nature of that full support in case there was a serious or a successful coup d'etat revolution against President Betancourt?

The President: Well, it would depend a good deal on the conditions and what our obligations might be under the Rio treaty. We strongly support President Betancourt's efforts in Venezuela in a good number of ways. But if you are asking me, I would have to see what the conditions were, what the responsibilities were under the Rio treaty, the OAS, if we knew we were going into a more substantial situation. If you are talking about aggression from outside, the answer is very clear. If you are talking about internal acts, we would have to judge those acts and depend a good deal on what the Government of Venezuela decided was the appropriate response.

Foreign Aid

Q: Mr. President, I think you've had a preliminary or tentative meeting with the Clay[4] committee on foreign aid. Can you tell us whether they're taking that hard and hardheaded look at foreign aid that you asked them to when you appointed them?

The President: Yes, they are, very definitely.

Q: Mr. President, the Mansfield committee, sent at your suggestion to the Far East and Europe, has recommended a thorough security reassessment in the Far East and a clamp down, if not a reduction in our aid to that part of the world.[5] Would you have any comment on this, sir?

The President: I don't see how we are going to be able, unless we are going to pull out of Southeast Asia and turn it over to the Communists, how we are going to be able to reduce very much our economic programs and military programs in South Viet-Nam, in Cambodia, in Thailand.

I think that unless you want to withdraw from the field and decide that it is in the national interest to permit that area to collapse, I would think that it would be impossible to substantially change it particularly, as we are in a very intensive struggle in those areas.

So I think we ought to judge the economic burden it places upon us as opposed to having the Communists control all of Southeast Asia with the inevitable effect that this would have on the security of India and, therefore, really begin to run perhaps all the way toward the Middle East. So I think that while we would all like to lighten the burden, I don't see any real prospect of the burden being lightened for the U.S. in Southeast Asia in the next year if we are going to do the job and meet what I think are very clear national needs.

Reporter: Thank you, Mr. President.

[1]Representative Leslie C. Arends of Illinois, ranking Republican member of the Armed Services Committee.

[2]Gen. Curtis E. LeMay, Chief of Staff, U.S. Air Force.

[3]Livingston T. Merchant, Special Representative for NATO Multilateral Force Negotiations.

[4]Gen. Lucius D. Clay, Chairman, Committee to Strengthen the Security of the Free World.

[5]See "Viet-Nam and Southeast Asia," Report of Senators Mike Mansfield, J. Caleb Boggs, Claiborne Pell, Benjamin A. Smith to the Senate Committee on Foreign Relations, committee print, 88th Congress, 1st session (Government Printing Office, 1963, 22 pp.).

THE PRESIDENT'S NEWS CONFERENCE OF

MARCH 21, 1963

The President: Good evening.

Last night I returned from a 3-day meeting in San Jose, Costa Rica, with the Presidents of the five Central American Republics and Panama. This was a most useful meeting. For the first time a President of the United States journeyed to Central America and conferred with all of the leaders of the vital area, which in terms of history, geography, common interest, and common goals is as closely allied with the United States as any area in the world. We agreed to continue our efforts under the Alliance for Progress to build and strengthen the machinery for economic cooperation with and among the nations of Central America and Panama, including the creation of a unified economic community in Central America. And we also agreed on the necessity for measures to halt the flow of agents, money, arms, and propaganda from Cuba to Central America.

Every nation present was determined that we would both protect ourselves against immediate danger and go forward with the great work for constructing dynamic, progressive societies, immune to the false promises of communism. This is the fourth Latin American country which I have visited. Here, as in all the others, we found a spontaneous outpouring of friendship and affection for the United States; and here, as in all the others, we saw impressive evidence of the work now being made and done under the Alliance for Progress.

Each trip makes it clear that Latin Americans, by an overwhelming majority are ready to work, to sacrifice, to fight if necessary, to maintain their own freedom and to build societies which serve the welfare of all their people. They lack only the full measure of resources necessary to build a hemisphere where all can be secure and free. They know that they bear the fundamental responsibility for their own welfare and progress, but the receptions we have received in Costa Rica, in Mexico, in Venezuela, and in Columbia demonstrate that they also know that we in the United States today have a deep concern for their problems, a common dedication to their aspirations, and a faithful commitment to help them in their efforts. For all these reasons, I return from San Jose with increased confidence that we will continue to live in a hemisphere of independent, firm, and faithful friends.

QUESTIONS

Soviet Withdrawal of Troops from Cuba

Q: Mr. President, did the Soviets honor their commitment on withdrawing troops from Cuba and where do we go from here?

The President: We estimate that they have withdrawn approximately 3,000 troops in these past weeks. We are waiting to see whether more will be withdrawn, as we would hope they would be. The month of March is not finished yet and we should have a clearer idea as to what the total numbers should be in the coming days.

The President's Travel Plans

Q: Mr. President, could we speak, for a moment, about your travel plans. One, on your forthcoming trip to Italy and Germany, do you plan to visit Berlin? And second, do you intend to make a trip to South America later in the year?

The President: I would hope that when I go to Germany that I would go to Berlin. I have no plans for any trip to Latin America this year. Though we have an agreement to visit Brazil, that trip has been postponed and no final date has yet been set.

The TFX Contract

Q: Mr. President, the TFX contract is causing a lot of controversy on Capitol Hill. Senator Symington told the Senate today that the investigation was affecting military morale and ought to be wound up quickly. How do you feel about it?

The President: I see nothing wrong with the Congress looking at these matters. My judgment is that the decision reached by Secretary McNamara was the right one, sound one, and any fair and objective hearing will bring that out. Mr. McNamara chose the plane he chose because he felt it most efficient, because he thought it would do the job and because he thought it would save the Government hundreds of millions of dollars. Everything I have read about the TFX and seen about it confirms my impression that Mr. McNamara was right. We have a very good, effective Secretary of Defense with a great deal of courage, who is willing to make hard decisions, and who doesn't mind when they are made that a good many people don't like it.

This contract involves a large amount of money and naturally some people would prefer it to go another place than the place which the Secretary chose. I think the Secretary did the right thing and I think this investigation will bring that out, and I have no objection to anyone looking at the contract as long as they feel that a useful function is served.

Q: Do you think the hearing that has been held has been fair and objective?

The President: I would think that - I am confident that we all know a lot more about the TFX than we did before, and that's a good thing. And my judgment is that the more this hearing goes on, the more convinced people are finally that Secretary McNamara is a very effective Secretary of Defense and that we're lucky to have him.

U.S. Interest in South Korea

Q: Mr. President, the United States has long had a deep interest in South Korea and its independence and democracy. Last weekend there was an announcement by the military government of a bid to continue its power for 4 more years rather than turn affairs back to a civilian government after an election. Would you give us your views on that?

The President: Well, as you know, the situation has been changing in South Korea very greatly in the last few days, and it's in some position of flux, so I don't think that it would be possible to make any final statement today.

We are continuing to maintain very close contact with what's going on there. We are anxious for stability in the area. We regard South Korea, of course, as an important interest in the security of Asia and therefore we are continuing to follow very closely the present discussions about the return of democratic government in South Korea. But as the situation is still not hardened, I don't think that anything I would say on it would be helpful, at least this week.

Status of Postmaster General Day

Q: Mr. President, is there anything to the reports that Postmaster General Day will be replaced before the next year's election campaign?

The President: No. No.

The Attitude of Central American Presidents on Cuba

Q: Mr. President, there were some reports in San Jose that the Central American Presidents wanted to take stronger action or decide upon stronger measures against Cuba than you were. I wonder if you could clarify whether that was the case or not.

The President: No, no proposal came in any of the meetings that I had with the Presidents. As you know, one of the conclusions reached at San Jose was to take effective measures, by the countries involved, and also to ask that other countries of Latin America to take effective measures to stem the flow of arms and particularly of men who move by subterranean means, frequently, without passports, from one country to another in Latin America, to Cuba, are trained and then come back for subversive activity. We are going to take effective means to attempt to control that traffic. There was no proposal.

I think they are quite aware that we have taken every conceivable action to isolate Cuba, that that's our ambition as long as Cuba maintains an association with the bloc, the Communists, and is used as a Communist military base.

I don't think that the Presidents of Latin America thought that further action, invasion, or blockade at this time would be fruitful. At least none of them made that proposal to me. And as you know, the burden of such an action would fall on the United States, and I think they're quite aware that the United States would have to carry out the action. We have responsibilities all through the world. You've just mentioned South Korea and Berlin, as an example of two areas where we have vital commitments, so that I think the Presidents of Central America are well aware that the United States is as anxious as they are to prevent flow of communism in this hemisphere and that we are taking every action that we believe to be responsible and effective to achieve that end.

They also recognize that one of the most effective ways is to meet conditions in their own countries, to make sure that communism doesn't get a grip because of the failure of the economies. In one of the countries that we visited, 400 out of 1,000 children do not attend any school. We cannot expect stable, democratic societies to develop in an atmosphere where half of the population is illiterate.

Now, that's the kind of problem which has traditionally affected and infected Central America. The Governments are attempting to meet these problems. We are attempting to help them through the Alliance for Progress. We believe that this is the most important step we can take now, combined with the actions we are presently taking against Cuba, which are well known.

The Olympic Games

Q: Mr. President, concerning effective action in another area, the Olympic games, some time ago you expressed concern that the amateur groups were bickering to such an extent that the U.S. might not be able to field a qualified team in the 1964 Olympics in Tokyo. Has that question been settled to your satisfaction?[1] And two, will the United States grant the usual Federal money to aid in the effort to get the Olympic games to the United States and to Detroit specifically for the first time since 1931, in 1968?

The President: Well, in the first place, as you know, General MacArthur did the arbitration, and did it most effectively; therefore, we feel that problem is going to be solved, in the question of accrediting amateur athletes.

Secondly, on the question of where the 1968 Olympics will be, that's a matter for the Olympics Committee. If there is a chance to get it to the United States, we will strongly support it, and if Detroit is chosen, I would certainly be wholly in favor of the United States doing everything it could to make it a success. I'm a strong believer in the Olympic games, and I hope the United States has a strong amateur team representing this country, because this is a vigorous society, and we would like to demonstrate it.[2]

Dangers of Recession

Q: Mr. President, you have been warning with repeated frequency lately about the possible dangers of a recession. Some of your supporters, both in and out of the administration, are expressing concern that your main thrust against it, namely, a large tax cut, may not get through this session. If that should happen to be the case or if you get an inadequate tax cut, do you have another alternative against recession?

The President: Well, in the first place we don't believe that there will be a recession this year. The most recent economic indicators seem to me to be more encouraging than the ones that we had in January when we stated that the chances were against a recession in 1963. But we also live with history, and we realize the rhythm of the 1958, and 1960, two recessions, and we don't want to duplicate that.

Now, our tax cut is predicated on the assumption of a $10 billion tax cut over a period of 18 months, which combined with the budget we had we felt combined thrust to the economy and also a degree of fiscal responsibility. If you are suggesting that I would look with equanimity upon the failure of Congress to act this year on a tax cut, that would be wholly wrong.

If we get through this year in good condition economically, we come into 1964. We know, as I said, something about the rhythm of the business cycle. We had two recessions in 2 years in the end of the fifties.

So I would think that merely because our prospects look good in 1963, I would think that that is all the more pressing for us to take action in time. Now, if we don't take action in time, and we move into a recession, we have to take a good deal more action than we would have if we had taken it before the recession came upon us, and we have to take action to put people to work. We already have too high a rate of unemployment, and if we get into a recession, it would go much higher than that.

So that I would think that everything, most of all common prudence, indicates and dictates that we get a tax cut this year which, combined with the expenditure level we have in the Government, we believe represents the best combination. So I would be very concerned if we did not get it this year.

Q: What I really meant, sir, was what do you plan to do if you don't get the tax cut?

The President: I plan to get the tax cut.

The Meeting Between the Pope and Mr. Adzhubei

Q: Mr. President, are you aware of any international significance to the meeting between the Pope John and Mr. Adzhubei, Khrushchev's son-in-law?

The President: No, some historic interest, but not any underlying international significance. As you know, Mr. Adzhubei stated when he got through that there was no coexistence between the ideologies of Pope John and Mr. Khrushchev, and that has been my view for a long time. But I think that what Pope John is interested in, of course, is seeing - and I think other religious leaders are interested in preventing a nuclear war. So that he believes, I think probably, that communication is one of the means by which we can achieve that objective.

Talks on the NATO Nuclear Force

Q: Mr. President, would you now give us a report on the exploratory talks on the NATO nuclear force, and what you see as the prospects for that force?

The President: Yes, I'm going to see Mr. Merchant[3] tomorrow. I understand he is encouraged by his trip. He is going back again in April. We are hopeful that it may be worked out. As I have said before, this is a proposal that we are making to the Europeans to meet a need which they've suggested. This is not a proposal which we feel essential to the security of the United States. It is a proposal which we have advanced to meet the security needs of Western Europe. So Mr. Merchant will travel again to the countries, the NATO countries, that he did not visit. Now we ought to know by May whether we are going to be able to make some progress.

In any case, by the Ottawa meeting[4] we should have made some progress on multinational nuclear forces, and we should have a clearer idea on whether we are going to carry through on multilateral nuclear forces.

U.S. Response to the USSR Launching Spacecraft

Q: Mr. President, sometime in 1963, the Soviets are scheduled to launch two spacecraft and perform a rendezvous and a docking and the men are supposed to change ships. Now I am told if this happens it puts them in a position of being able to mount a nuclear weapon in space, and if that happens, what would be the American response? Would we try to do likewise? Or would we try to shoot it down?

The President: These are all presumptions that I wouldn't be able to comment on. The United States is making, as you know, a major effort in space and will continue to do so. We are expending an enormous sum of money to make sure that the Soviet Union does not dominate space. We will continue to do it. And we will continue to take whatever steps are necessary to prevent any action against the United Nations.

The fact of the matter is the Soviet Union today with a nuclear weapon can reach the United States with a missile. So that I would have to know in more precise detail than you have described the exact nature of our threat before I suggested what our counter action would be.

Attack on Russian Ship by Cuban Exiles

Q: Mr. President, Radio Moscow said today that the Cuban exiles who say they shot up a Russian ship and an army camp on Monday, that these men were hirelings of the United States and that they were carrying out secret American orders. What have you to say to this?

The President: Well, as you know, our best information is that they did not come from the United States. We have already indicated that we do not feel that these kinds of raids serve a useful purpose. It seems to me in some way they strengthen the Russian position in Cuba, and the communist control of Cuba and justify repressive measures within Cuba which might otherwise not be regarded as essential. So that we have not supported this and these men do not have a connection with the United Staets Government. I think a raid which goes in and out does indicate the frustrations of Cuban exiles who want to get back home and who want to strike some blow, but I don't think that it increases the chances of freeing Cuba.

India's Military Needs and the U.S. Response

*Q: Mr. President, I believe the British Commonwealth - U.S. military sur-
vey team is back from India and has made its report to you. And I wonder what
your views are now, sir, regarding India's military needs now that the spring
is upon the country and the snows have melted and presumably the Chinese menace
can be looked at more realistically?*

The President: We haven't completed the report or our consultation with the
British as a result of the report.

Trade with Western Allies

*Q: Mr. President, the trade of our Western European allies, the four prin-
cipal ones, reportedly has quadrupled in the last 8 years in trade with the
Soviet Union. Is this alarming to the administration and, if so, are any
effective measures being taken to curtail it?*

The President: Well, we have attempted, in NATO, to maintain the Co-Com
list which is a list of those materials which are shipped from the free world
to the Communist world which would help them strategically and would help them
in the event of war.

There is pressure always to dilute this list, and a good many of these
countries depend upon trade and they want to trade with the Soviet Union. We
have kept our trade, as you know, to a minimum, particularly because the Soviet
Union does not show a great desire to trade in consumer items but instead wants
heavy industrial items which could be important strategically.

We strongly believe in supported the Co-Com list and we would continue to
do so. There are pressures against it. But so far there has been general observance by NATO.

Strike by Cleveland and New York Papers

*Q: Mr. President, as you know, the Cleveland-New York newspapers have been
out of operation for almost 4 months now. After your last rather strong statement on the situation[5] there was an improvement, but now it has lapsed back
again. Is there any comment that you care to make on this?*

The President: No, there seems to be some hope that in the next few days
that there will be an acceptace of the offer that Mayor Wagner made in the
New York case which I thought was a very fair offer. I understand that the
head of the printers is attempting to use his influence as well as the influence of others in attempting to have the printers accept it.

That also leaves the Cleveland strike which has gone on for a longer time
than the New York strike. I hope we can get that one adjusted, too, because
that city also needs its papers. I am hopeful that if New York moves in the
next few days that Cleveland will also.

Stemming Travel of U.S. Citizens to Cuba

*Q: Mr. President, the House Un-American Activities Committee has been try-
ing since last October to get some information from the Justice Department and
the State Department about traveling United States citizens who are going in
and out of Cuba by way of Mexico. They don't seem to be able to get any information on this, but some of these citizens come back and advertise lectures on
the advantages of Castro's Cuba.*

I am wondering how we can expect other countries to restrict this type of travel, as you say we plan to do in Nicaragua, I believe ——

The President: No, in Costa Rica.

Q: Well - I am wondering how we can expect other countries to stem this travel if we don't try to stem it by enforcing the McCarran-Walter Act?

The President: I would think the Justice Department would be delighted to give any information. We have taken action, as you know, against some people who have gone to Cuba without a permit, or without permission of the United States Government. There has been some criticism, as a matter of fact, of an action we took against a newspaperman. We would attempt to and I would be delighted - I would ask, if it has not already done so, and I would be surprised if it has not already done so - I would be very surprised if the Justice Department has not made available all the information that the congressional committee requested. But if they have not done so, I will be sure to instruct them to do so.

Q: Mr. President, at the Costa Rica meeting the Declaration of Central America[6] carries a rather intriguing phrase. It is that: "Cuba will soon join the family of free nations." I wondered if there is anything that you gentlemen know about that that you could tell us that we don't know.

The President: No, I think the strong conviction is that the people of Latin America want to be free, they don't want to live under a tyranny, and that Cuba will be free. That is the conviction of the people of Central America and Latin America. And that's the conviction of the people of the United States.

The Civil Rights Commission Hearing in Mississippi

Q: Mr. President, the Civil Rights Commission for months has been trying to hold a hearing in Mississippi. Do you feel that this hearing should be delayed any longer?

The President: No, that is a judgment the Civil Rights Commission should - any time, any hearing that they feel advances the cause or meets their responsibility which has been entrusted to them by the law, then they should go ahead and hold it.

The TFX Fighter Controversy

Q: Mr. President, the TFX fighter plane controversy has drawn more attention to Senator Case's criticism of those politicians who in recent campaigns have urged the public to elect candidates on the grounds that they can bring more big defense contracts into those particular States, the implication being that they could use political influence to do this. Now, do you feel that this sort of a proposition to the public builds confidence that these big defense contracts are being let fairly?

The President: I think the contracts are being let fairly. But of course, there's great competition, and it's no wonder because thousands of people, jobs are involved. The fact of the matter is defense contracts have been concentrated in two or three States, really, in space contracts, because those States have had the historical experience and also because they have a concentrated engineering and educational infrastructure which puts them in a successful position.

For example, a good percentage of the contracts traditionally in space have gone to the State of California, and in defense, because the great defense plants - for all the reasons, really, since the end of World War II. So Senators and Congressmen who are concerned about unemployment among their citizens, who are concerned about the flow of tax dollars, will continue to press. But the fact of the matter is that we have a Secretary of Defense who's making very honest judgments in these matters, and I know from personal experience that some Senators and Congressmen who recently visited Secretary McNamara, asking to present plans from being turned down, who happen to be members of my own party, and indeed, even more closely related, have been rejected by the Secretary of Defense.

Q: Mr. President, if I may follow that up, Senator Case has proposed that a watchdog committee be created to look into these ——

The President: To watch the Congressmen and Senators? Well, that will be fine if they feel they should be watched!

Hope for Arriving at a Test Ban Agreement

Q: Mr. President, after all of the years of failure in attempting to reach a nuclear test ban agreement at Geneva, and in view of the current stalemate at the Geneva conference, do you still really have any hope of arriving at a nuclear test ban agreement?

The President: Well, my hopes are somewhat dimmed, but nevertheless, I still hope. The fact of the matter is that the Soviet Union did accept in September a position which it had denied over the past 2 years or so, of inspection. Now, what we are disagreeing about are the number of inspections, but at least the principle of inspection is accepted. Now, the reason why we keep moving and working on this question, taking up a good deal of energy and effort, is because personally I am haunted by the feeling that by 1970, unless we are successful, there may be 10 nuclear powers instead of 4, and by 1975, 15 or 20.

Now, I am not even talking about the contamination of the atmosphere which would come when all of these nations begin testing, but as you know, every test does affect generations which are still away from us. So I think that when we are now talking, the Soviet Union and the United States, whether we will have seven or three, we've come this far, and I think that we ought to stay at it. So I am not disturbed at all by those who attack every effort we make to get a nuclear test ban.

The fact of the matter is that when the treaty is signed, if it ever is signed, and I hope it is, it must go to the Senate and it must be approved by two-thirds of the Senate. Therefore, it seems to me great protection to all of us. Now, the other point I want to make is that we test and test and test, and you finally get weapons which are increasingly sophisticated. But the fact of the matter is that somebody may test 10 or 15 times and get a weapon which is not nearly as good as these megaton weapons, but nevertheless, they are two or three times what the weapon was which destroyed Hiroshima, or Nagasaki, and that was dreadful enough.

So I think that we have a good deal to gain if we get a test agreement, and so we are going to keep at it. Now, Members of Congress, who may object to that will have their chance to vote "aye" or "nay" if we are successful in a treaty and we present it to the Senate. In the meantime, we are going to stay at it.

The President's Tax Program

Q: Mr. President, many, if not most, of the witnesses before the Ways and Means Committee and the members of the Joint Economic Committee say that your tax program is too little and too slow. Would you accept an immediate tax cut at the figure they are now using, around $6 billion or $8 billion, at once?

The President: Yes, but the only thing is they also then come out against the essential governmental programs. I have seen very few people who have said that they would support what I regard as essential programs, national security, domestic security, and all the rest, and a tax cut of the kind of figures you are talking about. What you are asking us to do is to choose between these programs, which involve, as I have said, the national security in many cases, or domestic welfare. They are asking us to choose between those programs and the tax cut. I think the best combination is the present figure that we have reached of our expenditure level plus the tax cut.

Now, if economic conditions warrant a speedup and the Congress believes it, I would accept that. But I don't think we ought to be under any misapprehension that when they talk about a speedy tax cut they are also talking about a decline in defense expenditures as well as space expenditures, as well as domestic. For example, a bill which I think is vital to this country, which is a bill to provide for building medical schools so we will have at least the same number of doctors in proportion to our population 10 years from now as we do today, is held up now in the Rules Committee seven to seven. I think that bill is very important, not so much for today, but 5 years from now, 10 years from now. It has the support of the doctors. We need doctors in this country. We don't have enough. They are reluctant to vote that out. It is tied seven to seven. I want this tax cut to stimulate the economy, but I also think we ought to have enough doctors. So I think the combination we've got is the best one.

The Monroe Doctrine

Q: Mr. President, there have been some published suggestions that you have amended the Monroe Doctrine in your statements made at Costa Rica. Would you care to comment?

The President: No, I have not heard that suggested and it isn't so. We did not amend the Monroe Doctrine in Costa Rica.

Q: Mr. President, at Costa Rica you agreed to support a number of projects for regional developments, but no figures, dollar figures, were mentioned in connection with any of them. Would you care to explain why we did not agree?

The President: Yes, because these countries are putting together an integrated economic plan, and they are then going to present it under the procedures of the Alliance for Progress at Punta del Este, to the Nine Wise Men, so called, who will then approve the plan. When the plan is approved, it will then be submitted to us, and we will, if it meets the conditions of self-help, reform, economic growth, and the rest, we will support it. What we have indicated to them is if their plan is sound, if they are making the necessary commitments themselves, the tax revenue, agrarian reform, and all the rest, and if it meets the approval of the Nine Wise Men, who are Latin Americans and North Americans, then we will support the plan. But I think we can decide what that figure of support will be better when we have seen the plan and gotten the approval. But we did not want to leave them in any doubt that they will have, and I think they should, our wholehearted support when the time comes. Anyone, as I have said, who has seen these countries and knows how much they want to do well, how vital they are, must feel that we should be of some help. We can't be satisfied to have the hard conditions of life which so many of them face. So we are going to support them, if the Congress agrees, but we first have to see the details of their plan.

The President's Role in the TFX Contract

Q: Mr. President, in regard to the TFX contract, would you describe your personal role, specifically. Did you make any suggestions as to who should get the contract?

The President: No, I did not. No. This was completely the Defense Department.

Q: Mr. President, do you share the view of some officials in the Pentagon that members of the McClellan committee, particularly those up for reelection next year, may have been politically motivated in attacking the award to General Dynamics?

The President: As I said, when a contract goes to one State, then the company may involve or the Senators may involve or the Congressmen want it to go to another. I would not get into that question, because I do not think that is the important point. I assume that the McClellan committee, on which I once served, will render a fair judgment.

Number 2, I am confident of the TFX contract because I am confident of Secretary McNamara. Therefore, as I've said, this hearing can go on as long as they feel it serves a useful result, and whatever the motivations may be – and I wouldn't attempt to explore them – I have confidence in the committee and the members involved.

Support for the President's Domestic Programs

Q: Mr. President, how do you explain the undue reluctance, it seems to me, in the large segment of Congress to support your domestic programs such as the support for medical schools, the youth service corps, and many of the other programs that you have advanced in order to help segments of our population?

The President: Well, the fact of the matter is the hospital plan came out of the committee and it came to the Rules Committee. In the Rules Committee, one of the members who supported the plan was sick, and so it came up for a vote. The five Republicans on the committee voted no. Judge Smith and Colmer, of Virginia and Mississippi, voted no. The seven Democrats voted yes. Mr. Madden was sick, so the bill is tied seven to seven. I hope he gets well. I hope he has an opportunity to vote on it again, and then maybe we will have some hospitals.

Reporter: Thank you, Mr. President.

[1] See 1962 volume of the *Public Papers of the President*, Item 546 (2). See also Item 7, above.

[2] On September 16, 1963, the President approved a joint resolution "favoring the holding of the Olympic games in America in 1968" (Public Law 88-124, 77 Stat. 156). The International Olympic Committee later announced that Mexico City had been selected as the site for 1968.

[3] Livingston T. Merchant, Special Representative for Multilateral Force Negotiations.

[4] NATO Ministerial Council meeting in Ottawa, May 22-24.

[5] See Item 35 of the *Public Papers of the President*, (1963).

[6] Printed in the Department of State Bulletin (vol. 48, p. 515).

THE PRESIDENT'S NEWS CONFERENCE OF

APRIL 3, 1963

The President: Good afternoon.

QUESTIONS

The Use of Lie Detectors

Q: Mr. President, when a Government department feels it necessary to check on a news story that is displeasing to that department, how do you feel about using lie detectors on men you've appointed to office?

The President: Well, are you talking about a hypothetical case or an actual case?

Q: I am talking about a case that started at the Pentagon, but was called off today.

The President: Well, I think that the case – Secretary McNamara was asked to investigate how this Air Force document was put out to the press. And at the suggestion of the committee, investigation was begun. I think that it was a mistake to suggest a polygraph. And I think Secretary McNamara, when he learned that in the investigation that a document was suggested which would indicate that the witness might be willing to accept a polygraph, I think he decided that that was in error, and he and Secretary Zuckert changed it. So I don't think we need concern ourselves in the future about it. The fact of the matter, no polygraph was given.

Support for SEC Staff Recommendations

Q: Mr. President, do you intend to support SEC staff recommendations for legislation designed to curb certain abuses in the securities industry?

The President: I will have to see the recommendations when they come to the White House. And then we will have a chance to look at it, and then I can give you a better answer, after we have examined it.

Soviet Troops in Cuba

Q: Mr. President, 2 weeks ago you said you wanted to wait until the end of March before taking another look and saying something about the Soviet troops in Cuba. Do you have any new information for us on how many have been pulled out and what can be done to get the rest of them out?

The President: Well, we estimate that 5,000 Soviet troops left in November, immediately with the missiles and with the bombers. And we estimate that in the last month approximately 4,000 Soviets have left. If we accept the figure, which was always a rough calculation, that there were 21,000, 22,000, Soviets there at the height of the crisis, we could get some idea of where approximately we think the figures are today. It is bound to be a generalized figure because it is impossible to take a detailed head count. That still leaves some thousands on the island. We hope they're going to be withdrawn. And we will continue to observe very closely in the next days, the immediate weeks ahead, whether there are going to be further withdrawals which, of course, we wish for.

The Situation in Korea

Q: Mr. President, again 2 weeks ago you indicated that the situation in Korea had not yet hardened to a point where any talk by you would be helpful. There does appear to have been a hardening situation in the meantime. Would you say how you feel now about the continuation of military rule in Korea?

The President: As you know, the conversations have been going on between the military group and the civilian opposition. It is our hope that a situation will develop which will permit the blossoming of democratic rule, in responsible and stable democratic rule in South Korea. These conversations have not finished. The United States Government feels that this is a finally - in a final sense, a decision for the people of South Korea. We've indicated what our hopes are, but this is a judgment which the people of South Korea must make, and the responsible officials in South Korea. In any case, it is our hope that an accord will be reached between the military group, its chairman, and the civilians, so that we will see in the future a merging pattern of democratic rule. But as of today, the situation is not clear.

The Difficulties of Preventing Raids by Cuban Exiles

Q: Would you be willing to discuss with us, sir, the political and military difficulties of preventing these hit-and-run raids by Cuban exiles who believe they are striking a blow for freedom?

The President: Well, obviously Florida is a long coast, and it is possible for some people to go from Florida and strike at a target and come back. We have attempted to discourage it for a number of reasons. We believe it is ineffective. There was a raid conducted in Cuba, left around the 17th, I think, the evening of the 17th or 18th, that shot at a Soviet merchant ship as a target of opportunity. It returned, a number of the people who took part in it came to Washington and held a press conference. It does not seem to us that this represents any real blow at Castro. It gives additional incentives for the Soviet Union to maintain their personnel in Cuba, to send additional units to protect their merchant ships. It is not controlled. No one in a position of responsibility knows about it. So that it will bring reprisals, possibly on American ships. We will then be expected to take a military action to protect our ships, which may bring a counteraction.

I think that when these issues of war and peace hang in the balance, that the United States Government and authorities should - and when American territory is being used - should have a position of some control in the matter. So we don't think that they are effective; we don't think they weaken Castro. We don't think a rather hastily organized raid which maybe shoots up a merchant ship or kills some crewman, comes back, holds a press conference, it doesn't seem to us that that represents a serious blow to Castro and, in fact, may assist him in maintaining his control.

Now, I want to contrast that kind of action with action of some other Cubans, and I don't criticize these men who took part in this. They are anxious to see their island free, but we just don't feel that this advances their cause. I contrast that with some others.

For example, between 400 and 500 members of the brigade who were prisoners, who were at the Bay of Pigs, have joined the United States Army, 200 as officers and 250 as men who are now in training, and who, I think, will be very fine soldiers, and can serve the common cause. The head of the - the commander of the brigade, Oliver, who is a Cuban, a Negro, got all of his marks at

100 in joining the service. So I think there are a good many very determined, persistent Cubans who are determined that their island should be free, and we wish to assist them.

We distinguish between those actions which we feel advances the cause of freedom and these hit-and-run raids which we do not feel advances the cause of freedom, and we are attempting to discourage those.

Federal Expenditures

Q: Mr. President, two weeks ago six Republican Members of the Joint Economic Committee, House and Senate, wrote you a long letter of suggestions about Federal expenditures, including a request that you establish a Presidential Commission on Federal Expenditures, somewhat similar to the Clay Commission on Foreign Aid. What would be your position on that suggestion?

The President: Well, I think we have the Bureau of the Budget which oversees and gathers together all of the recommendations which we wish to make for programs. We then submit it to the Congress - the House and Senate. And they finally appropriate the money; we do not. So that the House and Senate has its opportunities with its staff, the Appropriation Committee. We have probably the most effective staff in Washington, for the amount of work they do and the men employed, in the Bureau of the Budget. I am very satisfied with this procedure.

Defense Contracts and the TFX Situation

Q: Is it valid, sir, for the Government to give a defense contract to a firm in order to keep that firm as part of the production arsenal of this country? And, two, did that happen in the case of the TFX award to General Dynamics?

The President: No, to the last part. In the first case, if it is a hypothetical case, I would say it would depend on the circumstances, how great the need is. Is it for particular kinds of tools which we might need in the case of an emergency? I can think of cases where it would be valid. It has nothing to do with the TFX.

Accomplishments of the Congress

Q: Mr. President, even though this is a new Congress, hasn't it in its 3 months of life made a very low record of accomplishments, and what do you think is the trouble?

The President: Well, I must say that I am familiar with these stories in March and April that the Congress isn't doing anything, and I think this Congress is going to act on the major pieces of legislation.

The House Ways and Means Committee is now considering the tax bill. The House Rules Committee reported out the bill for aid for medical construction and education today in the House. The Senate this afternoon is considering the transit bill. It will be considering in the next few days the youth employment opportunities bill.

So I would say that you will see in April and May and June a good many important pieces of legislation coming to the Floor. But I think that this is, if I may use the word again, a rhythm of January and February, and then March the story starts to be written about the Congress not doing anything in April, and then in May we begin to get some bills to the Floor and some are defeated and then there are those stories about Presidential leadership. (Laughter)

The Settling of Labor Disputes

Q: Is there a lesson in the recent New York newspaper strike that might lead to the settling of labor disputes in this particular industry by means other than strikes in the future?

The President: No, I don't see it. I think that unless the unions and the employers are ready to accept compulsory arbitration, and there is no indication that either would be, I don't see that we are going to be able to set up any mechanical operation which would stop a city strike.

Now, a State may want to set up emergency procedures, which the Federal Government has in cases affecting the national health and safety. That's a State judgment. But I don't see any Federal actions that can be taken. I do feel, looking at that strike, that that strike could have been settled many days before it was, on conditions quite similar to what was finally accepted. But neither side was prepared to take those actions which would have brought it to an end. But I don't see any mechanical changes we can make in laws which could affect the situation.

Israel and Egyptian Manufacture of Missiles

Q: Mr. President, Israel has been evidencing growing concern over the manufacture of missiles in Egypt, and unofficially has asked the United States to use its good offices from Bonn to discourage the use of German scientists in this endeavor. Can you tell us anything about that point, and, secondly, can you tell us anything about Israel's requests for more armaments from this country?

The President: Well, as you know, the German Government itself has indicated its displeasure, and there is some question of whether it may be a breach of the law, the German scientists who are working on missiles, air engines, and airframes for the U.A.R. There is not a great number of them, but there are some of them, and of course they do affect the tensions in the Middle East. So I think this matter has been very strongly brought to the attention by the Israeli Government and by other interested parties who are seeking to diminish rather than increase the arms race in the Middle East.

Now, on the question of what military assistance we would give the Israelis; as you know, the United States has never been a supplier of military equipment directly to the Israelis. We have given economic assistance. The Israelis themselves have bought equipment, a good deal of it from France. We will just have to see what the balance of the military power may be in the Middle East, as time goes on. We are anxious to see it diminished rather than participate in encouraging it.

On the other hand, we would be reluctant to see a military balance of power in the Middle East which was such as to encourage aggression rather than discourage it. So this is a matter which we will have to continue to observe. We have expressed our strong opposition to the introduction or manufacture of nuclear weapons in the Middle East, and we have indicated that strongly to all of the countries. So we have to wait and see as the time goes on. At the present time, there is a balance which I think would discourage military action on either side. I would hope it will continue.

Eisenhower's Appraisal of the National Budget

Q: Mr. President, General Eisenhower has taken a crack at the national budget. He told Charlie Halleck in a letter that he thought it could be reduced by about $13 billion. The General was especially critical of your space *program. He said that there were enormous sums being wasted in that field. Would you care to comment?*

The President: Well, I think that President Eisenhower referred us to Maurice Stans, his budget director, for guidance, and I have examined that record. Under Maurice Stans, this country had the largest peacetime deficit in history. It took a $500 million surplus and put it into a $12.5 billion deficit. It had the largest outflow of gold in dollars in our history, 1959, about $3.9 billion. We had two recessions, 1958 and 1960, and we had the highest peacetime unemployment, 1959, since World War II. That is not a record that we plan to duplicate if we can help it.

Secondly, the United States Congress almost unanimously made a decision that the United States would not continue to be second in space. We are second in space today because we started late. It requires a large sum of money. I don't think we should look with equanimity upon the prospect that we will be second all through the sixties and possibly the seventies. We have the potential not to be. I think having made the decision last year, that we should make a major effort to be first in space. I think we should continue to do so.

Now President Eisenhower - this is not a new position for him. He has disagreed with this, I know, at least a year or year and a half ago when the Congress took a different position. It is the position I think he took from the time of Sputnik on. But it is a matter on which we disagree.

It may be that there is waste in the space budget. If there is waste, then I think it ought to be cut out by the Congress, and I am sure it will be. But if we are getting to the question of whether we should reconcile ourselves to a slow pace in space, I don't think so. This administration has concentrated its attention since it came into office on strengthening our military. That is one of the reasons why you could not possibly put in the cut which has been recommended, $9 or $10 billion, without cutting the heart out of the military budget. The fact of the matter is, when we came into office we had 11 combat ready divisions; we now have 16. We increased the scheduling on Polaris, nearly double per year. We've increased the number of planes on the 15 minute alert from 33 percent of our strategic air force to 50 percent. In a whole variety of ways - in the Navy we have added about 46 vessels, we've strengthened ourselves in defense and space.

The fact of the matter is, in nondefense expenditures we have put in less of an increase in our 3 years than President Eisenhower did in his last 3 years. I am concerned that we may not be putting in enough, rather than putting in too much, because the population of this country is growing, 4 million people a year. So that I think we ought to go ahead with what we are talking about. We ought to have effective, tight budget control, which we have tried to have. The Congress may be able to improve on it. But this idea that you can cut the budget wholesale without cutting very essential national programs, and, number two, taking $9 billion out of the economy, is just bound, in my opinion, to put you in an economic decline instead of a rise.

I think we ought to recognize that the percentage of our budget expenditures as a percentage of our gross national product are about the same as they were all through the fifties. The budget may have gone up because the country is growing and the population is growing, but so is our gross national product. And the debt as a percentage of our gross national product is steadily declining.

So I think we are in good position, providing we can prevent an economic decline of the kind we had very rapidly in 1958 and 1960. Then I think we can do that if we have effective programs of the dimensions that we are talking about, plus the tax cut, because we have to have, just to absorb the people coming into the labor market, we have to have a $25 billion increase in our gross national product just to absorb the people coming into the labor market, let alone cut down the number who are now unemployed. So that is my view of the matter.

U.S. Difficulties with Guatemala and Argentina

Q: Mr. President, as you know, we had difficulties lately in both Guatemala and Argentina, two countries which under the Alliance for Progress were making efforts to get on their feet economically and politically. I wonder how you feel about these developments? Do you regard these as symptomatic of the problem the Alliance is trying to attack? What are your views?

The President: Yes, I think so. That's right. I do regard it as symptomatic. There is instability, part of it through the hemisphere comes from maldistribution of wealth, part of it comes from inadequate wealth, part of it comes from the fact that they have been in a depressed state really since 1957 and 1958, because of a drop in commodity prices. Part of it comes from illiteracy and it is very hard to maintain a democratic form of government as we have seen even in Western Europe, which has many advantages. So that to do it in Latin America, with so many disadvantages, is extremely complicated. Great progress has been made, and a good many democratic governments now exist. I saw one of the finest in Costa Rica the other day. But I certainly would agree with you that what is happening in Guatemala and what's happening in the Argentine is symptomatic of the challenges which face us in this hemisphere and which the Alliance is trying to meet.

Q: Mr. President, Venezuela has said that it does not intend to recognize the new government in Guatemala because it took power by force. This is a recurring problem in various places. Are we going to have any consistent or uniform policy on whether or not to recognize governments that take power by force?

The President: No, we haven't got a consistent policy, because the circumstances sometimes are inconsistent. What we are interested in now is what assurances we get as to when a democratic government - or when elections will be held. This government which has taken over in Guatemala has indicated that it will provide a return to democratic rule. When we have a clearer idea of that and also what the position will be of the other Central American countries who are so intimately associated in the Common Market and other ways, we will then be able to make a judgment as to whether it is in our interest to proceed ahead.

The President and Governor Chandler

Q: Mr. President, we have a brand new issue in Kentucky in the Democratic primary. The question is: how much time Governor Chandler spent with you on Monday. Mr. Salinger and Mr. O'Donnell were there, and you popped out and shook his hand. Mr. Chandler got back home to Kentucky and said he spent more than half an hour with you and he says Mr. Salinger has quit managing the news and is now not telling the truth. Can you tell us how much time you saw Mr. Chandler? (Laughter)

The President: Well, I have never attempted to - Governor Chandler called up and talked to, I think Mr. O'Donnell on Monday morning and he said he was in town and he was there with his wife and two sons and his granddaughter and would like to pay a friendly call. And I was glad to see the former Governor - Senator - and one whom I have known for a good many years. So I was delighted to have him by and I wouldn't possibly clock him. (Laughter)

The President's Trip to Europe

Q: Mr. President, on your trip to Europe, there have been a lot of rumors about other cities than Rome and Bonn and Berlin wanting you to visit them. I wonder if there is anything you can tell us now about what other cities, you might visit, possibly London or even Paris, and also if you could tell us when you might be going?

The President: No, we have no plans to visit London or Paris. We will be going, I would think, the last half of June, to Rome and Bonn, and Berlin. That is our present schedule.

Increase in the Size of the Peace Corps

Q: Mr. President, we are told that the principal reason that you have ask-ed Congress to increase the size of the Peace Corps to 13,000 is because of the new emphasis on Latin America. But isn't there some danger that these countries will be disappointed if that goal isn't reached?

The President: Yes. We are going to attempt to make a major effort in Latin America in the Peace Corps. I would hope that this month, when we must really get our applications for the summer, when most of the students will be available, I would hope they would put their applications in, in April.

We need nurses, teachers, those who are knowledgeable in the mechanical arts, liberal art school graduates. I would hope that we would get a good, strong, volunteer group in April. We will concentrate on Latin America, and I think based on our experience already with them, it will be most useful.

The New Foreign Service Academy

Q: Mr. President, tomorrow they start hearings in the Senate on the new Foreign Service Academy. Why is this necessary? Why wouldn't it be better to have returning officers go to the schools in Pennsylvania, Harvard, or Chicago, and see something of the country to which they are returning, while they are doing their studies?

The President: Well, I think you might say "Why don't we eliminate the National War College?" I think that the problems which they face are very specialized, particularly those Ambassadors or Ministers or Foreign Serivce officers who go to Latin America, Africa, and Asia, the Middle East, where you have got a good many paramilitary, economic, social, political problems, all the rest. I think the Foreign Service Institute has indicated a response to that need, but we need a much stronger service in the same way that we need the National War College. Now that doesn't mean that some students may not continue to go to the places you named. But I think we need one here in Wash-ington which is directly tied to the work of the State Department, particularly the work in the areas which I have described, where an Ambassador - I just looked. I saw Ambassador Guillion this morning, from the Congo.

When you think of the decisions, for example, which our Ambassador in Guatemala must now make, our Ambassador in South Korea must have made over the last 3 weeks, and we depend heavily, of course, upon the judgment of the people there, the judgment that our Ambassador in Laos has had to make over the last year, the judgment of our Ambassadors in Pakistan and India, these are the most important, significant - the judgment of our Ambassador in Yemen and Saudi Arabia, I think we need this school, because I think these men deal with ques-tions which are so intimately related to the work of the Department, itself, that I think that the institute ought to be here, close to the Department and working with it.

The Railroad Strike

Q: Sir, do you plan to take any action to head off the threatened railroad strike?

The President: Yes, we will, and by this afternoon we are going to announce the appointment of a board.

Khrushchev's Present Status

Q: Mr. President, what is your evaluation of Khrushchev's present status, and the nature of the political struggle that is apparently now going on in the Kremlin? And is the uncertainty in the Kremlin affecting U.S. policy decisions right now, for instance, over Cuba?

The President: No, but I would think it is possible that Khrushchev is subjected to the same - I don't think we know precisely, but I would suppose he has his good months and bad months like we all do.

Q: By when do you think we will be first in space, and in view of Russia's current lunar probe, do you think we will beat Russia with a man to the moon?

The President: I don't know. We started well behind. Quite obviously they had a tremendous advantage in big boosters, and we are still behind, because obviously we haven't gotten our new boosters yet, which we won't get until 1964, '65 and '66. So that we will have to wait and see, but I can assure you it is an uphill race at best, because we started behind, and I am sure the Russians are making a major effort. Today's indication of what they are doing makes me feel that their program is a major one and is not spongy, and I think that we would have to make the same ourselves.

So I would say we are behind now, and we will continue to be behind. But if we make a major effort we have a chance, I believe, to be ahead at the end of this decade, and that is where I think we ought to be.

The Maintenance of Relations with the U.K.

Q: Mr. President, will we be able to maintain our special relations with the United Kingdom if Mr. Harold Wilson and the Labor Party win the next election?

The President: I don't see any reason why our relationship should change with Great Britain. It has existed with Labor governments and Conservative governments. I think it is a relationship based on history and common interest. And we also have strong relations with other countries of Western Europe, and we have special relations in Latin America. I think Mr. Wilson said, and I think probably Mr. Macmillan has said, that the word "special" is probably not the most appropriate word to describe it. It is a very strong, intimate, and reassuring relationship, and I think it will exist regardless of who is in power.

On a Double Standard for the Congress and the Exeuctive Branch

Q: Sir, I wonder if you think that there should be a double standard for Congressmen and one for men in the executive branch of Government. I am referring to these articles on cheating Congressmen which Jack Anderson wrote about the other day. And I wonder if you think that since you have been in Congress and the executive branch, if there should be the same standard for no conflict of interest and honesty as Congress insists upon for the executive, and if you think these should be the same thing for Congressmen?

The President: I think this is a matter where the Congress is the best judge of their own standards. As a matter of fact, I think the Constitution so states. And I would think that they would be jealous of their reputation as really any man or woman should be.

The Administration's Commitment of Resources

Q: Mr. President, you said a moment ago that your administration had no intention of emulating the record of the Eisenhower administration in a number of economic respects, and you have often stated your desires to move the country ahead in a number of social fields, education, for instance, and yet you say that in your first three budgets your nonspace, nondefense expenditures are less than in the last three Eisenhower budgets. My question is this: does this balance of resources, this commitment of resources, disturb you?

The President: Yes, I would like to see the United States able to do more in some areas, even though the programs we have suggested in education, if accepted by the Congress, would be very important, not only this year but also in the other years. That is a major program. So I think that we have a solid basis for action. But I do think it is.

On the other hand, I think the defense program is, in my opinion, essential, and I think the space program is vital. But what we are now talking about are those who wish to cut this program, the civilian and the nondefense expenditures, by such a substantial figure. For example, those who say that we should cut foreign assistance by a billion and a half, even though this assistance is vital to the maintenance of a good many countries' independence, while at the same time, as I have said before on other occasions, anti-Communist speeches are made, they want to prevent any Communists taking over in Latin America, they want to deny Latin America any economic assistance and they want us to do something about Cuba, because it is Communist. I don't understand that logic. I think the budget we have sent up is soundly based. I do think there is always a question of whether we are expending enough for civilian needs. But it still is a large budget, a large deficit, and I think that we have done about as much as we now can do. In other years we may have to do more, because this year we held our nondefense expenditures to the same figure as last year.

Dick Gregory in Mississippi

Q: Mr. President, yesterday according to reports comedian Dick Gregory was manhandled by police in Greenwood, Miss. Do you have any comments on the voter registration drive in Greenwood, and particularly do you think the Justice Department can do more in terms of speed and effectiveness to enhance the effort down there?

The President: We have had a suit there since last August against the registrar on the ground of discrimination in the voting. We have now a suit which we launched the other day against the denial of the rights of the voters themselves, and that is due for a hearing very shortly, perhaps this week.

Then I would hope that the court would find that there has been a denial of rights, which seems to me evident, but which the court must decide. Now if we secure the passage of the voting bill which we sent up to the Congress this week, in the case of the voter registrar case, a registrar would be permitted to sit during the period that the case was being considered, because what we now have is a registrar who is charged with discrimination in denying certain citizens the right to vote, and he has been sitting since last August when our suit was filed, and the suit, because of the law's delay, has not yet been settled. So that is an area where there is a vacuum in the law, and I would hope we could fill it. But on the subject, itself, we have two Federal suits and both of them are very important and both of them, I hope, will result in actions which will bring justice in Greenwood, Miss.

Reporter: Thank you, Mr. President.

THE PRESIDENT'S NEWS CONFERENCE OF

APRIL 24, 1963

The President: Good afternoon.

Prime Minister Pearson of Canada and I have agreed to meet at Hyannis Port, Mass., on May 10 and 11 for a first discussion of the many important questions that are of common interest to the two countries.

Secondly, Under Secretary of State for Political Affairs W. Averell Harriman, having consulted in Paris with French Foreign Minister Couve de Murville and in London with Foreign Secretary Lord Home, British Co-chairman of the International Control Commission for Laos, will proceed to Moscow tomorrow to discuss the Laotian situation with the Soviet Co-chairman, Foreign Minister Andrei Gromyko. He does have a short message for Premier Khrushchev from me, explaining the purposes of his trip.

QUESTIONS

Threats to the U.S. by the USSR and Red China

Q: Mr. President, with Laos boiling up, could you assess for us the relative threats posed to the United States by the Soviet Union and Red China?

The President: No, I think it would be a mistake to attempt to make that assessment on this occasion. We have difficult problems in Southeast Asia. They directly involve, of course, the Soviet Union, as the Soviet Union is the co-chairman and is also, as I have already said, a signatory to the Geneva accord. It has assumed in the past a special responsibility for the maintenance of a neutral and independent Laos, in the Vienna statement which the Chairman and I made in June 1961,[1] committing ourselves to that result. We have also of course been conscious of the threat to the security of independent countries of Asia and Southeast Asia, which has been made quite clear by the Chinese. So I would say that we have serious problems with them both. We would hope that the Soviet Union would make an effort to fulfill its commitments under the Geneva accord as the United States is attempting to do.

Proposals by British and American Diplomats Regarding Inspections

Q: Mr. President, there were reports from Moscow earlier today that the British and American Ambassadors during their meeting with Chairman Khrushchev had presented a new proposal on inspection in an effort to break the deadlock on the nuclear test ban treaty negotiations. Is it correct that the United States has presented such a proposal, and is there anything you can tell us about prospects now on this issue?

The President: The United States made proposals for intensification of the negotiations and suggested some procedures by which those negotiations might be speeded up. I am not overly sanguine about the prospects for an accord. We have been caught, really, since December, on the disagreement between the number of tests that should take place in any one year - the United States discussing seven and the Soviet Union three. No movement from the Soviet Union has taken place. In addition there are other details which are still unresolved, not so much the matter of tests but the area of inspection, the means by which the inspection will be carried out, the freedom of the teams, and what will be the composition of the inspection teams; all these questions are still unresolved.

As we feel time is running out, the Prime Minister and I wrote to Chairman Khrushchev in an effort to see if we could develop some means by which we could bring this matter to a climax and see if we could reach an accord, which we feel to be in the interest of the nuclear powers, the present nuclear powers, to prevent diffusion. But, as I say, I am not sanguine and this represents not a last effort but a very determined effort to see if we can prevent failure from coming upon us this spring.

The Attitude of the USSR

Q: Mr. President, back on Laos, it has been more of a testing ground for coexistence since the Geneva accord than perhaps any other place in the world. Would you interpret a Soviet refusal to go along with efforts to maintain peace in the government of national union there as a shift toward a hard line by the Soviet Union?

The President: Well, I don't want to say anything that will prejudice Secretary Harriman's trip. I think we will know a good deal more about the prospects after he has visited Moscow. Quite obviously, we regard the maintenance of the Geneva accord as very essential to the security of Laos itself, and also, as you quite rightly say, as a test of whether it is possible for an accord to be reached between countries which have serious differences, an accord to be reached and maintained.

If we fail in Laos, then I would think the prospects for accords on matters which may be geographically closer to us would be substantially lessened. But I think we will have an idea as to whether the Soviet Union is prepared to meet its commitments and whether the other countries who are also signatories - which include the Communist Chinese and the North Vietnamese, and others - are prepared to really see a neutral and independent Laos, or determined to try a military takeover. I think we should have a clearer idea of that after Governor Harriman's return.

Q: Could I ask just one more question on Laos? Do we have any evidence that the Soviet Union is not in control of the ground in Laos, as they seemed to be in control in 1961 and last year, when the Geneva agreement was signed?

The President: Well, that, I think, is a matter which I think time will tell us. There was a direct control because of the supply lines which were being maintained by the Soviet airlift. Whether the Soviets maintain the same degree of control now, whether they desire to maintain their influence, and whether their influence will be thrown in the direction of a maintenance of the Geneva settlement are the questions which I think we should find answered in the next 3 or 4 weeks.

What, of course, is happening in Laos is a struggle between the neutralist forces of Kong Le, who were allied with the Communist forces in 1961. So that it seems to me that the very nature of the **struggle** and the forces that are involved in the struggle are the best answer to the charges that have been made in the last 24 hours, that it is the United States which has disturbed the status quo. The struggle is not between the forces of Phoumi and the neutralists, but between the Pathet Lao and the Kong Le forces which, of course, are the army of Souvanna Phouma, whom the Communists themselves supported in 1961. So I think we have a very clear idea of where the responsibility lies, and it would be a distortion to attempt to place the burden for the breakdown upon the United States.

I think the world can tell very clearly who is struggling in the Plaine des Jarres and who, therefore, must bear the responsibility. Now, the solution is not to engage in polemics or debate, but to bring about a cease-fire, and to see if we can maintain what is a very fragile structure today.

Federal Involvement in the Attack on Uncontrolled Population Growth

Q: Mr. President, how do you feel about the recommendations of the National Academy of Sciences and also of Professor John Rock of Harvard, that the Federal Government should participate actively in an attack on uncontrolled population growth?

The President: Well, I don't know - I am familiar with the general thesis of Professor Rock. As you know, the United States Government today, through the National Institutes of Health, gives assistance to research in the whole area of fertility, biological studies, reproduction, and all the rest, which I think are important studies, and there are several millions of dollars of Federal funds involved, and I think they are very useful and should be continued.

Q: I think the recommendations are that our Government should take the lead and should participate much more actively and strongly than it has done before. You, sir, have never taken a position on this, I believe.

The President: Well, what is your question?

Q: The question is: Will you accept the recommendations of the National Academy that we should participate in international birth control studies - supply funds?

The President: Well, we are participating in the study of fertility and reproduction in the United Nations, which is an international study, at the present time. Now, if your question is: Can we do more, should we know more about the whole reproduction cycle, and should this information be made more available to the world so that everyone can make their own judgment, I would think that it would be a matter which we could certainly support. Whether we are going to support Dr. Rock's proposal, which is somewhat different, is another question.

Possibility of a Meeting with Khrushchev

Q: Mr. President, do you see any prospect for a meeting between yourself and Mr. President, any time in the next couple of months, in Europe, for example?

The President: No, I haven't heard any, and there is none planned.

Q: The British, according to reports from London, are hoping for a three-way summit perhaps on the test ban.

The President: There is none planned, and it doesn't seem to me that it would be useful unless we were in agreement upon a test ban, which we are not now.

Republican Criticism of the Administration's Attitude Toward Cuba

Q: Mr. President, would you care to address yourself to criticism express-
ed by some Republicans, including Mr. Nixon recently, about the administra-
tion's attitude toward Cuba, and suggesting, perhaps, that we are not taking as
firm a stand toward them as we should? Would you care to speak to that, sir?

The President: No. I know there is a good deal of concern in the United
States because Castro is still there. I think it is unfortunate that he was
permitted to assume control in the 1950's, and perhaps it would have been easier to take an action then than it is now. But those who were in positions of
responsibility did not make that judgment.

Now, as to what the present situation – we have, as you know, without going
through the entire list, we have – and the other countries of the free world
have – cut free world trade in the last 2 years from $800 million to $80 million. We are working with the OAS to set up an organization which will limit
the movement of potential guerrillas in and out of Cuba. We have – the OAS
have almost diplomatically isolated Castro in this hemisphere. I think the
members of the OAS have made it very clear that Marxist-Leninism and the Soviet
presence is not a matter which is acceptable to the people of the hemisphere.
We have been working through the Alliance for Progress to prevent a repetition
of the Cuba incident. We have made it very clear that we would not accept a
Hungary in Cuba. We have made it very clear we would not permit the movement
of troops from Cuba to another country for offensive purposes. We maintain
surveillance. We do a good many things.

Now, coming down to the question which is rather sidestepped, that is, if
the United States should go to war in order to remove Castro. That nettle is
not grasped, and it would seem to me that we have pretty much done all of those
things that can be done to demonstrate hostility to the concept of a Soviet
satellite in the Caribbean except take these other steps which bring in their
wake violence, and may bring a good deal of worldwide difficulty. If they are
advocating that, then I recognize that as an alternate policy, but if it is
merely a policy which says that we should do something without defining it, except perhaps as I have said, unleashing the exiles, which cannot do the job, it
seems to me that we deserve in a question of this importance a good deal more
precision in our prescriptions for its solution.

Q: Mr. President, now that the 21 Americans who were imprisoned in Cuba
have been released, what do you think that the U.S. policy will be toward
exile raids in the future if no U.S. laws are violated, and if these raids may
have some military value, perhaps done in conjunction with the underground
within Cuba?

The President: Well, I would think a discussion of that kind of a question, if the question is as you put it, is really not very useful to the exiles, or to the cause of Cuba. It does not seem to me that public dicussion
of these sorts of activities is worthwhile at this time, or beneficial.

The Dissemination of Information by the USIA

Q: Mr. President, I understand that at the request of the Defense Depart-
ment, the United States Information Agency is now supplying two 5-minute com-
mentaries daily on international affairs which are being broadcast by Armed
Forces Radio Service transmitters on both the East and West Coasts, and in
Germany. And I would like to respectfully ask you whether you feel it is the
business of an official Federal agency to be disseminating comment and opinion
to our citizen soldiers and their families overseas.

The President: What did these programs consist of that is objectionable?

Q: *Comment and opinion on international affairs.*

The President: Well, is there anything about the comment that is at all objectionable or slanted?

Q: *I am not overseas, and so I haven't heard them.*

The President: Well, I'll be glad - (laughter) - you and I share - (laughter) - I would be glad to check into it and find out if there is anything that is improper about it.

The Usefulness of a Talk with de Gaulle

Q: *Mr. President, France is not on your itinerary for this summer, and apparently no invitation has been extended, and certainly you have not solicited one, but I wonder in the light of Secretary Rusk's talk with President de Gualle if you think a talk between yourself and President de Gaulle would be useful this summer?*

The President: Well, I went to France last year. We are going to go to Italy and Germany and Ireland for good reasons in every case. We have not - I think actually according to protocol, which need not stand in our way, it would be the time for the French President to come to the United States. I think General de Gaulle would be glad to come or, protocol aside, I would be glad to go to France if there were some matters which we felt an exchange, a personal exchange would solve. I think that perhaps both of us feel that on those matters which concern us in common, France and the United States, that they can be best discussed at the diplomatic level.

Administration Support for a Cuban Exile Government

Q: *Another point on the exile problem, sir, rather in line with an admonition that you yourself made last December; the Attorney General suggested the other day that the Cuban exiles should compose their differences and speak with more of one voice, particularly in terms of their relationship with the Government. Is there an implication here, sir, of an approval or enthusiastic approval on the part of your administration toward the setting up of an exile government, a government in exile?*

The President: No, we supported the arrangement of the Revolutionary Council in order to give the exiles a voice which we hoped would be speaking for the exile community in all those matters which affect their relations with the United States and the United States Government. For us to agree and support a government in exile, however, is an entirely different question, because you have to - we would want to support a government which would strike a responsive chord in Cuba itself. The experience with governments in exile have not been particularly felicitous, historically speaking. There is no evidence that exiles themselves could develop a government which would necessarily be the government which the people of Cuba would freely choose.

It would seem to me what would be most valuable now would be a greater degree of cohesion among the exiles regardless of their political view, and there are substantial differences among them, so that they can negotiate with us, if that is the proper word, and bring their case before other Latin America countries, in the OAS, so that we can talk to someone about the many problems which we face and the exiles face with 200,000-250,000 people coming into our country. But a government in exile, I think that is a different question, and in my view it would be imprudent today and I don't think it would help the struggle.

Reduction of Russian Troops in Cuba

Q: Mr. President, Senator Keating says that according to his information there has been no reduction in the number of Russian troops in Cuba. He said several thousand have left, several thousand have arrived there, with no change in the overall number since November. Would you care to comment?

The President: Yes. I have already said that the best information we have from the intelligence community - and I rely upon the Director of the Central Intelligence Agency as chairman of the intergovernmental intelligence community for the information which I have given publicly. We attempt to ask any Congressman or Senator who has information to the contrary for his sources so they can be evaluated. I have stated that our information was, I think the last time we met, that 4,000, we thought, left in March, and that no substantial number had come in this winter. There is some evidence that some have left in April, but not a large number. Of course, the equipment itself seems to still be there, however, so that I would think there has been some reduction this winter in the number of Russian personnel on the island. There has not been a substantial reduction in the equipment. There has been no evidence, however, of any substantial introduction.

It is not, in my opinion, a grave question as to whether there's 17,000, 15,000, 13,000. There are still important elements on the island, and there's still Soviet equipment on the island. So I don't think Senator Keating and I are debating a serious question, unless there is a challenge on one side or the other of good faith, and I am sure there isn't. It is our best information that 4,000 or 5,000 have left since January and that there has not been an equal number come in. In fact, much, much less - 300 or 400 at the most. That's our best evidence and I repeat it as it has been gathered by our intelligence sources.

The Civil Rights Commission and the Abuse of Civil Rights

Q: Mr. President, you have rejected the Civil Rights Commission's proposal for the withholding of funds from the State of Mississippi in particular; yet Negroes and other persons in some Southern States are encountering violence and the withholding of some of their rights. Could you discuss with us what alternative steps the Federal Government might be able to take to bring some of these States into line with the law of the land?

The President: Well, in every case that the Civil Rights Commission described, the United States Government has instituted legal action in order to provide a remedy. The Civil Rights Commission gave a number of cases, the dogs, of a denial of equal rights at the airline terminal, and all of the rest. We are attempting through the established procedures set out by the United States Constitution to give protection, through lawsuits, through decisions by the courts, and a good deal of action has been taken in all of these cases.

Now, it is very difficult. We had outrageous crime, from all accounts, in the State of Alabama, in the shooting of the postman who was attempting in a very tradional way to dramatize the plight of some of our citizens, being assassinated on the road. We have offered to the State of Alabama the services of the FBI in the solution of the crime. We do not have direct jurisdiction, but we are working with every legislative, legal tool at our command to insure protection for the rights of our citizens, and we shall continue to do so.

We shall also continue not to spend Federal funds in such a way as to encourage discrimination. What they were suggesting was something different, which was a blanket withdrawal of Federal expenditures from a State. I said

that I didn't have the power to do so, and I do not think the President should
be given that power, because it could be used in other ways differently.

But I can just say to you that the Federal Government has been extremely
active in the State of Mississippi, from before Oxford and since, in an attempt
to provide for constitutional guarantees. We hope the State of Mississippi will
do it, we hope the local police will do it, we hope the mayors will do it.
Where they don't do it, the Federal Government will do it within the limits of
our authority.

Federal Employees

*Q: Mr. President, Budget Director Gordon says there are fewer Federal em-
ployees for every hundred people today than in 1952 or 1957. Much of the press
has always given the opposite impression. Hasn't the administration been making correct information available, or do you think this is an instance, perhaps,
of the press managing the news?*

The President: Well, I would not ever suggest that anyone would manage the
news. You have two kinds of statistics. One, you have Federal employment rising and therefore that's printed. That's news. Federal employment is rising.
Then you have the question of whether Federal employment is rising in relation
to the population, and it isn't. It is, as you suggested, declining. Federal
expenditures in relationship to the population - nondefense expenditures - are
declining. The Federal debt in relationship to the gross national product is
declining. The Federal debt has gone up in the last 15 years, but in relationship to the gross national product it is declining. It seems to me this is the
framework in which these statistics should best be put. If the population increases 3 or 4 million a year it's quite obvious you are going to have to have
additional services. But the question is whether this increase is excessive.
And, in nearly every case, in percentage of expenditures and in employment we
have gone down.

I hoped the budget would make that point, because otherwise the people get
an impression that there are excessive expenditures by the National Government;
that we are in a very difficult economic position, when the fact of the matter
is our **national** debt was 120 percent of our gross national product 15 years
ago, and today it's 53 percent. So we are far stronger economically than we
were 15 years ago. We are far stronger economically than we were 10 years ago
or 5 years ago. And we have every chance to be far stronger through this decade if we will follow monetary and fiscal policies that encourage the growth
of this country instead of stifling it.

And one of the reasons why I think we have such difficulty getting an acceptance of our expenditures and our tax policies is because people misread the
statistics or are misled.

Apathy at the Grass Roots

*Q: Mr. President, this has to do with the Wall Street Journal survey on
grassroots apathy which has just been published. Do you agree, sir, that such
apathy actually exists, and if so, how do you account for it, and if it does
exist, what do you plan to do about eliminating it?*

The President: Every April the Wall Street Journal writes a story on the
left-hand side of the paper, reporting that Congressmen who have come back
find great apathy about the President's programs. (Laughter) The fact of the
matter is that in the last month we have had five or six important votes on the
floor of the House and the floor of the Senate which I think indicates a

support of a program of expansion for the United States economy. Today we are going to pass in the House of Representatives, I am sure, a bill to assist us in building medical schools so we will have enough doctors.

We passed the other day in the Senate a bill on mass transit. We passed a bill yesterday to provide important research facilities for water, which we are going to need greatly in the United States in the next 20 or 30 years. We are going to pass other programs. So I don't accept that at all. If we can get a chance to get these bills on the floor of the House so that they can be voted upon - through the Rules Committee, and give the Members a chance to vote for them - in my opinion this program to a substantial degree will pass. The only thing that has ever concerned me is whether the Rules Committee of the House of Representatives will release it for a vote. But if they release it for a vote, I think that the Members of the House will make very clear that the American people are still committed to progress on all of these fronts, which I believe is essential if we are going to maintain a viable economy. So that I think that is the best answer to the Wall Street Journal.

Laos and the Domino Theory

Q: Mr. President, on Laos again, several years ago we heard a great deal about the "falling domino" theory in Southeast Asia. Do you look upon Laos in terms of that country alone, or is your concern the effect that its loss would have in Thailand, Viet-Nam, and so on? Would you discuss that?

The President: That is correct. The population of Laos is 2 million and it is scattered. It's very rough country. It's important as a sovereign power, the people desire to be independent, and it is also important because it borders the Mekong River and, quite obviously, if Laos fell into Communist hands it would increase the danger along the northern frontiers of Thailand. It would put additional pressure on Cambodia and would put additional pressure on South Viet-Nam, which in itself would put additional pressure on Malaya.

So I do accept the view that there is an interrelationship in these countries and that is one of the reasons why we are concerned with maintaining the Geneva accords as a method of maintaining stability in Southeast Asia. It may be one of the reasons why others do not share that interest.

The OAS and the Cuban Problem

Q: Mr. President, there has been suggestion in the Congress that the Government, the United States Government, might use more effectively the vehicle of the Organization of American States in the Cuban problem. I know there have been certain things done there already. And I understand that we are now prepared to go to the OAS shortly with a plan for intensified security measures. I wonder if you could discuss those and also whether you think there is general support among the Latin American countries for such a program?

The President: Yes. Out of the San Jose meeting some proposals came which were amplified by the Managua meeting for providing additional security, which we presented to the OAS. In addition, the whole Alliance for Progress will pass through the OAS machinery. The efforts we are taking on surveillance is a result of an action of the OAS. So I think that the OAS is very active, even though I think we recognize the particular responsibilities we bear because of our geography and also because of our military strength.

The Possible Withdrawal of Funds from the Civil Rights Commission

Q: Mr. President, you have no intention to withdraw funds from the Civil Rights Commission, do you?

The President: No, I don't. No.

Agreements with the USSR

Q: Sir, this regards the agreements with Soviet Russia, between the United States and Soviet Russia, regarding programs in outer space. We have two that are about ready. Those are not coming back to the Senate for ratification, I don't believe. I wonder why?

The President: Well, the kinds of agreements - the executive agreements to cooperate on weather? That is not a treaty.

Q: Well, should it not be a treaty?

The President: No, it doesn't seem to me that it involves issues which are substantive enough to warrant a treaty. The Congress has been kept fully informed. It is an exchange of information on weather and customarily that is not submitted to the Senate for treaty ratification. Any substantive agreement involving issues, for example, a test ban treaty, multilateral force, those sorts of issues, will definitely be submitted to the Senate.

The Wisdom of the "Man to the Moon" Program

Q: Mr. President, there seems to be a fairly lively debate developing on the question of the wisdom of our man-to-the-moon program and the amount of money that we have assigned to it. Have you had any cause at all to reconsider your commitment to that goal?

The President: Well, we are looking at - we looked at, of course, when we proposed our budget for this year. We are looking at it again in relationship to next year's budget. We are also looking at it because of the concern that has been raised in the Congress and out of the Congress. I have seen nothing, however, that has changed my mind about the desirability of our continuing this program.

Now, some people say that we should take the money we are putting into space and put it into housing or education. We sent up a very extensive educational program. My judgment is that what would happen would be that they would cut the space **program** and you would not get additional funds for education. We have enough resources, in my opinion, to do what needs to be done in the field, for example, of education, and to do what needs to be done in space.

Now, this program passed almost unanimously a year ago. What will happen, I predict, will be a desire perhaps, possibly, to cut it substantially, and then, a year from now or 6 months from now, when the Soviet Union has made another new, dramatic breakthrough, there will be a feeling of why didn't we do more. I think our program is soundly based. I strongly support it. I think it would be a mistake to cut it. I think time will prove, even though we can't see all the answers which we will find in space, that the overall expenditures have been worthwhile. This country is a country of great resources. This program in many ways is going to stimulate science. I know there is a feeling that the scientists should be working on some other matter, but I think that this program - I am for it and I think it would be a mistake to arrest it.

The Economic Picture and the Tax Bill

Q: Mr. President, there is reported to be a growing feeling on Capitol Hill that because of the brightening economic picture it might not be necessary to push your tax bill, that is, it might be all right to delay the effective date of your tax bill. Do you share that?

The President: No, I don't agree with that at all. The fact of the matter is that the economy today is moving along at relatively the same figure as was estimated by the Council of Economic Advisers. It might be about $2 billion more. But the fact is I think that one of the reasons why the economy has moved along has been partly the level of governmental expenditures, combined, of course, with the private vitality in the economy, and also the prospect of the tax cut. The tax cut would put $10 billion directly, in an 18-month period, into the hands of our people, which under the multiplier will mean $30 billion, and I think can make a very important difference in reducing our unemployment. We have to find a tremendous number of jobs in the next 2 years for new people, and, in addition, we have a 5.6 percent level of unemployment already.

So I think it would be a great mistake to stop the tax cut. It is a long-range program. And it would be a great mistake to delay it, because we have all been through experiences, even in the last 12 months, to know that no one predicts with certainty the level of the economy. And I think the prudent action is to go ahead with the program we suggested.

Reporter: Thank you, Mr. President.

[1]See 1961 volume of the *Public Papers of the President.*

THE PRESIDENT'S NEWS CONFERENCE OF

MAY 8, 1963

The President: Good afternoon.

I am gratified to note the progress in the efforts by white and Negro citizens to end an ugly situation in Birmingham, Ala. I have made it clear since assuming the Presidency that I would use all available means to protect human rights and uphold the law of the land. Through mediation and persuasion, and where that effort has failed, through lawsuits and court actions, we have attempted to meet our responsibilities in this most difficult field where Federal court orders have been circumvented, ignored, or violated. We have committed all the power of the Federal Government to insure respect and obedience of court decisions and the law of the land.

In the city of **Birmingham the Department of Justice some time ago instituted** an investigation into voting discrimination. It supported in the Supreme Court an attack on the city's segregation ordinances. We have, in addition, been watching the present controversy to detect any violation of the Federal civil rights or other statutes. In the absence of such violation or any other Federal jurisdiction, our efforts have been focused on getting both sides together to settle in a peaceful fashion the very real abuses too long inflicted on the Negro citizens of that community.

Assistant Attorney General Burke Marshall, representing the Attorney General and myself on the scene, has made every possible effort to halt a spectacle which was seriously damaging the reputation of both Birmingham and the country. Today, as the result of responsible efforts on the part of both white and Negro leaders over the last 72 hours, the business community of Birmingham has responded in a constructive and commendable fashion and pledged that substantial steps would begin to meet the justifiable needs of the Negro community.

Negro leaders have announced suspension of their demonstrations and when the newly elected Mayor who has indicated his desire to resolve these problems takes office, the city of Birmingham has committed itself wholeheartedly to continuing progress in this area.

While much remains to be settled before the situation can be termed satisfactory, we can hope that tensions will ease and that this case history which has so far only narrowly avoided widespread violence and fatalities will remind every State, every community, and every citizen how urgent it is that all bars to equal opportunity and treatment be removed as promptly as possible.

I urge the local leaders of Birmingham, both white and Negro, to continue their constructive and cooperative efforts.

Q: Mr. President, against the background or possibility of similar trouble developing in other Southern towns, I wonder if you could tell us how you regard the techniques that were used over the last few days in Birmingham by either side, dogs and fire hoses used by one side, and the use of school children and protest marchers by the other side?

The President: Well, I think what we are interested in now is seeing the situation peacefully settled in the next 12-24 hours. I think all of our statements should be devoted to that end. Quite obviously, as my remarks indicated, the situation in Birmingham was damaging the reputation of Birmingham and the United States. And it seems to me that the best way to prevent that kind of damage, which is very serious, is to, in time, take steps to provide equal treatment to all of our citizens. That is the best remedy in this case and in other cases.

Q: Mr. President, do you see any hope of Birmingham serving as a model for a solution in other communities facing similar problems?

The President: We will have to see what happens in Birmingham over the next few days.

QUESTIONS

Situation in the Mideast

Q: Mr. President, do you consider the situation in the Middle East, the balance of power there, to have been changed as a result of recent developments, and what is the U.S. policy towards the security of Israel and Jordan in case they are threatened?

The President: I don't think that the balance of military power has been changed in the Middle East in recent days. Obviously there are political changes in the Middle East which still do not show a precise pattern and on which we are unable to make any final judgments. The United States supports social and economic and political progress in the Middle East. We support the security of both Israel and her neighbors. We seek to limit the Near East arms race which obviously takes resources from an area already poor and puts them into an increasing race which does not really bring any great security.

We strongly oppose the use of force or the threat of force in the Near East, and we also seek to limit the spread of communism in the Middle East which would, of course, destroy the independence of the people. This Government has been and remains strongly opposed to the use of force or the threat of force in the Near East. In the event of aggression or preparation for aggression, whether direct or indirect, we would support appropriate measures in the United Nations, adopt other courses of action on our own to prevent or to put a stop to such aggression, which, of course, has been the policy which the United States has followed for some time.

Puerto Rico's Future Status

Q: Mr. President, a proposed commission to draw up legislation on Puerto Rico's future status consists of 12 members. Four would be from Congress and 4 would be named by you and the remaining 4 by the Governor of Puerto Rico. Republicans complain that there should be people on the committee only from Congress and the Puerto Rican legislature, and I wondered what are your own feelings on this?

The President: Are you talking about the commission that would be set up by the Puerto Ricans?

Q: That has been introduced in Congress.

The President: Oh, by Congressman Aspinall?

Q: Yes, the 12 men.

The President: Yes. Well we are going to take a look at that. It seems to me Congressman Aspinall's proposal might be useful in making more precise the alternatives before the Puerto Ricans. We'd have to make a final judgment on it later, but I would think it offers a basis for consideration. But I couldn't give you a final United States Government position on this at this time as yet.

The Crisis at Birmingham, Alabama

Q: Mr. President, in the Alabama crisis at Birmingham, according to your interpretation of the powers of the Presidency, was there power that you possessed either by statute or the Constitution that you chose not to invoke or did you use your powers in your view to the fullest in this controversy?

The President: There isn't any Federal statute that was involved in the last few days in Birmingham, Ala. I indicated the areas where the Federal Government had intervened in Birmingham, the matter of voting, the matter of dealing with education, other matters. On the specific question of the parades, that did not involve a Federal statute as I indicated in my answer. And that is the reason why Mr. Marshall has been proceeding the way he has – and we have not had for example a legal suit as we have had in some other cases where there was a Federal statute involved.

Q: Two Negro graduate students apparently plan to apply for admission this summer in the Huntsville branch of the University of Alabama, and the Governor of Alabama has said that he will physically bar their entrance. Is there anything the administration can do to avoid this collision?

The President: Well, we would hope that the decision of the court would be carried out – this is our continual view – in a way that maintains law and order. This of course does involve the Federal Government, because it's a Federal statute. But we would hope that all people would follow the dictates of the court whether they agree with them or not, and that law and order would be maintained by the local authorities and that all those who have a responsibility under any local or State constitution for the maintenance of law and order would meet their responsibilities. This is a matter of course, as I said, that does involve the Federal Government.

Admiral Anderson's Retention

Q: Sir, the fact that Admiral Anderson was not retained as Chief of Naval Operations has been written about in such a way as to imply that he did not measure up to your expectations as a head of the Navy, that he might have bucked reorganization plans, that he opposed Defense Secretary McNamara on the TFX, and other things which you probably are familiar with. Is it true that he was not retained as a sort of warning to others in the Navy to get in line with the Secretary and yourself?

The President: No, that isn't the reason. As a matter of fact, Admiral Anderson is going to continue to serve the United States Government. I am very gratified that he has. I talked with him today and he has agreed to accept - to continue to serve the United States Government in a position of high responsibility. So quite obviously, the reasons - if I did not have the highest confidence in him I would not want him to continue.

Q: Could you tell us what post, sir, he will serve in?

The President: No, I - he continues as, of course, head of the Navy through August and therefore at an appropriate time this summer we will make an announcement. But he has agreed to continue to serve and I am delighed because I think he will be a great addition to the Government in this new position which requires a good deal of skill, which requires a good deal of dedication, and to which I would appoint someone for whom I had only a high regard.

U.S. Relations with Canada

Q: Mr. President, in view of the strained relations that have existed with the former Canadian Government, would you be willing to share with us a discussion of the objectives of your meeting with Prime Minister Pearson at Hyannis Port?

The President: I think the central objective is to go over all the areas which involve the common interests of our country - defense, trade, the various matters of concern of distribution of natural resources, the flow of investment, and all the rest, which are of concern to either Canada or the United States. As close neighbors we have a whole spectrum of interests and problems in common and I am looking forward to going over them all with the Prime Minister. So we will, I think, cover the entire waterfront.

A Statue of Winston Churchill

Q: Mr. President, in the most prominent park in London, Grosvenor Square, with which you are familiar, there is a statue of President Franklin D. Roosevelt. Do you know of any plan for us to erect here a statue of Winston Churchill, our most honored honorary citizen?

The President: No, I don't know of any, although it seemed to me that the action which the Congress took by overwhelming vote, the ceremony which you witnessed, is perhaps really the best indication of our strong support for him.[1]

Q: Americans who go to London always go there, and every time there's Britishers laying little tributes and wreaths. And it seems to me we ought to have one of him here.

The President: Well, he is still very much with us, and I think we ought to lay our wreaths at his feet. (Laughter)

The Radical Right

Q: Mr. President, you have spoken out before against the dangers of the so-called radical right in politics. Could you update those observations today, in view of the fact that a dozen States or so, influenced in part by extremist groups, have given varying degrees of approval to legislation which would change the form of amending the Federal Constitution and would undercut the powers of the Supreme Court as well?

The President: Well, it has always seemed to me remarkable that those people, and organizations who are founded in order to defend the Constitution, should seek always to change it, and particularly to change it in such a basic way, either to affect the power of the Congress, to amend the Constitution and put severe limitations upon the Congress which after all represents the people most directly, or otherwise to affect the power of the Supreme Court, which is one of the most important protections of individual rights and one of the most important securities we have for an amicable settlement of disputes, and which, after all, became such a significant part of our American constitutional development under the leadership of an American who is usually heralded - Mr. John Marshall. So I would think that the efforts will come to nothing, and I will be glad when they do not.

Discussions Between Harriman and Khrushchev

Q: Mr. President, what conclusions, if any, have you drawn from the recent discussions in Moscow between Under Secretary Harriman and Chairman Khrushchev and between Ambassador Kohler and Chairman Khrushchev?

The President: Well, the conversation between Governor Harriman and Mr. Khrushchev dealt with the maintenance of the agreement of Geneva and also of Vienna that Laos should be neutral and independent. Mr. Khrushchev, at the time of the visit of Mr. Harriman, reaffirmed his commitment to a neutral and independent Laos. But that was in Moscow and now that commitment, we hope, will be implemented on the Plaines des Jarres. Quite obviously, the action a few days ago of attacking the ICC helicopters, action taken by the Pathet Lao, indicates that they are not at the present time living up to this commitment.

I would hope that the Chairman would be able to convince them that it was in the long-range interest of all concerned and most especially of the people of Laos and of peace in the area. So we are going to have to wait to see whether that happens. Now, Mr. Kohler did not have any direct conversations, except to deliver a message to the Chairman dealing with testing.

The President's Advisers

Q: Mr. President, back on the subject of Presidential advisers, Congressman Baring of Nevada, a Democrat, said you would do much better if you got rid of some of yours - and he named Bowles, Ball, Bell, Bunche, and Sylvester.

The President: Yes, he has a fondness for alliteration and for "B's". And I would not add Congressman Baring to that list as I have a high regard for him and for the gentlemen that he named. But Congressmen are always advising Presidents to get rid of Presidential advisers. That is one of the most constant threads that runs through American history and Presidents ordinarily do not pay attention, nor do they in this case.

Viet-Nam

Q: Back to the subject of Viet-Nam, could you explain to us, sir, why we have committed ourselves militarily in Viet-Nam, but have not committed ourselves militarily in Laos, depending instead upon this neutralist government?

The President: Because the situations are different. That's why the remedy has been different. We have had a commitment for a good many years to the integrity of South Viet-Nam. We are anxious to maintain the neutrality of Laos. It may not be possible to do so, and it may be necessary to seek other remedies. But we have adopted what we considered to be, considering the geography, the history, the nature of the threat and the alternate solutions - we have adopted for each country what we regarded as the best strategy. And we'll have to wait and see what happens on them.

The OAS and Haiti

Q: Mr. President, do you feel that the OAS should apply diplomatic or economic sanctions against the Duvalier regime?

The President: I think we ought to wait until the peace-keeping group which has just gone out with new instructions from the OAS, which are broader than the previous ones - I think we ought to wait and see what they are able to do in the next 2 or 3 or 4 days.

Q: Do you have the feeling that the OAS should take further action than it has?

The President: I think that the OAS action at the present is the proper one. I think it is very important that we proceed in company with the OAS, and therefore I'm supporting the action the OAS has taken in setting up this peace machinery.

The Wheat Referendum

Q: Sir, there has been a good deal of discussion about this forthcoming wheat referendum. The opponents have suggested that should the farmers reject the control plan, substitute legislation could be passed. Spokesmen for your administration and congressional leaders have said they oppose this. I wonder whether you could tell us whether the administration would not merely not support new legislation, but whether you would oppose the passage of a substitute?

The President: I'm sure there won't be new legislation, because the fact of the matter is, this legislation passed by the closest of votes. The legislation on the feed grains passed in the Senate by the closest of votes. We have not got a consensus on dairy legislation. We have not got a consensus today on cotton legislation. We may not have any cotton bill.

There is such a division among the farming groups themselves as well as among those in the nonfarming congressional groups that I don't think you could get a majority. If this legislation is defeated, I don't think you can get a majority in the House and Senate.

It is not a question of not wanting to do the best we could, but this seemed to us the best proposal. The farmers can vote it up or down. I think those who suggest that if this is defeated there will be some new bill that will come forward, I think they mislead the farmers. I don't think that you will see new legislation this year, because I don't think that there is an agreement on it. And if they will look at the record of the last 2 years and see the limited – in the last 5 or 10 years – how few agriculture bills have passed, they will come to the same conclusion that the Chairman of the House Agriculture Committee has come to, the Chairman of the Senate Agriculture Committee has come to, and the Secretary of Agriculture: that there cannot be a new bill because there is not a general agreement on what that new bill should be and this, therefore, represents the choice that the farmers will be faced with this year. And I think they should judge it on that, and not on some hope that some new bill will come which will solve all of the problems. There's just no such thing in the wings.

Improvement of Race Relations

Q: Mr. President, to try to improve race relations in a noncrisis atmosphere, last Sunday, according to the UPI, 160 Knoxville, Tenn., white and Negro families visited each other's homes. Do you feel it would be in the public interest for you to use the prestige of your office to encourage similar church- and civic-supported projects nationally?

The President: I think it would be very helpful, and I think it can start right here in Washington, D.C., where this is greatly needed. And all groups, it seems to me, can afford not only to concern themselves as they do with Birmingham but also to look into their own lives and their own eating habits, and all the rest, to see whether they are living up to the spirit you have expressed in your question.

A Tax Cut Program

Q: Sir, do you believe a tax cut program which does not directly benefit people in the lower income brackets will sufficiently develop the consumer demands, stimulate the economy, and overcome unemployment as you wish?

The President: Do I think it will?

Q: Yes.

The President: The total tax cut as estimated, I see, most recently by the Joint Committee on the Economic Report would provide a stimulation of nearly $40 billion to the economy. This would have a great effect upon employment and job security, as well, of course, as it would lighten the tax burden of those in all classes. But in the bottom classification it amounts to nearly 40 percent reduction, so that we've tried to provide a balance. The overall effect, of course, is what we are most looking at and a $40 billion increase in the economy I think would provide a substantial reduction in unemployment and a substantial increase in economic well-being.

Q: May I ask whether the Ford[2] committee, the businessmen's committee on tax cuts, has a program which meets with your approval?

The President: Well, as I said at the time, I disagree with some of their proposals. They don't agree with the reform section of our bill, but they are in favor of a tax cut of the same amount that we are. There is the exception, however, on reforms. This is a matter about which a good many members of Congress and citizens disagree, but the central point is that they are in favor of the 10½ billion tax cut which I am in favor of. They would redistribute it somewhat differently, but they have their views and I have mine. But we are in favor and join on the necessity for a tax cut for the economy.

The President's Wound

*Q: Mr. President, ever since you permitted the telecast of press confer-
ences, a great deal of attention has been paid to little things that occur,
especially in the home offices and newspapers. Would you save us a couple
of hours of work tonight and explain what the Band-Aid is doing on your left
hand?*

The President: Well, I cut my finger when I was cutting bread - unbeliev-
able as it may sound. (Laughter)

The Clay Report

*Q: Mr. President, in view of the Clay[3] report, do you think the Bokaro
steel mill project in India should be rejected on the grounds of public versus
private?*

The President: No. There is such a need for steel that is going to be un-
filled and providing it is an efficient project, I would think we could assist
if it meets what the economy of India requires. I must say that I don't quite
get the logic of those who so vehemently oppose this very much-needed project;
not just take possession of a steel mill already constructed but to build one.
So that there is an important distinction. At the same time, when we lend
hundreds of millions of dollars to Canada to join in the nationalization of the
electric lights in Quebec - in order to - private companies. Now I think that
this is a stimulus which will go up. All the evidence we have is that it will
not go up unless the United States joins in. The Soviet - I think we ought to
do it - I think we ought to do it. Now, the Congress may have other views, but
I think it would be a great mistake not to build it. India needs that steel.

Prospects for a Test Ban

*Q: Mr. President, on the test ban issue, are you - do you join what seems
to be the general feeling that prospects for a test ban at this time are zero,
that the Moscow atmosphere is so chilly, or is there something in your private
correspondence with Chairman Khrushchev which will give you some hope?*

The President: No, I'm not hopeful, I'm not hopeful. There doesn't seem
to be any sense of movement since December on the offer of two or three that
the Soviets have made. We have tried to see if they will change that figure.
We have, as you know, reduced our requirements. We have indicated a willingness to negotiate further. We have tried to get an agreement on all the rest
of it and then come to the question of the number of inspections, but we were
unable to get that. So I would say I am not hopeful at all.

*Q: Mr. President, would you assume that we will have another round of
testing by both the Soviet Union ——*

The President: I would think if we don't get an agreement that is what
would happen. And I would think that would be - personally I would think that
would be a great disaster for the interests of all concerned. If we don't get
an agreement this year - they almost had one in 1958 and 1959 - at least in
retrospect it seems it might have been possible. We thought maybe we were moving toward it in December. Now we seem to be moving away from it. If we don't
get it now I would think - perhaps the genie is out of the bottle and we'll
never get him back in again.

Race Relations

Q: Mr. President, on the matter of improving race relations in the United States, do you think a fireside chat on civil rights would serve a constructive purpose?

The President: Well, it might. If I thought it would I would give one. We have attempted to use all - what happens is we move situation by situation and quite obviously - and all these situations carry with them dangers. We have not got a settlement yet in Birmingham. I've attempted to make clear my strong view that there is an important moral issue involved of equality for all of our citizens and that until you give it to them you are going to have difficulties as we have had this week in Birmingham. The time to give it to them is before the disasters come and not afterwards. But I made a speech the night of Mississippi - at Oxford - to the citizens of Mississippi and others. That did not seem to do much good, but this doesn't mean we should not keep on trying.

Q: May I ask you a question on your statement on Birmingham? I believe you said that the results of the efforts by Mr. Marshall have been that the business community has pledged that substantial steps will begin to meet the needs of the Negro community. Could you expand on that? What kind of substantial steps?

The President: No, I said as the result of responsible efforts on the part of both white and Negro leaders over the last 72 hours, the business community of Birmingham, and so on. So it's their efforts and not the Federal Government's efforts. I would think that it would be much better to permit the community of Birmingham to proceed now in the next 24 hours to see if we can get some - and not from here.

Morale at the Pentagon

Q: Mr. President, a number of observers have noted that morale among the military at the Pentagon is particularly low and they ascribe it usually to the heavy-handed treatment by Mr. McNamara and his civilian secretariat, in addition to the wide dissatisfaction with the military pay bill. I understand that you recently went over to the Pentagon and spoke to an assemblage of military officers. I wondered whether you found any morale situation there that concerns you, or can you tell us the purpose of your visit?

The President: Well, I went over last year and this year and will go every year. I think the problem - pay is one of the problems. Housing is another. There are some shocking examples of inadequate housing for our military people. Obviously, there are bound to be some disappointments with the decisions of civilian leaders. Somebody has to decide whether we are going ahead with the Nike-Zeus or the Skybolt or one plane or another; or what the size of our conventional forces will be, our strategic forces, missiles. The military, as they always will agree, always feel more is needed. Mr. McNamara had to scale down their request some $13 billion even to reach the very hard budget figure and now there is some understanding that there may be a billion dollar cut in the budget we set up, which I think would be a serious mistake. That budget was very hard. As I say, $13 billion had been cut out of it. Now, any time you cut any amount of money some important interests are sacrificied. That causes some reaction. But I think this administration has put a good deal of attention in strengthening the military. We have increased the budget substantially. There have been those who said it could be cut 10 billion. I don't think it can be cut hardly at all, so that I would hope that we would be able to proceed ahead.

There are bound to be some frictions and differences of opinion. They're strong-minded men but I must say I have great confidence in their loyalty to their country and I think they will go on. I am sure there will continue to be disputes. But that is why we have the organization that we have. We have to have a Secretary to make the final judgment. You have four services. I think everybody will get along.

Q: Mr. President, aside from the top command, I was thinking more of a morale problem throughout the ——

The President: Well, I think that is a somewhat different problem. And I think part of that is pay; part of that is housing; part of that is the feeling that perhaps the military is not recognized for the service they are rendering at rather inadequate compensation; part is some disappointment or feeling of the Reserves that perhaps their services are not recognized, sometimes companies don't give them the kind of treatment that would permit them to carry on their Reserve activities.

I hope – as we depend very much upon our military and as we have been very well served by our military in the last 2 years, and as I said the other day, one of the things that impresses me greatly when I write letters on the death of servicemen – and 3500 lost their lives in the service from one action or fatalities of one kind or another in the last year – that the tremendously strong letters that come back from their families indicate a great interest in the love of their country. So this is a terrifically valuable asset for us. I would hope we can keep it and if there is anything we can do to improve the morale, I think we ought to do it.

Trade Talks at Geneva

Q: Can you tell us what our central objectives will be at the forthcoming trade talks at Geneva, and are you hopeful that they will lead to a big round of cuts in 1964?

The President: Yes. The objective of this, as you have described it, is to provide for satisfactory negotiations with the Common Market in 1964, and this GATT meeting is essential for that success.

Reporter: Thank you, Mr. President.

[1] See Item 126 of the *Public Papers of the President.*

[2] Henry Ford 2d, Chairman, Business Committee for tax reduction in 1963. See Item 145 of the *Public Papers of the President.*

[3] General Lucius Clay, Chairman, Committee to Strengthen the Security of the Free World. See also Item 111 of the *Public Papers of the President.*

THE PRESIDENT'S NEWS CONFERENCE OF

MAY 22, 1963

The President: Good afternoon.

QUESTIONS

Integration of the University of Alabama

Q: Mr. President, how do you regard the Alabama Governor's announced intention to block the integration of the University of Alabama? For instance, do you or does the Government plan to use Federal marshals as it did in Oxford, Miss., if the Governor does go through with his announced intention to prevent these Negro students from entering?

The President: Well, I hope that would prove unnecessary. I hope this is a matter that can be settled by the local authorities in Alabama. The university since last October has - the Board of Trustees have taken the position that they would accept a court order. They have now indicated that they will accept these students. The courts have made a final judgment on the matter, and I would hope that the law-abiding people of Alabama would follow the judgment of the court and admit the students. Every other State in the country has integrated their State university, and I would hope that Alabama would follow that example.

I know there is great opposition in Alabama, and indeed, in any State, to Federal marshals and Federal troops. And I would be very reluctant to see us reach that point. But I am obligated to carry out the court order. That is part of our constitutional system. There is no choice in the matter. It must be carried out, and laws which we do not like must be carried out, and laws which we like. This is not a matter of choice. If it were a matter of choice, it would not be law. So these decisions must be enforced. Everyone understands that.

Now, I cannot believe that the Governor wants us to send Federal troops there. I cannot believe he wants us to send Federal marshals there. I cannot believe he would not prefer to have the people of Alabama govern this matter and accept the order of the court and maintain law and order. The Governor has taken action against Federal troops who are now stationed at Federal bases in Alabama, and has taken the action to the Supreme Court. I said I welcomed that. This is where these disputes should be settled. So I would hope that the fact that the Governor has chosen to carry out our dispute in the courts indicates that in the final analysis he will accept the judgment of the court, in the cases coming up in June, as I would accept the judgment of the courts as to my powers to use - control Federal troops under certain conditions in various States. We are a people of laws, and we have to obey them.

Food Prices

Q: Mr. President, you have predicted a sharp drop in the price of wheat as a result of yesterday's referendum. I wondered if consumers can look forward to proportionate reductions in the costs of certain foodstuffs as a result?

The President: Well, as you know, the amount that the farmer gets in a loaf of bread is about 1 cent, so that you won't expect a very sharp drop. What

I am concerned about has been that you would have a drop in prices because you would have a great buildup of surpluses. A free market is regulated by supply and demand. If the supply is greater than the demand, then quite obviously it can be and will be because everyone is now free to plant what they wish.

Then, of course, that knocks the price down. So that we will have a combination of lower prices and larger surpluses. We sought to avoid that. But this is a free country and the farmers were offered their choice and they made the choice by - a great number of them voted for the free market and unlimited production. So we are going to be faced with the problem, but I don't think it will have much effect on the consumer. It might, but I think it is going to cause more difficulty to the economy, because it is going to provide these large surpluses and it is going to, I think, reduce farm income, particularly wheat farmers, and that is not to the interests of the consumers, of course, or the farmer.

Now, our feed grain bill will give him some relief. We will administer the laws that are now in effect in such a way as to give him maximum protection - the wheat farmer. We will cooperate in every way we can to maintain his income as high as we can. But I am concerned, as I said before the vote, that production will be increased and income will drop and prices will drop.

Q: Mr. President, if there is no legislation and the price of wheat does decline rather sharply, what would be the political consequence of that for you in 1964?

The President: I don't know. I have tried to make it very clear what the alternatives were and what I thought was in the best interests of the farmer, the wheat farmer. I felt that his best interests would be served by attempting to bring production in line with demand with an adequate income for him. Now the farmers have chosen to plant freely without controls and without that high support. We will have to see what the effects will be.

In any case, under the law that was passed, there is a chance for another referendum next year, and then we can see what the effect of this action has been. But we want to help in every way we can. But the farmers have made a choice, and even though I didn't agree with the choice, I recognize it and accept it and we hope that it does not have an adverse effect. I think some of the people who put material out to the farmers may have misled them on what the effect will be. We tried to make it as clear as possible.

India's Military Assistance Requirements

Q: Mr. President, a high-ranking Indian mission has been discussing with you and your advisers India's military assistance requirements. Can you say if the picture has clarified somewhat now and if there is any commitment by the United States to help India in this regard?

The President: Well, as you know, at the time of Nassau, we both - Great Britain and ourselves - agreed to proceed ahead with the program of assistance. The Indian Defense Minister is now proceeding on to Great Britain. We are going to be in consultation with the Commonwealth, and we will be giving further assistance to India.

The Mercury Flight

Q: Did the astronauts raise with you, sir, their desire for another Mercury flight? And do you have any opinion yourself tentative or otherwise as to the desirability of another Mercury flight?

The President: I think they feel that it is worthwhile. I haven't discussed it with Mr. Webb. NASA should make the judgment and will make the judgment, and I would not intervene, but they do feel that a flight is useful, and that the experience of Major Cooper has indicated that the time between the last Mercury flight and the new Gemini flight, which is a period of almost 18 months, they feel may represent a gap which could be filled very usefully by another Mercury flight. This will be a matter which I think they are going to be talking about this week with Mr. Webb and which I would discuss with them next week. But the final judgment must be NASA's.

The GATT Talks in Geneva

Q: Mr. President, how do you feel now about the compromise settlement that was reached at the GATT talks in Geneva? Don't we still have a very long and hard row to hoe, sir, before we start realizing any of the objectives of the Trade Expansion Act?

The President: Yes, I think we have a long road to hoe, but we have always known that. When you are talking about economic matters, and tariffs, these are all matters which involve very strongly the interests of countries, but I think that the settlement was satisfactory. We have got a situation where there are different tariff structures in many different countries, where you have great, contrasting economic interests not only between the United States and the Common Market, but between other newly emerging countries as well as those completely dependent upon agriculture. So I think it was a satisfactory settlement. But I quite agree with you that during the next year when this matter will be coming down to final negotiations, we will have a long road, but one that I think we can travel and should travel and must travel. And because that was a common realization by both the Europeans and ourselves is why I think finally an adjustment was reached and we didn't have a breakup. I think the fact that we did make that adjustment, compromise, final agreement, indicates that both sides realize that the West cannot possibly afford to have a breakdown in trade relations.

Corporal Punishment in Schools

Q: Mr. President, a recent lecture by Mr. Sorensen[1] disclosed that we apparently fell down on the job at a recent press conference when you had prepared - by recalling your own boyhood, apparently - your answer to a possible question about what you would think of corporal punishment in the District of Columbia schools. Could I make up for that slip now and ask you that question?

The President: Well, I didn't - I don't - (laughter) - I thought the idea was that that conference had passed into history, and that you would never have a chance to ask that question.

But as long as it hasn't, I think when we talk about corporal punishment, we have to think about our own children, and we are rather reluctant it seems to me to have other people administering punishment to our own children. But because we are reluctant to do so, it seems to me it puts a special obligation upon us to maintain order and to send children out from our homes who accept the idea of discipline. So I would not be for corporal punishment in the school, but I would be for a very strong discipline at home so that we don't place an unfair burden upon our teachers.

Meeting with the Pope

Q: Sir, on your forthcoming trip to Europe next month, can you tell us whether you plan or have any hopes of meeting with Pope John in Rome?

The President: Yes, I would hope to. I plan to, yes. We have a plan to and I am hopeful that we will.

The Base at Guantanamo

Q: Mr. President, Republicans have charged that some kind of agreement exists or may exist someday for our abandoning Guantanamo Bay Naval Base. Could you comment on that, please, sir?

The President: Well, I think that that charge indicates as some people have suspected before, that there was some political motivation in some of the attacks upon our policy with regard to Cuba. That of course is completely untrue. It has never been considered. It will not be done. And to raise that with no evidence merely because we happen to be putting in an acoustical center for improving our underwater detection system in Bermuda and strengthening a naval base in Puerto Rico from those two actions it was deduced that we must be giving up Guantanamo. I would hope that we would find a good deal more realism in the Republican conversations about foreign policy, because that is untrue. But it may be the sort of thing we are going to hear now for the next 18 months.

The Republican Candidate in 1964

Q: Mr. President, Governor Rockefeller, Governor Romney, and Senator Goldwater, none of these gentlemen are willing to admit that they are candidates in 1964. I wonder if to your experienced eye any of them looks like a candidate, and would you be a little more frank than they are about your plans? (Laughter)

The President: If I had to, I would say that if the party, if the spirit of the party comes to them that they will answer the call in all three cases, and I would say that is about my position, too. (Laughter)

Troops in South Vietnam

Q: Mr. President, the brother of the President of South Viet-Nam has said that there are too many American troops in South Viet-Nam. Could you comment on that, and give us some progress report on what is going on?

The President: Yes, I hope we could - we would withdraw the troops, any number of troops, any time the Government of South Viet-Nam would suggest it. The day after it was suggested, we would have some troops on their way home. That is number one.

Number two is: we are hopeful that the situation in South Viet-Nam would permit some withdrawal in any case by the end of the year, but we can't possibly make that judgment at the present time. There is still a long, hard struggle to go. We have seen what happened in Laos, which must inevitably have its effect upon South Viet-Nam, so that I couldn't say that today the situation is such that we could look for a brightening in the skies that would permit us to withdrawal troops or begin to by the end of this year. But I would say, if requested to, we will do it immediately. As of today we would hope we could begin to perhaps to do it at the end of the year, but we couldn't make any final judgment at all until we see the course of the struggle the next few months.

Assistance to Cuban Refugees

Q: Mr. President, are we providing any material assistance currently to any Cuban refugee organization, any Cuban exile organization?

The President: Well, we may well be, but you would have to make the question more precise.

Q: Any arms or financial assistance on a regular basis to any specific organization?

The President: Well, none that I am familiar with. In addition, I don't know whether it would be a matter I would want to discuss here, in any case. But to answer your question, I don't think as of today that we are. But I wouldn't want to go into details, if we were.

New Soil Bank Legislation

Q: Mr. President, I think new legislation is being introduced today by some of the people who opposed your wheat plan, providing for a soil bank arrangement of acreage retirement and other features. What is your attitude toward legislation of that kind?

The President: Well, I would have to take a look at it and see what effect it would have on production and how much it would cost. Of course, any plan that offered us a hope of reducing the surpluses, of maintaining the farmer's income, and that was not excessive in cost, we would certainly listen to. I don't know why - I am not familiar with any proposal which was made by any of the Republicans, if that is who is proposing it, at the time we proposed our wheat plan. But if there is any plan that offers us hope of accomplishing those three objectives, we would, of course, look at it. I think it would be difficult to get a bill by the Congress. As you recall, the bill which led to the referendum was very close. There is no indication that there is a concensus on agricultural matters in the Congress, between the House and Senate. The feed grain, itself, which I think has been very successful, passed by a very close vote. So we would have to take a look at the details of the bill. But as of now - I looked at the statement of Congressman Albert, the Majority Leader. He indicated that he did not think any bill would pass this year.

Jobs in El Paso

Q: Sir, in El Paso there are 900 jobs in the smelter dependent on some executive action by you. And according to the Mine, Mill and Smelter Workers and management there, and even the Chamber of Commerce, there are plants in Denver, Colo., and California and other States that are also dependent on executive action that you might take in reallocating lead quotas from South Africa. I wonder how you think this affects domestic mining and what you plan to do about it?

The President: I am not familiar with the matter. I will be glad to look into it, but I am not familiar with what the executive powers might be in regard to the importation of lead from South Africa, nor am I familiar with the exact quantity of lead we are receiving from South Africa. But I will be glad to look into it.

Military Buildup in Cuba

Q: Mr. President, there is still quite a lot of discussion in the Congress, Senator Lausche among others, on the increasing buildup militarily of Cuba. Is there anything you can say that would be in any way encouraging about the removal of the Russian troops there, or the military situation in Cuba?

The President: We do not have any evidence of increasing military buildup of the Soviet Union. I think in previous press conferences I have given an answer in response to the question of how many Russians were there and the comment in regard to the withdrawal of Soviet troops. We have no evidence that there is an increasing military buildup. There has not been a satisfactory withdrawal as yet. That is quite true, but we have no evidence that there is a number coming in larger than going out.

Q: Pardon me, sir. I was thinking more in terns of military equipment going into Cuba.

The President: Yes, I understand that. We have no evidence that there is an increasing military buildup in Cuba. The intelligence community has not found that.

Secretary Freeman's Effectiveness

Q: Mr. President, do you think Mr. Freeman's effectiveness as Secretary of Agriculture has been seriously impaired by the results of the wheat referendum?

The President: No, no; I think he is doing very well. If you compare farm income this year - the last 2 years, 1961, 1962 - it is higher than it has been any time since 1953 at the end of the Korean war. The farmers are better off today than they have been for 10 years. In addition, if we had not had the feed grain proposal, there would have been a much higher surplus and there would have been a much lower farm income.

So I think that while this is a very complicated problem, because automation has hit the farmers much harder than it has hit any other element in our community and their production is growing faster than our consumption, and therefore this has a tremendous effect on support prices and it has a tremendous effect, of course, upon the market price. Mr. Freeman is attempting to deal with them. My judgment is that he has met with some success, because he has prevented us from spending a lot more money than we would have spent.

We are getting rid of our grain surplus. We are hopeful in 2 years it will be gone. I think we could have made important progress with our wheat surplus if we had been successful. It may be that with the experience we are going to have now, the farmers may agree with that next year. But the fact of the matter is in 1963 the farmers are better off than they have been for 10 years, and I think Mr. Freeman deserves some of the credit for it.

A Formosan Attack on the Mainland

Q: Mr. President, there has been considerable discussion in the Far East that Chaing Kai-shek might be preparing to invade the mainland of China. How would our Government view an attempt of that sort?

The President: Well, the treaty relationship, as you know, provided by the 1954 treaty - the so-called Eisenhower Resolution - provides for very close consultation between the two governments before any such action would be taken.

As a practical matter, this of course does involve the United States, and we have expressed our views to the Government of Formosa on the matter.

Cigarettes and Cancer

Q: Mr. President, just a year ago we talked about the fact that several independent scientific studies have shown a causal connection between cigarette smoking and cancer. And the next week I think the Public Health Service appointed a blue ribbon panel to look into it, and you expected to hear from them in some months. I wondered, have you heard anything lately, and when do you expect a report from the panel on this problem?

The President: I would think very soon. We haven't received it yet, but I think it will be very soon.

Wheat and the GATT Negotiations

Q: Mr. President, how much will the negative vote on wheat affect the GATT negotiations at Geneva?

The President: Well, we will have to see. As you know, there was the agreement that agriculture would be included in those conversations, which I think was helpful. In addition I think the Secretary has indicated today - or if he hasn't he will - that we are going to do everything we can to sustain our international agreements on wheat, and to prevent dumping and all the rest.[2]

But quite obviously, we are in the process of attempting to persuade others to limit their agricultural production so we don't have a worldwide surplus and a worldwide depression in agricultural commodities. And when we make a choice for overproduction, which is what the choice was, and what the effect will be, it is bound to make it more difficult for us to persuade other countries not to open wide the gates themselves.

So that we have to operate the CCC and all of the other laws, and international laws, in such a way as to prevent worldwide results from the decision of yesterday.

Qualifications for Presidential Candidacy

Q: I would like to ask you a hypothetical question addressed to you as a politician of some considerable skill. Do you think that a potential presidential candidate who divorced his wife and married a recently divorced woman would damage his chances for the Presidency?

The President: Well, I must say that neither as a - if I occupied the position you described, or speaking personally, would I want to comment on it.

Civil Rights Legislation

Q: Sir, are you considering asking Congress for new civil rights legislation as a result of the recent developments down South?

The President: Yes, we are considering, as a result of the recent developments and as a result of the Supreme Court decision yesterday, we are considering whether any additional proposals will be made to the Congress. And the final decision should be made in the next few days.

As you know, we have several proposals up there now, dealing with voting, extension of the Civil Rights Commission and the Conciliation Service. But I think there may be other things that we could do which would provide a legal outlet for a desire for a remedy other than having to engage in demonstrations which bring them into conflict with the forces of law and order in the community.

I would hope that we would be able to develop some formulas so that those who feel themselves, or who are, as a matter of fact, denied equal rights, would have a remedy. As it is today, in many cases they do not have a remedy and therefore they take to the streets and we have the kinds of incidents that we have in Birmingham. We hope to see if we can develop a legal remedy.

Students' Demonstration

Q: Mr. President, a group of students in California are very perturbed because their prom has been evicted by your $1,000-a-plate dinner. I wonder if you might comment on the dilemma and offer any advice?

The President: Well, I just heard about it a few minutes before I came here, and I can assure you that if there isn't a satisfactory place for them we will postpone our dinner and I will come out on some other occasion.

Onsite Inspections

Q: Mr. President, I have a question about the nuclear test ban proposal. Mr. Harold Brown[3] has said before a Senate committee that we could accept as few as six onsite inspections. Do you think that there is further ground for us to move now to approach the Soviet Union in the test ban situation?

The President: Well, that is - the position we have taken more publicly - there've been seven. There has been discussion of six. Mr. Brown, whose judgment I value highly has not set the official Government position. He was giving his judgment as a scientist. There are a good many other questions that must be settled. We have suggested to the Soviet Union that we would consider the makeup of the inspection team, the rules under which the inspection team would operate, the area where there could be drilling, all these questions, and then if we can get those settled, we could then come finally to the question of the number of tests. The Soviet Union has refused, however to consider these other matters until we agree with their position of three. Now that has not been an acceptable negotiating position. We feel that we ought to try to wind up all the other questions which divide us. Then we could finally come and decide what would be - given the arrangements we have made for these other matters - what would be a responsible number of tests. But we are back and forth to the Soviet Union and we are still hoping that we can find a perhaps easing of their position.

Q: Where is the genie, sir? Is it out of the bottle or in the bottle?

The President: Well, it is neither in nor out right now. But I would say that we will know by the end of the summer whether it is finally out. I have said from the beginning that seemed to me that the pace of events was such in the world that unless we could get an agreement now, I would think the chance of getting it would be comparatively slight. We are therefore going to continue to push very hard in May and June and July in every forum to see if we can get an agreement which I regard as of - but I will say as of now, since December there has been no change in the Soviet position on the number of tests nor willingness to discuss in any way any of these other questions until we accept their position of December, which is not a satisfactory position for us.

Q: Are we about to move, sir?

The President: We are not going to move. On the question of the number of tests? As I indicated, what we are proposing is we settle the other matters and then come to the number of tests. So in answer to your question, we are not moving at this time on the number of tests.

Reporter: Thank you, Mr. President.

[1]Theodore C. Sorensen, Special Counsel to the President, had delivered the Gino Spernaza Lectures at Columbia University on April 18 and May 9, 1963. They are published with a foreword by President Kennedy as "Decision-Making in the White House: the Olive Branch or the Arrows" (Columbia University Press, 1963).

[2]On May 22 the President issued Executive Order 11108 "Delegating Authority Under the International Wheat Agreement Act of 1949, as Amended, to the Secretary of Agriculture" (28 F.R. 5185; 3 CFR, 1963 Supp.).

[3]Director of Defense Research and Engineering, Department of Defense.

THE PRESIDENT'S NEWS CONFERENCE AT THE FOREIGN MINISTRY IN BONN.

JUNE 24, 1963

The President: I want to take this opportunity to express the appreciation all of us feel to the German people for their very generous welcome. And I am delighted to accept the invitation of the German press corps to have this press conference here.

QUESTIONS

Relationship Between the U.S. and Germany

Q: Mr. President, would you please tell us of what importance you attach to the relationships between your country and Germany at the present time, and what you think the German role should be in the European development in the future?

The President: Well, I think we have consistently attached the greatest importance to the maintenance of a free Europe since 1945, and a whole series of collective actions have been taken by both of our countries and other countries since that time. That relationship is, I think, even more vital today because while I think the security of Western Europe against military attack is well guaranteed by the efforts that we have all made collectively, I think Western Europe and the United States, and Canada, Great Britain, and the Commonwealth, have a major role in serving as the center or the core of a great effort throughout the world to maintain freedom.

In addition, the Federal Republic and Berlin, are in the front lines of this struggle. It is a powerful country which has made an astonishing comeback. It has a great influence in Europe. That influence has been directed towards liberal, progressive, international monetary and trade policies. It is my hope that that policy will continue and, therefore, I am hopeful and I am confident that our countries will work in the closest relationship with each other.

Differences Between Kennedy and Chancellor Adenauer

Q: At the airport yesterday, there seemed to be a note of difference of emphasis between your remarks and those of Chancellor Adenauer. He seemed to be concerned mostly with your concern to defend Europe, while you were concerned with new approaches or approaches to a new peace. Has this difference manifested itself in your private talks with the Chancellor?

The President: No. I thought that the Chancellor was quoting - most of his remarks were a quotation from a speech which I gave at American University 2 weeks ago. He was quoting statements that I had made in regard to our commitment to Western Europe which, of course, is very basic to American policy. I also feel that the effort that we are making is in behalf of freedom and peace. That is the object of our policy, the policy of the United States. It must be, it seems to me, the object of every free country, and I am sure is the object of the policy of this country.

Pope Paul VI

Q: Mr. President, is there a possibility that you might attend the coronation of Pope Paul VI?

The President: No, I think the Chief Justice is leading the American delegation to that coronation, although I hope to see him during my visit to Italy.

Chances of Overcoming the Division in Germany

Q: You said yesterday that our common strategy had to be directed toward overcoming the division of nations and countries. In relation to that remark of yours I would like to ask you, do you specifically see any chance of overcoming the division of Germany, if nothing else, in the sense of perhaps reducing the pressures?

The President: Well, I would hope that - and it has been the policy of the United States for a great many years not to recognize in the juridical sense the division of Germany. Quite obviously, the German people wish to be reunited. If the people of the United States had lost a struggle, and the Mississippi River divided us, we would wish to be reunited. I think the people of the Soviet Union, if they experienced a comparable fate, would wish to be reunited. People and families wish to join together. So that is the object of our policy. Quite obviously there is no immediate solution. We hope that time, the desire of people to determine their own destiny, will be sufficiently strong, the policies that may be developed as time goes on, as events may change, will bring about that reunification which is, I think, the very strongly held desire of the German people, even though today that future may be uncertain, the date may not be possible to mark. There have been so many changes in the world in the last 18 years that I don't think anyone should despair.

Q: Mr. President, the allies have protested as illegal the most recent spread of the so-called Prohibitive Zone by the Communists in Berlin, but they have not tested that zone with controls. This has caused some to feel and to speculate that this means that we are letting the Communists take another so-called "slice" of salami. Could you clarify our position in that respect, sir?

The President: Well, I think that the commandants have made very clear what our view is of the action which has been taken. This matter does involve the interests of two other countries which bear responsibilities comparable to ours, and we work in consultation with them as to what would be the most appropriate steps. Therefore, I feel that it is a matter which should be dealt with by the commandants in Berlin in connection with their government, rather than by me on a unilateral basis.

Q: In the framework of reducing East-West tension, is there any intention of picking up the plan of April of last year for an international approach authority toward Berlin, international access authority?

The President: The matter which was - which came to the surface or was discussed last year was not considered to be a sound basis for negotiation. The Soviet Union did not respond favorably to it. Therefore, I would think it would lie on the table until such time as they might indicate some interest. My own feeling is that the - and I would say this in answer to this question and the previous one - that the position of West Berlin, the assurances we have given to it, are going to be fulfilled. And, therefore, in some ways it seems to me there is greater security in West Berlin - although, of course, the situation can always change - than there was, perhaps, in June of 1961. It is a continuing struggle because of the geographic location of West Berlin, but I think that the determination of those who have guaranteed Berlin is well known to the people of Berlin, to the other members of NATO who have joined in that commitment, and to those who make themselves our adversaries. So I expect West Berlin to continue to be free.

The President's Trip

Q: Why are you making this entire trip?

The President: Because I regard the relationship between the United States and Western Europe as vital to our security. This is a changing period in the West as well as in the East. We deal with problems of nuclear defense, of monetary policy, of trade policy. We are making decisions which may affect our relative positions through the world over the next decade. I think it is very appropriate that a President of the United States should come here to emphasize our strong convictions in these matters. The Chancellor of the Federal Republic has journeyed to the United States on 13 occasions. I think as a result of each of his visits the interests of the United States and the Federal Republic were served. I think it very appropriate that the President of the United States come to Western Europe. This is a matter of the greatest importance to us and I hope to the people here.

Objections to the German-French Treaty

Q: Does the U.S. Government still have any objections to the German-French treaty?

The President: The United States never registered any objections to the treaty. What I think we are concerned about is the maintenance of the integrity of NATO. And it seemed to me that the form in which the treaty passed the Parliament here in the Federal Republic took very important cognizance of the NATO obligation and the NATO responsibility and the NATO defense. I don't think that we can find strength in bilateral arrangements that we can in multilateral arrangements.

The reconciliation of France and Germany, I think, is essential to the security of the West. Europe has been torn by civil wars over a good many hundreds of years. To end that prospect, to bring France and Germany together, is a matter I would think of the greatest priority to the French and German people and a matter of the greatest interest to us. Twice the United States has been brought into war across the Atlantic because France and Germany were not friends. So I want to make it very clear that we support strongly the reconciliation and the effort at friendship which is being made and has been made over a number of years. We also want to be sure that NATO stays strong, because I think NATO is essentially the security of the Federal Republic, and we regard it as essentially the security of the United States. Those who do not place comparable importance on it, it seems to me, are ignoring history and are over-optimistic of the future.

Moscow Talks

Q: What meaning do the talks scheduled in July in Moscow have in relation to the Federal Republic's role in any multilateral atomic forces? Is there any possibility that these Moscow talks will be concerned with the nonspreading of the use of atomic weapons?

The President: Yes, I think they will be concerned with the nondiffusion of nuclear weapons. But we have felt that the organization of the multilateral force, as discussed between the Federal Republic and the United States, does not provide for a diffusion which would threaten this peace. In fact, I think it would give greater security and more satisfactory conditions of control.

The purpose of the talk basically, of course, is to get a test ban. I believe it essential that we get a test ban this year, or otherwise I think it greatly increases the prospect that there will be additional nuclear powers throughout the world in the months - in '64, '65, or '66. Now, I would regard that as a disaster. I do not regard the atomic weapon and the prospect of its spreading, and the realization that war has been the constant companion of mankind throughout our history and the conflict between the Communist system and the free system - when you mix all these factors together you have a highly explosive and a highly dangerous situation. When Pandora opened her box and the troubles flew out, all that was left in was hope. Now in this case, if we have a nuclear diffusion throughout the world, we may even lose hope.

European Trans-Atlantic Economic Cooperation

Q: After the failure of the admission of Great Britain to the Common Market, do you have any new ideas concerning European trans-Atlantic economic cooperation?

The President: I think the management, the successful management, of our monetary policies and our trade policy is essential. I would think the experience of the twenties, which helped lead to the disaster of the thirties, should be sufficient warning to us that we should be able to give this matter the highest priority. No nation, by itself, can maintain its own security and a successful management of its own fiscal affairs. There has to be the closest cooperation. I would hope that we would not, in 1963, when the trail is still uphill, when we have great challenges from the Communist world - that we would not break apart, that the Atlantic would not be regarded as a wall between us. I think we have to work in very close harmony; or otherwise, I think you will find successively in various countries deflationary policies which will lead to a lower standard of living at home; which will lead to each country managing its own monetary affairs with indifference to the affairs of others; which will lead finally to the breakup of our defensive alliances. Now that is the prospect which we face unless we are successful in working out the new round of talks, trade talks, that are coming up in 1964, and unless we can use other means of successfully solving our monetary challenges, or otherwise they are going to master us.

So I regard this matter of monetary policy, which deals with the standard of living of all of our people, as a matter of first priority. In addition we can't help but be concerned by the fact that the price of raw materials of the underdeveloped world has steadily declined relative to the price of manufactured goods. Therefore, their economic position in some ways is worse off in spite of all the aid we have given. Therefore, we may find ourselves, unless we work hard, and progressively, and with imagination, and idealism – we may find ourselves a rich area in a poor world, which is subject to all the influences that poverty brings with it, and ultimately we will be infected. So I hope that this is a matter which will not be left merely to those trade commissions, but, instead, will be a concern of presidents, chancellors, prime ministers, finance ministers, and defense ministers – and in fact the concern of all of our citizens.

France, Red China and Nuclear Weapons

Q: Mr. President, in regard to an earlier answer, if a test ban agreement were signed by the United Kingdom, the United States, and the Soviet Union, how can this prevent France, for example, China, or any other country who wasn't a signatory to the pact, how could this prevent them from going on and making nuclear weapons?

The President: Well, as you know, it is proposed in the treaty that those who sign the treaty would use all the influence that they had in their possession to persuade others not to grasp the nuclear nettle. Now, it is up to those countries. Quite obviously, they may not accept this persuasion, and then, as I say, they will get the false security which goes with nuclear diffusion.

German Views of the President's Trip to Italy

Q: Mr. President, a German newspaper wrote today that, about your next visit to Italy, you are giving more importance as a Catholic to the visit to the Pope than to the meetings with the President, mostly because we (Italy) had a recent crisis and our Government is only a technical one. Could you say anything on that?

The President: No, I wouldn't attempt to comment on that. I am visiting the President of Italy and the Government of Italy. I shall certainly look forward to paying a call on the new Pope. We have a good many matters of concern to us in relations with the Italian Government, not only defense but also economic and trade matters. I think the visit is important. Now, there is never a time when every country in the world is secure and is not having an election. There is no perfect time for visits, I suppose, but I think that this is not an inappropriate time, because I think that 1963 in the summer is the time of change. I would like to see the change be useful and in our favor.

The President's Speech at American University

Q: Mr. President, when you addressed the American University, you used the phrase that reads, "It is our hope to convince the Soviet Union that she, too, should let each nation choose its own future so long as that choice does not interfere with the choices of others." Could you say what you mean by "so long as that choice does not interfer with the choices of others"?

The President: Well, what we mean is that we cannot accept with equanimity, nor do we propose to, the Communist takeover of countries which are now free. What we have said is that we accept the principle of self-determination. Governments choose a type of government, if the people choose it. If they have the opportunity to choose another kind, if the one they originally chose is unsatisfactory, then we regard that as a free matter and we would accept it, regardless of what their choice might be. But what we will not accept is the subversion or an attack upon a free country which threatens, in my opinion, the security of other free countries. I think that is the distinction we have made for a great many years.

Talks with Chancellor Adenauer

Q: Mr. President, after your talks with Chancellor Adenauer today, do you have the impression that the Chancellor is no longer worried that there might be some arrangement between the Soviet Union and the U.S. at the expense of the Federal Republic?

The President: I am sure that the Chancellor never thought that there was any prospect, any more than we have considered the prospect, that other allies of ours would sell out the interests of the Free World. The United States has never had that intention, and I think the record of 18 years demonstrates it quite clearly. If anybody needed to be reassured, I am glad they are.

Possibility of Troop Pullout from Europe

Q: Senator Fulbright was quoted today in the newspapers as saying that it is obvious that the United States will have to pull some troops out of Europe unless the Common Market changes its trade policies. Is it also obvious to you - and would you explain, Mr. President?

The President: I have not seen all of Senator **Fulbright's statement.**

The United States, as I said yesterday - our troops are in Western Europe because it meets a very vital need of the United States. The security of Western Europe, the freedom of Western Europe, is essential to the security of the United States. That is why we are here.

Now, we keep 400,000 troops here in Western Europe. That is a burden to the people of our country. We would hope that in considering what use these troops are - and I think they have been useful - I would think that most Europeans would think they should stay. It is our hope that these matters which we may discuss, of trade and monetary policy, that some cognizance would be taken of the fact that the United States has carried a very heavy load around the world for 18 years. The United States put into assistance in Europe after the Second War over $50 billion - $100 billion around the world - and we are prepared to continue, as I said yesterday, to make this effort because we think it is essential to our security. But we regard our security as tied up with the welfare of others.

We hope that as these matters of monetary and economic and fiscal and trade policy are discussed, that every country will take a look at the general welfare and not merely at the very immediate and sure to be temporary advantage which might come from following a policy of restriction.

I think that Senator **Fulbright** is concerned that we are moving in the winter, spring, and summer of '63 backwards rather than forward toward a accommodation of all of our policies. Quite obviously if that happens, then it becomes far more difficult for all of us to sustain our welfare. The Federal Republic cannot do as much as it is doing, for example, in India and Pakistan, unless it has the resources to assist. The same is true with the United States.

The Harriman-Hailsham Talks

Q: Mr. President, when you said a moment ago that the Harriman-Hailsham talks will include the nondiffusion of atomic or nuclear weapons as well as a nuclear test ban treaty, will those topics be extended to include other topics in dispute?

The President: The primary purpose is the treaty, but I am sure the other matter may come into the conversation. They are dealing primarily with the treaty but, of course, relative to the treaty and the purpose of the treaty is nondiffusion, and therefore it is certainly going - I am sure will come up.

France's Withdrawal of Forces from NATO

Q: Have you any comments, sir, on the most recent notes that France is withdrawing additional naval forces from the control of NATO?

The President: No. They withdrew most of their forces in 1959. I think that Secretary McNamara said the other day that what concerns him most is the condition of the forces, land, sea, and air. We are confident that if an attack occurred that the French would certainly meet their obligations for the defense of Europe.

I am a strong supporter of NATO. Some others may not be. But what we are concerned about primarily is not only the command distribution, and organization, but also the condition of the forces. And we hope that the French will maintain their forces at peak strength, as we are, and we are confident that if trouble comes that General de Gaulle, as he has in the past, will definitely meet his responsibilities.

Possibility of the President Going to East Berlin

Q: On Wednesday, when you are at Checkpoint Charlie, sir, you will be just a few yards away from the entrance of East Berlin. If there were any thoughts given to your entering East Berlin, what was your reasoning behind not going, or are you planning to go?

The President: No, there wasn't; we had not planned to go into East Berlin.

Q: What is the reasoning behind the idea of staying away from East Berlin, where you have every legal right, of course, to go?

The President: Because the trip that we planned is to take us to West Berlin. I don't think that any gesture, however spectacular, of this kind would materially improve the lot of the people of East Berlin. This is why we are not going.

Talks with Mr. de Gaulle

Q: Do you have any intention this year to have any talks with Mr. de Gaulle about the strategic differences within NATO policy?

The President: No, we have no meeting planned.

The President's Desire to End the Cold War

Q: In your 10 June speech at American University, you spoke of the desire to end the cold war. Which role, in your opinion, could the Federal Republic plan in attaining this goal?

The President: Well, I think the role of maintaining our strength, of providing a better life for the people of the Federal Republic, joining in an effort in Europe to build a strong Europe, a Europe which can not only take on the burdens and responsibilities of partnership here in Europe but also play the role that its strength and its traditions entitle it to play throughout the world - Latin America, Africa, and Asia.

I hope, in other words, that the Federal Republic will, as it has for the past decade, look outward. I hope Western Europe will, as it has, look outward. I do not regard our effort as one that concerns only Western Europe and only the United States. I regard us as chosen by nature and our own decision to play a role throughout the world, or otherwise there is no security for any of us.

Exchange of Non-Aggression Statements Between East and West Berlin

Q: It has been said once in a while that there were some plans to exchange non-aggression statements between East and West, but this, in our opinion, would amount to a recognition of the zonal regime. Is any consideration still being given to such an exchange?

The President: I know of no consideration being given to any proposal which would involve the concern which the questioner expressed.

The African Conference in Addis Ababa and Plans for a Trip to Africa

Q: Mr. President, what is the feeling the West has towards the recent African conference in Addis Ababa, and have you any plans of visiting any of the African countries?

The President: No, I have no plans to visit the African countries. I welcome the effort which the Africans are making not only to meet their own problems but towards unity. I think it sets a good precedent - the unity of Africa - for the unity of Europe, a unity which is very encompassing in Africa and which may some day be in Europe, and I regard it as a very important step forward.

Reporter: Thank you, Mr. President.

THE PRESIDENT'S NEWS CONFERENCE OF

JULY 17, 1963

The President: I have two announcements.

I have a brief statement to make on the progress of the negotiations in Moscow. After 3 days of talks we are still hopeful that the participating countries may reach an agreement to end nuclear testing, at least in the environment in which it is agreed that on-the-ground inspection is not required for reasonable security. Negotiations so far are going forward in a business-like way. It is understood, of course, that under our constitutional procedures any agreement will be submitted to the Senate for advice and consent. It is also understood by our allies that the British and American representatives are not negotiating on other matters affecting their rights and interests. Any matter of this sort which may come under discussion will be kept open for full allied consultation.

Finally it is clear that these negotiations, if successful, should lead on to wider discussions among other nations. The three negotiating powers constitute the nuclear test ban subcommittee of the Geneva conference, and if the present negotiations should be successful, it will be important to reach the widest possible agreement on nuclear testing throughout the world. But all these questions are still ahead of us and today, while the negotiators are at work, I think we should not complicate their task by further speculation. And for that reason I do not expect to respond to further questions on this subject.

Second, I received a few hours ago the preliminary budget results for the fiscal year which ended June 30. The cash deficit was $4.1 billion, just half as large as we estimated some 6 months ago. The deficit in the administrative budget was $6.2 billion, $2.6 billion less than our January estimate. In both cases the deficit is below the level of the preceding fiscal year. The Treasury and the Budget Bureau will issue a more detailed statement later in the week.

Since the budget went to Congress, we have been able to reduce our request for 1963 supplemental appropriations by nearly $250 million.

Nearly every Federal agency reduced its expenditures below the figure estimated last January. Secretary McNamara announced last week that his campaign to cut costs in the Defense budget had produced 1963 savings of more than a billion dollars. We have also lowered net expenditures hundreds of millions of dollars by applying the policy of substituting private credit for public credit through the sale of Government-held mortgages and other similar assets.

Tax collections are also better than we estimated in January. But we still have too many idle plants and jobless workers. The recent improvement in business conditions has contributed to these higher revenues. This demonstrates again the point which I emphasized in my tax message to the Congress. Rising tax receipts and eventual elimination of budget deficits depend primarily on a healthy and rapidly growing economy.

The most urgent economic business before the Nation is a prompt and substantial reduction and revision of Federal income taxes in order to speed up our economic growth and wipe out our present excessive unemployment. A prosperous and growing economy is a major objective in its own right. It is also the primary means by which to achieve a balance in our Federal budget and in our balance of payments.

QUESTIONS

Communication Between the Vatican and the U.S.

Q: Mr. President, in view of the increased contact between the Vatican and the Iron Curtain countries, do you feel it would be fruitful at this time to consider setting up some regular channel of communication between the United States and the Vatican?

The President: No. It seems to me that the present methods of communication, which are the obvious ones and have been in effect, I suppose, for a great many years - any time anyone wants to get in communication, it's possible to get messages to the Vatican. The Embassy in Rome, I am sure, would be available. It doesn't seem to me that there is any need for changing procedures. I don't think there is any lack of information or communication back and forth.

Status of the President's Legislative Program

Q: Mr. President, referring back to your reference to the tax cut, we wonder, could you appraise the status of your legislative program in Congress today, particularly would you want the Congress to dispose of the civil rights proposals before they begin concentrating on the tax bill?

The President: I would - no, I think that the tax bill and the civil rights bill are both very important and also they are very complex pieces of legislation, and it is taking - Congress has been taking a good deal, amount of time, the Ways and Means Committee, in considering the tax bill, 6 months now. The civil rights bill, of course, in its latest form only went up about 6 weeks ago, 5 weeks ago, and that will take, I should think, a substantial amount of time. But they are both important pieces of legislation and I'm sure the Congress will be at it for a number of weeks to go. I would think - I would not attempt - this is a matter as to which bill should come to the floor first, and in which body is a matter for the leadership. It depends on the state of the hearings, it depends on the judgment of the committees involved, and of the Rules Committee. What I am interested in seeing is before the end of this year both bills enacted. That is what we will be judged on.

The Railroad Dispute

Q: Mr. President, do the reports from Secretary Wirtz and others give you any reason to expect a negotiated settlement of this railroad dispute before next Monday's deadline, or the report to Congress?

The President: No, but I think both groups should be much better off to reach a settlement in the remaining days than they will be to have a strike, which affects the national economy, and interest, and have this matter before the Congress. No one can be certain in what form it would come out. There are a few days left, and I think that they ought to reach an agreement themselves and not depend upon the Government to do it.

Status of the Moon Program

Q: Mr. President, there have been published reports that the Russians are having second thoughts about landing a man on the moon. If they should drop out of the race to the moon, would we still continue with our moon program; or secondly, if they should wish to cooperate with us in a joint mission to the moon, would we consider agreeing to that, sir?

The President: Well, in the first place, we don't know whether the Russians are - what their plans may be. What we are interested in is what their capabilities are. While I have seen the statement of Mr. Lovell[1] about what he thinks the Russians are doing, his information is not final. Their capacity is substantial; there is every evidence that they are carrying on a major campaign and diverting greatly needed resources to their space effort. With that in mind, I think that we should continue. It may be that our assumption - or the prediction in this morning's paper that they are not going to the moon - might be wrong a year from now. And are we going to divert ourselves from our effort in an area where the Soviet Union has a lead, is making every effort to maintain that lead, in an area which could affect our national security as well as great peaceful development? I think we ought to go right ahead with our own program and go to the moon before the end of this decade.

The point of the matter always has been not only of our excitement or interest in being on the moon, but the capacity to dominate space, which would be demonstrated by a moon flight I believe is essential to the United States as a leading free world power. That is why I am interested in it and that is why I think we should continue, and I would be not diverted by a newspaper story.

Q: What about the second part of my question?

The President: The second question is what cooperation we would be willing to carry on with the Soviet Union. We have said before to the Soviet Union that we would be very interested in cooperation. As a matter of fact, finally, after a good many weeks of discussion, an agreement was worked out on an exchange of information in regard to weather, but we have never been able to go into more detail. The kind of cooperation effort which would be required for the Soviet Union and the United States together to go to the moon would require a breaking down of a good many barriers of suspicion and distrust and hostility which exists between the Communist world and ourselves.

There is no evidence as yet that those barriers will come down, though quite obviously we would like to see them come down. Obviously, if the Soviet Union were an open society, as we are, that kind of cooperation could exist, and I would welcome it. I would welcome it, but I don't see it as yet, unfortunately.

Mrs. Murphy

Q: Mr. President, do you think that Mrs. Murphy should have to take into her home a lodger whom she does not want regardless of her reason, or would you accept a change in the civil rights bill to except small boarding houses like Mrs. Murphy's?

The President: The question would be, it seems to me, whether Mrs. Murphy had a substantial impact on interstate commerce.

Talks in Moscow

Q: Mr. President, if the talks in Moscow do go well, would you be receptive to the idea of a summit conference?

The President: The matter has never come up since Governor Harriman has been there. I have always said I would go any place if I thought it was essential to the making of an effective agreement. There is no evidence that a summit is indicated or needed. There seems to be every evidence if we can get an agreement that we can reach it in our respective capitals. So I must say in complete frankness that this matter has not been before us, and if it came before us, I would give it consideration in light of what the situation was. But as of yet there has been no talk about it.

The President's Travels

Q: Mr. President, there has been rising expectation since your visit to Europe that your next travels would take you to the Far East and South Asia. Could you tell us if you are considering such a trip, and, if so, if it could come by the end of this year or early next year?

The President: We have no plans for a trip. I would like to go sometime – to go to the Far East. I think it is an area of great importance to us, but we have no plans for it, and I would think that we have a lot of work to do here for a good many months.

Political Situation in Vietman

Q: Mr. President, there has been a good deal of public concern about the political situation in South Viet-Nam, and I would like to ask you whether the difficulties between the Buddhist population there and the South Vietnamese Government has been an impediment to the effectiveness of American aid in the war against the Viet Cong?

The President: Yes, I think it has. I think it is unfortunate that this dispute has arisen at the very time when the military struggle has been going better than it has been going in many months. I would hope that some solution could be reached for this dispute, which certainly began as a religious dispute, and because we have invested a tremendous amount of effort and it is going quite well.

I do realize of course, and we all have to realize, that Viet-Nam has been in war for 20 years. The Japanese came in, the war with the French, the civil war which has gone on for 10 years, and this is very difficult for any society to stand. It is a country which has got a good many problems and it is divided, and there is guerrilla activity and murder and all of the rest. Compounding this, however, now is a religious dispute. I would hope this would be settled, because we want to see a stable government there, carrying on a struggle to maintain its national independence.

We believe strongly in that. We are not going to withdraw from that effort. In my opinion, for us to withdraw from that effort would mean a collapse not only of South Viet-Nam, but Southeast Asia. So we are going to stay there. We hope with the great effort which is being carried by the Vietnamese themselves, and they have been in this field a lot longer than we have, and with a good deal more deaths and casualties, that behind this military shield put up by the Vietnamese people they can reach an agreement on the civil disturbances and also in respect for the rights of others. That's our hope. That's our effort. That - we're bringing our influence to bear. And the decision is finally theirs, but I think that before we render too harsh a judgment on the people, we should realize that they are going through a harder time than we have had to go through.

The President's Health

Q: A personal question, sir, if I may. It has been reported that you returned to playing golf again. I wonder if you could tell us how you feel and how you enjoyed returning to what has been reported one of your favorite sports.

The President: Well, I like it. I did not think I was going to play golf again until my trip. I don't want to get into a discussion of back difficulties, but my trip to Europe, I think, helped. Getting out of that office did something. So, I enjoy it.

The International Monetary Fund

Q: Mr. President, at Frankfurt you said the time has come for a common effort on the International Monetary Fund. Could you give us a more specific notion of what you had in mind?

The President: We are sending tomorrow a balance of payments message which will have a good many of our suggestions. Quite obviously, the dollar is international currency and has served us well, and served the West well, and with the sterling has been the basis for a good deal of international liquidity. I have every confidence that it can continue to be. I think we can still continue on the gold standard. We have had good bilateral relations with a good many countries of Europe, who by prepayment of debt, and by other rather technical transactions, have eased some of the burdens of the balance of payments difficulties which we have been undergoing.

But I would confine my remarks so that at this time, and recommend my statement tomorrow on the balance of payments. It may be that as time goes on, other suggestions may be made to provide greater liquidity and greater security for the various currencies. I think if the program we are recommending tomorrow is enacted, it will make a substantial difference to our balance of payments. And I think the long-range prognosis for us - for our balance of payments - I think is quite good.

Our costs in relation to other costs have remained relatively stable. Brookings Institution makes a judgment that by the mid-sixties and beyond we can be in perhaps even a surplus position again.[2] But what we want to do is prevent these large flows back and forth, which cause countries to adopt restrictive measures which affect adversely their domestic economy and therefore have a deflationary effect upon the entire Western monetary system.

But to be specific to your question, I have no proposals beyond the ones I am making tomorrow, which will be before you. But it is a matter which I think we ought to continue to talk to the Western European powers about.

Communist Chinese Policy

Q: Mr. President, the Communist Party of the Soviet Union in an official reply to the Chinese Communists this week described the Chinese Communists' policy as one which would lead to a conflict with the capitalist world in which both the victor and the vanquished would wind up under nuclear rubble. Do you share this view as to the apparent direction of Chinese Communist policy at this time?

The President: It would seem to be directed to that end, but, of course, if it came to that, the Chinese would be fighting with the Soviet nuclear arsenal. There are some countries which would like to have us fight a war with our arsenal of nuclear weapons, so I think the Soviet Union naturally is not anxious to engage in a nuclear struggle to carry out ideological doctrines that the Chinese Communists may develop. They have a natural reluctance to see their country destroyed for that reason, as do we.

Promotion of Conservation

Q: Mr. President, it's been reported that you hope to make a trip of 4 or 5 days' duration around the country in the fall in the interests of conservation. Could you tell us a little bit about that, and might you consider starting or ending your trip in the middle of the Potomac River to survey and perhaps to smell the sewage disposal problem in the National Capital?

The President: Well, if we do make that trip, I will certainly observe it, pass over it, and even go further than that.

U.S. Employment Service Activities

Q: Mr. President, the United States Employment Service is seeking jobs for both the unemployed and the employed, and some of these jobs solicited and advertised by the USES run from $10,000 to $22,500, which is a salary level of Congressmen and a level at which job seekers wouldn't be thought to need public assistance. Some of your critics have charged that the USES is competing with private enterprise, both in the business community and on the campus.

The President: What is your question - I didn't hear the first part of it?

Q: *The USES is soliciting jobs for people who have jobs and people who don't, and some of the jobs that they are soliciting for people who already have jobs run from $10,000 to $22,500 ——*

The President: What jobs are they talking about, for example?

Q: *They advertise in the papers ——*

The President: Was it because we need special skills, perhaps, in the Government?

Q: *Yes, sir.*

The President: I don't see anything wrong with that. We may need some skills. I am not familiar with the story, but just judging it from your question, I would assume that what they are talking about are certain skills which the Government needs, which may be in short supply, and therefore they are announcing that there are openings in the Federal Government for that purpose. That would seem ——

Q: *No, these are private jobs.*

The President: They are private jobs?

Q: *Yes, sir.*

The President: I would be glad to look into the matter, whatever it is. I would assume they are right, but I will be glad to check it.

Views of the Castro Government

Q: *Mr. President, do you see any indications that the Castro Government is seeking a more relaxed relationship with the United States, and, if so, are we prepared to meet him in that?*

The President: No. I have seen these verbal statements, but I have seen no evidence. As I say, I think the United States has indicated very clearly that we do not accept the existence of, and cannot coexist in the peaceful sense with, a Soviet satellite in the Caribbean. So I don't see that any progress is going to be made along these lines as long as Cuba is a Soviet satellite.

The Sino-Soviet Break

Q: *Mr. President, do you agree with Britain's Lord Home who believes that the Sino-Soviet breach cannot be healed?*

The President: I have always said that I thought it would be unwise for the United States to talk about a matter over which we have only limited control. Therefore, I have not commented and would not comment on it until the actuality becomes more obvious than it still is today. Quite obviously there are strong indications of pressure there, but I would not make any final statements because history has shown that they are frequently reversed.

The Country's Progress

Q: *Mr. President, in the 1960 campaign you used to say that it was time for America to get moving again. Do you think it is moving, and if so, how and where? The reason I ask you the question, Mr. President, is that the Republican National Committee recently adopted a resolution saying you were pretty much a failure.*

The President: I am sure it was passed unanimously. (Laughter)

I think that we have made significant progress on the economic front - in the increase in our gross national product of nearly $90 billion, in a 25-percent increase in profits, in farm income up 10 percent, and all of the rest. I think those statistics are available; they are obvious, and I think that they indicate that the United States has made substantial progress.

The only thing is that the United States has to move very fast to even stand still. We are going to have to find in the next decade 22 million jobs to take care of those coming into the labor market and those who are eliminated by technological gains. But we have been attempting to do something about the problem. In our tax program and in our various economic and legislative proposals that we have made in the last Congress and in this Congress, we have attempted to deal with some of the economic problems facing the country.

I must say that I found a scarcity of useful resolutions coming out of the source which you name, dealing with this problem of unemployment, tax revision, tax reform, minimum wage, social security, trade expansion. All these are areas where we have taken some action. But I am not satisfied at all, and I think we have to go a good deal further. Unemployment is still too high and it is particularly concentrated among the unskilled, which is the hard core, and among those who are structurally unemployed because of technological changes, and particularly in areas like the Appalachians which are very hard to reach even if the economy is going ahead at a strong rate.

I think the tax bill this year will make an important difference to the economic effect of the country. If the tax bill doesn't pass this year, a good many economic plans, and a good many inventory developments of the last months which have helped, I think, to stimulate the economy, will, of course, be disappointed, and I think the effect would be very adverse. This is a matter which I would hope we would have the support of Republicans and Democrats on. I think the argument about whether the country is moving or not will be, of course, a discussion next year, and I think we can get a better analysis of it after a 4-year period. I'll be prepared to say it is; they'll be prepared to say it isn't.

A Domestic Peace Corps

Q: Mr. President, getting back to legislation, some of your critics have charged that your proposed domestic Peace Corps will be, in effect, a large waste; that it would merely duplicate the work already being done by Federal, State, and local agencies. Would you care to comment?

The President: I don't agree with that at all. That's the same kind of argument we heard about the Peace Corps when it was formed; that this was a useless effort. I think it has been very successful. I think if you go to so many parts of this country - the difficulty is, and I have seen some interesting articles written about this, that there is a good deal of poverty in the United States, but not many people see it. There are a good many people who are mentally retarded, but not many people see it. After all, 3 percent of the population of the United States, of our children, are mentally retarded, and 1 percent of Sweden.

There are a great many areas where we need to do a good deal more - Indian reservations, parts of this country where school dropouts, slums, chronic poverty now exist. Millions of Americans experience it, but they are scattered and frequently not able to bring their views to bear. All of us move in a rather different atmosphere, so we are not as aware of it as we should be, except statistically. Now the fact of the matter is I think these young men and women would be proud to give a year of their lives to the service of their country. They are willing to go abroad - I think they'd be more willing to stay home. Their example, I think, can be a catalyst. We have millions of people who work in the various agencies, Boy Scouts, Girl Scouts, all the rest. I think they do a wonderful job. We want to supplement their work. Most of those who work in the field say more can be done. The District of Columbia is a prime example of where we need dozens of volunteers to work with young people. We get a lot of them. There are a good many people who work in this District, but we need a lot more.

What we want to do is to make it possible for people in this country to give a year of their lives without compensation, but with enough to live on, to service in these various areas where people do not enjoy the prosperity which so much of our country experiences. I think those opposed to it are wrong. I think the program is a good idea.

The Advancement of Civil Rights

Q: Mr. President, it's pretty generally acknowledged that your administration has done more for civil rights fundamental advances than any in many years. Do you find that the demonstrations which are taking place are a handicap to you, specifically the Washington march in August? Do you think that this will ——

The President: No. I think that the way that the Washington march is now developed, which is a peaceful assembly calling for a redress of grievances, the cooperation with the police, every evidence that it is going to be peaceful, they are going to the Washington Monument, they are going to express their strong views. I think that's in the great tradition. I look forward to being here. I am sure Members of Congress will be here. We want citizens to come to Washington if they feel that they are not having their rights expressed. But, of course, arrangements have been made to make this responsible and peaceful. This is not a march on the Capital.

Now, there are other places, of course, where demonstrations - where there are grievances, but where the demonstrations get caught up in a cycle. We've got it in Cambridge, Md., where there is no peace. They have almost lost sight of what the demonstration is about. You have an increasingly dangerous situation. You could have violence any night. You have 400 National Guardsmen there now. I am concerned about those demonstrations. I think they go beyond information, they go beyond protest, and they get into a very bad situation where you get violence, and I think the cause of advancing equal opportunities only loses.

But I do feel also - so I have warned against demonstrations which could lead to riots, demonstrations which could lead to bloodshed, and I warn now against it.

Secondly, some of the people, however, who keep talking about demonstrations never talk about the problem of redressing grievances. I would hope that along with a seccession of the kind of demonstrations that would lead to rioting, people would also do something about the grievances. You just can't tell people, "Don't protest," but on the other hand, "We are not going to let you come into a store or a restaurant." It seems to me it is a two-way street.

If the Congress will act, if, most importantly, individuals will act - and I am impressed by the fact that since May 22d we began our meetings at the White House, and Justice Department, and meetings have been held by Governors and Mayors all around the country, that there have been substantial gains made in areas of the country where before there was no progress in restaurants, movies, motels. So something can be done. So I would suggest that we exercise great care in protesting so that it doesn't become riots, and, number two, that those people who have responsible positions in Government and in business and in labor do something about the problem which leads to the demonstration.

Demonstration by the African States at the ILO Conference

Q: May I ask, sir, about the recent demonstration by the African States at the ILO conference with respect to South Africa? What is our American position with regard to South Africa's participation in the U.N. and many of its agencies?

The President: Well, we have condemned the racial policy of South Africa, which is inimical, I think, to the future of South Africa, as well as repugnant to us. We also do not believe that it is useful to begin to expel nations of the United Nations. I think you have enough pressures on the United Nations. The United Nations has every right to express hostility to policies which are pursued which are a threat to peace. But it would seem to me unwise to expel nations from the United Nations because if the hand were moved, others will come, and the United Nations will be fragmented. I think it ought to be as broad as possible a coverage. But I think we ought to be very clear in our hostility to the concepts of racial separation.

Raise of the Interest Rate

Q: Sir, I want to ask you something in view of yesterday's interest raise.[3] I want to read you a little bit from the Democratic Party Platform of 1960:

"A Democratic President will put an end to the present high interest tight money policy. This policy has failed in its stated purposes to keep prices down. The Republican high interest policy has extracted a costly toll from every American who has financed a home, an automobile, a refrigerator, or television set."

How can you reconcile this with what happened yesterday on interest rates?

The President: Because, as you study the statement made yesterday by the Federal Reserve, you will realize we are talking about short-term rates, and that under this administration, mortgage rates and other rates which affect business have dropped since this administration took office, and have dropped in some ways in a significant way. It is our hope that in the effort which the Federal Reserve is carrying out, which will be an increase in the short-term rates which primarily affect the short-term flow of the United States, they will also make an effort to maintain the stability of long-term rates. That is the policy of the Government, that is the effort of the Federal Reserve, and the Treasury, and, for that reason, the policy we took yesterday is in accordance with that statement you just read.

Coexistence with Cuba

Q: Mr. President, you stated that the United States would never agree to coexistence with Cuba as long as it was a Soviet satellite. If the Soviet troops left Cuba and if Cuba started moving towards a Titoist type situation, do you see the possibility of perhaps coexistence?

The President: It is very difficult to base a future policy on presumptions which are not today realized. The fact of the matter is the Soviet troops are there. The fact of the matter is that Cuba does follow a satellite role, and that is what we consider unacceptable to us. I would hope that the situation some day would change.

Attitude on Southern Segregationists

Q: Mr. President, Governor Rockefeller and Senator Goldwater are sharply divided on what sort of an appeal the Republican Party should make to the South in 1964. Perhaps this question will be faced by you next year, and I wondered whether you plan to either repudiate or reject the support and the votes of segregationists in the South.

The President: I think that the record of this administration on this matter of equal opportunity is so well known to everyone, North and South, that in 1964 there will be no difficulty in identifying the record of the Democratic administration, what it stands for. And my judgment is, based on history, that the Republican Party also will make a clear stand on this issue. I would be surprised if they didn't.

Integration in the South

Q: Mr. President, in the last week the Governor of Alabama, the Governor of Mississippi, and the Attorney General of Arkansas have all testified before the Senate Commerce Committee insisting that the integration move was Communist-inspired. And this has led to some fears on the part of some Senators that we may be entering into a period of McCarthyism that will submerge this issue. Will you comment on it?

The President: The fact of the matter is that the Communists attempt, and obviously, to worm their way into every movement, and particularly to worm their way into those movements where there is an obvious - where there is trouble. I would think that the relatively few remaining Communists in the United States, and they are very few, I would think that they would attempt to take advantage of whatever difficulties may arise in the United States. But I must say that we looked into this matter with a good deal of care.

We have no evidence that any of the leaders of the civil rights movements in the United States are Communists. We have no evidence that the demonstrations are Communist-inspired. There may be occasions when a Communist takes part in a demonstration. We can't prevent that. But I think it is a convenient scapegoat to suggest that all the difficulties are Communist and if the Communist movement would only disappear that we would end this.

The fact of the matter is, it is easy to blame it on the authorities in Washington, it is easy to blame it on the Attorney General or the President, and say, "If they would just stop talking about these things the problem would go away." The way to make the problem go away, in my opinion, is to provide for a redress of grievances.

Reporter: Thank you, Mr. President.

[1]Sir Bernard Lovell, British astronomer.

[2]The President referred to a study "The United States Balance of Payments in 1968" by Walter S. Salant et al. (298 pp., Brookings, 1963).

[3]To stem the flow of dollars overseas, the Federal Reserve Board raised its lending rate from 3 to 3½ percent. The raise was accompanied by authorization to banks to increase the interest paid to corporate depositors on short-term funds.

THE PRESIDENT'S NEWS CONFERENCE OF

AUGUST 1, 1963

The President: Good afternoon.

The end of this summer of 1963 will be an especially critical time for 400,000 young Americans who, according to the experience of earlier years, will not return to school when the summer is ended. Moreover, without a special effort to reverse this trend, another 700,000 students will return to school in September, but will fail to complete the school year. The greatest growth in labor demand today is for highly trained professional workers with 16 or more years of education. The second fastest growing demand is for technical and semiprofessional workers with 1 to 3 years of post high school education. Jobs filled by high school graduates rose 30 percent, while jobs for those with no secondary education decreased 25 percent in the last decade.

We must therefore combat, intensify our efforts to meet this problem. We are now talking about the lives of a million young American boys and girls who will fail to meet their educational requirements in the next few months unless we do something about it.

This is a serious national problem. A boy or girl has only a limited time in their life in which to get an education, and yet it will shape their whole lives and the lives of their children. So I am asking all American parents to urge their children to go back to school in September, to assist them in every way to stay in school. I am asking school principals, clergymen, trade union leaders, business leaders, everyone in this country, to concern themselves. Here is something that all of us can do in a practical way in the month of August and in the months to come.

One of the things which we are going to do here is to provide, out of the Presidential emergency fund, $250,000 on an emergency basis for guidance counselors in the month of August to see if we can get some of these boys and girls back to school. They will appreciate any effort we make for the rest of their lives.

QUESTIONS

The Nuclear Test Ban Treaty

Q: Mr. President, some Republican leaders, and some Democratic Senators as well, have expressed a "wait and see" attitude about the nuclear test ban treaty. Does this give you any concern about its ratification or about the size of the margin you expect?

The President: No. I think everybody ought to - I think there is nothing wrong with waiting and seeing. Sooner or later, however, if you wait long enough and you see long enough you have to do something and then you have to vote "yes" or "no."

My judgment is when the testimony is all in that this treaty will be ratified. I think it provides protection for the security interests of the United States and gives us some hope. Maybe that hope won't be realized but some hope of moving towards a more peaceful world. In my judgment, after the Senators - and they have a right to meet their responsibilities in a careful way, this is a constitutional power, as I said the other night, vested in them.

They have to study the matter carefully; they should hear from the Chiefs of Staff, the Defense Secretary, the State Department, and the rest, and make their judgment. I believe they will vote "yes."

Q: Mr. President, have you made any policy decision on whether we will continue testing nuclear weapons underground as the treaty permits us to do?

The President: Yes. Yes, we will.

Q: We will continue?

The President: Yes, that is correct.

Q: Mr. President, is the United States considering giving France some of its nuclear weapons secrets in order that that nation might stop testing?

The President: Well, France is a nuclear power and the United States and Britain have been in touch with the French authorities on this matter of how the interests of France, Britain, and the United States can best be protected in a test ban. At the present time, as you know, over a period of time, we have offered assistance to France on other occasions. After Nassau, we offered assistance to France on the Polaris program. That offer was rejected.

In Germany there are French aircraft with U.S. nuclear weapons, which are ready for the defense of the alliance which the United States has made available for sale, or tankers which could be used by the French military force, air tankers. So that we have been in some cooperation in this area. We have discussed – we have made some suggestions recently as to how that cooperation could be more satisfactorily developed if there were a test ban, but we have received no response from the French Government, other than the remarks of General de Gaulle at his press conference.

Q: Mr. President, Senator Dirksen and some West German officials have expressed concern that if the nuclear test ban is signed amongst others by this Government, by the Federal Republic of Germany, and by the East German regime, that this will amount to a tacit recognition of East Germany. What is your thinking on this point?

The President: No, that is not correct. This matter was discussed and the position of the United States and Britain was made very clear to the Soviet Union. As a matter of fact, the Soviet Union mentioned a regime which it did not recognize and did not wish to recognize. So that a procedure was developed whereby a regime which is not recognized by one of the other parties to the treaty can file its assent with one of the three parties. This act would not constitute recognition by the remaining signatories. The fact of the matter is that we signed a part of a multilateral treaty on Laos which the Red Chinese also signed, but we do not recognize the Red Chinese regime. This is a matter of intent. Diplomatic procedure, custom, and law provide that recognition is a matter of intent. We do not intend to recognize the East German regime and, therefore, the language which is in the treaty was part of the treaty when it was tabled more than a year ago. It has been before us for a year and it does not provide for recognition of East Germany, and we will not recognize it, and we believe strongly in the reunification of Germany as a free, democratic country. That is our policy in the past and our present policy and our future policy and would not be affected by this test ban agreement.

I do not think that it is important that we have as great a participation in this nuclear test ban agreement as possible. We have received no encouragement, but we would like the Red Chinese to come into the agreement. It looks like they will not, but it would obviously be in the interest of world peace, but that does not constitute recognition.

Situation in the Far East

Q: Mr. President, in view of the Red Chinese hard line, the recent flare-up of violence in Korea, reported troop movements along the Indian-Tibetan border, do you believe that the situation has taken a turn for the worse in the Far East? If so, what should we do about it?

The President: The potentiality is there for a turn for the worse. I don't think we can make a judgment as to what events will bring us. Broadcasts are very hard out of Peking. There has been a development of roads in the areas north of India's frontier. There are concentrations of troops. The potential for trouble is always there, and the same is true in other parts of Asia, but we have lived with a good deal of danger in Asia for a number of years. We have made quite clear, I think, our commitments, and we intend to carry out those commitments, and we would hope that there would not be a flareup which would bring a direct conflict. That's our hope, and we cannot say as of yet there have been any actions which would indicate that in a final way that hope would be denied at this time.

Nonagression Pact Between NATO and the Warsaw Pact

Q: Mr. President, General de Gaulle has pledged that France will not commit aggression against any other country, and he says that therefore there is no purpose in a nonaggression agreement. Is it possible, in view of his attitude, to proceed with other NATO allies now, to see if a nonaggression pledge or agreement or pact can be achieved with the Russians and the Warsaw Pact powers?

The President: Well, as I understood it, General de Gaulle has made a non-aggression pledge himself. It would seem to me that it might be advisable for the other members of NATO to meet together and discuss the matter. One of our interests in a nonaggression agreement would be greater security for Berlin. If everyone is going to unilaterally make a nonaggression agreement, then you have a nonaggression pact in a sense, and it does not seem to me that our interests have been adequately recognized. So I would feel, personally, for the United States, that we should consult with our other allies. We should, as Governor Harriman agreed to do, take up the matter of a nonaggression pact with our allies, consider their interests and our own interests, consider, as I said, for one matter, Berlin, and then go back to the Soviet Union and see what the situation looks like. That is the procedure we are going to follow. Every country, of course, is free to follow its own.

The Former Vice President's Comments on Foreign Policy

Q: Mr. President, former Vice President Nixon has been making a number of suggestions on the American foreign policy recently. In doing so, do you think he is sounding like a would-be presidential candidate again?

The President: No. I have taken him at his word, that he won't run again.

Abrogation of Miscegenation Laws

Q: Mr. President, in some 24 States all over the country, there are miscegenation laws in various forms. California courts once found them unconstitutional under the 14th amendment, and said that marriage is a fundamental right of free men. Now, in your crusade against racial discrimination for all races, will you seek to abrogate these laws, and how would you go about it?

The President: Well, the law - if there was a marriage of the kind you have described, I would assume - and if a legal action was taken against the party, then they would have a relief, it would seem to me, in the courts. And it would be carried, I presume, to the higher courts, depending on the judgments, so that the laws themselves would be affected by the ultimate decision of the Supreme Court.

I think there are legal remedies for any abuses in this field now available.

Q: Does not the Department of Justice take some discrimination cases to the courts themselves?

The President: I am not sure they could, as you describe it, because I am not sure they would be a party in the case. It would probably be - in order to have the case heard, and this is a legal matter which I am not familiar with, and I speak with some valor of ignorance as I am not a lawyer, I would think that they would have to be a party in interest, who would bring the suit. But this is a matter which I would be glad to have the Attorney General or the Solicitor speak to you about personally.

Civil Rights Policy

Q: There are indications lately that your policies on civil rights are costing you heavily in political prestige and popularity. Would you comment on that, and would you tell us whether civil rights are worth an election?

The President: Well, I assume what you say is probably right. On the other hand, this is a national crisis of great proportions. I am confident that whoever was President would meet his responsibilities. Crises come in different forms. I don't think anyone would have anticipated the exact form of this particular crisis. Maybe last winter we were dealing with other matters. But I think it has come and we are going to deal with it. My judgment is that both political parties finally will come to the same conclusion, and that is that every effort should be made to protect the rights of all of our citizens, and advance their right to equality of opportunity. Education, jobs, security, right to move freely about our country, right to make personal choices - these are matters which it seems to me are very essential, very desirable, and we just have to wait and see what political effect they have. But I think the position of the Government, the administration, is well known, and I expect it will continue to follow the same course it has followed in the past.

The Possibility of a Summit Meeting

Q: Mr. President, when Lord Hailsham returned to London, he said Premier Khrushchev had expressed an interest in a summit meeting in the fall. I wonder, sir, if you could give us your view on the issue of the summit, now that a test ban treaty has been initiated?

The President: No, I have not heard any discussion of the summit, and I don't really see at the present time it would serve a useful purpose. It seems to me that we have been able to conduct the negotiations, which are important, the matter of the hot line, for example, and the test ban treaty, the limited test ban treaty, through skilled negotiators, and that is really the best way unless there is an overwhelming crisis, or unless there is some new factor introduced into the international situation which is not now visible which would make such a meeting desirable.

The President on Adam Clayton Powell

Q: Mr. President, Representative Adam Clayton Powell has said that Negroes should retain the leadership of the civil rights movement in their own hands, excluding, for the most part, whites. This has upset a great many people, both

*Negroes and whites, who support the civil rights movement. Could you give us
your view of this position held by Mr. Powell?*

The President: Well, I haven't seen the statement that you attribute to
him, so it is hard to comment on it. I would think that this is a matter, of
course - when you are talking about 10 percent of the population - it is a matter which affects Negroes and whites and the relations between them are what
are at issue; not the relationship between the Negro community itself, but the
relationship between Negroes and whites. Therefore, it requires the work of
Negroes and whites. It seems to me quite obvious. But I don't know what he
said about it.

The Test Ban Treaty and Cuba

*Q: A two-pronged question, please: Do you feel that the relaxation of
cold war tensions resulting from the test ban treaty might in any way affect
relations between Cuba and the United States, and do you think that the United
States might take any action against the students who are now in Cuba?*

The President: That's really three questions. I don't know what the next
step in regard to relaxation of tensions are. We can't predict it. I described
it as the first step in a long journey, so I don't think we should make any
presumptions about what the future will bring. I think we should maintain our
strength. I don't think we should cut our defense budgets. I think we should
pursue, however, the next step and the next step, to see if we can bring about
a genuine *détente* - we don't have that yet - a genuine one, which covers a
broad area.

What we have now is a limited test ban agreement, and we should realize it
as an important step, but only a first step.

Now, secondly, our policy I described very clearly in regards to Cuba at
the last press conference.

Thirdly, in regard to the students, their passports are going to be lifted
when they come back here. Some of the leadership, it seems to me, are definitely Communists. The journey was paid for in cash by the Cuban Government. Some
of the students may be just young men and women who are interested in broadening their horizons. But I think that they should have some concern for the
security and foreign policy objectives of the United States.

In any case, their passports will be lifted, which may discourage their
travel for a period, and, in addition, other steps may be considered in regard
to a few who are not students but who are Communists.

The Threat of Communist China

*Q: Some reputable experts estimate that it will be at least 10 years be-
fore Communist China could become a full-fledged nuclear power. Against that
background, could you expand a little bit your answer to a previous question
on just how we assess the power and the threat of Communist China today?*

The President: Well, we assess its power at 700 million people, increasing
at 14 million or 15 million a year, surrounded by countries which are, in every
case but one, much smaller, which are faced with very difficult geographic and
social problems, which do not have a strong national history. So that we find
a great, powerful force in China, organized and directed by the government
along Stalinist lines, surrounded by weaker countries. So this we regard as a
menacing situation.

In addition, as I said, that government is not only Stalinist in its internal actions, but also has called for war, international war, in order to advance the final success of the Communist cause. We regard that as a menacing factor. And then you introduce into that mix, nuclear weapons. As you say, it may take some years, maybe a decade, before they become a full-fledged nuclear power, but we are going to be around in the 1970's, and we would like to take some steps now which would lessen that prospect that a future President might have to deal with.

I would regard that combination, if it is still in existence in the 1970's, of weak countries around it, 700 million people, a Stalinist internal regime, and nuclear powers, and a government determined on war as a means of bringing about its ultimate success, as potentially a more dangerous situation than any we faced since the end of the Second War, because the Russians pursued in most cases their ambitions with some caution. Even in the case of the most overt aggression, which was the North Korean invasion of South Korea, other forces were used and not the Russians.

So what we are anxious to do, and one of the reasons why we have moved into the limited test ban, even though we recognize its limitations, is because we don't want to find the world in as great a danger as it could be in the 1970's, for the reasons that I have described.

Negro Demonstrations

Q: Mr. President, it has seemed that as the summer has progressed, the vigor or some of the fever has gone out of the Negro demonstrations that we had around the country earlier in the year. I wonder, sir, how you feel, or why this might have come about, what effect it might have on the opinion of legislation, and in short if you could assess the demonstrations that we have had with the spring, and what we have accomplished?

The President: I think it is partly because an awful lot of work is being done in the local communities by biracial groups, by responsible officials, and this is true north and south, east and west, partly because I think that the Negroes are aware that the Congress is considering the legal remedies for some of the difficulties that they face.

It is partly because the responsible Negro leadership, I think, realizes that this is a long drawnout task to bring about, which requires jobs, which requires education, and all of the rest, and a quick demonstration in the street is not the immediate answer.

But merely because the demonstrations have subsided does not seem to me, those of us who are in a position of responsibility, does not mean that we should go to sleep and forget the problem, because that is no solution. So I think that it may be a good thing that the demonstrations, particularly in their extreme form, are subsiding. I think in some cases they were becoming self-defeating, and particularly demonstrations that I have seen, that I've read about recently, which seemed to me to be rather fringe actions. I thought that they were self-defeating.

But I would hope that if there is a period of quiet, we would use it and not merely regard it as an end of the effort.

Senator Dirksen's Concern About Cuba

Q: Mr. President, this is related to an earlier question. Senator Dirksen also expressed concern about Cuba, and he said that Cuba could become a party to the Moscow treaty, and then could test nuclear weapons in the caves down in Cuba. Do you share Senator Dirksen's concern about such a matter?

The President: If they did not become a party to the treaty, couldn't they test in the caves or in the atmosphere?

Q: Search me, Mr. President!

The President: Well, it seems to me that that doesn't - there is some logic, I am sure, to it. (Laughter) But the fact of the matter is that this testing underground is a very difficult business, very difficult, very expensive, and this will have a restraint on the development of nuclear weapons.

If you could get a complete, comprehensive test ban treaty, which we still are for, which I think we ought to pursue, then you would have an ending to all prospects. But to say that the test ban treaty itself is an encouragement to develop nuclear weapons, presents the problem in a way which does not add materially, it seems to me, to the illumination that I am confident that the debate will bring.

Evaluation of the Alliance for Progress

Q: Mr. President, this month we shall celebrate the second anniversary of the Alliance for Progress. With all of its frustrations and yours, and advancement in some areas, I wonder how you evaluate the movement during this 2-year period, since it was one of your inauguration ideas?

The President: Well, I am always depressed, to an extent, by the size of the problems that we face in Latin America, with the population increases, the drop in commodity prices, and all the rest. We sometimes feel that we are not going ahead. In addition, in nearly every country there are serious domestic problems.

On the other hand, there have been some changes in Latin America which I think are encouraging. I think there has been a common recognition that there is the necessity for revolution in Latin America, and it is either going to be peaceful or bloody. But there must be progress, there must be a revolution. In my opinion, it can be peaceful. In my opinion, given time and concentrated effort on behalf of all of us, in Latin America, and in this country, we can bring about success.

So I think the Alliance for Progress should be pursued, its efforts should be intensified. Wherever it has failed, if it has failed, and it has failed, of course, to some degree, because the problems are almost insuperable, and for years the United States ignored them, and for years so did some of the groups in Latin America themselves, but now we are attempting, we have a program, I think we should pursue it. I think we should do more about it. I am not sure that we are giving still enough attention to Latin America.

What I find to be almost incomprehensible are those who speak about Cuba all the time, and yet are not willing to give the kind of assistance and the kind of support to assist other countries of Latin America to develop themselves in a peaceful way. So I say on the second anniversary, we have a long, long way to go, and in fact in some ways the road seems longer than it was when the journey started. But I think we ought to keep at it.

The President's Authority under the Atomic Energy Act

Q: Mr. President, to go back to the French situation, you said, I believe, that you had made some suggestions with the British to the French in the nuclear field. Have you ever suggested or considered suggesting using the authority which I understand you have under the Atomic Energy Act, to treat France as we treat Britain, as a nuclear power, either under the present French policy or under a possibility of France joining with the U.S. and the U.K. and others in some form of Western or European nuclear force?

In other words, when you said the other night that France was one of the four nuclear powers, were you prepared to recognize it in the hard terms of the Atomic Energy Act as such?

The President: Yes, I do recognize it in terms of the Atomic Energy Act. As a matter of fact, at the time of the Nassau agreement, we thought that it would be profitable to enter into a dialog with the French, and as you remember in the Nassau accord, it said we would make a similar offer to the French. That offer was rejected. It was rejected because, while the British were prepared and have placed their V-bomber force under NATO and Polaris under NATO, their Polaris force under NATO, I think that the French regarded that condition as unsatisfactory, or that proposal as unsatisfactory. I think that is a more precise word, proposal, not condition.

Now, we have the question of where we should go from here. As the General made clear in his press conference, he has a somewhat different view of NATO than we do, and its importance, and he has suggested on several occasions that it should be reorganized. He also has some objection to the word "integration," which we think is a good word. But he does not. So that the problem does not rest solely with an interpretation of the McMahon Act. The problem really goes to the organization of the defense of the West, and what role France sees for herself, and sees for us, and what kind of a cooperative effort France and the United States and Britain and the other members of NATO - and this is important, the non-nuclear powers of NATO - could join in.

Now, that is a very complicated political problem and this is a matter which we opened up for discussion some months ago, and which I would assume that we should continue to discuss. And, of course, we are always prepared to, and have indicated as much to the French.

The Nassau Talks

Q: Mr. President, apropos the Nassau talks, we haven't heard much about the multilateral nuclear force lately. During your talk with Prime Minister Macmillan, he apparently gave you some rather discouraging answers about their interests. I wonder if you still have a timetable for the development of that force, or whether you have decided to abandon it, at least temporarily?

The President: No, there has been a meeting - since my trip there has been a meeting of some of the interested parties and there will be another meeting in the next few weeks in which other countries will join. What we have to concern ourselves with, though this may not seem very pressing, is the problem of the countries which do not have a nuclear capacity. How are they going to be included in? I think as the General said in his press conference last January, those who have a monopoly position always regard it as the wisest organization, and as the most beneficial. Well, we have a strong nuclear position, the British do, the French are developing theirs. What about those who do not have a nuclear capacity? How can we include them into this cooperative effort so that we do not break up the alliance? That is what we have been attempting to deal with.

Now, there are many shortcomings to our proposal, but my experience has been that there are shortcomings to every proposal, and those who do not like our proposal, it seems to me, should suggest one of their own. We hear frequently, for example, there should be a European deterrent. It seems to me that the General discussed that when he said that there was not the political organization of Europe that would permit the organization of a deterrent in a European sense. There may be someday. In the meanwhile, we think the multilateral force represents the best solution to hold the alliance together, which we believe to be essential, and I know of nothing that has happened which in my opinion lessens the need on both sides of the Atlantic for the closest cooperation on military matters, on economic matters, on political matters, on foreign policy matters.

Now, we don't have always that viewpoint and cooperation, but we intend to work at it. We intend to work at it.

America's Status in the Anti-Missile Missile Race

Q: Mr. President, one of the concerns voiced by some of the critics of the partial nuclear test ban agreement involves the relative status of the anti-missile-missile programs of the Soviet Union and the United States. And these critics point to last year's massive series of Soviet tests in which very large warheads were detonated as probably giving the Soviets an advantage in this area. Now have our scientific and technical intelligence people examined those tests, and can you give us your estimate of where we stand relatively?

The President: I don't think that the problem is solved by the explosion of a large megaton bomb. The problem is really one, as you know, of discrimination, of being able to prevent saturation, of having to protect many targets while the adversary can select a few.

The problem would not be solved if the United States exploded a 100-megaton bomb. The reason that the United States did not explode or develop is because we had no military use for it.

When you talk about 100 megatons, which we do rather casually, we should realize what we are talking about. What is the blast effect? Would three 30-ton megaton bombs do more damage? Well the fact of the matter is they would, because the effect of a 100-megaton as opposed to a 50-megaton does not move up in arithmetical progression. So we have felt that lesser yields, combined with the means of delivery, provided the United States with the greater security.

The problem of developing a defense against a missile is beyond us and beyond the Soviets technically, and I think many who work in it feel that perhaps it can never be successfully accomplished, because the whole problem, as you know, is to have 100 objects flying through the air at thousands of miles an hour, to be able to pick them out. And if you can do that there is an advantage, it still seems to me, to the offense, because they can pour in 200 or 300. And therefore, the problem is not the size of the bomb, but rather the problem of discrimination and the problem of selectivity, targeting, and all the rest.

On those matters we can continue to work, but I must say those who work the longest are not particularly optimistic that a scientific breakthrough can be made, and polluting the atmosphere by further tests will not materially advance our security.

Reporter: Thank you, Mr. President.

THE PRESIDENT'S NEWS CONFERENCE OF

AUGUST 20, 1963

The President: Good afternoon.

The House of Representatives begins this week consideration of legislation vital to the security and well-being of the United States and the free world, the mutual defense and assistance bill of 1964. I hope the House will give support to the authorization recommended by the Foreign Affairs Committee. Our foreign aid program is essential to the continued strength of the free world. It gives us increased military security at a cost far lower than if we had to carry the entire burden alone. It gives protection against Communist internal takeover to free people who are yet not able to build solidly without outside help. It provides essential assurances to the new nations of the world that they can count on us in their effort to build a free society. Only with this assurance can they continue to maintain against the pressures that are brought upon them.

This does not represent an impossible burden for the United States; indeed, it is only half as heavy as it was during the Marshall plan. Then about 2 percent of our gross national product was allocated to foreign assistance. The program today costs only 7/10 of 1 percent. The bill before the House has already been cut $850 million from our original estimate last January. Fortunately, the bill now has bipartisan political support. More than half of the Republicans on the House Foreign Affairs Committee are in favor of the $4.1 billion authorization now before the House.

This program is not an abstract set of numbers, but a set of concrete and continued actions in support of our national security. No party or group should call for a dynamic foreign policy and then seek to cripple this program.

One wonders which concrete actions critics would like to stop. Should we scrap the Alliance for Progress, which is our best answer to the threat of communism in this hemisphere? Should we deny help to India, the largest free power in Asia, as she seeks to strengthen herself against Communist China? Do we wish to dismantle our joint defenses in Korea, Taiwan, Pakistan, Iran, Turkey, and Greece, countries along the very rim of Communist power? Do we want to weaken our front in Southeast Asia?

This is no time to slacken our efforts. This fight is by no means over. The struggle is not finished. And therefore, as has been said on many occasions before, however tired we may get of this program, our adversaries are not tired. I don't think this country is tired and the cause of freedom should certainly not be fatigued. Therefore I think it is necessary that we continue to make this effort. I hope the House will support it. Eighty percent of these funds are spent in the United States and I think it is necessary and essential - as the Secretary of State, the Secretary of Defense, General Clay, and others - that the House figure be passed.

Experience shows us that the appropriations traditionally has been less. I think it is incumbent upon us to support the action of the House Foreign Affairs Committee, and I hope the House of Representatives will.

QUESTIONS

Safeguards and the Test Ban Treaty

Q: Mr. President, the Joint Chiefs of Staff have approved a series of safeguards that they say will maintain our security under the limited test ban treaty, but there seems to be some feeling in Congress that perhaps these safeguards won't be carried out as vigorously and as fully as some of the Members of Congress would like. What do you have to say to that, sir?

The President: I don't know where that feeling would arise.

Q: It has been raised.

The President: In view of the fact that the four safeguards they suggested, the Chiefs of Staff, were all mentioned in my address to Congress which preceded their meeting – there is a letter going to the Congress in response to a request from the Senate Armed Services Committee, the Foreign Relations Committee, and we are going to describe in detail what steps we are going to take to implement the four safeguards.

Now, the four safeguards consist of: one, that we should keep our laboratories activated and vital. I have already met with Dr. Foster and Dr. Bradbury[1] – we have talked with others. We are going to do that.

Secondly, we should prepare a standby so that if the treaty should be breached, abrogated, or if we should have what the treaty language describes as an imminent threat to our security we would be prepared to resume testing. Already, we have begun to prepare Johnston Island for that unhappy eventuality if it should occur. Twenty-two million dollars has been already allocated; $11 million has already been put out in contracts. We are dredging the harbor; we are building some piers. There are two dredges already out there. So I can assure you that we are going ahead very rapidly in that area.

Third, I think they wanted or suggested a vigorous series of underground tests. We have already – in the last 2 years we've conducted 97 tests underground. That is quite vigorous. We are going to continue to carry on, as I have said, a vigorous series of tests. So that I think that the areas of concern, the feeling of the Joint Chiefs, when they endorsed the test ban, that these areas should be met. I think – oh, and the fourth area, as I remember, was that we improve our methods of detection. And on that we have additional recommendations to make which will be unanimously endorsed, I think, by the Joint Chiefs of Staff.

So we are just as anxious – we appreciate the concern of the Members of Congress, but this matter is of concern to us also and I can assure them we are going to do the job.

August 28th Civil Rights Demonstration

Q: Mr. President, this is probably the last time we will have a session with you before the August 28th civil rights demonstration here. I wonder if you have any new thoughts on that march, and whether you intend to participate or be involved in the activities that day, beyond conferring with a group of leaders of the movement?

The President: No. I have already given my view at a previous press conference, and I will, as I have said – I have been asked for an appointment, and I will be glad to see the leaders of the organizations who are participating on that day.

Curtailment of Atmospheric Tests

Q: Mr. President, Dr. Teller[2] has charged that the administration curtailed a number of the atmospheric tests last year for what he called political reasons, in order not to alienate public opinion. Senator Humphrey has called this a very serious charge. Could you say whether those atmospheric tests were curtailed and why?

The President: No, we had set up a committee in the National Security Council headed by Dr. Seaborg,[3] and we heard recommendations from the various laboratories, Los Alamos and Livermore, from the AEC, from the Department of Defense, and others, what tests would be most valuable. Obviously, we don't like to test in the atmosphere unless the test is essential. Every test in the atmosphere produces fallout and we would, it seems to me, be remiss in not attempting to keep the number of tests to the minimum, consistent with our national security.

As you remember there were 28 atmospheric tests; 28 atmospheric tests, 97, as I have said, underground tests. That is quite a lot of tests. Before that there was a 3-year moratorium where there were no tests, underground or in the atmosphere.

In addition, as you recall, we have to proceed with some care in deciding what tests. You remember one test went out and built an artificial Van Allen belt, which was far different from what had been imagined, which could have endangered our whole space program and indeed that of any other country.

So we kept a careful eye, and we in fact did more tests, several more tests than we had originally planned 6 months before. So I don't think that the charge is valid. Quite obviously, we didn't test unnecessarily. Quite obviously there may have been tests that Dr. Teller would like to have run. I don't know about that.

But every test was considered by the National Security Council, was considered by the group of principals, of which Dr. Seaborg was the chairman. We carried out, as I say, several more tests, as I recall, than we had originally planned. We carried out in all 28. There may have been, as I say, several tests that different scientists wanted to run at one point or another, but I think we did the major tests, and I think that they were an impressive series. But it would be very difficult, I think, to satisfy Dr. Teller in this field.

A New Postmaster General

Q: Mr. President, have you narrowed your search for a new Postmaster General, and are you seeking a man with a business background or a political background?

The President: The search is narrowing, but we haven't - there are other fields that are still to be considered, including even a postal background.

A Secret Atomic Energy Agreement

Q: Mr. President, the ranking House Republican expert on atomic energy says that in spite of all administration denials, he is sure that there was a side agreement at Moscow. Is there some way that you can present any proof positive?

The President: No. I cannot. There is nothing I can say other than to say it isn't so. There is nothing the Under Secretary of State can say other than that it isn't so. There is nothing Governor Harriman can say than it isn't so.

There is nothing the Prime Minister of England can say, who participated in it, Lord Hailsham, Lord Home, except that it isn't so. No, we can't prove it.

The Civil Rights and Tax Bills

Q: Mr. President, this promises to be a very long session of Congress. There is talk of it running into Thanksgiving dinner or Christmas dinner, and there is beginning to be talk heard among some of the rank and file that possibly it would be a good idea to put over both the civil rights bill and the tax bill into the next session. Do you think, sir, it will be possible for the leadership to keep Congress in town long enough to pass both of these major bills?

The President: I don't see why not. What is the advantage of putting it over until next year? We have other problems. We have the whole new appropriation series. We have an election year. There are a good many excuses next year to get out of town. It seems to me this is the year for us to consider these pieces of legislation. I think there should be a vote on both of them this year, and they are both very important. The civil rights legislation represents a response to a very serious national crisis. I don't think it is a matter that should be put off to next year.

The tax bill was recommended in January. It has not come to the House floor yet. It will come in early September. It should be possible for the Congress of the United States to dispose of this issue this year - 12 months. This is a matter which affects employment, jobs, our economic prospects, the struggle against a recession. We are talking about a tax cut beginning in January '64, and we are talking about the state of the economy through the next 6 months, which I think is predicated in part upon a possible tax cut. If that proved to be disappointing, and we started all over again in January, when would you get it to a vote then - May, or June, or July of next year? What would happen to the economy in the meanwhile?

I think it is very important that we get a vote on both of these issues this year, and I think most Congressmen will agree that they should meet their responsibilities on two very vital matters before they go home, and should have voted on these matters. I hope "up," but at least voted on them.

Signing of the Nuclear Test Ban Treaty

Q: Sir, there has been reports that if the limited nuclear test ban treaty is ratified, that you and Prime Minister Macmillan and Soviet Premier Khrushchev might go to the United Nations and register it there. If the treaty is ratified, do you see a possiblity of conferring with them there, and with other leaders, such as Marshal Tito?

The President: No, there has been no such plan. It has been suggested that I might speak at the United Nations, but I know of no decision which has been made on that. But as far as any ceremony of ratification or summit meeting involving ratification at the U.N., I would think that would be very unlikely.

Effect of the August 28th March

Q: Mr. President, in your view, what do you think the effect of the August 28 march will be, both on the country and on the Congress?

The President: I wouldn't - I think the purpose, of course, is to attempt to bring to the attention of the Congress and the country the strong feeling of a good many thousands of citizens. I don't know, of course, how many are going to come. What we are really talking about is a problem which involves 180 million people. That 180 million people, it seems to me, have elected a Congress and elected some of us to attempt to deal with that matter. So that this issue does not stand or fall on the August 28th. The August 28 is a chance for a good many people to express their feeling, but it is hard for them - a lot of other people - to travel; it costs them money, they all - many of them have jobs.

So that I think that what we are talking about is an issue that concerns all of our people and must in the final analysis be settled by the Congress and by the executive branch, working with 180 million people. This is an effort, however, to bring focus to the strong concern of a good many citizens. So that I think, as I said before, it is in that tradition that I meet with the leadership and in which I think it is appropriate that these people and anyone else who feels themselves - who are concerned - should come to Washington, see their Congressmen, and see any of us if they feel that it is in the public interest.

British Guiana

Q: Mr. President, I would just like to ask a three-part question. Do you feel that Cheddi Jagan, Prime Minister of British Guiana, is a Communist? And what do you think of the possibilities of British Guiana becoming another Cuba should the British leave very soon? And is the United States exerting any - trying to exert any influence on the British to stay in British Guiana, or to suspend the Guiana constitution?

The President: Well, I don't think it would be useful to respond, really, to any of those questions. With regard to Mr. Jagan's political philosophy, I think he has made it clear himself, and his associates have made it clear. The British still exercise a responsibility in the matter. I think we should leave it to them to exercise that in a responsible manner.

As to what might happen under hypothetical conditions in the future, quite obviously the United States Government is concerned about what happens in this hemisphere and observes matters in this hemisphere closely. But I think it is very important that we point out that this is primarily a British matter and we should leave the judgment to them.

The Question of Stationary Control Posts

Q: Mr. President, in case serious negotiations will be started with the Russians around the proposal to place some stationary control posts on both sides of the Iron Curtain, in what area should these control posts be stationed according to the United States point of view, and could it be only in both parts of Germany?

The President: No, I think we are a good, long way from reaching any conclusions or any position on the question of posts. This is a matter which I think would have to be discussed. I think it is a matter that has been discussed since it was first put forward 4 or 5 years ago. It is being discussed today in NATO Council. It is a matter on which I don't think the United States will have a United States view. But I think that there will be a NATO view. And that view, I think, will be evolving after a good deal of consultation.

So that in answer to your question, there is no - I don't think it would be proper to refer to an American view. I think this is a matter which we will have to work out in consultation, and then after the Allies have consulted about it, and come to conclusions, then I would imagine there may be conversations between the Allies and the Soviet Union. But we are a good, long way from that right now.

Special Consideration for Negroes

Q: Mr. President, some Negro leaders are saying that like the Jews perse-cuted by the Nazis the Negro is entitled to some kind of special dispensation for the pain of second-class citizenship over these many decades and genera-tions. What is your view of that in general, and what is your view in particu-lar on the specific point that they are recommending of job quotas by race?

The President: Well, I don't think - I don't think that is the generally held view, at least as I understand it, of the Negro community - that there is some compensation due for the lost years, particularly in the field of educa-tion. What I think they would like is to see their children well educated so that they could hold jobs and have their children accepted and have themselves accepted as equal members of the community.

So I don't think we can undo the past. In fact, the past is going to be with us for a good many years in uneducated men and women who lost their chance for a decent education. We have to do the best we can now. That is what we are trying to do. I don't think quotas are a good idea. I think it is a mis-take to begin to assign quotas on the basis of religion, or race, or color, or nationality. I think we'd get into a good deal of trouble.

Our whole view of ourselves is a sort of one society. That has not been true. At least, that is where we are trying to go. I think that we ought not to begin the quota system. On the other hand, I do think that we ought to make an effort to give a fair chance to everyone who is qualified - not through a quota, but just look over our employment rolls, look over our areas where we are hiring people and at least make sure we are giving everyone a fair chance. But not hard and fast quotas. We are too mixed, this society of ours, to begin to divide ourselves on the basis of race or color.

Senator Goldwater

Q: Mr. President, there have been charges that Senator Goldwater could become a captive of the radical right. Do you see any indications that the influence of the radical right is growing to proportions where it might be a major factor in the 1964 campaign, and could in effect get enough strength to make any candidate a captive?

The President: Well, I don't know. I don't know who has captured who. I would think that this is a matter which can best be handled by the Republi-cans at this time. Then after we have a convention and a candidate, then I would discuss it in some detail.

Compulsory Railroad Arbitration

Q: Mr. President, the railroad management and unions have reached what appears to be an impasse by submitting differing proposals for arbitration pro-cedures. Does this mean that the administration will now revise its proposals for compulsory arbitration in Congress?

The President: No. I understand that there is going to be a meeting to-morrow morning at 9 o'clock of a select group of the Senate Commerce Committee, who will meet with the parties with a proposal for settlement of the dispute. Then we will have a better idea, if this proposal is accepted by both the parties, or one of the parties. If it is not accepted by the parties, then the Senate Commerce Committee must make a judgment as to whether they will ac-cept the legislative proposals that we sent up or some proposal of their own. But I think we ought to have an answer to your question by tomorrow morning.

Appraisal of the Economy

Q: Mr. President, you mentioned the economy in reply to a question about the tax bill. Could you appraise the economy at this stage: how we are doing, and how is the economy going - is it good, sluggish, bad?

The President: I would say good. I think it is slightly better, although not much better, but slightly better than was estimated in January. So that looking over - I think, the Federal Reserve Board statistical comparisons based on the '57-'59 base as 100; it was 119 in January, and it is 127 now, and it rose, I think, a point in the last month. So that unemployment is 5.6 percent, and factory hours are strong. So, I would say that the state of the economy is good.

What we are concerned, of course, is about what's going to happen for the rest of '63 and '64, because we have now run from the winter of '61 - the fall of '60 and the winter of '61 - when we had our downturn, and in '58 the downturn, and then '60 and '61. And we have now run pretty steady with the exception of the difficulties of June of '62, and we have had a pretty steady rise.

Of course, you have to have a very substantial rise in order to take care of the number of people coming into the labor market. What I am concerned about therefore is that the tax bill be passed if we are going to see '64 another good year.

But to answer your question, standing as we do right now, I would say the state of the economy is good. What we must be concerned about always, of course, is the future. That is why I consider the tax bill so essential.

Soviet Troops in Cuba

Q: Can you bring us up to date, sir, on the Soviet troop strength in Cuba? Has there been a net reduction in recent weeks and months?

The President: Yes, there has been a decline in the last - since my last conference, I think - when we discussed it, about 2 months ago. The intelligence community judges that there has been a decline, and the primary emphasis of those who remain now is in training, and not in concentrated military units.

But there are still Russians there, and this is still a matter of concern to us.

Dr. Teller's Criticism of the Test Ban Treaty

Q: Mr. President, Dr. Teller, in urging the Senate to reject the nuclear test ban today, said that it weakens American defenses and thus invites attack, because the information that is necessary to develop a sure-fire antimissile missile can only be developed through atmospheric tests. What do you have to say to this?

The President: I think Mr. McNamara answered that very clearly.[4] Other scientists have answered it. I recognize Dr. Teller has made it very clear that he is opposed to it. He opposed it all last week and this week. Now, there are a good many other scientists with comparable experience - we have a Scientific Advisory Committee to the President, we have other scientists who work in nuclear matters, we have Nobel price winners and others, we have members of the military and others - who think that the test ban is a source of strength to us.[5]

I understand Dr. Teller is opposed to it. Every day he is opposed to it. I recognize he is going to continue to be opposed to it. I think that the question was very clearly answered by Mr. McNamara on what effect the atmospheric test ban would have on the development of an antimissile weapon.

Now just let us think of the other side of it. If we begin to test again and the Soviet Union tests again, and others begin to test again, how much security do we have? As I said before, in my message I sent to Congress, we needed only one test to develop the Hiroshima weapon. To anyone who works in the laboratories today, a 30-megaton weapon is perhaps not as sophisticated as a 60- or 70- or 80-megaton weapon. But it's still many, many, many times, dozens of times, stronger than the weapon that flattened Hiroshima and Nagasaki.

How many weapons do you need and how many megatons do you need to destroy? I said in my speech what we now have on hand, without any further testing, will kill 300 million people in one hour. I suppose they could even improve on that if it's necessary.

So on your specific question, I refer you to Mr. McNamara's answer, which I think is the clearest and most specific answer that you could possibly get on what effect the atmospheric test ban will have on the development of this weapon.

Exposure of Utah Children to Radioactivity

Q: Mr. President, in this connection, Utah scientists have announced that Utah children under 2 years have received from 2 to 28 times as much radioactive iodine-131 last year in less than a month as our Government says is safe for an entire year. Does the Government have any plans to examine some of these children to detect possible damage?

The President: Well, I have seen the report about the radio iodine and it is a matter of concern. As you know, the report is not unanimous. There is some controversy about it. In addition, the standards that were set do not - I don't think we should mislead the people there, that there is evidence on hand of a serious deterioration there. But, of course, it is a matter of concern to us that we not continue. But we are looking into it. But I would say that as of now that we do not believe that the health of the children involved has been adversely affected. But it does tell us - though of course these matters require further study - what it does tell us is that it is very desirable to get a test ban.

U.S. - USSR Collaboration on a Moon Shot

Q: Mr. President, apparently there is some consideration being given to the United States and Soviet Russia collaborating on the moon shot. I wonder, in view of that, if there is any plan to have Soviet observers when the Apollo moon shot tests start at White Sands, N. Mex.?

The President: No. We haven't had any success in reaching any agreement. The kind of agreement to really be meaningful would require a good deal of inspection on both sides, and there is no evidence as yet that the Soviet Union is prepared to accept that. All we have ever gotten was an agreement to exchange weather information. We haven't had anything more substantial.

Secretary Korth and the TFX

Q: Mr. President, do you see anything in the relationship of the Secretary of the Navy Korth to the TFX contract which would suggest a conflict of interest?

The President: No, I don't. I have the highest regard for Mr. Korth, Mr. Gilpatric, Mr. McNamara, and it seems to me the matter has been looked into for many months and I think they have emerged in a very good position.

George Kennan on Arms Control

Q: Ambassador George Kennan the other day said he thought the most promising area for further exploration in East-West negotiations was President de Gaulle's idea about controlling means of delivery rather than nuclear warheads. Does this Government have a position on that possible approach?

The President: No. As I said, I think we would be interested to hear what General de Gaulle might propose. How you are going to control the system. Without inspection we can detect atmospheric tests. The Soviet Union has been reluctant to have the kind of inspection which would permit us - which after all, would be very limited inspection - to have underground tests detected. Is there any evidence that they would accept the kind of very detailed inspection that control of a delivery system would entail when it gives out no signal as a nuclear explosion does?

But General de Gaulle has not indicated the details of his proposal. We would be very interested in it. We would be delighted to join with him in any meeting to discuss it. But we have not had it described and I have not yet seen evidence that the Soviet Union would accept that kind of inspection. However, we will be very responsive if the proposal is put forward.

Withdrawal of Soviet Troops from Cuba

Q: Mr. President, going back to your earlier answer on Cuba, can you say what our estimate is of how many troops have been withdrawn?

The President: No. I think it's difficult - as we can't call the roll - for us to say precisely. But based on the information we have about outward movements and inward movements it is the judgment of the intelligence community that there has been a reduction in the last 2½ months.

Balance of International Payments

Q: Mr. President, in view of the figures released yesterday by the Commerce Department on the balance of international payments, does the administration have any further measures it is going to recommend? It looks as though the deficit could be the largest since the war.

The President: No, I don't think it will be. The second quarter was particularly difficult. Since then the indications are better. In addition, as you know, we have taken two important steps - really three. One is the equalization tax. Two is the interest rates. And three is the reduction in military expenditures and trying our foreign aid expenditures here in the United States. So we think that is going to make an important difference. Quite obviously, we will have to look at the effect of all of those proposals.

Q: Do you see an end in sight when there will be a balance?

The President: Yes, I do, because I think that by one means or another we are going to bring it into balance. Quite obviously we would not accept it. But we are reluctant - quite obviously we are not going to devalue, because there is no necessity for it. It would be a defeating measure. So I eliminate that. It may not be necessary for us to proceed any further.

You can see already the effect of even the rather limited steps we have taken - two effects. One, the effect in Canada and Japan of the equalization tax, which shows the deflationary effect of this kind of restriction, and therefore we were reluctant to do it.

Secondly, there was an article in the paper, in the Times on Sunday about the effect on the Euro-dollar of our interest rate rise. So that everything we do shakes the West – the monetary system – so we proceed with care. We are still in good shape. A good deal of this outflow represents assets abroad. The United States, while a good deal of money is going out, has also picked up a good many assets in Western Europe and all around the globe.

While it means our position may not be as liquid as it might, it does mean that we are in a strong position in regard to our ultimate balance sheet.

Q: Will that call for any action at the next meeting of the I.M.F.?

The President: Not that we have planned. But I think – let's see what effect the interest rate increase has on the short term flow. This tax can be important and this cut down on defense and our foreign aid can be important, and there are other steps we may be able to take. We feel that with the rising cost in Europe that we are going to begin to come into balance. We are going to bring it into balance. The question is, we would like to bring it into balance in a way that does not shake – as I have said, we don't want to have a 1928 situation where you take an action to protect your problem here and you cause a far greater problem.

I think this situation can be brought under control. What we are now do-ing, I think, is an important step in that direction.

Reporter: Thank you, Mr. President.

[1]Dr. John S. Foster, Jr., Director, Lawrence Radiation Laboratory, Liver-more, Calif.; and Dr. Norris E. Bradbury, Director, Los Alamos Scientific Lab-oratory, N. Mex.

[2]Dr. Edward Teller, professor at large and associate director of the E. O. Lawrence Radiation Laboratory, University of California, Berkeley, Calif.

[3]Dr. Glenn T. Seaborg, Chairman, Atomic Energy Commission.

[4]See "Nuclear Test Ban Treaty," Hearings Before the Senate Committee on Foreign Relations, 88th Congress, 1st Session, August 12-27, 1963 (Government Printing Office, 1963).

[5]On August 24 the White House released a statement by the President's Science Advisory Committee expressing "strong support" for the treaty. "Public discussion of the treaty raises many important questions other than those of a technical nature," the statement declared. "However, the questions raised with regard to the potential effects of the treaty on the future military capabil-ities of this country relative to the Soviet Union are primarily technical.... The Science Advisory Committee, drawing upon the assistance of outstanding scientists and engineers throughout the United States, has long been engaged in independent detailed examination of military technology as it affects our national security in broad aspects. The Committee believes that the continued unrestricted development and exploitation of military technology by both the Soviet Union and the United States would in time lead to a new decrease in our real security."

THE PRESIDENT'S SPECIAL NEWS CONFERENCE AT HYANNIS PORT ON THE

MUTUAL SECURITY PROGRAM

AUGUST 30, 1963

The President: Good morning, ladies and gentlemen.

General Clay and Mr. Bell, the director of the mutual security program, and I have met this morning to consider what actions we could take to strengthen the mutual security programs to be sure that they are adequately financed and to make every possible effort to assure that the security of the United States and the effectiveness of its foreign policy will be maintained in the coming months.

This matter is now before the Congress but, in a very real sense, it is before all of the American people.

This program of mutual security has helped protect the independence of dozens of countries since 1945.   Most importantly, it has protected the security and the best interests of the United States.   This effort is by no means over.   We are going to have a difficult struggle in the 1960's.   The peaceful coexistence which is frequently talked about will be very intense in Asia, Africa, the Middle East, Latin America.   This struggle is going on every day, and I think that the United States has a part in it, as do other free countries, and I am confident the American people will recognize this effort involves their security, the maintenance of freedom, and our peace.

I am particularly glad General Clay came up this morning, as he studied this program very carefully and he continues to be head of the committee which oversees the aid program and advises with us on it.   He might have a word to say on the matter.

General Clay: We are, of course, fully aware of the action that has been taken with respect to the foreign aid bill.   We on the committee are greatly concerned in two fields particularly.   It has endangered the whole program, and that is in the reduction of the funds available for our military aid and, further, in the reductions in the Alliance for Progress.   We think these reductions in the authorization have gone too far and that they could seriously endanger these programs.

We are certainly most anxious that these programs continue; that there be sufficient authorization for the appropriations to permit the jobs to be done. Above all, we hope that they will be considered as in the best interests of the American people on a nonpartisan basis.   It is to this end that certainly we on the committee are going to work, Mr. President.

The President: Thank you very much, General.

Q: Mr. President, what strategy are you going to try to use to get the total amount increased now?

The President: It is not a question of strategy.   We are trying to point out very clearly how significant these programs are.

General Clay has already pointed out the effect of these cuts on Latin America, which is perhaps the most critical area in the world today, the effects on our military assistance programs in Greece, Turkey, Iran, Pakistan, South Viet-Nam, Thailand, South Korea.

I think that it is important that the American people understand that this is a matter which involves the security and the balance of power all over the world. So we are going to continue to work with the Congress.

General Clay and his committee will continue to make an effort to bring this home to the American people as well as to the Members of Congress.

This is a matter which involves very greatly the security of our country. This is the same view that was held by President Eisenhower, the same view that was held by President Truman, and it is no accident that three Presidents in a row, sitting where they do and bearing particular constitutional responsibilities for foreign policy, should all feel that this program is most important, most effective, most essential, and we hope that the American people will come to share that view.

QUESTIONS

Public Support for Foreign Aid

Q: Mr. President, do you feel there has been a significant swing in the public's move away from support for foreign aid?

The President: I think people don't enjoy carrying this burden. I never thought they did. I always thought in the forties, and the fifties, and the sixties that there were reservations about it. I think that is quite obvious, but I think in the final analysis most of them realize that it is as essential a part of our effort as the appropriations for national defense. This money is spent, nearly all of it, in the United States, and it helps keep the freedom of this country of ours. It represents much less of a percentage of our wealth than it did during the Marshall Plan days. I think the American people realize that freedom does not come cheaply or easily.

The Authorization Bill

Q: Mr. President, the Senate Foreign Relations Committee has not completed its action on the authorization bill. Is there any possibility of getting a higher figure and then out of conference getting a fairly reasonable floor?

The President: We hope so.

Q: Mr. President, are you going to seek the restoration of the entire amount cut by the House from the Senate, or is there some new figure that you gentlemen have agreed upon?

The President: No, we are going to try to get a figure as close to the recommendations. Obviously we won't get all the recommendations, but as close to the recommendations as we can in the Senate Foreign Relations Committee and in the Senate. Then there must be a conference. After that, there must be consideration by the Appropriations Committee. So, I think it is important that the State give us as much help as it can in this program.

Q: Mr. President, does this program look different to you now that you are in the White House than it did when you were in Congress?

The President: No. I supported it very strongly in the Congress as a member of the Senate Foreign Relations Committee.

Obviously, a President has a particular responsibility in the field of foreign policy, as I have said, constitutionally. Therefore, as I see very clearly how vital this program is in all of the countries of Latin America –

you can see it week in and week out - as well as in these other countries, I perhaps feel it more strongly in the same sense that General Eisenhower did. But I supported this program in the Senate, and I think it is essential. I think it is essential. I think, as I say, I put it right alongside of our defense appropriation.

Q: Mr. President, in your meeting this morning, was there any discussion of revamping the program in terms of what the House has done?

The President: No. This program we set up. Then General Clay and his group, which included Mr. Eugene Black of the World Bank, Mr. Lovett, and others, looked at it. They made some proposals. We reduced our request of the authorization after their report came in. They recommended a figure of over $4 billion. This figure now, of course, in the House is almost $600 million less than that.

As I say, we have not even gone through the appropriating procedure, which is usually less than the authorization. This will mean, as Mr. Bell pointed out, that the United States will not fulfill its commitments under the Alliance for Progress, and we are going to say to the Latin American people that we are not going to do what we said we were going to do. It will mean that we will have to cut back on our military assistance to countries which are right on the firing line, and it will mean that a good many of these programs in countries of low-term development loans will come to an end. I think it will limit very much our ability to influence events in these areas. That is why I am very anxious to see the program restored.

THE PRESIDENT'S NEWS CONFERENCE OF

SEPTEMBER 12, 1963

The President: Good afternoon.

Ladies and gentlemen, I want to stress again how important it is that the United States Senate approve the pending nuclear test ban treaty. It has already been signed by more than 90 governments, and it is clearer now than ever that this small step towards peace will have significant gains. And I want to commend to the American people the two distinguished and outstanding speeches made by Senator Mansfield and Senator Dirksen, the Majority and the Minority Leaders, who in the great tradition of American bipartisanship and national interest I think put the case most effectively.

This treaty will enable all of us who inhabit the earth, our children and children's children, to breathe easier, free from the fear of nuclear test fallout. It will curb the spread of nuclear weapons to other countries, thereby holding out hope for a more peaceful and stable world. It will slow down the nuclear arms race without impairing the adequacy of this Nation's arsenal or security, and it will offer a small but important foundation on which a world of law can be built.

The Senate hearings and debate have been intensive and valuable, but they have not raised an argument in opposition which was not thoroughly considered by our military, scientific, legal, and foreign policy leaders before the treaty was signed.

This Nation has sought to bring nuclear weapons under international control since 1946. This particular kind of treaty has been sought by us since 1959.

If we are to give it now only grudging support, if this small clearly beneficial step cannot be approved by the widest possible margin in the Senate, then
this Nation cannot offer much leadership or hope for the future.

But if the American people and the American Senate can demonstrate that we
are as determined to achieve a peace and a just peace as we are to defend our
freedom, I think future generations will honor the action that we took.

Secondly, I would like to say something about what has happened in the
schools in the last few days. In the past 2 weeks, schools in 150 Southern
cities have been desegregated. There may have been some difficulties, but to
the great credit of the vast majority of the citizens and public officials of
these communities, this transition has been made with understanding and respect
for the law.

The task was not easy. The emotions underlying segregation have persisted
for generations, and in many instances leaders in these communities have had
to overcome their own personal attitudes as well as the ingrained social attitudes of the communities. In some instances the obstacles were greater, even
to the point of physical interference. Nevertheless, as we have seen, what
prevailed in these cities through the South finally was not emotion but respect
for law. The courage and the responsibility of those community leaders in
those places provide a meaningful lesson not only for the children in those
cities but children all over the country.

QUESTIONS

Resumption of Nuclear Testing

*Q: Mr. President, last year when you discussed resumption of nuclear test-
ing in a public speech, you anticipated difficulty in being able to keep top-
flight scientists operating on standby preparations; you doubted that large-
scale laboratories could be kept fully alert. And you said this wasn't merely
difficult or inconvenient, but that after thorough exploration you had determined that keeping laboratories fully alert on a standby basis would be impossible. Could you tell us, sir, what has happened since then to change your
mind about this?*

The President: Yes. I believe that what I was talking about then was a
comprehensive test ban treaty. Obviously, if you had no underground testing,
the laboratories would atrophy. I stated at that time, or on other occasions,
that if we could get a responsible, comprehensive test ban treaty that I would
be willing to take that risk. But we didn't get a comprehensive test ban
treaty, but only a limited one. Under that limited agreement it is possible
to carry on underground testing, and, therefore, we will not have the deadening
of the vitality of the laboratories. Instead, the underground testing will
continue, free from fallout, but the scientists will be able to engage in their
work. They will be maintained, the laboratories will be maintained, and therefore I think that we are faced with a different situation than the one that I
responded to earlier in the year.

Meeting with Mr. Gromyko and the Possibility of an Address to the U.N.

*Q: Mr. President, do you plan to address the U.N. General Assembly session
later this month, and will you meet with Mr. Gromyko there or here?*

The President: Well, I plan to address the United Nations General Assembly later this month. The meeting with the Foreign Minister - and I am going to meet with other foreign ministers when they come - I assume will be in Washington.

U.S. Policy Toward Vietnam

Q: Mr. President, in view of the prevailing confusion, is it possible to state today just what this Government's policy is toward the current government of South Viet-Nam?

The President: I think I have stated what my view is and we are for those things and those policies which help win the war there. That is why some 25,000 Americans have traveled 10,000 miles to participate in that struggle. What helps to win the war, we support; what interferes with the war effort, we oppose.   I have already made it clear that any action by either government which may handicap the winning of the war is inconsistent with our policy or our objectives. This is the test which I think every agency and official of the United States Government must apply to all of our actions, and we shall be applying that test in various ways in the coming months, although I do not think it desirable to state all of our views at this time.   I think they will be made more clear as time goes on.

But we have a very simple policy in that area, I think.   In some ways I think the Vietnamese people and ourselves agree: we want the war to be won, the Communists to be contained, and the Americans to go home.   That is our policy.   I am sure it is the policy of the people of Viet-Nam.   But we are not there to see a war lost, and we will follow the policy which I have indicated today of advancing those causes and issues which help win the war.

The Test Ban and Limitations on the U.S.

Q: Mr. President, some opponents of the test ban treaty have expressed the fear that once the treaty has been ratified it might then be possible later by Executive action to amend the treaty so as to further limit the freedom of action of the United States. What is your reaction to these suggestions?

The President: No, I can give a categorical assurance that the treaty, as you know, cannot be amended without the agreement of the three basic signatories.   The treaty cannot be changed in any way by the three basic signatories, and the others, without the consent of the Senate.   And there would be - of course any proposal to change the treaty would be submitted to the usual ratification procedure followed by or prescribed by the Constitution.   In addition there would be no Executive action which would permit us to in any way limit or circumscribe the basic understandings of the treaty.   Quite obviously this is a commitment which is made by the Executive and by the Senate, operating under one of the most important provisions of the Constitution, and no President of the United States would seek to, even if he could - and I strongly doubt that he could, by stretching the law to the furthest - seek in any way to break the bond and the understanding which exists between the Senate and the Executive and, in a very deep sense, the American people, in this issue.

Books on the President

Q: Mr. President, two books have been written about you recently. One of them, by Hugh Sidey, has been criticized as being too uncritical of you, and the other, by Victor Lasky, as being too critical of you.[1] How would you review them, if you have read them?

The President: I thought Mr. Sidey was critical, but I have not read all of Mr. Lasky, except I have just gotten the flavor of it. I have seen it is highly praised by Mr. Drummond and Mr. Krock and others, so I am looking forward to reading it, because the part that I read was not as brilliant as I gather the rest of it is, from what they say about it.

Busing

Q: Mr. President, as a parent, do you think it is right to wrench children away from their neighborhood family area and cart them off to strange, faraway schools to force racial balance? I notice you said that you did not approve of racial quotas in employment. Now, do you approve of forcing racial quotas in schools?

The President: Well, the question, as you described it – I would not approve of the procedure you described in your question. Now, a lot of these, of course, depend on the local school districts, and I would have to see what the situation was in each district. But I would not have any hesitancy in saying no to your question. I would not approve it. But this in the final analysis must be decided by the local board. This is a local question. But if you are asking me my opinion, faraway strange places and all the rest, I would not agree with it.

Discrimination in Housing

Q: Mr. President, there are consistent reports that you are about to consider a more sweeping Executive order dealing with an end to discrimination in housing. Have you any comment on that?

The President: No. The order we now have is the one we plan to stand on.

The Part to be Played by the U.N.

Q: Mr. President, in the past you repeatedly stated that the United States strongly wished the United Nations to develop as an instrument of strengthening the peace and cooperation among the states. What concrete new efforts is your administration going to take toward that goal at the forthcoming session of the United Nations General Assembly?

The President: That is going to be really one of the, I suppose, central matters that I will discuss when I speak before the United Nations in just a few days. Perhaps that will be the best place to discuss it.

Ngo Dinh Nhu and our Policy Toward Vietnam

Q: Mr. President, in your statement of just a few moments ago on South Viet-Nam, would you consider that any significant changes in the policy of South Vietnam can be carried out so long as Ngo Dinh Nhu remains as the President's top adviser?

The President: I think that, aside from the general statements which have been made, I would think that that sort of a matter really should be discussed by the Ambassador – Ambassador Lodge – and others. I don't see that we serve any useful purpose in engaging in that kind of discussion at this time.

Governor Rockefeller's Statement on Taxes

Q: Mr. President, Governor Rockefeller says that he may have to withdraw his pledge not to raise taxes in New York State. The grounds he gives is that you had promised to achieve a certain economic growth rate in the country and you failed to keep that promise and therefore he feels relieved of this pledge. Could you comment on his statement?

The President: I saw all of those campaign statements that were made in the fall of 1962, about how New York had moved ahead, and all of the rest, and I didn't see any acknowledgment that it was due in any way to the economic measures we have taken since 1960 to provide for an increase in economic growth.

I think there has been a substantial increase in the economic growth, and New York has shared in it. I don't know what grounds on which Governor Rockefeller categorically made an assurance to the people of New York in the fall of 1962 that is now impossible to fulfill. If he feels it is my fault, then I am prepared to accept that.

I must say he is not really the only one. I got, I suppose, several thousands of letters when the stock market went way down in May and June of 1962, blaming me, and talking about the "Kennedy market." I haven't gotten a single letter in the last few days about the Kennedy market now that it has broken through the Dow-Jones Average. So Governor Rockefeller is not alone in his disappointment.

The Naming of Mr. Gronouski to the Cabinet

Q: Mr. President, speaking of letters, there have been suggestions that you are putting Mr. Gronouski into the Cabinet to pay some old political debts in Wisconsin as well as to lay the basis for future political support elsewhere. Would you tell us your reason for naming him?

The President: Yes. I met Mr. Gronouski in 1960 in Wisconsin. He was - and he is - a distinguished public servant, and he has had a fine war record, and he was a Ph.D. of the University of Wisconsin, and he is in charge of taxation, and he was highly recommended, and is a very good administrator. I don't know why it causes quite so much excitement when the name is Gronouski as opposed to when it may be Smith or Brown or Day. I think that - or even Celebrezze.

I think that - the issue is whether he is of Polish extraction and therefore it must be political, but if he is not of Polish extraction, it is not political. And I am not sure that I accept that test. I think Mr. Gronouski is a fine public servant and I am glad to have him here, and I think we just happen to be fortunate that his grandparents came from Poland.

Senator Goldwater's Comments on Cuba

Q: Mr. President, in a Chicago speech last night, Senator Goldwater said there are not 10 men in America who know the full truth about Cuba, all the facts of the test ban treaty, or the commitments made on behalf of this Nation with governments dedicated to our destruction. He seems to be hinting that you made secret agreements both in the Cuban settlement last fall and to obtain the test ban treaty. Could you say unequivocally that there were no commitments, or would you care to comment on Senator Goldwater's comments?

The President: There are no commitments, and I think that Senator Goldwater is at least one of the 10 men in America who would know that is not true. I think there are a good many other men. The fact of the matter is, as you know, we offered to have the correspondence on the test ban treaty made available to the leadership of the Senate. It stands on its own. So I can tell you very flatly there were no commitments made that have not been discussed or revealed. I think most people know that.

Q: Would you care to comment further on this type of attack by Senator Goldwater?

The President: No, no. Not yet, not yet.

Information on Vietnam

Q: Mr. President, some persons in criticizing your policies and your comments on Viet-Nam say that you are operating on the basis of incorrect and inadequate information. What do you have to say about it?

The President: I am operating on the basis of, really, the unanimous views and opinions expressed by the most experienced Americans there – in the military, diplomatic, AID agency, the Voice of America, and others – who have only one interest, and that is to see the war successful as quickly as possible. I would say that I understated their concern about the matters in Viet-Nam. We have no other interest.

In addition, I think we are fortunate, as I have said before, to have Ambassador Lodge there, and I will say that any statement I have made expressing concern about the situation there reflects his view, and reflects it in a very moderate way.

American Legion Comments on the Cuban Problem

Q: Mr. President, the American Legion meeting in Miami adopted a resolution today asking the United States to "proceed boldly alone" to end the Communish rule in Cuba if the other hemisphere nations do not assist us, and they say that we cannot have coexistence with communism in this hemisphere, and that there has been a lack of effective action by our Government since the Castro regime began back in 1959. Could you comment, sir?

The President: Yes. Well, we have taken every step we could short of military action to bring pressure on the Castro regime – shipping, trade, all the rest. It has been relatively isolated in this hemisphere. It is quite obvious now that it is a Soviet satellite – Mr. Castro is a Soviet satellite.

Finally, though, once you get beyond these words, you finally talk about military invasion of Cuba. That I do not think is in the interest of this country. I regard that as a most dangerous action, an incendiary action which could bring a good deal of grief not only to the people of the United States, but to Western Europe and others who are dependent upon us. I do not think that is wise. Those who advocate it should say it, but I don't agree with it.

Opposition to the Test Ban by the Air Force Association

Q: Mr. President, the Air Force Association yesterday openly condemned the test ban as a danger to this country. How do you feel about the propriety of an appreciable proportion of its members, being serving officers of the United States Air Force under your command, and thus contradicting their Commander in Chief and their Secretary of Defense?

The President: Well, I wouldn't – I think the Air Force Association is free to give its views. I am sure – I don't know exactly the membership of its resolutions committee, and I do not know how the vote ran and who took what position. But the fact of the matter is that the Joint Chiefs of Staff favored this treaty, and the Secretary of Defense favored it, and General Lemnitzer favored it, and the Unified Command has favored it, and I think that the treaty is in our interest.

Of course there are going to be people that are opposed to these actions, but I think the greater risk is to defeat it. So I would not suggest any reproof in any way of those who made their judgments. I just don't agree with it.

Senator Church's Proposal on Vietnam

Q: Mr. President, how do you feel about Senator Church's proposed resolution that you withhold further aid to Viet-Nam if certain changes in policy and personnel are not forthcoming?

The President: I think his resolution reflects his concern. He is particularly interested in the Far East, as is Senator Carlson and some other Senators. I have indicated my feeling that we should stay there, and continue to assist South Viet-Nam, but I have also indicated our feeling that the assistance we give should be used in the most effective way possible. I think that seems to be Senator Church's view.

The Stand of the "Young Democrats"

Q: The Young Democrats out in the West have taken some unusual stands on Red China and East Germany, Cuba, and Viet-Nam. Have you seen them and would you care to comment on them?

The President: Yes. I didn't agree with any of them. I don't know what is happening with the Young Democrats and Young Republicans, but time is on our side.

Withdrawal of American Dependents from Vietnam

Q: Are you giving any thought, sir, to the withdrawal of American dependents from Viet-Nam?

The President: As I have said, I think that any matter which we are now considering should best be considered by the Government, and any conclusions we come to should be made public when it is the appropriate time.

Improving the Press Conference

Q: Mr. President, have you given any thought to some of the proposals advanced from time to time for improving the Presidential press conference, such as having the conference devoted all to one subject or to having written questions at a certain point?

The President: Well, I have heard of that, and I have seen criticisms of the proposal. The difficulty is - as Mr. Frost said about not taking down a fence until you find out why it was put up - I think all the proposals made to improve it will really not improve it.

I think we do have the problem of moving very quickly from subject to subject, and therefore I am sure many of you feel that we are not going into any depth. So I would try to recognize perhaps the correspondent on an issue two or three times in a row, and we could perhaps meet that problem. Otherwise it seems to me it serves its purpose, which is to have the President in the bull's-eye, and I suppose that is in some ways revealing.

Negroes and the President

Q: Mr. President, a Negro leader who helped organize the March on Washington says that he feels you are greater than Abe Lincoln in the area of civil rights. Apparently a lot of other Negroes support you. The latest poll showed that 95 percent probably would vote for you next year. Now, in your opinion, Mr. President, does this political self-segregation on the part of the Negroes, combined with continued demonstrations in the North, pose any problems for you as far as the electoral vote in the North is concerned next year?

The President: I understand what you mean, that there is a danger of a division in the party, in the country, upon racial grounds. I would doubt that. I think the American people have been through too much to make that fatal mistake. It is true that a majority of the Negroes have been Democrats, but that has been true since Franklin Roosevelt. Before that a majority of them were Republicans. The Republican Party, I am confident, could get the support of the Negroes, but I think they have to recognize the very difficult problems the Negroes face.

So in answer to your question, I don't know what 1964 is going to bring. I think a division upon racial lines would be unfortunate - class lines, sectional lines. In fact, Theodore Roosevelt said all this once very well way back. So I would say that over the long run we are going to have a mix. This will be true racially, socially, ethnically, geographically, and that is really, finally, the best way.

Q: Mr. President, this is a related question. It is about the Gallup poll. It has to do with a racial question. Agents of Dr. Gallup asked people this question: Do you think the Kennedy administration is pushing integration too fast or not fast enough? Fifty percent replied that they thought you were pushing too fast. Would you comment?

The President: No, I think probably he is accurate. The fact of the matter is, this is not a matter on which you can take the temperature every week or 2 weeks or 3 weeks, depending on what the newspaper headlines must be. I think you must make a judgment about the movement of a great historical event which is taking place in this country after a period of time. You judged 1863 after a good many years - its full effect. I think we will stand, after a period of time has gone by. The fact is, that same poll showed 40 percent or so thought it was more or less right. I thought that was rather impressive, because it is change; change always disturbs, and therefore I was surprised that there wasn't greater opposition. I think we are going at about the right tempo.

Q: Mr. President, in a related area of civil rights, after the events in Alabama this week, we have the situation now where the schools have been desegregated in Alabama, Mississippi, Georgia, South Carolina, practically all of the States of the Deep South. Do you have a feeling that perhaps a milestone has been reached in this area, or do you see a continued really step-by-step progress from one city to another?

The President: Step by step, I would think. What is impressive, as I said - and I don't think we realize the full significance of it - is that most of the work really has been done by southerners themselves. In the case of Alabama, the five Federal judges who signed that order were all from Alabama - all grew up in Alabama - and I am sure shared the views of the majority of Alabamians who, I think, are not for desegregation, but, nevertheless, met their responsibilities under the law, which we are trying to do. And I think what has happened in South Carolina, Florida, in the last few days, Georgia - I think it is an impressive story. It is slow, step by step, but it will continue that way. But this Nation is passing through a very grueling test, and with the exception of a few aberrations, I think we are meeting it. And I say "we" in the national sense. We, as a country, are doing quite well. We have to do better, but I think there is some cause for satisfaction in most of the events that happened in the last 2 weeks.

Richard Russell on the Test Ban

Q: Mr. President, in your view, what impact will the Senate Armed Services Committee Chairman Richard Russell's opposition to the test ban treaty have on the Senate vote on the pact?

The President: I think he is highly respected, probably the most individually respected, perhaps, in the Senate, and therefore what he says is going to have some influence. On the other hand, it seems to me the whole weight of opinion makes this essential. I think the Senate is going to approve this. We can't turn our backs and tell 90 nations who have now signed it that the lid is off, the atomic age has come in all of its splendor, and that everyone now should begin to test in the atmosphere - which, of course, everybody would have to do if this treaty fails. This would be the green light for intensive atmospheric testing by a number of countries. You couldn't possibly stop it. This would be the end of an effort of 15 years. I don't think the United States would want to take on that responsibility.

Q: Mr. President, what significance do you see in the failure of Cuba so far to sign the treaty? Do you think, specifically, that this reflects any new friction between Cuba and Russia? And also I was wondering whether it is satisfying to be called more imperialistic by Castro than Eisenhower was.

The President: Well lately, I have had so many things said about me that I thought what Castro said was not particularly bad. He is attempting to demonstrate he is an independent figure. That is what he is attempting to do. I think probably he may sign finally, I don't know. We made it very clear in my letter to Senator Dirksen that if there is any breach in the treaty which involves Cuba, that appropriate action will be taken.

Therefore, this is a gesture of protest against what is obvious. But I don't put much significance on it. As far as what he says, I think it would be - I don't know.

Admiral Anderson's Speech on Public Confidence in the Military

Q: Mr. President, last week, Admiral Anderson expressed concern that there is too little trust and confidence between civilian and military officials in the Pentagon. Also, the Admiral said that he favored legislation introduced by Congressman Vinson to fix the tenure of members of the Joint Chiefs at 4 years. I wonder if you would comment on these points in the Admiral's speech.

The President: He felt very strongly about the matter and made his speech, and that was all right. Now secondly, on the question of the 4 years, I am not for that. I think that any President should have the right to choose carefully his military advisers. I think the 2-year term fits very well. I am for the 2-year term. I think, not just in my case but I would think for those who come afterwards, I think they will be better served.

Fear of the Pakistanis of American Support for India

Q: Mr. President, the President of Pakistan said yesterday in his interview that he may have to make an alliance with the Chinese because of his fear of our arming India further. Is there any way this government can, or has it been able to give assurances either to the Indians or to the Pakistani which would quiet this mutual fear which seems to plague both of them?

The President: I can tell you that there is nothing that has occupied our attention more over the last 9 months. The fact, of course, is we want to sustain India, which may be attacked this fall by China. So we don't want India to be helpless – there's a half billion people. Of course, if that country becomes fragmented and defeated, of course that would be a most destructive blow to the balance of power. On the other hand, everything we give to India adversely affects the balance of power with Pakistan, which is a much smaller country. So we are dealing with a very, very complicated problem because the hostility between them is so deep.

George Ball's trip was an attempt to lessen that. I think we are going to deal with a very unsatisfactory situation in that area. My judgment is that finally Pakistan would not make an alliance with China. I think she will continue to make it very clear to us her concern about the rearmament of India and her strong conviction that she must not be put at a military disadvantage in relationship to India. But that would be much different, I think, than a formal alliance, because that would change completely, of course, the SEATO relationship and all the rest.

So we are trying to balance off what is one of our more difficult problems. This is true, of course, in other areas, in the Middle East, but I would say it is most complicated right now in India. We had hoped that a settlement of the Kashmir dispute would bring about an improvement in the relations between the countries, but Kashmir is further from being settled today than it was 6 months ago. So I think we are just going to have to continue to work with this one.

Thank You.

Reporter: Thank you, Mr. President.

[1]Sidey, Hugh, "John F. Kennedy, President" (New York, Atheneum Publishers, 1963); Lasky, Victor, "JFK, the Man and the Myth" (New York, The Macmillan Co., 1963).

THE PRESIDENT'S NEWS CONFERENCE OF

OCTOBER 9, 1963

The President: I have a statement to make. The Soviet Union and various Eastern European countries have expressed a willingness to buy from our private grain dealers at the regular world price several million tons of surplus American wheat or wheat flour for shipment during the next several months. They may also wish to purchase from us surplus feed grains and other agricultural commodities.

After consultation with the National Security Council, and informing the appropriate leaders of the Congress, I have concluded that such sales by private dealers for American dollars or gold, either cash on delivery or normal commercial terms, should not be prohibited by the Government. The Commodity Credit Corporation in the Department of Agriculture will sell to our private grain traders the amount necessary to replace the grain used to fulfill these requirements, and the Department of Commerce will grant export licenses for their sale with the commitment that these commodities are for delivery to and use in the Soviet Union and Eastern Europe only.

An added feature is the provision that the wheat we sell to the Soviet Union will be carried in available American ships, supplemented by ships of other countries as required. Arrangements will also be made by the Department of Commerce to prevent any single American dealer from receiving an excessive share of these sales.

No action by the Congress is required, but a special report on the matter will be sent to both Houses tomorrow.

Basically, the Soviet Union will be treated like any other cash customer in the world market who is willing and able to strike a bargain with private American merchants. While this wheat, like all wheat sold abroad, will be sold at the world price, which is the only way it can be sold, there is in such transactions no subsidy to the foreign purchaser; only a savings to the American taxpayer on wheat the Government has already purchased and stored at the higher domestic price which is maintained to assist our farmers.

This transaction has obvious benefit for the United States. The sale of 4 million metric tons of wheat, for example, for an estimated $250 million, and additional sums from the use of American shipping, will benefit our balance of payments and gold reserves by that amount and substantially strengthen the economic outlook for those employed in producing, transporting, handling, and loading farm products.

Wheat, moreover, is our number one farm surplus today, to the extent of about 1 billion unsold bushels. The sale of around 150 million bushels of wheat would be worth over $200 million to the American taxpayer in reduced budget expenditures. Our country has always responded to requests for food from governments of people who needed it, so long as we were certain that the people would actually get it and know where it came from.

The Russian people will know they are receiving American wheat. The United States has never had a policy against selling consumer goods, including agricultural commodities, to the Soviet Union and Eastern Europe.. On the contrary, we have been doing exactly that for a number of years, and to the extent that their limited supplies of gold, dollars, and foreign exchange must be used for food, they cannot be used to purchase military or other equipment.

Our allies have long been engaged in extensive sales of wheat and other farm products to the Communist bloc, and, in fact, it would be foolish to halt the sales of our wheat when other countries can buy wheat from us today and then sell this flour to the Communists. In recent weeks Australia and NATO allies have agreed to sell 10 million to 15 million tons of wheat and wheat flour to the Communist bloc.

This transaction advertises to the world as nothing else could the success of free American agriculture. It demonstrates our willingness to relieve food shortages, to reduce tensions, and to improve relations with all countries. And it shows that peaceful agreements with the United States which serves the interests of both sides are a far more worthwhile course than a course of isolation and hostility.

For this Government to tell our grain traders that they cannot accept these offers, on the other hand, would accomplish little or nothing. The Soviets would continue to buy wheat and flour elsewhere, including wheat flour, from those nations which buy our wheat. Moreover, having for many years sold them farm products which are not in surplus, it would make no sense to refuse to sell those products on which we must otherwise pay the cost of storage. In short, this particular decision with respect to sales to the Soviet Union, which is not inconsistent with many smaller transactions over a long period of time, does not represent a new Soviet-American trade policy. That must await the settlement of many matters. But it does represent one more hopeful sign that a more peaceful world is both possible and beneficial to us all.

Q: Mr. President, do you have any misgivings about possible political repercussions from your decision?

The President: Well, I suppose there will be some who will disagree with this decision. That is true about most decisions. But I have considered it very carefully and I think it is very much in the interest of the United States. As I said before, we have got 1 billion bushels of this in surplus, and American taxpayers are paying to keep it, and I think we can use the $200 million or $250 million of gold which will help our balance of payments. I think it is in our interest, particularly in view of the fact that the sales are being made by other countries.

QUESTIONS

CIA Activities in Vietnam

Q: Mr. President, could you discuss some of the recent public accounts of CIA activities in South Viet-Nam, particularly the stories or reports of how the CIA has undertaken certain independent operations, or independent of other elements of the American Government, that are in South Viet-Nam?

The President: I must say I think the reports are wholly untrue. The fact of the matter is that Mr. McCone sits in the National Security Council. I imagine I see him at least three or four times a week, ordinarily. We have worked very closely together in the National Security Council in the last 2 months attempting to meet the problems we faced in South Viet-Nam. I can find nothing, and I have looked through the record very carefully over the last 9 months, and I could go back further, to indicate that the CIA has done anything but support policy. It does not create policy; it attempts to execute it in those areas where it has competence and responsibility. I know that the transfer of Mr. John Richardson, who is a very dedicated public servant, has led to surmises. But I can just assure you flatly that the CIA has not carried out independent activities but has operated under close control of the Director of Central Intelligence, operating with the cooperation of the National Security Council and under my instructions.

So I think that while the CIA may have made mistakes, as we all do, on different occasions, and has had many successes which may go unheralded, in my opinion in this case it is unfair to charge them as they have been charged. I think they have done a good job.

Objective of Talks with Gromyko

Q: Mr. President, you are meeting tomorrow with Soviet Foreign Minister Gromyko under somewhat different conditions than you met a year ago. I am wondering if you would care to give us your assessment of the principal objective of your talk tomorrow with him?

The President: Well, this continues to be an exchange of views on those matters which are at issue between the Soviet Union and the United States. In my speech before the General Assembly, I indicated those areas where the Soviet Union and the United States had disagreement. It is my hope that those disagreements will not lead to war. I am hopeful that what has happened in the last months will lessen that prospect. Really, what has happened since a year ago when I saw Mr. Gromyko will lessen the prospect of a military clash. But the differences go on. The systems are very different.

Mr. Khrushchev has said that there is no coexistence in the field of ideology. There are bound to be very severe matters which concern us on which the Soviet Union and the United States have very different views. As we don't want these disputes and frictions to escalate into military clashes, it is worthwhile to have consultations. The Secretary of State has been having them for several weeks, and I will see Mr. Gromyko this afternoon to just go over the ground which has already been laid by the Secretary of State.

Q: Mr. President, will you discuss with Mr. Gromyko the joint moon project proposal that you made before the U.N., and, if not, will that be pursued through some other channels?

The President: We have received no response to our - to that proposal, which followed other proposals made on other occasions. As I said, our space program from the beginning has been oriented towards the peaceful use of space. That is the way the National Space Agency was set up. That is the position we have taken since my predecessor's administration. I said this summer that we were anxious to cooperate in the peaceful exploration of space, but to do so, of course, requires the breakdown of a good many barriers which still exist. It is our hope those barriers, which represent barriers of some hostility, some suspicion, secrecy, and the rest, will come down. If they come down, of course, it would be possible for us to cooperate. So far, as you know, the cooperation has been limited to some exchange of information on weather and other rather technical areas.

We have had no indication, in short, that the Soviet Union is disposed to enter into the kind of relationship which would make a joint exploration of space or to the moon possible. But I think it is important that the United States continue to emphasize its peaceful interest and its preparation to go quite far in attempting to end the barrier which has existed between the Communist world and the West and to attempt to bring, as much as we can, the Communist world into the free world of diversity which we seek. So the matter may come up. But I must say we have had no response which would indicate that they are going to take us up on it.

Verification of the Ban on Nuclear Weapons in Outer Space

Q: Mr. President, in the reported agreement in principle between Russia and the United States to ban nuclear weapons from outer space, has the issue of verification come up in any way, and if so, in what way?

The President: No, there is not an agreement. The United States has stated it would not put weapons in outer space. We have no military use for doing so, and we would not do so. The Soviet Union has stated that it does not intend to. We are glad of that. There is no way we can verify that, but we are glad to hear the intention. We must recognize that there is no secure method of determining that someday they may not decide to do so. So we obviously have to take our own precautions. But we do not intend to, although we intend to protect our security, and we are glad to hear the Soviet Union does not intend to.

This is a matter, it seems to me, that can be best handled not through any bilateral agreement, but as a General Assembly matter, because other countries may someday have the capability, and I think every country should declare that they are not going to put atomic weapons in the atmosphere, which could threaten not only the security of a potential adversary, but our own security, if for some reason the weapons should miscalculate and descend on us. I think it is a good thing to keep them out of the atmosphere.

A Shorter Work Week

Q: Mr. President, last week in California, you said something that led some people to believe that you had changed your opposition to a shorter work-week. Is that correct?

The President: No, no, I am still opposed to it. What I was talking about was that inevitably as the century goes on, in my judgment, as machines increasingly take the place of men, that we will have more leisure, and there-fore we should take those steps in the field of conservation, resource develop-ment, and recreation, which will prepare us for that period. But that is not talking about today or tomorrow. It would be a great mistake for us to reduce our 40-hour workweek now. It would affect our competitive position abroad, and I think that the needs of American production are such that we ought to stick with our 40-hour week. I see the time coming, as I was saying, at the end of the century, perhaps sooner than that, when there may be a change in that, but not now.

Vietnam Policy

Q: Could you say, sir, how our policy is progressing in Viet-Nam in meet-ing what you established as desirable last month, a change of personnel and a change of policy that would help the government there better get on with the war?

The President: I don't think that there have been significant changes of the kind that ——

Q: For better or worse?

The President: I say I don't think there have been changes in the situa-tion in the last month. I think we are still dealing with the same problems we were dealing with a month ago.

U.S. Policy on Dictatorships in Latin America

Q: Mr. President, was Assistant Secretary Martin's statement cleared with you, and if so, does it represent a reversal of your policy on dictatorships in Latin America?

The President: No, I was informed generally of what Mr. Martin was saying, and in fact, I re-read it this afternoon. In the first place, our policy is not reversed. If attention could be drawn to Secretary Rusk's statement of Friday evening[1] in regard to the coups in the Dominican Republic and Honduras, we made it very clear that we are opposed to an interruption of the constitu-tional system by a military coup, not only because we are all committed under the Alliance for Progress to democratic government and progress and progressive government, but also because of course dictatorships are the seedbeds from which communism ultimately springs up.

So we are opposed to military coups, and it is for that reason that we have broken off our relations with the Dominican Republic and Honduras. It is for that reason that we attempted to work on the situation in Peru, which led, I think in part because of the American effort, mostly because of the Peruvian people's effort, to free elections.

Mr. Martin was merely attempting to explain some of the problems in Latin America, why coups take place, and what problems they present us with. But we are opposed to coups, because we think that they are defeating, self-defeating, and defeating for the hemisphere, and we are using our influence and I am sure the other countries of the hemisphere are using their influence in those areas where coups have taken place to provide for an orderly restoration of constitutional processes.

Q: Beyond the immediate action, sir, in relation to the Dominican Republic and Honduras, does the United States plan any general enunciation of policy in regard to military regimes, or does it contemplate asking any general hemispheric action in regard to this?

The President: Well, I have just described, I have just attempted to describe what our policy is towards coups. And as far as our national policy, it was described on Friday, with the withdrawal of our diplomatic - our Ambassadors, our aid, our military assistance, and all the rest. So I think we have made very clear our policy and our interest in providing for a return to, as I have said, constitutional processes in those two countries.

We are working with the other members of the Organization of American States so that together we can bring about a return to order in those countries and a return to peaceful procedures. This is the policy of the United States. I have just enunciated it again.

Q: I was asking specifically, sir, whether the United States contemplated any broader hemispheric action in terms of general action by the OAS in this respect.

The President: Not at this time. This is a matter which I think all the other countries of the OAS have to decide what they are going to do. I think the United States has made its position very clear.

Q: Mr. President, are you satisfied in retrospect that the United States did all it could, short of the use of force, to prevent the Dominican and Honduran coups?

The President: Yes, I am. I have looked over the conversations, the minutes, of cables and so on, and I think we did. This idea that we ought to send the United States Marines into Honduras, which, of course, we couldn't have done under the conditions, because of the time gap, I think is a very serious mistake. That is not the way, in my opinion, and I think Mr. Martin was attempting to explain that that is not the way for democracy to flourish.

So I think we did the best we could. It may be possible to always do better, but we did the best we could, and we are going to continue to do so.

Senator Goldwater's Candidacy

Q: Mr. President, there is a widespread impression that you expect Senator Barry Goldwater to be the Republican nominee for President next year. I think your speech in Salt Lake City had something to do with that. Is that your expectation?

The President: I think he can do it. I think it is possible for him to do it. But he has a long road to go, recalling the situation in September 1959, October 1959. I think Senator Goldwater has a trying 7 or 8 months which will test his endurance and his perseverance and his agility.

Q: Are you basing that on your own experience in 1960?

The President: Yes.

Q: Former President Eisenhower wrote recently in an article that he was unclear about Senator Goldwater's views on certain major issues. I wonder, sir, whether you share this uncertainty and if so how you think Senator Gold-water should better express himself.

The President: Senator Goldwater is speaking frequently, and he is saying what he thinks as of the time he speaks, and I think, therefore, we have an opportunity to make a judgment of where he stands. I don't think Senator Goldwater has ever been particularly deceptive. I think he has made very clear what he is opposed to, what he is for. I have gotten the idea. I think that President Eisenhower will, as time goes on.

Other Democratic Candidates

Q: Mr. President, to keep the ball rolling, there are a couple of obvious candidates in another party who say they are going to make their announcement of their decisions in December or January. Have you set a timetable for yourself or are you already a candidate?

The President: No, no, I think I will wait - this next year - I can wait longer.

The Valachi Crime Committee

Q: Mr. President, the Valachi crime committee hearings are getting very mixed reviews. As a former congressional investigator, I wonder whether you feel they are serving any useful purpose?

The President: No, I wouldn't want - I haven't commented on the Senate procedures and I wouldn't now on this hearing or other hearings. That is a judgment for Senator McClellan and the committee. I do think that we shouldn't get a distorted idea from the hearings. I think - particularly as Columbus Day comes up I think there may be some feeling of some people that the name Valachi perhaps causes embarrassment to other American citizens. I don't think it should. These difficulties occur in a good many different racial groups, and I think that they ought to feel a good deal of pride in what they have done and not be concerned because a Valachi or an Irish name or some other name may occasionally get in trouble.

Labor Statistics

Q: Mr. President, Congressman Pucinski of Illinois has said to me, and I think he has proposed to Secretary Wirtz, that we should have three categories instead of two in our labor statistics, general statistics. He is proposing that we have employed, unemployed, and unemployables, because of their lack of skills. Would you agree with the Congressman that this would be helpful in highlighting the problem we have in employment and education?

The President: I wouldn't want to put it in that kind of a category. I think I can see there might be some merit in trying to mark out those who are unemployed because of structural unemployment, those who are unemployed because of the seasonal nature of their work, those who are unemployed because of illiteracy or lack of motivation - we have a good deal of it - a good deal of technical information, but I don't think I would label anybody in the United States unemployable.

A CIA Watchdog Committee

Q: Mr. President, how do you feel about Senator Gruening's proposal to set up a congressional committee as a watchdog over the CIA?

The President: I think the present committees – there's one in both the House and Senate which maintains very close liaison with the CIA – are best, considering the sensitive nature of the Central Intelligence Agency's work.

As you know, there is a congressional committee in the House, one in the Senate, composed of members of the Appropriations Committee and the Armed Services Committee. They meet frequently with Mr. McCone. He also testifies before the Foreign Relations Committees of House and Senate and the general Armed Services Committee. And I think the Congress has through that organization the means of keeping a liaison with him.

In addition, I have an Advisory Council which was headed by Dr. Killian formerly, now Mr. Clark Clifford, which includes Jimmie Doolittle and others, and Robert Murphy, who also served as an advisory committee to me on the work of the intelligence community. I am well satisfied with the present arrangement.

The Senate Internal Security Subcommittee

Q: Sir, there seems to be some connection between the attempt of the State Department to discharge Mr. Otto Otepka, the Security Officer, there seems to be some connection between the fact that he gave much information to the Senate Internal Security Subcommittee about various employees of the State Department - William Arthur Wieland and Walt W. Rostow and many others. Also Secretary Rusk has now put forth an order that employees of the State Department cannot talk or give information to this congressional committee. Isn't that a direct violation of law?

The President: No, it isn't.

Q: That Government employees are allowed to give information to Members of Congress and to committees?

The President: By what means? You mean secret dispatches?

Q: Well, any information. The law doesn't say what it will be. It says that any Government employee can give information to Members of Congress or to the committees.

The President: Well, let me just say that the Secretary of State has been prepared to testify since August before the Internal Security Committee and discuss the case very completely ——

Q: Well, but ——

The President: Excuse me. There was a hearing scheduled for early September, but because of the Labor Day weekend that hearing did not take place. The Secretary of State stands ready; he is the responsible officer. Now the best thing to do is to give the Secretary of State a chance to explain the entire case, because in all frankness your analysis of it is not complete.

Q: Would you like to complete it, sir?

The President: Well, I will be glad to have the Secretary of State talk to the Internal Security Committee about what it is that has caused action to be taken, administrative action within the Department of State, to be taken against the gentleman that you have named, the kind of actions he carried out, what the law said, how he met the law, how he didn't meet the law. This is all a matter which is going to be heard by the State Department board. Then it will be heard by the Civil Service Commission for review. Then it can be discussed in the courts.

In the meanwhile the Senate subcommittee can have all the information that it requires as to why Secretary Rusk has taken the action that he has. I think that is the best procedure. And I can assure you that I will examine the matter myself, when it comes time, as the Secretary of State will, who bears the responsibility, when it comes time to take any disciplinary action, if such a time does come.

Price Increases in Steel

Q: Mr. President, last spring there were selective price increases in steel, recently there have been price increases in steel. Are you concerned about these increases, sir, and do you feel you are going to take any action about them?

The President: Well, we are watching very carefully the rises which have taken place in certain industries. This country has avoided an inflationary spiral. We see no reason why there should be one now. The Wholesale Price Index has remained relatively constant for 5 years. We are concerned that price increases in one or two basic areas may stimulate other price increases which will affect adversely our competitive position abroad, and therefore affect our balance of payments, therefore affect our national interest.

In addition, profits are at a record high now – they have never been higher in history. The whole year of 1963 looks very good and, therefore, we should be concerned also with reducing prices as well as increasing them. For the time being we are watching the matter with concern and will continue in the days ahead to do so.

Giving Commercial Credits to the USSR

Q: Mr. President, has there been an official ruling that giving commercial credits to Russia would not violate the Johnson act?

The President: Yes, that is correct, because it is not a government transaction.

Q: Is it not a government-to-government?

The President: It is not a government-to-government. These are private traders that will be involved and the credit will be granted by banks. In the case of Canada, as you know, the terms were 25 percent down, 25 percent then for every 6 months for a period of 18 months. But because the interest rate was of a certain figure, I think 4 7/8 percent, the Soviets decided to pay cash and, therefore, paid something like 80 percent cash. We will be dealing on the same matter with them on interest rates. Our interest rates would be slightly higher than the Canadian rate, possibly, under the private commercial system, and it may be that they will decide, therefore, to pay a very large percentage in cash.

But I have gotten a ruling from the Department of Justice that this does not contravene existing laws, particularly the Johnson act.

Q: Will the grain dealers take the risk, then?

The President: The grain dealers will take the risk with the private banks.

Allen Dulles' Comments About the CIA, State Department and Vietnam

Q: Mr. President, former head of the CIA Allen Dulles said in an interview in the Journal American today that reports of disputes between the CIA and the

State Department and various branches of the government in South Viet-Nam have arisen because "of a lack of a clearcut operational policy in Washington." And he goes on to say that he thinks what is needed is less backbiting between U.S. agency officials. In view of the defense you just gave CIA, would you care to agree with the Dulles charge or contest it?

The President: I would agree with the last part of it, that the agencies – as we all know, they are faced with a very difficult problem in South Viet-Nam, which we are all familiar with, both on the military and political side. Men have different views about what actions we should take, and they talk to members of the press, to all of you, in Saigon and here in Washington. But I must say that as of today, and I think this is particularly true since General Taylor and Secretary McNamara came back, I know of no disagreement between the State Department at the top, CIA at the top, Defense at the top, the White House and Ambassador Lodge, on what our basic policies will be and what steps we will take to implement it. Now if down below there is disagreement, I think in part it will be because they are not wholly informed of what actions we are taking. Some of them are necessarily confidential. But I think our policy, though we can't say what effect it is going to have, I think we are in agreement about what we ought to do. I would think that Saigon, and personnel in the various agencies, should support that policy, because that is the policy we are going to carry out for a while.

U.S. Wheat Shipment to the USSR

Q: Mr. President, if I understood you correctly on the wheat statement, you said the Russian people will know they are receiving American wheat.

The President: That is correct.

Q: Is that by some agreement with the Soviet Union or how would that come about?

The President: No, but we have our own means of informing the Soviet Union. As you know, for many months the Voice of America has not been blocked, for example, and therefore we believe that we have adequate means to inform the Russian people of the arrangement.

In addition, I am not sure that there is any reason for the Russians themselves to keep it quiet as it is a commercial transaction. But in any case, we have the means to provide that knowledge.

Administration Assets and Liabilities

Q: Mr. President, as the election year approaches, there is an unusual amount of political activity already, as the questions reflect. I wonder if you would give us your thinking as an experienced politician as to the prime assets of your administration next year, and the prime liabilities of your administration?

The President: I think that you would not want to – as we only have a relatively short time, I think we ought to make a judgment on that in 1964. And I say that without any – a lot of these matters we will have to decide whether the United States is better off economically than it was before, and whether our position in the world has improved, and whether our prospects for peace are greater, and whether our defenses are stronger, and whether we are making progress at home and abroad. That is a matter which it seems to me will be argued very strongly in '64. For example, we can't make a judgment about the state of the economy in '64. I think if they pass our tax bill, we are going to be able to demonstrate a very successful, ebullient economy for a period of 4 years. If they do not, we will have a different situation.

I cannot tell what our relations will be in Southeast Asia a year from now. I know what results our policy is attempting to bring. But I think that result ought to be judged in the summer of '64 and the fall of '64, and I have hopes that the judgment will be that the economy is moving ahead, that the rate of growth has been almost $100 billion, will have been from about $500 billion to $600 billion, that we are substantially stronger militarily, that the chances of war have been reduced over Berlin and perhaps in other areas. But I would not want to make these judgments now, because I think we still have a long way to go before next summer, and I think that to say that this is the end of the road would be a mistake. I think we ought to be judged by what we do over a 4-year period, and that is the way it is going to be. It is too early now.

Impressions from the President's Trip to the West and South

Q: Could I ask one final thing, sir? Have you brought back any dominant impressions from your two recent trips in the West and South, political impressions?

The President: I would say we are going to have a hard, close fight in 1964. But that has been my impression for a good many months.

Reporter: Thank you, Mr. President.

[1]Secretary Rusk's statement of October 4 is published in the Department of State Bulletin (vol. 49. p. 624). The statement by Edwin M. Martin, Assistant Secretary of State for Inter-American Affairs, is also published therein (vol. 49, p. 698).

THE PRESIDENT'S NEWS CONFERENCE OF

OCTOBER 31, 1963

The President: Good afternoon.

QUESTIONS

Removal of American Forces from Europe

Q: Mr. President, I wonder, could you tell us something about this Government's policy toward reports we hear from Europe and from here about removal of American forces from Europe, or reduction in the size or the strength of American personnel in Europe?

The President: Yes. I think that Secretary Rusk explained quite clearly the American policy last weekend, as he reaffirmed it. The policy of the United States is to maintain 6 divisions in Germany, as long as they are required. In addition to these 6 divisions, and over and above our NATO commitments, we sent to Germany as temporary reinforcements during the Berlin crisis of 1961, 6 combat units consisting of 3 artillery battalions, 2 armored battalions, and 1 armored cavalry regiment.

This augmentation of U.S. forces in Germany was made to help meet the deficiency of other NATO members in fulfilling their commitments at a very crucial time when the buildup of West Germany's own forces was incomplete. Although some of these deficiencies have been corrected, and the German force buildup is progressing, we are prepared to keep these additional combat units in Germany as long as there is a need for them.

Thus, we are not planning any reduction in United States combat units in Germany. As part of the reorganization of the Army's European logistic forces, we are planning some reduction in noncombat personnel, a matter on which of course we are in touch with our allies.

But we do not intend to bring back any units or personnel whose return would impair the military effectiveness of our forces in Germany. In short, we intend to keep our combat forces in Germany as they are today - that is, more than 6 combat divisions.

Q: Mr. President, that being so, how many human beings are we going to bring back from our European stations now?

The President: Well, any we bring back may include some supply forces or ——

Q: As much as a regiment, sir?

The President: Well, we have over, I think, 240,000 or 250,000, so a regiment is a very small - less than a percent of that, so I am sure that there will be movements in and out. But we are talking about the whole European theater. But, in the case of Germany, I think it is important to make this clear, the 6 divisions which are our NATO commitment, are being kept. In addition, these other combat units are being kept in Germany also. If there is any change in personnel, and I am sure there will be some, it will be in logistic forces. There have been some changes, for example, in our logistic supply lines in France. There may be some changes in headquarters units and all the rest. They are relatively small. They may be spaced over a period of time. But our combat effectiveness, of course, is increasing as our material increases.

Q: Will these 6 divisions, sir, be kept at conventional divisional strength?

The President: That is correct. There will be no change, no change in the number of combat forces in Germany; no change in the number of these extra forces which, as I have said, are beyond our NATO commitment but which will be also kept in Germany.

Q: Mr. President, you spoke of some deficiencies. Who is falling short?

The President: We are talking about deficiencies in 1961, when we were having a serious crisis in Berlin and where the NATO forces were inadequate. And, as you know, I think the Secretary of State made a reference to the fact that a number of our allies had not, and in some cases have not, met their NATO commitments today, with the number of forces that should be stationed in Germany for the defense of Germany.

Q: But we still have to keep these troops there, although apparently, because ——

The President: There has been a buildup since 1961, particularly among the German forces, whose target is 12 divisions. Some other countries have not met their quota. But we are keeping our forces there primarily because we believe that it emphasizes the commitment of the United States to the defense of the Federal Republic, and our concern about the defense of Europe. In addition, it should be pointed out that the Federal Republic, West Germany, is purchasing military equipment in the United States which provides an offset to our gold losses for our forces in the Federal Republic. So they are making an effort and so are we, and we are going to continue to do it.

Senator Goldwater's Accusation

Q: Mr. President, Senator Goldwater accused your administration today of falsification of the news in order to perpetuate itself in office. Do you care to comment on that?

The President: What was he referring to?

Q: He was making a speech here at the Women's National Press Club, and his point was that you and your administration are mismanaging the news, and using it to perpetuate yourself in office.

The President: Well, as I have said before, I think it would be unwise at this time to answer or reply to Senator Goldwater. I am confident that he will be making many charges even more serious than this one in the coming months. And, in addition, he himself has had a busy week selling TVA and giving permission to or suggesting that military commanders overseas be permitted to use nuclear weapons, and attacking the President of Bolivia while he was here in the United States, and involving himself in the Greek election. So I thought it really would not be fair for me this week to reply to him.

Troop Reductions in the Far East

Q: Mr. President, back to the question of troop reductions, are any intended in the Far East at the present time, particularly in Korea, and is there any speedup in the withdrawal from Viet-Nam intended?

The President: Well, as you know, when Secretary McNamara and General Taylor came back, they announced that we would expect to withdraw a thousand men from South Viet-Nam before the end of the year, and there has been some reference to that by General Harkins. If we are able to do that, that would be our schedule. I think the first unit or first contingent would be 250 men who are not involved in what might be called front-line operations. It would be our hope to lessen the number of Americans there by 1,000, as the training intensifies and is carried on in South Viet-Nam. As far as other units, we will have to make our judgment based on what the military correlation of forces may be. We are becoming increasingly mobile, as the Big Lift Operation suggests.

What is important in the case that Mr. Smith was talking about, we not only have these divisions that I described there, but we have - after the '61 experience, we moved equipment for 2 more divisions. So during the Big Lift, we actually have 7 divisions. So that we are able to move around the world much faster, and with new planes which are beginning to come off the production line, particularly the ones in Marietta, Ga., out of Lockheed. And so we are going to have increased airlift capacity over the next 2 or 3 years. So naturally our force will be more mobile.

The Philadelphia Mayoral Election and Civil Rights

Q: Mr. President, on the basis of your experience in Philadelphia, yesterday and last night, will you regard next Tuesday's mayoral election as a test of how civil rights will affect the voting?

The President: In Philadelphia, or just —

Q: In Philadelphia, yes - as well as in other large northern cities.

The President: I am sure that that may be a factor in the election, although I am not sure that the two candidates have taken different positions, but I suppose this is a matter of major concern in the country today, and it may be reflected in the voting. As I say, I am not aware, although it may be, that the candidates have taken different positions on it. My guess would be that they have taken relatively the same position on the question.

Q: The question is whether or not there will be some backlash from white minority voters against the Democrats because of their pushing of civil rights.

The President: Well, I - it is possible. We will have to wait and see, though, as I have said from the beginning, it seems to me both parties have taken a clear position historically and at present on civil rights. But there may be. We will have to wait and see Tuesday, and I am sure that a good many things will be written into it.

The Yemen Situation

Q: Mr. President, the United Nations Secretary General U Thant has withdrawn the mission from Yemen, which was supposed to secure peace and the withdrawal of Nasser's troops from Yemen. Since you are sponsoring this effort, could you tell us what further steps you have in mind?

The President: Well, he is keeping his political people there and we are still hopeful that the governments of Saudi Arabia and the U.A.R. will come to some conclusion, either bilaterally or with the Secretary General, which will permit the cease-fire to be maintained, and the withdrawal which has been limited to be expanded. So, I have not given up on the hope of keeping that cease-fire.

Q: (Inaudible). — is not thinking of any bilateral moves?

The President: No. We have expressed our great interest in seeing that fighting does not break out along the border, and I think it would be unfortunate if it did. We have indicated that to the countries involved. I am hopeful, as I say, that perhaps they will be able to work it out bilaterally, or at least keep a cease-fire.

The Resignation of Secretary Korth

Q: Mr. President, do you think the letters that Secretary of the Navy Korth wrote made his resignation advisable, and was it requested?

The President: I think the letters which Mr. Korth and I exchanged explain the situation as I would like to see it explained.

Mr. Korth, I think, worked hard for the Navy and he indicated his desire to return to private life and I accepted that decision. But I think he worked hard for the Navy.

The Dehumanization of Work

Q: Mr. President, thousands of jobs are lost every week to automation. The Federal Government is one of the leaders in automation. Do you think it is good for us, as human beings, to dehumanize work and sacrifice people to machines and money?

The President: Well, I think it is all a question of degree and how it is done. Obviously, most of the comforts we now enjoy are the result of automation, technology over a period of 100 or 150 years, and there were, historically, efforts at various times to stop the introduction of machines which made the labor of men easier.

So automation does not need to be, we hope, our enemy. What is of concern now is this combination of a rather intensive period of automation, plus the fact that our educational system is not keeping up, so that we are graduating or dropping out of high school so many millions of young men and women who are not able to operate in this new society who have only physical labor to perform and they can't find enough jobs.

So that is what concerns us. Now, as you know, job retraining is important in that area, vocational training. We are trying to combat school dropouts, trying to urge families to keep their children in school, and all the rest of these efforts with which you are familiar.

We have a proposal before the Congress for a new analysis of automation. In answer to your question: I think machines can make life easier for men, if men do not let the machines dominate them. And it is our intention to try to see that life is easier. The fact is, life is easier because of machines, and I think it can provide new jobs, but I think it is going to take a good deal of wisdom by those of us in the Government as well as labor and management.

Sale of Wheat to the USSR

Q: Mr. President, last week there was a certain amount of optimism that a sale of wheat would soon be reached for the Soviet Union. And a lot of this optimism seems to be gone in the last couple of days. I wonder if you could tell us quite precisely what seems to be holding up the sale and whether you are optimistic that the sale will go through?

The President: We are involved in negotiations which, of course, are very intensive and it seems to me that this is the week when these negotiations are reaching a critical phase. I don't think that it would be useful for me to comment on them. I think we ought to know in the next days whether we are going to be successful in completing our sale. But obviously this is a matter in which the seller and the buyer have interests which are not always harmonious and we have to reach the best bargain possible. That is what they want and that is what we want, and so I think we ought to let the negotiators negotiate.

General David Shoup

Q: Mr. President, do you expect to use General David Shoup's services in the Government after he leaves?

The President: I would hope so. I would hope so - if he will - I would like to have him stay.

The President's Appraisal of His Job

Q: Mr. President, just shortly after the Bay of Pigs I asked you how you liked being President, as I remember you said you liked it better before the event. Now you have had a chance to appraise your job, and why do you like it and why do you want to stay in office 4 more years?

The President: Well, I find the work rewarding. Whether I am going to stay and what my intentions are and all of the rest, it seems to me it is still a good many, many months away. But as far as the job of President goes, it is rewarding. And I have given before to this group the definition of happiness of the Greeks, and I will define it again: it is full use of your powers along lines of excellence. I find, therefore, the Presidency provides some happiness.

Negotiations with the Dominican Junta

Q: Mr. President, there have been persistent reports in recent days that the State Department is negotiating with the Junta in the Dominican Republic looking toward a resumption of full diplomatic relations. Are these reports true, and is there some basis on which we would be willing to recognize the present Junta?

The President: Well, there have been conversations in the Dominican Republic to see what assurances can be given regarding the restoration of democratic rule, constitutional rule in the Dominican Republic. We have a chargé d'affaires there, and quite obviously we are interested in that restoration. Those assurances are of free elections, so we are continuing to carry out these discussions, although actually they are relatively informal, and they have reaped no harvest as yet. But that would be our policy to attempt to see if we can resume relations with the Dominican Republic under assurances of a restoration of constitutional government. As yet we have had no success.

USSR Wheat Sale

Q: Sir, when you approved the sale of wheat to the Soviet Union, you placed a condition on the sales that the shipments be in U.S. flagships to the extent that they were available. I wonder if you could explain to us how you came to place this condition on it; what the genesis of that condition was.

The President: No, I think we ought to let the negotiators negotiate this week. I don't mean to be evasive, but I think we ought to let those who are representing the United States point of view, we ought to give them a free hand. So I would rather not get into a discussion of the wheat deal. Next week I am sure we can.

Russian Troops in Cuba

Q: Mr. President, could you tell us how many Russian troops there are in Cuba now and what you ——

The President: No, I don't think we can ever give a precise figure. All I can say is that the numbers have steadily been reduced, and in the last 2 months there have been further reductions and since the first of January there has been a marked decrease in the number of troops in Cuba, according to all our intelligence estimates. I couldn't give you a precise number that are still there, but I can give you a - the general trend is outward.

Expansion of Trade with the USSR

Q: Mr. President, since you approved the wheat sale, other groups have come along and suggested we sell other products to the Russians, too, surplus butter, for example. And Congressman Cooley says maybe if we send them some tobacco it will quiet their nerves a little bit. Would you favor expanding this list to other farm surpluses, if they are interested?

The President: They have shown no interest in anything else, but they may show interest if this deal is consummated, and I would be responsive to any further request they made for farm commodities. But first, we have to get this deal. I think this is the bellwether.

Secretary McNamara's Rejection of the Atomic Power Plant

for the New American Carrier

Q: Mr. President, can you explain Secretary McNamara's rejection of the atomic power plant for the new carrier in the face of the experts, like Admiral Rickover and Chairman Seaborg, and others who think it is necessary? And will the same policy go over to the other warships that the Navy wants, of over 8,000 tons, with the atomic energy power?

The President: No, we are going to build a conventional carrier, which has already been announced at this time. That is what we think that the Navy needs. Now, we are not going to make any final decision until a later date on whether we are going to have nuclear power for important ships of the Navy.

As you suggest, there is no use having a nuclear carrier unless we have the ships that accompany it - and after all, there is a large train with a carrier - unless they have nuclear power. So that it requires a rather large investment. In the case of the nuclear carrier, it is about $160 million or $170 million more. If you add up the other ships that might have to accompany, it, it gets into a large sum of money. What is the mission of the carrier? What is it going to be used for - limited war or strategic attack? What is the best use of that extra money? I think I am supporting Secretary McNamara in the decision that he has made so far in this matter.

Race Relations in Birmingham

Q: Mr. President, the United States Steel Corporation has rejected the idea that it should use economic pressure in an effort to improve race relations in Birmingham, Ala. Do you have any comments on that position and do you have any counsel for management and labor in general as to their social responsibility in areas of tension of this kind?

The President: Actually, Mr. Blough has been somewhat helpful in one or two cases that I can think of in Birmingham. I don't think he should narrowly interpret his responsibility for the future. That is a very influential company in Birmingham, and he wants to see that city prosper, as do we all.

Obviously, the Federal Government cannot solve this matter, so that business has a responsibility - labor, and of course every citizen. So I would think that particularly a company which is as influential as United States Steel in Birmingham, I would hope would use its influence on the side of comity between the races.

Otherwise, the future of Birmingham, of course, is not as happy as we would hope it would be. In other words, it can't be decided, this matter, in Washington. It has to be decided by citizens everywhere. Mr. Blough is an influential citizen. I am sure he will do the best he can.

Conflicts of Interest

Q: Mr. President, you have signed one Executive order and one law banning conflicts of interest on the part of executive branch employees. In the light of recent events on Capitol Hill, do you think that that law should be broadened to cover members of Congress and congressional employees?

The President: Well, I think that we ought to wait until the investigation is over. It has only begun, and it is a matter which Congress of course would have to consider. But I think that perhaps out of the investigation there may come a decision to develop new rules, procedures, or laws, but I would rather wait until the Congress has had the hearing and then we can make a better judgment about that.

The Moon Race

Q: Mr. President, do you think that Premier Khrushchev has actually taken the Soviet Union out of the so-called moon race, and in any case do you think that the United States should proceed as if there were a moon race?

The President: I didn't read that into his statement. I thought his statement was rather cautiously worded and I did not get any assurances that Mr. Khrushchev or the Soviet Union were out of the space race at all.

I think it is remarkable that some people who were so unwilling to accept our test ban treaty, where there was a very adequate area of verification of whatever the Soviet Union was doing, were perfectly ready to accept Mr. Khrushchev's very guarded, careful, cautious remark that he was taking himself out of the space race and use that as an excuse for us to abandon our efforts.

The fact of the matter is that the Soviets have made an intensive effort in space, and there is every indication that they are continuing and that they have the potential to continue. I would read Mr. Khrushchev's remarks very carefully. I think that he said before anyone went to the moon, there should be adequate preparation. We agree with that.

In my opinion the space program we have is essential to the security of the United States, because as I have said many times before, it is not a question of going to the moon. It is a question of having the competence to master this environment. And I would not make any bets at all upon Soviet intentions. I think that our experience has been that we wait for deeds, unless we have a system of verification, and we have no idea whether the Soviet Union is going to make a race for the mood or whether it is going to attempt an even greater program.

I think we ought to stay with our program. I think that is the best answer to Mr. Khrushchev.

Q: Mr. President, it still continues to be the fact that we have had no responses to your proposal for a joint moon exploration?

The President: That is correct. In addition, the two astronauts of the Soviet Union earlier that week had made a statement saying the Soviet Union was prepared to go on lunar expeditions, so I think that we should not disregard our whole carefully worked out program which is being carried on very impressively in Huntsville, Ala., and in other places, merely because Mr. Khrushchev gave a rather Delphic interview to some correspondents.

Castro's Alleged Capture of American CIA Agents

Q: Mr. President, Fidel Castro claims to have captured some Americans whom he says are CIA agents, and he says he is going to execute them. Is there anything at all that you can tell us about this.

The President: No, no.

Bilateral Air Transport Agreement

Q: Mr. President, what is the status of the bilateral air transport agreement between the United States and Russia?

The President: It was initiated some months ago, more than a year ago, in fact a year and a half ago, and there are still some technical matters which have to be discussed before it can be formally signed.

Q: Are you optimistic of it being signed, and if so, when?

The President: I think there is a good chance it will be signed; yes.

The Building of a National Environmental Health Research Center

Q: Mr. President, as you know, the plan to build a National Environmental Health Research Center has been hung up in Congress. Apparently they can't decide where to build it. Now there is a report that you would like it built in North Carolina. Would you?

The President: North Carolina would be very acceptable. I think the Budget recommendation was Maryland, but North Carolina does have the facilities. But I think in our recommendations we made, HEW made, the first recommendation was Maryland. The site in North Carolina is a good one, as there is a triangle there of colleges and hospitals and medical facilities. And I have indicated that that would be satisfactory, if that was the judgment of the Congress. I think our first choice was Maryland.

The Vice-President's Status

Q: Mr. President, in spite of something you said here in May 1962, there is talk that Lyndon Johnson will be dumped next year. Senator Thruston Morton used the word "purged." Now, sir, assuming that you run next year, would you want Lyndon Johnson on the ticket, and do you expect that he will be on the ticket?

The President: Yes, to both of those questions. That is correct.

Secretary Korth's Problems

Q: Mr. President, Navy Secretary Korth had some correspondence which indicated he worked very hard for the Continental National Bank of Fort Worth while he was in Government, as well as for the Navy, and that during this same period of time that he negotiated, or took part in the decision on a contract involving that bank's - one of that bank's best customers, the General Dynamics firm. I wonder if this fulfills the requirements of your Code of Ethics in Government, and if, in a general way, you think that it is within the law and proper?

The President: In the case of the contract - the TFX contract - as you know, that matter was referred to the Department of Justice to see whether there was a conflict of interest and the judgment was that there was not. That is number one.

Number two, the amount of the loan to the company. That bank was one of a number of banks which participated in a line of credit and it was relatively a small amount of money, as bank loans go. So in answer to your question, I have no evidence that Mr. Korth acted in any way improperly in the TFX matter. It has nothing to do with any opinion I may have about whether Mr. Korth might have written more letters and been busier than he should have been in one way or another.

The fact of the matter is, I have no evidence that Mr. Korth benefited improperly during his term of office in the Navy. And I have no evidence, and you have not, as I understand it - the press has not produced any, nor the McClellan committee - which would indicate that in any way he acted improperly in the TFX. I always have believed that innuendoes should be justified before they are made, either by me, in the Congress, or even in the press.

Debating Senator Goldwater

Q: Mr. President, Senator Goldwater also said today that if he is nominated, the Republican - for the Republican President - if he is the Republican Presidential nominee, he will gladly debate you. Would you accept this challenge?

The President: Well, I have indicated that I was going to debate if I were renominated.

The Quality Stabilization Bill

Q: Mr. President, a number of your congressional leaders have said they favor the so-called quality stabilization bill, but all of your executive departments are opposed to it. Can you tell us what your views are on this legislation?

The President: Well, that hasn't come to me as yet. I am not - I have never been for the quality stabilization bill. I will have to look at the bill when it finally comes and the form it is in. I can't comment on the legislation before it finally comes to the desk of the White House, but the administration witnesses have spoken my views.

The Accelerated Works Program and Unemployment

Q: Mr. President, unemployment is just about as high today as it was a year ago, but there are rumors that the administration has given up on getting Congress to extend the accelerated public works program. Is this a fact?

The President: No. The amount of money that is in the public works program runs through July so that there is still a good deal of money that is available for public works under that program.

Q: Doesn't the act, sir, expire in January?

The President: The amount of money, though, given the pipeline runs through July. So this is not a matter for immediate decision before us.

Decision on Otto Otepka

Q: Sir, would you please tell us what is going to be the final decision on Mr. Otto Otepka, the Security Officer of the State Department, who is up for firing? And would you please, in a related question, tell us what was the final decision on whether the State Department employees can go before the Senate Internal Security Subcommittee and answer questions?

The President: Well, I don't think any final decision has been made on Mr. Otepka. I think there is a hearing scheduled in the next few days on the matter. And I have said to you before that the Secretary of State would study the matter and so would I before any final decision is reached. Of course, if a decision is reached of the kind you described, it would be possible for him to appeal to the Civil Service Commission.

Now, the question of - I have no objection, and I think it would be perfectly appropriate, for any employee of the Federal Government to appear before any congressional committee. I would think it would be proper that the head of the department would be notified, but I am sure that they will give permission.

The Decision for Troops to Remain in Germany

Q: Mr. President, a little while ago you said that our present force of combat troops would remain in Germany as long as they are required. I wondered whether you planned to be the sole determiner of that or whether it would be a bilateral or a NATO-wide proposition.

The President: I would think it would be a NATO - well, it would certainly be discussed in NATO, and, of course, the country particularly affected, in this case the Federal Republic. Its views would have very heavy weight, very heavy weight. I am sure that no action would be taken which would not meet the needs of the country involved, the Federal Republic as well as our own.

International Inspection and the Test Ban Treaty

Q: Mr. President, in negotiating the limited nuclear test ban treaty we and the Russians avoided the issue of international inspection by limiting it to the three environments in which that, theoretically, was not required. Now we have joined at the U.N. in proposing a wider ban, including underground tests. Is there anything new in the state of the art of detection or in our understanding of the Soviet position that leads us to hope we can get anywhere with this approach?

The President: I am doubtful that we can get any place. We are still insisting on inspection. The Soviet Union is still resisting inspection. And therefore, unless the art of seismology improves, I would think we would not get an agreement. Sometime it may improve so that it is not necessary for us to have the kind of detailed inspections that we believe necessary or perhaps the Soviet Union will change its policy. I would hope either event would occur. For the present, I am not optimistic.

Reporter: Thank you, Mr. President.

THE PRESIDENT'S NEWS CONFERENCE OF

NOVEMBER 14, 1963

The President: Good morning, gentlemen and ladies.

QUESTIONS

The Cambodian Situation

Q: *Mr. President, how menacing do you regard the Cambodian threat to re-ject our foreign aid, and can that country be slipping into the Communist orbit?*

The President: Well, I regard it as serious. It is my hope that Prince Sihanouk, who must be concerned about the independence and the sovereignty of his country - he has after all been involved for many years in maintaining that independence - will not decide at this dangerous point in the world's affairs to surrender it. I would think that he is more concerned about Cambodian in-dependence than we are. After all, he is a Cambodian. So my judgment is that in the long run he would protect that independence. It would be folly not to, and I don't think he is a foolish man.

Professor Barghoorn

Q: *Mr. President, how do you regard the case involving Professor Barghoorn, and what are we doing about getting his release from the Russian Government?*

The President: As you know, the American Ambassador - the United States Embassy has made six protests to the Soviet Government in the last 48 hours. Ambassador Kohler has been to the Soviet Foreign Ministry personally. The United States Government is deeply concerned about the unwarranted and unjus-tified arrest of Professor Barghoorn, by the fact that he was held for a number of days without the United States being informed of it, and that the United States officials in the Soviet Union have not had an opportunity to visit with him. He was not on an intelligence mission of any kind. He is a distinguish-ed professor of Soviet affairs, he has played a most helpful and constructive role in arranging cultural exchanges, scientific exchanges. We are concerned not only for his personal safety, but because this incident, I think, can have a most serious effect upon what we understood the Soviet Government's strong hope was, certainly our hope, that we would find a widening of cultural intel-lectual exchanges. We have heard from a good many universities and private organizations, which have expressed their alarm - been taking part in these exchanges - and it is quite clear that the Professor's early release is es-sential if these programs are to be continued.

I can assure you that the Department of State, our Embassy in Moscow, will do everything it can to effect the early release of the Professor. His arrest is unjustified. I repeat again: he was *not* on an intelligence mission of any kind. I am hopeful that this will become quickly obvious to the Soviet Union and that they will release him.

Q: *Mr. President, some persons view Professor Barghoorn's arrest as a sign the Soviets are now deliberately seizing innocent Americans with the aim of later swapping them for some of their convicted espionage agents or that the Soviets may be doing this with the hope of somehow extracting political concessions from us. How would you view any such tactics?*

The President: I wouldn't think - obviously they would not be successful. I wouldn't attempt to make a judgment as to the conduct of the Soviet Union, or what may motivate it from week to week, day to day, but I am certainly - it is quite obvious that if it is based on the presumptions you state, that it will not be successful.

Resumption of Trade with Red China

Q: Mr. President, what are the prerequisites or conditions for resumption of some sort of trade with Red China?

The President: We are not planning to trade with Red China in view of the policy that Red China pursues. When the Red Chinese indicate a desire to live at peace with the United States, with other countries surrounding it, then quite obviously the United States would reappraise its policies. We are not wedded to a policy of hostility to Red China. It seems to me Red China's policies are what create the tension between not only the United States and Red China but between Red China and India, between Red China and her immediate neighbors to the south, and even between Red China and other Communist countries.

The Tax Bill and Civil Rights Bill

Q: Mr. President, it now seems unlikely that you will get either your tax bill or your civil rights bill in this session of Congress. Does that disturb you?

The President: Well, I think that the longer the delay, I think – yes, I think it is unfortunate. The fact of the matter is that both these bills should be passed. The tax bill has been before the Congress for nearly a year. The civil rights has been there for a much shorter time; it didn't go up until June. I am hopeful that the House will certainly act on that in the next month, maybe sooner. The tax bill hearings have been quite voluminous. It would seem to me that it might be possible to end those hearings and bring the matter to the floor of the Senate before the end of the year. Otherwise, the civil rights bill will come over after the first of the year. There may be a very long debate. The tax bill may be caught up in that. I suppose some people are hopeful that that is so, but I am not. And I think that the economy will suffer. The economy will suffer and I think that – I certainly would not want to be responsible for that. Therefore, I would like to get the tax bill out of the way quickly and this important piece of legislation. I would think the Members of Congress would.

General Harkins in Vietnam

Q: Mr. President, there have been published reports that General Harkins may have lost his usefulness in Viet-Nam because of his identification with the Diem regime and lack of contacts with the new generals running the country. Would you care to comment on that?

The President: I think it is wholly untrue. I have complete confidence in him. He was just doing his job. I think he said in the interview yesterday he had seen Mr. Nhu, I think, only three times. He had seen President Diem on a number of occasions. That was his job, that is what he was sent for – to work with the government in power – that is what he will do with the new government. I have great confidence in General Harkins. There may be some who would like to see General Harkins go, but I plan to keep him there.

Q: Following up that, sir, would you give us your appraisal of the situation in South Viet-Nam now, since the coup, and the purposes for the Honolulu conference?

The President: Because we do have a new situation there, and a new government, we hope, an increased effort in the war. The purpose of the meeting at Honolulu – Ambassador Lodge will be there, General Harkins will be there, Secretary McNamara and others, and then as you know, later Ambassador Lodge will come here - is to attempt to assess the situation: what American policy should be, and what our aid policy should be, how we can intensify the struggle, how we can bring Americans out of there.

Now, that is our objective, to bring Americans home, permit the South Vietnamese to maintain themselves as a free and independent country, and permit democratic forces within the country to operate - which they can, of course, much more freely when the assault from the inside, and which is manipulated from the north, is ended. So the purpose of the meeting in Honolulu is how to pursue these objectives.

Q: Mr. President, Madam Nhu has now left the United States, but indicated that she intends to return. Will we renew her tourist visa?

The President: Yes.

Q: And if she asks for it, will we grant her permanent residence ——

The President: I think we'd certainly permit her to return to the United States, if she wishes to do so.

The Foreign Aid Program

Q: Mr. President, year by year, the foreign aid program seems to encounter more and more resistance in the Congress. And this year we are seeing Senators who ordinarily in the past have gone along with the program ——

The President: Yes. This is the worst attack on foreign aid that we have seen since the beginning of the Marshall plan.

Q: In the event that one of these years the Congress, the arguments for foreign aid notwithstanding, surprises itself by voting the program out, what would we then do?

The President: I think it would be a great mistake. Of course, some of the difficulty is where the President sits and where the Members of the Senate sit. It has been said very many times, and I have never questioned it, that the Senate and the Congress have every right to decide how much money should be appropriated. That is their constitutional right.

But on the other hand, the President bears particular responsibilities in the field of foreign policy. If there are failures in the Middle East, Africa, and Latin America, and South Viet-Nam, Laos, it is usually not a Senator who is selected to bear the blame but it's the administration, the President of the United States.

I regard this - President Eisenhower regarded it, and President Truman - it is no coincidence that all three Presidents since this program began, and Presidential candidates - Mr. Nixon, Mr. Stevenson, Governor Dewey, that all of them, Governor Rockefeller today, others - it seems to me all recognize the importance of this program. It is because it is a very valuable arm of the United States in the field of foreign policy. I don't think it is recognized what an important influence this has.

Now, we spend $51 billion or $52 billion on defense. We spend $2½ billion on the atomic energy program. We spend $5 billion on space, of which at least a good percentage has a military implication in the sense of our national security. We spend all of this money and yet we are going to deny the President of the United States a very valuable weapon in maintaining the influence of the United States in this very diversified world.

I can't imagine anything more dangerous than to end this program. I can assure you that whoever is President of the United States succeeding me will support this program.

Now, the second point I want to make is that what we are now talking about is only a fourth of what we tried to do in the early fifties. What I said in the - I don't understand why we are suddenly so fatigued. I don't regard the struggle as over, and I don't think it is probably going to be over for this century. I think this is a continuing effort, and it is not a very heavy one. It is a fraction of our budget, a fraction of our gross national product. The gross national product of the United States has increased $100 billion, will have by the end of this year, in a 3-year period.

So what we are asking is a billion dollars less than in the average program since '47. The need today is greater, these countries are poorer, there's a good many more of them; and yet we are being denied, the President of the United States is being threatened with denying him a very important weapon in helping him meet his responsibility. The Congress has its responsibility. But in the field of foreign policy there are particular burdens placed on the President, whoever he may be.

The Supreme Court in the Curtis Rider case said that the President is the organ of the country in the field of foreign policy. I just want to say personally as President, and my predecessor said the same, this program is essential to the conduct of our foreign policy, and therefore I am asking the Congress of the United States to give me the means of conducting the foreign policy of the United States. And if they do not want to do so, then they should recognize that they are severely limiting my ability to protect the interest. That's how important I think this program is.

Q: Before you leave the subject, sir, would you comment just a bit further? It is still a fact that a negative action by a Congress is something that an administration has great difficulty in coping with. Has the administration, has the Government, looked ahead to that possibility and prepared against it?

The President: No, I can't believe that the Congress of the United States is going to be so unwise unless we are going to retreat from the world. Are we going to give up in South Viet-Nam? Are we going to give up in **Latin** America?

I have said before that what we are talking about in the case of Latin America and the Alliance for Progress, for all of Latin America, is what the Soviet Union and the bloc are putting into Cuba alone. Now, can you tell me the United States is not able to do that? In addition, these amendments which are passed because they don't like a particular leader or a particular national policy as of the moment - it is a very changing world. Because they don't like the fishing policy we are going to decide to end all aid to the three countries in Latin America that are hardpressed, rather than permitting us to negotiate the matter out. But anyway, as I say, they have their responsibilities and I have mine. I am just trying to make it very clear that I cannot fulfill my responsibility in the field of foreign policy without this program.

Now, the most important program, of course, is our national security, but I don't want the United States to have to put troops there. What's going to happen in Laos if it collapses? Are they going to blame the Senate or are they going to blame me? I know who they are going to blame. So I need this program.

The Possible Candidacy of Margaret Chase Smith

Q: Mr. President, as a possible candidate for President, would you comment on the possible candidacy of Margaret Chase Smith, and specifically what effect that would have on the New Hampshire primary?

The President: I would think if I were a Republican candidate, I would not look forward to campaigning against Margaret Chase Smith in New Hampshire - (laughter) - or as a possible candidate for President. I think she is very formidable, if that is the appropriate word to use about a very fine lady. She is a very formidable political figure!

Professor Barghoorn and the Exchange Agreement

Q: Mr. President, getting back to Professor Barghoorn for a moment, the negotiations for renewal of the exchange agreement with the Soviet Union were scheduled to begin next Tuesday, and now as I understand it have been postponed.

The President: That is right.

Q: Do these negotiations depend upon the release of Professor Barghoorn?

The President: I don't think it is helpful to the Professor to try to put these conditions upon it. I just say that there's no sense having a program if a man who is innocent of any intelligence mission, which is true in this case, is subjected to arrest without means of defense. How can you carry on that kind of a program? I am sure that everybody would agree that it would be hopeless under these conditions.

Wheat Deal with the Soviet Union

Q: Mr. President, would you comment on the wheat deal with the Soviet Union, and tell us whether the Export-Import Bank, or whether any other agency of Government is doing more in this deal than it would for any friendly country?

The President: No, it will not do more than it would for any friendly country. The matter is now in private negotiations, and I don't know what is going to happen on the deal.

Changes in Travel Restrictions for Soviet Diplomats

Q: Would you expand, sir, on the changes in the travel restrictions for Soviet diplomats? For example, in Oregon there were five counties that were off limits during the last 2 years, and now it has been expanded to 13 counties. Could you expand on that?

The President: In the case of the Soviet Union, 26 percent of their country is off limits to the United States, and we have put the same percentage of ours. If they would be willing to change that percentage and drop it, I think we would be willing to. Now, in the case of the bloc, we have attempted to put some limitations on the travel of bloc military attachés, because we feel that it is important to the security of the United States, and to the alliance. The base of the alliance rests upon the nuclear forces of the United States. I think we have to protect their security. And the Defense Department felt very strongly that this was important to the security of the United States, or otherwise it would not have been done.

The Status of Legislation on the Hill

Q: Mr. President, I think a few minutes ago you said it would be unfortunate if the tax bill and the civil rights bill don't get through. You just said also it is the worst attack on the foreign aid bill since its inception.

Several appropriations bills are still hung up in Congress, the first time in history this late. What has happened on Capitol Hill?

The President: Well, they are all interrelated. I think that there is some delay because of civil rights. That has had an effect upon the passage of appropriations bills. There isn't any question. On the other hand, of course, what we are talking about in both the civil rights bill and the tax bill are very complicated and important pieces of legislation, in fact more significant in their own way than legislation which has been sent up there for a decade. My judgment is that by the time this Congress goes home, in the sense of next summer, that in the fields of education, mental health, taxes, civil rights, this is going to be a record that is going to be - however dark it looks now, I think that "westward, look, the land is bright," and I think that by next summer it may be.

Q: In view of what you just said, sir, you listed certain items. You didn't mention medical care for the aged. Now, even though Chairman Mills has promised to hold hearings this month, there doesn't seem to be any immediate prospect of clearing it. Since he was so helpful on the tax bill, are you prepared to ask him to cast his vote to get that out of committee so the House can vote on it?

The President: I think that we are going to get that bill out of committee - not this year, but next year - and I think we will have a vote on it, and I think it will pass. But I don't think it will pass this year, but I think it will next year. I did not mean to make an exclusive list. I am looking forward to the record of this Congress, but it may not come until - this is going to be an 18-month delivery!

Sponsorship of a Bipartisan Measure

Q: Mr. President, the bill - the program put forward by this distinguished committee of private citizens seemed to go farther than your bill on medicare. Would you be prepared to sponsor a program, say, if Senator Javits joined with Senator Anderson in a bipartisan measure?

The President: Yes. I am going to meet with them, and I think that that bill recognized the principle of social security. I thought it was a very valuable job because it was a bipartisan - the committee[1] had distinguished Republicans on it as well as Democrats. I am meeting with Senator Anderson and Senator Javits, and I think that this offers a good deal of hope for that bill. I think they have given it new life.

Foreign Aid and Executive Flexibility

Q: Mr. President, part of the disenchantment on Capitol Hill over foreign aid seems to be the feeling that the administration has not fully used the flexibility it asks. For example, no aid to Indonesia, when President Sukarno was threatening Malaysia.

The President: Well, we have suspended the aid to Indonesia.

Q: But you have not suspended it, have you, Mr. President, to the United Arab Republic, which is defying the U.N.?

The President: Well, now, in the case of Indonesia, though, we are suspending it.[2] It seems to me it is much better - I don't know what the situation is going to be 3 months from now in regard to the relations between Indonesia and Malaysia. I hope they are better. But it is the possible use of passing a prohibition for assistance to Indonesia, because of its attitude toward Malaysia when 3 months from now it may or may not be the same as it is today. That's the point.

Now on the United Arab Republic, the United States, as you know, 80 percent of its assistance consists of food, surplus food. We have been working to try to get a withdrawal, an orderly withdrawal, in the case of the Yemen. There has not been a conflict – I think a good deal as a result of effort which we and others have made – between Saudi Arabia and the UAR. I am concerned about the Yemen because the rate of the withdrawal, of course, has been quite limited.

There are going to be further withdrawals by January, but unless those withdrawals are consistent with earlier statements. I would think that the chance of increased tension between the UAR and Saudi Arabia would substantially increase. But I don't think that the language that the Senate adopted, which calls upon me to make a finding which is extremely complicated to make, is particularly – strengthens our hands or our flexibility in dealing with the UAR. In fact, it will have the opposite result.

These countries are poor – I am not talking now about the UAR, most of them – these threats that the United States is going to cut off aid is a great temptation to Arabic countries to say, "Cut it off." They are nationalist, they are proud, they are in many cases radical. I don't think threats from Capitol Hill bring the results which are frequently hoped. A quiet work may not bring it. But I think there is a great temptation to say – at the time the Aswan Dam was cut off, that produced – that did not bring the Arab Republic to follow us. It produced the opposite result. I am afraid of these other threats. I think it is a very dangerous, untidy world. But we are going to have to live with it. I think one of the ways to live with it is to permit us to function. If we don't function, the voters will throw us out. But don't make it impossible for us to function by legislative restraints or inadequate appropriations.

Argentina and U.S.-Owned Oil Companies

Q: Mr. President, in view of congressional sentiment towards the Alliance for Progress program, is your administration going to make any special effort to persuade the Government of Argentina not to nationalize American-owned oil companies?

The President: Well, as you know, Governor Harriman visited the Argentine, discussed the matter. It is now in negotiation. What we are concerned about is that if action is taken there will be adequate machinery for compensation, fair compensation. We can't deny the sovereign right of a country to take action within its borders, but we can insist that there be equitable standards for compensating those whose property is taken away from them.

We are attempting to work this out with the Argentine, but the Argentine is faced, as are all of the Latin Americans, with staggering problems. They have emerged from a military junta, Peronism, and all of the rest, and democratic election, and this was one of the commitments that was made. So now we attempt to adjust our interests. But we are concerned about the oil in Argentina and in Peru.

The Vote in Philadelphia

Q: You have been reported as saying you were very satisfied with the vote in Philadelphia. Why were you satisfied?

The President: Because Mayor Tate was elected. As John Bailey said, the Republicans had the statistics and we, the offices. So that is why I was satisfied.

The Moral and Ethical Climate in Washington

Q: Mr. President, the Fred Korth and Bobby Baker cases have prompted some serious questions about the moral and ethical climate in Washington. What is your assessment of today's climate in Washington?

The President: I think it is always - in the first place I don't lump the two cases together. I think that there are differences between the two cases. I want to make that clear. So there are differences between the cases.

Now, if you are talking about - there are always bound to be in the Government, the newspaper business, labor, and so on, farmers - there are always going to be people who can't stand the pressure of opportunity, so that - but the important point is what action is taken against them.

I think that this administration has been very vigorous in its action, and I think that we have tried to set a responsible standard. There are always going to be people who fail to meet that standard, and we attempt to take appropriate action dealing with each case.

But Mr. Baker is now being investigated, and I think we will know a good deal more about Mr. Baker before we are through. Other people may be investigated as time goes on. We just try to do the best we can. And I think that - the governmental standards, let me say, on the whole I think compare favorably with those in Washington, with those in some other parts of America.

The Russian Anti-Missile Missile

Q: Mr. President, last week the Soviet Union in Moscow showed what they claimed was an anti-missile missile. I wonder if you could tell us what you know about that missile. Is it what they claim it is supposed to be, and also what is the effectiveness of their anti-missile system?

The President: Well, I don't think it is probably useful to discuss it in detail here. I don't think there is any doubt that they have an anti-missile missile, as do we. The problem, of course, is what you do with saturation. I don't think that the Soviet Union or the United States have solved the problem of dealing, as I have said before, with a whole arsenal of missiles coming at us at maximum speed, with decoys. That's the impossible. That, up to now, has been an impossible task.

On Recognizing the Dominican Republic and Honduras

Q: Mr. President, we seem to be in somewhat of a stalemate on recognizing the new regimes in two Latin American countries, the Dominican Republic and Honduras. I am wondering - the administration perhaps has been reluctant to tell these countries precisely what they had to do to get recognition.

The President: Well, we have had discussions with both countries. As you know, this is not just a matter of the United States. This is a matter of nearly the whole hemisphere. In fact, by a vote of 18 to 1, the OAS voted to have a meeting on the problem of military coups.

We have attempted to indicate or inquire what steps each of these two countries, the governments of the two countries, are prepared to make to return to constitutional government, which we regard as the most desirable form of government and also the one that would be most effective in meeting the challenges of the hemisphere. So we have inquired of both of them what steps they are prepared to take, when elections would be, who would be in the government. So we have been working very assiduously.

Q: In general terms, sir, could you say whether we would be prepared to accept the same conditions for recognition there that we did in the case of the junta in Peru, elections within 1 year, for example?

The President: Well, I think it would be unwise to attempt to negotiate it out here, but we did recognize the junta in Peru on the assurances that they would hold elections. They did hold them and the result was very fair. So it shows that it can be done. That is what we would like to see done in these countries.

Pressuring the Russians

Q: Mr. President, to go back to the Russian-American problem, given the fact that our relations seem to alternate between hot and cold - the Barghoorn case and the autobahn at the moment - what do you say to those Americans who say that in such a situation we should not sell wheat to the Soviet Union, certainly not without trying to use it as a method of, say, negotiating some better arrangement on the autobahn?

The President: Well, I think the wheat deal is desirable for us. It is desirable for the Soviet Union. I am not convinced - it may mean $200 million in balance of payments for us. It means wheat to the Soviet Union. But in view of the supplies that the Soviet Union has in its own country, in Australia, in Canada, I am not sure that the wheat can carry other loads. I think it pretty much stands on its own. It is of some benefit to us, some benefit to the Soviet Union, but this idea that other things can be hitched onto it - but obviously this kind of trade depends upon a reasonable atmosphere in both countries.

I think that atmosphere has been badly damaged by the Barghoorn arrest. In the case of the autobahn, this is a continuing matter over a good many years. We are going to maintain our rights in Berlin and we have made that quite clear. I expect that we are going to have difficulties, and the Soviet Union may have difficulties in other matters. But Professor Barghoorn I regard as a very serious matter.

The Compromise Bill

Q: Mr. President, do you feel that you have a firm commitment from the Republicans and the House leadership to back and support in the Rules Committee and on the floor every provision in the compromise bill approved by the House?

The President: I wouldn't want to speak for them. I think they ought to speak for themselves. I will say that a substantial part of that bill bears Republican language and imprint. It wouldn't have been passed without their support. It is a bill which is Republican and Democratic. I think it is a bill which is bipartisan. I would hope it would have - it can't pass without bipartisan support. I would hope it would be able to maintain it on the floor of the House, because if we don't we are not even going to get it through the House.

Bringing Troops Back From Vietnam

Q: Mr. President, in view of the changed situation in South Viet-Nam, do you still expect to bring back 1,000 troops before the end of the year, or has that figure been raised or lowered?

The President: No, we are going to bring back several hundred before the end of the year. But I think on the question of the exact number, I thought we would wait until the meeting of November 20th.

The Alliance for Progress

Q: Mr. President, we will soon be getting some distressing news from São Paulo in Brazil in relation to the Alliance for Progress. Now the Post had a piece - this morning - saying that an idea has been circulated by which the Alliance would be made worldwide with the participation of Eastern European countries and the Soviet Union in this to help the Alliance reach its goals. Can you tell us in principle what you think about it?

The President: No, I have never heard of that, and we are not proposing to engage in a joint effort with the Eastern Europeans. That is a matter, of course, of sovereign decision. But I don't regard them as interested at all in the Alliance because the Alliance and the charter of Punta del Este is based upon the development of free, democratic societies in Latin America, which is our objective. Their objective, of course, is different. So I don't see how you can join them in the Alliance.

The Nomination of David Rabinovitz

Q: Mr. President, several months ago you nominated David Rabinovitz to be a Federal judge in western Wisconsin. Since that time the American Bar Association has opposed this nomination and a majority of lawyers polled by the State Bar Association said that he was unqualified. Do you still support this nomination, or in view of this opposition are you going to withdraw?

The President: No, I am for David Rabinovitz all the way. I know him very well, in fact for a number of years. And the American Bar Association has been very helpful in making the judgment, but I am sure they would agree that they are not infallible. Mr. Brandeis was very much opposed. There are a good many judges who have been opposed who have been rather distinguished. And I am for David Rabinovitz.

Professor Barghoorn and the Wheat Deal

Q: Sir, do you mean to leave the implication by your remarks on the wheat thing that if the Barghoorn case is not satisfactory —

The President: No, I wouldn't attempt to. I want to get Professor Barghoorn out of prison and it seems to me the best way to do it is to confine my remarks to what I have said. I am merely saying - in fact, I won't say it - any more!

Help for New England

Q: Mr. President, the Senators from New England met this morning in the office of Senator Kennedy and agreed to renew their annual appeal for relief on wool and for the lifting of restrictions on residual oil. What can you do and what will you do to help the people in New England on these problems?

The President: Well, as I understand it, in one case there is a desire to limit imports and the other is to encourage imports. I used to take part in those meetings myself.

On the other hand - and there is a matter of concern - as a matter of fact, yesterday I met with the head of the coal producers - the coal association - they're very concerned about the imports of residual oil. But it is a fact that the imports of woolens and worsteds have gone up from about 15 to 22 or 23 percent. So there has been a sharp increase, and it is a matter of concern. In the case of residual, we are attempting to - that is a matter of great interest, as you know, to Venezuela, which is a country that is under Communist attack and, therefore, we have to consider that obligation as well as our obligations to the domestic coal industry. So we have not forgotten New England.

Reporter: Thank you, Mr. President.

[1]National Committee on Health Care of the Aged (see Item 460 and note).

[2]As explained by the State Department immediately following the news conference, the President did not mean that existing aid programs to Indonesia had been suspended. He had in mind the fact that the United States has suspended consideration of a large additional aid program which, until Indonesia's recent actions against Malaysia, was being developed in cooperation with other members of the Development Assistance Committee of the Organization for Economic Cooperation and Development.

1961

Act of Bogota
    82 (264), 93 (394)

Africa
    and commitment of troops to
        the Congo - 40 (98)
    and the Congo problem - 1 (8),
        15 (34), 16 (34), 27 (70), 33 (92)
    and U.S. roving Ambassador -
        45 (139)
    import of food from China - 9 (15)

Aged
    and Medicare prices - 79 (261)
    medical care for - 158 (703)

Agriculture
    new progress of - 19 (37)

Algeria
    CIA involvement in - 108 (435)
    peace talks on - 44 (138)
    U.S. intervention in - 104 (431-2)

Armenia
    and missing U.S. fliers - 10 (16)

Arms Control
    and disarmament - 46 (140)
    negotiations - 38 (96)

Asia
    and commitment of troops to
        the Congo - 40 (98)

Atlantic Community
    participation in defense and
        foreign aid - 49 (142)

Atomic Energy Commission
    and regulatory responsibility
        for the Atomic Industry - 67 (190)

Atomic Power
    development of by the
        states - 66 (189)

regulatory responsibility for the
    Atomic Industry - 66 (189)

Automobile Industry
    negotiations in - 141 (576)

Azores
    U.S. air rights in - 20 (37)

Berlin
    access to the East - 144 (578),
        155 (663-4)
    four power talks on - 137 (572-3)
    methods for financing - 122 (515-6)
    negotiations on - 138 (573-4),
        145 (580), 170 (761)
    possibility of war over -
        124 (517-8), 133 (558)
    prospects for a settlement -
        147 (657)
    public opinion on - 127 (520)
    Republican criticism of Adminis-
        tration's handling of - 141 (576)
    situation in - 122 (515), 151 (660),
        157 (702)
    Soviet attitude on - 129-30 (554),
        141 (576), 147 (657)
    Soviet exacerbation of tension
        in - 110-1 (476), 143 (577)
    U.S. mobolization of forces
        in - 113 (478)
    U.S. on the Wall - 153 (662)
    U.S. role in - 106 (433),
        118 (483), 141 (576)
    the Autobahn in - 167 (458)

Brazil
    and Castro - 143 (578)
    and distribution of American
        food - 43 (138)

Budget
    a balanced - 154 (663)

*The index numbering system should be read as follows: The first number repre-
sents the page in the* Kennedy Presidential Press Conferences. *The number in
parentheses is the source from the* Public Papers of the President.

administration policy - 9 (15),
17 (35)
military requests - 18 (36)

Business Community
assurances to - 163 (708)

Caribbean
relations with the U.S. - 4 (11)

Central America
relations with the U.S. - 4 (11)

Central Intelligence Agency
involvement in Algiers - 108 (435)

Civil Defense
policy on - 170-1 (761-2)

Civil Rights
administration policy - 15 (33)
and executive action in -
55 (156-7)
and school desegregation - 25 (69)

Civil Rights Commission
recommendation on Federal
funds - 43 (137)

Civil War Commission
and Southern Blacks - 72 (217)

Colonialism
U.S. role in - 107 (434-5)

Communications
funds for - 91 (313-4)

Common Market
and Britain - 128 (553)
importance of - 162 (707)

Communist Bloc
increased power of - 25 (68-9)

Communist China
American imperialism in - 20 (38)
belligerency of - 25 (69)
normalization of relations
with the U.S. - 108 (436)
strength of - 18 (36)
U.S. relations with - 58 (159) -

Communist Systems
durability of - 79 (261)
U.S. military role in educating
the public on - 131 (556)

Community Facilities Administration
and broadening of eligibility
requirements - 12 (31)

Conflit of Interest Laws
President on - 97 (357)

Congo
and U.N. troop involvement -
40 (98)
impact on Soviet-American
relations of 35 (93)
pro-communist government
of - 42-3 (137)
situation in - 15 (34), 27 (70)
Soviet agitation of - 38 (97)
unilateral intervention
in - 33 (92)
U.S. aid to - 1 (8)
U.S. proposals on - 16 (34)

Congress
and a new agricultural
program - 19 (37)
and abuse of executive
privilege - 7 (13)
and the education bill - 126 (520)
and electoral reform - 11 (17)
and problem of unemployment -
16 (35), 140 (575)
and school legislation - 123 (516)
appropriation of funds
question - 82 (264)
conflict of interest laws -
96 (357)
federal aid to schools - 54 (155),
61 (184)
legislative priorities - 171-2 (762)
medicare funds - 88 (310)
on textile imports - 114 (479-80)
President's domestic program
and - 89 (312)
rules committe vote in - 17 (35)
support for the tax investment
incentive program - 90 (313)

Conventional Forces
increase of by U.S.
allies - 121 (515)

Cuba
and American policy
toward - 82 (264)
and American prisoners in - 20 (38)
and the problem of tyranny -
31 (73)
and the refugee problem - 5 (11-2)
exiles from - 96 (357)
import of food from China - 9 (15)
possibility of state department
collusion in the Cuban
operation - 38 (96)
re opening of diplomatic relations
with the U.S. - 4 (10)
the Cuban operation - 114 (479)

the tractor deal - 113 (479)
U.S. support for an invasion
of - 76 (258-9), 146 (580)
U.S. trade policy - 36 (95),
97 (358), 159 (704)

Cuban Refugees
training of - 84 (307-08), 96 (357)

Defense Department
and the anti-missile missile -
21 (39)
and the missile gap - 24 (67)
expenditures of - 154 (662-3)
policy planning in - 133 (558)
strategy of - 42 (136)

Democratic Party
in New York - 7 (13)

Dependents, Military
preparation of overseas - 99 (360)

Desegregation
of public schools - 25 (69),
137 (572-3)

Development Lending
commitments for - 142 (577)

Diplomatic Relations
with Cuba - 4 (10)

Diplomacy
Rusk's statement on - 8 (14)

Disarmament
and planning for negotiations -
47 (140)
debates on - 2 (9)
U.S. position on negotiations -
2 (9)

Domestic Interest Rates
and Presidential authority -
28 (71)

Dominican Republic
situation in - 164-5 (756)

East Europe
self-determination in - 126-7 (520)

East Germany
refugees from - 132 (557)
relations with West Germany -
173 (762)

Economy
and import competition - 58 (158-9)
public attitude on - 81 (263)
state of - 69 (215)
upturn of - 42 (136)

Education
aid for bills on - 126 (519-20)
financing of program of - 48 (141)
President's educational
program - 90 (313)
segregation in 56 (157)

Elections
in New York - 157 (701-2)

Electoral reform
proposition for - 11 (16-17)

El Salvador
U.S. recognition of - 33 (92)

Eskimos
status of school age children -
51 (152)

Executive Privilege
abuse of - 7 (13)
and Dick Goodwin - 139 (574)

Exports
and the iron curtain - 56-7 (158)

Extremism
financial contributions to
extremist groups - 171 (762)

Fallout Shelters
President on - 147-8 (657),
160 (705)

Farm Bill
and title III section - 65 (188)

Federal Aid
and the Everson case - 49 (142)
for highways - 60 (183-4)
for the unemployed - 7 (13)
to schools - 49 (142), 53 (154-5),
66 (189)

Federal Funds
withholding of - 43 (137)

Federal Housing
segregation in - 73 (218)

Federal Housing Administration
and FHA insured loans - 12 (31)

Federal Reserve Board
and domestic interest rates -
28 (71)

Food Stamps
distribution of - 12 (31)

Foreign Aid
and long term borrowing - 73 (218)
and NATO - 49 (142)

expanding populations, aid
for - 125 (518)
to Laos - 133-4 (558)
to Peru - 133-4 (558)

Foreign Policy
and Senator Fulbright - 96 (357)
criticism of - 149-50 (659)
information on - 90 (312)
military support - 13 (32)
status of - 98-9 (358-9)

France
and alternatives to changing
strategy of the U.N. - 82 (264)
and Atomic tests - 105 (432)
and reconciliation with
Germany - 162 (707)
Kennedy impression of - 108 (435-6)
President's trip to - 91 (313)

Freedom Riders' Movement
President's opinion of -
132-4 (517)

Fuel
limitation in import of - 44 (138)

Geneva negotiations
and the Atomic test ban - 1 (8)

Government Spending
waste in - 45 (139)

Great Britain
and Laos - 10 (16)

Harvey Aluminum Company
sale of Government's aluminum
extrusion plant to - 94 (355)

Hijackings
by Frenchmen - 134 (559), 136 (560)

House of Representatives
increase in size of - 130 (555)

Housing
passage of housing bill - 158 (703)

Immigration Laws
legislation on - 136 (560)

Inaugural Address
re America's position in the
world - 9 (15)

India
persuasion of the Prime
Minister - 161 (706)

Indians, American
and changing of treaties with -
55 (157)

Indonesia
and dispute with Netherlands on
West New Guinea - 83 (265)

Inflation
danger of - 18 (36)

Inspection sites
within the USSR - 66 (189)

Intelligence Community
reorganization of activities
of - 114 (479)

Inter-American Affairs
President's handling of - 117 (482)

International Control Commission
and Laos - (10 (16), 96 (356-7)

Japan
and protest on trade barriers -
173 (763)
and visits by Eisenhower -
100 (360)
and U.S. trade with - 156 (701)

John Birch Society
President's view of - 88 (310)

Justice Department
and private and public business
practices - 30 (73)

Labor
management conference on - 65 (188)
relations with management -
65 (188)

Labor Unions
attitude on the work week -
62 (185)

Laos
action in - 70 (215)
and buildup of conventional
forces - 74 (219)
and possibility of SEATO
intervention - 72 (217-8)
and Soviet attitude - 74 (219)
cease fire in - 78 (260),
85-6 (308)
communist intervention in -
15 (34)
crisis in - 10 (16), 27 (70)
importance to the U.S. -
71 (216)
neutrality of - 106 (433-4)
North Vietnamese troops in -
70 (216)
policy in - 69 (215)
problem of - 67-8 (213), 150 (660)

situation in - 52 (154),
  118-9 (483-4)
U.S. aid to - 61 (185),
  133-4 (558)

Latin America
  and self-help measures - 136 (561)
  five point program on - 21 (38)
  President on - 62 (185), 117 (482)
  relations with the U.S. - 4 (11),
    82 (264)

Management
  relations with labor - 16 (34)

Maritime strike
  policy on - 115 (480)

Medical Care
  for the aged - 63 (186)

Meteorology
  funds for - 91 (313-4)

Mexican Americnas
  support for Kennedy - 27 (71)

Mideast
  U.S. foreign policy in -
    99 (359-60)

Military
  and criticism of Eisenhower
    policy of - 18 (36)
  and dependents - 16 (35)
  and organization of side-bar
    corporations - 63 (186)
  cut back in abroad - 6 (12-13)
  deterioration of - 156 (701)
  role of in educating the public
    regarding communism - 131 (556)

Minimum Wage Bill
  compromise on - 71 (216)

Missile Program
  acceleration of - 21 (39)
  air force program - 45 (139)
  gap between U.S. and USSR -
    23-4 (67), 52 (153)

Monroe Doctrine
  U.S. position on - 99-100 (360)

Mortage rates
  reduction of - 41 (135)

Mutual Assistance Act
  amendment of - 135 (560)

National Guard
  call-up of - 121 (515)

NATO
  and support by European members -
    104 (432), 143 (578)
  and U.S. foreign policy - 98 (359)
  Kennedy on - 23 (67)
  meeting of leaders of - 25 (68)
  nuclear weapons and - 28 (71)
  relations with Warsaw Pact -
    167 (758)
  responsibilities of members -
    122 (515), 130 (555)

Negro Photographers
  in White House Photographers
    Association - 81 (263)

Neutron Bomb
  development of - 135 (560)

New Orleans, La.
  desegregation of schools in -
    25 (69)

News Media
  and President's conference on
    Russian TV - 47 (141)
  and press conferences - 52 (153),
    159 (704)
  news briefings - 24 (68)

New York
  Democratic party in - 7 (13)

Nuclear Power
  nuclear weapons and NATO - 78 (71)
  our nuclear deterrent - 149 (658)
  possibility of atomic test -
    152-3 (661)
  resumption of testing - 115-6 (481),
    131 (556), 158 (703-4)
  test ban conference at Geneva -
    93 (354)
  testing of - 142 (577), 163 (708)
  U.S. forces - 149 (658)

Organization of American States
  proposal of convocation - 93 (354)

Paris Conference
  results of - 130 (555)

Peace Corps
  and Charles Kamen 140 (575)
  establishment of - 41 (136)
  possibility of a U.N. corps -
    58 (159-60)
  progress of - 84 (307)

Pentagon
  and the RB-47 fliers

Peru
  foreign aid to - 133-4 (558)

Poland
    and frontier with Germany –
      81 (263)
    Warsaw talks in – 21 (38)

Portugal
    seized ship of – 5 (12)
    the liner Santa Maria – 19-20 (37)

Press Conferences, Presidential
    instantaneous broadcast of – 4 (10)

Price Supports
    increase of – 19 (37)

Public Schools
    desegregation of – 25 (69)

Punta del Este
    agreement at – 132 (557)

Radio Free Europe
    President's support for – 50 (152)

Railroads
    financial problems of – 73 (218)

RB-47 Case
    and relations with the USSR –
      27 (70)
    fliers' status – 1 (8)
    Kennedy role in the release of –
      2 (9)
    Khrushchev role – 6 (12)
    Pentagon on – 13 (32)
    release of fliers – 3-4 (10),
      10 (16)
    restrictions on fliers – 13 (32)
    Soviet view of – 2 (9)
    U.S. view of – 2 (9), 57 (158)

Recession
    legislation on – 42 (137)
    President's feelings about –
      35 (94)
    Republican criticism of President's
      program on – 39 (97)

Reconnaissance Overflights
    Soviets on – 10 (16)
    the U-2 – 2 (9)
    U.S. policy on – 2 (9)

Red China
    and book publishing – 74 (219)
    and the U.N. – 77 (259-60)
    and the USSR – 46 (140), 160 (705)
    attack on Laos – 106 (433)
    surplus food to – 9 (15)
    U.S. talks with – 148 (658)

Regulatory Agencies
    Congress' investigation
      of – 26 (69)
    oversight of – 26 (69)

Republican Party
    criticism of Berlin policy –
      141 (576)
    criticism of President's
      economic program – 39 (97)

Rules Committee
    expansion of – 4-5 (11), 17 (35)

Schools
    aid measure – 139 (574)
    aid to private – 53 (154-5),
      127 (520)
    desegregation of – 137 (572-3)
    federal aid to – 49 (142),
      60 (184), 61 (184), 66 (189)
    legislation on – 122-3 (516)

Scientific Advisory Committee
    and the anti-missile missile –
      21 (39)

SEATO Agreement
    and intervention in Laos –
      72 (217-8)
    and Vietnam question – 75 (270)

Segregation
    in federal housing – 73 (218)

Senate Foreign Relations Committee
    President's influence on – 7 (13)

Small Business Administration
    and attitude on eligibility of
      business for defense contracts –
      34 (93)

South Africa
    racial policies in – 171 (762)

Southeast Asia
    U.S. foreign policy in –
      99 (359-60)

Soviet Union
    and access to East Berlin –
      144 (578), 155 (663)
    and aid to Laos – 61 (185)
    and attitude on Laos – 52 (154),
      74 (219), 86 (308)
    and availability of space
      knowledge to U.S. – 101 (361)
    and book publishing – 74 (219)
    and disarmament – 45-6 (139)
    and Gary Powers – 10 (16)
    and inspection sites within –
      66 (189)

and negotiations on arms control -
38 (96), 60 (183), 74 (219),
93 (354), 111 (477)
and nuclear testing - 118 (483),
142 (577), 153 (661-2),
158-9 (703-4), 163 (708),
and RB-47 fliers - 3 (10), 7 (13),
10 (16)
and Red China - 46 (140), 160 (705)
and reflections on history -
109 (436)
and rocket launch - 28 (71)
and space gap with U.S. - 36 (95)
and summitry with U.S. - 27 (70)
and the situation in the Congo -
38 (97)
and U.S. relations - 46 (140),
74 (219), 89 (311)
formal agreement with the U.S. -
92 (314)
impact of Congo on relations
with U.S. - 35 (93)
invitation of space scientists
to U.S. - 47 (141)
on Berlin - 110-1 (476-7),
119-20 (513-4), 141 (576),
143 (577), 167 (758)
reconnaissance flights, opinion
on - 2 (9)
Soviets in space - 37 (259),
134-5 (559)

Space
and availability of Russian
knowledge on - 101 (361)
and coverage of space shot -
101 (361)
and launch of astronauts -
98 (358)
as an area of war - 35 (93-4)
gap between U.S. and USSR -
36 (95), 80-1 (262), 86 (309)
program acceleration - 26-7 (70),
86-7 (309), 94 (355), 125 (518),
133 (558)
progress in sending a man to
the moon - 153 (662)
Soviets in - 77 (259), 134-5 (559)
task force report on - 9 (15)

State Department
policy planning in - 133 (558)
possibility of collusion in
Cuban operation - 38 (96)

Steel Industry
price hike in - 142 (576-7),
154-5 (663)

Succession
to the Presidency - 11 (17)

Summitry
developments prior to - 27 (70)
possibility of - 116 (481),
136 (561)

Supreme Court
and rulings on American Indians -
55 (157)
and the Everson case - 49 (142)

Taxes
increase of - 154 (663)
investment incentive program -
90 (313)
tax cut - 14 (33)

Ten-Nation Conference
resumption of - 60 (183)

Texas
election in - 83 (265)

Textile imports
distribution of - 114 (479-80)

Thailand
U.S. forces in - 150 (660)

Trade
barriers and the Japanese protest -
173 (763)
reciprocal trade agreements
act - 6 (12)
U.S. policy - 162 (707),
172 (762-3)

Troop Movements
by navy and marines - 70 (215)

Underdeveloped areas
West German aid to - 29 (72)

Unemployment
and Americans on relief - 34 (92)
and closure of military
installations - 78 (260)
and methods for cutting - 101 (361),
140 (575)
distribution of food to
unemployed - 3 (10)
federal aid for - 7 (13)
federal compensation for - 16 (34),
42 (136), 48 (141-2)
food stamp aid - 12 (31)
level of - 64 (187), 154 (663),
158 (703)

United Nations
and French attempts to change
strategy of - 82 (264)

and Red China question –
    77 (259-60)
and the Congo – 1 (8), 33 (91),
    38 (97), 40 (98), 43 (137)
and U.S. attitude – 33 (90)
Khrushchev visit to – 2 (9),
    13 (31-2)
liabilities of membership in –
    40 (99)
troop commitments to – 40 (98)

United States Information Agency
    President's direction of – 7 (13)

U.N. Food and Agricultural Organization
    U.S. participation in – 84 (307)

Venezuela
    possibility of Kennedy visit
        to – 72 (217)

Veterans Administration
    and payment of national insurance
        dividends – 12 (31)

Vice-President
    responsibilities of – 44 (138)

Vietnam
    and SEATO pact   75 (220)
    criticism of U.S. – 165 (756)
    participation of North Vietnam
        in Laos – 70 (216)
    U.S. forces in – 95 (356),
        150 (660)
    U.S. initital support for –
        146 (656), 155 (701)

War
    public attitude on possibility
        of – 148 (657-8)

Warsaw Pact
    relations with NATO – 168 (758)

Ways and Means Committee
    and hearings on extention of
        unemployment compensation –
        34 (92)

West Germany
    aid to underdeveloped countries –
        29 (72), 47 (141)
    and Soviet intentions – 119 (513)
    crisis in – 161 (706)
    policy on – 119 (484)

Women
    and administration's efforts
        re – 164 (709)

World Council of Churches
    distribution of food – 38 (96)

1962

Acoma Indians
    peace corps assistance for -
    372 (678)

Aerospace Industry
    negotiations with - 280 (337)

Aged
    health care for - 246 (232)
    medical care for - 186 (63)

Argentina
    events in - 257 (272)

Agriculture
    and dairy price supports -
    245 (231)
    and the free market - 397 (712)
    control and management of
        farm production - 179 (19)
    farm bill - 331 (512), 365 (632)
    meat and grain prices - 376 (649)
    support for dairy farmers -
        262 (276)
    two-price system in cotton -
        397 (714)
    withdrawal of grain from Billie Sol
        Estes' warehouses by the agri-
        culture department - 305 (434)

Algeria
    and U.S. policy - 234 (200)
    cease-fire in - 223 (153)
    recognition by USSR - 251 (258)
    revolt in - 180 (20)

Alliance for Progress Program
    Latin America and - 325 (495),
        386 (676)
    progress of - 198 (94), 313 (460),
        364 (597)
    submission of reforms to -
        244 (230)

Amalgamated Clothing Workers
    wage decision by - 298 (406)

American Medical Association
    and medical care - 302 (432)

Arms Control
    inclusion of Red China in
        negotiations - 213 (135-6)

Atomic Energy Commission
    funds for - 239 (226)

Azores
    U.S. air rights in - 187-8 (62)

B-70
    funds for - 236 (202), 244 (230)

Berlin
    access to - 290 (381)
    and the USSR - 258 (273)
    Adenauer on - 223 (153)
    consultation with Khrushchev
        on - 376 (650)
    discussion of at Geneva - 233 (200)
    four power meeting on - 377 (651)
    progress on question of - 200 (96),
        280 (338), 343 (545)
    situation in - 377 (651)
    Soviet attitude on - 209 (126),
        284 (376), 346 (568-9), 385 (676)
    Soviet involvement in - 381 (652)
    Soviet planes in Berlin air
        corridor - 224 (154), 242-3 (229)
    U.S. efforts in - 208 (125),
        225-6 (155-6), 290 (381-2)

Billie Sol Estes Affair
    President on - 291-2 (400),
        303 (433)
    the Estes' defraud - 307 (436)

*The index numbering system should be read as follows: The first number repre-
sents the page in the* Kennedy Presidential Press Conferences. *The number in
parentheses is the source from the* Public Papers of the President.

Brazil
    effect of economic problems
        of - 417 (871)
    food shipments to - 306 (435)
    seizure of American telephone
        company - 237 (203)
    urge for a ban on nuclear
        arms - 408 (836)
    visit of the President of -
        260 (275)

Budget
    balancing the 260 (275), 315 (461),
        316 (462)
    the 1963 - 297 (405-6)

Business Community
    administration attitude on -
        334 (515)
    administration sensitivity to
        business world - 396 (711)
    Democrats and - 342 (544)
    President's efforts re
        321-2 (491)
    President's view of businessmen -
        287 (379)

Cambodia
    guarantee of neutrality of -
        380 (653)
    treaty relations with - 305 (434)

Capitalism
    Khrushchev on - 407 (835)

Carpetbagging
    rules on - 257 (272)

Castroism
    checking the advance of -
        179 (19)

Central Intelligence Agency
    and Cuba - 249 (256)
    budget of - 213-4 (136)
    supervision over - 197 (94)
    U-2 incident and - 231 (198)

Chamizal Zone
    solution to - 344 (545)
Chile
    visit of the President of -
        416 (870), 418 (872)

Christmas Island
    and nuclear testing - 209 (126),
        212 (134-5)
    use of by the U.S. - 205 (123)

Civil Rights
    black rights in Albany, Ga. -
        358 (892)

legislation on - 198 (95)
Cold War
    policy in - 220 (141)

Common Market
    and U.S. trade expansion
        bill - 263 (277)
    British difficulties with -
        308 (436)
    growth of - 177 (17)
    Kennedy opinion on - 349 (571)
    negotiations in - 183 (22)
    relations with U.S. - 308 (436)
    trade agreements with the
        U.S. - 229 (196)

Communism
    and Vietnam - 215 (137)
    Communist countries, aid to -
        312 (459), 323 (492), 350 (571-2),
        366 (632)
    competition with - 400 (715)
    fragmentation of the communist
        bloc - 192 (266)
    freeing Cuba of - 241 (228)

Communist China
    and American surplus food
        to - 301 (431)
    and flow of refugees to Hong
        Kong - 310 (431)
    and movement into Taiwan
        straits - 327 (509-10)
    and relations with the USSR -
        409 (837)
    confrontation with India -
        403 (832)
    export of wheat to - 243 (230)
    possibility of an attack by
        Formosa - 261 (275-6)

Congo
    airlift to - 207 (124)
    situation in - 182 (22), 350 (572),
        370 (636) 381 (653)

Congress
    and a transportation tax -
        310 (457)
    and consideration of a tax
        reduction - 227 (157)
    and exchange of delegations with
        the USSR - 217 (139)
    and funds for the B-70 - 236 (202)
    and President's authority in the
        Cuban affair - 391 (679)
    and refugee problem in Hong
        Kong - 301 (431)

and the decision to send troops to
    Vietnam - 241 (228)
and the problem of division of
    powers - 187 (62)
and the urban affairs problem -
    223 (153)
and U.S. purchase of U.N. bonds -
    233 (199-200)
campaigning by - 333 (514)
legislation in - 313-4 (460)
pace of - 344 (564)
results of races for - 373 (638)
support for administration's
    domestic program - 253 (260)
trade fight in - 191 (66)

Construction Industry
    in California - 285-6 (378)

Cost of Living
    and steel price increase -
    269 (320)

Cuba
    and the Monroe Doctrine -
        382 (654)
    and no-invasion pledge by U.S. -
        404 (832), 407 (835), 411 (866)
    and Soviet threats - 389 (678)
    and the CIA - 249 (256)
    communist troops and supplies
        in - 372 (638), 375 (639),
        381 (653), 382 (653)
    crisis in - 402 (831)
    differences between Castro and
        the Cuban Communist Party -
        259 (274)
    expulsion of from Inter-American
        Defense Board - 193 (90)
    freeing of from communism -
        241 (228)
    Kennedy role in Cuban affair -
        391 (679)
    Khrushchev's speech on - 410 (866)
    Latin American assistance in
        the Cuban situation - 340 (543)
    military strength of - 251 (258)
    offensive weapons in - 416 (870)
    prisoners in - 415 (869)
    ransom for POWs - 333 (514)
    reintroduction of trade by
        U.S. - 196 (93)
    release of POWs - 271 (321)
    role of Latin America in -
        390 (679)
    Senator Capehart on - 380 (652)
    shipping to - 415 (869)
    situation in - 384 (674), 388 (677),

Soviet involvement in - 384 (674),
    388 (677)
trial of POWs - 250 (257)
U.S. presence in Guantanamo
    Bay - 254 (260)
withdrawal of Soviet bombers
    from - 401-2 (830-1)

Defense Department
    and contracts - 245 (231)
    censors in - 219 (140)
    Eisenhower on defense spending -
        334 (515)
    ICBM warning system in the
        south - 296 (404)
    U.S. strategy - in nuclear
        engagement - 363 (597)

Democratic Party
    vote on medical bill - 355 (376)

Desegregation
    of schools - 277 (335), 296 (376)

Dhahran
    renewal of U.S. air rights
        at - 216 (138)

Disarmament
    and influence on the economy -
        206 (123)
    and nuclear testing - 202 (120)
    British-American draft agreement
        on - 216 (138)
    progress at Geneva - 206 (124),
        272-3 (333), 278 (336)
    prospects of - 235 (201)

Drugs
    drug bill - 365 (632)
    President's opinion on
        pharmaceuticals - 364 (597)
    thalidomide problems - 355 (590),
        356-7 (591)

East Germany
    and access to West Berlin -
        279 (337)
    trade with USSR - 351 (572)

Economy
    administration policy - 353 (575)
    and unemployment - 315 (461)
    congressional support for adminis-
        tration's domestic program -
        253 (260)
    debt limit - 326 (496)
    effect of deficits - 320 (491)
    gold drain - 347-8 (370), 362 (596)
    influence of disarmament on -
        206 (197)

meat and grain prices - 376 (649)
outlook for - 309 (456-7)
recovery of - 230 (197)
state of - 240 (227), 348 (570),
   359 (594), 371-2 (637),
   394-6 (709)
two-price system in cotton -
   399-400 (714)
White House conference on national
   economic issues - 305 (434)

Ecuador
   aid to - 349 (571)

Education
   bill to aid - 329 (511)
   bill on educational TV - 192 (60)

Egypt
   U.S. and British aid to - 314 (461)

Election (November 1962)
   goals for - 354 (575)
   results of - 406 (834)

Europe
   growth rate of Western - 306 (435)
   nuclear force for - 345 (546)
   political and economic integration
     of - 191 (66)
   possiblity of as a 3rd force -
     298 (406)
   Rusk's trip to - 332 (513)
   U.S. troops in - 330 (511)

Executive Privilege
   use of re the military
     204 (122)

Extremism
   and radical right organizations -
     190 (64-5)
   and the John Birch Society -
     207 (124)

Fallout Shelters
   funds for - 341 (543)

Far East
   review of policies in - 322 (492)

Federal Aid
   college aid bill - 203 (121)
   farm bill - 324 (493)
   for state hospitals - 264 (278)

Federal Bureau of Investigation
   activities of - 277 (334)

Federal Flood Insurance Act of 1956 ,
   revival of - 275 (333-4)

Federal Housing
   segregation in - 342 (544),
     182 (21)

Food for Peace Program
   expansion of - 177 (18)

Foreign Affairs
   negro conference on - 414 (869)
   Republican criticism of leadership
     in - 317 (463)
   Rostow on - 336 (516-7)

Foreign Aid
   bill for - 336 (539), 378 (651)
   funds for - 239 (226)
   limitations on bill for -
     323-4 (493)
   to countries doing business with
     the Soviet Bloc - 366 (632)

Formosa
   and possibility of an attack on
     the mainland - 261 (275-6)
   U.S. policy on - 262 (276)

France
   aid to nuclear force of - 275 (333)
   and Berlin talks - 280 (338)
   creation of a defense community
     apart from NATO - 295 (403)
   differences with the U.S. -
     293 (401)
   help to underdeveloped countries -
     232 (199)

Freedom Rides
   reverse - 288 (380)

Free Market
   significance of - 397 (712)

Geneva
   summit conference in - 231 (198),
     240 (227), 247 (255), 256 (272),
     278 (336), 361 (595)

Great Britain
   aid to Egypt - 314 (461)
   and agreement to terminate
     decision on Thor missiles -
     357 (592)
   and Hong Kong's refugee problem -
     301 (431)
   and the Atlantic Alliance -
     338 (540)
   differences with the Common
     Market - 308 (436)
   joint agreement with the U.S. on
     disarmament - 216 (138)
   trade agreements with U.S. -
     229 (196)

Hanna Nickel Company
    Stockpile investigation and
      profits of - 374 (639)

House of Representatives
    size increase of - 216-7 (138)

Housing
    housing order - 406 (835)

Hong Kong
    refugee problems - 301 (431),
      303 (432), 324 (494)

H.R. 10
    President on - 400 (714-5)

India
    and confrontation with Communist
      China - 403 (832) 404 (833)
    dispute with Pakistan over
      Kashmir - 215 (137-8)
    purchase of Soviet jets - 360 (594)
    relations with Pakistan -
      187 (61-2)
    weapons for - 319-20 (490)

Indonesia
    and dispute with Netherlands on
      West New Guinea - (176 (17)
    and the Bunker proposal -
      308 (436)
    economic survival in - 374 (639)
    U.S. position on Netherlands and -
      270 (320)

Industry
    tax benefits to - 271 (321)

International Access Authority
    membership in - 289 (381)

Japan
    and U.S. intentions toward
      Okinawa - 234 (200)
    invitation to build plants in
      U.S. - 341 (543)

John Birch Society
    and the Republican Party -
      207 (124)
    criticism of - 419 (872-3)

Judiciary
    conduct of - 180 (19-20)

Kashmir
    and the influence of India -
      180 (20)
    dispute over - 186 (61-2),
      215 (137)

Katanga
    military action against - 370 (636)

Labor
    and the union shop - 398 (713)

Laos
    agreement on - 357 (592)
    disengagement in - 222 (153)
    infiltration of Vietnamese
      units into - 198 (95)
    Kennedy and Khrushchev on -
      325 (495)
    possible attacks on - 300 (407-08)
    situation in - 195-6 (93),
      218 (140), 222 (153), 258 (273),
      294 (402-3) 336 (517)
    U.S. policy in - 285 (377),
      317 (463)
    U.S. treaty relations with -
      305 (434)

Latin America
    and assistance in the Cuban
      situation - 340 (543)
    and the alliance for Progress
      Program - 325 (495), 386 (676)
    role in Cuba - 390 (679)
    U.S. efforts in - 208 (125)

Legislation
    Eisenhower criticism of
      297 (405)
    support for the President's
      program - 331 (512)

Literacy
    test bill for - 291 (382)

Malaysia Federation
    formation of - 357 (592)

Medical Care
    and the AMA - 302 (432)
    and the Kerr-Mills law - 315 (461)
    King-Anderson bill on - 301 (431)
    legislation on - 184 (23),
      301 (431), 315 (461)
    medicare bill - 344 (546),
      355 (576)
    medicare compromise - 304 (433)
    plan for - 249 (257)

Mexico
    and the Chamizal Zone - 344 (545)
    President's visit to - 239 (226)
      335 (516)

Mideast
    Republican sentiment in -
      351 (573)

Military
    and service depnedents - 225 (155),
      227 (157)

censorship issue in - 185 (61),
189 (64), 214 (136
muzzling of - 204 (122)
release of reservists - 219 (141)

Military-Industrial Alliance
influence of in the defense
program - 183 (22)

Milk
fallout in - 364-5 (597)
price of - 188 (63)
strontium levels in - 190 (65)

Monroe Doctrine
and Cuba -   383 (654), 385 (675)
status of - 217 (139)

National Security Council
Life article on - 419 (873)

National Stockpiling Program
purpose of - 193 (91)

NATO
and a declaration of interdependence - 338 (540)
and France's decision to create a
defense community apart from -
295 (403)
and Great Britain - 338 (540)
nuclear force for - 345 (546)
nuclear independence of - 208 (125)
question of a commander for -
352-3 (574)
strength of - 186-7 (62)
treaty relations with - 305 (434)
use of NATO ships as transports of
Soviet goods to Cuba - 381 (653)
U.S. responsibility to 239 (226),
293 (402)

Netherlands
and dispute with Indonesia on
West New Guinea - 176 (17)
and the Bunker proposal - 308 (436)
U.S. position on Indonesia and -
270 (320)

New Guinea
settlement of Indonesia Dutch
problem - 357 (592)

News Media
flow of the News - 419 (872)
information policies - 408 (836)
newspaper strikes - 283 (375)
public support of TV networks -
198 (95)
suppression of the news -
405 (833-4)
the press - 283 (376)

Nuclear Power
aid to France's nuclear force -
275 (333)
a NATO or European nuclear force -
345 (546)
and Project Rover - 415 (869)
atmospheric tests - 181-2 (21),
202 (120), 206 (124), 209 (126),
254 (260), 274 (333), 388 (677)
Brazil's urge for a ban on
weapons - 408 (836)
Christmas Island - 209-10 (126),
212 (134-5)
collapse of test negotiations -
199 (96)
extention of timing for additional
testing - 358 (593)
inclusion of Red China in test ban
agreement - 217 (139)
international nuclear control
stations - 357 (591-2)
Khrushchev on U.S. threat -
320 (490)
NATO as an independent nuclear
power - 208 (125)
negotiations at Geneva -
229-30 (197),   235 (201),
256 (272)
nuclear control posts - 360 (594),
361 (595)
nuclear tests and fallout -
335 (516)
on-site inspections for -
210-1 (127), 242 (228-9),
244 (230), 246-7 (254), 256 (272),
356 (591), 360 (594), 361 (595),
379 (652)
Prime MInister McMillian on -
212 (134-5)
role of Britain in Atomic
defense - 413 (867-8)
secret testing - 231 (198),
377 (650)
Soviet proposal for test ban -
278 (336), 375 (649)
studies on - 209 (126)
success of U.S. nuclear
submarines - 365 (631)
test ban and production of
delivery vehicles - 361 (595)
test ban, agreement on - 347 (569)
test ban, possibility for -
298 (406)
testing by U.S. and USSR -
205 (122-3), 241 (228),
264 (278)

testing, resumption of –
226 (156), 281 (338)
testing, U.S. security and –
382 (654)
U.S. initiative in a nuclear
war – 261 (276)
U.S. position on nuclear free
zones and non-nuclear clubs –
231-2 (198)
U.S. strategy in nuclear
engagement – 363 (597)
violation of test ban treaty –
381 (653)

Okinawa
and U.S. intentions in – 234 (200)

Organization of American States
exclusion of Cuba from
deliberations – 217 (139)

Pakistan
and dispute with India over
Kashmir – 215 (137-8)
relations with India – 186 (61-2)

Panama
renegotiation of treaty with –
325 (495)

Patents
uniform policy for – 289 (381)

Peru
developments in – 363 (597)

Petroleum
reduction of oil imports –
200 (96)

Poll Tax
outlawing of – 365 (632)

Pornography
in the mails – 377 (650)

Post Office
and censor of communist
propoganda – 188-9 (63)
postal rate increases – 218 (140)

Profit Sharing
– 281 (338-9)

Punta del Este
and the Alliance for Progress –
198 (94)
conference at – 192 (66), 193 (90),
179 (19)
criticism of Rockefeller –
213 (136)
U.S. ambitions at – 195 (92)

Quemoy and Matsu
and U.S. commitment – 330 (512)

Race
anti-negro terrorism in the
South – 387 (676)
racial representation in the
administration – 369 (635)

Racketeering
government's investigation of –
192 (66)

Railroads
pay raise for – 289 (381)

Reapportionment
President's participation in the
decision – 262 (277)
Supreme Court and – 259 (274)

Recession
tax cut as an anti-recession
measures – 201 (97)

Red China
and a nuclear test ban agreement –
217 (139)
inclusion of in arms
negotiations – 213 (135-6)

Republican Party
and the John Birch Society –
207 (124)
criticism of Berlin policy –
181 (20-1)
criticism of leadership in foreign
affairs – 317 (463)
criticism of White House
authority – 316 (462)
Eisenhower on – 344 (545)
on Vietnam – 214 (136-7)
sentiment of in the Mideast –
351 (573)

Reservists
demonstrations by – 252 (259)
scholarship aid for – 190 (65)

Schools
desegregation in – 277 (335),
296 (404)
public school bill – 203 (121)

SEATO Pact
signing of – 214 (137)
treaty relations with – 305 (434)
U.S. obligations to – 299 (407)

Segregation
in federal housing – 342 (544),
182 (21)

State Department
    and security risks - 189 (64)
    censors in - 219 (140)

Stock Market
    help for - 304 (433)
    status of - 296 (405)

Stockpiling
    information on - 208 (125-6)
    investigation into - 370 (636),
        374 (639)

Southeast Asia
    coalition governments in -
        178-9 (18-9)
    developments in - 357 (592)
    discussion of at Geneva -
        633 (200)
    policy in - 304-5 (434), 322 (492)

Soviet Union
    and Berlin - 209 (126), 258 (273),
        279 (337), 284 (377), 290 (382),
        346 (468-9), 377 (651), 380 (652),
        388 (676)
    and collaboration with U.S. on
        space - 221 (151-2), 233-4 (200),
    and collapse of test ban
        negotiations - 199 (96)
    and direct communication with the
        White House - 415-7 (871)
    and exchange of delegations with
        the U.S. - 217 (139)
    and Geneva negotiations - 375 (649)
    and inspection systems in test
        ban negotiations - 242 (229),
        246-7 (254), 256 (272), 356 (591),
        360 (594), 361 (595)
    and nuclear testing - 181-2 (21),
        202 (120), 241 (228), 254 (260),
    and planes in Berlin air
        corridor - 224 (154), 242-3 (229)
    and relations with Red China -
        407 (837)
    and Robert Kennedy's visit -
        215 (138)
    and the race in space - 366-7 (633)
    and the situation in Laos -
        198 (95), 285 (377)
    cooperation with U.S. on weather
        information - 306 (435)
    desertion of command office in
        Berlin - 366 (632)
    involvement in Cuba - 383 (674),
        388 (677), 389 (678)
    Kennedy on tensions with -
        342-3 (544)
    Kennedy visit to - 197 (95)

military significance of space
    shot - 368 (634)
proposal for a test ban -
    278 (336)
recognition of Algeria - 251 (258)
relations with U.S. - 194 (91),
    200 (96), 253 (261), 338 (541)
sale of jets to India - 360 (594)
strength of vs the U.S. -
    205 (122-3)
surplus food for - 230 (197)
treaty with East Germany -
    351 (572)
use of NATO ships as transports
    for goods of to Cuba - 381 (653)
withdrawal of bombers from Cuba -
    401-2 (830-1)

Space
    and Project Rover - 415 (869)
    and spy satellite - (263 (277)
    aerospace dispute - 392 (680)
    communications satellite bill -
        361 (595)
    Glenn's flight - 220 (151)
    military significance of Soviet
        space shot - 368 (634)
    postponement of Glenn's flight -
        218 (139)
    progress of program - 208 (125),
        326 (495-6)
    race in - 228 (157-8), 366-7 (633)
    U.S.-USSR collaboration -
        221-2 (151), 233-4 (200),
        391-2 (679
    uses of - 221 (151), 249 (256),
        288 (380), 388 (678)

Steel Industry
    agreement on a contract for -
        257 (272), 260 (275)
    and increase of prices -
        265 (315-6), 268-9 (318),
        233 (332)
    and wage price controls -
        267 (317-8)
    assurances from - 277 (335)
    bargaining timetable in - 178 (18)
    direct procurement of steel -
        270 (320)
    negotiations on - 210 (126-7),
        229 (196)
    price increase and the cost of
        living - 269 (320)
    response of to the President -
        234 (201)
    victors in the steel situation -
        275 (333)

Strategic Air Command
    false alarm of - 268 (318)

Strikes
    and the President's labor
        message - 352 (574)
    Chicago Northwestern Railway
        strike - 387 (677)
    of flight engineers - 318 (459)
    the missile strike at
        Huntsville - 371 (637)

Students
    foreign opposition to U.S. -
        226 (156)

Sugar Act
    and conflicts of interest -
        339 (541)

Summitry
    agreements - 231 (198)
    practice of - 213 (136)

Supreme Court
    and pornography - 377 (650)
    and reapportionment - 259 (273)
    declaration on prayer in schools -
        328 (510), 335 (516)

Taiwan
    and Chiang Kai-shek's decision
        to return to the mainland -
        333 (514)
    U.S. position on a return to the
        mainland by - 329 (511)

Taxes
    benefits to industry - 271 (321)
    President's program for -
        415-6 (870)
    reduction of - 227 (157),
        327 (496-7), 335 (516)
    tax bill - 282 (375), 310 (457),
        312-3 (459), 370-1 (636)
    tax cut - 316 (462), 337 (540),
        343 (544), 347 (569-70),
        358 (593), 409 (837), 412 (868)

Technology
    need for more scientists -
        414 (869)

Thailand
    dispatch of troops to - 294 (403)
    legal basis for troop presence -
        299 (407)
    possible attacks on - 300 (407-8)
    situation in - 302 (431),
        322 (492)

Third World
    European aid to - 349 (571)
    U.S. help to - 232 (199)

Trade
    agreements with the Common
        Market, etc - 229 (196)
    and appeals in the office of
        emergency planning - 180-1 (20)
    and protection of textiles -
        191 (66)
    development of the trade program -
        186 (62)
    import of crude oil - 399 (715)
    liberalization program -
        176-7 (17)
    reintroduction of with Cuba -
        196 (93)
    reduction of oil imports -
        200 (95)
    trade expansion bill - 263 (277),
        328 (510), 365 (632)
    tariff classification act -
        397-8 (712-3)

U-2 Incident
    - 231 (198)

Unemployment
    and defense contracts - 243 (229)
    and layoffs - 216 (138)
    effect on of stockpiling -
        210 (126-7)
    rise of - 212 (135)
    state of - 240 (227), 315 (461)

United Nations
    and relations with the U.S. -
        247 (254-5)
    and the Congo - 207 (124),
        350 (572)
    and the use of space - 249 (256)
    bond issue in - 182-3 (21-2),
        197 (94), 207 (125), 210 127,
        233 (199-200), 248 (255),
        356 (591), 365 (632), 370 (636),
        382 (653)
    Herbert Hoover's suggestion on -
        372 (637)
    relationship with the U.S. -
        407-8 (836)
    senate foreign relations committee
        plan on - 250 (257)
    U.S. payments to - 233 (199-200)

Urban Affairs
    and criticism by Governor
        Rockefeller - 205 (123)
    and the race question -
        200-01 (96)

bill on - 184-5 (60-1)
President's program on - 195 (92)
proposal on - 223-4 (153-4)
Urban Affairs Department -
    187 (62)

Vietnam
    administration reforms in -
        225 (155)
    American deaths in - 272 (322)
    and infiltration into Laos by
        North Vietnamese - 198 (95)
    fighting in - 204 (121-2)
    news of - 233 (199)
    situation in - 195 (93), 222 (153),
        322 (492), 416 (870)
    treaty relations with - 305 (434)
    U.S. efforts in - 207 (125),
        214 (136-7)
    U.S. troops in - 241 (228),
        177 (17)

Wages and Prices
    administration role in discussions
        on - 319 (490)
    increase of - 273 (372), 276 (334)
        287 (378)
    price controls - 279 (337)

Wilderness Bill
    status of - 399 (714)

Weather
    cooperation between U.S. and
        USSR on information on -
        306 (435)

West Germany
    relations with U.S. - 298 (406)
    U.S. misunderstanding with -
        304 (433)

Women
    demonstration in favor of
        disarmament - 183 (22)

Yugoslavia
    aid to - 312 (459)

1963

Africa
    and the conference in Addis
        Ababa - 521 (511)
    demonstration by African states
        at the ILO conference - 530 (572)
    President's travel plans to -
        521 (510-11)

Africa, South
    demonstration by African states
        re - 520 (572)
    import of lead from - 510 (422)

Agriculture
    and the wheat referendum -
        501 (376), 511 (422)
    and willingness of USSR and East
        Europe to purchase grain -
        562-3 (766)
    food prices - 506 (418-9)
    grain surplus - 511 (422)
    new soil bank legislation -
        510 (421)
    wheat shipment to USSR - 570 (774),
        575 (829), 576 (830), 586 (848)
        591 (852)

Alabama
    abuse of civil rights in -
        492 (347)
    crisis in Birmingham - 498 (373)
    integration of the University
        of Alabama - 506 (418)
    segregation ordinances in -
        496 (372)
    voting discrimmination in -
        496 (372)

Alliance for Progress
    evaluation of - 538 (617)
    state of - 468 (244), 592 (852)

Argentina
    relations with - 428 (98)

U.S. differences with - 482 (308)
U.S.-owned oil companies in -
    589 (849)

Atlantic Alliance
    problems of - 443 (175)

Atomic Energy Act
    President's authority
        under - 538-9 (618)

Atomic Energy Commission
    and Atomic tests - 543 (631)

Balance of Power
    in Mideast - 481 (307)

Bay of Pigs
    CIA involvement in - 459 (237)
    U.S. participation in - 421-2 (92)

Berlin
    establishment of international
        access authority over -
        516 (506)
    exchange of non-aggression
        statement between East and
        West - 521 (510-11)
    possibility of President going
        to East - 520 (510)
    settlement on - 443 (175),
        456 (208)
    spread of prohibitive zones
        in - 515 (506)

British Guiana
    political state of - 545 (633)

Budget
    Republican assessment of cuts
        of - 460 (238)
    results for year 1962-63 -
        522 (567)

Business Community
    and opportunities for the negro
        community - 504 (378)

The index numbering system should be read as follows: The first number represents the page in the Kennedy Presidential Press Conferences. The number in
parentheses is the source from the Public Papers of the President.

support for the tax bill –
447 (179)

Busing
President's opinion on –
556 (674)

Cambodia
and effect of Laos on – 494 (349)
situation in – 583 (845)

Canada
relationship with the U.S. –
463 (240), 499 (374)

Central America
attitude of presidents of on
Cuba – 470 (275)

Central Intelligence Agency
activities in Vietnam – 564 (768)
Allen Dulles on – 570 (774)
involvement in Bay of Pigs –
459 (237)
knowledge of Soviet missiles
in Cuba – 462 (239)
watchdog committee on – 568-9 (772)

Civil Rights
abuse of – 492 (347)
and the Philadelphia Mayoral
voting – 575 (828)
civil rights bill – 544 (632),
584 (846)
consideration of by Congress –
523 (567)
demonstrations on – 529 (572)
542 (631), 544-5 (632)
legislation on – 512 (423)
policy on – 535 (615)
possible withdrawal of funds from
Civil Rights Commission –
495 (349)
President on communists in
Civil Rights movement –
531 (574)

Chamizal Zone
transferral of to Mexico –
464 (241)

Civil Service
President on employees of –
427 (97)

Cold War
President's decision to
end the – 520 (510)

Common Market
and Great Britain – 427 (97),
431 (148), 455 (207)

and trade policies of – 519 (509)
U.S. policy on – 427 (97)

Communist China
and nuclear weapons – 518 (508)
break with USSR – 527 (571)
Kennedy on – 435 (151)
policies of – 526 (570)
resumption of trade with U.S. –
584 (845)
Stalinism of – 536-7 (616)
threats of – 487 (343), 535 (616)
threats of to India – 562 (678)

Communism
foreign aid for – 423 (94)
publication of propaganda
through U.S. – 448 (178)
spread of in Mideast – 499 (374)
strength of – 421 (92)
threat of to Western Hemisphere –
446 (178)

Congress
accomplishments of – 480 (306)
and agricultural bills –
502 (376)
and appropriation for American
warheads – 457 (208)
and approval of the nuclear test
ban treaty by the Senate –
553 (672)
and civil rights legislation –
512 (423), 544 (632)
and compulsory railroad
legislation – 546 (634)
and consideration of civil
rights proposals – 523 (567)
and disenchantment over foreign
aid – 588 (849)
and legal remedies for black
Americans – 537 (616)
and the authorization bill –
552 (647)
and the compromise bill –
591 (852)
and the President's hospital
plan – 451 (203)
and the mutual defense and
assistance bill of 1964 –
541 (629)
and the nuclear test ban treaty –
475 (280)
and the quality stabilization
bill – 581 (833)
and the tax bill – 426 (96),
454 (206), 459 (237), 543 (632)
and a watchdog committee on
the CIA – 568 (772)

and youth employment opportunity
  bill - 458 (236)
consideration of education bill -
  480 (306)
consideration of medical
  construction bill - 480 (306),
  494 (348)
consideration of transit bill -
  480 (306)
decision on space race - 482 (308)
double standard for the executive
  and - 485-6 (310)
limitation on terms for
  representatives - 425 (95)
state of legislation in -
  523 (567), 587-8 (848)

Conservation
  promotion of - 526 (570)

Costa Rica
  meeting at - 473 (278)
  President's visit to - 463 (240)

Cuba
  American legion on - 558 (676)
  and coexistence with U.S. -
    530 (573-4)
  and presence of Soviet troops
    and weapons in - 455 (206)
  and resumption of trade relations
    with the U.S. - 466 (243)
  and Soviet weapons
    in - 439 (155), 458 (209)
  and Soviet assistance - 423 (93),
    432-4 (149), 445-6 (177),
    450 (203)
  and statement of the Declaration
    of Central America - 474 (278)
  and the OAS - 494 (349)
  and the test ban treaty - 536 (615)
  and U.S. base at Guantanamo -
    509 (420-1)
  and U.S. shipping orders -
    444 (176)
  as military threat to U.S. -
    437 (153)
  attacks on U.S. shipping by
    planes of - 449-50 (202),
    452 (204), 457 (209)
  attitude of Central American
    Presidents on - 470 (275)
  economic condition of - 456 (207-8)
  elimination of communism from -
    435 (151)
  Everett Dirkson on - 537 (617)
  farm aid to - 447 (178)
  failure of to sign the test ban
    treaty - 561 (678)

Goldwater on - 557 (625)
military buildup in - 511 (422)
Republican criticism of administration's attitude on -
  490 (345)
Russian troops in - 461 (238)
  478 (304), 547 (634), 577 (830)
shipment of soviet oil to -
  465-6 (242)
threat of - 431 (148), 444 (176)
withdrawal of Soviets from -
  434-5 (151), 437 (153-4),
  468 (274), 549 (636)
withholding of information on
  situation in - 462 (239)

Cuban exiles
  aid to - 510 (421)
  American support for a
    government of - 491 (346)
  attack on Soviet ship by -
    472 (278)
  difficulties of preventing
    raids by - 479 (305)

Defense
  and Soviet underground tests -
    459-60 (237)
  funds for - 482 (308)
  need for a new strategic
    bomber - 428 (98)

Democratic Party
  stand of the "Young Democrats" -
    559 (676)

Demonstrations
  by blacks - 537 (616)
  on civil rights - 529 (572)
  riots in Washington, D.C. -
    426 (96)

Desegregation
  at University of Mississippi -
    429 (99)
  of schools in Atlanta, Georgia,
    and South Carolina - 569 (677)
  of southern cities - 554 (673)

Discrimination
  in housing - 556 (674)

Dominican Republic
  coup in - 567 (870-1)
  negotiations with - 577 (830)
  U.S. recognition of - 590 (851)

Domino Theory
  and Laos - 494 (349)

Economy
    administration's commitment
        of resources to - 486 (307)
    and budget cuts - 469 (238)
    and President's tax program -
        454 (205)
    appraisal of - 547 (364)
    budget resolutions for 1962-63 -
        522 (566)
    dangers of recession - 471 (276)
    economic picture and the tax
        bill - 496 (350)
    federal debt - 493 (348)
    federal expenditures - 489 (306)
    food prices - 506-7 (419)
    jobs in El Paso - 510 (422)
    national budget, Eisenhower's
        appraisal of - 481-2 (307)
    policy on 35-hour work week -
        453 (205), 566 (769)
    progress of - 528 (571)
    raise of interest rates -
        530 (573)
    support for the President's
        domestic programs - (427 (281-2)

Egypt
    and manufacture of missiles -
        481 (307)

Employment
    employment services act -
        526 (570)

Europe
    and economic cooperation with
        the U.S. - 516 (508)
    and GATT talks - 506 (420)
    de Gaulle on - 435 (152)
    interdependence and partnership
        with U.S. - 442 (174)
    possiblity of U.S. troop pullout
        from - 518 (509), 572-3 (826-7)
        447 (179P
    President's trip to - 483 (309),
    role of Germany in development
        of - 513 (505)
    U.S. policy on - 441 (173),
        461 (238)
    U.S. relations with - 421 (92)
    U.S. support for unification
        of - 431 (148)

Extremism
    the radical right - 500 (374-5)

Far East
    situation in - 534 (614)
    troop reductions in - 574 (828)

Foreign Aid
    and the Most-Favored-Nation
        clause - 423 (94)
    and the Congress - 585 (846-7)
    economic and military programs -
        467 (243)
    importance of - 541 (629-30),
        585 (847)
    public support for - 552 (647)

Foreign Assistance Act
    amendments to - 465 (242)

France
    and allegation of non-aggression
        attitude - 534 (614)
    and Nassau Pact - 435 (152)
    and nuclear weapons - 518 (508)
    and the test ban - 457 (208)
    and U.S. donation of nuclear
        weapons to - 532 (613)
    nuclear force for - 443 (174)
    nuclear deterrent of - 430 (99)
        431 (148)
    objections to treaty with
        Germany - 516 (502)
    withdrawal of forces from
        NATO - 520 (510)

Free Market
    regulation of - 507 (419)

GATT talks
    and wheat question - 512 (423)
    at Geneva - 508 (420), 512 (423)

Geneva
    and GATT negotiations at -
        508 (420), 512 (423)

German-French Treaty
    objections to - 516 (507)

Germany
    and U.S. forces in - 573 (827),
        582 (834)
    chances of overcoming division
        in - 515 (506)
    differences between Kennedy
        and Adenauer - 515 (555)
    objections to treaty with
        France - 516 (506)
    relations with the U.S. -
        514 (505)
    role of in European development -
        514 (505)
    spread of the prohibitive zones
        in Berlin - 515 (506)
    tacit recognition of East -
        533 (613)

view of Kennedy trip to
   Italy - 518 (508)

Great Britain
   and commitment of troops to
     NATO - 435 (152)
   and Common Market - 427 (97),
     431 (148), 455 (207), 517 (508)
   maintenance of relations with -
     485 (310)

Guatemala
   U.S. differences with - 483 (308)

Haiti
   economic sanctions against by
     the OAS - 501 (375-6)
   differences with - 455 (206)

Honduras
   coup in - 567 (770-1)
   U.S. recognition of - 590 (851)

Hospital Plan
   President's - 451 (203)

Housing
   discrimination - 556 (674)

I.G. Farben
   relationship with Interhandel
     463-4 (240)

Immigration Laws
   liberalization of - 425 (95)

India
   air support for - 452 (204)
   and the Bokaro steel mill
     project - 503 (377)
   military needs of - 473 (278),
     507 (419)

Indonesia
   foreign aid to - 588 (849)

Integration
   criticism of as inspired by
     communism - 531 (574)
   rate of - 560 (677)

Interhandel
   relationship with I.G. Farben -
     463-4 (240)

International Monetary Fund
   common effort on - 525 (569)

International Payments
   balance of - 549 (637)

Israel
   manufacture of missiles by -
     481 (307)

U.S. policy toward - 496 (373)

Italy
   President's trip to - 517 (508)
   withdrawal of U.S. missile
     bases in - 428 (98)

Jordan
   U.S. policy toward - 497 (373)

Korea, South
   situation in - 479 (805)
   U.S. interest in - 469 (275)

Labor
   settling dispute of - 481 (306)

Laos
   and the domino theory - 494 (349)
   cease-fire in - 489 (344)
   lack of U.S. military
     commitment - 501 (375)
   situation in - 487 (343)
   USSR on - 488 (344), 500 (375)

Latin America
   dangers to - 437 (153)
   need for revolution in - 538 (617)
   policy on dictatorships in -
     566 (770)

Legislation
   state of President's program -
     523 (567), 587 (848)

Lie Detectors
   use of - 478 (304)

Malaysia
   form of - 448 (179)

Merchant Mission
   progress of - 464-5 (242)

Mexico
   transferral of the Chamizal Zone
     to - 464 (241)

Mideast
   balance of power in - 481 (307)
   situation in - 497 (373)
   spread of communism in - 498 (373)

Miscegenation Laws
   abrogation of - 534 (614)

Mississippi
   and voting discrimination in -
     486 (311)
   abuse of civil rights - 492 (347)
   desegregation at the University
     of - 429 (99)
   Dick Gregory in - 486 (311)
   Nike-Zeus and Skybolt programs -
     in - 504 (378)

Missiles
America's statement in Anti-missile
missile race - 540 (619)
manufacture of by Israel and
Egypt - 481 (307)
polaris - 425 (95)
Soviet missiles in Cuba -
433 (149), 462 (239)
the Soviet anti-missile missile -
589 (851)
withdrawal of some U.S. bases -
428 (98)

Monroe Doctrine
status of - 476 (281)

Nassau Pact
- 435 (152), 443 (175), 456-7 (208),
539 (618)

NATO
and Nassau Pact - 435 (152),
456-7 (208)
British commitment of troops to -
435 (152)
France's withdrawal of forces
from - 519 (510)
General Norstad on - 443 (175-6)
non-aggression pact with Warsaw
pact - 533 (614)
nuclear force of - 464 (241),
472 (277)

Negroes
and quota system - 546 (633)
special consideration for -
546 (633)
support for Kennedy - 560 (677)

News Media
falsification of the news -
574 (828)
importance of the press
conference - 559 (677)
management of the news - 438 (154),
452 (204)
New York and Cleveland newspaper
strikes - 425 (95), 434 (150),
449 (202)

Nuclear Power
and Harriman-Hailsham talks on
non-diffusion - 519-20 (510)
and Nassau talks - 435 (152),
443 (175), 456-6 (208), 538 (618)
and secret atomic energy
agreement -543 (632)
and talks in Moscow - 517 (707),
521 (566)

control posts in East and
West - 545 (633)
curtailment of atmospheric
tests - 543 (631)
de Gaulle on - 435 (152)
France and - 518 (508)
France and the test ban -
457 (208)
French nuclear deterrent -
439 (99)
George Kennan on arms
control - 549 (636)
inspection systems - 424 (94),
487-8 (241), 513 (424)
international inspection and the
test ban treaty - 582 (834)
McNamara's rejection of Atomic
power plant for U.S. Carrier -
578 (831)
multi-national nuclear force -
446 (178)
nuclear weapons in space -
565 (769)
nuclear force of NATO - 464 (241),
472 (277)
Red China and - 518 (508)
resumption of nuclear testing -
554 (673)
Richard Russell on the test
ban - 561 (678)
Soviet underground tests -
459-60 (237)
Teller's criticism of test ban
treaty - 547 (634)
test ban and limitations on
U.S. - 555 (673-4)
test ban treaty - 422 (93),
453 (281), 487-8 (343),
503 (377), 532 (612-14),
542 (630), 544 (632), 547 (634)
test ban treaty and Cuba -
536 (615)

Olympic Games
funds for - 470 (275)

Organization of American States
and economic sanctions against
Haiti - 501 (375-6)
and limitation of movement of
Cuban Guerrillas - 490 (345)
and the Cuban problem - 494 (349)

Organized Crime
and the Valachi crime committee -
568 (771-2)

Otepka, Otto
decision on - 581-2 (833)

Pakistan
    fear of for U.S. support for
        India - 561-2 (678-9)

Peace Corps
    a domestic - 528 (571)
    increase in size of - 484 (309)

Pentagon
    morale at - 504 (378)

Poland
    aid to - 423 (94)

Pope John
    meeting with - 508 (420)

Population Growth
    government involvement in the
        attack on - 489 (344)

Protest
    student demonstrations -
        513 (423-4)

Puerto Rico
    future status of - 498 (373)
    voting rights for - 423 (94)

Race relations
    and busing - 556 (674)
    importance of - 502 (376)
    in Birmingham - 578 (831)

Radioactivity
    exposure of Utah children to -
        548 (636)

Railroad
    and compulsory arbitration -
        546 (634)
    dispute of - 523 (567)
    strike by - 485 (310)

Recession
    dangers of - 471 (276)

Republican Party
    and candidacy in 1964 - 509 (421)
    and the candidacy of McNamara -
        429 (98)
    assessment by of budget cuts -
        460 (238)
    criticism by - 444 (176), 490 (345)

Rockefeller, Nelson
    criticism of - 445 (177)

Schools
    corporal punishment in - 508 (420)

Segregation
    ordinances for in Birmingham -
        496 (350)

South
    attitude of southern
        segregationists - 531 (574)
    integration in - 531 (574)

Southeast Asia
    dangers to - 448 (179)
    maintaining security in -
        494 (349)
    threats to security of - 487 (343)

Soviet Union
    agreements with U.S. - 495 (349)
    and bilateral transport agreement
        with U.S. - 580 (832)
    and collaboration with U.S. on
        Moon shot - 548 (636)
    and expansion of trade with
        U.S. - 578 (830)
    and nuclear testing - 503 (377)
    and nuclear weapons in space -
        565 (769)
    and resistance to inspection -
        582 (834)
    and the Barghoorn problem -
        583 (845), 587 (848)
    and underground testing -
        460 (237)
    and U.S wheat shipment to -
        571 (774), 576 (829), 577 (830)
    and willingness to buy U.S.
        grain - 562-3 (766)
    attack on ship of by Cuban
        exiles - 472 (277-8)
    break with Red China - 527 (571)
    buildup in Cuba by - 423 (93)
    extention of commercial credit
        to - 570 (773)
    negotiations with U.S. -
        591 (851-2)
    on Laos - 488 (344), 500 (375)
    position on inspection sites -
        513 (424)
    response to proposal of
        International access authority
        over Berlin - 516 (506)
    shipment of oil to Cuba -
        465-6 (242)
    significant changes in - 466 (243)
    Soviets in Cuba - 432-3 (149),
        445-6 (177), 455 (206),
        461 (238), 479 (304), 479 (305),
        577 (830)
    space program of - 523 (567-8)
    state of anti-missile missile
        race and - 540 (619) 590 (851)
    supply of weapons to Cuba -
        439 (155), 451 (203)

threats to U.S. - 487 (343)
travel restrictions for Soviet
  diplomats in U.S. - 587 (848)

Space
  ban on nuclear weapons in -
    565 (769)
  mercury flight - 507-8 (419)
  moon race - 579 (831)
  race in - 485 (310)
  state of moon project - 523 (567-8)
  U.S. response to Soviet lanuch
    of space crew - 472 (277)
  U.S. - USSR collaboration on
    space shot - 548 (636)
  wisdom of the "Man to the Moon"
    program - 495 (349)

Steel Industry
  price increase in - 570 (773)

Strikes
  New York and Cleveland newspaper -
    425 (95), 434 (150), 449 (202),
    454 (205-6), 473 (278), 481 (306)
  railroad - 485 (310)
  dock workers' - 437 (153)

Summitry
  prospects of a summit
    conference - 524 (568), 535 (615)

Supreme Court
  and the Curtis Rider case -
    586 (847)

Taiwan
  attack on the mainland -
    511 (422-3)

Taxes
  and the business community -
    447 (179)
  resistance to tax reform -
    441 (173)
  Rockefeller on - 556-7 (675)
  tax bill - 426 (96), 454 (206),
    496 (350), 502 (376), 544 (632),
    584 (846)
  President's plan on - 440 (172-3),
    476 (280)
  tax cut - 440 (173), 441 (173),
    459 (236-7), 475 (280)

TFX
  Admiral Anderson on - 498 (374)
  and Secretary Korth - 548 (636),
    580 (830)
  contract on - 469 (274), 480 (306)
  controversy over - 474 (279)
  President's role in the contract -
    477 (281)

Thailand
  and effect of on Laos - 494 (349)

Trade
  expansion of with USSR - 578 (830)
  policy of U.S. re. USSR -
    563 (768)
  restrictions on imports of
    wool textiles - 455 (207)
  resumption of with Red China -
    584 (845)
  trade expansion act - 438 (154)
  with Western allies - 473 (278)
  zero tariff authority - 438 (154)

Turkey
  withdrawal of U.S. missile
    bases - 429 (98)

Unemployment
  and TFX fighter controversy -
    475 (279)
  level of - 581 (833)

United Arab Republic
  and foreign aid - 589 (849)

United Nations
  and participation by South
    Africa at - 530 (572)
  participation of - 556 (674)

United States Information Agency
  dissemination of information
    by - 490-1 (346)

Vatican
  communication with U.S. -
    522 (567)

Venezuela
  and refusal to recognize
    Guatemala - 483 (308)
  U.S. relations with - 466 (243)

Vietnam
  Allen Dulles on - 570 (774)
  and Ngo Dinh Nhu - 556 (674)
  CIA in - 564 (768)
  Church on - 559 (676)
  effect of Laos on - 494 (349)
  information on - 558 (675-6)
  political situation in - 525 (569)
  return of troops to - 591-2 (851)
  troop withdrawal from - 574 (828)
  U.S. military commitment -
    501 (375), 509 (421)
  U.S. policy toward - 555 (673),
    556 (674), 566 (770), 586 (847)
  withdrawal of American dependents
    from - 559 (676)

Warsaw Pact
    non-aggression pact with NATO –
      534 (614)

Washington, D.C.
    riots in – 426 (96)

Yemen
    situation in – 575 (824),
      589 (849)

Yugoslavia
    aid to – 423 (94)

Accelerated Works Program and
    unemployment - 581
Acoma Indians, request for peace
    corps assistance by - 372
Adam Clayton Powell, President on - 535
Adenauer, differences between Kennedy
    and - 515
Adenauer, letter from - 145
Adenauer, talks with - 519
Administration aid and Massachusetts
    primary - 299
Administration appointments, favoritism
    or negligence in - 299
Administration assests and
    liabilities - 571
Administration members, club
    memberships for - 152
Administration priorities - 420
Administration success - 29
Admiral Burke's speech - 30
Aerospace dispute - 392
Aerospace field, report in - 399
Aerospace industry, negotiations
    with - 280
Africa, plans for trip to - 521
Africa, the conference in Addis
    Ababa - 521
Aged, health care for - 246
Aged, medicare for - 188
Aged, price of medicine for - 79
Agriculture, effect of automation and
    technical improvements on - 85
Agricultural progress, new - 19
Aid program, reorganization of - 313
Air Force association, opposition to
    the test ban treaty by the - 558
Air Force missile program, status
    of - 45

Air transport agreement,
    bilateral - 580
Alabama, crisis at Birmingham - 498
Alabama, integration of the
    University of - 506
Albany, Ga., events in - 358
Alger Hiss' TV appearance - 408
Algeria, cease fire in - 223
Algeria,U.S. intervention in - 104
Algerian government, Soviet
    recognition of - 251
Algerian government, U.S. policy
    toward a new - 234
Algerian peace talks - 44
Algerian problem - 180
Algiers revolt, CIA involvement
    in - 108
Alliance for Progress - 592
Alliance for Progress, evaluation
    of - 538
Alliance for Progress, Latin America
    and - 325, 386
Alliance for Progress, progress
    of - 198, 364
Alliance for Progress and submission
    of reforms to - 244
Almond, nomination of Governor - 374
Amalgamated Clothing Workers, wage
    decision by - 298
Ambassadors - 22
Ambassadors, financial status of - 359
American Legion comments on the
    Cuban problem - 558
American-owned telephone companies,
    Brazil's seizure of - 237
American Republics, cooperative action
    with other - 30
Anderson's retention - 498

Anti-missile missile race, America's
status in - 540
Anti-recession measure, tax cut
for - 201
Argentina, events in - 257
Argentina, relations with - 428
Argentina, U.S. differences with - 483
Argentina and U.S. oil companies - 589
Arms accord, possibility of - 60
Arms control, George Kennan on - 549
Arms control negotiations - 38
Arms control negotiations, inclusion
of Red China in - 213
Assessment of issues of President's
1st year - 157
Astronaut, launching of - 97
Atlantic Alliance, a declaration of
interdependence and the - 338
Atlantic Alliance, major problems
of - 443
Atlantic Alliance, sharing the burden
of defense and foreign aid - 49
Atlantic partnership and deterrence
to aggression - 339
Atlantic partnership as a political
unit - 340
Atmospheric tests, curtailment of - 543
Atmospheric tests, possiblity of - 152
Atmospheric tests, resumption of - 274
Atomic energy agreement, a secret - 543
Atomic Energy Act, President's
authority under - 538
Atomic defense, role of Britain
in - 413
Atomic industry, development by the
states - 29
Atomic industry, regulatory
responsiblity for - 66
Atomic power plant, McNamara's
rejection of - 578
Atomic testing, continuation of - 388
Attorney General's overseas trip - 236
August 28th march, effect of the - 544
Authorization bill - 552
Automobile negotiations - 141
Azores, American bases in - 187

Barghoorn, Professor - 583
Barghoorn and the exchange
agreement - 587
Barghoorn and the wheat deal - 592
Bay of Pigs, CIA involvement in - 459
Bay of Pigs invasion - 421
B-70 - 236
B-70, funds for - 244
B-70 question - 254
Belasco theater - 199

Berlin
Adenauer on - 223
air corridor and USSR - 242
air corridor and Soviet
planes - 224
an international administration
on the Autobahn to - 167
consultations on - 145
crisis in - 157
exchange of non-aggression statements between east & west - 521
fighter escorts for transport
in and out of - 225
negotiations with the USSR
on - 284
possibility of ground war in
Europe over - 124
possiblity of war over - 133
possible mobilization of forces
in - 113
public opinion on - 127
question of - 138, 176, 343
Republican criticism on - 141
settlement - 443
settlement, prospects for - 147
situation in - 122, 151, 377,
situation, methods for
financing - 122
Soviet abandonment of command
office in - 366
Soviet announcement on - 386
Soviet intervention in - 346
Soviet involvement in - 380
Soviets in - 209
state of western readiness for
negotiations - 170
talks, status of U.S. as
spokesman on - 280
the Soviet Union and - 258
threat - 118
U.S. proposals on - 279
Wall, destruction of - 181
Wall, U.S. attitude on the
building of - 153
withdrawal of forces from - 333
Billie Sol Estes
affair - 291, 303
defraud, stockpile investigation
and the - 307
warehouses of and removal of
grain from by Agricultural
department - 305
Bipartisan measures, sponsorship
of - 588
Birmingham, race relations in - 578
Bond issue - 210

Bond issue, foreign relations committee's plan on - 250
Brazil, visit of the President of - 260
Brazil's economic problems, effect of - 417
British admission to the EEC - 431
British Guiana - 545
Brown, meeting with Governor - 345
Budget, the - 9, 17
Budget, 1963 - 297
Budget, balancing the - 160
Budget cuts, Republican assessment of - 460
Budget, our GNP and the possiblity of a balanced - 316
Burke, President's comments on - 36
Business and Democrats - 312
Business community - 447
Business community, assurances to - 163
Business community, control of - 369
Business, President's efforts regarding - 321
Business slump and a tax cut - 14
Business and the administration - 334
Business world, administration sensitivity to - 396
Businessmen, President's view of - 287
Busing - 556

Cabinet, naming of Mr. Gronouski to the - 557
California, construction industry in - 285
Cambodian situation - 583
Cambodia's neutrality, guarantee for - 380
Campaign in the South - 376
Campaign promises - 86
Canada and the U.S. - 463
Canada, U.S relations with - 498
Candidates, equal time requests for - 341
Carpetbagging, rules on - 257
Carpets and glass, duties on - 326
Castro and Brazil - 143
Castro government - 527
Castroism, checking - 179
Chamizal Zone to Mexico, transmittal of the - 464
Chamizal Zone, solution to - 344
Chandler, President and Governor - 483
Charles Meriwether, nomination of - 44, 58
Chicago Northwest Railway strike - 387
Chile, discussion with the President of - 418
China, Americans imprisoned in - 20

China, reopening of diplomatic relations with - 4
Christmas Island - 209
Christmas Island, agreement with Britain on the use of - 205
CIA activities in Vietnam - 564
CIA budget - 213
CIA agents, Castro's alleged capture of - 580
CIA, Allen Dulles' comments about the,

CIA involvement and Bay of Pigs - 459
CIA, supervision over - 197
CIA watchdog committee - 568
Cigarette smoking, federal action against - 307
Cigarette smoking and killer diseases - 317
Cigarettes and cancer - 512
Citizen participation - 53
Civil defense policy - 170
Civil Rights - 15, 55, 544
Civil Rights, an advance of - 527
Civil Rights bill - 584
Civil Rights, Civil Rights Commission and the abuse of - 492
Civil Rights Commission, possible withdrawal of funds from - 498
Civil Rights demonstration, August 28th - 542
Civil Rights legislation - 55, 198
Civil Rights, Philadelphia mayoral election and - 575
Civil Rights policy - 535
Civil Service employees, pressure on - 427
Civil War Commission and Southern Blacks - 72
Clay Report - 503
Cold War, President's desire to end the - 520
Cold War, President's policy in - 220
Colonel Glenn's flight, postponement of - 218
Common Market, Britain's entry into - 107
Common Market, Great Britain's differences with - 308
Common Market, negotiations in - 183
Common Market, U.S. relations with - 308
Communications Act, amendment of section 15 - 19
Communications and Meteorology, funds for - 91
Communications satellite bill - 361

Communist and Capitalist blocs,
  non-intervention between - 272
Communists, competition with - 400
Communism, freeing Cuba from - 241
Communism, U.S. military role in edu-
  cating the public re
Communist bloc, fragmentation of - 192
Communist China, export of wheat
  to - 243
Communist Chinese policy - 526
Communist Chinese, problem of - 58
Communist Chinese relations with
  West, normalization of - 108
Communist Chinese, threat of - 536
Communist countries, aid to - 312
Communist propoganda, publication of
  in the U.S. - 447
Communist publishing and the book
  gap - 74
Communist systems, durability of - 29
Compromise bill - 591
Conditions in the country - 15
Conflict of international laws - 96
Congo airlift - 207
Congo, future developments in - 40
Congo, situation in - 42, 350
Congo, U.S. proposals and - 76
Congress, accomplishments of - 347, 480
Congress and the Executive, double
  standard for - 485
Congress, campaigning by - 333
Congress, increasing the quality
  of - 344
Congress, legislation in - 313
Congress, pace of - 235
Congressional races, results of - 373
Congressmen, limitation on terms
  for - 425
Conservation, promotion of - 526
Conservative trends of the
  President - 192
Conventional forces, increase of - 121
Corporation profits, Secretary Dillon's
  estimate of - 75
Costa Rica, President's visit to - 463
Cotton, two-price system in - 399
Cuba
    American policy on - 82
    Americans imprisoned in - 20
    and Governor Stevenson - 412
    attitude of Central American
      Presidents on - 410
    Cuba-based planes, attack on U.S.
      ship by - 449
    coexistence with - 530
    communist troops and supplies
      in - 372
    embargo of imports from - 159

Cuba (Cont'd)
    freeing of from communism - 241
    General Taylor's findings
      on - 114
    Khrushchev's speech on - 410
    military buildup in - 510
    military threat of to U.S. - 437
    NATO ships as transports of
      Soviet goods to - 381
    offensive weapons in - 416
    payment of farm aid to - 447
    prisoners in - 415
    reduction of Soviet troops
      in - 492
    reintroduction of trade
      with - 196
    Republican criticism
      tration's attitude on - 490
    resumption of friendly
      relations with - 469
    Russian troops and weapons
      in - 455, 461, 477
    Senator Capehart's allegations
      re - 379
    Senator Dirkson's concern
      re - 537
    Senator Goldwater's comments
      on - 557
    Shipment of Soviet oil to - 465
    shipping orders of - 444
    shipping to - 415
    Soviet criticism on - 388
    Soviet implied threat on - 389
    Soviet military buildup in - 423
    Soviet military personnel
      in - 432
    Soviet nationals in - 445
    Soviet troops in - 478, 547
    Soviet weapons in - 450
    Soviet withdrawal of troops
      from - 468
    stemming travel of U.S. citizens
      to - 473
    supplies to - 374
    U.S. support for an invasion
      of - 76
    the test ban treaty and - 536
    threat of - 444
    trade embargo on - 97
    trade policy toward - 36
    trial of POWs in as war
      criminals - 250
    troops in - 380
    withdrawal of Soviets in - 434
    withdrawal of Soviet troops
      in - 549

Cuban affairs, President's authority
    in – 391
Cuban air attack – 456
Cuban Communist Party, differences
    between Castro and – 259
Cuban exile government, administra-
    tion support for – 491
Cuban exiles, attack on Soviet ship
    by – 472
Cuban exiles, difficulties of
    preventing raids by – 479
Cuban exiles, training and arming
    of – 96
Cuban invasion and Secretary Rusk – 146
Cuban military strength, buildup
    of – 251
Cuban operation, President and – 249
Cuban problem, American Legion
    comments on the – 558
Cuban problem and the OAS – 494
Cuban refugees, assistance to – 510
Cuban refugees, training of – 84
Cuban release of POWs – 271
Cuban situation – 388
Cuban situation, Latin American
    assistance in the – 340
Cuban situation, Latin American role
    in – 390
Cuban situation, withholding of
    information on – 462
Cuban tractor deal – 113

Dairy farmers, support prices
    for – 262
Dairy price support program – 245
Dangers to the U.S. – 25
Day, status of Postmaster General – 469
Debt limit, pressure for a positive
    vote on – 326
Defense community apart from NATO,
    France's creation of – 295
Defense contracts – 245
Defense Department, censors in – 219
Defense, Department of – 133
Defense expenditures – 154
Defense funds, requests for – 123
Defense matters, decisions on – 145
Defense spending, Eisenhower on – 334
Defense strategy, reappraisal of – 42
Deficits, effect of – 320
de Gaulle and the President – 303
de Gaulle, meeting with – 311
de Gaulle on Berlin, understanding
    with – 106
de Gaulle, talks with – 520
de Gaulle, usefulness of talks
    with – 490

Democratic candidates, other – 568
Democratic convention in South – 424
Democratic Party in New York – 7
Democrats and business – 342
Democrats "young", the stand of – 559
Democrats, Republican efforts to
    unseat – 196
Dependents going overseas – 268
Dependents of servicemen, transferral
    to Europe – 373
Desegregation of public schools – 25
Desegregation of schools – 277
Development lending, commitments
    for – 142
Dhahran, renewal of U.S. base rights
    at – 216
Dick Goodwin – 139
Disarmament – 206
Disarmament and its influence on
    the economy – 206
Disarmament and Peace, women's
    demonstration in favor of – 183
Disarmament and the plan for
    negotiations – 47
Disarmament, joint U.S.– British
    agreement on – 216
Disarmament negotiations, U.S. position
    on – 2
Disarmament progress, zonal – 252
Disarmament, prospects of – 235
Disarmament, Soviet concept of – 45
Disputes in other countries, U.S.
    policy on – 83
Distressed areas, President's
    position on – 39
Division of Powers – 187
Dock Workers' strike – 436
Dollar, status of – 37
Domestic economy – 81
Domestic interest rates, President's
    authority over – 28
Domestic issues, Kennedy and
    Eisenhower on – 308
Domestic program, congressional
    support for – 253
Domestic program, President's – 189
    151
Dominican junta, negotiations
    with – 577
Dominican Republic, recognition
    of – 590
Dominican Republic, situation in – 164

East Berlin, access of West to – 155
    144
East Europe, self determination of the
    peoples of – 126

East German refugees - 132
East Berlin, possibility of President going to - 520
East Germany, Russian peace treaty with - 351
Economic Community, U.S. and - 426
Economic myths and realities - 371
Economic picture and the tax bill - 496
Economic policy - 353
Economic recovery - 230
Economic recovery and unemployment - 154
Economic review - 84
Economic upturn, views on - 42
Economy - 359
Economy, disarmament and its influence on - 206
Economy, appraisal of the - 547
Economy, evaluation of - 348
Economy, state of - 69
Economy, state of - 240
Economy, strength of - 80
Economy, unemployment and a balanced budget - 315
Educational bills, aid to - 126
Educational program, financing of - 48
Educational TV, bill on - 192
Edward Kennedy's candidacy - 332, 371
Edward Kennedy in Massachusetts - 378
Egypt, manufacture of missiles by - 481
Egypt, U.S. and British aid to - 314
Eisenhower's criticism of legislation - 297
Eisenhower, Kennedy's talk with - 259
Eisenhower's military policy, criticism of - 18
Eisenhower's participation in the administration - 67
Election results - 283
Election results, effect of - 406
Elections, recent - 157
Elections, upcoming - 392
Elections, goal in November for - 354
Election reform, proposal for - 11
Electrician's Union's contract in New York - 191
El Paso, jobs in - 510
Emergency Planning, appeals in the office of - 180
Employment Services Acts - 526
Estes case, Eisenhower suggestion on - 295
Europe, aid to 3rd world - 349
European allies and the U.S. - 447
Europe, American troops in - 330
Europe as a third force, possibility of - 298

Europe, interdependence and partnership in - 442
European nuclear force - 345
Europe, political and economic integration of - 191
Europe, possiblity of U.S. troop pullout from - 518
Europe, President's trip to - 484
Europe, removal of U.S. forces from - 572
Europe, U.S. policy toward - 441
Europe, U.S. policies in - 461
Europe, withdrawal of troops from - 448
European situation, de Gaulle on - 435
European trans-Atlantic economic cooperation and - 517
Executive Privilege, abuse of - 7
Export licenses for American manufacturers to the Iron Curtain - 56
Extremist groups, financial contributions to - 171

Fall campaign - 373
Fallout detection and survival and monitor systems, funds for - 317
Fallout, protection against - 174
Fallout shelters - 147, 160, 341
Far East policies, review of - 322
Far East, situation in - 534
Far East, troop reductions in - 574
Farm bill - 65
Farm production, control and management of - 179
Federal aid for the unemployed - 7
Federal aid to schools, President's view of - 66
Federal employees - 493
Federal expenditures - 14, 490
Federal food Insurance act of 1956, revival of - 275
Federal funds, withholding of from universities - 43
Federal judgeships in South - 462
Federal housing projects, segregation in - 73
Federal housing, segregation in - 342
Fidel Castro as Communist - 77
Floyd Patterson and Sonny Liston - 199
Foreign affairs, Republican criticism of leadership in - 317
Foreign Aid - 125, 467,588
Foreign aid and long term borrowing - 73
Foreign aid and the Most-Favored-Nation clause - 423

Foreign Aid bill – 152, 378, 323,
Foreign aid funds, request for – 239
Foreign aid program – 585
Foreign aid, public support for – 552
Foreign Assistance Act, amendment
    to – 465
Foreign dignitaries, possibility of
    meeting with – 18
Foreign policy and the military – 13
Foreign policy, assertion and support
    of – 98
Foreign policy information – 90
Foreign policy, negotiations on – 414
Foreign policy, Rostow on – 336
Foreign policy, status of – 98
Foreign policy, Fulbright on – 96
Foreign policy, the President's – 149
Foreign policy, Vice-President's
    comments on – 534
Foreign Service Academy – 484
Food distribution, to the unemployed –
    3
Food for Peace program, expansion
    of – 177
Food prices – 506
Food surplus, U.S's – 250
Formosa, possibility of an attack on the
    mainland by – 261
Formosa, U.S. policy on – 262
France and General de Gaulle,
    President's impressions of – 108
France and nuclear weapons – 518
France in Europe, role of – 106
France, nuclear equipment for – 314
France's withdrawal from NATO – 520
Francis Gary Powers and missing U.S.
    fliers – 10, 231
Frankfurter, Felix – 379
Franklin D. Roosevelt Jr. – 442
Freedom Riders' Movement – 123
Free elections, majority will in – 263
Freeman's effectiveness – 510
Free market, significance of – 397
French Atomic Tests – 105
French nuclear deterrent – 430-1
Fuel, limitation on import of – 44

Gary Powers, location of 224
Gary Powers, release of – 78
GATT negotiations and wheat – 512
GATT talks at Geneva – 508
George Romney's criticism –206
General Clay's return, significance
    of – 269
Geneva, Ambassador Dean's statements
    at – 349
Geneva, discussions about Berlin and
    Southeast Asia at – 233

Geneva, discussions at – 247
Geneva negotiations – 229
Geneva, summit conference in – 240
Geneva, talks at – 505
Germany, U.S. relations between – 514
Germany, chances of overcoming
    divisions in – 515
Germany, decision for troops to be
    removed and – 582
Germany, public support for – 119
Germanies, President on ties
    between – 173
German and Berlin question – 20
German crisis, recent – 161
German-French treaty – 516
German views of President's trip to
    Italy – 518
Glenn's achievements – 222
Gold drain – 347
Gold flow abroad, reduction of – 362
Goldwater's accusation – 574
Goldwater's candidacy – 567
Goldwater, Senator – 546
Goldwater, the debating of – 581
Government, problems involved in
    influence in – 300
Government supervision of the TV
    networks – 198
Government waste question, public
    response on the – 45
Grass roots, apathy at the – 493
Great Britain, maintainance of
    relations with – 485
Gromyko, meetings with – 75
Gromyko, meeting with and the possibi-
    lity of an address to the UN – 554
Gromyko, objective of talks with – 564
Gromyko, Rusk's talks with – 258
Gromyko, talks with – 150
Growth rate, country's – 116
Guantanamo Bay – 254, 509, 483

H.R. 10 – 310, 400
Haiti, and the OAS – 501
Haiti, differences with – 455
Harriman and Khrushchev discussions –
    500
Harriman-Hailsham talks – 519
Herbert Hoover's suggestion – 372
HEW, filling the post of secretary
    of – 343
HEW, new head of – 292
Higher Education, bill to aid – 329
High school children, request
    from – 164
Highways, money for – 60
Hijacking – 134

Hong Kong, refugee problem in - 301, 303, 324
Honduras, recognition of - 590
Hospital plan, President's - 451
House of Representatives, increasing the size of - 216
House of Representatives, proposals to increase the size of - 30
Housing, discrimmination in - 556
Housing order - 406
Houston, President's trip to - 393
Hungry people, food to - 43

ICBM warning system in the South - 296
ILO conference, demonstration by African states at - 530
Immigration laws - 136, 423
Import competition, economic boycott as an answer to - 57
Inaugural address - 9
India, air support to - 452
India, militaty assistance requirements in - 506
India, military needs and the U.S. responsibility - 473
India, persuasion of Prime Minister of - 161
India, purchase of Soviet jets by - 360
India, weapons for - 319
Indian situation - 404
Indian treaties, changing of - 55
Indiana Dunes, preservation of - 237
Indo-Dutch dispute - 176
Indonesia and Netherlands, U.S. position on - 270
Indonesia, economic survey in - 374
Industrial countries, invitation to build plants in U.S. - 341
Industry, effect of Automobile and technical improvements on - 85
Industry, tax benefits to - 271
Inflation - 18, 398
Information policies - 408
Information to the public - 22
Inspection sites within the USSR - 66
Inspections, proposals by British and U.S. diplomats - 486
Inspections, Russian position on - 246
Inspection systems, U.S. proposal for - 210
Items which are understocked - 199
Intelligence activities, reorganization of - 114
Interest rates, rise of - 530
Inter-American proposal - 314
Inter-American affairs, President's handling of - 117

Interhandel and I.G. Farben, relationship of - 463
International access authority - 289
Interests, conflicts of - 579
International Control Commission, Indian chairman of - 96
International inspection - 582
International Monetary Fund - 525
International nuclear control stations - 357
International payments, balance of - 549
Israel, manufacture of missiles by - 481

Japanese officer, Legion of Merit to - 272
Japan, U.S. ties with - 100
Joel Broyhill's comments - 387
John Birch Society - 88, 419, 207
Judicial system, control of - 180
Juvenile delinquincy, policy on - 21
Kamer, Charles - 140
Kashmir - 180, 215, 186
Kennedy and Khrushchev, exchange of letters between - 325
Kennedy and Khrushchev, meeting between - 71
Kennedy appearance at UN - 59
Khrushchev, aim of meeting with - 105
Khrushchev and Harriman, discussion between - 500
Khrushchev and the German problem - 129
Khrushchev, Ambassador Thompson's meeting with - 61
Khrushchev, communication with - 404
Khrushchev, consultation with - 376
Khrushchev, conversation with Ambassador Thompson - 3
Khrushchev, meeting with - 35
Khrushchev on capitalism - 407
Khrushchev, possibility of meeting with - 7,13, 369, 488
Khrushchev's present status - 485
Khrushchev, President's message to - 56
Khrushchev's remark re the U.S. threat - 320
Khrushchev's responsibility in setting off a nuclear war - 143
Khrushchev, Robert Frost's visit with - 390
Khrushchev's speech on Cuba - 411
Khrushchev's visit, possibility of - 2
Khrushchev's willingness to release the fliers - 6

Korea, situation in - 478
Korea, U.S. interest in South - 469
Korth's problems - 580, 575
Kremlin, direct communication with - 416

Labor disputes, settlement of - 481
Labor management conference - 65
Labor management relations - 16
Labor message - 352
Labor unions and the work week - 62
Labor statistics - 568
Latin America - 62
Latin America and self-help
    measures - 136
Latin America, 5 point program on - 21
Latin America, U.S. policy on
    dictatorships in - 566
Laundry workers - 100
Laos - 198
Laos and Thailand, possible attacks
    on - 300
Laos and the buildup of conventional
    forces - 74
Laos and the domino theory - 494
Laos and the prospects of improving
    relations with the USSR - 74
Laos, cease-fire in - 78, 85
Laos, crisis in - 10
Laos, importance of a free - 71
Laos, foreign aid to - 133
Laos, neutrality of - 106
Laos, possibility of increased U.S.
    aid to - 61
Laos, situation in - 52, 195, 218, 258,
    294, 222,
Laos, U.S. backing for a coalition
    government in - 317
Laos, U.S. policy in - 285
Laotian question - 69, 118
Legislative program, support for - 331
Legislative program, status of
    President's - 523
Legislative priorities - 171
Legislation, status of - 587
Lie detectors, use of - 478
Lincoln Park problem - 196
Literacy test bill - 291

Mainland China, possible attack on -
    329
Mainland, Chiang Kai-shek's decision to
    return to - 333
Manned strategic bomber, need for - 428
Man to the Moon, progress in sending
    a - 153, 495
Margaret Chase Smith, possible
    candidacy of - 586
Maritime strike - 115

Maritime strikes, food shipment to
    Brazil and - 306
Martin Luther King, impression of - 340
Martin Luther King's comments on
    the President - 350
Meat and Grain prices - 376
Medical Care program - 88, 249, 315
Medical care bill,
    on - 355
Medical Care amendment - 302
Medicare compromise - 304
Medical bills, legislation on
    payment of - 301
Medicare legislation - 184
Merchant fleet - 507
Mexican-Americans, recognition
    of - 27
Mexico, President's visit to - 239,
    335
Mideast, Republican sentiment in - 351
Mideast, situation in - 497
Military abroad, cutback in - 6
Military, Admiral Anderson's speech
    on public confidence in the - 561
Military aid - 350
Military at the Pentagon, muzzling
    of the - 204
Military censorship issue - 189
Military dependents, repeal of
    directive on - 16
Military dependent's travel - 227
Military figures, limitations
    on public statements of - 185
Military-Industrial Alliance, influence
    of in the defense spending
    program - 183
Military reservists, release of - 219
Military speeches, censorship
    of - 214
Military strength, deterioration
    of - 156
Milk, discovery of fallout in - 363
Milk, price of - 188
Milk, strontium levels in - 190
Minimum wage bill, compromise
    on - 71
Miscegenation laws, abrogation
    of - 534
Missile bases, withdrawal of some
    U.S. - 428
Missile gap - 23, 52
Missile program, acceleration of - 21
Missiles, Israel and Egypt manufacture
    of - 481
Missile strike - 371
Mississippi, desegregation at the
    University of - 429
Mississippi, Dick Gregory in - 486

Mississippi, Civil Rights Commission
hearing on - 474
Moon project, status of - 523
Moon race - 579
Mobilization powers, President's
request for reserve - 391
Monroe Doctrine - 99, 382, 476
Monroe Doctrine, status of - 217
Mortgage bankers and the FHA
system - 119
Moscow talks - 517, 524
Most-Favored-Nation clause and
foreign aid - 423
Mutual assistance Act, Amendment
of - 135

Nassau Pact and NATO - 456
Nassau talks - 539
National Auto show - 388
National budget, Eisenhower approval
of - 481
National Economic issues, White House
conference on - 305
National Guard, call-up of - 121
National health Institute, budget cut
of the by HEW - 167
NATO Alliance's European members,
force goals of - 104
NATO allies, part played by our - 143
NATO commander, question of - 352
NATO and Nassau pact - 456
NATO and Warsaw pacts, non-aggression
pact between - 534
NATO, France's withdrawal of forces
from - 520
NATO, Geneal Norstad's suggestion re. -
443
NATO, meeting leaders of - 25
NATO nuclear force - 345, 464
NATO nuclear force, talks on - 472
NATO, nuclear weapons of - 28
NATO, strength of - 86
Navy and Marines, troop movements
by - 70
Negro demonstrations - 537
Negro Photographers in the White House
news photographers associaiton - 81
Negroes and the President - 559
Negroes, special consideration for - 546
Netherlands and Indonesia, U.S.
position on - 270
Neutron bomb - 135
New York, Democratic primary in - 145
New York, grand jury investigation
in - 274
New York, gubernatorial election
in - 369
New York printers strike - 454

New England, help for - 592
News briefings - 24
News, flow of - 419
News, management of - 438, 452
Newspaper strikes - 283
New speaker of the house - 151
News, suppression of - 405
Ngo Dinh Nhu and our policy toward
Vietnam - 556
Nixon, Mr. - 140
Nixon on the administration - 116
Nixon, President's talk with - 84
Nixon's prospects in California - 317
No-invasion pledge, possibility
of - 403, 407
Nuclear arms, Brazil's urge for a
ban on - 408
Nuclear control posts - 360
Nuclear deterrent - 149
Nuclear energy, U.S. strategy on - 363
Nuclear force, aid to France's - 275
Nuclear force, a multi-national - 446
Nuclear free zones and non-nuclear
clubs, U.S. position on - 231
Nuclear on-site inspections - 424
Nuclear power, de Gaulle on - 435
Nuclear power, NATO as an indepen-
dent - 208
Nuclear preparation, inspection
against - 379
Nuclear test agreement - 453, 347, 582
Nuclear test ban - 298
Nuclear test ban agreement and Red
China - 217
Nuclear test ban and limitations on
the U.S. - 555
Nuclear test ban and U.S. security -
382
Nuclear test ban, opposition to by
the Air Force association - 558
Nuclear test ban, prospects for - 503
Nuclear test ban, Richard Russell
on the - 561
Nuclear test ban, Soviet proposal
for - 278
Nuclear test ban treaty - 241, 422,
532
Nuclear test ban treaty and Cuba - 536
Nuclear test ban and production of
delivery vehicles - 361
Nuclear treaty, Dr. Teller's
criticism of the - 547
Nuclear test ban treaty, safeguard
and the - 542
Nuclear test ban treaty, signing
of the - 544
Nuclear test ban treaty, violation
of the - 381

Nuclear test question, completion of studies on - 209
Nuclear test situation - 135
Nuclear testing - 163, 206, 226
Nuclear testing, justification of the resumption of - 158
Nuclear testing, next step in - 142
Nuclear testing, McMillian's statement on - 212
Nuclear testing, extending the timing of additional - 358
Nuclear testing, resumption of - 115 (131), 281 (554)
Nuclear testing, underground - 264
Nuclear tests in Atmosphere, ban on - 209
Nuclear tests in Atmosphere, Soviet - 181
Nuclear tests, inspection against clandestine - 242, 244
Nuclear tests and nuclear fallout - 335
Nuclear tests, resumption of in Atmosphere - 254
Nuclear tests, safeguards against secret - 231
Nuclear tests, secret - 377
Nuclear war, U.S. initiative in a - 261
Nuclear weapons and NATO - 28
Nuclear weapons in outer space, verification of the ban on - 565

Oil import program - 400
Oil imports, reduction of - 200
Okinawa, U.S. intentions toward - 234
Olympic games - 470
Onsite inspections - 361, 513
Organization of American States, and the Cuban problem - 494
Organization of American States, Mexican Ambassador on - 315
Otto Otepka, decision on - 581
Outer space, U.S. cooperation with USSR in - 233
Outer space, verification of the ban on nuclear weapons in - 565
Over population and poverty - 320
Overseas dependents, preparation of - 99

Pakistanis, fear of the on American support for India - 561
Panama Canal treaty, renegotiation of - 325
Papers, President's official - 414
Paris Conference, results of - 130
Paris and Washington, differences between - 293

Patent policy, uniform - 289
Pay raise, implications of the government's - 308
Peace Corps - 58
Peace Corps, a domestic - 528
Peace Corps, increase in size of - 484
Pentagon, morale at - 504
Personnel changes - 168
Peru, developments in - 363
Peru, foreign aid to - 133
Pharmaceuticals, Kennedy opinion of - 364
Philadelphia, vote in - 589
Polaris missile - 425
Polish-German frontier - 81
Political Philosophy of the President - 17
Pope and Adzubei, meeting between - 471
Pope Paul VI - 515
Pope, meeting with - 508
Population growth, federal involvement in the attack on - 488
Pornography in the mail - 377
Port and Lake Michigan area, confrontation between - 341
Porter Hardy's subcommittee and the State Department - 251
Portuguese liner Santa Maria - 19
Postal rate bill, House amendment to - 188
Postal rate increase - 218
Postmaster General, a new - 543
Postmaster General's statement - 160
Powell, Adam Clayton - 451
Prayer in schools, President on - 335
Prayer in schools, Supreme Court on - 328
Presidency, Kennedy view of - 577
President, book on the - 555
President, satire on - 416
President, vicissitudes of - 127
President's advisors - 500
President's answer to Martin Luther King - 387
President's attitude on his office - 261
President's conference of Governors, establishment of - 429
President's domestic programs, support for - 477
President's 1st hundred days - 100
President's 1st year - 178
President's health - 113, 359, 525
President's illness, arrangement in case of - 130

President's news conference on Russian TV - 47

President's popularity and congressional support - 62

President's political past - 173

President's retreat, the - 26

President's speech - 124, 518

President's travel plans - 165, 468, 369, 524, 91, 516, 170, 572

President's wound - 503

Press conferences - 52, 559, 159, 4, 283

Price controls - 279

Price supports, increase of - 19

Prisoners of war, ransom for Cuban - 333

Private business, morality in - 30

Private diplomacy, Rusk's statement on - 8

Private schools, aid to - 53

Property loss, federal insurance against - 242

Public business, morality in - 30

Public school bill - 203

Public sacrifice, need for - 15

Puerto Ricans, voting rights for - 423

Puerto Rico's future status - 498

Punta del Este, agreement at - 132, 192, 195

Quality stabilization Bill - 581

Quemoy and Matsu, reduction of commitment to - 330

Rabinovitz, David, nomination of - 592

Race relations - 502, 504

Racial policies, U.S. and South Africa's - 171

Racial representation in the administration - 369

Racial segregation in Federally assisted housing - 182

Racketeering, investigation of - 192

Radical Right organizations - 190

Radical right - 500

Radioactivity, exposure of Utah children to - 548

Railroad arbitration, compulsory - 546

Railroad pay raise - 289

Railroad strike - 485

Railroads and unions - 295

Railroads, coordination to save - 73

Railroad dispute - 523

RB-47 fliers - 13

Reapportionment decision - 259, 262

Recession - 39, 471, 35

Reciprocal trade agreements act - 6

Reconnaissance overflights, the RB-47 case and - 2

Red China and USSR, relations between - 409

Red China, inclusion of in arms negotiations - 213

Red China and nuclear weapons - 518

Red China, resumption of trade with - 584

Red China, surplus for to - 9

Red China, talks with - 148

Red China, threats to U.S. by - 487

Refugee problem, Cuban - 5

Regulatory Agencies, oversight of - 26

Release of fliers, Kennedy role in - 2, 3

Religious prejudice - 63

Republican Party and the John Birch Society - 207

Republican Party, Eisenhower on - 344

Republican Presidential candidate in 1968, MaNamara and - 429

Reservists and National Guardsmen, scholarship aid for - 190

Reservists, demonstrations by - 252

Reservists, morale among - 169

Resources, administration's commitment to - 485

Reverse Freedom Rides - 288

Riots in Washington, D.C. - 425

Robert Kennedy's decision not to visit Moscow - 186

Rockefeller, criticism by - 205, 213

Rockefeller, John Bailey's statement on - 313

Rockefeller, Nelson - 445

Rover project - 415

Roving Ambassador to Africa, statements of - 45

Rules committee, expansion of - 4, 17

Rules fight and the President's action - 27

Rusk's trip to Europe - 332

Russia and Red China, rift between - 160

Russian anti-missile missile - 590

Russian people, President's address to - 165

Russia, pressure on - 591

Russian rocket launch - 28

Russians, administration's dealing with - 89

Russians in orbit - 134

Russians in space - 80

Russians, negotiating with the - 141

Russian spy Melekh, charges against - 91

Russian troops in Cuba – 577

Sales tax, national – 64
Salinger, criticism of – 201
Sargent Shriver, role of in the
   Peace Corps – 43
Satellite, price of stock in the
   communications – 251
School aid, Cardinal Spellman and – 61
School aid fight, constitutional
   issues in – 60
School aid legislation – 122
School aid measure – 139
School desegregation, progress in –
   296
Schools, aid to private –127
Schools, Corporal punishment in – 508
Schools, federal aid to – 49
Schools, need for more – 414
SEATO, intervention in Laos,
   possibility of – 72
Secretary of State Bowles, President's
   confidence in – 125
Secretary of State, role – 432
Securities and Exchange Commission,
   staff support for – 478
Security Council, *Life* article
   on – 418
Segregated clubs and the President –
   166
Segregation in federal housing – 342
Segregationists, attitude in
   South – 531
Segregattion, religion and education –
   56
Seized ship, Portuguese – 5
Senate Internal Security Subcommittee –
   569
Senator from Massachusetts, Democratic
   candidate for – 238
Senior Service Corps, proposals for –
   324
Servicemen, ban on uniting dependents
   with – 275
Servicemen overseas, dependents of –
   225
Set-asides for labor surplus areas
   in selected civilian agency pro-
   curement contracts – 228
Shipping, attitudes on U.S. – 452
Shoup, David – 576
Side-bar corporations, military
   organization of – 63
Sino-Soviet break – 5
Soil bank legislation, new – 510
Southeast Asia, coalition government
   in – 178

Southeast Asia, developments in – 357
Southeast Asia,   in – 304
Southeast Asia, possibility of Vice-
   Presidential trip – 92
South, integration in the – 531
South Vietnam criticism of U.S. – 165
South Vietnam, news of – 233
Soviet-American relations, impact
   of Congo on – 35
Soviet bloc, foreign aid to countries
   doing business with – 366
Soviet criticism on Cuba – 388
Soviet diplomats, changes in travel
   restrictions for – 587
Soviet implied threat on Cuba – 389
Soviet intentions on Berlin – 346
Soviet jets, Indian   of – 360
Soviet proposal for a test ban – 278
Soviet recognition of the Algerian
   government – 251
Soviet space scientists, invitation
   to U.S. – 47
Soviet space program, U.S. receipt of
   data from – 222
Soviet space shot, significance
   of – 368
Soviet testing, acquisition of infor-
   mation on – 118
Soviet troops in Cuba – 547
Soviet underground tests – 459
Soviet weapons in Cuba – 451
Soviets in Berlin – 209, 258
Soviet Union, collapse of test ban
   negotiations with – 199
Soviet Union, formal agreements
   with – 92
Soviet Union, relations with – 338
Soviet Union, significant changes
   in – 466
Soviet Union, wheat deal with – 587
Soviet Union's man in space – 77
Space, availability of Russian
   knowledge on – 101
Spacecraft, U.S. response to Soviet
   launch – 472
Space efforts – 133
Space field, efforts in – 94
Space, peaceful uses of – 389
Space progress – 86
Space progress, acceleration of – 26
Space program, progress of – 125, 208
Space program, status of – 326
Space, race in – 228, 366
Space shot – 101
Space, task force report on – 9
Space, uses of – 249, 288

Spanish representatives in Caracas,
    meetings with - 314
Spending proposals - 19
Spy satellites - 263
Standards for memberships in clubs -
    184
State Department, Allen Dulles'
    comments about the CIA and
    Vietnam - 569
State Department, censors in - 219
State Department collusion, possitility
    of in Cuban operation - 38
State, Department of - 133
State Department, security risks
    in - 189
State of the Union Message - 14
Stationary control posts, the question
    of - 543
Steel, assurances for - 277
Steel, bargaining timetable in - 178
Steel Companies and Union, response of
    to President - 234
Steel contract, agreement on - 257
Steel contract negotiations - 210
Steel, direct procurement of - 270
Steel price hike - 142
Steel price increase and the cost
    of living - 169
Steel price increase, action on the
    possible - 144
Steel, price increases in - 570
Steel price increase, possibility
    of - 154
Steel prices, decision to increase -
    268
Steel question - 260
Steel situation - 267, 275
Stock market, help for - 304
Stock market, status of - 296
Stockpile information - 208, 370, 194
Strike by Cleveland and New York
    newspapers - 425, 473, 434
Strategic Air Command's false
    alarm - 268
Students' demonstration - 513
Succession, problem of - 11
Sugar act and conflicts of interest -
    339
Summit meeting, developments prior -
    to - 27, 231, 116, 136, 213, 535
Surplus Air Force metal extrusion
    plant, disposition of - 67
Surplus food, distribution of - 38

Tariff Classification Act - 397
Tax benefits to industry - 271
Tax bill - 426, 447, 584, 495, 312, 370
    544

Tax cut - 337, 358, 409, 413,
Tax cut and defense spending - 343
Tax cut, hearings on a proposed - 347
Tax cut possibility - 459
Tax cut program - 502
Tax cut, range of - 316
Tax cut, resistance to - 441
Tax investment incentive program - 90
Tax plan - 415, 440, 434, 476
Tax reduction - 227, 327, 335
Taxes, Rockefeller statement on - 556
Ted Kennedy in Massachusetts - 187
Ted Walker incident - 86
Telstar transmission - 354
Tenant farmer problem - 3
Texas vote, significance of - 83
Textile imports, distribution of - 114
Textiles, wider trade protection
    of - 191
TFX contract - 427, 469, 474, 548,
    480
Thailand and Laos, possible attacks
    on - 300
Thailand, legal basis for sending
    troops to - 299
Thailand, situation in - 302
Thalidomide, problem of - 356
Thirty-five hour week, policy of - 453
Thor missiles, British decision to
    terminate agreement on - 357
Thurgood Marshall's nomination - 367
Trade barriers and the Japanese
    protest - 173
Trade expansion bill - 263
Trade, expansion of with USSR - 578
Trade liberalization program - 176
Trade policy - 172
Trade program - 186
Trade, resumption of with Red
    China - 584
Troop commitments to the U.S. - 40
Troop withdrawals, Washington and
    Moscow - 455

U-2 Aircraft, export of - 385
Unanticipated problems - 70
"Union shop," the - 398
Underdeveloped areas, West German
    participation in aiding - 29, 47
Underdeveloped countries, help to -
    232
Unemployment - 216, 243
Unemployment and the closing of
    military installations - 78
Unemployment compensation - 16
Unemployment, expected level of - 64
Unemployment problem - 140

Unemployment, prospects of rising - 212
Unemployment, spending in public works
    as an attack on - 101
United Nations (U.N.), and the problem
    of Red China - 77
U.N. and the U.S. - 247
U.N., bond issue of the - 182
U.N. bond proposal, criticism of - 245
U.N. bonds, purchase of - 197, 370, 381
U.N., French attempts to change
    strategy of - 82
U.N. membership, liabilities of - 40
U.N., the part to be played by
    the - 556
U.N., U.S. payments to - 233
U.S. and the U.N. - 247
U.S., foreign students opposition
    to - 226
United States Information Agency,
    dissemination of information by
    the - 490
United States' main adversary - 94
U.S. prestige abroad - 444, 450
U.S. relationship with the U.N. - 407
U.S. role in the world - 107
U.S. society, Myrdal's comments
    on - 354
U.S. strategy vs Soviet strategy -
    205
U.S. - USSR collaboration on a moon
    shot - 548
U.S. - USSR cooperative ventures in
    space - 390
U.S. and USSR, exchange of delegations
    between - 217
U.S. - USSR, prospects for settlement
    of issues of concern to - 194
U.S. - USSR, talks between - 253
Urban affairs proposal - 223
Urban Affairs bill - 184
Urban Affairs Department and the race
    question - 200
Urban Affairs program - 195
Urban Affairs and Housing,
    Department of - 187
USSR, agreements with - 495
USSR and Berlin air corridor - 242
USSR and the U.S., space gap between -
    36
USSR and Red China, relations
    between - 409
USSR and Red China, split between - 46
USSR, attitude of - 488
USSR, Attorney General's visit to - 215
USSR, expansion of trade with - 578
USSR, giving commercial credits
    to - 570
USSR, possible agreement with - 200

USSR, sale of wheat to - 576
USSR, surplus food to - 230
USSR, tensions with - 342
USSR, threats to U.S. by - 487
USSR - U.S., talks between - 253
USSR, U.S. wheat shipment to
    the - 571
USSR, visit to - 197
USSR, wheat sale - 577

Valachi crime committee - 568
Vatican and U.S., communication
    between - 522
Venezuela, possibility of a visit
    to - 72
Venezuela, U.S. relations with - 466
Vice-President Johnson and the 1964
    ticket - 288
Vice-President, responsibilities
    of the - 44, 580
Vietnam - 501
Vietnam, administration reforms
    in - 225
Vietnam, Allen Dulles' comments about
    the CIA, State Department and -
    570
Vietnam, American deaths in - 272
Vietnam, American troops in - 177
Vietnam, bringing troops back to - 591
Vietnam, CIA activities in - 564
Vietnam, committing troops to - 241
Vietnam, extent of the battle
    in - 204
Vietnam, forces in - 95
Vietnam, General Harkins in - 584
Vietnam, information on - 558
Vietnam, Ngo Dinh Nhu and our policy
    toward - 556
Vietnam policy - 566
Vietnam, political situation in - 525
Vietnam, progress in - 416
Vietnam, Senator Church's proposal
    on - 559
Vietnam, situation in - 150, 222
Vietnam, troops in - 509
Vietnam, U.S. involvement in - 214
Vietnam, U.S. policy toward - 555
Vietnam, withdrawal of American
    dependents from - 558

Wage increases, guidelines for - 287
Wage price discussion, administration
    role in - 319
Wage-Price increase - 276
Wagner, the President and Mayor - 318
War, public attitude on possibility
    of - 148

Warsaw talks — 21
Washington, moral and ethical climate
    in — 590
Weather information, cooperation
    between U.S. and USSR on — 306
West Europe, growth rate of — 306
West Germany, misunderstanding with —
    304
West Germany, relations with — 298
Western allies, trade with — 473
Wheat and the GATT negotiations — 512
Wheat deal and Barghoorn — 592
Wheat reform — 501
White House authority, Republican
    criticism of — 317
Whittaker, successor to — 260
Wilderness Bill — 399
William Blakley, support for — 79
Winston Churchill as U.S. citizen — 424
Winston Churchill, statue of — 498
Women, administration's efforts
    regarding — 164
Wool textiles, restrictions on — 455
Work, dehumanization of — 576
Work week, shorter — 565
World peace, President's thoughts
    on — 286

Yemen, situation in — 575

Zero tariff authority — 438

PUBLIC FIGURE INDEX

Abel, Rudolf - 211
Acheson, Dean - 23, 28, 119
Achilles, Theodore - 133
Adair, E. Ross - 237
Adenauer, Konrad - 41, 145, 157, 161,
    284, 290, 368, 427, 447, 515, 519
Adoula, Cyrille -350
Adzhubei, Aleksei - 167, 193, 201, 470
Aiken, George - 248
Albert, Carl - 253
Alger, Bruce - 201
Almond, J. Lindsay - 374
Anderson, Clinton - 451
Anderson, George - 236
Anderson, Jack - 485
Anfuso, Victor - 47
Annis, Edward - 315
Arends, Leslie - 462
Aspinall, Wayne - 498
Atwood, Rollin - 133
Auchincloss, Bayard - 37

Bailey, John - 313
Balderston, Canby - 430
Ball, George - 181, 397, 500, 562
Barghoorn, Frederick - 583, 587, 592
Baring, Walter - 500
Barry, Joseph - 108
Belt, Guillermo - 465
Benson, Ezra Taft - 3
Berle, Adolf - 21, 31
Betancourt, Romulo - 466
Bethune, Mary - 196
Black, Eugene - 76, 186, 197, 215
Blakeley, William - 79, 83
Blough, Roger - 267, 578
Blum, Robert - 76
Boggs, Hale - 253, 284
Bowles, Chester - 85, 125, 168, 500
Brandt, Willy - 269
Brown, Edmund - 345
Brown, Harold - 513
Broyhill, Joel - 387
Bunche, Ralph - 500

Bunker, Ellsworth - 270, 308
Burke, Arleigh - 13, 30, 36, 185, 219
Burns, Arthur - 201

Cabot, John - 323
Cadett, Thomas - 107
Capehart, Homer - 379
Carroll, John - 433
Case, Clifford - 474
Castro, Fidel - 77, 82, 99, 143, 146,
    259, 271, 333, 384, 490, 527, 580
Celler, Emanuel - 79
Chandler, A.B. - 483
Chaing Kai-shek - 333, 511
Chiari, Roberto - 325
Chidester, Larry - 374
Childs, Marques - 322
Church, Frank - 498
Churchill, Winston - 424, 498
Clay, Lucius - 137, 269, 551
Clayton, William - 186
Coerr, Wymberley - 51
Coffin, Frank - 76
Collins, Leroy - 405
Colmer, William - 477
Connally, John - 284
Corbett, Jacob - 51
Craig, May - 22, 188, 452
Crommelin, John - 49

Dale, William - 76
Day, J. Edward - 160, 496
Dean, Arthur - 60, 66, 92, 93, 247,
    278, 357, 361
de Gasperi, Alcide - 427
de Gaulle, Charles - 18, 82, 91, 105,
    107, 108, 180, 191, 243, 295, 303,
    311, 431, 435, 443, 447, 491, 520,
    534, 549
Diefenbaker, John - 23
Dillon, Douglas - 6, 82, 90, 126, 271
Dirkson, Everett - 533, 553
Dixon, Paul - 79

Dobrynin, Anatoly - 285, 343, 351, 456,
Douglas, Paul - 37
Dowling, Walter - 137, 144
Dryden, Hugh - 246

Eisenhower, Dwight - 11, 14, 18, 36, 41,
    54, 67, 100, 155, 183, 186, 189,
    259, 295, 297, 308, 327, 334, 378,
    388, 392, 481, 567
Ellis, Frank - 200
Engle, Clair - 370
Erhard, Ludwig - 47
Erlander, Tage - 51
Estes, Billie Sol - 291, 295, 299, 303,
    305, 307
Farbstein, Leon - 465
Fascell, Dante - 283
Finletter, Thomas - 23, 28
Fisk, James - 147
Fleigers, Serge - 105
Fogarty, John - 167
Foster, William - 247, 353, 362
Fountain, L.H. - 292
Frankfurter, Felix - 375, 379
Freeman, Fulton - 177, 179, 292, 299
Frost, Robert - 390
Fry, Franklin - 38
Fulbright, J. William - 96, 131

Gagarin, Yuri - 98, 135
Gavin, James - 359
Gilpatric, Roscoe - 163, 389
Glenn, John - 218, 220, 222
Goldberg, Arthur - 34, 94, 198, 210,
    228, 245, 375
Goldwater, Barry - 172, 509, 546, 557,
    567, 581
Gomulka, Wladyslaw - 81
Goodwin, Richard - 117, 139
Gordon, Robert - 493
Gore, Albert - 269
Goulart, Joao - 272
Gregory, Dick - 486
Gronouski, John - 557
Gromyko, Andrei - 75, 147, 150, 194,
    253, 258, 285, 346, 422, 554, 564
Gruening, Ernest - 568

Hailsham, Lord - 535
Halleck, Charles - 481
Hammerskjold, Dag - 42
Hardy, Porter - 251
Harkins, Paul - 574, 584
Harriman, Averrill - 198, 500, 534, 543,
    589
Harris, Oren - 355
Hartsfield, William - 137
Hatcher, Andrew - 139

Hayes, Sam - 76
Hebert, F. Edward - 37
Heller, Walter - 64, 84, 343
Herter, Christian - 186
Hickenlooper, Bourke - 248
Hightower, John - 78
Hiss, Alger - 408
Hitch, Charles - 24
Hobby, Oveta Culp - 205
Hodges, Luther - 94
Holland, Elmer - 85
Home, Alec - 487, 527
Hoover, J. Edgar - 21
Horsky, Charles - 427
Humphrey, Don - 76
Humphrey, Hubert - 9, 253, 370, 453,
    543

Jackson, Henry - 247
Jacobsson, Per - 413
Jagan, Cheddi - 545
Jenkins, Herbert - 137
Johnson, Christopher - 107
Johnson, Lyndon - 44, 92, 93, 95, 288,
    580

Kasavubu, Joseph - 33
Keating, Kenneth - 367
Kefauver, Estes - 79
Kekkonen, Urho - 166
Kelsey, Francis - 355
Kennan, George - 27, 323, 549
Kennedy, Edward - 332, 371, 378, 592
Kennedy, Jacqueline - 50
Kennedy, Robert - 226
Kharlamov, Mikhail - 194
Khrushchev, Nikita - 2, 3, 6, 7, 8, 10,
    13, 27, 35, 45, 56, 60, 61, 92,
    105, 106, 109, 112, 116, 119, 127,
    129, 143, 212, 221, 230, 238, 246,
    258, 320, 325, 342, 343, 369, 376,
    390, 401, 403, 404, 407, 410, 424,
    434, 437, 456, 485, 489, 500, 503,
    535, 544, 565, 579
King, Martin Luther - 340, 350, 387
Knebel, Fletcher - 66
Kohler, Foy - 338, 500, 583
Korth, Fred - 548, 575, 580
Kosaka, Zentaro - 156
Koterba, Edward - 110

Labouisse, Henry - 76
Landis, James - 26
Lasky, Victor - 555
Lausche, Frank - 511
Lawrence, William - 123, 243
Lemay, Curtis - 156, 462

Lemnitzer, Lyman - 146, 185, 236, 272, 352, 558
Letson, John - 137
Lippman, Walter - 92
Lodge, Henry Cabot - 186
Long, Russell - 134, 237, 393
Loser, Carlton - 373
Lovett, Robert - 361

Madden, Raymond - 477
Magnusen, Warren - 151
Malraux, Andre - 411
Mann, J. Keith - 21, 117
Mansfield, Mike - 167, 253, 291, 322, 553
Marsh, Thomas - 368
Marshall, Burke - 497, 504
Melekh, Igor - 91
Menshikov, Mikhail - 127
Merchant, Livingston - 443, 457, 465, 472
Meredith, James - 429
Meriwether, Charles - 44, 49, 59
Micey, L.E. - 108
Miller, J. Clayton - 189
Millikan, Max - 76
Mills, Wilbur - 413, 476
Minow, Newton - 198
Morgenthau, Robert - 369
Morse, Wayne - 54, 55, 58, 61, 140
Morton, Thurston - 580
Moscoso, Theodoro - 418
Moss, Frank - 450
Myrdal, Gunnar - 354
Macmillan, Harold - 18, 77, 118, 238, 274, 444, 539, 544
McClellan, John - 94, 292, 295
McClendon, Sarah - 63, 189, 279
McCloy, John - 1, 2, 45, 47, 60, 404, 411
McCone, John - 197, 462, 569
McCormack, John - 253, 450
McDonald, David - 257
McDermott, Edward - 208
McGovern, George - 38, 43, 177
McMurray, Joseph - 41
McNamara, Robert - 6, 12, 23-4, 86, 126, 145, 146, 204, 215, 236, 241, 265, 342, 357, 362, 413, 429, 433, 434, 458, 469, 478, 498, 504, 520, 547, 571, 574,

Nasser, Gamal - 314
Nehru, Jawaharlal - 33, 161, 215, 360
Neuberger, Richard - 11, 97
Nitze, Paul - 24

Nixon, Richard - 84, 86, 116, 140, 141, 245, 249, 257, 317, 345, 490, 534
Norstad, Lauris - 16, 28, 352, 443
Noyes, Crosby - 106

O'Brien, Lawrence - 27
O'Donnell, Edward - 51
Olmstead, Freeman - 1
Otepka, Otto - 581
Owen, Bernis - 274

Parsons, Graham - 133
Pastore, John - 19
Patman, Wright - 369
Pauling, Linus - 163
Pearson, Drew - 487
Penobos, Manuel - 421
Phouma, Souvanna - 61, 258, 489
Plimpton, Francis - 246
Pope John XXIII - 421
Pope Paul VI - 515
Powell, Adam Clayton - 203, 451, 535
Powers, Francis Gary - 10, 78, 211, 224, 231
Prado, Senora Manuel - 363
Prettyman, E. Barrett - 224
Pryor, Frederic - 211
Puchinski, Roman - 568

Rabinovitz, David - 592
Radford, Arthur - 330
Radziwill, Lee - 333
Rayburn, Sam - 4
Reuther, Walter - 287
Ribicoff, Abraham - 23, 343
Rickover, Hyman - 578
Roberts, Chalmers - 66
Rock, John - 489
Rockefeller, Nelson - 60, 205, 213, 275, 313, 445, 509, 556
Romney, George - 206, 509
Rooney, John - 359
Roosevelt, Franklin D. - 200, 442
Roosevelt, Theodore - 11, 30
Rostow, Walter W. - 336, 569
Rubin, Seymour - 51
Rusk, Dean - 8, 23, 30, 74, 85, 126, 145, 146, 147, 214, 233, 238, 243, 249, 253, 256, 258, 284, 346, 437, 456, 566, 569, 572
Russell, Richard - 41, 450

Salinger, Pierre - 1, 8, 30, 194, 201, 238, 239, 261, 483
Schuman, Robert - 427
Seaborg, Glenn - 543, 578
Sheppard, Harry - 45

Shoup, David - 576
Sidey, Hugh - 555
Sihanouk, Norodom - 380
Smathers, George - 238, 253, 283
Smith, Margaret Chase - 586
Smithies, Arthur - 76
Sohn, Louis - 361
Sorenson, Theodore - 508
Spellman, Richard Cardinal - 203
Spivak, Lawrence - 141
Stans, Maurice - 482
Stennis, John - 185
Stevenson, Adlai - 13, 33, 60, 118, 207,
    402, 411, 415, 419, 420
Sukarno, Achmed - 83, 374
Sylvester, Arthur - 399, 438, 500
Symington, Stuart - 193, 469

Tannenwald, Theodore - 76
Taylor, Maxwell - 125, 146, 150, 155,
    197, 392, 398, 574
Teller, Edward - 543, 547
Thomas, Albert - 393
Thompson, Lewellyn - 3, 6, 16, 27, 56,
    61, 141, 147, 176, 194, 199
Thirpe, Willard - 51
Timberlake, Clare - 16
Tsarapkin, Semyon - 278
Tshombe, Moise - 182, 350
Turk, Joseph - 164

Udall, Stewart - 51, 97
Ulbricht, Walter - 120
U Thant - 176, 350, 575

Van Allen, James - 288
Vandiver, Ernest - 137
Vanocur, Sander - 90
Von Brentano - 29, 47, 49
Von Eckhart, Felix - 280

Wagner, Robert - 286, 318, 369, 473
Walker, Ted - 86
Walter, Francis - 136
Watkinson, Harold - 357
Webb, James - 91
Weisner, Jerome - 414
Welsh, Matthew - 341
Wexler, Harry - 390
Whitney, John - 27
Whittaker, Charles Evans - 255
Wieland, William A. - 189, 569
Wilson, Harold - 485
Wirtz, Willard - 453, 523, 568,
Woodward, Robert - 117

Yarborough, Ralph - 190, 284, 393